The Way We Were
Growing Up French-Canadian in Woonsocket, RI
"Le Canada en bas"

Rene M. Tellier

At Long Last Publishing
A subsidiary of Thought I'd Never See It
46 Yearlong Dr., Tellfont Haven, RI

Cover design: Christine Reale-Strauss
Front cover photo – The Tellier Family – circa 1945
(L to R) Robert, Alphonse, Suzanne, Rachel, Rene,
Léopoldine, Bernard
1944 map, Woonsocket, RI. (Courtesy of Woonsocket Historical Society)
Edited errata update.
Copyright © 2023 Rene M. Tellier, Bruce J. Tellier, Janine Reale
All rights reserved.

ISBN 979-8-9877491-0-4

DEDICATION

To my parents, Alphonse and Léopoldine (Fontaine) Tellier, brothers Robert and Bernard, sisters Suzanne and Rachel, relatives, friends, and other French Canadians in Woonsocket and elsewhere, I have shared your proud heritage in our march to the fullness of American life in this glorious land where the lady of liberty forever beckons those who seek a new life. Gracious thanks to my late wife Patricia for her encouragement, son James for his expert advice on word processing, and Carolyn Faubert for her librarian advice on works cited.

ADDITIONAL ACKNOWLEDGEMENTS

When author of this book Rene Tellier passed away, this project, his magnum opus, was not yet ready for publication. Fortunately, Rene's son Jim had worked with his dad to transcribe what had originally existed only on paper to digital format. These files were shared with us, the book's editors, so we could undertake preparing it for publication. Our work in tasks like fact checking, translating French passages, picture gathering and editing, required the help of many who contributed to this project beyond those recognized by the author in his original Dedication. We would like to acknowledge them here.

Christine Reale Strauss, Rene Tellier's great niece, re-designed the book's cover, created the family tree diagrams and one of the maps. Rachel Tellier Clark, the author's youngest sibling, was a great help translating the patois French they spoke and with fact-checking. Her son Christopher was her technical support. Patricia Savoie Benoit, sister-in-law to Rene's brother Bob, also assisted in translations. Eugene (Gene) Peloquin (a first cousin of the Tellier family), assisted us with his amazing memory which helped with names, facts and family recollections. Gene also provided his impression of the book for the back cover. Anne-Marie Tellier Bibeault, Bob Tellier's youngest daughter, helped transfer edits between Gene Peloquin and Janine Reale. Ray Bacon, retired Woonsocket HS history teacher, historian and Founding Director of Woonsocket, RI's Museum of Work & Culture was invaluable in proof reading, fact checking and commenting on the book. Rene's cousin Claude Trottier allowed us to reference the Fontaine family genealogy in his book *Trottier and Fontaine Family History*. Also, cousin Robert Brunelle helped with the Tellier family genealogy. Mount Saint Charles Alumni Coordinator Gail Bryson aided in accurately listing the school's original alumni association as well as confirming other Mount facts. Finally, we'd like to thank Irene Blais and her staff at the Woonsocket Historical Society for providing historical maps and photos that made it possible to give the reader a glimpse of what the St. Ann neighborhood of Woonsocket looked like when the Tellier family lived on Gaulin Avenue in the early to middle 20th century.

Our happiness in completing this book is only tempered by the fact that Rene and his oldest brother Bob, our father, passed away in 2019 before they could experience the joy of seeing this long-anticipated work of love come to light. We are proud to have been entrusted with brining this story of our family and the city they called home for so long into being.

Bruce Tellier & Janine Tellier Reale
(Rene Tellier's nephew and niece)

CONTENTS

PREFACE xiv
1 - "LITTLE CANADA'S" CULTURAL AND ECONOMIC TIES 1
   Little Canada: "Gone with the Wind"..1
   Poverty in "Frenchville" 5
   French Roots in American Soil..14
   "Qui perd sa langue, perd sa foi" 18
   The Greeks Had a Word for It 25
   The Echoes of Our Patois..28
   Cultured Pearls in a French Wasteland..53
   The Longest Peaceful Border in the World 62

2 - LA BONNE VIE DE FAMILLE (THE GOOD FAMILY LIFE) 69
   "Eight is Enough" – Families and Others 69
   That Suit's for Sunday 79
   The Sacred Trust of Parenting 94

3 – THE TELLIER ODYSSEY 108
   Travails in a New Land..108
   "But o for the Touch of a Vanished Hand"..................................119
   The Daily Trek to the Mills..127
   Ceaseless Drudgery and Unremitting Toil..................................140
   A Day in the Life of a Mill Worker 147
   Un bon père de famille..155
   "How Came He by That Knowledge?".......................................164
   A Day on the Farm..173
   From Those Agrarian Days of Yore to Urban Life.....................177

4 - THE FONTAINE SAGA 184
   Femmes de Maison: Homemakers 184
   Homemaking Amid Chill Penury 189
   Nurturing at Mother's Knee...199
   Cochrane Inferno Routs the Fontaines..206
   Coins of Despair in Cochrane Ashes 210
   Can You Spare a Dime for the Fontaines?..................................217
   Misfortune a Constant Traveler 226

5 - NEIGHBORHOOOD AS EXTENDED FAMILY 237
   Tenement House: High-Rise of the Poor 237
   The Piazza or Porch Culture 247
   That Wonderful Gang of Mine...253
   The Playing Fields of Eton They Were Not................................259
   Babes in Toyland 268
   Peddler for the Fourth Estate 276
   Newspaper Carrier Days: A Blessed Seedtime..........................283
   St. Ann's Park: Wake Up the Echoes of Yesteryear...................288

Quoits: Pursuit of the Perfect 35 298
Comment ça va? - What Ails You? 303
The Unnamed Hurricane of 1938 312
'*Le guy des vues*' in the Theaters of Yesteryear 318

6 - WORLD WAR II AND THE AMERICANIZATION OF FRENCH-CANADIAN WOONSOCKET 325
The Nazi Peril 325
Woonsocket in the Depths of War 371
Woonsocket as a Homefront in the War 386
War-Weary Woonsocket Longs for Peace 401

7 - CATHEDRAL OF THE SPIRIT 410
Church Wasn't Just a Building 410
Sermon in Stone 423
The Cult of the Living Dead 436
Death Ushers in New Life 445
Joyeux noël 454
Father Roussel: A Treasured Friend of Youth 465
Guido Nincheri: St. Ann's Michelangelo 471

8 - THE ASCENT TO TRUTH IN THE OLD SCHOOLHOUSE 484
Parochial School: "The Bishop Tells Me So" 484
The Mission of Catholic Education 489
Baby Room: "*Bébé rum*" 503
Discipline: A Gauntlet of Steel Under a Velvet Hand 510
The Fourth R: Religion in the Curriculum 517
The Good Nuns: Lifeblood of the Parish 526
Encounter With the Gendarmes 534

9 - HILLTOPPER BLUES 540
Scaling Bernon Heights 540
The Melting Pot Boils 555
The 'Sting of French' at the Academy 568
Teachers as Bilingual Role Models 577

10 - SCOUTING AS A FRENCH-CANADIAN KID 599
A Rite of Passage 599
Monday Night 'Not the Loneliest Night of the Week' 609
Father Moreau: Black-Robed Scout 620
Camp Yawgoog: The Call of the Wild 638
Finis Coronat Opus: The End Crowns the Work 647

GLOSSARY 656

BIBLIOGRAPHY 658

FAMILY TREE 666

ABOUT THE AUTHOR 673

NOTES ON THE TEXT

During the nearly five decades the author dedicated to writing this book, he frequently interjected his first language, a patois dialect of French, into his discourse. These passages have been translated for the benefit of readers who don't speak French. One exception, however, is the frequent use by the author of some simple, common French words within an otherwise English sentence. For example the French words for "and," "the," "my," "father," and "mother," are often the only French word in a sentence. When they first appear, they've been translated, but we felt it uneccesary to continue doing so since their meaning should be easily remembered by the reader. Nevertheless, we've compiled a list of translations of these common French words in the glossary for your convenience.

The author also assumed that readers would be knowledgable of the Catholic religion and his professional field of education but to make the book accesible to all, we've also included definitions and explanations of terms used in those vocations in the glossary and in footnotes.

Additionaly, a decision was made to explain many references the author made to media personalities, radio and television programs and events from the mid-20th century that may no longer be common knowledge by adding explanatory footnotes. All editor generated footnotes not part of the author's original manuscript have been concluded with: - *ed.*

Finally, it may be prudent for the reader to have a dictionary available when reading this book. As an English scholar, the author had an affinity for utilizing vocabulary that may not be common knowledge for most. To restate this as our author Rene Tellier might - he was besotted with a propensity for magniloquence.

Bruce Tellier
Janine Tellier Reale
-*Contributors & Editors*

Joseph and Angelina (née Durand) Tellier Family
Front row (l – r): Joseph, Alice, Diana, Marie-Rose, Annette
Back row: Marie-Louise, Napoléon, Alphonse (author's father), Marie-Anne, Philibert / Joseph's wife Angelina and infant Joseph-Romeo were deceased when the picture was taken.

Louis and Emerance (née Morvan) Fontaine Family, c. 1919
Front row (l – r): Léopoldine (author's mother), Yvonne, Emerance, Laurence, Marie-Ange
Back row: Urgel, François, Louis, Auray, Edmour

ANCESTORS

The song that surfaces
Is impulse from which one of you?
Who willed that I should dance
To melodies I never knew?
What fragment of myself
Shall I bequeath those yet to be?
What seeded evidence
Will prove them still a part of me?

-Louise A. Nickerson, Cushing Academy,
Ashburnham, MA

PREFACE

THE EXODUS OF French Canadians into New England has been chronicled several times since Francois Proulx was reportedly the first circa 1814. Without any pretension or attempt to revisit this historical phenomenon in detail, I've attempted, on the contrary, through remembrances, vignettes, and shared happenings to flesh out some of their transplantation and acculturation histories from inside out as it were, as I heard it largely from my mother and learned from research. What I found lead me to believe there was a great story, awe-inspiring in its scope and courage, far beyond mere genealogy. Call my attempt a kind of socio-genealogy, uncovering as it were the inner wellsprings of its vitality, uniqueness, and indomitable will of these immigrants not to lose their faith and identity.

As a progeny of those *émigrés* (emigrants), I had an excellent vantage point to be participant and chronicler, since I shared their feelings and faith; spoke their language at home and in our community; agonized in their struggles during the Depression; shared their dread during the war over the fate of their sons in the military; rejoiced in their postwar triumphs and prosperity; and finally, saw their total assimilation into the American culture and language and rightful place with other Americans in the new postwar industries of the country. This is my attempt to uncover their full acculturation and its epochal moments.

Francos felt intense nostalgia for their former homeland and shed copious tears in the dust bowl of *La Grosse Depression*: The Great Depression.[1] They also dealt with the deprivations of World War I and II, and the eventual flight of the source of their livelihood, the mill trade, to southern climes. For many, migrating to a new country meant leaving loved ones behind. There's no doubt family separations made the immigration experience more painful.

My narrative stems largely as a member of the family of Alphonse and Léopoldine (née Fontaine) Tellier. This focus, not because my family pretends to any noted historical or biographical significance, but because of its common saga. Facetiously, if you will, it had all the earmarks of your typical "run-of-the mill" family among the 800,000 who came down from Canada: "*descendus*," said mom. She seemed to have total recall of the details of the story of our family and others she knew. In how many other homes did the *femmes de maison* (housewives) also tell their immigration and acculturation story to their children and grandchildren?

---

[1] French speakers may consider *"Grande"* preferable to *"Grosse,"* but the patois French spoken by the author's family used "Grosse." – *ed.*

In her limited sphere, our mother became like the oral chronicler for this great migration of her people, at least those whose lives intersected with hers and ours. We had little reading material in the house, except some French magazines, like *Le Samedi,* and an occasional *La Presse* paper from her sister Yvonne in Canada. But in college parlance, she was like "an endowed chair," or a local historian with prodigious recall. Dad was more into current affairs. He was like an economist, factotum, political savant, and predictor of local, state, and national events, all from his rocking chair next to *mémère* (grandma) and our big, black coal stove.

Except where historical research was needed to authenticate certain facts, like the ruinous Cochrane, Ontario fire of 1916 which drove mom's Fontaine family to America, the reader must keep in mind the following pages are reminiscences. As such, many of those stored memories were not only implanted in me, but enlarged almost daily by her, truly as extraordinary a "griot" or storyteller as the one who informed Alex Haley in *Roots* about the coming of his African ancestors to America.

Where my book departs from recollections and reminiscences, I share extensive research of those historical, economic, political, and educational events whose vortex swirled around them and eventually undermined, to a large degree, the life, language, and faith they brought here from Canada. I list numerous books read and cite many statistics from newspapers and magazines whose objectivity, bias, or veracity the reader should exercise the usual prudence.

If any part of this narrative departs from historical veracity, the fault lies either in my or someone's recollection of events, and not in our disregard or careless neglect of the facts as they are known. I beg the reader's indulgence if this chronicle states, restates, and enlarges on certain elements. Faith, family, neighborhood, school, church, and work were all important influences in the life of this community. Their impact was like encircling benevolent forces creating a remarkable and unique culture. Perhaps it will never be seen again but in its time, it always held its center, was like no other, and is a major theme of this work: *The Way We Were: Growing Up French-Canadian in Woonsocket, RI: Le Canada En Bas (The Lower Canada).*

I found a diversity of opinion about "French Canadian" versus "Franco American" to describe immigrants from Canada. Those who prefer the latter think it's important to remember they are now fully Americans. Those preferring "French Canadian" also stand firm in their choice, but the appellation can only be applied to those who came to the United States strictly by way of Canada. Unless I'm quoting, I use both and also "Francophone," "Franco," and "Francophonish," but with no particular rhyme or reason.

Because nearly all the people we knew worked or were supported in some way by the city's mill culture, I speak volumes about its impact on families like mine. My father was proud of his work at the mill, so no willful denigration of that way of life is meant when I speak of its negatives. Our very lives hung on those threads, not of gold, but of cotton and wool. In defense of this sporadic negativity, bear in mind that working conditions in that bygone era were largely unhealthy at a time when no one had health or unemployment insurance. By the ages of 50 to 60, wrote an author, many, like dad and his family, had developed serious respiratory problems and some deafness. They commonly lived long, fruitful lives, however.

I make frequent use of italics if a word is proper French, or patois, or Latin. I also do it at times for emphasis, ethnic fit, or humorous touch. Patois, as I soon enlarge on, is a corruption of true French with many borrowings from English, with preceding French articles *le* or *la*, meaning "this" or "that," or "*er*" (ey) at the end of English verbs. As my etymology professor told us about the history of words in the West, when William the Conqueror's Norman Conquest of England occurred in 1066, there began this voluminous intermingling of English and French. In England, both the educated and the poor melded the two languages into one as did Francos here in reverse and in a more limited way. Ingenious Francos also became wordsmiths when new words were needed for unfamiliar experiences, objects, and events.

Since Francos, like other ethnicities, served numerously and bravely in the war, and because to me that epochal event greatly hastened our total Americanization, I give it the attention it deserves as the biggest event of the century, perhaps history. I also often refer to my going to Mount Saint Charles Academy (aka: Mount, MSC, the Academy) as well as the 25 years I spent as a religious. My entrance into the Brothers of the Sacred Heart followed my graduation from the Academy. The order provided me with a superior education while I was in training at Spring Hill College, Mobile, AL, St. Michael's College, Colchester, VT, and Boston College, Chestnut Hill, MA. All prepared me for a rewarding 42-year career in education.

As is said to be the privilege of a chronicler who has seen, heard, or read copiously of the people and events in this narrative, I offer comments and comparisons, as I reflect on "the way we were" compared to today's modern realities, especially in those facets that once defined the glories and aspirations of French-Canadian life in matters of faith, family, manners, and education or lack thereof. Once you've read the forthcoming thought of a Belgian/French writer, the reader may reflect during the book how much my thoughts, reflections, and comparisons disclose the influence, thought patterns, and sentiments of my primitive language.

The following then is perhaps the greatest revelation I encountered in my research. Not only French Canadians, but readers of all ethnicities who have gone through the immigration experience may discover why at times their thoughts, and reactions may arise from a subconscious past. For me, Luc Santé's "*Living Tongues,*" as appeared in The New York Times in 1996, explains best why my book is from my essential, inescapable self as a French Canadian, née American, engendering so many "we-they" comparisons. He wrote, "**French is a pipeline to my infant self, to its unguarded emotions and even to its preserved sensory impressions. / There are states of mind, even people and events, that seem inaccessible in English since they are defined by the character of the language through which I perceived them.**" One can aver he was also, if unknowingly, speaking of our *patois* when he said of his Belgian Walloon French, "It is a good-humored, long-suffering language of the poor, naturally epigrammatic, ideal for both choleric ("heated") fervor and calm reflection, wry ("grimly humorous") and often psychologically acute." In Bible-speak, doesn't the mouth speak what the heart is full of? No matter how serious, light, tragic, or comical is the material in this book, the reader should always bear in mind that Santé's words may in some way have infused my thinking and writing. Novelist Willa Cather said, "We write what we are" ...but that changes every day.

Lastly, I confess I sometimes depart from a singular thought or topic to engage in a "flight of fancy," a humorous or serious anecdote, or a literary line, because someone said or wrote something better or more appropriate about the subject. Mine does not pretend to be a great scholarly effort or divine prose, but more of a diary-like, "I-was-there" narrative from my mother's fabled memory and my own observations, experiences, and reading.

What underlies this effort is to present the intimate, day-to-day life of Francos. I reiterate that because some aspects of their lives are constants, I come back to them again and again adding still further insights and observations as appropriate. We teachers know the value of repetition to bolster memory. Personally, I always hate to go back in a book I'm reading, because the author presumes too much of my retention. David McCullough, the nation's eminent historian, said we're too ignorant of history. Hopefully these pages will shed light on the French-Canadian experience in one vibrant corner of America and a bit of the world at large. As James Joyce in *Ulysses* says, "Hold to the now, the here, through which the FUTURE plunges to the past." NOW 2015, will this humble effort help the reader do that? I invite you to go back in time and discover or relive a storied past in the history of Francos here.

1 - "LITTLE CANADA'S" CULTURAL AND ECONOMIC TIES

Little Canada: "Gone with the Wind"

WITH THE NEAR total Americanization of Woonsocket after WWII, I've often thought the movie preface of Margaret Mitchell's novel *Gone with the Wind* a fitting epitaph for "the Lower Canada" (*le Canada en bas*) French-Canadian Woonsocket once was. The nostalgic movie preface extols "There was a land of cavaliers and cotton fields called the Old South. Look for it only in books for it's no more than a dream remembered, a civilization gone with the wind." A reminder that nostalgia and the transiency of the human experience are two of the most recurring themes in writing about life and people, like the Franco culture we speak of. But as "every comparison limps," the obvious here is that the city was of course industrial, not agricultural, harbored no landed gentry or slaves, but just hard-working lower middle class millworkers with many children. (But one tenuous link is that so-called "Negro cloth" was once made in New England mills and perhaps in Woonsocket.)

As is "the way of all flesh" some of the feel and cultural face of Woonsocket of the last half of the 19th Century and first half of the 20th Century may be gone, but as *Boston Globe* staffer Jack Thomas wrote about moviedom's best-remembered film, 'Gone' doesn't mean forgotten. And so, just as the novel's portrait of the changing South is now a national cultural remembrance, so locally is the memory of the Woonsocket of yesteryear, especially to the old and middle-aged Franco population in the city, with perhaps ties of blood still with Canada. An ever growing and insatiable thirst for research continues to propel people of French-Canadian descent to unearth long-forgotten ancestral roots, not only to discover one's forbears, but to get a sense of life in Canada and here at one time. It only happens when a people's ethnic self-worth is in full bloom. Among many manifestations, this curiosity is evident in the founding of the city's Museum of Work and Culture to memorialize mill labor centers in and around Woonsocket where the industrial revolution of this country was born and immigrant Americans like Francos toiled to make Northeast America a budding industrial giant, leaving their imprint forever in its mosaic. Further evidence is the annual celebration of *la francophonie*, which continues to bind the cultural heritage of French-speaking Canada *et le Canada en bas* in New England's Franco centers.

In this revival, personally I extol the research done by my former teacher and the now departed religious, friend, librarian, and Saint Jean Baptiste archivist Brother Felician, SC, and of course the researchers and patrons in the city of the famed American-French Genealogical Society with its thousands of documents, reels of microfilm of birth, marriage, and death records from the Province of Québec and other areas. Our past, which had been waiting to be unearthed, recalls *les bons vieux temps* or good times.

Many also like fellow teacher and lifelong friend Patrick Martin-Beaulieu, have traveled to *La Belle Province de Québec* (The Beautiful Province of Quebec), as cousin Robert Brunelle and I did, where parishes and universities abound with information about the New France forbears of our grandparents or parents who came to Woonsocket or other centers in New England before or at the turn of the century. Cousin Claude Trottier, retired Ciba-Geigy executive, PhD chemist, and serious genealogist, came across a WWI Memorial in Montreal bearing the name of our war hero uncle, Auray Fontaine, who like his brother Urgel, did not expatriate with the family in 1916 after a disastrous forest fire in Ontario.

When my wife Pat and I visited the little town of Contrecoeur, P.Q., where my mom Léololdine was born in 1898, the pastor of *la paroisse* (the parish) *Sainte Trinité* instantly recognized her maiden name of Fontaine (at times just Pion or with dit; most other variations are preceded by *la*). Not only did he show me a handwritten entry in an old baptism registry, but as a genealogist, he boasted he could easily trace back the family's Canadian origin some 300 years. Fortunately, because of the Catholicity of *les Québécois* (the people of Quebec), their genealogical history has been preserved in parish records. Priests and functionaries called avocats (somewhat like lawyers in English) were as assiduous in preserving these vital statistics, as are the Mormons in unearthing the roots of the entire American family as well as copying all Canadian records. Another important source are *les notaires* who kept important documents in addition to their function as notaries.

Personally, I hinted that only since French Canadians became fully assimilated into the mainstream of American life, customs, and language have they felt such an innate pride to proclaim their heritage, boast of its glories, and draw cultural vitality from roots once dormant or suppressed. For example, at one time the joy, pride, and participation evident in the festive *Jubilé Franco Americain* with its epiphany of dance, music, food, songs, and French liturgy were all nostalgic and joyous, as was the Museum of Work and Culture's *Jour de l'an festivities* (New Year's Day festivities), and other celebrations in the city and state.

Born in Woonsocket in 1930, I consider myself fortunate to witness this new cultural vitality. Equally so because I was to know the Woonsocket of the 1930s and '40s, in many ways the same Little Canada my parents and thousands of other expatriates knew before and after the turn of the century. Gary Gerstle in "Interpreting Woonsocket History, 1875-1955" says even in 1925, three-quarters of French-Canadian youngsters still attended French-speaking parochial schools, and a majority still spoke only French and would eventually marry French-Canadian spouses. Nostalgia and a kind of *survivance* (survival), overt or subdued, are still here for us in the valley, like an unstoppable current running alongside the Blackstone River with the same power and persistence.

Personally, it's been rewarding to recall or recapture those days of yesteryear - "*les rêves d'autrefois*" (dreams of the past) as mom often said - and to give them life again in this chronicle. Comparing America's history with the great European, Middle East, and Far East cultures of the world, in jest or serious reflection, some have said America has no past, only a future. But the trend in genealogical research, especially with Francos, belies that perception and undermines the wisecrack "there's no continuity or second act in American life," except for baseball, as was once humorously thought!

But without a doubt, to anyone focusing on Woonsocket where we lived, the most awesome and catastrophic event, with a global reach, was *La Grosse Dépression* (The Great Depression) of 1929 thru the next decade. Indeed, the Roaring Twenties, a decade in which financial empires were hastily built, crashed like the cotton plantation culture of the Old South during and after the Civil War. The suicidal fall of many financiers in New York City during those critical years especially remains a graphic scenario of the descent of millions of workaday Americans from relative prosperity into an abyss of economic ruin. (On a smaller scale for Americans was the 2008 Recession, which dropped 60 million people from the middle class.) But worse for the Depression, for almost ten years workaday mill bound Woonsocket saw many of its wool and cotton machinery sitting lazily like the sometimes-placid Blackstone River. Yes, for men and women and the river, there was no work. Since the coming of the first European to the area, there had always been a symbiotic or close relationship between the two. Each needed the other to be productive.

The city where thousands like my parents had come to find a better life keenly felt the ravages of that sinkhole. It severely tested the mettle of all Americans, especially those unskilled foreign-born and their first-generation offspring whose share of the American pie was still miniscule. According to our domestic seer (mom), if you couldn't make it during the Depression, especially in a mill town, you only had two choices: lie down and die or go back to Canada: "*mourir ou s'en r'tourner au Canada.*"

No subject of conversation in our home was more recurrent. If my parents didn't always say *"La Grosse Dépression,"* it was *La Crash*, its pulverizing effects on families, relatives, neighbors, and city peppered almost every adult conversation. If today's child is not always cognizant of the economy enabling his parents to provide the good life, how different it was with us. Every day for a decade, we were reminded graphically how bad things were and why. For my family, except for my siblings Bob and Sue who were born in the mid-1920s and so "pre-Doomsday," Ben, Rachel, and I were all Depression arrivals. Was it a classic case of "the rich getting richer and the poor getting children?" Later in postwar, how dad chuckled when at the birth of Ben and Rachel he had received from Relief[2] a sack of flour and a blanket. I was seven when Rachel was born and walked downtown with him to get our handout. Knowing so well the poignancy and bittersweet humor of the human condition, for the first time I noticed his trademark single guffaw as he got those freebies, because the family now had a beautiful little girl nicknamed Coucou. And ironically, from Roosevelt, who he was convinced would lessen people's sense of self-sufficiency.

When mom and we children heard dad say Hitler put him back to work, she heaved a sigh of relief, "I'll never know how I ever managed to bring all seven of us through that decade *avec ton père* (with your father) often out of work from 1930 to 1939." As I elaborate later, she held the purse strings co-jointly with him, perhaps a bit unusual in patriarchal Franco families. Since she had no choice but to be frugal, she confided people thought she was a rather stingy, plain Jane, and conservative-looking. In her defense, however, "conservative" was a trait of *femmes de maison* or homemakers. Like most, no way could she afford the fine dresses, shoes, bling and rings, she once preened herself in as a salaried mill girl before marriage in 1923. We knew she didn't always look like a washerwoman *le lindi* (*lundi*) *jour du lavage* (Monday washing day). I've never forgotten the image.

About women's appearance especially, there was this great ethnic consciousness of morals, behavior, and modest attire. But she didn't mind a plainer look if it meant more for us kids. For nine years, she replicated "the multiplication of the loaves and fishes" to keep the slim bodies of the Telliers from being more skeletal. Like the Old Testament woman using her last flour to feed a prophet with an oven cake, I like to think God never allowed hers, and others' larders (cupboards) to go empty. In school, the nuns often told us Christ's Father even fed the birds of the air. Yes, God heard their million *Pater Nosters* (Our Fathers) prayers for "daily bread" in

---

[2] "Relief" is a shortened, commonly used name for the Federal Emergency Relief Agency established in 1933 by President Roosevelt to combat the adverse economic and social impacts of the Great Depression. – *ed.*

the 1930s version of Meals on Wheels from Our Father in Washington, as a wit said, like manna for the Jews in the desert.

Perhaps this was one of their pillow-talk resolutions: "Your dad and I vowed to give you *un bon chez eux* (a good home) with good food (*une bonne table*), if nothing else." Oh, before marriage she had dressed so well in the 1920s fashions of the day, as Fontaine family photos show. She was no longer, as it were, the daughter of a Canadian businessman with five failed enterprises or the survivor of a ruinous fire in Ontario. This, after her family had finally been able to afford a place of their own and older children worked in the mills: *travailler à factorie*. Oh, those halcyon days when she was like one of those Lowell mill girls in their best feature and her social life was *"les filles de ma factorie!"* (the girls of her factory) (I submitted a 1920s mill photo of her with her sister Marie-Ange and other girls as a possible choice for the wall of the Museum of Work & Culture entrance. It wasn't chosen but when it appeared in our city newspaper, *The Call*, a woman told me she recognized her mother.)

The Depression or "The Crash" came up so often I thought it was strictly my family's hang-up. Imagine my surprise when entering the Order in 1947, I heard old-time monks (*les vieux mwènes: moines*) speak of everything as "*Avant* (Before) *la Crash*" and "*Après* (After) *la Crash*." It reinforced my notion that financial devastation had been a pivotal time in our history. Something as dramatic to people's existence (if you pardon the vastly unequal comparison) like the birth of Christ, of course a blissful event, which later temporized all happenings as B.C. or A.D.

At one time I really thought BC and AD meant "Before the Crash" and "After the Depression." Language-wise we Francos were expert mixologists, a natural outcome, because we lived in two worlds and I didn't know the Bard's advice: "Neither a borrower nor a lender be." Linguistic purity existed only in the rarefied enclaves of academe and those professions beyond the reach of new immigrants.

Poverty in "Frenchville"

DESPITE AN ECONOMIC respite during the war, in the 1930s and '40s Woonsocket, RI was still in continuous decline as a national or regional textile power. But the northernmost city of RI, which once boasted 100 mills or more, was still a typical southern New England mill enclave. Its historic locus was at the heart of "The Golden Triangle," that is, about 25 minutes from Providence, one hour away from Boston, and roughly 35 minutes from Worcester.

Spawned by the horsepower from the rush of the Blackstone River as it wound its way southward, the city had risen to its textile greatness because of the genius, vision, and industry of men like Samuel Slater, Dexter and George Ballou, Edward Harris and later, Aram Pothier, and enterprising French and Belgian families. In fact, so successful were the efforts and mechanical genius of those early industrial pioneers that soon Woonsocket became one of the major textile centers of the United States around the Civil War and afterwards. Hoping to make it the veritable Queen of the Blackstone Valley, Aram Pothier, mayor of Woonsocket and seven-time governor of RI, attended the Paris Industrial Exposition in 1889 and 1900 and convinced French manufacturers, like two Lepoutre families to build, among others, the Argonne, Lafayette, Rochambeau, and Verdun mills. They were followed by Charles Tiberghien (Masurel Mill), Provost Lefebvre (Branch River, later T.D. Burns), and Cavedon, an Italian family (Falls Yarn). He also convinced trades and businesses to follow suit. Soon between 1,500 and 2,000 French and Belgian families came to Woonsocket to work in the mills as well as 800,000 from Canada who not only settled in Woonsocket but in other New England mill towns. To help preserve their Canadian Catholic faith, religious educational institutions soon came on the heels of industry as Monsignor Charles Dauray of Precious Blood Church, with the backing of the Lepoutre and Tiberghien families, played an active role in the founding of *Le Petit Collège du Sacrè Coeur*, Mount Saint Charles Academy, Jesus-Marie Convent and School, St. Clare High School, St. Francis Orphanage, St. Francis House for the Ages and Hospice St. Antoine. It was an unprecedented boom in the cultural, industrial, commercial, and educational life in the city's history, buttressing its already existing public education institutions

Added enticements for those industrialists were avoiding tariffs and tapping an available immigrant labor force with a great work ethic and docile temperament. All told, banker, industrialist, mayor and RI governor Pothier could never have imagined his industrial vision would literally transform the city into one of the "dyed-in-the-wool" (cotton included) prominent Little Canadas of the Northeast. The city's touted French-Canadian immigrant labor force and the Irish who preceded them provided its strength and sweat for numerous decades despite arduous working conditions and a modicum of education. Even though most mills left after World War II, its textile imprint would forever shape the city's character and image as a Little Canada south of the border *(en bas)*.

So initially, a trickle of Canadians in search of a better life became like a veritable flood in Woonsocket and other New England cities. Indeed, their sheer numbers along with staunch adherence to their language, religion, and customs created one of the great sociological phenomena in the Northeast. That is, a completely transplanted culture existing in New England like ethnic islands frozen in time, as a Spring Hill College, Mobile, Alabama, sociology professor said. Until WWII, many of those enclaves remained mostly unaffected in various degrees by the lapping waves of the American way of life all around them. For example, Woonsocket's Social *Coin* (variably called The Flatlands, Mill River Square, and *Coin Sochelle*), (*coin*: corner) where it is said that at one time a person could live his entire life without hearing a word of English, achieved perhaps one of the highest forms of this Francophone isolationism or *survivance* (survival) in southern New England. But the winds of change could not be held back and as the 20th century progressed, the city would find itself enmeshed in the numerous challenges these changes would bring. Especially economic.

In his 1751 poem "Elegy Written in a Country Churchyard," English poet Thomas Gray mentions how the chill of poverty choked the innate genius of its inhabitants. What similar terror did the Depression wreak upon Woonsocket and its people? Once a thriving mill city whose promise of steady work, if not great wages, lured my mom's and dad's families and others from Canada. The city of our youth, however, seemed at times as still and unproductive as those unused spinning/carding/ weaving machines in the mills. Before, then, and after, their children's education was, as Sherlock Holmes often said to Dr. Watson, "very elementary." That meant grades 1 to 9 for most providing a bit of literacy sufficient for the men's lifelong toil in the mills and for women, "domestic engineering" and frequent childbearing, and hopefully, a faithful Catholic life. So, no need to warble *Que sera! Sera* (Whatever will be, will be) about one's life and work destiny, as now is the case.

Workers of the Depression era have largely passed from the scene. But for those still here, how do they compare their lot to the present threat now again facing the American worker about keeping a job? In my book, I marvel how insightful and prophetic dad was about the American scene and international events. Amazingly, as he endured joblessness during the 1930s, he predicted a greater calamity for Joe and Josephine Worker: outsourcing. In his day it was the mills moving south where raw materials and weak unions, if any, were the draw; and a good work ethic, a surprise for many. As poorly paid as he was at the Lafayette mill, he theorized Americans beginning to chase the inflationary spiral might ask too much for the work they did. Imagine a millhand saying that! He reasoned when poor countries acquired our know-how and machinery, jobs would soon follow. I realized he was right when auto pitchman Lee Iacocca in his autobiography flagellated that same cycle in his suggestions on how to improve the nation's competitiveness. But sadly, now almost everything, like home ownership, heat, food, transportation, medicine, education, is too expensive for the worker not well educated or not well remunerated.

Joblessness in the city weighed heavily on the well-being of families like mine. As a youngster, whenever I walked with dad and met an acquaintance the first question was always about work. In *franglais*,[3] *C'est dull. J'loaf.* (Things are slow. I'm laid off.) Without war, joblessness was a constant like the Bard's North Star. I thought a job was something a man like him was always trying to get and keep. Was this my unpromising future? Would it happen to me?

A lot of mill working French-Canadian families in the city 'begot' numerous children. After an elementary education, they were expected to support their families and contribute to their parents' retirement. Parents spoke about *la fin de mes jours* (the end of my days) and *le baton de ma viellesse*: (the walking stick of my old age): a thinly veiled but loving wish that grown-up children would take them in and support them in their declining years. As mom and *tante* (aunt) Laurence did for *mémère* (grandma) Fontaine and our unmarried aunt, Marie-Ange Fontaine, and the Peloquins who had a second story apartment for *pepère* (grandfather) Joseph Tellier.

Unemployment played cruel havoc with this economic plan, as children, however wanted and loved, were mouths to feed and clothe, if not educate. Handouts given by Relief at the birth of a child during the Depression reminded parents there was no other support agency, like unemployment coverage or the welfare we know today. Also, no health services for the young, old, and disabled. Few could fall back on savings since salaries were hand-to-mouth. As the Irish learned from their cruel English landlords during the Great Famine in the 1840s, self-reliance was their only support. And sadly, upon crossing the ocean, many Irish died on so-called "coffin ships." In one statistic, 20,000 America-bound Hibernians died out of 100,000. Like Syrian refugees now.

For the single or married members of mom's family *les Fontaines*, want and misery were like "*déjà vu* all over again." More later, but in the aftermath of losing their farm and home in a forest fire in Cochrane, Ontario, the government only provided tents and $10 for transportation to where, hopefully, extended family would help. You get the feeling that until Roosevelt's New Deal policies, it's almost as if governments were not rich or concerned enough in people's quest for those basic ends of life, liberty, and the pursuit of happiness ... or a full stomach and a place to stay! The New Deal was new.

In retrospect, the one "bright spot" about the Depression for us Francos is it may have hastened our march into the mainstream of American life in the 1940s and postwar. Why? Root causes of wars are very complex, but politically astute dad always saw a connection between the Depression

---

[3] A form of French that borrows many words and idioms from English.

and WWII, which forever broke the isolationism of Francos in the city and other enclaves. Right or wrong, he reasoned that since nine years of Roosevelt's New Deal policies had not helped the nation's well-being that much, **a wartime economy would.** However, Harry Hopkins, Roosevelt's confidante in work projects for the unemployed, had reported "the President is loath to get us into this war." Given the nation's pacifism and his upcoming fourth presidential bid, historians say he did not want "to fire the first shot," but only to react strongly. I discuss later a sampling whether he knew or didn't about the Dec. 7 (surprise?) attack, a question still debated today.

So long before "that day in infamy," dad was sure the President would send us to war against Japan. I remember when Roosevelt died in 1945, a wild, unsubstantiated rumor circulated that he committed suicide, still depressed over the tremendous loss of life at Pearl Harbor. I listened carefully for a comment from dad, but none came. Extremely well-informed about local and world events, both my parents commented on the news of the day. I heard him say FDR was a sickly man when he ran for his fourth term and wouldn't last the term! But as a sacrificial lamb, he ran to save the White House for the Dems. My scoutmaster Walter Jannell's Troop 4 Scouts heard the news while camping indoors at Camp Yawgoog in RI. One theory about Roosevelt not knowing about Japanese intentions was that no way could he have risked the eventual loss of so many men (2,200) and all those ships if the Japanese struck first. So some are convinced that complacency, underestimation of the so-called yellow races and unbelievable administrative bungling led to our disregard of so many intercepted messages. We had broken their naval code, J-25, but no mention of Pearl Harbor, a great target on a Sunday because of shore leaves and even on-board services. For a whole year, a known Japanese had been amassing notes.

Living in an open society, vigilance at one time was not our strong suit. But providentially in our history, manpower and massive retaliatory armor trumped our lack of preparedness, as seen in books on WWI and II. Yes, Nazi subs couldn't believe our initial complacency and inattention when they sank 259 ships off the eastern Atlantic Coast in 1942. One submariner had tickets to a dance in Maine! We finally met the challenge and the last U-boat was sunk off the coast of RI. Whether Roosevelt "wanted war" to boost our economy, the History Channel in its three-part series on the Battle of Britain reported he did and he did agree to the Lend Lease Act to help China, Russia, and England. Adding credence to dad's theory that war brings jobs and prosperity, he often cited Hitler's promises to the German people for "work, bread, and order." About the motive of revenge or retribution for the total cost of WWI and the loss of all German territories at the Treaty of Versailles, he told me no way could Germany pay its war debts. But I was too young to know what that meant. In one oddity, General

Heinz Guderian in *Blitzkreig* (lightning war creator) wrote some soldiers were again fighting in the same places their fathers did in France in The Great War (WWI), the cause of the second. But Hitler canned him and twenty other generals when they gave up ground in Russia. Didn't he know, "He who has only himself for counsel is a fool."

We've hinted that sociologists once thought this cultural isolationism of Francos would never end. In fact, at Spring Hill College, Mobile, Alabama, in the early 1950s, our professor, Father Majoli, said Woonsocket (he didn't know some of us Sacred Heart Brothers were from there) and other mill cities "up Nawth" were cultural ethnic islands that would remain isolated from the mainstream of American life. Fancifully, another spoke of us as "*ces ilots français dans une mer anglo-saxonne*" (French islands in an Anglo-Saxon sea). Geographic poetry I thought! I'd never heard the Blackstone River and "Anglo Saxon" in the same breath, even if the English were the first to see and harness it.

So because of this isolation, kids like me would savor fully the city's Francophone culture, learn French before English, experience the everyday struggle of a family on a millhand's pay, and adopt its strong family, neighborhood, school, and church values. But eventually develop a greater sense of Americanism during and after the war, along with mastery of the language, high school and college education for many, and better wages.

If world events such as WWII and mass media influences had not occurred, it would have been possible for people like us to live our entire lives in the ambiance of the French-Canadian language and culture, as if still in *Québec*. (Mom said she learned "a lot" of English from TV's Milton Berle after we got them a set.) In his historical account of Woonsocket and those French-Canadian pioneers from Canada, author Dr. Alton Thomas in his *Woonsocket—Highlights of History* alludes to this phenomenon.

On two occasions we were reminded the only language we knew well was not that of our country. But first I should mention that nearly all our experiences occurred while my family lived for over 20 years in a typical six-family (eight counting the rear units) tenement house, a typical "high rise of the poor," owned by the Carle Bakery family. My very first job ever was delivering bread and pastries for 50 cents a day and a pastry. We lived at 309 Gaulin Avenue, later an unfortunate victim of urban renewal, which precipitated the demise of St. Ann Church, so a priest told me. Our hilltop section of the street overlooking Woonsocket Hospital and the Hamlet Avenue mills was called *la Grosse Gaulin*[4] (Big Gaulin), as Roger Petit, volunteer *extraordinaire* said, setting it apart, as it were, from *la Petite Gaulin*

---

[4] As seen earlier, the patois of the author's family preferred the use of *"Grosse"* rather than *"Grande." – ed.*

(Little Gaulin: same street), which rose more gently behind St. Ann Church towards Elm Street (*Ellem* in patois), where the nun's convent was. Since by dad's count our neighborhood was comprised of 40 or more kids, nobody's yard could hold all of us at play. Like the Jewish, Italian children in the streets of New York at the turn of the century, we often played on its macadam. At night, it was by the light of a dim streetlight swarming with moths. Since only a family or two owned a car in those days, traffic rarely disturbed our street games. Home plate was a manhole cover. Fences, rocks, and an old glove were bases. (Woonsocket Village off Cass Ave. and Cumberland St. now occupies our Gaulin Ave. location.)

Our game naturally was baseball, a game we played six months a year, even shoveling snow in early spring to find pavement or dormant grass in an open field near the hospital. When I was eight, one day the rare sight of a motorist wanting directions interrupted our game by stopping beside me at the plate. But from my wide-eyed disturbed look, he must've thought I was peeved for breaking up our game. Or perhaps stupid because he didn't get an answer to his question! I hadn't understood a word. After the motorist from the *Twilight Zone* left, a kid, who lived down the street and knew a bit of English, came over from third base and said, "Rene, that was English the guy was speaking. It's what they teach you in public school." So someone from America had driven into our *Canada en bas* where rubber wheels were largely for peddler wagons (if not pulled by horses) and our balloon-tire bikes. In winter, cars were even rarer, since owners put their cars in storage to avoid snowy roads and car taxes before Jan. 1.

Later, even if learning some passable English in school, we still weren't sure at age 12 about the status of the King's English. After I joined the scouts, Mr. Jannell, scoutmaster, boosted my pride one day at his house. "Setting me up," he said I passed my Tenderfoot test in the fastest time ever in the troop. In English, if you please, "minus a few t-haitches," he teased. Bob, an officer, had prepared me well. For me, everything came down from him: scouting apparel, bike, baseball glove, clothes, as if I was a second-hand Rosie. Then a question he asked all of us kids: "What is your native tongue?" As soon as I said French, he guffawed good naturedly with that broad, infectious smile, which filled his entire round head with its patted-down hair and a few gold teeth. "Rene," he said, "even if you know French better and your folks were born in Canada, you're a first generation American and your native tongue is English." Hello! Had someone forgotten to tell me that? Welcome to America! No wonder Camp Yawgoog scouts and boarders later at the Academy licked their teasing chops when we young Americanized Maple Leafers arrived.

But later, I was amused and shocked when in the 1980s Senator S.I. Hayakawa, R-Calif., proposed an amendment to make English the country's official language. So, it wasn't after all, and Mr. Jannell had overstated his case in his efforts to fully Americanize us. Only in just more than twenty states, excluding RI, is it the official language. Now fueled by security and job issues, the debate continues unabated in our immigrant-based country. ESL programs (English as a second language) in schools, government publications, and other polyglot or multi-language things would be casualties. It's a touchy issue, and politicos are reluctant to alienate a growing voting bloc whose vote was crucial in 2012, when the previously insignificant Hispanic vote became critical for the Dems' victory presidentially, said a columnist. In 2016, minority children are more populous than whites for the first time, said a report. And by 2050 the now-minority will be the majority. But their dropout rate raises fears about our industrial, academic, and commercial superiority in the world, one wrote. Of course, they could've said that about us Francos too at one time, locally and throughout New England.

Ma tante (My aunt) Alice Brunelle, dad's sister who died at 101 in 2004, said her son Robert experienced a similar culture shock when the family moved to New York in the 1930s to find work in the Geffin Textile Mills. His first day in public school was like stepping off the boat at Ellis Island or crossing *les lignes* (the lines) at the border. He didn't know or understand a word of English! Were Gothamites then, despite their many ethnicities, more familiar with Yiddish, Italiano, and Gaelic, besides the King's English? My cousin quickly mastered the Bard's language, and great Irish novelist, Frank O'Connor, became a favorite. At the museum, he related parts of his *American Story*. We also share an interest in American novelist, Willa Cather, who wrote about French and Scandinavian pioneers in our early history: *Death Comes for the Archbishop, My Ántonia* (her masterpiece), *A Lost Lady, O Pioneers!, The Song of the Lark, Lucy Gayheart,* and short stories. She was the subject of my M.A. thesis at St. Michael's College, especially her artistry and vivid character creations, all done with an admirable economy of words still admired today. Hers was not, a critic said, "A deluge of words in a desert of ideas." Betty June Steinshon, dressed as Cather, captured her essence at the city library in 1992 with "The Second Coming of Willa Cather." She signed my thesis. I was attracted to Cather because her immigrant stories resonated with me and the Francos' Canada-to-America saga, complete with the same travails of poverty, language deficiencies, discrimination, old world religions, and lack of education.

So our French language was a bond of unity with our own, but also a cultural abyss across the shores of the American mainstream. Since we hardly ever heard a word of English in the inner sanctum of our homes, neighborhood, and church, did we think we'd ever cross that Great Divide? Did it really matter if we didn't get much education as long as the city remained Spindle Heaven? *Ici on parle le français* (Here we speak French).

The Way Woonsocket Was in 1944...

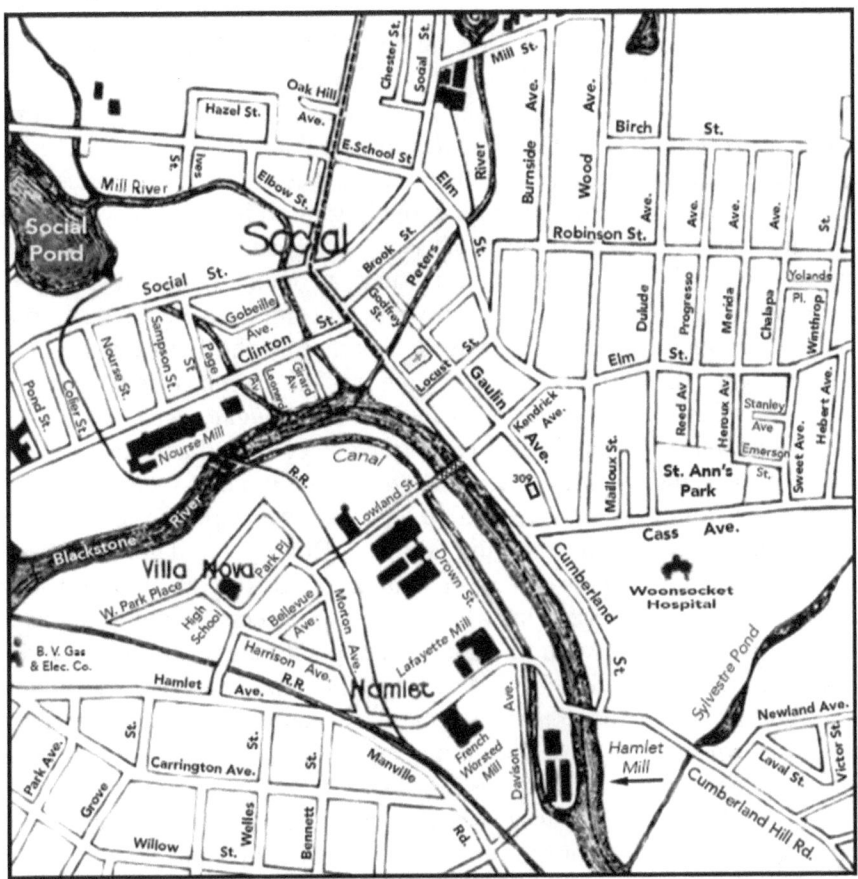

Woonsocket was very different during the author's childhood. Significant landmarks shown here that are now gone include: Social Pond, all the mills, the tenements and streets between Social and Clinton Streets (only two renamed streets remain), the railroad extension (R.R.) that veered north at Hamlet Ave. and crossed the Blackstone River via a covered bridge to the Social District and St. Ann's Park where baseball and football were once played across the street from Woonsocket Hospital. Gaulin Ave., where the author's family lived at #309, once extended to Cass Ave. but now stops at Locust St. The catastrophic flooding caused by Hurricane Diane in 1955 led to major changes to Woonsocket's three rivers. Mill River was rerouted and both it and the Peters River were partially covered over and now flow through the Social district in underground conduits to the Blackstone River. The portion of the Blackstone Canal seen here was filled in and the Hamlet Bridge was rebuilt further north from where it is in this map. A final note: the Lafayette and French Worsted Mill complexes were much larger than this map shows. – *ed.*

French Roots in American Soil

WAS THE CANADIAN who said abandoning the French language meant loss of faith a front man, so to speak, for the late Marshall Mcluhan, the cultural anthropologist who dealt with folklore and linguistics? Mcluhan's famous belief is the medium is the message. That is, the way knowledge or a message is transmitted often has a greater impact than the thought itself, so I was told. Thus, he perceived television, regardless of its myriad messages, as a kind of electronic village or glue, binding us all into one way of speaking, thinking, getting, and living. So it seemed to Francos that language itself was the faith and they couldn't be separated, a contentious point later in the *survivance* struggle to keep our culture pure, or somewhat adjusted to America's, or completely integrated with it. Apart from the faith for a minute, some thought, like Francos, that language was the essence of our culture.

Similarly, did the author of *Qui perd sa langue, perd sa foi* (Who loses his language, loses his faith) think that since Canadian provinces outside of Québec and the United States didn't speak French, at least before the mass Franco immigration of 1,800,000, you should stay put for fear of learning another language and becoming faithless? But if you did go, was French seen as a kind of religious or cultural Master Card, so you shouldn't leave home without it? Or give it up when you arrived there. Would media, for example, paganize you with its materialism, godlessness, irreligion, and its ultraliberal stance on very basic faith matters (fetal life, man-and-woman marriage), at least in comparison with world established thought and religions. Elsewhere, we report that in media, print and speech, the Northeast, and young people are the most liberal.

Again, about that "lose your French..." saying, did the same Canadian falsely reason that only French conveyed the Catholic Faith? Did he make too much of France's place in the Catholic Church? In church history, the French even removed the Roman Papacy to their own shores (Avignon: 1305-1377), justifying the transplantation by a kind of heretical belief called Gallicanism. That is, France - her language and culture - was Catholicism. Not Rome! Called the Great Schism or Babylonian Captivity, like the Jews exiled to Babylon in Old Testament time. St. Catherine of Siena, later named doctor of the church, helped resolve the break.

At St. Ann, you detected strong echoes of that linkage between faith and French from the pulpit in the 1930s and '40s. In late August especially, the pastor no less reminded parishioners of their duty to send children to the parish school where, of course, religion and French were joined at the hip, *"comme deux gouttes d'eau,"* like two drops of water, said commentator mom, who always put a finishing cap on a debatable issue.

This emphasis on attending Catholic school stemmed from a Baltimore Bishops' Conference in the 1880s. Said their Excellencies, a Catholic school made for a good parish, because children were instructed in the faith, a seminal belief on which the latter-day Sentinellists in the city grounded their defiance of the bishop who wanted diocesan schools where English would be the prime language (as if that would be non-Catholic?). Faith-wise, in varying degrees, it must have been the same in Irish, Polish, Italian churches, and others "about the value of a farm system." But the difference with us was that the message about the Faith and French seemed far more intertwined. In one instance, parents protested when catechism was not being taught in French in school. This because English was making inroads in the city, and fewer teachers were fluent in French. Like priests later who didn't learn Latin in the seminary. Could the faith be transmitted in any other language?

Consequently, in our parish and in other churches, there was only a small need for a CCD[5] program of catechism outside of school. For example, until my sister Sue went to Woonsocket High School in the early 1940s, I never knew anyone else who ever did. When I enrolled at Mount Saint Charles (MSC) after St. Ann's the following year, a student friend went to public school. Not only were he and his family faithful parishioners, but he was also a member of our Catholic Boy Scout troop. Quickly scout chaplain *Père* (Father) Moreau visited the family, and my friend promptly showed up at the Academy with tuition help. Even though the curriculum at MSC wasn't all French, religion was, of course, compulsory, and in French for us native speakers. Thus, the implied safeguard was there. The Sentinellists of 1924 - 1928 had lost the war but won a round or two in their battle with Bishop William Hickey and his non-parochial high schools and territorial churches, no longer national.

If you misbehaved in school, your parents threatened to send you to public school. This bred a fear in us (about salvation?) since you picked up from your parents and teachers a vague foreboding about those Horace Mann institutions. *Père* Moreau also emphasized that the YMCA was of Protestant origin so you shouldn't be in it because you were counted as one of them in their annual survey. Wow! That was scary for us kids who were told it was practically impossible to make it to heaven if we didn't comply. Of the four characteristics of our church, it was the mark of ONE, as in the ONLY ONE, that was sacrosanct. So if you weren't a Roman Catholic, you were like *extra gratiam*, that is, outside the pale of grace, and not "predestined," as we and the Calvinists believed. (But in the latter religion, some

---

[5] CCD: Confraternity of Christian Doctrine or catechism. Religious instruction for catholic public-school students.

supposedly had the gift from birth, and private morality was not crucial, which mom didn't like. She thought all had a chance and reminded us our creation was *"pour gagner son ciel"*: to gain heaven.)

As Küng laments in *The Church*, differing churches were not into fellowship, but, shades of the Reformation, they were more like competitors, until Pope John XXIII and church renewal. But even if Pope John Paul II emphasized only the Catholic Church has the full faith and doctrine of its founder Jesus Christ, and others only partly, we should share faith elements and display Christian togetherness. Holy Family Pastor Edward Saint-Godard also touted this in his *Call* newspaper articles and Lenten retreats where he invited ministers to speak. Didn't the apostles at one time want Christ to do something about some who were preaching in a nearby town, but not part of "the College of Apostles.": He told them that those who were not against Him were for Him. If only adherents of differing faiths had not forgotten that for hundreds of years! Now with the Christian retrospection of ecumenism, simple charity, and tolerance, I regret boyhood chum Paul Ducharme and I mocked public school kids when they came up Gaulin from Cass Avenue on their way to Kendrick School or the former high school over a bridge by that name. If not just boyish deviltry, was it that vague feeling they were *ex cathedra*, that is, not of our church? That meant they were probably Protestant, English-speaking, and of course went to a school where no religion was taught. And the nuns reminded us religion was the reason for our school. Why, a school without religion was like no school at all! In those schools, you were instructed, Brother George-Aimé later told us in the Order, but not educated in a moral, religious sense. Imagine, in winter our derision turned to meanness as we pelted them once with snowballs as we sang this little ditty, "Go to school. Go to school. Tell the teacher she's a fool." I guess we figured no one was a teacher who wasn't a nun. Those assaultive times were usually days when we had no school due to a holy day of obligation when Mass was *de rigueur*. Our missals had turned - you guessed it! - to missiles. It struck us as *un sacrilège* to go to school, say, on the Feast of the Immaculate Conception, December 8; the Ascension of Christ into Heaven (always on a Thursday, 40 days after Easter); and Holy Thursday of Holy Week (institution of the Holy Eucharist), and the following Easter Week, off for us. Of course, we also threw at each other all winter in "snowball fights." Our Troop 4 scoutmaster and my mom stepped in to halt the mischief.

Obviously Catholic and public-school kids didn't have the same school calendar, and busing was still a long way off. Would our bus rides have been like the Crusades, "the Christians" versus "the infidels" in our narrow view? Understandably, my becoming a public-school teacher late in my career conjured up a seminal regret for my youthful behavior. As the poet said, "Those who came to scoff, stayed to pray" or tolerate. And we did learn to respect their faith, especially after Church Renewal.

Even though only one of us five children ever went to public school, dad especially recognized the value of learning English well to get ahead. It crossed his mind when he heard us speak, so mom allowed Sue to go with friend Madeleine Carle, as did *cousine* Estelle Tellier. Dad often said of all the nationalities in the state, we progressed the least because we spoke neither French nor English. Like educational theorist John Dewey, for one, he thought public education was the democratic assimilator and equalizer, especially for non-English-speakers like us. But perish the notion in the formidable unison of language and faith! And "the threat" of *Père* Moreau at our door?

In jest, also in connection with the faith, you often heard the phrase, *Il faut faire ce que le prêtre nous dit*, about doing what the priest told you. It was a standard comical reply whenever *un père de famille* (a father) with a large family justified why he was so fecund: fruitful. It was either the result of trying to produce more progeny than the English in Canada – the "Revenge of the Cradle" - or a millhand's conviction that many children were needed to boost family finances.

Even if Peck's law to make English compulsory in schools like ours was passed, but later weakened, it was taught in our school, but more as one curricular subject rather than the total medium of our education. Thank God for that inclusion since I learned all my English grammar at St. Ann's. Practically, French was what you heard from teachers and students on the playground, hallways, and classrooms. And speaking of consistency, one of the inevitabilities of school life was that you always got disciplined in French, like at home. We prayed in French too. But as said later, camping at Yawgoog we didn't know how to go to Confession in English, nor the meaning of *Ego te absolvo*: I forgive you.

As long as we stayed in our milieu, our English deficiency was no barrier. Obviously, we were culturally and linguistically insulated, living our lives in a city (excepting largely the Irish North End or the Diamond Hill Italian section) that was like Québec Revisited … or Never Left, truly making Woonsocket a kind of lower Canada *en bas* or *la ville plus française aux États Unis* (the most French city in the U.S.).

My first serious exposure to English came after I joined the scouts. But as we rose in leadership and attended meetings with other troops who knew English well, I experienced my first feelings of language inadequacy. When I started at Mount in 1944 and attended classes with fluent-speaking boys from all over New England and beyond, that feeling of verbal deprivation and social *gène* (uneasiness) grew even larger. As our horizons expanded more and more beyond the city after the war, were we the first generation to experience greater culture shock? Highly insulated as immigrants often are, our parents, however, lived in a somewhat impermeable cultural cocoon, except for a few occasions, like citizenship, class at night, shopping on Main Street, reading the city newspaper *The Call*, or taking in a movie at one of the six city theaters.

The conversational lack of many Francos gave me my first insight into the academic and career reticence I began to see in many people. Somewhat like the people in Québec who, living in an anglicized Canada, generally paid a heavy price for their "splendid isolation" and *survivance* mentality, combative or pacific, especially in education, economics, and politics. Like us, a cultural island in a sea of Anglicism!

Sociologists point out it takes at least one or two generations in a new land before complete assimilation, language proficiency, and economic sufficiency can be achieved. Of course, there are exceptions, depending on myriad factors. Since nearly all the parents I knew were Canadian born, my siblings, relatives, friends, schoolmates, and I were some of those first-generation children. But because of our seemingly cultural siege mentality, fortified by the weight of our sheer numbers and the French-faith influence of our church and school, we came very close to missing the timetable. But outside forces we never imagined were headed our way with the speed of a bullet, "one fired in anger in a foreign field." Dad's prediction of war against Germany and Japan. Edmund Morris in *Colonel Roosevelt* (Theodore) said he also predicted the war as far back as the early 1900s because of the Axis' (Germany, Japan, Italy) imperialistic stances. Later, we'll share intimate details of the everyday French-Canadian life in multiple chapters. But for the moment, I want to explain more in depth those elements of isolationism that for one defined our Francophone culture, while on the other also enveloped us in a seemingly impregnable grip, somewhat largely of our own making.

"Qui perd sa langue, perd sa foi"
(Who Loses His Language, Loses His Faith)

HAVING TOUCHED upon it, we discuss here more in depth why and how Franco-Americans were among the most adamant of all turn-of-the-century immigrants in holding on to their language and customs. Of course, the fact that Canadian-born families tended to cluster around other families who immigrated before them accounts for some of this mill town preservation. This happened in Woonsocket, Central Falls, West Warwick, Manville, and Albion, RI; Nashua and Manchester, NH; Lowell, MA, Lewiston and Biddeford, ME, Putnam, CT, and others. One article said there were hundreds of mill centers in New England, (I once saw 440!) but, of course, not all strictly Franco, even if our DNA was often predominant.

Using a time-honored strategy, Canadian families counted on relatives as stepping-stones in the states. Mom's family arrived in the city after a short stop in Derry, NH, 1916, at granduncle Médéric Fontaine's house to recuperate from their tragedy in Canada. In Woonsocket, they stayed with *mémère* (Morvan) Fontaine's two married sisters: Julienne Duguay and Sédulie Girard, hitting *le coin Sochelle* (Social corner) almost dead center in a four-story tenement in the back of the now Fournier Funeral Home parking lot. Earlier in 1904, dad's Tellier family was welcomed by *pepère* Joseph's relatives on Brook Street. Fortunately, the city's tenement houses accommodated large families. For example, our own apartment on Gaulin Avenue had four spacious bedrooms, a huge kitchen, parlor, and a front and rear hallway, the latter used for access and storage. There was also a cellar space, good for dad's winemaking and storing wood, coal, and bike. All for less than $5 a week! No wonder homelessness was rare. Weren't flop houses in large cities just $1 a night back then? These were times when "Don't let the bedbugs bite" was a common expression!

But don't most incoming ethnic groups initially live with their extended families in their new country? So what else explains the long-standing adherence of the French Canadians to their language and customs? We hinted this cultural and linguistic stick-to-it-iveness had for them its roots in salvific[6] history. Worried about Canadians who moved to English-speaking sections of Canada or *aux états* (to the states), Catholic prelates preached that menacing phrase with salvific overtones. To the untutored did it seem Bible-derived? *Qui perd sa langue, perd sa foi*: lose your language, lose your faith." For example, the pastor of the Fontaines' Cochrane, Ontario parish objected strongly to their leaving, even if they were in rags: *guenilles*.

The caution, I discovered, went as far back as France, seedbed of Québec's faith. Records about the time of explorers and warriors relate how King Louis XIV of France, *le Roi Soleil* (The Sun King) himself, insisted first Canadian bishop Francois de Laval foster religion and French customs as one. So by royal decree, if you will, *les émigrés* and the clergy and religious (Jesuits, Recollects, nuns, Samuel Champlain, Jacques Cartier, Louis Hébert, and others) were given "their marching orders" to keep France's faith of a 1,000 years. Mom boasted France was *"la fille ainée de l'église"*: the oldest daughter of the church in Europe. So their challenge was from the beginning to minister to the first 60,000 who settled in Canada, stayed, or who crossed the border: *"traverser les lignes,"* mom said. Several times we

---

[6] Salvific – leading to or bringing salvation.

record 800,000 did come to New England; a million or so the rest of the country.

True, we never felt any "church imperative" to speak French in our home, even if it was strictly the vehicle of our beliefs. But prayers at mom's or *mémère's* knee; the Baltimore Catechism and most subjects at school; and Mass and sermon on Sunday were all in French. Praying and believing in English just wasn't "Catholic" for us. In scouting, I recall I experienced some chagrin at Yawgoog at the Feast of the Assumption in August when I told the chaplain in Confession I didn't know the Act of Contrition in English. Father William Delaney, pioneer scout chaplain, told me to say it the way I knew how, as Mr. Jannell said. So our small sins "were committed in French," their absolution in English, and back to French for the Act of Contrition! Hail Marys for penance became *Je vous salue, Marie*. At the birth of Christianity, Pentecost (the Feast of the coming of the Holy Spirit), the apostles heard people speak in 15 to 20 languages, so a little bilingualism in the 1940s didn't upset the Irish American cleric, a friend of *Père* Moreau. Except for *The Woonsocket Call*, *The Providence Journal* on Sunday, and a rarely used radio, practically no English was read or heard in our house in our earliest years. Our Motorola radio didn't get much use because dad worked the first shift and retired early. In later grades we had an English text or two for grammar and literature, but the latter, to my chagrin, we rarely used in class since memorization and recitation took most of the day. But I had a scout manual and a *Boy's Life* magazine with its last page of jokes. Bob was a pharmacist's mate in the war and sent his manual home, and dad had his 22 medical volumes - a Rialto movie house giveaway. I gave up on both.

In the 1920s and '30s, mom said our newspapers were occasionally Montreal's *La Presse* and the city's *La Tribune*. With postage cheap, Canadian relatives, like mom's sister Yvonne *au* (in) Canada, occasionally sent an issue. This aunt, whom we never saw, married Edez Villemure and raised a large family. On average, families there had eight children. Even with our modest means, mom collected our used clothing for her. With *tante* Laurence Trottier also providing discards from her Claude and Ronald, mom shipped the stuff out. At the time, Canada was trying to fill its vast territories with stipends for each new birth. So my aunt was "right on the money." Since all five of us were born in desperate times, yes, she told me it would've been nice to get money for doing their Christian duty. Rarely heard was the statement: "We've got a pair, we've done our share." Dad, who knew the income tax laws well, beefed about the vastly inadequate child deduction amount. Like 25 other things, he of course did his own taxes and helped relatives with theirs. He knew to the penny what each one of us cost to raise in a year, as he told me. But about lack of material comforts, mom had a very egalitarian outlook, "*Yon tous à peu près la même chose.*" Meaning we all had no more or no less than others.

Quickly becoming an avid reader of newspapers, a lifelong habit (we never went to the library and couldn't buy books), I for one liked *La Presse's* sports page. The Montreal baseball team was a Triple A affiliate of the Brooklyn Dodgers. In the 1940s I was reading about the heroics of a rookie named Jackie Robinson, later the first black player to integrate the majors. A movie biography, *42,* came out in 2013. It gave me an "I'm-with-him" feeling when a future teammate was reliever extraordinaire Clem Labine, whom I saw pitch a couple of times at St. Ann Park on Cass Ave. I also saw future Soxer Lou Lucier there. I never missed a sports event at the park in 12 years, amateur or semi-professional. Mom knew if we weren't spectating, we were playing in its vast confines. Hey, where else in "factorized" Woonsocket could you find two blades of grass to play on? To accommodate millworkers, houses had been stacked *comme des sardines* (like sardines). Except for the park, I never saw a homeowner need or use a lawnmower. *A Tree Grows in Brooklyn* could not have been written about most places in the city.

Expressions like *coupe marquerite*: sharp groundball; *voltigeur*: outfielder; *balle*: ball; *prise*: strike; *lanceur*: pitcher; *coup de circuit*: circuit smash or homer were as familiar to me as American baseball lingo. Boy, how much more un-American could a French-Canadian kid in the city be than to talk about America's game in French?

But this Canadian lingo served me well when I reached the second stage (the Novitiate) of my training with the Brothers. Since French was the official language of the Order, *le Frère* (Brother) George-Aimé Lavallée, Master of Novices, made it de rigueur we sometimes play our Sunday morning baseball games in French. We were right at home. Besides daily prayers in French, he decreed during the annual French Week all conversations except our collegiate studies be in *Gallois* (Welsh). Saturation learning! Only in French did they pass you a dish at the table. ("Ma, how do you say 'beans' in French?")

Besides the Montreal paper, mom relished a weekly magazine, *Le Samedi*, a kind of *Saturday Evening Post*. On weekends, I sometimes got the magazine at the little corner store on Wood and Cass Avenues that is still there. She, *mémère* Emérance and *tantes* Laurence Trottier and Marie-Ange Fontaine passed it around and enjoyed its romantic short stories. They used the word *roman* (romance) to describe these stories. Imagine, even in her late 70s *mémère* walked once or twice about one mile to Gaulin if *mon oncle* Henri was not available. So *mémère* was sometimes the courier of this precious feuilleton in her black bag along with her knitting paraphernalia for her woolen creations. Canadian by birth, she knew how to keep us warm in winter for outdoor play.

Tante Laurence, *ma marraine* (my godmother), also recalled a Cyril Lafleur, who ran a small Social Street store for *La Revue Populaire, La Revue Moderne*, and *l'Almanac du Peuple*." This infusion of French reading material perpetuated their hold on their language and culture. It kept English at bay, if you will, as Spanish and Portuguese newspapers and radio and TV programs now do for other older immigrants. If typical for people of little formal education, you must admire their extreme reading curiosity. And as print-starved Francophiles, they just didn't look at magazines, they read them cover-to-cover. Chores done by mid-afternoon ("*ma grosse besogne finie*"), looking like Whistler's Mother she sat in a small rocker by the window through which the afternoon sun flooded our third floor living room. Only then was she incommunicado to those requests kids make every day to their mothers, especially if they're sitting down for a second! If annoyed at our ill-timed interruptions, she said, "*Lâche-mwé, j'ai mon feuilleton*," meaning this was HER quiet reading time: her literary flight of fancy to the land, people, and stories of the country of her birth. We learned to respect that, and totally immersed in reading she was almost oblivious to the din (*le bruit*) of us five children. Like dad, reading was her muse.

Mom never read us English fairy tales on her knee, but in a powerful manner, she passed along the reading habit. And despite her asthma, she sang French in a nice, clear voice. It was often either "Au clair de la lune" or, as I write later, songs from the Nelson Eddy-Jeannette MacDonald flicks like *Maytime*, for one. Only when in high school and college, I realized I didn't know the popular fairy tales of children's stories of America or world literature. *Jack and the Beanstalk, Little Red Riding Hood, Cinderella* were all creations of other unknown ethnics. We just didn't have those books, which of course my wife Pat and I quickly got for our little Jimmie, her "little tykie." Monolingual and from New York, she of course knew those stories. She had a great memory of poems and songs she learned growing up, in school, and in her Saint Joseph Order. Her dad, a sports bibliophile, had that noticeable Brooklyn accent I liked and had often seen 'Da Bums' (the Dodgers) play before they moved to the West Coast.

I was at Norton HS when Jimmy was growing up and he always wanted me "to find him" when I got home. Like I saw in a TV commercial, he'd be stifling his laughter while "I searched," pretending not to know where he was. If I found him too soon, he said, "Dad, find me again." He also liked to do "uppa shoulders" (mine) while Pat chased us around the dinner table. One time he made us laugh when he said, "Don't make me caught." Then he floored us with his first unintended "flight of fancy" when we told him TO BE-HAVE. His interpretation of that lead him to say "No," because he was Jimmy. (A speech expert said for a very short time a child learning to speak goes through a very unique, original way of saying certain words. Verbal facility comes so well and quickly, one author wrote "the miracle of speech" may have its origin in the womb, along with a natal memory of the mother's voice.) Saint Thomas Aquinas said every creature on earth communicates. I received my first lesson in avoiding objectionable reading material when one day mom and sister Marie-Ange talked about how risqué the romantic interludes in the magazine had become. I didn't understand what they were saying, but I knew it was about one of those things people didn't talk about: "*On n'en parle pas*," she said. It was the same feeling nuns gave us in school when they told us to avoid sins against the 6th and 9th Commandments (purity of body and mind) without ever explaining or detailing what they were. It was like "Ignorance is bliss," a thought once prevalent in the Middle Ages before education became everyone's right. Did it stem from people's fear of Adam and Eve's misadventure, because of their curiosity about The Tree of Knowledge?

In those days, it would never have occurred to my parents to explain to us what salacious literature was. No more than the nuns or priests! In many respects, because of the strong religious ties of families and an all-pervasive cultural ethic, St. Paul's admonition about evil not even being mentioned among the faithful was the way our parents raised us. Of course, she didn't know English Cardinal John Henry Newman's observation that sin finds its way into literature because man (and woman) is of course a sinful creature. Or the principle that one immoral character or scene doesn't vitiate a whole piece of work. And that if there is evil in a piece, there must be a counterbalancing conscience in one of the characters about it. Newman (1801-1890) whose cause for sainthood is progressing is already given credit for one American miracle. Two are needed for canonization unless there's a papal dispensation. He helped initiate the Oxford Movement, mentioned later, where English writers and converts produced works of great merit with salvific overtones and values. People born and raised in the faith can't help but admire the élan, fervor, and oftentimes apostleship of those called to the banquet or wedding feast later in life, while we, chosen from birth, may grapple with "weariness in well-doing." Constancy is a will-of-the-wisp virtue!

French on the radio was pure delight to my parents. To them, it was the feeling you get when you meet someone who knows you (or doesn't) and talks your language in a setting or place unfamiliar to you both. Their favorite was a 7 p.m. Monday transmission from Canada called *L'Homme et Son Péché*: (Man's Frailty or Sinfulness). It was about the misadventure of a miserly farmer named Séraphin, a seminal prototype of the latter-day

Archie Bunker.[7] Speaking in an exasperated, gravelly voice, he was always belittling his pitiable wife (color in Edith) or life in general. Especially the cost of things, a raw nerve for poor Canadian farmers. At one point, I understood enough French to laugh when he berated her for losing a $200 ring in a storm. "*On aura pu acheter deux vaches pour c'montant-la,*" he wailed about losing the price of two cows. That was the classic line when my folks teased each other about losing something of value. Both liked to laugh and had a cheerful disposition, which amazed people who knew their stories. Like for Roosevelt's fireside chats during the war, they gathered close to the radio because of the infernal static and even gave up listening one time because of it.

Shades of Roger and Claudette Laliberté's French radio program, *Le Programme Français* for them was as "obligatory" as Sunday morning Mass. Narrated by *monsieur* Albert Foisy, it often featured a romantic crooner named Tino Rossi. He sang French songs she knew as a girl in Canada. Whenever, on Mother's Day especially, he sang, "*Ne fait jamais pleurer ta mère car tu ne l'auras pas toujours,*" about not making your mother cry because you won't have her forever, well, with her ready wit, she called our attention to the lyrics. Dad did his typical one-chuckle and piped in his support. A precious family moment!

Our English vocabulary grew every day, but out of respect we always spoke French to them, even in our adult life. I wrote to them in French in the Order, as Rachel did from convent school. But Bob and Ben wrote in English when they served in the military while Sue kept the home fires burning until she married. Even if every time we went outside the house, we Americanized more and more, returning home we effortlessly slipped into our parents' native culture and language. We were citizens of two worlds, the one they brought with them from Canada, and the one whose dim surrounding light and urgency always sought to break through to us, as if whispering, "We're going to get you, sooner or later."

I don't know if they did, but if they believed speaking French was a safeguard to remaining Catholic, they must have been pleased to hear us speak it most of the time, at least in their presence! If for us at home the link between French and the faith was perhaps only an understated force, it had the force of law in the very Canadian family of *les* Bérubés (more later) who one day moved into our tenement. Rachel, closer to them because of youngest daughter Pierrette, still remembers their mother Marthe's conviction on the matter: "*Qui renie sa langue maternelle n'est pas loin de renier son Dieu.*" The old equation in more flowery, passionate, or ominous language:

---

[7] Archie Bunker was a character in the hit 1970s sitcom *All in the Family*. He was irritating, opinionated, bigoted, and often condescending towards his wife Edith.

lose your French; lose your faith, and even your God. Did God or some Canadian bishop send them to 309 Gaulin as the "dogma police," because we were melding our patois with English?

The Greeks Had a Word for It

I SAID MY DAD often chided us for speaking neither French nor English, but a mixture of both. After I joined the Brothers, I heard the same criticism from Provincial Brother Bartholomew, a religious superior who fled from anticlerical France in 1903.

One day he lashed out in a provincial letter sent to Brothers' schools for using "hybrid expressions," as he called it, like *un* truck, *une* tin can, and the like. He said such usages were not worthy of teachers in the New England Province. Like my folks, since *les premiers habitants* (the first inhabitants) in New England were natively ingenious but with little formal education, their speech was a patois, a linguistic usage devoid of most of the grammatical and esthetic niceties of the beautiful and precise French language. Because of this patois limitation in providing new words for their ever-widening American experience, or not knowing an existing French word, like renowned Greek wordsmiths, they made up their own words. Not shy about improvising, recall they took the English word and put *un* or *une* (a or one) or *le* or *la* (the or that) before it, while also adding *er* (ey) at the end of English verbs. I thought about that when in college I read Lady Macbeth's line: "A little water clears us of this deed," about the murder of a king.

Examples were *le* toaster (*grille-pain*); *un* truck (*un camion*); *un* coat (*un pardessu ou manteau*); *un* wrench (*une clef*); *les* brakes (*les freins*), and the untoward use of *mwé* and *twé* for the more grammatical *moi* (of Miss Piggy fame) and *toi* (you). But my friend who tried to slip by the watchful eye of *Père* Moreau to attend Woonsocket HS instead of Mount used to say *té* (you), a worse grammatical aberration. Is that because, as my professor at St. Michael's College said, "There's always a simplification process (a dumbing down!) in speaking and writing a language." Today, internet speak and texting are howling examples! Before African Americans were given an equal chance at education, he said many in the South substituted the verb "to be" with "am" for all three singular and plural personal pronouns. While there I did hear "Do you know where they am?"

A humorous anecdote about this unholy mixture of French and English came up at gatherings where my parents and relatives poked fun at their own speech. A pompous Franco ("*y s'en fa crère*," she said) insisted he wanted to be waited on in a grocery store only by someone who spoke impeccable French. His wish granted; he started his shopping list with "*J'veux une can de bines et met-ça sa slip.*" No less than three English words in his request for a can of beans (*bines*) on credit! Would the guardians of the French language - *l'Académie Francaise* - have guillotined him for his linguistic *gaucherie* (awkwardness)? Mom added, "*Yava l'nez (nose) dans l'air*" (He had his nose up in the air). Cousin Frank knew the story.

Our life was lower middle class rather than abject poor, but the community had its pride and unwritten rules about a lot of things, especially language, dress, and moral practices. A lot of religious "LePage Glue" held the culture together. But the center (the basic public concept and practice of morality) never weakened or collapsed, like now. Dominican Rev. John Lennon of Providence College wrote about this impending moral collapse: "Presently, the Catholic Church in America is embroiled in a culture war, the outcome of which will determine whether the values of Christianity or secularism will prevail in our country." Believers in the Fatima miracles say secularism will prevail, especially from Russia, if it isn't totally consecrated to the Immaculate Mary. But Lennon also cites Father Neuhaus about the present time also being a "Catholic moment, a golden opportunity for the Church to make relevant to the contemporary world its traditional wisdom." Like it once was in Canada and Europe. This before the Western World splintered into many religions in a spirit of questionable accommodations, bolstered by the nation's beliefs in modernism (science the only knowledge), secularism (no spiritual world), and consumerism. Catholicism, on the other hand, has always boasted it has never changed its divinely inspired truths, as it was reiterated in the Synod of 2014. At times newspapers gave you the impression the church was relaxing them. It was not, but it now advocates a more compassionate understanding of people's failures, natural inclinations, and weaknesses, while not embracing their lifestyle. As Christ did, "Love the sinner but not the sin." Pope Francis is beloved for that mentality.

Brother Josephus, founding principal of Mount Saint Charles in 1924, once told me the French language is sometimes known as *Le Verbe*. (Even if Irish, he wrote about French grammar!) Is it because, as with all languages, the verb, action, or state-of-being word (is, was) is the most communicative and expressive in human speech? Anyone who has ever studied French knows the unbelievable intricacies of French verbs with their hundreds of exceptions and spelling variations. We Francos fractured verbs even more. But again, with their love of conversation, the locals found a way to enlarge their meager store of *les verbes*. Recall they simply added *er* (pronounced: EH) to any English verb they borrowed. So to brake became *braker*; to dive: *diver*; to lead: *leader*; to lift: *lifter* - often used by dad who was not always the language purist. He, like my brother Bob and me, groaned about toting or lifting coal from the cellar up some thirty steps.

(Fancifully, the laws of gravity are not absolute: they weigh more heavily on those with simpler means. Missing are the machinery and people to thwart the pull of the earth's iron core for them. It's why the poor man seeks "to repeal" gravity more than others. In Mobile, AL before integration in the 1950s, we sometimes heard the ballad, "Tote that barge, lift that bale; You gets a little drunk and you lands in jail." A writer recently said gravity accounts for close to 80 percent of our setbacks.)

I was surprised to learn the literati of the French language condemned the above verbal and spoken concoctions. The nuns told us that in France some 40 French language savants - *les Quarante Immortelles* from the above *Académie Francaise* - always stood ready to expunge such Anglicisms from the language. But who cared? They never stepped foot into Woonsocket! As I later learned about English, the ultimate test of a language is its ability to communicate meaning. Ours did. Yes, the whole gamut of our culture: its humor and pathos, follies and fancies, despair, and triumphs.

Our parents had more reasons for their crude French speech because their education was "elementary." We, however, had more opportunity to learn proper French with the nuns and more schooling. But our daylong instructions in correct French profited us little. First, since the age of learning by doing or conversing had not yet dawned, our study of French was more cerebral than practical. The assault on our memory was tremendous, and practice was limited because of large classes. I joked in late elementary grades I knew every French grammar rule and exception in the big, blue French grammar book. But I did not use any of its correct rules in everyday speech. Our milieu sorta' forbade it. If anyone had used proper French, he or she would've been laughed off the block, as were initially *les* Bérubés, the Canadian family. For example, I was pleasantly surprised in college in Mobile to be called "Renay" instead of "Rainy," as I was in the city. Like Eliza Doolittle in *My Fair Lady*, anyone in our world speaking good French risked being stranded between the city's own French cockneydom and its gentility and refinement. We wanted to belong too much for that. For us, "the rain in Spain" didn't stay "mainly in the plains" despite our hilly mill town. Eliza Doolittle-like, our speech was more the "bloomin' arse" type. Even if not sexual, our patois, however, could be racy ("*parler gras*," mom said) and mildly biting, if not satirical or crude.

Because of respect, we spoke more grammatically to our parents, avoiding *toi, tu, té* in speaking to them, using instead the respectful *vous*. But what a surprise when Ghislaine (Bérubé) Parenteau, lifelong friend and Our Lady Queen of Matyrs parishioner, told me they also respectfully "*tutoyer*-ed" their parents, according to their Canadian custom. But I felt that besides showing them respect by speaking to our parents in the language of their birth and culture, we also made them feel good in their role as transmitters of the faith-language ideal in English-speaking America. And helped them continue dwelling nostalgically in spirit with brothers, sisters, relatives from whom they became separated by their expatriation. Of course, those letters coming from Canada were all in French, like those going there. Only during the war, did I hear her quick, scratchy Spencerian scrawl directed away from Canada and towards Bob in the South Pacific.

We also used our school "blue-book" language when speaking to priests, nuns, adult relatives, and parents of friends. You never wanted to be called un *p'tit polisson* or *mal élevé*: a bad-mannered or ill-brought-up kid. Respect for older people was sacrosanct in our culture. As much as children were loved and wanted, it wasn't like America today with its youth-oriented culture and uneasiness at times with elders who now live in a separate world. They were all at the top of the pyramidal foundation of authority and respect in homes and society. It's probably why juvenile delinquency, especially towards them, of a serious sort was practically unknown. You got the impression parental law was, well, next to God's law. Besides the 6th and 9th Commandments about purity, the 4th Commandment to honor thy father and they mother was practically the whole Law of Moses for us, along with the 5th about not getting angry, mouthing, and quarreling with siblings. Killings were unknown. I only recall Jack Letendre whose murder was never solved. But so ingrained in our DNA was Sunday Mass, our 3d Commandment to keep holy the sabbath day didn't seem an obligation, as attested by over a thousand people in attendance at Sunday Mass. As repeated later, is that why *Père* Moreau with his great memory actually knew the 600 men who didn't attend? Did they hide during the biennial parish visit? I swear women had perfect attendance.

The Echoes of Our Patois

AS FAITHFULLY AS my memory and ear allow, I sprinkle bits of our patois in this narrative. Hopefully in the same pithy and picturesque manner it was written and spoken to express the hopes and fears, sadness and joys, triumphs, and failures of those early comers. But what was this patois and what was America's native tongue? Did I need later to grovel at the shrines of Presidents Jefferson and Wilson, the two best masters of the English language - my college major - with the latter said to have the second largest vocabulary after Shakespeare?

Webster defines patois as "a dialect other than the standard literary dialect; illiterate or provincial speech; the characteristic special language of an occupational (like mill work!) or social group; jargon." If so, all three parts of his definition bear very faithfully on the speech that passed through the lips and pen of mine and the families we knew. But hard to believe, Graham Robb in *Discovery of France* says, "except for Paris, patois was also spoken by most people up to the middle of the 19th Century, even by the elite." But a priest wrote a book to dissuade people from using it instead of Parisian French. Did he think patois a little too earthy or rough at one time, like what I heard once from a poolroom on lower Cumberland St? About the paysans of the many little towns and hamlets, Robb said the locals (like Francos in Canada and here?) married only local people of the Roman Catholic faith and were generally satisfied with what they had, and not driven like others. Is that why the English, for one, hated them in Canada and here? But is it partly because of that docility that Pothier "sold" French mill owners about coming here?

But foreign language teacher Domenico Marceri said, "The standard language will open doors to opportunity. The home language is who we are." He also spoke about the present adjustment problems of the greatest number of immigrants: people who speak Spanish. Just as our mélange was called "Franglais," theirs is "Spanglish." He says the task is to tell them their language is good but different, without bruising their pride, as ours was. And isn't it rapidly becoming the nation's second language? With help from French and Latin, I took a semester of it in college in the South and read it in my Spanish missal. The grammar is just a couple of pages, not a whole book like French.

Because it was the speech of our parents, it was the first language we children learned. Eventually we became bilingual, however very imperfectly. In his book *The French-Canadian Heritage in New England*, Gerard Brault mentions efforts are in progress to preserve or codify this speech. The expressions recorded in my book were by and large spoken in our milieu. Since mom, her sisters, and relatives read some good French, some words or expressions claim a rightful place in the dictionaries of Cassell or Larousse. And, of course, *les bonnes soeurs et les prêtres* (the good sisters and priests) used correct French, which we picked up in school and sermons. Those proper words became *les enfants adoptés de notre patois* (adopted words of our patois) and gave it some patina of academic respectability. Like in the anecdote about the guy buying a can of beans!

For us children, parents, and forbears in Canada, this speech was a kind of oral tradition. Except for all those letters mom wrote to us, I never saw it written. At least not in the French texts we used at school, our church missals, or in the French newspapers and magazines in our home. Proper French, if you will, was always trying to bring down the almost impregnable walls of our defensive patois stronghold. "*S'faire gogner la tête*," getting hit on the head, was mom's take about that battle royal. Dad especially didn't like how our speech was a mishmash of English, some good French, and patois.

In my study of true Canadian French in the Order, occasionally I'd depart from the newsiness of mom's letters to notice how purely phonetic her patois spelling was. After all, you learned it by ear, you spelled it by ear. But I liked her rather flamboyant Spencerian strokes, like John Hancock's. She often piped, "*Il faut s'faire aller*," about doing things with flourish and style. If ending your letters with a high curving upsweep indicates optimism, her glass was always half full. Webster defines sangfroid as imperturbability under strain, a quality her family showed in Canada during a disastrous forest fire; dad with the death of his mother and sister; and, of course, the Depression. But the Fontaines, especially, had that grittiness about them, an indomitable will to survive despite, as the Bard wrote, "the slings and arrows of outrageous misfortune." What mom called "*la misère noire*," as in darkness and despair.

Our speech was remarkable for its endurance. Consider the moment you entered school, teachers tried gamely to change us - male and female Eliza Doolittles - into scrubbed, educated, lower middle class paysans. But their efforts fell on deaf ears since our milieu was a mill town workaday world. Imagine what little success if Professor Higgins in *My Fair Lady* tried to change the hood Eliza came from (her dad's "Get-me-to-the-church-on-time" crowd), instead of using his own patrician or highbrow abode. Location - the essence of gentrification. If you have to ask what it cost, you can't live there!

Mom, who for one read a lot of good French, told me how her entourage gasped once when she said dad was *un fileur à l'usine* (a spinner at the factory) instead of one *qui runned les mules à la factory* (who ran the mules at the factory.) I never heard it again. Pretension was an unwelcomed guest in our culture. Most of us had little, so we shouldn't pretend we had more, either in fact or speech. Not initially understanding the Bérubé family was Canadian in manners and speech, did we think they were putting on airs, as if cut from better cloth? So, we derided them slightly behind their backs. Isn't it human nature to suspect snobbery and condescension in better-educated people? It reminds us of our educational shortcomings, merited or not.

I thought our patois hung on because the people continued to speak it. Their numbers easily prevailed over the linguistically few of academe, priests, and professionals in the city and Northern RI. In time I grew fond of hearing older folks speak it. Because of their age and Canadian origins, their jargon was "the real stuff." Ours, mingled anglicisms and was not as ancient or colorful. Education and our gradual assimilation into the American mainstream were responsible for that. Our schooling was getting in the way of our French Canadianism. From its once dominant position in the city (especially *au Coin Social*: at Social corner), you only hear it now when the elderly gather. Is this, sadly, the price of assimilation? Someday it will be no more. As in my extended family, we first generation American children understand, speak, and write it, if very imperfectly. Our children understand it very little but don't speak it and our grandchildren neither understand nor speak it unless they've studied it in high school or college. Grandniece Jenna Bouffard while at Mount Saint Charles even told her class how to make crêpes. I begged my Irish Gotham wife to learn how to do them. My brother Ben's wife Gloria is famed for hers.

But gone or vanishing fast, in many ways I still hear faint echoes of my folks' patois in what already-quoted author Luc Santé (*Living in Tongues*) says about his parents' dialect of Walloon (similar to French), heard in southern Belgium. Because of its importance in reading my notes, bear with me as I repeat it: "Walloon is a good-humored, long-suffering language of the poor, naturally epigrammatic (a single catchy phrase like many of mom's), ideal for both choleric (as in heated) fervor and calm reflection, wry (a bit teasing) and often psychologically acute..." He also added, "French is a pipeline to my infant self, to its unguarded emotions and even to its preserved sensory impressions. Also, that there are states of mind, even people and events, that seem inaccessible in English since they are defined by the character of the language through which I perceived them." How many born Francos know or say yes to that?

I especially agreed with the above when it came to our faith and prayers. I recall *Soeur* (Sister) Sainte Émilie who reminded us God was *le bon Dieu* (the good God), instead of "Almighty God" for English speakers. To this day, His goodness resonates more with me than His Omnipotence. I do, however, like those great English hymns: *"The Battle Hymn of the Republic"* and sentimentally *"How Great Thou Art"* for its beautiful natural imagery and majestic sweep; my German Irish wife Pat's (née Smith) final musical blessing and farewell.

Dad couldn't wait for us to speak English or French well. He hated to hear us speak a language hodgepodge that was neither English nor French, convinced that our mélange might prevent our equal progress with others in education, business, industry, and, yes, even higher clerical leadership in the diocese. He was pleased when Bishop Louis Gelineau ascended from Vermont, simply because it proved Francos could. Today from Québec we also know the price of true and separate bilingualism can only be paid with the coin, real or threatened, of disunification and intrusive or nettlesome language laws. (Coincidentally, Pat and I were in the legislature the week Québec was still debating some part of it). But in a negative context, I was shocked when Hitler justified invasion or annexation if people in neighboring countries were of German descent and spoke the language (*anschluss*). The one nation, one speech thing! Once very European.

Mom flashed a quick wit, apt phraseology, and comedic timing that a Jack Benny or George Burns would've praised. That's why I now want to recall some of those expressions and their English equivalent. Anyone knowing French or any language for that matter knows a word-for-word translation does not convey their whole meaning, since those expressions are sayings or idioms where the meaning is more or different than the sum of the words in a grammatical or literary sense. Think of author Santé's use of "epigrammatic" to convey that ... and my mom's upcoming one-liners.

Even if the reader has no knowledge of our patois, I thought it useful, perhaps valuable, to record some of them, because their speech was their life and their persona in America, a country whose own identity, so poignantly evoked in Emma Lazarus' poem about the Statue of Liberty, is a nation of immigrants and of course different languages, at least initially. The criticism today is that American speech is full of stock phrases revealing little thought of the speaker and requiring none of the listener. Young adolescent speech is especially mindless as a college professor wrote, even from perfect SAT scorers. (For example: "whatever," "like," the ubiquitous "cool," or texting in fractured-English.) In comparison, it seems to me that French-Canadian speech, however unlearned, conveyed so much more. As Santé said about Walloon, it was replete with their faith, philosophy of life, human experience, work, and family, loves and fears, compassion, and their precarious grasp on life.

Because of poverty and a difficult life, their speech often had shades of resignation, but also a sense of hope undergirded by their great faith. And as true *pèlerins* (pilgrims) on a lifelong journey to heaven, how often they spoke of that grand design, *le salut éternelle* (eternal salvation). If indeed "the mouth says what the heart is full of," I thought the reader, knowing French or not, might gain insight into the deep recesses of their faith. I said she wrote all those letters, but despite his encyclopedic grasp dad never wrote anything, other than a shopping list. In a sense he was more steeped in that oral tradition than mom. Was he typical of thousands of millworkers who "writ large" on their looms and machines rather than paper? Don't education, opportunity, and career create what our canvasses are?

I've heard the word *joual* in reference to Canadian or French slang. I don't know if it's synonymous with patois or an even worse departure from correct speech. I never heard its meaning as a kid, except for "horse" ... *un cheval*, corrupted to *joual*. Some of these coming expressions are a story in themselves, as I elaborate later in my concentric style. Consider them "talking points" for the moment. Those who still remember some of their high school French may rise to the challenge of trying to mouth them.

1. *Avec tout ça.* With all that! Finally! Perhaps their most used resignation statement.
2. *Il éta sur cinq épingles.* He was on pins (five) and needles. Mom, who always told you where a person was from and their family constellation, often described a person's appearance and emotional state, if in the grip of pain or loss. Unknowingly, she and dad helped me in my later counseling work. And before that in my interacting with my *Call* newspaper customers.
3. *Ya baim tournée.* He turned out okay. There was always the concern whether someone was living a good life and earning salvation. It seemed no one died without the community passing judgment whether the departed had died in God's graces. Had he received the Last Rites, done the nine First Fridays, or gone to Confession regularly? These were all positive signs he or she had "the heavenly ticket." I heard Bishop Sheen once lament that unlike some of the more evangelizing Protestant religions, Catholics were complacent about spreading the faith as lay people. But on the contrary, French-Canadian faith was communal. Good or bad, if someone didn't live up to the faith he professed to be in, the community was shocked and concerned. It promoted a level of public decency whose absence is lamented today. Authors believe morality doesn't hold up without the underpinning of religion, as Cardinal Newman said. And recent popes.
4. *J'laisse tombé ça.* I'm overlooking or accepting that. Another comment of resignation. At a time when social critics think anger and violence are now rampant in our culture, generally French Canadians and other immigrants in a slower time were more self-controlled, more accepting, and less prone to irrational behavior like mass shootings. Is it because there was less sense of entitlement, that someone owed you a living? A lower standard of living with less public or personal wealth may have kept most envy at bay. I cited her labeling the sin of envy useless, since most Francos had no more or no less than their neighbors.
5. *Il éta en travers du chemin.* He was different or off the beaten path. In a culture of sameness and conformity, this was a critical judgment. Just the opposite of the Romantic poets' thinking: "We're born originals, but we died copies."

6. *Il lui manque un bardeau.* He's missing a roofing shingle. She made me laugh when she said it. It's today's "someone's a quart low," "the elevator doesn't go up to the top floor," or "not the sharpest knife in the drawer." All figures of speech about not measuring up.
7. *Un bougonneux.* A malcontent or in Christian thinking, one lacking a sense of that resignation Francos had in the face of adversity. A correct French expression.
8. *J'men sacre baim.* Clark Gable's "I don't give a damn" in patois. Often heard when adversity won over patience.
9. *On sma* (for *se met*) *l' nez dans.* Nosy or involved! Again, you had to balance privacy with that communal circle and spirit we all lived in. True, she for one knew a tremendous amount of stuff about people (kings and queens too), but it wasn't derogatory, and didn't intrude into other people's inner sanctum, beyond the decorum of privacy. Illnesses, for example, were not a matter of privacy like today. She knew about it because French-Canadian life in Woonsocket was her beat, as it was for many, and most especially for *les femmes de maison*: homemakers. And, as someone wrote, in their pedestrian culture, they were far more attuned to the people of the community than us in our fast-moving media-driven lifestyle. Nobody was a nobody.
10. *Cé baim simple.* To tell you the truth! Real easy! Poverty exacerbated life, but the gods favored even the poorest Francos at times. But when they said, *"Le diable s'en mêle"* - "the devil's in the details" - that was Murphy's Law: what could go wrong, did.
11. *Sauver ma peau.* Save my hide. Get away with something. Even with a great sense of personal responsibility, Francos thought themselves lucky every now and then to catch a so-so break, even if many thought that without bad luck, they had no luck at all.
12. *Mon beausoleil est fini.* Literally, the sun's going down on me. A strong resignation comment when a good thing came to an end, like dad's job. But the joy of living on the third floor was seeing the sun going down behind the Hamlet mills: *"le soleil va s'coucher"* (the sun's going to bed), mom said. A gorgeous canvas! I still visualize it. Once farmers, they knew the poetry of the earth, which they missed in mill towns, what with few trees, little greenery, and the absence of flowers and vegetation.
13. *On va jouir d'la vie.* Like the Apostle Paul, they put up with bad times, but rejoiced with the good. (Speaking of a good time, when in training with the Order in Mobile at Spring Hill College, Director Brother Ignatius hired an African-American cook, telling her to watch her speech with us impressionable trainees. Said the cook

Bella with a devilish twinkle in her eye: "I can be good with the good and wicked with the wicked."

14. *Elle éta méchante de santé*. Mom was so sympathetic if a woman's poor health prevented her from managing her household well and having children. Dad's sister Marie Rose, most afflicted with the family's bronchiectasis curse and who died at Wallum Lake Sanitarium, evoked that comment from her. I recall dad, also afflicted, showed me her autopsy report. With the Telliers and the Fontaines, it always seemed to be the lungs, *les poumons*, a kind of genetic curse, like the breast cancer gene today. The poor were more often victims because they were not as protected like others. How often I heard her say *le climat du Canada* was colder and healthier for her, besides less humid. And millwork where unfiltered wool-or cotton saturated the air was injurious to millworkers, as well as causing a loss of hearing.

15. *A toujours été de cérémonies*. A woman who always did things in a grand style. Said in a praising or critical manner.

16. *Ya faite baim des bontés*. A truly giving person whose generosities poor people immensely appreciated during hard times when charity was largely private. For example, she lauded *monsieur* Bérard who gave us free lodging on Mailloux St. during the Depression. Dad in turn admired grocer *monsieur* Belhumeur for his gifts to the poor, besides reserving real butter for us during the war. As *mon oncle* François Fontaine did, grocers allowed customers to put purchases on the bill: "*Met-ça sa slip*" in the 1930s. Some never paid it back, even in good times, but he never lost his *joie de vivre*. St. Paul said, "God loves a cheerful giver," like our uncle was. The perfect public servant.

17. *On ai (est) toujours en l'envers*. If things could go wrong, they did, as Frank McCourt wrote in *Angela's Ashes*. Rachel was bemused by mom's complaint that God always seemed to be after the Fontaines: "*Cé(e) comme-çi le bon Dieu nous en voula.*" If you get past her lament for a second, see how much the notion of God or Divine Providence was in their lives. He alone allowed things to happen. If not Him, then the devil, if evil.

18. *A perdu sa façon*. To lose one's composure. Heard if a highfalutin person got snuffed or got hit with "the perfect squelch." When frustrated artist Nincheri was "forced" to cover up more of the risen Christ behind our church altar, she said it about him, but he won the tempest about unadorned Eve.

19. *Yé dans l' champ d'patates* (in the potato field). Crazy. Or "in left field." The expression spoke to her agricultural roots in Canada.

20. *Yéta un p'tit peu lâché.* A bit lazy! Loose morals. Given their work ethic and moral sense, this was another severe indictment. Since the welfare state was not what it is today, if you didn't work, you couldn't survive or deserve to. I speak of dad worried about the growth of the welfare state mentality, now very entrenched, due to our great population. The $19 trillion-dollar federal debt, the battle line of today's Washington debates.
21. *Y travaille baim son affaire.* The community's approval for a good work ethic. Initiative and get-up-and-go were highly prized because they were handmaids to survival itself, not just a better life. A reflection that we were once a producer nation, not a service one, though it too requires commitment and effort.
22. *On tomba sur l'dos.* Figuratively, crushed or falling on one's back! With most millworkers living a hand to-mouth existence, most setbacks were critical. *Tomber sa paille* ("drop his straw" or "to be penniless") was also Depression-speak. Today's "I'm collecting."
23. *Toujours est-il.* Perfect French, it's another summation or resignation expression, like Walter Cronkite's "And that's the way it is."
24. *C'é(e) ça qui ai (est) notre richesse.* Our happiness or treasure. That's how she weighed life's real values, like family, health, goodness, children, etc., against the material things we lacked. She said it with Christian resignation and pride.
25. *Donner satisfaction au travail.* Do an honest day's work at the job. In this, they both reflected the immigrant work ethic of years ago, when having a job was a bonus, as is now the norm again. Dad said some youngsters lacked it at the mill.
26. *On ava seulement nos quenilles* (rags). Only the clothes on our backs! During the 1938 Hurricane when eight families were all with the Carpentiers on the first floor, comically she said they could lose even their rags. They all roared. Mom could work an audience.
27. *Ça ma faite vieillir.* A costly learning experience! One that took years off your life.
28. *Quand on grouille pas, on mouve pas.* No pain, no gain. Getting the lead out. *"mouve"* is *franglais*.
29. *A jama été dans l'argent.* She never had a cent. Not a *économe* (thrifty) housekeeper.
30. *Ta pas besoin d'avyerre* (*avoir*: have) *peure.* No need to worry. Or "worry *pas* (not)," vestige patois that still survives in today's speech.
31. *Questqu'a chante d'bon?* How's what's her name doing? Because of the insularity and inclusiveness of their lives, what seems like nosiness today was in its best sense the "coffee klatch" exchange of

our mothers. Because of hard times, there was always the curiosity whether people you knew were making it. It was concern for survival, not prosperity.

32. *En twé ca.* For all intents and purposes. I must've heard it a hundred times a day.
33. *Yé pas d'bonne humeur.* Sad sack. Out of sorts. She used the expression also for a baby waking up, crying, disoriented, or wanting to be picked up.
34. *On va l'remettre sur pied.* To help someone get back on his feet. Even though dad thought Francos were sometimes too critical or jealous of each other, they both admired their mutual support in times of crisis. They lauded the Jews especially.
35. *Cé t'après virer en peine.* Things taking a turn for the worse! Said when a sick person wasn't getting better, like with incurable cancer or heart disease, two illnesses they feared most. *La consomption* - TB or related lung diseases - was a close third, or for my parents a primary concern. It's why dad made his own cough syrup, and we wore her little camphor sacks against *la grippe espagnol* (the Spanish flu). And with *mémère's* woolens, we never went outside in winter without being dressed from head to toe: mittens, woolen stockings, sweaters, and knitted caps. They attacked incipient illness with a vengeance. We loved his potion (*une ponce*) for a cold: warm milk, honey, and a spot of French (of course) brandy.
36. *Ya raison d'avyerre soin.* He's got to be careful. With no health coverage at work, they dreaded a prolonged illness. Dad always preached eating good food and avoiding strenuous exercise, like mom did: "*Pa(s) travailler dépasser* (beyond) *ses forces*" (Not working beyond your strength). Like the Latin idiom - *In medio stat virtus,*" virtue stood in the middle of two opposing forces. But out of his earshot, she told me that he and the Tellier clan didn't know when to stop and worked until they dropped. Another fault of his many virtues.
37. *Yava l'air triste.* Someone looked down in the dump. Sad. Mom always picked up on people's emotional look or state, as women are more attuned to do from raising kids.
38. *On été faire les* stores. (We went to the store) Instead of *aller au marché,* they used the word "store." Living with inefficient refrigeration, people marketed often for perishables. Families usually set aside a day to go. For us it was usually Thursdays. We'd pull our homemade wooden wagon from Mailloux St. to Belhumeur store on Cumberland St.

39. *Elle s'en fa craire.* She's putting on airs, a strict no-no in our culture, especially for women. An English writer said women look at each other more critically than men do.
40. *A sé (sait) pas l'tour.* Incompetent. A severe indictment if *une femme de maison* (housewife) was not raising her children and managing her household well. Since it was a full-time role for many, the community judged women that way. It's amazing that with women entering the workforce for good during and after the war, those who stayed at home were sometimes demeaned by others. Presently over seven million who can afford to are full-time homemakers. But like Michelle Moran Zide in Fitchburg, an engaged woman at the time with a PhD, once told me, "I didn't go to college for close to ten years for nothing. I'll raise kids, but I'm working outside the home too." She studied at Fitchburg State College in education. I, with her folks, witnessed the PhD defense of her thesis on the rise of the drug culture. I submitted an article about it to *The Fitchburg Sentinel*. When she spoke to parents of our Crusader Club, the gym was packed.
41. *Bord mwé pas.* A frustrated or exhausted Franco was likely to dip into English to express annoyance. If for no good reason you disturbed mom during her afternoon reading break that was her zinger.
42. *Y'éta toute au contraire.* Confused. Out of sorts.
43. *A sé faite dévorer par les autres.* She was bamboozled. Taken in. It was shocking and sad if someone compromised a woman's virtue through deceit or culpable flattery. It took time for the law to catch up to this abominable crime. Even to this day, one of five coeds in college is molested. Colleges like Dartmouth and Brown are zeroing in on drinking as causative.
44. *On voula s'réchapper.* Hoping to make it. An often-repeated mantra about getting through the 1930s decade especially. In 1940, mom told me she couldn't believe she and dad saved the family. The agony of (or near) defeat had turned into the thrill of victory," as Jim McKay, Olympics announcer, said at the start of ABC's *Wide World of Sports* program.
45. *On y fera d'la façon.* To be nice to someone. Because of tenement living, multiple families, and lack of mobility, life was very much "in your face," good or bad. She used the expression when despite some frostiness with a tenement dweller (always over kids in the neighborhood), she tried to be sociable. For us Francos, living in dense neighborhoods in the second densest state (after New Jersey) in the nation, social tolerance was an absolute necessity. Privacy is

now said to be the last true bastion of wealth with our nation's current level of congestion. But our population was only 125 million back then.

46. *On a seulement ça à faire.* Only one thing to do! Whether she talked about salvation or success in life, she usually predicated success on *s'faire aller*: to get going. Since immigrants quickly realized nothing (or much) was given them, they resorted to sweat, elbow grease, smarts, and prayer to do it.

47. *Ça pa(s) été question.* Cut and dried. Not debatable. In an age when morality and standards of conduct were rather absolute, that was the final word on what was good or bad. No situational ethics or moral relativism. I've read it was once easier to be good, because there were more absolutes and far fewer false prophets. Today a reader is bombarded by scores of differing opinions on all matters of the human condition, even morality. Old Hickory President Jackson said self-interest always intersected with the common good. Treasurer Hamilton and Roger Williams did too; it's why he didn't want the body politic with its questionable morality dictating church matters.

48. *On va vwerre (voire) la beauté.* We're going to see something beautiful. Her optimism and love of life were so evident in that expression. She was *une ricaneuse* (a happy, smiling person). People who knew the Fontaine saga couldn't believe her optimism. Her eyes would tear up with happiness, infusing the whole house.

49. *On peut toujours envoyer.* We can always give it a shot, so typical of her usual grittiness in the face of obstacles. *J'envoyé fort* (I gave it my best shot), she also said.

50. *Tout d'aincoup on nava rien.* Lost it all in a flash, like in the disaster in Canada. We see that often now when television shows us victims of fires, tornadoes, earthquakes, hurricanes, and viruses. (It's why I think often-spared New England is one of the safest places to live in terms of catastrophic destruction, not forgetting the 1938 hurricane and Sandy.)

51. *Ça roder ça.* The word on the street! Or rampant illness! Mom always knew the beat of the neighborhood and city. Hers and *ma tante* Marie-Louise Peloquin's information hotline amazed everyone.

52. *Ça baim (bien) n' été.* Everything went well. Even good fortune smiled on them at times.

53. *Fa pas l'mauvais.* As the Elvis song says, "Don't be cruel...." If we children got mad at each other, she reminded us to be kind. But even with a passel of kids, serious inter-family squabbles were rare. And kids almost never ran away from home, like a million kids now do every year.

54. *Ya pas grand chose à gagner.* Nothing much to gain, so she said, especially if a temporary gain compromised one's eternal salvation. In our more secular, worldly outlook, it may strike us funny or obsessive that this otherworldliness or vision of the grand design was always on their minds or lips. How was our Church so successful in implanting that kind of faith in them? In that sense, they perfectly mirrored Christ's rejection of indulgence, power, and riches in his three temptations in the desert.
55. *On l'wé souvent.* We see him often. (*L'wé* is from the French verb *voir*: to see.)
56. *C'ta pa(s) funné.* Not funny. Francos sometimes used *drôle* instead of the anglicism.
57. *En fin d'compte.* In the last analysis. To make a long story short.
58. *Ya baim d'laction.* A lot of action. Almost never going to movies (unless it was a Nelson Eddy-Jeannette MacDonald flick), she never used it as people did about movies.
59. *Oter* (take away) *l'fancy.* Make it simple. Another Anglicism.
60. *Y senta sa fin.* Death encroaching. Always said with sadness. Because death sealed one's fate, a person's last moments on earth were most precious, like many Shakespearean characters who mostly reflected a moral dimension of good or evil at their demise. (All religions, of course, tout the morality of good works. One recent article spoke about the Bard's Catholicity in his actions and writings, even if he had to be circumspect during England's Reformation. Married Catholic, Henry VIII had 70,000 of his subjects killed, including Thomas More, now canonized, because he didn't sign the King's Oath of Supremacy despite his wife's pleas not to leave her a widow and his children orphans. Catholics like More who refused were called "recusants" from 1570 to 1791. But when Queen Bloody Mary tried to bring Catholicism back, she also condemned refuseniks: martyrs in the Anglican faith. I enjoyed Jesuit John Gerard's book *The Autobiograhy of a Hunted Priest*, who escaped the Tower of London and cheated death, unlike many of his fellow priests during those assaultive times.)
61. *Ya pas gagner diable.* He or the devil didn't win much. Notice the implied relationship between earthly riches and the tempter. Because we depict Lucifer as a buffoon in silly apparel, some theologians think we underestimate his influence for evil in our world. Francos, however, generally had a true notion of his fallen angelic nature and power to seduce. Christ delivered many from the devil.
62. *On pourra baim.* It may be possible to do something. Another example of her unfailing optimism.

63. *Pourquoi s'en faire?* Why get hot and bothered? A "worry *pas* (not)" person, people said she achieved an admirable kind of let-live outlook about things she couldn't control. She reflected the motto of Mother Cabrini, first American Saint: "If God be with us, who can be against us?"
64. *Falla baim prendre ça.* Still another resignation expression where people learned, as the Serenity prayer says, "God, grant me the serenity to accept the things I cannot change; Courage to change the things I can; and wisdom to know the difference." I put it up in my kitchen when I had to learn to run a home, cook, and shop after my wife Pat died. Back from our honeymoon, she had told me, "The kitchen is my domain." All I had to do is show up and do dishes after. A fabulous cook, financial manager, and shopper; I was the chauffeur, repairman, painter, investor, gardener, and vacuum-er. I also took care of son Jim's sports activities. My sociology prof in college said that ideally, partition of household duties should equal 100 percent, but usually not 50-50 due to specific skills, work circumstances, health, and other factors.
65. *Yé smatte.* Smart or learned. This anglicism was the best compliment for good manners and academic achievement. Not many had a chance to better themselves academically, but those who did received that acclaim. See #73 also.
66. *Bavasser latsu*, Talk about something. A woman, however, who spoke too much or didn't keep a secret, was *une bavasseuse*: a gossip. (Men were spared that castigation.)
67. *Manger* (Eating) *d'la misère nwère* (noire: black). Hard times. Spoken when things couldn't get worse.
68. *Il falla à tout casser.* Something had to be done. For example, my jobless father's disapproval notwithstanding, Roosevelt's New Deal was Washington's response to the Depression. We took free rent from our landlord (for some property maintenance) and handouts from the government, even if depressing for him. William Shirer in *The Nightmare Years: 1930 - 1940* said before the war: Mussolini and Hitler as well as Hitler's predecessor Bismarck had not made the mistake of neglecting to help the poor. Did Roosevelt wisely learn from them? Is there some good in evil people?
69. *A pas bonne mine* (pronounced like MIN). Bad complexion or looks. She made Bob, Ben, and I laugh one day when she suggested if we weren't lucky enough to marry a good-looking woman (*une bonne mine*), we should find a good homemaker: *une bonne menagère*. Like other women, she had the matchmaker gene. See also #71 and #72. "Good looking" was also "*des beaux traits.*"

70. *Ya travaillé comme un fou.* Worked like a dog. Very much a cause-and-effect person, she had a definite reason for most illnesses. For example, you got *la maladie d'coeur* (heart disease) or *un mal au dos* (backache) if you worked too hard. If you ate a lot of *gras* (fat), you got stomach problems or became obese (*pesant*). All that medical talk in our house was a reflection on their concern for health, especially their lung problems. They took their own advice and lived long. They both said if you had an ailment in adult life and took care of it, it took care of you.
71. *Y'éta striker d'ssus.* He fell head over heels for her. Notice the anglicism "strike": attracted to. If mom (our society page reporter!) said that about a couple, they had something going.
72. *Shez pa(s) ousquia trouver ça!* He married badly. When I heard it, she was telling *tante* Laurence what a bad marriage this man had made. Where had he met her? Catholic marriages just didn't dissolve, so you had to get it right the first and only time: "*un bon choix*" (a good choice). Is it why a yearlong courtship was an unwritten rule, besides marrying Franco?
73. *Ya faite des études poussées,* A smart person. Academic degrees. Priests, doctors, dentists, lawyers, and teachers received this accolade.
74. *Ya mangé d'la vache* (cow) *enragée* (tough). Something bad he ate. Teed off. If talking food, it was "meat between the horns," like during the war or a steer that walked all the way from Texas! (Dad knew all his cuts and tried to teach me once.)
75. *Ya travaillé son métier.* Made himself a good worker. A trait so much admired by the community. Before the New Deal, the only sure safety net was your work, if any. You saw jobless mendicants at Social *Coin* where down-and-outers sat cup in hand, like one legless man in front of the A & P store.
76. *J'loaf.* Out of work. Another anglicism instead of *chomer* (unemployed), which mom knew.
77. *A gagner notre respa.* She won our respect, If you began a sentence with A (Ah), as I did, your subject was feminine; if you began with Y (EE) or Ya, the person was masculine. Il (he) and Elle (she) were the correct usages.
78. *A serré la cenne.* Penny-pincher. It's a slur she thought some people used against her, but she justified herself, because she was between a rock and a hard place. I recall she told me she hardly wore cosmetics, never took a vacation, made a lot of her own clothes (hats too) and ours, downsized older siblings' outfits, prepared our des-

serts, and canned a hundred jars of edibles every year, besides putting out 20 meals a week. Laundry on Mondays, hanging it out, and ironing (*repassage*), a 2 to 3 days chore. And, of course, keeping our six-room apartment clean: *un beau logis*. When someone once criticized her housekeeping, she told me we always came first, since she could put off something for a day. She would even get on her knees to do the living room floor. No wonder men outlived their wives at one time.

79. *Ya enduré son calvaire*. He suffered a lot. A reference to when Christ died. Priests and nuns taught us to see the religious dimension of suffering.

80. *Manger du vieux*. Dipping into "old money," your savings, if any. This was a serious step because it meant you weren't working. Now a common ailment. Poorly paid people, or not trained to save, begged for help. Dad often used the expression. My folks had little money in the bank, but he boasted he had one of the first books from the Woonsocket Institution for Savings. They started a bank book for all five children. Hey, twenty-five cents a week really piled up! Mom died in 1988 and fifteen years later, my brother Bob told me the *Providence Journal* listed $62 to my name. Parents often opened an account for a newborn.

81. *Cta un ivrogne*. A drunkard. Curiously, she thought a lot of nationalities were known to have a particular failing (our lips are sealed). If so, was it genetic, cultural, environmental? But French Canadians too, she thought, were a bit too bibulous for their own good. But married for good or worse, women with drunkards nearly always stayed the course, enduring "*de la misère*" (misery), she said. With no car, drunks bobbed and weaved walking home, with us ruffians trying to get money from them. I relate one such story later.

82. *Bwère (boire) sa paye*. A corollary of #81: "drink" your wages. It was considered one of the worst things a man could do to his family, because it meant nothing was left for the week in their hand-to-mouth existence. When so, it was the mother who practically went without food, sparing what little there was for the kids. One local wrote a book about it.

83. *Faire du pousse* (thumbs up!) or *prendre une brosse* (sweep clean with a brush?), that is, to lift a few tankards, especially to excess. Dad's comical expressions for a drinking spree. He made whiskey during the Depression and wine after that, but he drank very little and never went to a bar: "abstemious." Like his garden produce in Bellingham, it was his calling card. How often I heard a relative say, "*du bon vin à Ti-Phonse*" (good wine at Alphonse T.'s).

84. *Ses enfants ont viré mal.* A sad commentary about one's kids turning out badly. It was one of the worst outcomes for a family, since parents thought imparting the faith and teaching good behavior to their children were their callings. (Mom, a wordsmith in her own right, told me *virer* was nautical for *tourner*, as in "to turn." Also used by Arcadians in their own version of French. I loved those little tidbits from her.)

85. *J'nassey pour m'enterrer.* Enough money for my burial. Poor people wanted to be buried properly in their faith. Dad in his old age referred to his best suit as *mon habit d'enterrement*, his burial suit. Not maudlin or depressed, he stated a fact of life for which he was prepared. Mom's burial insurance, purchased in 1920 matured in 1951 at $297! It was, she thought, enough to cover expenses. They both paid for their insurance on a dime-a-week or monthly basis to a collector who always came to the back door on Saturday. *Monsieur* Mailloux was a jovial, talkative person who loved small talk. Mom got a lot of news from him about the community. But actually, her own demise in 1988 cost $3000. The History Channel said until modern times people were much more preoccupied with death than we are now with our longer lives. Do we now think more about prolonging life? But if their life was short, was it perhaps due to disease, malnutrition, hard labor, and lack of today's medical care? But when I read 60 million people died in WWII and 15 million in WWI, I wondered if more people since the dawn of history have died from violence. In the Bible's first family, Cain slew his brother Abel! When God questioned him about it, he, flippantly, said, "Am I my brother's keeper?" About burial insurance or financial readiness for it, are more people now not doing it? But charitably, is it because they have barely enough to live? Or that growing sense of dependency? The latest: Americans have a $14 billion deficit in savings. Women who live longer and retire longer are more at risk.

86. *Ya pas entré dans l'église.* Not allowed in church at death. A family's worst outcome was for a pastor to deny a deceased a church funeral service. It meant he or she was a well-known public sinner whose Christian burial would've scandalized the faithful. (Like the mafia Don Gotti of recent memory, but, as said elsewhere, not his lifestyle, but his non-membership.) It's why, not only public sinners, but even suicides didn't have a church service before depression was better understood! One of the earmarks of a great culture is its devotion to the dead. The French-Canadian community had it. Going to Mass on All Souls, Nov. 2, was like a day of obligation.

People visited cemeteries and had Masses said. Now some are buried without a religious ceremony and not interred in holy ground. Urns, said a writer, are sometimes forgotten, abandoned, or improperly disposed when families move.

87. *Yé mort comme un chien.* Died like a dog. As #86 suggests, it alluded to a misspent life, not worthy of salvation. It's how she described the lot of well-known fallen-away Catholics who had been *lachés* (immoral). So no church burial was in the offing. Like Mussolini, she said, when the Italians hanged him and his *signorina* Clara Petacci by their heels, as I saw in *The Call*. Mom, a reader, liked three things about him, but not his lack of faith. He secured the Vatican for the Pope, filled the swamps around Rome, and made trains run on time, but people turned against him when Italy caved in.

88. *La vache aime son veau* (calf). Again, a good French saying. It meant people, like animals, prefer their own. She said it when naturally one chose kin over strangers whether right or wrong. When I entered the Order, *Frère* Floribert, our formation master, often said negatively, "Birds of a feather, flock together." Elsewhere I cite the poet's witticism: "Home is where they have to take you, when you have to go there."

89. *Chaque quenille a son torchon.* Humanly speaking, a dirt bag loves another. Among others, Rachel liked this one of mom's expressions too. It also meant you liked your own, good or bad, as #88 shows. "Thick as thieves" in English. Mom used it when she saw an instance where "misery loved company." *Quenille et torchon* were rags used to pick up dropped food or dry a wet floor. There were no paper towels then, so those rags, black like the stove, spread dirt and germs in equal measure!

90. *Mon p'tit trou d'cu.* Asshole. (Excuse the indelicacy). From the French *trou de cul* (tail), I suspect. Used like the word "bastard." An angry parent might use it towards a recalcitrant child. Boys did a lot with each other, but not within earshot of their moms, the guardians of public decency. I recount that a couple of families on our street "*parla gra(s),*" that is, they swore a lot. It's the 2nd Commandment that we watched out for or had to tell the priest in Confession. Arthur Milot in *Childhood Memories* makes you split a gut when he relates how an Irishman in Lowell thought his French-Canadian buddies at the mill praised him when they called him that. He went around praising others, saying, "true to key."

91. *Les yeux plus gros qu'la panse.* Overstuffed. Literally, your eyes are bigger than your stomach! Mom used it a couple of times at the

table. Siblings to each other said "*safre.*" Bear in mind the table was sometimes meager, especially during the Depression. With many mouths to feed, children were told to take only what they could eat "*pour en garder pour les autres*". But because of mom and dad's wise husbandry, we always had a fairly plentiful table. His bible was "*You Are What You Eat.*"[8] I liked seeing him tell the grocer exactly what piece of meat he wanted. In jest, if mom didn't have what we wanted to eat, she said, "*Mange ta main, et garde l'autre pour demain,*" about eating only one hand today, the other the next day. If she asked, I always wanted Shepherd's pie, often misspelled Shepard's pie by vendors. (Another peeve of mine is a corpse laying there instead of lying, as in reclining. But it's a lost cause, as police, academicians, professionals all falter. "Laying" is only for putting down something.)

92. *A sé faite démancher*. She had an abortion. I heard her say that to *tante* Blanche in almost inaudible tones. I had no idea of its meaning until adolescence, or that it would launch "a holy war" between pro-life and abortionist forces often masquerading as pro-choice, as stats reveal. (I defer to prophet Jeremias' "I knew you before I formed you in the womb") With mothers having as many children "as the good Lord sent them," aborting was considered unnatural, unmentionable, and extremely sinful. It was long the law of the land and nations and in the bible of even the first feminists. So sacred a calling was motherhood, mom believed a mother dying in childbirth went straight to heaven, like dying for the faith, neighbor, and country. In defense of a fetus, I liked reading it has its own genetic code independent of its mother. And sadly, the irony that passing or not through the birth canal determines whether fetal violence is murder or allowed abortion. The U.S. total now 56 million! What a loss of human capital! In history, nations, like France for one, who experienced a lower birth rate after WWI, lamented a loss of manpower later in war especially. "The civil rights issue" of our times. Abortion in French is *avortement*, which LAROUSSE describes as expulsion, *spontanee ou provoquée avant l'époque* (before delivery). No nation can allow that without somehow paying for it.

93. *Ya baim pleurer sa femme*. Felt deeply the loss of his wife. Also, *J'ai perdu mon gros morceau*, about someone in the married state losing the most precious thing in his or her life, a spouse. The pathos

---

[8] While there are several recent books with the title *You Are What You Eat*, the editors were unable to find a similarly titled publication from the appropriate time period. – *ed.*

was so obvious when someone said it. It was the face of absolute pain. My lot in 2000. Like a widow said on television, so much in life is built on two. But as C.S. Lewis wrote, "Love stories do end in tragedy in life."

94. *Ya pas d'chaire chez os.* Skin and bones! Said of a thin man somewhat like dad. Or more seriously of a cancer victim pining away to nothing.

95. *Yé pas bon en chaire.* Poor pulpit speaker. My folks hated not being able to hear the Sunday sermon well and two of our priests had rheumy, frog-throated voices. (Smokers?) While it's beautiful with artist Nincheri's awesome Last Judgment frescos, our church dome was also extremely vaulted, and like most Catholic churches at the time, the sound system, if any, was poor. Not much better now. The faithful often listened in stony silence and some, like the Apostles in the Garden of Gethsemane, slumbered and slept. But they always came. (In the Order we had more than two hours of prayers and Mass before breakfast, so we too sometimes dozed. To keep the troops awake, a superior in Canada told the Brothers to pray and meditate standing up. One fell asleep and fell forward, wiping out three rows of chairs. Studying Saint Paul in the morning at Sharon, MA for my master's degree and certificate in religion from the Order, I kept one eye open and the other shut while I tried to read. Theology at 6 a.m. does that to you. Paul is very profound. The test was in French, so I couldn't believe it when the Provincial, a Frenchman, praised my style. Properly humble, I didn't tell him that was only half of me!

96. *J'lui envoyer une bean (bin).* Throw someone a zinger. A merited put-down. Protective like most mothers, she was at her best if someone needed to be put down a peg or two. "Bean" was another anglicism.

97. *Té v'nu au monde chez les indiens.* Literally, born on the reservation. It's how the miracle of birth supposedly occurred. For us, it was the extent of sex education. Ignorance was bliss in matters of procreation and sexual morals in general. It was their version of the stork story. Good or bad, Indians, like Russians during the Cold War, got blamed for everything. Misbehaving kids in school were sometimes called *"une bande d'indiens"* (a band of Indians). (One time a Canadian teacher in Canada told his unruly "Indians" all they lacked were feathers. A clever tyke told him they had them, because in French *"plumes"* (pens) also means "feathers." But a lot of Canadians and Francos do have Indian blood evident in traits like deep-set eyes, high cheek bones, and good noses. It's because of

those *coureurs de bois* or beaver hunters who could not survive in the wilds without a squaw. It's estimated Charbonneau of Lewis & Clark fame had around five!)

98. *Ta baim changé, Willé.* Wow! Have you changed! Supposedly said by a woman who after a long separation was reunited with the wrong child instead of her son Willie in one of our Canadian boarding schools. Relatives, neighbors, or friends who hadn't seen you for a long time said that to you in jest if you had gone through a growth spurt, say, in their absence, as I did in my two years in Mobile. It caused mom not to recognize me when I finally returned home. Seeing me in a black suit, she called me "reverend." Then she recognized me and cried.

99. *J'fa ma r'traite.* Doing one's annual parish retreat. These weeklong renewal exercises in Lent, still somewhat in vogue today, featured visiting preachers who in successive weeks spoke to different age groups and genders. It almost had the force of law to attend if you were no longer in school. My parents never missed.

100. *La mort avec ses bas d'laines.* Death as a feared stalker creeping up on its victim in noiseless, woolen socks. To counter this, the good nuns advised us to live as if death came at any moment. They told you about these young future saints - Stanislas? and Berchmans? - who, unlike their playmates, said they would continue playing if death was imminent, because they were ready. That's why for Francos monthly Confession on Saturdays and before Mass was a regular practice for many, along with an Act of Contrition at bedtime. I still do. When, during the Cold War, the Russians had a warhead aimed at every American city with at least 50,000 people, a priest was asked which state was best to live in. He said, "the state of grace." If there was ever a culture anchored on the notion that "we have no lasting dwelling place here," Francos, Irish, Poles, Spaniards, and Austrians did. As surely do other devout faithful in their religions. In the history of mankind, how far back is the belief in the hereafter found?

101. *Ya ambitionné sur l'pain bénit.* Christian imagery (blessed bread) used to mean vaulted ambition in the overuse of a good thing. Mom used it a lot.

102. *Comme un diable dans l'eau bénite.* Literally, like the devil in holy water, that is, extremely uncomfortable and agitated. When she used it, I laughed as I pictured the devil in the holy water font at the entrance to St. Ann's. The nuns taught us never to enter without making the sign of the cross. But the excess water went "to bless" a friend ahead of you in the neck. I broke a font once by pressing too

hard to get enough water from a sponge. The last of the big dippers! Every family had holy water in their home from the Holy Saturday services for the last rites if a priest came for a very sick or dying person.

103. *Fière comme un pape.* Happy or proud like the pope. Favored by my godmother, *tante* Laurence, she meant how proud someone was because of success. *Fière comme un coq* (proud as a peacock) meant the same.
104. *Y çée faite chauffer la coine.* Someone on the hot seat! Never found out where *coine* came from, but she used the expression to describe a narrow brush with the law, humiliation, or the embarrassment of failure.
105. *S'tunne frotteuse.* Over meticulous homemaker. Even though women prided themselves on keeping a neat home, they poked fun at anyone obsessive about it. The afflicted husband could not find his spot. Archie Bunker would never have stood for this at home: "*Y sava pa(s) ou se mette*," mom said about one discomfited husband.
106. *Un catholique à gros grain.* A perfectly good French expression for a lukewarm Catholic, a pick-and choose "cafeteria" believer. On the other hand, a holier-than-the-pope type was *plus honnête que l'pape.* She teased dad about that, like returning change to the market, like at Lavergne's Market one time with Mr. Choquette in disbelief.
107. *Ya faite* (made) *son purgatwère* (*purgatoire*) *sa terre.* Atone for one's sins on earth. Nuns and priests said few ever went to heaven directly after death. You spent some time in Purgatory - a kind of delaying or purifying station - to burn the dross and refine the tainted gold of imperfect deeds, as the Old Testament says. Earthly sacrifices and indulgences for good works and prayers shortened the time. (Indulgences were a sore point with Martin Luther, who saw abuses.) If someone suffered a lot on earth like a martyr, she said, "*Ya souffert comme un martyre.*" Saints are believed to go to heaven directly, like Sainte Thérèse de Lisieux and the Good Thief, so Christ said, and still some are canonized sooner than church custom, as was John Paul II (*subito*), and John XXIII and others recently.
108. *Ya gagner sa vie avec ça.* He made a living with this or that. That too was one of the highest praises she gave, because it meant someone had beaten the odds, especially during the 1930s. Economic talk was never about prosperity or how one's investments were doing, but more about making it. Like today's immigrants, they did jobs better-educated Americans didn't, like millwork, mining, and track

laying. Their work was often done under brutal conditions, as my Boston College magazine said, especially the Irish. It reported most Boston Irish kids at one time lost their fathers in their fifties.

109. *Une mémwère (mémoire) à tout cassée.* Unbelievable memory. Given their oral culture, they highly praised any person with great retentive powers. I was too young to remember, but she told me about a homeless mendicant with a huge repertoire of stories begged for a meal in exchange for interesting and funny stories. I suspect he didn't have too many takers, because she said you just couldn't fill him up. *Tout cassée*: they broke the mold (when they made him).

110. *Ya passé pour bel homme.* Handsome man. After saying who someone was and where he or she came from, mom told you whether he or she was considered good-looking. *Belle femme* was an attractive woman. We all thought this was a woman thing, this fascination with people's looks. She thought *pepère* Tellier with his beguiling forelock (like dad's and Bob's) and woodcutter (*bucheron*) build, "*un joli homme*" (a pretty man).

111. *Ya faite le fou.* Behaved badly. Said with an undertone of sadness if someone was headed to jail or died badly and denied church burial. Always, there was the community's ethical judgment whose disappearance many think ushered in today's weak standards of conduct, private and societal. Media has made foolhardiness hot news, as in "bad news is good news." Or how you get famous, often not by achievement, but by notoriety.

112. *Ya pas calculer son affaire.* He didn't think things out. For dad who carefully thought out what he wanted to do, this was a faux pas. A self-made efficiency expert, he always told you how you saved time with forethought. He never made *soupair* or superintendent at the mill (or in proper French: *le patron*), but back home he told you who was a good or bad operative.

113. *A lui a faite un bon chez eux.* A good homemaker. This was one of the nicest compliments *une femme de maison* (a housewife) gave another. Otherwise, an unflattering comment was *A garde un logis sale* (Keeps a dirty home).

114. *Ya couraillé* (running after) *sa fin.* Someone digging his own grave. Or merited punishment. Like poet Walt Whitman said, you were captain of your own ship (soul) in terms of good and evil. If you came to a bad end (*la fin*) because of your own actions, they said that. A notorious ne'er-do-well was called a "public sinner."

115. *J'espère que Saint Pierre lui en passe.* Again, perfectly good French and a humorous reflection on your judgment after death. Catholics are taught you have a private accounting at your death,

ahead of the Last Judgment at the end of the world when all will be reunited with their bodies. The expression speaks of a decedent who might need a boost or oversight from St. Pete at the pearly gates, which engendered funny stories. One was about a sinner who hoped to go in unnoticed with the bishop's luggage (*le baggage de l'évêque*); another, a tight-lipped sinner who wasn't going to bring certain things up unless St. Pete mentioned it first: *avant que Saint Pierre le mentionne*.

116. *Ya une forte constitution*. Strong person. Good health. With dad battling bronchiectasis and mom asthma, how she envied those with good respiratory health. With the way she wished it, I feared it wasn't a sure thing for us kids. Gratefully, with postwar prosperity and medical advances, like antibiotics, all five of us averted pulmonary problems; I, after two infant pneumonias. We avoided the three curses that "bedeviled" their lives: lung problems, little work, and lower middle-class retrenchments.

117. *A la mode de Bretagne*. Like in a unique fashion. Perhaps a valid French expression and a favorite. She used it for someone who did things with a flourish or unusual manner. Perhaps people in her part of France (Northwest near Normandy) were once considered flamboyant. Like Texans?

118. *Att'lée comme la chienne à Jacques*. Attire outside the strict canons of French-Canadian dress, "like Jack's dog." Living so close to so many people, comments, good or bad, were inevitable. Something now back in vogue with the internet and Facebook.

119. *Ça ya*. Another resignation comment. Her cry - "So it is" - when I broke the news to her at Saint Antoine of dad's death at Fogarty Hospital (now the Rehabilitation Hospital of RI) on Father's Day in 1982.

120. *D'la créature*. Women. A friend of mine also used "*de la brebis*": lamb or ewe. The implication is one of gentleness. (Forget about the Lady Macbeths and Ma Barkers.)

121. *Mitaine*. A Protestant church in patois. We thought it came from "meeting house," but I think it has another derivation, wrote a local pastor in an article.

122. *Ai adrette* (adroit)). Skillful, especially with the sewing machine. Dexterity was a valued skill with immigrant women who made or altered clothes. A next-door neighbor, *madame* Bernadette Beauregard, was absolutely super in her estimation. Generally, instead of taking in wash as some poor Irish immigrant women did, these women were "*faiseuses de butin*," or home-based *couturiers* (seamstresses). Mom loved the gift of *un patron* (a clothing pattern). To

me they looked like membranous cutout dolls. If you saw a new one on her Singer sewing machine, *tante* Laurence was often the giver.

123. *On va faire la noce*. Going to have a blast. Because good or prosperous times were infrequent, people revved it up at New Year's Day, Easter, Christmas, weddings, baptisms, and family get-togethers. Conviviality was second nature. About a convivial person, she said, "*Ya beacoup d'entregent*." Like people in the Middle Ages, a lot of their celebrations were church based, now most are secularized and commercialized.

124. *S'casser la tête*. To rack your brains. She often goaded us to work hard to succeed, praising men and women - inventors, scientists, doctors, and others - who worked hard to discover things to make life easier. She had a fascinating notion that God had purposely kept secrets of nature hidden, so his creatures could discover them throughout time with their creativity: *leur génie*. Was it a private revelation or from her *feuilleton* (serial) or magazine? I admired my factotum and omniscient father, but I found her absolutely fascinating too, because she was always thinking or saying things I thought no one else knew or said. For me, she was the books we never had. She could generate knowledge from knowledge. Elsewhere I call it *la théologie selon Léopoldine* (theology according to Léopoldine). Again about the curse of limited means, for her too it meant "Many a flower is born to blush unseen and waste its sweetness upon the desert air." But luckily, we children benefited from her sweetness and light. Yes, she and dad not only raised us, but brought us up in the full meaning of that term. And because parenting was their first and biggest calling in life, they never seemed unfulfilled.

125. *Mon p'tit torrieux*. You mischievous brat! An epithet you often heard an angry or frustrated parent say to a child. I'm not sure of the origin of *torrieux*.

126. *La fin est venue avec tout ça*. One of our favorites and a good translation for *Finis Coronat Opus*: The End Crowns the Work, or Shakespeare's "All's Well That Ends Well." A fitting epitaph for French Canadians and others like them who often lived into old age and died peacefully in the grace of their God. And this despite a life severely tested by the stress of immigration, World War I and II, the Spanish Influenza, the Great Depression, the mills leaving, and the travails of becoming citizens in a country that largely, at first, didn't share their faith and customs and mocked their language. It even questioned their loyalty at times. But most Francos lived their entire lives in His grace and echoed dad's dying words: "*J'veux m'en aller. C'est mon tour*": I wish to go. It's my turn. Like St. Paul's wish:

Cupio dissolvi et esse cum Christo: "I wish to die and be with Christ." If you love life, as most of us do, think of the faith required to say or wish that either as a dying mill worker or as the Apostle of the Gentiles did. It was also the wish of St. Theresa of the Child Jesus. And without a mention of Christ, from deist Quaker Ben Franklin, who knew his aging body would be renewed in the afterlife.

Cultured Pearls in a French Wasteland

IT'S SOMEWHAT ERRONEOUS to say our milieu was a complete linguistic wasteland. There were several sources or opportunities to learn good French. We did *un peu* (a little) by cultural osmosis or exposure. Real French and our patois culture vied for ascendancy.

Even if by today's collegiate training standards, our religious teachers (*Les Soeurs de la Présentation de Marie*)[9] probably had few advanced degrees, but I suspect no more nor less than many religious Orders like mine at the time before college degrees. But our nuns spoke a clear, grammatical French devoid of our crude anglicisms and patois. But by dint of their teaching status, membership in a French-speaking Order, and their birth in Canada, they were, like our priests and some professionals in our world, part of the local intelligentsia. "Birth in Canada," since mom told me, if known, where in Québec most of them were born. How in the world did she know? But she didn't know *Soeur* (Sister) Donat who was a Rhode Islander.

If we stayed longer in school, in smaller classes, and the city more amenable to correct French, they probably would've emphasized usage rather than rote memory of French grammar and exposed us more to French literature. But our mill culture forbade it, and language labs and other learning tools were still eons away. And after all, we were just grammar school kids, and language study has always been largely a high school subject, except for a few school systems. In fact, my wife Patricia, a reading teacher, told me how the mind's ability in a young child to learn a language as fluently as a native person is quickly over. High school is way too late. Prosperous school systems with language saturation programs in the early grades (2nd or 3rd) achieve dramatic results. A teacher in Bellingham and resident of North Smithfield once tried to start it in town, but was it too prohibitive? Holliston, MA, has it, I believe. For a whole year a young child is taught only in a foreign language and becomes fluent in it with no loss of English proficiency.

---

[9] The Sisters of the Presentation of Mary.

But now let's recall more in detail how it happened that we were once presented with a golden opportunity to hear and learn proper Canadian French in our tenement house. That linguistic tsunami was the arrival of that family - *les* Berubés - into the first-floor apartment next to *les* Carpentiers. Mother, father, six daughters and son all spoke French purely as we thought educated Canadians or Frenchmen did.

However, with that characteristic suspicion (and mild derision sometimes) of the unknowing toward the knowing, initially nearly all of us mocked them for their savoir- faire. Their purity of language confirmed they just hadn't fallen off the proverbial turnip truck like the rest of us with our mishmash of crude French or patois and bad English. So all of a sudden our patois seemed hick. And since we felt bad, we wanted to get even "for showing us up." They were different and that was unpardonable. Wasn't it an unwritten cardinal rule of our life that we were all cut from the same cloth and shouldn't try to be what we weren't? What were Professor Higgins of *My Fair Lady* and his minions doing in our "ethnic ghetto?"

Also, even though we were in the main rather well-behaved children (parents tolerated no less than that), the Bérubé children's respect for their parents also engendered those put-down feelings in us. They were polite and obedient in a way we were uncomfortable with. It's why dad even pointed them out as examples.

Even the names of some of the girls, like Pierrette and Ghislaine, were too Canadian, not Woonsocket-ish. You swore most families in the city picked their children's names from the same list of about 30-40 choices. Of boys, our eight-apartment tenement had at least four Roberts and at least two Renés. My brother Bob had his complete namesake down the street. The Christian practice of choosing a saint's name at baptism for heavenly protection limited the list. Greatly adding 20th Century saints to the list, Pope John Paul II hopefully lessened the selection of faddish or Hollywoodish monikers, which made mom cringe after the war. "*Des noms a coucher d'hors,*" - names not domestically French or "Catholic" - she sighed.

But soon, our initial derision was replaced by toleration, acceptance, and finally friendship. Even though our own speech never improved by exposure, we gradually appreciated the modicum of true Canadian culture they brought to the hood. Did we look better by association? Faith-wise, I cited how *madame* Bérubé rendered the link between French and Catholicity in what seemed French poetry.

They also brought the sound of piano music to the tenement. None of the 41 residents played any instrument besides the radio, a wit said. In fact, my sister Rachel learned to play the piano by ear, sitting next to Pierrette (the youngest, the neighborhood would soon call her Perry) when she practiced. Now a Michigander with husband John, she worked so hard to speak English without an accent, she never tried to teach her children any French. Is this the inevitable price of total acculturation in a new country? And the end of the put-down, "You're French, aren't you?" Even majoring in English in Mobile, I still didn't have the accent down pat, my southern Brothers said. Was it that last accented syllable in French speech sneaking into our English parley? The" Rebs" (not all; some from N.Y.) also caught me mispronouncing "yacht." We Gaulinites were all landlubbers; our parents came to America by train, not by boat.

Several real French families also lived next to Lavergne's Market at the bottom of Gaulin. Whenever you saw them, they always had two huge dogs, black and brown, trailing them. Tenement dwellers like us usually had no pets. Since they had no children playing in the hood, attending school, or attending our church, they didn't enter our everyday world. No one on our hilltop ever spoke to them. Only about them, kindly. Their perfect French heard at the market also set them apart from us. Hard for us kids to figure out how someone spoke French and was not a parishioner. Had they lost the faith, as some thought: *perdu la foi*? Or did they go to a Protestant mitaine (church)? Or were they Frenchmen who came here as union activists, as I once read?

Of course, many lost the faith during the French Revolution, but mom showed her erudition when she told me about French Protestants called Huguenots, aka Calvinists, led by "the Father of the French Protestants," Jacques Lefêvre. In Champlain's bio, one of the early Canadian settlers was sent back to France because he was a Huguenot and created tensions between him and all Catholics there. But I was surprised to learn Champlain himself had once been one and his wife too but converted to Catholicism when they married. Those practitioners came mostly from La Rochelle, so recruiters for Canada shunned that town. The first Québécois came from above the Loire River; the Acadians below it. That one faith, one nation thing! Many Huguenots who had great artisan skills (a great loss to France), like the Dupont family, came to America or England to avoid religious intolerance from the French king. Some settled in East Greenwich during the Colonial Period. And Gabriel Bernon, who never lived here but after whom a Woonsocket district/village was named, was one of them.[10] A house bears his plaque. In France, there were no less than seven internal

---

[10] Woonsocket was once six villages with Woonsocket Falls the largest. The others were Bernon, Globe, Hamlet, Jenckesville, and Social. The Eastland woodland Indians - mainly Nipmucs, Wampanoags, and Narragansetts - were the first inhabitants.

clashes, some bloody and criminal really, between them and Catholics. An invitation to a wedding was a slaughter.

No one ever questioned mom about her knowledge of her own people. But if you asked her why she was so interested in other countries and cultures, especially royalty, she said she liked knowing "*Comment les autres vivent ou ont vécu*": how the other half lived. Like other reformers, those Huguenots were shocked by the luxurious life of prelates, excessive fees for church services, harsh regulations, and the "sale of indulgences." Unfortunately, they chose to break away from the one church that had united Europe for about 1,500 years, rather than reform it, as the Council of Trent did later.

To give them their due, Dorothy Mills in her *Renaissance and Reformation Times* said reformer religions with their insistence on local church control, as opposed to centrist Rome and bishoprics, unknowingly influenced the notion of self-rule in government-by-the-people, away from autocracy, royalty, and oligarchy. But unfortunately, says Mills, Martin Luther, for one, lived during the papacies of two less-than-admirable popes which may have helped his severance and the start of his own religion. (An article compared these breakaways to a baseball game. They didn't like the umpire's calls, (the teachings of the Pope and church), so they let the batter call the pitch: self-interpretation of the Bible, which spawned a multiplicity of religions, weakening Christ's call of *Ut unum sint*: That they all might be one. Some left the faith completely when these new religions had conflicting beliefs.

In the Brotherhood I lived in Mobile for two years and thought it was a city of churches. But Woonsocket, the northernmost city of Rhode Island, deserved that designation no less since at one time it had 11 Roman Catholic and 3 Baptist churches as well as Apostolic-Pentecostal, Assembly of God, Church of Christ, Eastern Orthodox, Episcopal, Jewish, Lutheran, Ukrainian Catholic, United Methodist, and Universalist congregation. As RI historian Patrick Conley wrote, "Roger Williams and Dr. John Clarke sought separation, not to free civil society from religious influences and expressions of religious faith, but to prevent the states from interfering with a person's private religious beliefs." Williams' ordeal to obtain "religion free" is chronicled in John M. Barry's *Roger Williams and the Creation of the American Soul*. "In secular America this intention has been disregarded and reversed over the past three generations." In the book Barry relates what the Dutch in New Amsterdam (later New York), fearful of business competition, thought of Rhode Islanders as: "scumme" and "riff-raff" and the colony as a "sewer" and "*latrina*." Some Bay Staters shared those sentiments and wanted to take away what exiled Williams bought from the Indians. Because its first settlers were all like Williams with their resistance to any government control of religion, like Puritanism, Calvinism, Anglicanism, they were despised initially. Some think their reactionism and stubbornness became part of the RI soul! Is this a fair assessment of Rhode Islanders? Do Ocean Staters ascribe to a belief system of "Do not be the first to try something (like using seat belts; giving up smoking; and avoiding single party politics), nor the last to leave the old aside?" (Historian Conley laments the Cranston West prayer mural objection, as well as the Woonsocket military memorial objection by outsiders.)

Inevitably some of the 30,000 habitants like my parents who generally came to RI from 1860 to 1916 would come out of their severe religious and ethnic immigrant view. Through education, both world wars, media, and interaction with others, assists from their better educated children, church renewal, and more overall civic tolerance; they embraced a more multiracial outlook, both local, state, and national.

There was also a Lepoutre French family living at the top of Kendrick where it meets *Ellem* (Elm St.). Even if extremely devout churchgoers, they were upper crust industrialist people who owned, for one, the Lafayette mill where dad worked for close to 40 years. He spoke well of their conservative black dress, piety, and pursuit of education. He admired any nationality or family that prized education, chiding Francophone families for their reluctance in this regard, not forgetting, however, their meager means, millwork, and farming heritage in Canada. Some of those Lepoutres also attended the Academy and even owned a small mansion below Academy grounds which the Order eventually bought to train recruits before reselling it. They were among the families encouraged by Aram Pothier to build mills locally when he met with them twice in France. Avoiding President McKinley's tariffs was a motivation. Even though the city was already a burgeoning textile endeavor, said industrialist Jacques Staelen, his ambition was to make the city "The Queen of the Blackstone Valley." No doubt the governor was largely responsible for the Tellier and Fontaine related families and thousands like them coming to Woonsocket to find work in those French-like *usines*: mills. With French Canadians willing to work for less ("the Chinese of the East," as they were disparagingly called), resentful earlier-come Irish plied arduous jobs like track laying and canal building. They also worked in the Millville rubber shop over the MA border.

In *Nothing Like It in the World*, Stephen Ambrose said thousands of Irish also signed on to build the Transcontinental Railroad from 1863-1869. But "with gold in dem thar hills," when they got out west, many worked just a few weeks to build a stake and then ran off to dig in the bowels of California for gold or silver. (*Mémère's* own brother in Canada went twice to Alaska - the Yukon Gold Rush for one - along with 160,000 others.) With the rush to the gold mines, the Chinese arrived by the thousands to finish the railroad, displaying an incredible work ethic, while enduring thousands of fatalities due to horrendous working conditions. Since, as a wit said, no good deed goes unpunished, they later suffered the indignity of being refused admission to California and the country. (A lot of our immigration policies used to depend on whether Americans were willing to do certain jobs! This was revived somewhat in the 2008 recession.)

The Lafayette mill complex was on Hamlet Ave. where the city's middle schools are now located. Only two structures survive. The small building below the left smokestack was the administration building and the smaller structure near the now gone train tracks was the guest house. Today it is often referred to as the guard house but that is incorrect.
(Courtesy of Woonsocket Historical Society)

So, in union-speak, the mills were almost like "language shops," since you practically had to know the language or quickly learn it to talk to someone, at least in totally French enclaves. As dad did, I offered a *bonjour* if we met those Lepoutres on our way to church, since they walked as we all did. They also attended every morning Mass during Lent, and the Marian devotions in October and May. No family ever "bought" (reserved) a pew, like in some Protestant churches at one time, but no one ever denied them theirs up front on the people's right side of the nave. Like us from *la grosse* (big) Gaulin and the nuns, they came in from the door on the right attired in their somber, almost funereal-looking outfits. As people once did in the presence of "gentility" or "their betters," we kinda' stood still and gaped if they walked by you. Our closest brush to wealth, glad rags, or perfect French. Mom spoke of their *"moyenne taille"*: medium height, just like us Francos.

Our parish priests - the pastor and his three or four curates - delivered their sermons in good French. But however much we listened, or dad quoted this or that line from sermons, our patois remained entrenched. When they came to the house for the parish visit, we were in awe not only "of the cloth," but also of their speech and educated ways. For the Irish and us, they were our nobility, long before the Kennedys were saddled with that role nationally, if not as nobly. Remember that Francos lived in a kind of theocracy or government by God or his emissaries like Jews did in Moses' time. Church pronouncements or regulations had great importance in their lives, but those were never in conflict with legitimate temporal authority, contrary to what the Know-Nothings (aka the American Party) and Maine's KKKs thought. These radical nativist anti-Catholic, anti-immigration groups espoused an exaggerated patriotism as neo-Nazis do today. Active in Maine at one time, said a Museum of Work & Culture speaker, they even scared parents from teaching French to their children. Their oppression also caused some to anglicize their names, until the threat was over.

In a French-Canadian home, if you did anything wrong, parents and teachers were more likely to tell you which Commandment you broke, not the law of the land. Mom frequently used Moses' Decalogue[11] to keep us in line. She knew we went to Confession every month as she and dad did. That's why *Père* (Father) Moreau in his chaplain's minute at scout meetings told us juvenile judge Jalbert couldn't remember when he last saw a French-Canadian kid in his court, which I repeat several times. There's no greater praise about our culture's genius in raising children! Hillary Clinton's conviction that it takes a village to raise a child was embedded in those structures we stress in this book: home, neighborhood, school, church, and for us boys, scouting. Each unit had at least four guardians watching its back. It's why their center never gave way.

On the national scene, presidential hopeful Alfred E. Smith (1873-1944) battled to disprove Catholics like him weren't citizens of Rome first and the U.S. second. Amazingly, rumors circulated that if Smith defeated Hoover in 1928, the pope would move to Washington! A capital, mind you, surrounded by church sites that were really gun emplacements, bigots thought, wrote Bragdon McCutchen in *History of a Free People*. Was I reading fiction? He later said the same prejudice that hurt Smith might hinder Kennedy's bid against Nixon in 1960. His victory, however narrow, laid to rest the notion a Catholic could not be elected president. (When I toured the Air Force Academy as a counselor, a teacher-guide told us there was talk about too many Catholics on the staff. Upon scrutiny, they realized our religion taught and upheld the same principles, like other faiths, of conduct they wanted in their cadets.)

I personally like to think that because some of that Irish animosity was due to their faith (for us, more our language), they deserved Christ's

---

[11] Decalogue is another term for the Ten Commandments. – *ed.*

own praise for that Roman soldier whose daughter he healed: "Truly, a greater faith in all of Israel I have not seen." Hardened by "the slings and arrows" of bigotry, is that why "Keep the Faith," was an everyday greeting for the Irish? In college as a future Latin teacher, I found it amusing when I heard that the phrase "Hocus Pocus," referred to the supposed dark, mysterious rites of the Mass, and is actually a corruption of *Hoc Est Corpus Meus* (This is My Body), said at Consecration. They couldn't even get the Latin right! When my sister Rachel's family moved to the Deep South many years ago, she heard it too and was shocked, if I recall correctly, when asked if Catholics still had "Black Masses" in which children were sacrificed!

Recall that this reverence for the clergy was why every Francophone family, mom said, aspired to have one of its male children called to the altar or any other religious life. For daughters the convent was a preferred life path. Large families made that happen more often. Humorously, in the South I once tried to explain to a little boy in a watermelon patch what a religious Brother was. Nothing worked. Finally, I told him we were "men-sisters" and he understood.

Mom spoke with pride about members of *mémère's* family, *les* Morvans, in the priesthood (Gabriel) and religious life (Edgar) with the Oblats in Canada. *Père* (Father) Gabriel visited us and promised to return later and entice me to become a member of founder "Mazenod's Army," as boyhood friend and fellow scout Vincent Auclair did. Sadly Vinnie, Mount Saint Charles '48, died young as a missionary in Haiti, soon after I emceed festivities for his 25th year of ordination. He served his far-flung, 75-mile parish on a motorbike. MSC grad, priest, and friend, Normand Demers '50, greatly aided his missionary work in education with a new school. When Gabriel came back many years later, I had said no to *Père* Moreau's invitation to ascend the altar and had joined the Brothers so I could teach. I never thought I would ever counsel, as my dad did so superbly. If I had known, I would've asked God to confer a *Talis Pater, Talis Filius* blessing on me, meaning "like father, like son."

When my family lived on the corner of Mailloux St. and Cass Ave. across from the hospital, I befriended a tyke who was French and I found his mother's speech so Parisian in its purity and inflection. Come afternoon, she offered us a sandwich (*une tartine*) and money to buy candy at the little store, corner of Wood and Cass: "*Quelques sous pour acheter des bons-bons.*" But alas, we moved and I lost my first Gallic oracle as well as a young girl playmate who one day suggested I steal matches when mom was napping. I lit my short pants and mom put out the fire when she heard me scream! I then got the warning all misbehaving mill town kids got from their mothers: "*Attend qu'ton père arrive d'la factorie,*" about dads meting out domestic discipline after their shift at the factory. Boy, that's all dad needed to hear after a day at work! Kids aren't that sophisticated but it was so obvious to the guys that mill workers like dad lumbered rather than walked and were stoop-shouldered rather than erect when they marched up *la* Gaulin after their work shift. It's no wonder men plying that trade were not generally corpulent or *"gras"* (fat). But dad, *le grand maigre*, seemed thinner and taller than most, like an actor I liked in my first movies in the 1930s: Slim Summerville. Or *Barnaby Jones* and *Beverly Hillbillies* star Buddy Ebsen, whom I once spoke to in Newport. I say later that homebound women with many children put on weight as they got older, but not the men. Eating a dry sandwich while chasing the mules or other machines kept them lean, but not mean.

But did we think good French was strictly the reserve of our parish church, school, or *les* Berubés? What a surprise when Sue enrolled at Woonsocket HS in the early 1940s and had difficulty with her French course. Mom said a teacher chided her for a meager vocabulary, poor grammatical sense, and especially her non-Parisian pronunciation. Her patois just didn't cut it at the school with its trained French teachers. Gerard J. Brault in his book mentions a continuing tug-of-war in academe between Canadian and Parisian French. But there's no mention our patois has ever been in the ring for legitimacy or supremacy among them. Like so many disappearing dialects all over the world, is it struggling now to hang on? But that's why I was so pleased two Ph.D. college professors, Cynthia Fox of the University of Albany and Jane Smith of the University of Maine at Orono, undertook a study and conducted recorded interviews of Ghislaine (Berubé) Parenteau, cousin Eugène, myself, and others. Their goal was to validate the continuing status of our patois as a valid language of a distinct group of people. A form of speech that expressed so well the totality of our lives, with some word-pilfering from the King's English. And who knows, is it still extant in parts of New England found especially among the elderly? Can it also be found in France where it was once the dominant parley in hundreds of little hamlets?

But locally because we remained impervious to all the above good French influences ("cultured pearls"), we continued to savor and use our patois, good or bad. More later, but about *l'Académie* in France's mission to keep the language pure, Cardinal Richelieu said his purpose was "to clean out the garbage from the mouths of common folk and also to rein in the nation's elite thinkers." Today language cops provide instruction manuals in French. But Victor Hugo, 19th Century novelist, wrote, "The word is a living thing," meaning the nature of language is fluid and almost defiant of regulation, as we now see with English becoming just staccato electronic beats for many. But our speech was colorful, convenient, and often humorous. It's only when I was in college that I learned our patois wasn't the only word borrower. England in its empire heyday also assimilated words from its vast colonial possessions, like those 90,000 words from its defeat by the Normans and their Latin-enriched culture in 1066. The Romans also bequeathed words too from Caesar's conquest some 600 years earlier. Now ours is a million-word language understood by half of the world's 8-9 billion people! In my visit to Sweden with the Cerrone family and the Andover Prep hockey team in the 1970s, every native we spoke to understood English. (But they didn't like their pro hockey players wanting to play here. One man I spoke to remembered Jim King, Mount Saint Charles grad '70, for his hard shot the year before. He played on one of the great lines at MSC with Bob Cooper '70, and John Harwood '70.)

The Longest Peaceful Border in the World

AGAIN, IF PERHAPS I've created the impression our French-Canadian language and culture may have harbored more limitations for us than benefits, I'd like to even the score a bit more. Our language and culture did prove an invaluable continental legacy for the vast immigrant bands that continued to speak French here or learned it here. In playing softball in the Charles Baldelli League, I spoke to several non-Francos who learned to speak our patois because they married French-Canadian girls to fit in better in the city.

Doesn't the border between Canada and the states constitute the longest and most peaceful stretch between two countries in the world? George Russell in his *Time* magazine review of Andrew Malcom's book *The Canadians* cites him, "In fact, the 49th parallel is like no other border in the world: some 70 million people casually cross it every year, and at any one time each winter, roughly 4% of the Canadian population is living in Florida. Canada and the U.S. share everything from electrical power networks to deep ties in blood and marriage." Alexander Moens, international politics teacher, noted $700 billion Canadian dollars in bilateral trade amounts to 75 percent of Canada's gross domestic product. Wow! A curious anomaly, however, is while America is turning more conservative (?), Canada is going liberal on life issues. Does it mean "never the twain shall meet?" Historians say that often the mother country goes liberal first, while "the provinces" remain more conservative. For example, the faith has seriously eroded in Québec compared to us. Catholics are less than 20 percent of the population now; 90 percent decades ago. But Robert Lecke in *A Few Acres of Snow* waxes ecstatic about the relationship of the two countries: "The disparity of population and climate between these two neighbors - both enormous in landmass - living amiably side by side, speaking or at least understanding the same language and enjoying the same liberties as neither enjoyed in their infancy, is nothing short of incredible." Do we appreciate what having a good neighbor means?

I've always found Cape Cod a good place to hear Québecois. Once I enjoyed a touching Canadian family scene at Nauset Beach (a family favorite) in Orleans. A family waded in, leaving a forlorn *jeune fille* (young girl) on shore. Crying out, *"Papa, viens me chercher"* (Daddy, come get me), her *paterfamilias* came back to bring her *"au sein de la famille"* (within the bosom of the family), as mom used to say. A couple of decades ago, many Francos in the city had those "deep ties in blood" with Canada, as few still do today, but tenuously I suspect, like my family with never-seen first and second cousins on the Fontaine side. One first cousin, Paul Villemure died in 2013 in Cochrane where the Fontaines were routed in 1916. I was grateful for sharing his research on the fateful forest fire of 1916, which niece Patsy (Bouffard) Severson has done too.

I expressed admiration for dad's insights. Once he said, "There was something in the Canadian mind at one time that didn't like aggressiveness or promotion in oneself or others, as if you had to know your place." If so, is it a little chink in the armor of the Catholic, cultural, and linguistic oneness of Canadians and French Canadians? I guess he knew instinctively what I only learned in the Order, that envy or jealousy, as a saint said, is a useless sin, since it doesn't help its agent at all, either in the short or long term. On the other hand, besides their love of education, he admired the Jews for their great mutual support, perhaps a result of their history of persecution and discrimination. But in my latest trip to Canada, I read many think our influence is too encompassing, and that Canada is slipping into a kind of satellite status vis-à-vis us, however unfailingly friendly. Many nations think it's a role our country has taken on after becoming the world's only superpower after the war causing us to become "the world's policeman." An author has also written that our consumer excess, need for more energy, and borrowings have all prompted our nation to develop an aggressive foreign policy stance to ensure those sources stay out of enemy hands, like in The Middle East. But self-sufficiency in energy is finally in hand in 2015. Low gas prices mean billions of dollars can be spent on other family necessities. (My first car after I left the Order in the early 1970s, could be filled with gas for less than three dollars. Now, just one-gallon costs me more than that. Hybrids and electric cars are alleviating that.)

Also, how quickly in life we in the city, New England, and beyond learned the truism of *Qui sait deux langues, vaut deux hommes*: speaking two languages is like doubling your worth or influence. Mom knew and told us which cousins and acquaintances, especially in the European theater of war, doubled as interpreters and translators. More later, but among my five soldier Peloquin cousins who served during or after the war, Normand *et*

Raymond were often called upon in WWII or after because of their fluency in French. An army careerist, Normand spent five years in France with a military intelligence unit, keeping in touch with French agencies and finding time to visit un *orphélinat* (orphanage) to give kids *un bon Noël* (a good Christmas). In Hawaii in 1971, he was one of five interpreters helping Lon Nol, the U.S-rescued Prime Minister of Cambodia who was brought there with his family by President Nixon. Since Nol and his entourage spoke little English, Normand and his group translated during his visits with doctors and military briefers. When Nol was well enough, a pleasant duty was to drive him around to see the sights and get him to his therapist. Raymond, who with his brother-in-law Eugène Godin and Norman Malo, was in a post-June 6 Normandy landing with the 83rd Infantry Division and the 329th Infantry Regiment, respectively, returned to France no less than 15 times until his death in 1996. Because he had been one of their liberators and *parlait leur langage* (spoke their language), he, like others, were always welcomed like conquering heroes. According to his brother Gene, he had a role in one or more of the 50th anniversary celebrations of the invasion, helping local officials with, *sacré bleu* (damn it), those Anglo-Saxon, Irish, and Italian names.

I also had five Lebel first cousins in WWII. Imagine 10 first cousins from only two families in the military in or postwar. And the Lapierres (names later) from Burrillville, cousins removed, were another quintet! Historians also have lauded the numbers and patriotism of the immigrant Irish who so quickly volunteered to fight in the Civil War. But in it also and subsequent wars, Francos were no less patriotic or numerous, given the size of those habitant families. In my extended family, this zeal for military service is historically fitting since the first Tellier *et* Fontaine in North America had been in one of these regiments of the French king: LaFouille, Froment, Chambly, Rougement, Carignan-Salières especially. These regiments fought the Turks in their forays in Europe and their victory gave rise to a feast day in honor of The Most Holy Name of Mary, celebrated September 12. Thousands of Canadians fought in the Civil War, many as paid replacements for Americans, and were given lands in northern New England and New York in gratitude. Many too in the Revolutionary War, but not without incurring the wrath of their countrymen still angered by our attempts to invade Canada (three times all told) and our nation's anti-Catholic sentiment at the time. Some Catholics were threatened with excommunication for serving in our military! More later, but one of my Lowell, MA, cousins even married a French girl he found hiding from the Germans in Berchtesgaden in or near Hitler's own retreat at war's end! When he spoke French to her, Jeanine Serer from La Rochelle near Cherbourg knew soldier Joseph Morvan was a friendly rescuer. Delivering the paper, I met a few French war brides in the city after the war. Their speech was so cultured. What did they think of our patois? But *Je t'aime* (I love you) is universal, isn't it?

When I've traveled to Canada, I've not been able to overlook the mild envy of Canadians hearing our command of both English and French (however imperfect from lack of use). For all their fierce cultural pride to retain their French language and culture, people living in Québec Province know the priceless advantage of bilingualism. Apart from discrimination and racial absolutism, it's their lack of fluency at one time in predominantly English-speaking Canada that long caused them to lag behind their countrymen educationally, economically, and politically. In an article about the Separatist Movement,[12] a Washington Post columnist summed up Charles de Gaule's thinking on the subject: *"Vive le Québec Libre!"* ("Long live free Québec!") Charles wished to revive the historical bonds between *la belle France* (beautiful France) and the province founded by Champlain *et* Jacques Cartier. When I spoke French in a Versailles bookstore, *le commis* (the clerk) said, *"Ce que vous voulez, cadeau."* What you want is free, so overjoyed was he and amazed my ancestors left France 300 years ago.

Mom told me that Canadian French was really 16th Century French frozen in expansionist history. It stirred a kind of pride in me, thinking my ancestral and linguistic roots lay so far back. But isn't that true of all languages, especially English with its foundation in Old and Middle English, all shaped or enhanced by Latin, Scandinavian, French, and German words? Long before our relative *Docteur* Auray Fontaine had the family genealogy done, mom knew her *Pion dit LaFontaine* family went back 12 generations to a Nicolas Pion, who was born in 1575 in Tours. Now my research centers on France itself and time long, long past. About many claiming Canada's first and permanent habitant Louis Hébert is hopefully in their ancestral tree, I hope it isn't like what a comedian said about Washington. If he slept in as many places as they say he did, no wonder "he's the father of our country!" But Hébert was a great moral man and friend of the Indians, whom he wished to convert.

Mom was delighted many Fontaine men were named Louis like her father. Was it because the name in French history resonates with royalty, one of her interests? Where Lafontaine sometimes occurs as a *dit pion* name, she fancied the family might have once lived next to a church tower or a fountain in Tours. In her book, Bonier says the Fontaine name was at times changed to "Spring" by others. And changed back to French later, if the name change was not voluntary: as when in an English neighborhood or, as we said, pressured by the Maine KKK.

---

[12] Known as the Québec Sovereignty Movement, its goal is to separate Québec from Canada to maintain its distinctly French culture. – *ed.*

One ancestor in 1796 shows up solely as Félix Pion. With little education among its members, family names changed often, and not only in spelling. In a similar and interesting vein, friend and family genealogist Patrick Martin-Beaulieu, whose ancestors once lived by a beautiful meadow (hence Beaulieu) in Canada, found relatives in Blackstone, MA, who kept only the original Martin name. I also mention elsewhere the story of a Bellavance, for whom I did translations in Norton; his family name was changed because of some earlier "good fortune" or *belle avance*. Names were derived from one's occupation especially, location, unique happenstance, physical appearance, achievement or even fancy. In 7th grade I never forgot the German named Barbarossa was the red-bearded one. And before William the Conqueror's famous victory of 1066, he was *Guillaume le Batard* (Bastard). This long before all agreed a child's birth is a perfect, natural phenomenon, with no taint stemming from his or her conception. Other name changes I came across are Boies (Woods), Boisvert (Greenwood), Dupont (Bridges), Dupuis (Wells), Lapierre (Stone), Leblanc (White), Lebrun (Brown), Létourneau (Blackbird), Lévesque (Bishop), Poisson (Fisher), Racine (Roots), and Roy (King). In training I had the lead role in a play of mistaken identity where a Greenwood was really a Boisvert.

Mom's encyclopedic memory for current, genealogical, and historical details simply amazed people. When she fell, broke her hip, became disoriented, and lost that great retentive memory in her mid-80s, many people, especially *tante* Laurence, all expressed the pity of it. I had recorded her discussing our history that day until we went to a restaurant. Walking unattended, with little Jimmy behind her, I could not prevent her fall when she tumbled to her right. Mount Saint Charles classmate, Dr. Jean Guay, '48, repaired her hip, but her memory and health declined after that. It's something doctors have noticed in the elderly who fall; their hip often broken before the fall; hers, however, was just impacted. I worked on her memory when I visited her at St. Antoine Hospice. Once she recognized my siblings' names, but about mine, she said, "Who gave you that funny name?" Why is it the messenger is often the one who gets the shaft?

As said elsewhere, Dad's forbears were also from France and a Jean le Tuillier is the first recorded ancestor for us, so to speak. As the name implies, he was a tile maker. Our family name has an English counterpart - Tyler - as in John Tyler (1790-1862), our 10th president. If there had been a family connection, mom would've known. The first Canadian Tellier forbear was Jean-Baptiste Letellier dit Lafortune (yes, a soldier of fortune, as military history records) who disembarked in 1665.[13] He came from Coutances, Normandie, an area, coincidentally, liberated by our American soldiers in WWII, with cousin Ray Peloquin, Gene Godin, and friend Norm Malo fighting in the area. Gratefully, our academic life as a schoolboy at the Academy was easier because of our knowledge of French. While other kids had to struggle with six subjects to get on the honor roll, we "day hops" or "frogs," as we local French Canadians were called, barely had to touch our religion and French books.

I restate the invaluable legacy of the French language and culture has never been more evident than in the last two or three decades or so. With no question in anyone's mind that Francos are now fully in the mainstream of the American culture and language, what a source of pride to boast of our ancestry, speak of the riches of our dual culture, and avidly search all we can of its challenging but glorious past. No wonder Yvonne Beaudry, a New York-based writer who frequently visits France and French Canada, said, "Franco-Americans are homeward bound. These Franco-Americans, together with six million Canadian residents, descend from the 60,000 Gauls who dwelt in New France when it was ceded to England in 1763."

How many English-speaking Franco-Americans felt justifiably concerned when President Jimmy Carter called the lack of language study a national disgrace in this country? How often it's been documented this omission is hurting our international, commercial, and political interests in the global arena? But now with many students hoping to attend colleges who require two or three years of language study, the problem is being addressed. Hopefully it will eventually erase the serious indictment of our nation's very insular mono-linguistic habit.

But no doubt Spanish is now the ascending second language of the country, especially south of the Mason-Dixon line. (I took it in college after years of French and Latin.) If the country turns bilingual, it'll be English and Spanish, as immigrants in the main no longer come from Western Europe.

Our France and Canada origins and links established, let's now explore how this culture once thrived in America, *le pays en bas* (the country below), especially in Woonsocket and a bit in other French-Canadian centers. Our effort is to portray it as personally, intimately, and profoundly as possible in resurrecting the day-to-day story of their lives. House Speaker Tip O'Neil once said, "All politics is local." It's the same for immigrants in their day-to-day experiences with a new language, customs, and manners,

---

[13] Genealogical research following the author's death has found no direct connection to Jean Baptiste LeTellier. A family tree at the end of this text provides updated information regarding the author's ancestry. - ed

not to mention, as it was for us, the tensions of our Catholic faith in a Protestant country. As said elsewhere, I relate the story as an observer, participant, reader, and researcher, with objectivity, or interested participation. With emotion and feeling, wonder, joy, hilarity, sadness, and hope about the whole experience, which I welcome the reader, Franco or not, to share, since every non-Native American is here because of an immigrant story.

2 - LA BONNE VIE DE FAMILLE
(THE GOOD FAMILY LIFE)

"Eight is Enough" – Families and Others

ONE OF THE MOST endearing aspects of French-Canadian life we grew up in was family life. And *cette vie de famille's* (this family life's) most obvious features were its size, mutual affection, *ameublements* (possessions), joys, and values. Whether parents bred children for mill-based economic reasons or surely more for the love of children and the Christian duty of procreation, Francos raised large broods.

I stated unmarried aunts, uncles, and grandparents, often enhanced the size of those families. Given the tenor of the time and because senior rest homes were rare (no need with mothers always at home), it would've been unseemly to displace elders who held a seat of wisdom and place of honor in their children's homes.

With mom and dad, five children, and our *mémère* (grandma) on weekends, we were an "Eight is Enough" family, recalling the TV series of the late 1970s. When not with us, *mémère* lived with *oncle Henri et Laurence Trottier's* family, children Claude *et* Ronald, and our spinster *tante* Marie-Ange Fontaine. Considered by mom a miraculous cure of the now sanctified Frère André of *l'Oratoire Saint-Joseph*, Montréal, she was like "our rich aunt" who helped you get things our parents couldn't afford, like your first bike, private school tuition, Easter outfit, wedding money, your first TV, etc. In French she was *une vieille fille* (an old maid.) A photo of mom at the Alsace mill in 1919 with other mill girls shows a very healthy working girl. But that was before her respiratory ailment and later cure by "*le travailleur de miracle de l'Oratoire*," (the Oratory miracle worker) mom said. At home there was always a booklet, pamphlet, or magazine about Brother André, who got a ton of favors (and quite a few miracles) through his favored saint, Saint Joseph, patron of Québec and carpenters.

Imagine, every day he found time to visit 10 to 15 Montreal families! No wonder a million people came to his wake! Mom was amazed every time he was running out of money to build the Oratory, miraculously some benefactor came forward. Did she hope as she and dad "built" their family during the Depression, the same godsend would occur? *Le Frère André*, whose surname was Béssette, really endeared himself to her because of his prayer life, good works, the Oratory, and miracles. And he also cured dad's sister, Alice Brunelle, who moved to New York with her family in the 1930s. Imagine two divine favors in our related families! Sensitive to people on crutches, these now hang by the hundreds at the Oratory, so-called *ex votos en mémoire d'une grâce obtenue*: proof of favors obtained. A million visit the shrine each year. I've been several times.

Before entering religious life, he was a millworker in New England, but in poor health. In his religious life, most of his followers were as poor as he was. People identified with his meager education, simplicity, poverty of hand and spirit, and work ethic. His devotion to the saints, especially to Jesus' earthly father, Joseph, was also their very own devotion, as with the Brothers of the Sacred Heart, which pleased mom when I entered the order. No matter how exhausting his day as a porter or visitor, he often prayed hours before retiring, saying God was on your lips when you prayed. *Cousine* Lucille (Fontaine) Langlois told me he was once seen levitating several feet off the floor, as he prayed one evening. His heart, which is encased at the Oratory, was once stolen but returned.

Saint André of Montreal. Brother André cured two of the author's aunts: Marie-Ange Fontaine and Alice (Tellier) Brunelle

About big families in our culture, our tenement house had at least three large families among the eight renters: *les* Carpentiers *et les* Bérubes, each with nine members, and *les* Turcottes with 10. You never came in or out without meeting someone in the stairs or hallways, our Grand Central Station. My speedy manner of scaling handrails or jumping stairs precipitated near collisions. One unfortunate consequence of our dense situation was little privacy. We were some 41 people in our three-decker house with its eight cold water flats, six in the front and two more sunless ones in the rear below street level. How I remember with the warm afternoon sun flooding into our front apartment, mom felt bad for families in the rear deprived of it. As meager as the rent was ($4.50 a week at one time), mom thought it was too much for a cold, dank place. Someone once started a potato chip business in one of those apartments.

For my parents, health issues revolved mainly around three things: the cold, (*le fraite*), humidity (*l'humidité*), and of course germs (*les jarmes*.) Both mom and dad were not stout people - "*pas du gros monde*," she said – so mom and her sisters always sought *d'la chaleur* or warmth. In contrast, dad worked in 100 degree heat at the mill. In winter, thick ridges of ice formed on our windowsills, illustrating how cold our apartment was with no central heating. Insulation was largely unknown but thankfully, coal and wood were cheap. What a job it was keeping our third story apartment heated. Eventually dad and Bob added insulation in the crawl space below the roof. Mom always feared that a cough (*un rhume*) might turn *chronique* (chronic), like her asthma and dad's bronchiectasis. If you had a cough, they attacked it with a vengeance, since they thought medical ignorance, neglect, and poverty brought on their conditions.

Our living situation then, despite its socializing plus, caused people wittingly or unwittingly to trespass occasionally on each other's living space because there was so little of this precious commodity. But necessarily and charitably, our close quarters did generate more humor than irritation. I rarely watch TV sitcoms but on the rare occasion when I do, I reflect how our tenement house remains to me a great untapped source of material for a TV series. Providentially, Franco family size provided a rich source of wisdom about everyday life in general. With grandparents aboard, families mirrored the whole age spectrum of life, as each generation served as role models and domestic counselors for the next. Eight was generally the size of Canadian and Franco families then.

But when I began studies at Boston College for a degree in Counseling Psychology, our teacher said its practice became necessary in schools when the old-time American family of parents, children, grandparents, single aunts and uncles began to change. With homes for the aged, 50 percent divorce rate, single relatives living by themselves, and one-parent families (now home for 44 percent of all school kids), his contention was those rich conduits of life's wisdom passed out of the home. If so, also damaging was the veritable necessity of two-worker parents to make ends meet, becoming "like two ships passing in the night," so there was a high degree of parent absenteeism in their children's lives.

When General Colin Powell, a strong advocate of mentoring programs, spoke at the annual Providence Business Convention in 1998, son Jim and I heard him say most juvenile mayhem occurred between 3 to 7 p.m. when parents were not yet home from work. Living in New York with his two-worker parents in tolerable poverty, he avoided trouble because of close-by relatives and a nearby Y. For us, the only time mom wasn't home was the day of the 1938 Hurricane when she walked back from a whist party at St. Louis Parish, uttering *"Le diable s'en mêle,"* about Lucifer being on her case again. Recall that often in their faith, all good came from God and bad from the devil. As chief malefactor, he got blamed for a lot, starting with our primal mother Eve who dumped on the serpent that was in cahoots with the devil.

Having two working parents seemed unusual, and I heard them talking about it, as touched upon later. Always concerned with economics, dad thought some women, usually with smaller families or older children, worked "*pour payer ses taxes*," that is, to offset what the man paid to Uncle Sam. But she, however, countered "*pour d'la luxure*," for a few extras, the good life. Hers was a more insightful reflection than his, said Froma Harrop, *Providence Journal* contributor. In 1943 at the height of Rosie the Riveter's wartime fame, an editor in *Catholic World* said that not having full-time homemakers was fraught with danger. Hard to grasp in our present day and I think overly conservative even for its times, he said, "Women who maintain jobs outside their homes weaken family life, endanger their own marital happiness, rob themselves of man's protective capabilities, and by consequence decrease the number of children." It's hard to believe it was written just some 70 plus years ago. It's possible that to avoid concerns like the above, the War Department emphasized those wartime jobs were only for the duration. But like our soldiers, "How ya' gonna keep 'em down on the farm after they've seen Paree?" One working lady on TV said she had money for the first time and didn't have to ask her hubby how to spend it. Tensions arose because of independence.

Despite the desirability, usefulness, and often the necessity of women's work, the debate still rages on today, as women working outside the home are said to really work two jobs putting in 40 hours at work and 60-plus at home for more than a 100-hour week (110, if they have a husband, said the report humorously). This results in strain and tension. Men are doing more now at home, research shows, but women still do most domestic chores, either by necessity or frustratingly convinced they can do them better and faster. Working parents whose work shifts are at opposite ends of the day face even greater marital and family stress. There's no easy answer. One prominent TV woman from RI said, "A woman can have it all, but not at the same time." Didn't we say some seven million now stay at home voluntarily? And growing. But apart from their natural creative and nurturing roles and given their now equal education, why should women have to make that choice about working or not outside the home? But also, not uncommon now are wives as the sole breadwinners, with their men taking the role of "homemakers." Not having to cook is a big plus some women have told me.

About the benefits of the extended family, how I remember the wisdom, piety, and love of learning *mémère* dispensed to us by word and example. As did many elders, she sat in her favorite chair next to the stove, her aged and smooth-skinned fingers often gliding over her dark wooden rosary or her knitting needles as she worked on *un gilet* (a sweater) or *tuque* (hat) or *bas d'laines* (socks)! Otherwise, she was flipping the pages of a French magazine or devotional book! How she was a tower of strength and composure for us during the 1938 Hurricane! Seemingly unperturbed, she sat there reciting her beads while we children hid our heads under the tablecloth in the kitchen. With two forest fires in Ontario, five failed businesses, the loss of her husband, and separation from some of her children who stayed in Canada, did *l'ouragan* (the hurricane) seem like the proverbial piece of cake? Mom's comment was "*Ça lui bord pa(s)*" (It doesn't bother her). She never complained about "the slings and arrows of outrageous fortune."

As kids were then, we five were naturally *grouilllant* or active, but *mémère's* calm demeanor and soothing voice helped resolve our quarrels, reminded us of household tasks, and encouraged us to habits of piety and industry in school. From a prosperous land-owning family in St. François-du-lac, P.Q., recall she was a teacher before marriage in the 1880s. Naturally my parents appreciated the time she spent with us. She loved to walk. Her old family farm had been six walking miles from their home in downtown Cochrane, Ontario, so she had a lively gait. She died in 1949 in her eighties. In training, Brother Frank and I as novices were allowed to attend the funeral.

With what we know about walking and health, is that why Francos lived long in Canada and in *marche-à-pied* (walking everywhere) Woonsocket? Every weekend, mom waited for her, walking or driven from Rathbun near Precious Blood Cemetery: "*Ta grandmère arrive*" (Your grandmother's coming), mom announced. It was good for us to see that filial devotion. Soon the aroma of hot blueberry pies and doughnuts by the hundreds wafted through the house. Except for cream puffs from Belisle Bakery at Easter and an occasional pastry of our choice from Carle Bakery, my folks rarely allowed store-bought confectioneries in the house. For one, too much sugar, dad said. Women tell me they don't bake much nowadays, but those full-time moms did, with or without their mothers' help. The kitchen looked like a bakery. Mom's pride and *mémère's* joy radiated throughout the house. For us, the prize was to lick the bowl! Oh, the simple joys of family life of yesteryear!

Born Emérance Morvan in 1864, she went to convent school as a young girl, since her comfortable family eagerly sought education for its sons and daughters. She married Louis Fontaine in 1888. Her niece, Florentine Maher, wrote an award-winning book, *Florentine Raconte* about the family in Canada. You can imagine with what pride and joy, mom, *tante* Laurence, *et mon oncle* François enjoyed the book. I read it too and only a few French words escaped my comprehension. It deepened my admiration for the family's industry, pristine rural values, and love of education when they all lived in Canada. Since I don't think she ever learned a word of English, she taught us all our prayers and letters in French. Once a teacher, always a teacher! With many single-parent homes now or two-working parents, wouldn't a *mémère's* role be invaluable to today's families. In fact, some seven million grandparents are now raising their grandkids because, as one wrote, parents are into serial monogamy, in trouble with the law, into drugs or alcohol, or gone. The evaporation of the nuclear family of yesteryear!

But, if it's their wish, how rewarding for grand folks who finally have time for leisure, travel, or volunteerism secure in the knowledge they raised their families well. I read where at one time the mark of a good parent was how much money you left the kids "to fight over," a wit said. Having been a teacher, I'm glad education and gainful employment in their working life now allow them a blessed, enjoyable retirement, with or without grandkids. "Old age hath yet its honor and its toil," wrote Tennyson, with fellow Victorian poet Robert Browning adding "The last of life for which the first was made."

The family meal, especially *le souper* (dinner), revealed the size and cohesiveness of the family. Unlike today's households, inescapably splintered into so many directions and unable to partake in that time-honored meal, families then were the picture of togetherness in breaking bread. Like us, if you ventured into any home at suppertime, you saw the whole family at table. Eating, yes, but observably reaffirming each other's love and interest in their lives through the sharing of the day's happenings, joys, and mini tragedies.

One the most "serious faux pas" against the social canons of family life was to be absent or late for any family meal, unless prevented. Mom occasionally reminded us we'd go without eating even if just late: "*Si té en r'tard, tu passera endsu la table*," about winding up under the table if AWOL. That is, to go without. Of course, it was observed more "in the breach (not enforced) than in practice." What helped is that at one time, societal units, mercantilism, organizations, sports especially, all respected and honored family-time meals, especially Sundays and holidays. There was also a measure of compassion in eating what mothers prepared, because they rarely got a "McDonald's break," preparing three meals every day, except Sundays perhaps like mine, when members went to different Masses. Living at home until 17, I don't remember ever having a meal in a restaurant with the family; only on scouting trips or in a small diner when I delivered bread. We even came home for lunch from elementary schools. Now Americans eat nearly half of all meals out, a major culprit in the nation's obesity. Eating foods from God knows where is responsible for more malaises and stomach discomforts than we suspect, a report said. We now have too many outbreaks of e-coli or salmonella. The profit motive for businesses dealing with consumables and useful products is so strong that some put greed ahead of humanitarian concerns sometimes resulting in loss of life.

About large families, the largest we knew was *la famille Bérard* on Dulude Ave. Counting non-survivors, there were more than 15 children, four of whom I was to know in religious life with the Brothers. Very athletic and generally robust, the boys made up their own unbeatable softball team. A double play was Berard to Berard to Berard, as I saw once in Sharon. I first met them by volunteering a few times to help with their *Woonsocket Call* route. Our Lebel cousins were almost as numerous. Deaths in childbirth or early infancy were or were not counted in family numbers. As mom said, "*Si toute ava vécu…*" which is to say: "If all had survived …." We Telliers and Fontaines had 58 living cousins at one time.

Since some of the Berard children were born in Canada, as I presume, or more imbued with its culture, the family exemplified to a high degree its joie de vivre, love of song and laughter, and warm camaraderie. Barrel-chested Brothers Fernand *et* Louis (Rodolphe) also had superb voices. They regaled our religious community soirées and solemnized church services, especially with their rendition of "Minuit Chrétien," ("O Holy Night") at Midnight Mass.

I never forgot the time Brother Louis invited me to taste 150 proof whiskey someone had given him at Notre Dame High School. I was surprised I didn't explode. This was after night prayers and Grand Silence. The Superior, whose room was below, knocked on the door. We didn't move and he went away. I repaired to my room and "slept the sleep of the just." But spirituous drinks were a rare treat in the Order.

Loyalty, as in many cultures, was another outstanding trait. Francos ran tight in good and bad times. Even if their culture had been written and not oral, I don't think literary "tell-all" memoirs of the members' shortcoming and failings would have seen the light of day. No *Mommie Dearest* by "a local Joan Crawford" ever ripped a parent apart in print. People like mom were keenly interested in people's lives, but never to the prurient or invasive levels seen in today's supermarket rags. Dad chided us sometimes for not sticking up for each other in scraps with neighborhood kids, oblivious of blood being thicker than water. But he never asked us to condone misconduct or illegality, no matter who did it. About Jews' strong community bonds and education, Ed Berman, one-time *Call* newspaper editor, told me: "Rene, with us it's been like that for thousands of years." Mom also spoke about their cohesiveness: "*Les Juifs s'tiennent ensemble*" (Jews stand together). If dad spoke first, she often threw out that unforgettable line, good for Bartlett's Quotations. Women are more vocal, and in her case, generally speaking, she was generally speaking!

At family soirées women, especially dad's sisters, talked themselves hoarse, with their cheeks reddening and their lungs gasping for air. Of course, oxygen was always in short supply in our Tellier *et* Fontaine respiratory systems. Mom was so convinced of that, she told me one day we weren't as likely to die of cancer or heart disease, as most people did, but of respiratory malaises. But dad's self-taught medical practice (from those 24 medical books), his expert knowledge of nutrition, and new miracle drugs also played a large part, because respiratory infections were now cured before becoming chronic. She lauded "*les remèdes d'aujourd'hui*" (today's remedies). She had known people who died of a burst appendix in Canada before antibiotics. René Beauregard, boyhood friend whose family once shared the same floor with us, survived a burst appendix because of them. So, a salient part of this loyalty was the way a family closed in on itself in times of trouble. A family's "dirty laundry" was kept on the back clothesline, she told me: "*sa corde.*" However, if a member's conduct was bad enough to merit banishment from the house by family or law, the paterfamilias did at times decree the name of the recalcitrant never be mentioned again in the house! But that was more in once ultra-Catholic Québec, she said. Like "shunning" with the Amish! Homes were generally paternal in style, not democratic or child driven. Banishment was also a domestic version of the church's own excommunication edict called *ex cathedra*, for a dogmatically serious and scandalous public failing. I relate later some 60 Sentinellists in defiance of the bishop over the use of parish funds for English speaking diocesan schools were excommunicated. About that kind of "capital punishment," I learned in the Order it meant "you now had to work out your salvation by yourself, without Mother Church."

But in one case of "more sinned against than sinning," twice I mention a daughter who left forever, because her tyrannical father's anger vented itself at her relationship with a man who was separated or divorced by civil law, but not annulled by our church. And was it that long ago the late actress Ingrid Bergman became persona non grata and told to stay out of the country when, still married, she had a child with a man not her husband? Or that baseball's Leo Durocher was banished from the game for a spell because of his questionable dalliance with actress Larraine Day? Until it became a public conviction you couldn't legislate morality. There was a civic and legal attempt to uphold public decency that's now being resurrected in part to sanitize media vulgarities with delayed transmissions. "Public sinner" described a person's scandalous lifestyle, almost like an adulteress wearing a capital A on her dress like in Hawthorne's "*The Scarlet Letter.*" No one misses that severe public judgment nowadays. But with a loss of faith, family disunity, and lack of school and domestic moral or religious instruction, communities are shocked by the horrendous and completely illegal, immoral actions of some its citizens, young and old.

Sometimes tragedies, especially impending death, had a way of annulling some family estrangements. Mom told me she witnessed or had been told about several of these deathbed reconciliations. About those *in extremis rapprochements* (on the edge rapprochements), especially those coming back to the faith when at death's door were indeed the stuff of high drama because salvation was in the balance. Death scenes in Canadian paintings always seemed to have a crucifix-holding priest at bedside, either for conversion or last confession. Often, she reminded us that life's goal was to go to heaven: "*gagner son ciel.*" I beg the reader's tolerance if I often repeat this salvation principle because it was the essential note of their life and faith which validated their beliefs and very existence. One can't understand them without that. Its lessening probably explains why the faith of Francos today is diminished so visibly. C. S. Lewis wrote some people don't want to think about the hereafter because it would change the way they act, especially about hell, mentioned nearly 20 times in the Bible. An angry person often says, "Go to hell."

In the wake of this disintegration, isn't it a source of envy or admiration to know their life and *raison d'être* (most important purpose) had this single unifying principle? Like the Irish, whose history was so strife-driven, life didn't make sense without faith and the afterlife. Even if not a favorite, I admire President Andrew Jackson for the same conviction. It's no wonder "Why did God create you?" was one of the first questions asked in the Baltimore Catechism! Yes, if Christ hadn't risen, as Paul said, and if Francos didn't think they would, their long suffering and staunch faith would've been for naught. (Humorously, without that faith, would their lot have been like the atheist who insisted they dress him "to the nines" for his burial? On his tombstone: "All dressed up and no place to go!")

One day mom told me a wife hid a religious patch inside her wayward husband's hatband for conversion before his death. (Men always wore hats then, except for church and fight scenes in the movies.) Mom didn't tell me whether "he headed off" the conversion plot, or the faith penetrated his hard heart ("*son coeur endurci,*" was her memorable line). God only knows if he died in the faith. "*Se repentir à la fin*" (Repent at the end) was a deathbed conversion, she said. When confession was a regular practice, some priests told you the impact of having a penitent unload the burden of a sinful life of 20 or more years.

The classic one of course is the Crucifixion story of the Good Thief on Golgotha (*le bon larron* in French). Wittingly, Saint Augustine said, "The thief stole all his life and at the end stole heaven." A divine caper! Grand larceny! We read *The Lives of Saints* before supper in the Order, and he's Saint Dismas and patron of prisoners. Imagine, with just one final thought rebuking the bad thief for jeering at the innocent Christ and asking mercy merited him salvation and sainthood. In Latin class, I liked Christ's words to him, "*Hodie eris mecum in paradiso*," about his being with Him in Paradise that very day. Our in-house biblical guru knew the story from Holy Week but cautioned the "artful dodger" had called it pretty close to the vest: "*un peu juste*." Another unforgettable one-liner with a touch of humor.

In the same vein, mom, who read about the life and knew the miracles of the sainted *curé d'Ars* (St. John Vianney), said he once consoled a widow who thought her husband was damned (*damné*) because he jumped to his death from a bridge. Reassuringly, the sainted pastor told her that her husband asked for forgiveness of his sins before hitting the water and was thus saved. Like us in the Order, she too read spiritual books and the lives of the saints! But a few of these so-called hagiographies were later found to be pure fiction, like the blarney of St. Patrick reading his breviary in the Irish Sea while seals licked his feet! We muffled our laughter in the dining room, surprised fiction had found a way into our religious house. You could be questioned, so you listened. For example, we were forbidden to lean on our elbows when we prayed. Once when the lector read a saint had scabby elbows (to make a point about his many hours of prayer while prostrate on a cold floor), Brother Benedict said, "He must've leaned on his elbows." However chagrined by our laughter, our religious CEO didn't deny him his supper. (No one ever was.) We were told tales of "misbehaving monks" ordered to scrub floors with a toothbrush in Canada or elsewhere in early Christendom. We bristled (oops!) at that, but it never happened, even though someone said religious orders weren't just a collection of goody-goody guys: *des bons garçons*. Nobly intentioned recruits came in with their character and personality well formed. It made life interesting. Once a Brother at the Academy stood up in the dining room to complain about being teased. So, we took him "off our list." Two weeks later he whined no one talked to him!

When I hear priests and religious getting knee operations later in life, it must be all that kneeling and genuflecting and not from doing floors, which the staff did at Sacred Heart School, Sharon, MA when the 200 boarders were on vacation. (My first teaching assignment.) And when you knelt in church, you had to touch the floor, not just curtsy. But now Brothers live longer. I also see older priests get a pass on that. Abbot St. Columba, 600 A.D., meted six lashes if a monk forgot to say Amen; ten for notching a table with his knife; and six for singing out of tune.

That Suit's for Sunday

IN ADDITION TO its mutual affection and size, simplicity was another obvious feature of family life. There was a kind of ordinariness in material possessions, manners, and general lifestyle. Don't the poor usually have only two choices: slim and none?

Typical of a family of our size and means, our furnished apartment with its four large bedrooms and equally large family room and parlor was very unpretentious in appearance and décor. And thank God, very affordable for a millworker's family! A Saturday morning chore was bringing the $4.50 rent to the family across the street that owned Carle Bakery. Still, for a salary of $44 at the mill, that was 10 percent *"de ses gages pour la semaine,"* (of his wages for the week) said mom, who twice had faced homelessness.

Our cold-water flat was heated with hard anthracite and soft bituminous coal and wood. Dad liked the first and cursed the second for its dustiness, despite its quick ignition. Our big black stove contained the all-important *fourneau* or oven. How I admired dad's operation of the stove, the biggest thing we owned and easily the most discussed thing in the house! Women like warmth, and mom often asked dad about its inner fire: *Comment ai (est) ton poêle?* (How is your stove?) As a child, that roaring fire awed me when dad opened one plate with a curved ring-topped instrument, too hot for a child's hand not yet callused by millwork. Since it was our only heat source, on cold winter mornings we rushed out from under the covers of our chilly bedrooms. But oh, the labor to keep it fed and its hazards!

A stove's biggest threat was chimney fires which were very common on our street. News of one spread fast, and we ran to them like fire trucks. One day my fear grew when we found out a young woman had died and we went in to pay our respects in her lower Gaulin Ave. home. Her silk-draped body covered her burns, the family said. Greatly moved by the sight of my first dead body, I had nightmares for a year, but never told my parents. Curious and good-hearted, we kids saw the funeral wreath on the door of the first-floor home. I don't recall how we were dressed (we wore overalls all the time, save school and Sunday Mass), but the family let the gang in. The nuns were always telling us about those corporal or spiritual acts of mercy. We recited them in class, and the nuns said we'd hear them at the Last Judgment from Christ himself: "I was hungry and you fed me; thirsty and you gave me to drink; in prison and you visited me; in sorrow and you comforted me," et al. If you were a St. Ann parishioner, you could hardly forget the Last Judgment at the end of the world and the one at your death. Every time we entered our church, artist Nincheri's tour de force fresco of it loomed above us in the vaulted ceiling. But if our church was a "sermon in stone" or fresco, it re-enforced the notion you wanted to be "in that number," and not like Lucifer and his minions being ousted by St. Michael, the Sword of God. The bad folks hanging on for dear life before their hellish descent. Back to the stove, I watched with fascination as he struck a wooden match, threw it into *le kindlin'* and yesterday's paper, adjusted the damper, and added coal with a small metal shovel. Until he had a good fire, he often checked by lifting a ring. Mom did this only in his absence. Occasionally he shook the grates and emptied the embers in a bucket kept behind the stove or in the hallway. When cooled (*"ton feu ai mort,"* said mom), he covered them with old newspapers. One evening they went to pay their respects to a deceased and Bob being out, he asked me to watch it. I was nervous like it was my first time at the wheel of a car.

Outside of germs and constipation, he thought dust was public enemy number one. You can imagine how swirling woolen dust impeded his breathing at the mill, especially with the incipience of his bronchiectasis disease. Except perhaps for the Irish who were among the first, Franco workers faced the worst respiratory and auditory shock of all those immigrants in New England mill towns.

The coal was stored in two bins, one along the back wall of the rear hallway and one in the cellar. What a backbreaking job Saturday to tote the coal in canvas bags up the 30 or more steps! Dad, Bob, and I (Ben was too young) performed that manly chore, which strengthened our backs beyond compare. It took 3-4 trips to fill the upstairs bin. Only around 1950 when he lost his coal haulers did he switch to oil heat. He couldn't get an oil burner during the war but put his name in at a store in Social for peacetime.

Even though we had a one-sided pyramid-shaped toaster, most of our breakfast and bedtime toasts were made on the stove. They were done more quickly, if only on the surface. Pity the "toastmaster" who left this task to attend to something else! Soon rising plumes of smoke and the odor of burning bread, not to mention the frantic yells from the living room, brought the peripatetic one back to the stove's burnt offerings. (I laughed when a husband said of his Catholic cook that: "Everything is a burnt offering!")

Often in the evening, dad, for whom good nutrition was a hobby and passion, asked who wanted to share an apple. (I've had one almost every day of my life.) He peeled an apple in an unbroken strip and threw the intact peel on the stove, sending a rugged, woodsy aroma to the living room. He also cored apples, put brown sugar in them, and put them in a metal dish with water. They were like candied apples, but the pulp was very hot. Always thrifty, he bought apples and oranges by the bushel (*"un minot et en gros,"* mom added) from Gardella's in the city. He told you how much he saved compared to three pounds at a time from Lavergne's Market. He was famous for his *compote aux pommes* or applesauce, which we and later his grandkids, especially the Clark grandchildren, loved. And of course, we always started our day with a fresh-squeezed orange for *"Vitamine Cée,"* her favorite health booster.

Une bonne cuisine (good food) was homemaking's highest order. They were always talking about good nutrition for our own housekeeping someday. These *mères de famille* (mothers) were legendary for teaching daughters the art of cooking *"pour élever une famille de bonne santé"*: to raise a healthy family. Consider that despite major respiratory diseases, he lived to be 86, she, 90. Dad especially astounded the medical profession, outliving his disease timetable sevenfold. Isn't it ironic today's affluence and rushing lifestyle have Americans eating poorly, largely because meals no longer come from home? America lost two big health plusses when cooking and eating "left the home," which once fed the body and nourished the family's soul. Now we see the government stepping in as obesity threatens to be a $58 billion disaster. Sugary drinks are one target. Isn't the nation's body mass index for those over 30 highest on earth? One pundit said we have "No girth control."

On the opposite wall from the stove was the second most important appliance in our house: the icebox. For ice, Ben and I went to Lemonde's, corner of Sweet Avenue and Cass next to the Dupras' Bakery, where I was born. Because I was a third child, mom said the childless Dupras couple wanted to adopt me. I wondered later if the Dupras would've had to pay them a reverse ransom to take me back like O'Henry's mischievous, kidnapped child in *"The Ransom of the Red Chief."* Anyway, even allowing for the half-mile trek and melting, it was a better deal because his ice pickings were generous and cheap. You rang at the corner house and went to his icehouse in the yard, a cool treat in summer. Some of the melting in our wagon occurred because we sometimes dilly-dallied at St. Ann Park if we saw the gang there. *"Il nous faut d'la glace"* (We need ice), mom whined "icily" if the bottom pan was full of water. But if like Christ at the Wedding Feast of Cana we gave her that look, "Woman, what does that have to do with us?" she wore you down with persistence, as women have done since housekeeping came out of Eden. A child psychologist told Pat and me a child feels he exercises power over you by having you repeat. But with so many kids, mothers didn't listen. The funniest thing was to hear a woman, on the porch or window, go through four or five of her children's names before hitting the one she wanted.

So, refrigeration was a constant concern. If we had a meltdown during the night dad, who had the nose of a wine connoisseur, decided what to discard in the icebox. Even if we weren't buying, the iceman's arrival in the neighborhood was always an event on hot days. The more placating vendors ice-picked pieces for us, preferring to appease us rather than fight us off.

Others didn't, so you waited until they trudged up to an apartment with the pincered ice piece in hand or canvas-shielded shoulder. They knew what size to bring from a multi-colored or numbered card customers placed in the window. Ray Bacon of the Museum of Work & Culture gave me one. I displayed it for fun. Most third-floor apartment dwellers were customers, even us when dad worked *steadé* (steady) during the war. Mom called them "*des vendeurs de glace*" (ice vendors). She labeled everyone's job.

With the vendor gone, we used a fist-sized rock to chisel pieces to lick. Naturally, you always cut a piece for the guy who stood watch during the ice caper. Mothers objected to our ice treat for three reasons: one, it was petty thievery, a venial sin; two, it's not healthy to put something that cold in your mouth; three, it's unsanitary. The whole drama was our version of "The Iceman Cometh." As the truck upped the hill, it drew a wet straight line. If not around, you missed cooling off. There was no ice cream at home or money to buy a cone for a nickel. Summer was hot because, as she often said, "*l'air conditionée cée pour les riches*" (Air conditioning is for the rich.)

Street collectors of discarded clothing and vendors of fruits and vegetables also brought the kids out in numbers. Equally annoying for the ragman in his horse drawn wagon was our hanging on to the rear. If two or three of us did it at the same time, we slowed the horse almost to a dead stop. Those equine creatures were a breath away from the glue factory. When the wagon slowed, the rider turned around to shout at us, or he got off to shoo us away. Like domestic gnats, we came right back.

Fruit peddlers inched along on small trucks easily mounted from the rear bumper. We learned to do that from watching our favorite cowboys at the Laurier Theater on Cumberland Street. In those westerns, our heroes mounted stagecoaches with bravado and speed. But we had to move fast not to be caught by the peddler or your mother on the porch.

I recall in a college class on morality where some were skeptical about a person always acting "for the good." When I asked Father Jansens, our Jesuit moral philosophy teacher, he said we blinded ourselves with the notion the forbidden fruit was actually "a good." Like the self-duped kid stealing a car, he added. After all, didn't Adam, assisted by persuasive Eve, see "that the apple was good or desirable to know good and evil," as the serpent proposed? Was any other generation brought up with the Ten Commandments so indelibly written on its forehead? Perhaps we weren't "better kids," just better informed, so perhaps more culpable. For us "ignorance of the law is (was) no excuse." The only sin was to get caught, so we thought. Like sneaking in at St. Ann's Park for a game Sunday afternoons or fight nights. Or the Laurier Theater on Saturdays! Does poverty write its own catechism? Deep down we probably knew it really wasn't right to bag a pear, plum, or apple. But we rationalized, so we didn't have to tell *Père* (Father) Moreau in the confessional. For example, "So-and-so wouldn't miss it"; "he doesn't give honest measure" ("*la mésure exacte*," said mom, but not in defense of our actions); "some portion of what my mom buys always goes rotten soon." It's what we call situational ethics today. Or "It's only bad if you think it is"; and, "I exercised bad judgment there," now clearly the winner, with the notion of sin outdated, as Bishop Tobin wrote. Respect for people's property made life so much easier. Aren't break-ins and petty thievery the rage today? After prison, the pesky thieves, most with little education, a broken family, and no moral compass, come right back. Silly I know, but when I see a criminal use violence, I wonder why he doesn't think it's wrong! Moral insanity said one.

For us, these produce vendors were also the first McDonalds or Burger Kings, that is, our first jobs. Mothers yelled their order from their porches. The vendor weighed the produce and you legged it up there. As the truck inched along, besides a small base pay, you also got a percentage of what you sold if you made a sale by rapping on doors to alert mothers. I was encouraged by my first sale. But walking in the heat, the frequent no-sale, the unfamiliar neighborhoods, the gang playing ball at St. Ann's Park or cooling off at some swimming hole quickly made me a homebody again.

Fortunately, kids really didn't need much money then. It blew my mind when I heard recently that teens spend about eighty dollars a week and earn about two-thirds of it themselves! Madison Avenue's advertising quickly makes consumers out of kids. As college author Taine wrote, "Ours is an acquisitive society." Other stats are also impressive: kids 4 to 12 help spend or influence $3 billion in spending; those 12 to 19, $170 billion; and 87 percent of car sales are influenced by kids. You can spot a sophomore in high school by the driver's manual in his or her pocket. But car makers are in trouble if couples continue to downsize their families. Also, young people, a recent study said, find electronic communication easier and cheaper than financing a car. It costs $8,000 a year now to drive a car: depreciation, gas, repairs, insurance, taxes, etc. Additionally, there's the danger of texting at the wheel.

Called *quenilloux* (old-clothes man) by our parents, the rag picker caused excitement with his cry. If a person's job somehow defines his appearance and speech, how true of those who plied that long-vanished method of commerce, now replaced by depositories on church grounds et al. Even to us poor people, the unshaven, ill-dressed driver, the tired, drooping horse, and the rickety wagon all bespoke a greater poverty than ours. But dad gave me "the rest of the story," as radio legend Doug Harvey said daily.

Trundling up Gaulin Avenue at a snail's space, the rag picker's cry of "Rags" turned everybody out. Unless dealing with him that day (we got more money on Elbow Street), we ruffians made his life harder by also hanging on to his wagon, mimicking his cry, and spooking his horse. Only when dad said rag pickers were not ashamed to ply that trade to send their children to college, did I begin to respect them more. Later, I even saw one of them as a salesperson/owner in one of the Social *Coin* stores mom went to. It always struck me that dad, a well-read man with little formal education, believed the noblest thing a person could do was to invest in his children's education. He didn't demean the ragman's profession because he knew why he did it. He had his information sources but was no match for mom's. They were easily the "Current Events" news sources of Gaulin Avenue. He never forgot anything he read; she, what she heard. "A match made in heaven."

Our oracle father often said education was an investment he'd never lose money on, like buying a house and losing it, as some did in the Depression. Or winding up with useless mining stocks like he had in his closet strong box. He had invested during his bachelorhood, with the rest of his nest egg going to his brothers to buy farms. Unfortunately, the Depression, millwork, Christian generosity, the size of our family, and the incipience of a serious lung disease at the "top" of his earning power in the late 1940s all prevented him from pushing us far up the academic ladder. But he did bequeath us his unbridled curiosity, love of learning, doing, and reading especially. If at one time he chided Francos for not getting enough education for themselves and their children, how proud he became when they did so after the mills left. But I repeat often he never demeaned the mill trade. He loved his work, did it superbly, and it supported his family. His frustration was it didn't pay well, work was slack, it undermined lungs for some, and didn't really "allow" education for workers and their children. One must read Dunwell's "*The Run of the Mill*" for a comprehensive indictment of the industry and what it did (or didn't) to its people in New England. But a Museum of Work and Culture speaker thought the author's indictment too severe. True, they didn't have much in Canada either, but farming was of course "*au grand air*," (in the open air) said mom. Their home was their own and they grew a lot of their own food, so no government help was needed. In 2018 one-third of RI is being fed by SNAP: Supplemental Nutrition Assistance Program or other sources. Forty percent of Woonsocket families.

In home furnishings, basic functionality and rugged usefulness were standard features. Once a family had its furniture in place, very few pieces were brought in. However, since newly married couples usually bought only what they had money for, it took years sometimes before a family acquired everything needed or desired. Mom told me it was foolish to court credit with unemployment always a threat before the war. The "enjoy now and pay later," approach that is now wreaking solvency problems with many was not in vogue. But now a report in 2014 said insolvency is coming down. Was the recession of 2008 a lesson!

Since people were geared into buying for life (no built-in obsolescence like today), people like dad just kept repairing and painting furniture, using, for example, wood glue and wire to reattach chair rungs or table legs. Wood or coal stove heat continually dried up furniture glue as well as your nostrils. When my folks entered Hospice Saint Antoine and I inherited a few pieces of their furniture, I had to strip four or five layers of paint on pieces I refinished.

If I'm right, he took two-bedroom night tables, united them with a top board, and created a small dresser or chiffonier. Always in the living room, it served as a repository for handkerchiefs, bobby pins, and other sundries. It's now metamorphosed into a stationery stand. As a tree says in a poem, *"Je suis mort mais je porte encore,"* about being "dead" but still serving the living. But if our "rich aunt" bought a bedroom set or furniture piece, then a poorer (or lucky) relative inherited the old. The master bedroom in our house was uniform in style, but other rooms, save perhaps the room where my sisters slept, were furnished in Early Hodge-Podge style. Mom said, *"On vit comme les pauvres"* (We live like the poor). She always knew our standard of living but was never morose about it. It's as if she knew poet Pope's line: "Whatever is, is right." What made it easier was that everybody was like us, she said. If early Christians all lived in common by choice, Francos did it by necessity. But it wasn't a poverty seared by marital tensions, substance abuse, violence, or illegal strivings. But some were inebriated at times: "the psychiatric couch of the poor," a prof said. A solution sought at the bottom of a bottle!

Judging by their joie de vivre, they accepted their lot in life exceptionally well. Was it Christian resignation or because millwork for all its shortcomings was still better than dirt farming in land-wasted Québec? They made a virtue of making do. Tersely, she added, *"On a ce qu'on a"*: what they had was it and not likely to change much. Psychologists might call that a defense mechanism to cope with the material futility of their lives, but they were fortunate to live at a time when acquisitiveness was not the driving force it is now. Recent popes have praised that kind of Christian spirit of moderation and detachment, blaming its opposite for the incredible divide between rich and poor nations. Now two percent of the people have 80 percent of the wealth.

Since parlors were still used for courting and extraordinary company, ours had some cushioned comfort in the sofa and soft chair. Ordinary friends and relatives (often too numerous) didn't qualify for that inner sanctum, but clergy did for the biennial visit. But there was no carpeting! Always that dull linoleum, well trafficked and without the glow of those never-need-to-wax creations of today. It was *"du prélard* (linoleum)"

In our kitchen or living room, only attached thin cushions softened two rocking chairs. The dining room *chaises* (chairs) were barren. We often straddled those rocking chairs, causing broken armrests, so another glue job: *de la colle*. Besides the big black stove and icebox, the only three other pieces of note were her Singer sewing machine, a shelf radio, and a clock we had to wind. When we finally went electric, it added a few cents to our three dollar-a-month bill! Mom spoke of her sewing machine or *moulin* with possessiveness and even affection. But about the clock, pity the one who didn't put the winding key on the clock shelf after performing that occasional chore! The crime remained undetected for a day at least. Were we better for it, not being programmed as we are today to "fill the unforgiving minute with sixty seconds of work," as poet Kipling wrote? Nobody had a watch, so it was everyone's timepiece. As a Christian community, church bells announcing Masses, May and October devotions to Mary, and funerals served as our Big Ben with spiritual "overtones." (I always liked the witty observation a stopped clock is right twice a day. "Relentless time," as a poet said, made to stand still. Like everyone, I too wrestled with the definition of time, such as "Time is a river I go a-swimmin' in.") Kitchen cabinets were huge and triple-tiered, but with no recessed door features. Mom used recycled material to line the shelves. And beneath the cold-water tap was a heavy, chipped white porcelain sink accommodating a large family. Unlike us, in homes without a bathtub, family members washed babies and splashed themselves there daily until the housing code made *le baim* mandatory. We only had one small bathroom, complete with a wooden medicine cabinet, bathtub, and a pull-chain toilet. With no ventilation or exhaust, I practiced holding my breath for the longest time if waiting on someone. It's why my lifeguard instructor Brother Edgar at Camp Sacred Heart, Sharon, was dumbfounded with my time underwater. If someone was waiting on you, you raised one or two fingers before you went into the bathroom. If in there too long, you heard a bang on the door or a cry to our "Judge Judy."

Ben remembers the toilet plumbing was almost like a telephone line to the bottom floors. One could be heard while in there but fortunately, not seen. We bathed only once a week, usually Saturday night! Other nights we washed our faces and hands in the sink before going to bed. Mom said parsimonious landlords didn't take kindly to renters taking daily baths. More later, but we heated the water on the stove in a pitcher called *un canard* (like "a duck") and brought it to the tub. If we were all taking baths on a Saturday, dad hauled out the copper tub used also for Monday laundry. Since we boys had never known anything else, we didn't miss hot water faucets, but mom, Sue, and Rachel did. Another luxury only *"pour le monde riche,"* (for rich people) said mom. She married a factory worker, and since he did his best to provide for us, she set the tone for the family. That's why I liked hearing ours was a happy family. My first revelation as a counselor was not all families were like the one I was brought up in or like others in our neighborhood. Our moms were all full-time homemakers, but in 2014, women were the breadwinners in 42 percent of the homes.

Except for an occasional mirror (like on dressers), wall adornments were usually of a pious or religious sort. Music cabinets, movie star photos, scenes of natural wonders, or *objets d'art* (art works) rarely graced anyone's living rooms, at least in our 'hood. Family portraits hung in the parlor. This barrenness is why I remember so vividly *mon oncle* François' print of a young lady holding a furry cat like the family's own Tabby. Visiting mom's brother and family on Ross Street, I enjoyed how at feeding time *ma tante* Blanche told her cat, "*Fait ta belle*": beg or purr nicely. This as she brushed against her leg, making pleading sounds for a morsel. (My family cat, named Brooklyn in Pat's memory, did the same to me in the kitchen. Seemingly healthy, he died of an aneurysm on the vet's table. We cried all the way home, with him in a box on the back seat. He's buried in our yard. Our dog Benji who kept vigil over my cancer-stricken wife for a whole year, was also buried among flowers there. Is he the only dog buried with a written eulogy? Niece Christine (Bouffard) Spielberger gave him to us after her "and his" graduation from Bryant College. He was a hit when he visited the elderly at Hospice St. Antoine. In the new catechism, I like the section devoted to the care and attention we owe God's creatures that share the earth with us and give us unrequited love. About "salvation" for animals, a college teacher of mine said that when an animal died, it was now reduced "to the potency of matter": what Nature does with enduring matter. Many would like pets to share heaven with them!

About those pious or religious icons, like medieval people whose churches and lives were replete with Christian art, Francos faithfully displayed the artifacts of their faith. These were crucifixes, de rigueur like in the Order in many rooms; pictures of saints in prayer or in the act of martyrdom; Old or New Testament events, like Mary's Assumption into Heaven; statues of the Sacred Heart; the ever-popular St. Anthony (the Finder), Moses with the Ten Commandments, and St. Francis, lover of animals. A nun told us he attracted them, because the creatures knew he meant them no harm, and we would too if we projected the same affection. I tried it that very afternoon, but they didn't get the message. Few ever came close to our yard except sparrows, cats, and pigeons, but not dogs. Perhaps there were too many kids who didn't project the mendicant saint's mantra of love and affection.

The Laferrieres who lived in the rear basement apartment of the next house had a big, raised wooden stoop which we often broad jumped. But cats a few times had their litters underneath. I was so excited when I first noticed it, I ran up three flights to tell mom. The first thing she said was the cat didn't "make" kittens but "had" them, and she was not impressed. Did she think we'd once again ask if we could have an animal? In the two tenement houses, none of the 14 renters had a pet. Only one family across the street bred dachshunds, and two Frenchmen down the street had some big dogs. Dad spoke about a dog on their Saint Cuthbert farm in Canada who developed a taste for chickens. They gave him to somebody 50 miles away. Guess who showed up later lookin' for "that paw-lickin' good poultry?" As usual, dad guffawed once.

A lot of us in the Order wore a cloth scapular[14] or one or two medals on our neck. In summer the joke was their weight might cause you to drown. A former lifeguard who still swims in the summer, I feel nostalgic for some of those practices whenever an older person like me blesses himself before going in. It's one more pious act barely surviving our less devotional time. If you didn't make the sign of the cross before going in, you risked a watery grave, the warning was, but worse, the holy indignation of our vigilant moms. "*Oublie pas ton signe de la croix*" (Don't forget your sign of the cross), she said before we went out to swim. Mothers had so many kids it was like watching "over their flock." Like Christ did, they could boast to the Father, "I have not lost any of those you gave me." But it's been much harder for the WWII generation to see their kids keep the faith, since education and jobs have taken them far from the protective cocoons of faith their parents had, a writer theorized. But I'm convinced faith waxes and wanes. I often read the Bible and can't believe how often in the Old Testament His chosen people turned away from Him, the prophets, and the message. And how swift His retribution! I'm glad it's more tempered with mercy now, unless war and worldwide atmospheric and oceanic conditions are signs of His displeasure, as some favored with Mary's visions said.

No Catholic woman was without rosary beads in her purse. The good nuns who wore them as part of their religious habit wanted us boys to carry them too. But like our dads, whose physical work negated that, our rough play made wearing the penny rope-stringed beads impossible. The nuns rewarded us with rosaries for attending Mass during Lent, knowing catechism, or selling taffy. Many Catholics said their rosary every day, some say the 15 decades.[15] They give faith "portability," said one. Many also have

---

[14] The monastic scapular is a panel of cloth suspended both front and back from the shoulders, often to the knees.

[15] Each group of ten rosary beads separated by a larger bead is a decade. – *ed.*

a rosary around one of their bedposts, like me. I get many from religious groups raising money.

Recitation, now in revival with the Medjugorje, Yugoslavia, apparitions, had receded a bit with church renewal under Pope John XXIII. Liturgy, rather than devotional practices favored by Francos and Italians, for example, was re-emphasized. When a priest asked an old lady why she hid behind a column at Mass, she replied, "The Mass interferes with my saying the Rosary." This reflected the simplicity and everyday practicality of their faith, especially with Mass in Latin and the priest with his back turned towards the faithful. Many were buried with their rosaries. Like *mémère* and dad in their last years, you couldn't always go to church, but you could say your beads at home and read the Mass in a missalette. The church has now added *The Luminous Mysteries*, recalling Jesus's Baptism, Wedding at Cana, Proclamation of the Kingdom, Transfiguration, and Institution of the Eucharist. I like what "the Rosary Priest" (Father Peyton in Mobile) said about prayer: "The family that prays together, stays together." In my WWII notes, I recall how mom had us pray on our knees after supper to bring Bob back alive. Would it help to re-integrate Catholic families now sundered apart at the same rate as the nations? Did Mary spare mom another tragedy when a kamikaze plane just missed Bob's ship in the Pacific?

The faithful have always had a special devotion to Mary. Her apparitions at Lourdes and LaSalette, both in France, Fatima in Portugal, Our Lady of Guadaloupe in Mexico, and in Ireland, and other places give witness to that. In my chapters on the church, I mention evening devotions to Mary in October and May (*les mois de Marie:* the months of Mary) were jammed with people just like Sunday Mass! We knew devotional songs to her as well as we did Canadian Gisèle McKenzie's Top Ten Hit Parade songs heard Saturday night on the radio and later TV. So many churches in Christendom honor her name and role in leading people to salvation. The best argument I heard against feminists who decry the non-ordination of their sisters as delimiting is that Christ chose her to be His Mother. There's no greater role this side of heaven. Think of it! Mother of Christ God! About Fatima, Mary asked the three children, especially Lucia, to have Russia consecrated to her to restore world peace. Some aver it has not been done, at least fully, prompting criticism of the Cardinal Secratariat in Rome. Is the fear of alienating Russia or their religion the cause? Because not done, Mary said Russia's threat would be diminished but not abolished. She also predicted war in Spain.

About the kitchen, mom said a new bride received cutlery and dishes as wedding gifts. Long after we kids arrived, you still discerned traces of the silver and decorative lines that once adorned her wedding dinnerware and silverware from 1923. But rough handling, more than a thousand washings a year, heavy detergents, and an occasional breakage had left their imprint. The knives especially fared badly. Unlike today's one-piece construction, the blade was in a separate handle. Water eventually seeped into the connecting socket, undermining the junction, resulting in a loose blade and a possible germ source, dad warned.

A standing family joke was her special dinnerware set. On Gaulin Ave, it was always stored on the last inaccessible kitchen cabinet shelf. As the years went by, we always heard it was for special company, but none ever qualified for us to haul it down and use it. Rachel made us laugh one day when she avowed not even the King of Sweden, as the expression went, was special enough *pour descendre le set*: to bring down the set. Clinging as women do to mementoes of treasured events - weddings, baptisms, and anniversaries - she knew the delicate light blue china would not survive a week with us five kids. Our everyday china was more unbreakable. But pieces of that special china still survive in my sisters' homes. Are they still waiting for Scandinavian royalty? Personal clothing also mirrored the simplicity and lower middle-class station of our lives and was far removed from the fashions of the day. Besides cost, plainness and durability dictated most purchases, not "keeping up with the Joneses." Until you were a teen, if you had older siblings of the same sex (and who didn't?), your wardrobe consisted of hand-me-downs or homemade stuff. But there were a few purchases from Eisenberg and Tickton in *Sochelle Coin*, Jewish merchants who spoke French. "*Ils parlent notre langage*" (They speak our language), mom told me several times.

But how I sulked all the way to the church rail when she didn't buy me my first suit for First Communion! A good seamstress, she had downsized Bob's former black suit. Quite tall for a Franco, he was always much bigger than me at a comparable age. But she didn't touch his Boy Scout shirt which hung on me like the skin of an old man's withered face. Wearing my altered suit, you could tell it had been resewn. People said I looked good that day, but I deeply envied friends preening themselves in their store-bought sartorial splendor. It struck me funny we practiced sticking our tongues out to receive the host because we often did it in sibling verbal fights. Our nun warned us not to touch the host if it dropped. Remembering how the Israelites were warned if they touched the Ark of the Covenant they would die, as two did, we wondered if that would be our fate. Despite the altar boy's paten (a plate), when there was a drop, we just stared at it on the floor. But nowadays, doubt has crept into some Catholics' wavering belief about the Real Presence of Christ in the host! In 2012, two-thirds of the faithful in *Eire's* (Ireland's) former "land of saints" said they didn't believe it. But none of us doubted that was Christ hitting the floor. And *Noli Tangere*: don't you dare touch it.

In the supper reading in the Order about the saint of the day, we heard some holy people saw a bleeding host in the uplifted hands of a priest. One Jesuit teacher even told us a physicist was attempting to prove a substance change - transubstantiation - really was taking place at the Consecration, despite the visible physical appearance of bread (the host) and wine in the chalice. But isn't faith "belief in things the evidence of which appears not?" Unfortunately, acts of desecration, fueled by curiosity or hatred, have occurred since the Last Supper. Other faiths believe Christ is only in the bread and wine – a belief that is called impanation – or they are just a memorial or recollection of what Christ did that one time. Christ's multiplication of the loaves and fish which fed thousands was a foreshadowing of the Eucharist, a writer opined. Christ was very direct about one's salvation chances if not partaking of his body and blood. But one good outcome compared to ages past is that communion is way up, even if confessions are way down.

In attire, boys usually wore corduroy pants to school. You could gauge the age of the pants from the bare and shiny knee section, continually scraped from rough schoolyard play or praying on our classroom hardwood floors. Some were gouged with pens and had nail heads showing. Girls wore a white blouse and a blue/black jumper with stockings and leather shoes.

Outside of school, we were always dressed in railroad jeans, endlessly patched, and patched again, not with store-bought patches, but from usable discards. We wore baseball caps with the visor forward, not backwards as is often seen today. But during the war I wore the navy hat Bob brought home. It was my trademark in my *Call* newspaper deliveries in downtown Social. Like in that Frank Sinatra and Gene Kelly flick, I gave it a kind of rakish angle like all sailors did. But boys didn't wash their hands except when told by their moms at meals, so our hats were dirty. It didn't qualify as family clothing so it had no place in the heaping Monday wash.

Like in movies of that time, men wore soft hats, changing to straw ones after Memorial Day. Women were rarely without them, bowing to St. Paul's admonition to cover their heads as a sign of submission to the Lord, they kept their hats on in church. But women's equality and hatlessness for both sexes, even in frigid weather, eventually became the style. But it was considered a serious health hazard in my family. Dad read in his medical books you could lose 90 percent of your body heat and suffer from sinusitis by going *nu tête* (bareheaded) in winter. Always they watched over our lungs and potential malaises like all-seeing surgeon generals. So, we wore hats most of the year, even in summer. I've got many caps today, but kids then had only one. They cost a quarter and no team ever gave them out like candy. But in winter the Tellier children wore woolen tuques knitted by *mémère*. Like *pepère* Tellier, dad and Bob were lucky with their curly forelock and manageable hair, but Ben and I always had the look of unruly, flattened-out hair from wearing a hat, almost like the tonsured look of cloistered monks!

Franco women in our 'hood were always dressed modestly. Our culture was not exhibitionistic in any form. Only once or twice do I recall priests in the pulpit, and mom, speak about women who dared to go to church in an inappropriate manner and even receive Communion! Showing even the slightest cleavage was definitely the worst canonical faux pas a woman could commit. Mom told me about a priest who denied Holy Communion to a "Cleavage Cleo": "*a pa eu de respa*," (she who had no respect). In 2012 a Catholic paper said a priest also denied Communion to a parishioner in a lesbian relationship. She wanted him transferred, protesting she should've been told before! The bishop is leaving it to the discretion of the pastors. Rare and illegal then, the status of same sex married couples never came up. How did it also happen in RI, once the most Catholic state in America? The liberal leadership at the state level didn't let the voting public decide. These acts are no longer criminal in the eyes of human law. As said already, the feeling is you can't legislate morality, but it does leave a society that is basically pagan, amoral, and devoid of the values and traditions of past Christian traditions. Since some families no longer inculcate morality in their children, we see unspeakable acts in the public domain, since no one has taught them. My belief is that since crimes are against the laws of the land, their prohibition should be taught in the classroom. Even the ACLU could not object, since no moral/divine prohibition would be mentioned, as it is in Catholic schools and churches. It's how our consciences were formed.

Most of us owned but one good Sunday outfit. *Pour le dimanche* (for Sunday) was the label. As a youngster, God, how you got in trouble if in a playful mood like playing catch after church, you dirtied or ripped those duds. Ditto for our Sunday shoes! Since grass was rare, it was easy to scuff shoes in our pebbly gravel backyards. Even if our Sunday fineries were ordinary by today's standards, we wore those outfits with some awkwardness and gee-whiz air, not being to the manner born like rich kids. There were no Fauntleroys in Woonsocket! Being squeaky clean after your Saturday night bath was your Sunday attire's first requirement.

Easter was a time for new fineries. How you wished that Sunday was late enough in spring to show off your new duds. If only light zephyrs blew, there'd be no need to wear a winter coat over your "glad rags." Most times it was nippy, but as we got older and wanted to impress, we braved the cold hoping to be warmed by the admiring glances of peers and parishioners. "*Yé fier*," (proud) mom intoned if you felt good about your get-up. Like at the Oscars now, girls were the Easter mass show with a new wardrobe of dress, hat, shoes, stockings, and purse. From the choir loft where many girls sang, the church looked like a meadow splashed with springtime colors. At least for that one day, our drab world was in Technicolor, like rare big budget movies at the theater.

About special attire, oftentimes you also saw the difference in men's getup at Sunday ballgames at St. Ann Park. Of course, they weren't in suits, but with dress shirts, ties, and hats. Sunday was a kind of dress-up day where rest and relaxation, a victim now of our ruthless economic engine, were prime. It's hard to fathom, but recent stats indicate Americans work 180 hours more a year than at one time. The nation's production is up 50 percent, but wages only 20. We're the workaholics of the industrialized world, and yet indebtedness keeps rising. We spend more than we make. There's an old saying: "A fool and his specie (money) are soon parted." It's why someone also said, "We've never had it so fast, nor lost it so quickly."

But with today's affluence, who needs to wait for Easter "to walk the red carpet?" It's still America's biggest church day, and churches, like Our Lady Queen of Martyrs (now Holy Trinity) must add chairs. A reminder of the past. But "Sunday special" now plays to a lot of empty seats the other 51 Sundays or Saturdays. Church attendance for Catholics, once as high as 75 percent, has dropped below 20. It's encouraging that 59 percent in America say religion is very important in their lives. But it's lower in Canada and especially France, "the oldest daughter of the church" in Europe. It's a victim of the godless French Revolution that even then turned the stomach of rich Parisian families who took refuge in Philadelphia and hoped to make it French. The French leader when the European Union was created did not even allow the mention of the historic contribution of the church to faith and learning in drafting its constitution.

So, families we knew mirrored the prewar Franco-American family and tenement living in its most pristine, simple, and conservative features. Pity it would never be the same in postwar America, as we inescapably became strictly "American families," if you will, in all their good, yes, but sometimes fragmented, materialistic, modernistic ways. Now finally educated, well employed, and well spoken, we Catholics, like the Irish, are no longer an immigrant church. Like Humpty Dumpty, has the American family, religious or not, fallen from its once lofty perch? Can it be put back together? Does the blueprint exist only in the Smithsonian?

The Sacred Trust of Parenting

ALMOST A NORMAN ROCKWELL painting in subject matter if not in touch, the depiction of a Franco family kneeling at a father's feet for the New Year's Day blessing is an endearing and memorable scene that was once commonplace. (*La bénédiction du jour de l'an* - The blessing of the new year.) We did it in our family. Not every year, but a few times are etched in my memory. It was in the parlor where the couch was our one good piece of comfortable furniture. The rest of the room was used for the annual Christmas tree and, as a bow to domesticity. It was where dad gave us haircuts, repaired shoes, and kept his spinning jenny for *mémère's* knitting. On the walls was mom's Fontaine family photo and one of our family taken just before I joined the order in 1947.

The author with his parents and siblings in 1979.
Front: Léopoldine and Alphonse Tellier
Back: (l – r) Rachel, Bernard, Rene, Suzanne, and Robert
The 1947 photo of the family appears on the front cover.

The good nuns prompted us to do it. We boys felt a bit *gêné* (uncomfortable,) but also a deep sense of awe and respect for him. Like offspring asking the patriarch's blessings in the Old Testament, we knelt and listened to his few words of endearment and wishes. Typically altruistic, he exhorted us to be good to our mother during the New Year. How proud he must have felt about our doing this! But he never asked anything of us for himself! The family in its best loving moment. I suspect mom in the kitchen was taking it all in. In their pillow talk, did they say, "We're blessed with our children. They know we love them, even if we can't give them more." In school, we often recited the Ten Commandments, including the Fourth to honor and obey our parents and all lawful authority. We felt we were doing that with our simple ceremony, especially the honor part. Sister *Sainte* Émilie quoted us a "selfish" reason to obey our parents. From Prophet Sirach I later learned: "He who reveres his father will live a long life; he obeys the Lord who brings comfort to his mother." Later, a theology professor of mine in college said it's one of the few exhortations promising a temporal reward.

As far as family authority went, even if I hinted it was patriarchal, I can't say for sure to what degree. There was a wonderful symbiosis in most parents' governance, since begetting and rearing children were, besides mutual affection, the very essence of their matrimonial union. When old enough, I was impressed with those time-honored emphases in Catholic weddings. The degree of permanence in their marriages at the time was a terrific example as well as security for children. It gave credibility to the most abused phrase, said or implied, in the marriage contract: "till death do us part." Revealing was a recent study that over 40 years, 67 percent of all marriages wind up in divorce; 40 percent within the first seven years. The bloom on the rose withers quickly! "The twenty-year fracture" is also critical I read. Especially if a couple's attention and affection have been mostly towards the children to the detriment of their own relationship. AARP magazine in 2012 said divorces in people over 60 have increased. A reflection of greater longevity and financial status of men and women in retirement.

Expanding further on overall family governance, I did sense there was a wonderful complementarity in everyday decision-making between fathers and mothers. In our home, for example, the power to discipline physically (however mild and rare, it was still in vogue) rested in him, but her wishes or commands we considered no less imperative. Occasionally she wielded a yardstick (aptly called *"la mesure"*) that hung next to an old barber strap at the end of the kitchen cabinets. Because of its rare usage, like the cop on the beat, it had a sobering effect. Whether for my edification or compunction, one time she broke a yardstick on my bedpost while I was under the bed. While physical punishment was rare enough, when patience was worn to a frazzle, our parents used it. Expectedly, in a Catholic household, "divine retribution" that invoked names of saints, Mary, Communion vessels, Confession, and even Christ and Tabernacle was common. So, however rare, "Spare the rod and spoil the child" - a 19th Century adage still in vogue in England - had its devotees in the task of raising large broods. But never did a situation rise to the level of abuse.

Also, knowing the catechism by heart and parts of the Bible, mom, like Moses, was more likely to hurl a Commandment at us rather than wield the yardstick. Luckily her "Commandments" were not on stone tablets. She even suggested this or that slippage in our conduct was a matter for monthly confession! This spouting of moral law was an indication of how well they knew we knew the Decalogue (Commandments). In a family of five children like ours, Catholic education meant a tuition bill of $5 a month, but they wanted us to grow up to be good, practicing Catholics. The best feeder system ever.

When house discipline had an outdoor venue, it was grand theater to see moms yelling through an open window at their misbehaving kids in the backyard. Like bad actresses in a tragicomedy, they ranted at their own children's misbehavior, like throwing sand, wrestling, mouthing off, girls pulling hair, or the boys a cat's tail. They even lashed out at the conduct of other children, even in the presence of their own mothers. They were always at home, if not at the market, church, or relatives. Thus, you were almost always under their watchful eye, a classic prescription against delinquency. Undoubtedly, those outdoor vocal fulminations were really a bit of turn-of-the-century Rockwellian Americana, long gone with the wind. In summer especially, it was sometimes WWII in the yard. If a gallery goddess was known for mouthing off or jawing, I referred to her as *"la gueule,"* an anatomical animal word for jawbone or *la bouche*: the mouth. If angry, it's how you told someone to shut up: *"Ferme ta gueule"* (Shut your mouth). Even without Anatomy 101, we knew the difference, so the reply was automatic: *"J'ai* (I have) *une bouche, pas* (not) *une gueule."* Usually, women found it more difficult to be objective about their children than fathers. Mothers tended to defend their own in backyard fights, no matter who was at fault. In French it's *la vache aime son veau*, about cows favoring their own offspring, something natural in any maternal creature. But more than once I heard *messieurs* Carpentier *et* Houle *et notre père* (our father) chide their own for culpable stupidity or anger. But I never heard a father telling a recalcitrant child's mother his behavior stemmed from her side of the family. Or tell another child his mother "wore army boots," as I heard later in Fitchburg near Fort Devens where GIs were billeted during WWII and some of their children attended Notre Dame HS.

The degree of self-control in neighborhood men was exemplary in disciplining children or in dealing with each other. It's well documented the absence of fathers is the reason for teen violence today, as President Obama said about the Baltimore riots. For our dads, did their self-control stem from obeisance to the 5th Commandment against anger, or was it because after a long day at the mill, they were too exhausted to fight? Mom told me that a couple of times: *"Ton père est fatigué quand ya arrive d'la factorie* (Your father is tired when he arrives from the factory)."

Even though our all-day guardians of the hearth naturally spent more time with us, dads were not as absent from our lives as today's studies indicate about *padres*. Jobs were scarce, but even when the eight-hour shift became the norm, overtime and moonlighting were not common. An unemployed millworker might try to pick up menial jobs, as dad did during the Depression, but that didn't amount to a 40-hour week. One man in our neighborhood seemed to mom like a workaholic, and I could see she felt a bit negative about that. Besides mill working, he had carpentry skills. I wonder if envy undermined her judgment, thinking dad was without a job during the 1930s. Even though dad could do scores of things, he wasn't handy like a rough carpenter, mechanic, plumber, electrician, and the like to generate income. But yes, if opportunity had knocked, he had a lot of skill, as we reveal. Mom said he basically had *"seulement un métier,"* only his factory work. True, our uncles said as a mule spinner he was among the best, and that skill was top shelf in the textile kingdom. Hey, they didn't give you $44 a week for unskilled work! But you couldn't get him to take side money for his homemade wine, whiskey (during Prohibition), applesauce, tomato flats, etc. He was the "Al" as in "Altruism."

But if you omit the war years when the pay was better, the other times were a struggle and a restriction on his creative mind, curiosity, and ambition. A mill town did that to you, limiting your educational and vocational opportunities. As a young boy you were almost 100 percent factory-bound and no skills were needed when machines were perfected. One day, as we both looked out of the living room window at the Lafayette mill on Hamlet, I recall my wounded pride when he told me it was going to be my work destiny. Paying my way through Mount, I was studying hard and getting good grades, but he was telling me the way things were. Economics 101 in mill towns like Woonsocket, Central Falls, Pawtucket, and West Warwick, RI, - Uxbridge, Lowell and Lawrence, MA, - Putnam, CT, - Lewiston, ME, and others. New England was Spindle Heaven!

After all, isn't that why they came from Canada? So, parents pointed out our working future, just like a miner to his son in Appalachia, or a guild *meister* (master) to his son in medieval times! Of course, the mills eventually went that-a-way long before northerners also went south to catch more rays, protect their retirement income from taxes, Social Security pension, and jobs for the young. My dad's "outsourcing" of jobs prediction was a difficult concept for a child to understand. Newspapers had to be the source of his foresight and wisdom. We're still losing people, and one report said 1,100 people leave every week (?) for reasons too well known: the high cost of doing business, high taxes, the flight of industry, underperforming schools, and pollution. In "Charity in Truth," - Pope Benedict XVI said the drive to outsource work to the cheapest foreign bidder has endangered the rights of workers and he demanded they be allowed to unionize to protect their rights, including continuing employment. I'm not surprised many papal encyclicals and letters deal with the economic subjugation of the worker, an endearing struggle. It's why communism was one misguided attempt to solve that problem. Pope Francis quickly spoke about the disparity between the have and the have-nots and "the idolatry of wealth." (Didn't a wit say, "Money is the root of all evils, but we still root for it?")

At St. Michael's College, Vt., I spoke to a nun from Pennsylvania who said her father died young. When I said, "black lung disease?" her shoulders drooped in acquiescence. Similarly, has the heroic story really been written of the immigrant French-Canadian millworker, the Irish canal and railroad builder, the German or Polish mineworker and others who literally gave up their lives for their family when they worked in generally unhealthy conditions for starvation wages? In the Order we called that *le martyre de chaque jour* or *le dur quotidien*: a kind of daily martyrdom while donning "the tools of ignorance," as catcher Yogi Berra once said jokingly of his trade and look. Also, a 2013 report added, "Unhealthy air that makes its way into New England from coal-fired power plants in the Midwest is a major reason why such states as Rhode Island continue to struggle with air pollution that threatens health." But good news, one of the nation's largest electricity producers, AEP, will reduce dangerous sulfur-dioxide emissions from several Midwest plants. Of all the possible causes of cancer, isn't environmental pollution among the most causative, along with a sedate lifestyle, poor nutrition, and smoking?

Speaking of the Irish, my Boston College magazine said because of dangerous work conditions at one time, many Irish kids became orphans before their dads turned 50. For millworkers, the threat was not so immediate or catastrophic, but slowly progressive. Just as there was a kind of residential gentrification among nationalities in our early history, also in the kind of work a person did. There was little thought and little pay given the poor laborer, as if he alone bore Adam's curse: "By the sweat of your face shall you get bread to eat until you return to the ground from which you were taken." Fortunately, unions did ameliorate that, as I relate later. Workers my dad's age (born 1896) had initially known workweeks of around 60 hours for about seven or eight dollars, said Joseph Plante. Luckily for them and us children in the 1930s and early '40s, they worked fewer hours when the 40-hour week came in 1940. Factory owners liked our people's docility but wouldn't have gotten far challenging their strict sense of justice and native stubbornness. I repeat later Plante was able to help a man keep his job and get *le soupeur* (supervisor) fired to boot. In his 17 years as union boss at the mill, he butted heads with bosses who didn't want to give up anything. Was he an earlier male counterpart of the cinematic union organizer Norma Rae, played by Sally Field?

There were other laudable traits on par with the simplicity, size, and mutual affection of the French-Canadian family: its integrity and honesty. A tight ethnic neighborhood, proximity to church (priests) and school (nuns), a 1,500-year heritage of deep-rooted faith, and a total acquiescence to the precepts of God and Mother Church, all helped shape parents of strict moral persuasion. By example and word, they asked and accepted no less from their children. It was understood that if you were under their roof, you lived by their standards. I enlarge on it later, but the late Senator Patrick Moynihan sounded the alarm about the casualty of fatherlessness: "A community that allows a large number of young men to grow up in broken homes, dominated by women, never acquiring any stable relationship to male authority, never acquiring any set of rational expectations about the future - that community asks for and gets chaos." Written in 1965, it begs the question of our day about crime among young men, and young women also with missing parents. This of course is not to question the valiant efforts of single parents, but more to pinpoint their challenge. Kids from single-parent homes drop out more and have more delinquency. His predictions resurfaced in 2015 with the riots. Nearly 70 percent of black kids are born out of wedlock; whites near 25 percent. One said recently, "If you don't want to be poor, don't have children before marriage, job, and home. Sociologists also agree how difficult it now is when adult singles, or once married and now divorced, have returned or are still at home past their mid-twenties. This is often due to protracted education, career building, and college debts or simply the inability to pay those high rents for the pad they thirsted for to escape their parents' domestic sphere. Short of being thrown out for disgracing the faith or family, the pre-WWII generation always married from home, never leaving home for academe or a distant job, but more for the College of Hard Knocks. The marrying age was about 20. Today it's 27 (women) and 30.1 for RI men.

A bit unusual, my parents married in their mid-twenties in 1923. Was it because both were adamant you never spent money you didn't have, or that dad, as someone told me, was a bit shy around women, even if raised with six sisters? Well read, did my parents know the advice of Francis Bacon on when to marry? - "A young man not yet, an elder man not at all." About the young part, a survey revealed most early twentyish marrieds said they should have waited. Have many divorced persons leaned too late? - "Marry in haste, repent at leisure." A lady at the Ice Cream Machine in Cumberland split a gut when I told her that. Revealingly, she stood in a long line while hubby sat nearby. (A wit said never get in line behind a woman if you can help it. She's usually buying for others. Is theirs the burden of Milton's literary line? - "They also serve who stand and wait.") The Bible says fear is the beginning of wisdom. The fear of parental punishment, possible rejection, and the loss of their affection were all sturdy planks in our moral platform. Generally, authority at home, school, and society was considered inviolable, before it crashed and burned around the Vietnam War era. Legitimate authority had long been the glue that held a well-ordered society and families together. But even though I've spoken of parental authority in terms of our submission to it, parents we knew in the neighborhood ruled more, as did our teachers, "by a hand of velvet than by the gauntlet of iron beneath it." I love that maxim.

In large families, older children were expected to be like stand-in or surrogate parents. The oldest daughter was like the second mother, *la seconde mère*. Sometimes, like in Irish families, the oldest girl even subordinated her marital ambition to care for the folks in old age: *Prendre soin dans leur vieillesse*. If, on the other hand, older parents begot a child, he or she was *un enfant pour ma vieillesse*: a child for my old age. Or *un baton de vieillesse*: a walking stick. Always there was that sense of self-sufficiency, connectedness, and perpetuity in family life. Did America's liberalism, redefinition of marriage, the constant buffoonery of TV family values help undermine that sacred institution? In a thousand years of history, one wrote nothing like the nuclear family did a better job in raising kids! Women are the worst victims of the family dissolution, also stemming initially from a live-in situation without commitment, creating a mindset not favorable for a lasting marriage later if trouble comes along. Also, a British study said there's far more violence and murder of women and children when the man is not a spouse or related to her children. It happens too often in RI.

Fortunately, the chill penury of millhand salaries didn't prevent parents from properly nurturing their many children. Poverty today, as a writer said, is made more oppressive by its juxtaposition to so much wealth and affluence. But since poverty then was a very common phenomenon in our city, mom for one said it invited no harmful comparison, nor did it seem a special curse visited on any family or ethnic group. As my sister Rachel is fond of saying, "Whatever difficulty that doesn't hurt you, will make you stronger." Naturally there were degrees of poverty or comfort as I saw on my paper route in the Social District. But generally, in our world, outside of the Lepoutre family and a few professionals, we couldn't name one so-called very affluent family. Her *mot juste* (final word) was that some were just less dispossessed than others: "*Cette famille-là est moins sa paille*," meaning "straw," the bedding of the poor. Capitalism today has been touted as one of the best economic systems ever, but it creates gross inequalities of wealth. Yet even the very rich can be larcenous. *Cupidas radix malorum*: cupidity, larceny, and envy are all synonymous as the root of all evils, says the Good Book and one Church Father. The recession of 2008 revealed CEOs who once had salaries 40 times that of their workers, now have a 400 margin. Times also were better when wealth was generated by industrialists or individuals, not by market speculators, especially if not regulated. Presidents "Bull Moose" Teddy Roosevelt and Woodrow Wilson, we said, started combating corporate greed. But it came back recently. Naturally there will always be disparity between rich and poor, but studies in 2010 showed the rich now have far more in purchasing power than the middle and bottom classes.

Judging by today's level of comfort or acquisition, few then owned their own home, drove a car, had a great wardrobe, or took annual vacations. The accretion of wealth or the personal advancement of its members was usually not within reach or their primary objective. But *la famille et son bonheur* - the family and its happiness - were *la raison d'être* (the reason for being.)

About family ethics, dad's legendary honesty (like returning too much change to the store) once cost me a bicycle, prolonging my pedestrian lifestyle. You generally didn't see two bicycles in a family, so I waited for Bob to hand me down his Schwinn bike. Since it costs $26, our "rich spinster aunt," *tante* Marie-Ange, helped him.

But one day an itinerant young man offered to sell us an almost new bike for six dollars. We didn't know him, but his needing money for something else sounded credible enough. Bob and I didn't know that if it's too good to be true, it is too good to be true. Also, not knowing him should have raised our suspicions, because in those days we knew or knew about most kids in and out of our turf. That's because we walked or biked all over creation. The Negro spiritual said it best: *"All God's Chillun Got Shoes."*

Back from his work shift, dad was curious about the "new bike" in his wine cellar. Its newness didn't square with what we paid. Mom said he knew the price of everything. Once when I asked him what salt cost 25 years ago. He told me. We told him we came up with the six dollars from both our banks, mine a metallic Woonsocket Institution for Savings account. Since Bob already had a bike, it was either altruistic of him to chip in or he just wanted me off his back. Anyway, dad said to check the paper if it was stolen. Disaster! It was! We returned it to the owner somewhere in the Elm Street area. They say it's not real charity unless it hurts but we only got two dollars from the grateful victim. So, I had to wait until Bob went into the navy to finally get his bike.

Mom always praised dad's honesty, which we kids thought was nice, but this time it hurt me. I grumbled, "Why did he have to be *plus honnête que l'pape*: holier than the pope? For us, "the coin of the realm" largely came from our nickel-a-week allowances, selling rags on Elbow Street, and picking up two-cent returnable bottles at St. Ann Park. When I later taught Virgil's "The Aeneid" to my Latin-4 seniors at Notre Dame HS, I identified with "being wary of Greeks bearing gifts," a famous adage about that Trojan Horse story. It reminded me of our run in with that bike thief. The Trojan War is the only war ever fought over a woman (Helen) and it inspired a great line: "the face that launched a thousand ships / And toppled the topless towers of Ilium?" (Troy) (A teacher friend wondered what Grecian facial cream she used?")

Some forty years later, I tried "to recapture" my youth when a neighbor moving to Florida promised to sell me his classic Schwinn bike when the time came. When it did, he said he sold it to someone else. His wife, a witness to his promise, gave him the worse withering look I've seen. Facetiously I've often wondered which of poet Dante's ("Divine Comedy") nine levels of hell is reserved for promise breakers? Mom would've said, "*Ya pas d'coeur*": He's heartless. In William Shirer's "*The Nightmare Years*" 1930-1940, he paints Hilter as the worst promise-breaker ever. He promised peace, but forcefully took gigantic pieces of Europe bit by bit until the timid English and French finally put their foot down about Poland. Ministers Chamberlain and Daladier (France) could've conceivably prevented WWII and the death of 60 million people if they had opposed his first land grab since Germany was not yet war ready. Appeasement, say historians, rarely works. Can you believe dad in our home rebuked Chamberlain for "his peace in our time" cave-in to Hitler? It made his war prediction a sure thing.

Like a minister's or policeman's children, we could've complained that we too, at times, lived under a double standard of morality. But he wasn't at all puritanical or unbearably moralistic. Just the reverse, he was a classic example of "the truth setting a man free," allowing his faith to lie easy and peaceful on him. An immigrant and orphan at an early age who later lived with a friend because of his dad's second and ruinous marriage, one would think he should've cursed his lot and become "sicklied o'er with the pale cast of thought," (think depressed), as Shakespeare said. His situation is an example why child psychologists ponder why a difficult childhood sometimes produces a troubled or criminal person, or, *au contraire*, a person like dad "who was the very salt of the earth in his personal, family, and community roles. One writer opined no matter how bad circumstances are, if a child feels loved, he or she will prosper. As the Rat Pack crooner Dean Martin lyricized, "Everybody loves somebody sometime...." So, both our parents came from stressed backgrounds which somehow, some way, made them the beautiful human and moral people they became. They were loved by their big and great families, no matter their tragedies.

Even though mom was no less ethical, she did tease him for being so upright and never taking a penny that wasn't his: "*Il volera pas même une cent.*" (He won't even steal a cent.) She added that what he didn't have in the way of material things, he wasn't going to get unless he worked for it. But she wasn't downplaying his industry or ambition. She knew too well the vagaries of the mill profession, so she ran the household with the little he brought in. Amazingly, later in life when disabled, if he had a dime to his name, he was still uncomfortable with government programs and handouts, as Sue told me. He was convinced there was "no free lunch." Politicians only returned money you gave them, he said. He believed big government meant big taxes and those programs nearly always grew wasteful, costing more than their original estimate. Knowing something about human nature, he told me one day how personal initiative and industry would be undermined, as did happen, by too much bureaucratic largesse. Even though he was a poor millworker who stood to benefit he still had misgivings about some of Roosevelt's New Deal programs. Poet Robert Frost did too, saying if you didn't provide for yourself, someone else would, and you might not like that. As filmmaker Moore said, "While forced sharing is good to some, a system built on excessive redistribution inevitably leads to special benefits to a few insiders while making the poor, poorer, shrinking the middle class, and reducing median incomes." President Wilson added, "We do not want a big brother government; I do not want a government that will take care of me. I want a government that will make men take their hands off so that I can take care of myself." Were the above men echoes of the Advent Season line: *Vox clamantis in deserto...* A voice crying in the desert, i.e., unheard? Until Franklin D. Roosevelt, all presidents didn't want to spend money.

Somewhere, somehow, he had bought into the 19th Century philosophy of Self-Reliance, as immigrant America once did: "Trust thyself; every heart vibrates to that iron string." Not that he knew anything about the likes of fiercely independent writers like Thoreau and Emerson, author of that quote, to name but two conservatives of the 19th century. People then, I believe, did have a higher degree of self-initiative, self-reliance, and readiness to help when disaster struck and created situations of untold misery for individuals and groups, like the Irish famine (1845-51) and the Depression at first. But realistically, with the great disparity of wealth among people now, and because "we hear the cry of the poor," as the song says, churches, private organizations, and all levels of government are all attuned now to the welfare of all, as they must to some degree. Roosevelt said it wasn't virtue, but a necessity to help the poor. So, despite dad's wish for self-reliance in his case and for others, within my narrow perspective I thought no one helped individuals more in our 'hood. We said people living in large, congested cities, instead of on their own lands in rural areas, magnified today's problems. And no one is more generous in times of need than Americans. So even if stats about murder and larceny are unbelievably high in this country, it's comforting to know "Charity does cover a multitude of sins." Is it ironical we are, yes, rather violent, yet extremely charitable! "No seamless garment," as the Catholic Church advises us about the difficulty of choosing our political figures, especially about the abortion issue and its specter of fetal violence. Also, the destruction of the historical and divinely ordained human family with same sex marriage. Can you imagine one pol said we should approve same sex marriage because it would boost his state's economy? But one study cited how children raised without a father experienced depression and emptiness more.

About violence and thievery, I was amazed during a hockey jaunt to Sweden with the Andover Prep School in the early 1970s, when officials said players could leave their stuff unattended, and we could walk the streets at night, as I did on Christmas Night for its fabulous light displays. No homelessness, no joblessness, and the highest literacy in the world. Perhaps an exception as a successful socialist state where taxes, Swedes told us, take 52 percent of one's pay. But reports say our governments take out as much! But despite the riots of a couple of years ago in England, Spain, and France it is believed that unique ethnic cultures are generally more law-abiding than cosmopolitan ones since the violence was caused by racial segments. But no matter what the kings of France or elsewhere thought centuries ago or Middle East radicals today, nations now are a hodge-podge of races, nationalities, cultures, and religions, the oneness of us all despite our differences under the Fathership of one God. Again, *"Ut Unum Sint,"* (To be one) as Christ said. Jared Diamond in his book *Guns, Germs, and Steel* speaks about the movement of people from one continent to another since the dawn of human history. The items of the title bear on the success or failure to do so because of those influencers, plus written language. It's hard to believe our nature doesn't always accept the incredible variety of life.

*The author's family
and the families of his siblings…*

Rene Tellier Family
Rene, James, Patricia (Smith)
Jimmy's First Communion, May 3, 1987.

Robert Tellier Family
Front: Mildred (Savoie), Anne-Marie, Robert
Back: R. Kenneth, Janine, Bruce

Guilbert Bouffard Family
Front: Christine, Julie, Patricia, Claude
Back: Denis, Suzanne (Tellier), Guilbert, Guilbert Jr: deceased

Bernard Tellier Family
Front from left: Marc, Michael
Back: Alan, Gloria, Exilina & Eugene Landry (Gloria's parents), Bernard

Donald Clark Family
Donald, Rachel (Tellier), Christopher, David, Donald Jr.

3 – THE TELLIER ODYSSEY

Travails in a New Land

LIKE THOSE EARLY American pioneers who undertook a courageous trek to find their El Dorado (City of Gold, i.e., a better way of life), so did my grandfather Joseph Tellier, wife Angélina, and their nine children when they left Saint Cuthbert, P.Q., to come to Woonsocket in 1904. Their exodus was another chapter in their ancestors' first transplantation story from France. Like nations, families too have their Manifest Destiny.

My grandfather's first forefather in the New World (New France to him) was a 21-year-old soldier named Jean-Baptiste Letellier, son of Nicholas Letellier and Elisabeth Delespine from Coutances, Normandy. He sailed to Québec in 1665 with 1,000 men in the Lafouille Company of the Carignan-Salières Regiment. Renamed several times, it survived to see action in the French Revolution in 1791. Many of his mates eventually returned to France, but he stayed, and once at Contrecoeur interacted with one of mom's ancestors (Louis Jean dit LaFontaine) in a real estate transaction, a copy of which I have. Under the leadership of Lt. General Alexander de Prouville, Sieur de Tracy, the regiment established forts along the Richelieu River, cementing friendship with the Mohawks to keep the other warlike Iroquois at bay. But in one of their forays, they attacked Contrecoeur where the Fontaines lived and were once rescued.

Because Letellier was a soldier, he was in the pay of no less than King Louis XlV himself, the fabled *Roi Soleil* or Sun King. He reigned under absolute rule, proclaiming *"L'état c'est moi,"* meaning he was France, the country. (In the Order, we mispronounced *"l'état,"* to *"le tas,"* meaning His Corpulence or Immensity.) Jean-Baptiste first married Marie Grassiot, one of the first *filles du Roi* (Daughters of the King) sent to marry single Frenchmen. But Job-like, later he lost his wife, daughter, and son in the space of two months, leaving him with one child. "In disguise," the grim reaper was either an epidemic, accident, or Indian attack. Longevity for women especially was like a misnomer. He next married Anne Chenier, who died childless. He married a third time to Marie-Renée Lorion in 1691 after her husband Jean Delpué and 44 others were killed in a battle with either the English or *les* Iroquois. No less than most in fecundity, they had six children. He was 60 when he died in 1704 at Varennes. His widow then married a Jean Tifroy. As was the custom, widows and widowers with children remarried quickly from the sheer necessity of needing spousal support to raise large families in a harsh environment. There is a Fort Gratiot (an alternate spelling), north of Detroit, named after our ancestor.

No less fascinated with dad's family tree than her own, mom, who loved genealogy as well as royalty, left a handwritten note that a LeTellier was Secretary of State in France, and his son a courtier. She left no other indication, however, that our mill state was once connected to those Parisian blue bloods. If we were, how did we get off the gravy train or become more "red" than "blue" in our sanguinary or rather financial makeup? Ah well, I did read the poet's line in college about coming to earth "trailing (emphasis on trailing, as in losing ground) clouds of glory." If like Plato's believers we had a pre-existence somewhere else in the cosmos, we "crashed and burned" from our once galactic, supernova-rich origin. "Lost in transit," as they say. (About the Latin word "transit," I recall when a new pope is chosen, he's immediately told to remain humble: *"Hic transit gloria mundi,"* that is, the glory of your crowning in this world passes away quickly. After the election of a recent pope, a New Yorker graffitied that thought on a subway wall to remind Gothamites to be less mundane or ambitious. But a wit countered, "Gloria Mundi doesn't live here anymore; she moved.")

Like his ancestors, *pepère* Joseph tilled a small farm in St. Cuthbert, P.Q. When Pat and I visited dad's birthplace, the local priest genealogist (like the one who knew about the Fontaines in Contrecoeur) showed us a handwritten baptism registration in a timeworn leather-covered book. He knew about *pepère's* family and the location of their small, rented farm. When we stopped at a little mom-and-pop store for a soda, the lady knew *"les* Durands," my grandmother Angélina's family, and had been to Woonsocket a long time ago to visit them. They lived close to us on Wood Avenue near *la* Gaulin Ave. Unfortunately, not one photo of hers survives in the family albums. In fact, none from the family's years in Canada! Only after she died here was a family photo taken. It's a pity because judging by her six gorgeous daughters, she must've been *un dix*: a Ten.

To digress for a minute, the Fontaines, however, loved to take photos, but they lost all but three in that forest fire before coming here. But they went at it with a vengeance once they moved to *la* Gaulin where we kids mostly grew up. Perhaps because the street was close to church, school, mills, and market, mom's own ambulatory family and ours lived there three separate times. Unfortunately, the demolition later of the neighborhood (in the name of renewal?) scattered nearly a thousand long-standing parishioners, ushering, as a cleric told me, the eventual decline and demise of St. Ann's parishioner base of 3,200. The city did not achieve a commendable record in preserving a unique piece of French-Canadian Americana that was *le coin Sochelle*. No grand vision; only piecemeal additions. Reasons given were the growing and chronic economic woes of the city when the mills went south, lack of highway access and available commercial real estate, and a legacy, at least by detractors, about its lack of an educated workforce.

Some genealogy studies given me by *Frère* Hermenegilde Tellier, SC, from a Canadian Province of the Order, reveal the family name came from *un Jean LeTuillier*, a tile maker (*tuile*), or as another source says, "one who was a weaver of linen or wool." He had three sons whose perpetual motion he symbolized by three lizards on his coat-of-arms. Mom would've agreed with that active reptilian moniker when siblings Bob, Ben, and I were a noisome trio whose romping angered two Turcotte old maids below us in our tenement. Brother said there are at least six Tellier lines, all related to some degree. When I read about poet Chaucer's life, author John Parker said the English version of Tellier is Tyler, the surname, I said, of our tenth president (John - 1841-45). How did that prestigious tidbit of coattail genealogy escape mom's detection? Maybe it's only written in English books! A Michel le Tellier (Marquis de Louvois) was a trusted minister of war, a position considered loftier than the king's generals. Louis XlV also had a Jesuit confessor named LeTellier. But how did the king justify having a wife and a mistress (*une affaire du coeur* - an affair of the heart)? Was it because it was common since marriages were often arranged for territorial and political reasons? Gallantly, he spent some time each day with them, but at night with his paramour. One night his wife peeked! And later, finally gave birth.

A Paul Bunyaneske type, *pepère* Tellier worked his little but unproductive farm. But, said mom, he knew from a previous short stay in RI *les états* (the states) had jobs like mill work, hauling (with horses), and merchandising. Also, with his brother-in-law and family already living here on Brook Street, there was *un pied-à-terre* or a jumping-off point. Throughout history pilgrims have relied on that. The idea that "When you're here, you're family."

Unknowing Ben Franklin's adage that "Fish and visitors stinketh after three days," newcomers stayed on until they got their first mill jobs and first-ever paychecks. However burdened, in their magnanimity relatives echoed the great line of the Boys Town tyke carrying his brother: "He ain't heavy, he's my brother." About work, in his book Dunwell cites an instance before the Civil War when Irish immigrants began to replace those first Yankee mill girls in Lowell. He writes, "Seventy-two persons were sheltered in one-half of a house." Salary was seventy-five cents a day and a "numbing" three jiggers of whiskey! Was that to dull the mindless drudgery of their work or ward off microbial invasions from their unhealthy living and working sites? Or perhaps simply to boost their spirit(s)? About the jiggers, did prospective jobbers say, "I'll drink to that?"

About that temporary stay before 1900, he feared conscription into the Spanish-American War. So, he bade farewell to his Pascoag, RI, *demeure* (abode.) He wasn't an American citizen (were non-American citizens drafted?), so he wasn't draft dodging. Like Vietnam refuseniks, did he croon, "Hell no, I won't go?" Or was he labeled "a Chinese of the East?" Or as seen recently: "Industrial flotsam (waste) from Canada." But oh the "charitable dilemma" of his brother's family when the family came down *pour bon*: for good. They took in all eleven of them (two others had died in infancy) for more than a few months. Pity the poor landlord and his water bill! Did people have any idea what they were in for when they yelled, "Come on down?" No doubt when families were all intact, this mutual help worked so much better than today's more impersonal methods, public or otherwise.

But not to be outdone, he later hosted either his or his wife's relatives *"quand ils ont descendus"* ("when they came down") said mom. The family lived on the streets of Social, Rathbun, (Francos said Rathburn) and Page after their stay on Brook. Dad said a lot of immigrant families lived on those streets, like *les* Gignacs (more than 20 members), two were later in the Order with me, like *le Frère* Blaise, national African Violet champion grower, who also created his own special growing medium. He displayed his beauties every year at the Academy, rewarding "his publicist" with an All-American plant with twenty or more blooms. His brother Leander Order was our cook at Notre Dame HS. Challenged with difficult English, he tore off labels from cans and gave them to *économe* (thrifty) Brother Adelard to re-supply. But a true Franco, he was a great conversationalist. Dad knew the family and said it was too poor to afford education. Apart from having relatives here, I can't imagine a more familiar place than *le Coin Sochelle* for those immigrants. Except for mills instead of *les terres* (farms) and tenement houses instead of *leur proper chez eux* (their own home), all seemed the same. Commenting, mom said, *"C'ta comme autrefois,"* it's like old times. One writer said they just moved to *"un Canada en bas"*: a Canada south of the border, as our book title recalls. Benedict Arnold and others failed to conquer Québec! Now it was their turn to take the offensive, like Mexicans inexorably retaking California nowadays. Including my grandparents, the gang of eleven was my dad Alphonse, Napoléon, Philibert, Annette, Marie-Anne (they said Marionne), Marie-Louise, Marie-Rose, Diana, *et* Alice. Joseph Romeo, born here, died at 3. A private man like his brothers, dad never told me as much about his family like mom did. Besides his natural reticence, a taciturn trait natural in someone born on the farm where people toiled from dawn to dust "in splendid isolation," he harbored two painful episodes.

About one episode, it's from mom and *tante* Alice I learned how and why Diana died. (Alice kept a photo of her sister's monument.) After coughing for a whole year from the effects of a cold she contracted swimming at a picnic with the sodality of *Les Anges de Marie of St. Ann's Parish*, she died at 19 in 1919. Fortunately, because of that photo, Bob, and I, with the help of Precious Blood Cemetery Director Angelo Romano, found the aged monument and severed cross, now restored. Mom kept her photo'd mortuary card, as she did of so many relatives and friends whose lives intersected with hers and our family. These photos are precious mementoes and a source of valuable family history. They were more likely to be kept, as she did. Newspaper obits with a photo are also precious. If Diana had lived, would she too have endured the family's bronchial curse? Again, does her death show a kind of susceptibility to chronic respiratory malaises in the Telliers, like the Fontaines? Like *tante* Alice - the second Tellier centenarian ever (as I read in a worldwide Tellier book) - would they all have lived longer without that affliction? Later I relate another painful episode, which mom told me in adolescence because of its painful, personal, cultural, and ecclesial burden at the time. (Statistical facts from 1945 about the number of Telliers worldwide are France, 12,153; Canada, 4,479; United States, 1,850; Belgium, 490; Netherlands, 130; Great Britain, 20; Germany, 18; and Italy, 6. The Provence of Québec had 1,026, and Montréal, 173.)

With the city becoming a national textile giant at the turn of the century, the family fortunes improved with the older children's millwork after a few years of schooling at St. Ann's. Four of my aunts worked in these local mills at one time. Living in a mill town, the little education they possessed and lack of skills didn't hinder them at all. It was to be their way of life in "Textile (Woonsocket) U.S.A." Yes, like other Canadians in Québec, they too at one time possessed lands, houses, herds, and farm equipment, but their buying power had been almost nil since money was rare. That first paycheck was an ecstatic high, wrote Arthur Milot about one textile-working forbear in *Childhood Memories*. Covered with the residue of his work, he was almost unrecognizable, like a mannequined Mr. Cotton. But he had money for the first time ever! Quite adept at handling horses as a farmer, *pepère* Tellier drove a team, picking up bales at the railroad station and delivering them to mills in the city and Manville. There were no 18-wheelers in those days, only oat-burners! *Tante* Alice recalled the New Year's Day paternal blessing and *gros déjeuner* (He-Man breakfast) didn't occur before he had risen at 5:30 to feed and water his team of horses at the company stalls. He taught dad well, who had the same solicitude about feeding and caring for birds and dogs. There was tenderness for all of God's creatures in the way he and mom said, "*une petite bête*" (a little beast.)

Besides those snarling cats at night, only those plentiful plebeian sparrows with their drab color showed up in the yard. But dad always fed them. In Bellingham, when Ben had a German shepherd and Sue's family a dog or two, you could see dad loved animals, as he gardened or watched them from their second-floor apartment.

(I also say later that one writer opined humanity has misunderstood God's biblical order to Adam and Eve "to fill the earth and subdue it," thinking the latter meant "to wipe out" in its worst sense. In the last 100 years or so, our species has been especially destructive, making us the agents of the world's fourth greatest extinction ever! Another author said of all the five orders of creation - mineral, vegetative, animal, human, angelic, none like Homo Sapiens has been so destructive and unable to live with the earth as is or should be. In one of his specials on the country's national parks, Ken Burns records a naturalist telling how crass commercialism and destructive greed have been causes. Ninety-seven percent of modern-day creatures have disappeared because of us. Will we have to live on another planet after we've made ours uninhabitable, wrote a naturalist? Recall that Plato thought we came to earth from outer space. Was this after our galactic damage? Is it why no one communicates with us?)

In scouting, there was a Bird Study merit badge, but only through pictures did we learn about the beautiful plumage of other birds, and that sparrows weren't the only avian creatures on the planet. Lincoln commented how God must've loved the common man, He made so many of them. The same about the sparrow! Dad gave them crusts we didn't eat (our fussiness had some hidden magnanimity to it!). If too many crusts piled up, mom made bread pudding, *d'la poutine au pain*, if she beat him to it.

More later on the jollity and fraternity of Francos, but New Year's Day - *le Jour de l'An* - was one of the biggest feast days of the year for them. Adding to the joy and hope of a new year was the continuation of the Christmas Season. New Year's is now the Solemnity of Mary, Mother of God. The Christmas Season now lasts until early January. In the Order, it was more like Feb. 2.

My folks said you extended greetings to all your near and dear ones on New Year's Day. In those pre-telephone days, it meant visiting or welcoming relatives all day. Living close, some came on foot since cars were rare. It was quite a feat for the men (often with their wives for physical support, as I'll explain) to make the rounds: "*faire le tour*," she said. You quaffed a drink at every house, exchanged wishes, and hoped to be ambulatory (a euphemism for "standing up") at day's end. Since these drop-ins were short, the company often kept their winter coats on. Mom said dad didn't have the stomach ("*une forte constitution*") for those bibulous marathons. He only made the rounds once. The smell of hard liquor was obvious. It was not as the poet said, "The cup that cheers but does not inebriate."

Prof Doc Fairbanks at St. Michael's College told us in an etymology or history-of-words class that English has some 40 words or more for drunkenness. Dad had a few, but one of his favorites was "*La mère est haute*," about the tempest-tossed waves of inebriation. But only wine was his calling card; not homemade Johnny Walker Red, except during Prohibition, mom said. In the summer, it was garden produce. So only at one time did he figure in the city's reputation of hills, mills, and stills.

Everyone on that day wished others eternal salvation at life's end: *le paradis* (heaven) *à la fin de vos jours*. In my last visit to Montreal over the holidays to accompany niece Cathy Reale back to McGill University with her mom Jan and her grandfather Bob, I was surprised a young Montrealite, coincidentally named Paradis, had no clue when I wished him eternal felicity with that traditional greeting. As cited elsewhere, faith declines first at home or the center "before the provinces." France, from where French-Canadian faith originated is now at 5-7 percent in the importance of God in the lives of people. Father John Randall, who was pastor of St. Patrick and St. Charles in Providence in his lifetime and a great evangelist of the Pentecostal and Marian Movements, revealed the Spirit told him only one-third of all faithful would remain. His book *No Spirit... No Church...* was given me by a Turkish-American woman, Behiye, from Barrington at the annual St. Theresa celebration in Nasonville, RI. I recall the late Bishop Sheen's prediction during his famed TV talks that missionaries would someday "return" to evangelize the West. About Italy, a recent article said people may hold the papacy in high esteem, but apart from contact with the church for epochal events (baptisms, marriage, death), there's a disconnect common in all the Western world between church teachings, church affiliation, and practice. Once faithful, a Sunday morning jogger boasted he got more from his exercise than attending Mass and prayers. No longer "an athlete for Christ," will he not "win the race" or be at the finish line, which St. Paul said you must be in your last sprint? Or will he be an also-ran, like the Gospel's wedding feast guests who failed to show and were replaced? Recent brief world cataclysms saw a limited return to the faith, now again waning. Will it take another bloodbath like WWII to bring people back?

Always boisterously comical, my *tante* Marie-Anne's husband, Jules Hantis, who made these rounds, almost met his maker one New Year's Day. Why? He came down with acute indigestion after drinking whiskey (*du fort:* strong) on an empty stomach. That diagnosis of course came from dad, our own family doctor. As a result, I've always been cautious about imbibing hard liquor on an empty stomach. But doesn't everyone? Always convivial, *oncle* Jules made the assembled relatives roar with laughter during one Sunday night gathering which we Telliers often hosted. He bellowed the overflow from the icebox pan on our tan linoleum floor was from the bladder of someone who drank too much beer. From his capacity, he surely believed Franklin's "sober" observation that "Beer is proof that God loves us and wants us to be happy." (When I made a cross-country trip one year, I couldn't wait to drink a Coors, so I could get "a Rocky Mountain high!")

Keeping the tradition of family gatherings alive in 1992. Present in this photo are members of the Tellier, Bouffard, Bibeault, Reale, and Clark families.

But drinking was extremely modest at family gatherings. *Passer la 'traite* (giving out drinks) consisted of a small beer and a chaser for uncles, and Ti-Phonse's wine for aunts. Seen but not heard, it was our chance to shine, as he put the drinks on a serving plate for us to serve. You got some nice compliments, and one time I got a nickel, a whole week's allowance. Unknowingly we were learning moderation.

Like the Fontaines, a strong, affectionate bond existed among husbands, wives, and children of the Tellier clan. Often, *tante* Alice recalls, they gathered at the drop of a hat for homemade food, good cheer, and amateur entertainment. As mom said of her family, *"On faisa notre propre fun"* (We made our own fun). Notice the anglicism "fun" instead of *bonheur*, used more for "Heaven."

Very often on the Tellier entertainment bill was my grandmother Angélina's singing. She cut a nice figure with her gorgeous hair and hour-glass form, said her daughters. Also on the card were violin pieces from *mon oncle* Napoléon's wife Maria and magic tricks by dad and friend Noé Tessier. They had learned them from a book they bought. One of their favorite acts of prestidigitation was making water come out of a wall, or so *tante* Alice thought. But she realized later that while she watched with almost "blind amazement" during the performance, one of them was pouring water on her.

Either by natural talent or his work (binding broken strands on the mules at the mill), dad always had quick, well-coordinated hands, however nicked and gouged they were by those machines. Today, he'd be Bandaid Al. We loved it when he showed us how to juggle three balls at once; cut leather cleanly for his shoe repairs; trimmed our hair so professionally (no bowl-over-the-head operation for us); made medicine, wine, ice cream, toys, and woolen baseballs. One of his sisters - with no link to his behavior! - said he was one of the fastest runners in the city. Walking those eight miles a day at the mill certainly kept him in shape. In the Bambino – Babe Ruth's bio, I read the trick to foot speed was a big body or power source and skinnier legs. Like his boys he had the skinny legs, but not the big body, so how did he become "the little engine that could?" I've said my dad Alphonse was called Ti-Phonse. In her book "*Florentine Raconte*," about life in Canada, Maher wrote that nicknames like Ti, Quéton, la Zoune, José, Coq (rooster), and others were common. Like today, physical characteristics, mannerisms, and familiarity spawned those monikers. In the Order, Joseph Phaneuf, whose religious name was Brother Alfred, was Ti-Fred and I was Ti-Phonse to some. A Brother who complained about a sore arm became *Bras Mort* (Dead Arm) and a biology major was dubbed "Bugs."

Friends and relatives loved to meet at a Franco-Belgian hall in the city to dance *la quadrille*, a kind of square dance for four couples cavorting through a series of steps. Mom's eyes always lit up with sweet rêverie when she recalled that dance. Even with us five kids and that "O Mom!" look on our faces, she went into an almost girlish swoon when she recalled "tripping the light fantastic," as poet Milton called it. (Kids, I've read, don't think their parents were once young lovers, or danced, and had fun.) I cherish those moments when I saw the young woman in her. For too many young men and women married in the 1920s, the next song was "After the ball is over…" ushering in the Depression, joblessness, war, food rationing, and their sons in harm's way. Like most families in the Social District, *les* Telliers had absolutely no language problems. Everyone spoke French in the house and to everyone else in the neighborhood, school, church, and work, even up to the 1940s. First generation children in school learned a bit of English as a subject, but daily living provided limited practice. As one of the oldest children, *tante* Marie-Anne, for example, never schooled in the city and knew less English than the others. I never heard a word of English from any of dad's sisters at those Sunday night soirées. But how they could talk, as was *l'habitude* (the habit) of Franco women then. They didn't discuss ideas or abstractions, but as domestic divas with apron strings they talked about things that happened, were happening, or going to happen. Existentialists all! Here-and-now people. Yes, not culture, art, music, planned trips, faith questions (not debatable!), or the latest book read or movie to see, but more the Bard's "life with its petty pace," like her letters to us.

The Romans had household gods, *lares et penates*, who watched over things in the house. In turn we had our moms and dads who for reasons of culture, domesticity, mill working, little travel, and no car spent so much time with each other, us, and homemaking. It was almost like at the turn of the century where over 90 percent of work was in homesteading, agricultural or related endeavors until Henry Ford and others left domestic America behind the Model T's tailpipe exhaust, so I read. The birth of the automobile culture came about, with Eisenhower given credit for connecting east and west and north and south, and "from sea to shining sea."

Tante Alice, who lived in New York since the mid 1930s and bemoaned that no one around her spoke French, got the best opportunity to learn English and Yiddish to boot in the city. As immigrant or au pair foreign girls still do, at 18 she hired out with a prominent Sadwin family who were factory and curtain store owners. During her two and one-half years with the family, she helped raise five boys and one daughter, learned quite a few Yiddish words, and felt part of the family. She remembered the almost parental affection of Louis and Edith for her.

My aunt delighted in conversing in French with Mrs. Sadwin whose dry-good parents of Fall River had sent her to a French-speaking convent school. She was a prototype of the many Jewish merchants in the city who learned to speak French passably well. Alice recalled that on his frequent buying trips to New York, Mr. Sadwin brought back dresses and coats for her wardrobe. Mom said that was "*du swell*." "Really Special."

In an age of strong ethnic unity when interracial marriages were not common, Mrs. Sadwin, sensitive to *pepère* Tellier's wishes, urged her to date only French-Canadian boys. But most in the city were Irish, Italians, Poles, Romanians, and English, et al. Francos were far less numerous. Besides, did she also know from the nuns about our obsession with faith and language? So, my aunt's friendship with an Irish salesman died on the vine or shamrock! But what a touch of real class when Mrs. Sadwin insisted she return home by taxi after a date. That was "putting on the Ritz," a familiar expression then. "*Prendre le taxi*," mom said, cost 25 cents, somewhat of a luxury. Often as we came back from playing ball at Cass Park we made a bogus call to Standard Cab at the corner of Cass and Wood. The only number any of us knew! But our Peloquin cousins down the street also had a phone, and a few times they yelled from the bottom of *la* Gaulin "to come on down" for a call from Canada. Now phones are literally people's third ear. (Recently, some young women on television were lamenting their addiction to electronic devices. Providence police verified at one time over 40 percent of crimes involved cell phone thievery. My church advises people to shut their devices.

My parents were always telling us what things cost: 3 lbs. of bananas - 25 cents; a taxi - the same; a bus ride - 7 cents; bread - 11 cents, etc. With no buying on credit, they kept a mental checklist of what his $44 paycheck could afford. You couldn't go over or have the bottom fall out; "*en dessous un point final*" (under an endpoint). One "bitter critic" indicted Americans today for "knowing the price of everything but the value of nothing." If so, people then seemed to share the first part of that indictment but for a different reason. As for the second, their tight grasp on economics, faith-filled lives, and unshakable belief in the hereafter ("the economy of salvation?") rejected it. Recall that she said what we didn't have today, we weren't likely to have tomorrow. Not exactly poet Pope's "Hope springs eternal" was it? Always the slippery slope undergirding the quotidian and uncertain equilibrium of millwork! Except for the war, the Dow Jones index for millworkers was "a bear market" all year long.

After my aunt picked up some conversational ease in the language and even sang a few Jewish songs, she was often mistaken (no blondes among the Telliers!) for a Sadwin when she brought the children to Cold Spring Park to play. Her most grateful memory of Mrs. Sadwin stems from her approval of the man, Hervé Brunelle, whom she married after meeting him at a policeman's ball in Fairmount. (He wasn't one.) The "Matchmaker-Matriarch" approved of him immediately and encouraged her "to set her cap for him." From Manville - a Northern RI community once more French than Woonsocket - *la famille* Brunelle was renowned for its musicality and inventiveness. One of her precious mementos was a picture of Mrs. Sadwin and four of the boys when they were young. One of the boys reminisced with me at a specialty auto show in North Smithfield. He was displaying a three-wheeled Isetta car with great mileage. Over the years I sent her newspaper clippings of the extended surviving family, especially Larry whom I also knew. I spoke of dad's esteem for the Jews, so his sister's experiences enhanced that admiration. And mom's too, who, of course, knew the story.

Like other immigrant nationalities, because of their faith, customs, and language, turn-of-the-century Francos were pegged as insular or not American enough in this or that way. Much like how Yankees initially thought about the Irish, virulently. But my aunt's story with the Sadwins is a touching foretaste of the growing toleration and respect among immigrant groups that became precious threads in the racial tapestry of the city as the

20th Century unfolded. Nationally, but sadly, it will always be a never-ending struggle as immigrants now from different parts of the world still come pouring in, sometimes illegally. How do we integrate some 14 million illegals?

It was so obvious mom's life had practically all been with only her own people, more than dad's. Without malice or prejudice, if someone entered her orbit and was not holding *une Fleur de lis* in hand, she said, "*Il (ou elle) ai (est) pas du monde comme nous autres*": he/she is not like us. Was it instinctual immigrant behavior to feel comfortable only with your own? Or again was it *survivance* with them, that is, their cultural organism of faith and language trying to remain intact and unalloyed by ethnic diversity? For her, like others, the expression "melting pot," if they knew the word, must've been nothing more than *un creuset*, a cooking pot for the stove or *fourneau* (furnace). In that American pot, they may have put some ingredients in there, but ethnically, religiously, or geopolitically, they never wanted initially to put too much of themselves into it and come out not recognizable. How do you say "simon pure" in French? Without knowing the word "miscegenation," they wanted their Francophone genes unalloyed, something not unique in the history of peoples on this earth. They didn't want to be what she called "*un Canadien manqué*," (an unrecognizable Canadian).

They came here primarily to find a job and to live and not to undergo a life-altering existence per se. But also, not fully realizing that with or without their assent, the transforming experience of American citizenship and life was inevitable. Unlike biblical Ruth, a Moabite in a mixed marriage to an Israelite, they couldn't continue forever "shedding tears amid the alien corn" (produce not from their own native soil). Hopefully they would eventually reap America's own "amber waves of grain." Is it because the Mayflower's English progeny often didn't make them feel welcomed, so like a wounded organism turning on itself in stress and pain, it took much longer to assimilate than today's newcomers? Practically, I thought of myself French-Canadian before American, or at least a French-Canadian American.

"But o for the Touch of a Vanished Hand"

SHORTLY AFTER THEIR ARRIVAL, the Telliers felt the pang of loss. Some 70 years before, England's Tennyson in "Break, Break, Break" had best expressed the poignancy of the loss of a loved one, when his friend Arthur Hallam died: "But O for the touch of a vanished hand, / And the sound of a voice that is still!" Mom said, "*La mort avec ses bas d'laines*" (Death with his woolen stockings) had stalked my grandmother Angélina Tellier in a quiet, "woolen-stockinged" way three years after they arrived.

Moving from one cold water flat to another in the Social District, *pepère* Joseph's large brood was making modest economic strides. But if life had been hard on a dirt-poor Canadian farm, there had been many helping hands as the family lived and toiled together. Somehow a large family in an agricultural setting seemed easier in some ways, because wants and needs were simpler. And expectations and pressures on the family were also less because it was more self-contained and less dependent on others. Now thrust into an urban industrial setting in somewhat cramped quarters, initially the family lacked modern conveniences: a washing machine, floor coverings instead of cold wooden floors, an oil-or-gas fired oven, gas or electric fixtures, a multiplicity of cooking gadgets, means of transportation, and a whole support system from dealers providing services unknown in farm life. Children were of limited help because of age or employment in the mills, a necessary support for the family now and for the parents' old age: *la vieillesse des parents*. Scott Molloy in *Irish Titan, Irish Toilers*, wrote immigrant families considered children, however loved, a source of wages, working sometimes even before the age of ten. Yes, unlike children born today who may cost $400,000 or more to raise (the latest: $800,000), they were actually an economic boon (however small) rather than an expense. Contrariwise, reasons for today's smaller families, besides the high cost of living, are education, college loans (19 percent or more American families have college debts around $30,000), family instability creating two households, and huge costs for housing, clothes, transportation, food, entertainment, emergencies, and health care.

Running a home the size of the Tellier household was a backbreaking task: *"une grosse besogne,"* mom said, and we were "only seven." But the family bore its relative poverty well because they were happy in their togetherness, a strong Franco earmark. But the steadily deteriorating health of dad's mother Angélina threw the family into a vortex of despair in 1907. She was dying of a lung disease whose name would become just as familiar as the common cold in the extended families: bronchiectasis. According to dad, who died of it some 75 years later, he said it put a stress on the heart. Incredibly he endured it for some 40 years. It affected nearly all his siblings. Among his sisters, only Aunt Alice escaped its moribund clutches, but her sister Marie Rose had it worse, dying at Wallum Lake Sanitarium, her lungs totally ravaged. I don't know to what extent dad's two brothers were afflicted, but mom diagnosed them all the same way.

Defined in Webster's New Collegiate Dictionary as a "chronic dilatation of bronchi," the disease, Dr. Catello Scarano told me, is caused by repeated lung infections (severe pneumonia also) that never healed completely due to inadequate medicine or care. Mucus accumulates in the dilated, flabby sacs, causing a haven for germs and eventually shortness of breath, fatigue, and the necessity of expectorating yellow sputum in excess. One bright note I gathered is the disease, unlike emphysema, is on the wane because antibiotics cure most infections completely. (The preceding medical assessment is my understanding of what I heard when I brought dad to his doctor's office.)

Never a big or strong woman but obeying the dictates of the church to bear as many children as the Good Lord sent her, Angélina raised a large French-Canadian family. But immigrant women like her, fatigued from almost annual birthing during their productive years, the laborious if willful uprooting from the country of their birth, and the travails of making a home in a new land, often left husbands widowers and children orphans. Saddened her death was going to leave her two littlest ones (Alice was three; Joseph Romeo, younger) more motherless than the others, she had them lie next to her whenever she rested during her last year. She was never to see any of her children marry, or caress her grandchildren, as mom told me tearfully. *Tante* Alice also recalled her mother occupied an equal place of authority in the family. Forceful but loving, her word was like a commandment. And as a deeply religious woman, she filled her home with religious objects, pictures, and statues. Resigned and trusting in God, at 46 (1861-1907) she embodied the long-suffering pioneer woman risking and losing all for a better life for her children in a new land. Recall my graduate thesis about American novelist Willa Cather and her novels about immigrants, like *My Ántonia* about pioneer women. No, my grandmother didn't face hostile indigenous people or the harshness of extreme climatic conditions of the Southwest or Northwest, but like them, her struggles were no less titanic in her own immigrant journey. After her death, the older girls each took turns being *la seconde mère* (second mother) to the younger ones, until the mills or marriage intervened. Mothers will always be everything to their children, and I loved mom saying that. Because of sickness, tragedy, or natural death, it was common in an age when poor, immigrant married women didn't live as long as their men. She added "the second mother" oftentimes stayed in that role until marriage intervened (if at all) or had her own "*chez eux*" (home.) In old age, a surviving *mémère* or *pepère* often moved in with one of the married children. It reflected the unbroken family unity so characteristic "*de la famille d'autrefois*," (of the old family) said mom, who so loved sharing her mother with *tante* Laurence. One day, grateful dad whispered to me mom couldn't have coped running our home without *mémère's* huge help. A big tenement and five kids took a toll on a 105-pound *femme de maison*. Especially since "*l'argent éta rare*" (money was scarce) as she said, so you couldn't hire help or purchase energy-saving facilities.

But speaking about the ills, wants, and tragedies of life in dad's or her own family, mom, the faith-filled incurable optimist, always saw the human and divine redeeming dimension of personal and family misfortune. Because her people never lost their center or focus in life, nothing really didn't make sense to them. It was all one big continuum in their Pilgrim's Progress (John Bunyan: 1628-1628) towards eternal life after death, as I read in the faith-filled lives of the first martyrs, Robert E. Lee, President Jackson, and most of the Founding Fathers. About Francos, how had the church succeeded so well in transmitting the love of God, a sustaining faith in the hereafter despite hardships, and the Gospel's message of good works in their lives? One hopes the wealth of the last half of the 20th and now the recovering 21st Century, despite the penurious first decade, doesn't usher in the dire prediction of the new industrial age of England centuries ago: "Ill fares the land, to hastening ills a prey, / Where wealth accumulates, and men decay." Does this sound like the increasing gap between the rich and the poor now? No matter what economic system prevails, isn't the gap between the rich and the poor, as seen in Christ's day and throughout the ages, an inevitable outcome? Pope Francis spoke about the idolatry of wealth when not shared. So what is it about prosperity that often corrupts, as Christ said, "How hardly will the rich enter heaven?" He talked about the rich man, Dives, who didn't share with a beggar.

Near six feet, with a rugged woodcutter's build, blue eyes, and light curly hair, *pepère* Joseph Tellier, born in 1866, wasn't a typically short, somewhat dark-complexioned, and slightly built French-Canadian man. Aunt Alice and mom told me he commanded attention and respect wherever his big feet tread. He always wore high tops, the first thing I noticed. When he lived in his daughter's two-story home (*tante* Marie-Louise *et* Armand Peloquin, 205 Gaulin) and sometimes walked up the hill to sup with us, I watched dad looking at his father. You know how kids take their cue from their parents, and I saw pride, admiration, and affection in dad's eyes; the same deference we tried to have towards him. You know as a kid you have no real understanding of the way your parents were at your age. You think they were born your parents and never had parents of their own or a childhood. Like we thought about our teachers at St. Ann's. So it was good for us to see that, as it was for mom and her mother when she came on weekends. It's like all of a sudden our parents weren't authority figures, but more like us towards their parents, that is, reverential and grateful for all they had been to them. For a moment, it's as if they had regressed into childhood. I found it fascinating.

Dad "warned" us to behave when *pepère* came and not to shame him before his dad. You know, the usual family mini-temper tantrums among siblings at table, like on TV. However, *grouillant* (active) the five of us were at times as a family, he didn't have to worry. We were awed by his physical presence, his now all white hair with that beguiling and curling *toupet* (forelock), and even his slightly trembling hands. Dad told us not to stare at the tremor, noticeable when he ate his soup. Francos nearly always started every big meal with soup, and my parents were superb at making *la soupe du jour*. Dad deferred his place at the head of the table and we all dropped down one chair on one side. Was anything more beautiful in immigrant times than to see a large family breaking bread in their common affection and togetherness, especially with grand folks on board at times? Is this the biggest loss of our modern culture? Everyone is now out "making the donuts," instead of eating them from the family oven, as people once did.

Pepère Joseph Tellier (seated) poses proudly with his sons (l to r) Napoléon, Philibert, and my dad, Alphonse.

The decibel level among us kids was low at those meals. If you permit the vastly unequal analogy, every now and then as I raised my eyes to look at him, it was almost with the same reverence the nuns advised us when the priest raised the host at Mass. A man who could barely read and learned late to write his own name (he began his working life around 12, she said), he nevertheless had great faith in education. A faith he conveyed to dad, whose formal education was also stymied by penury and his workfare. *Pepère* insisted all his children attend school for as long as they could, obey all school rules, and accept school discipline without complaint. How fortunate we were to have grandparents so intimately involved in the fabric of our family life, since it mirrored the perspective of three generations. Society, did we say, has never found a better societal unit for spousal happiness and raising kids than the nuclear family of yesteryear.

An extremely generous man (the source of dad's legendary altruism?) who like the widow in the Gospel was ready to give his last mite (the biblical one-tenth of a penny) to the church, he especially valued his reputation above all else. This at a time when a person's word was his bond, rather than his position or standing like today. And in an age when poverty was a little easier because everyone was poor, he bore it well, always content with what the Good Lord provided. *Tante* Alice remembered his credo was contentment, a roof over your head, and loved ones to share it with. Profound in its simplicity! And on her wedding day, he told her a cardinal precept for successful parenting: "If you give an order to your children, make sure it's important and stick to it, so you never weaken your authority."

Also, a man who prized self-control and peace within himself and others, he evolved a piece of wisdom worthy of emblazoning on the walls of the UN building and in every disarmament talk among warring nations: "It's not a question of who is right, it's a question of the wisest one making peace." Profound stuff from someone who, as the poet said, the written word never shared its pearls of wisdom. Like for dad, he's the man I thought of when I first read Thomas Gray about uneducated villagers in "Elegy Written in a Country Church-Yard": "But Knowledge to their eyes her ample page / Rich with the spoils of time did ne'er unroll; / Chill Penury repressed their noble rage, / And froze the genial current of the soul." But fortunately, he like dad dodged the malediction of missing out on "the genial current of the soul." *Pepère* was indeed the epitome of congeniality, a trait dad and his brothers, strong, silent types, and their loquacious and loving sisters, were renowned for. It's why they loved us, as we did them. So for a man with such love, peace, and harmony in his household, it was indeed a heavy cross when he became a widower at 41. He had lost his *gros morceau*: the biggest part of his life. He didn't remarry "in haste," but he did "repent at leisure."

Unlike today when most women outlive their men (but leveling is occurring due to less smoking cessation in women, weight, blood pressure, and enduring workplace tensions once "reserved" for men), it was commonplace for men to marry again after their wives died. It's so obvious in genealogy research. None of us children knew until our teens that *pepère* was married twice and his second wife lived apart from him. It was probably an emotional issue with dad. At that time, living apart from one's spouse was a hush-hush affair. And a legal divorce was never mentioned, as well as a marriage annulment from Rome, a situation now more common, but troubling to the Vatican because of its greater occurrence in America. His was neither of those two options. I recall my mom said poor people didn't have the money to divorce.

Because of the unsettling experience of his getting married again and moving to his wife's home, his children began to leave after trying to live there. Even easy-to-live-with dad went to live with his friend Noé Tessier. Why? They were angry their stepmother deprived them of food, used dad's money without his knowledge to finish paying her house, and threatened to throw him out. The problem? For his kids, was it just the adaptive travails of getting used to an instant stepmother? Or the reverse, an instant stepfather for her boy? (I've read where it may take five years for these "instant" families to mesh, especially if in the new mélange there are his children, hers, and sometimes theirs, as I saw in my counseling career in Norton. Hence the divorce rate is even higher than in first marriages, close to 70 percent rather than 50. But one study said second and third marriages are proof Americans still believe in the institution.)

Or was there more to it in this new ménage? *Les* Telliers doubted her son's integrity. Things began to disappear and blame put on them, like her washing machine motor, money, and Marie-Rose' skates, to name a few things on the hot sheet, as cousin Brunelle wrote with a touch of humor. At that point he realized his loneliness and fear of coping single-handedly with a large family without a wife and mother for his kids had caused him to make a marital mistake. They separated. Tight-lipped dad never said anything about his stepmother or his father's remarriage. But mom, who told me the story, did not spare the woman. She loved *pepère* and could not understand how she treated such a good man and his children so badly. Her final point: "*Elle lui a pa(s) faite une bonne femme*": She was not a good wife for him.

I've never forgotten in teaching the Bible that Peter asked Christ why people married if it's such a stressful state. He said it was given to some to know why not! Since it was not a commandment from Christ for His disciples (except for John, all were married anyway before He called them), the church's position on celibacy for its priests, for example, stems from a later council decision. When asked, Paul said he too had no commandment from the Lord but said a married man's attention is naturally directed towards his wife and family, a celibate priest towards his mission exclusively. Both marriage as a sacrament and the single life are esteemed by the Church. And true friendship too, as writers have written about King David and Jonathan in the Old Testament. But marriage in the United States is nowhere as popular or common as it once was. Cost? Cohabitation? Job search? Education debt? Divorce in half the marriages.

Pepère Joseph never married again and died in 1950. But when his second wife's obit appeared, the folks exchanged glances and words. Their sighs seemed to say the thing was finally over. It's one wake they didn't go to. I enjoyed their comments about a decedent (*un disparu*) when the paper came in around suppertime. Dad and mom read the obits first, and if she knew someone, she reminisced about the deceased. My ears went up. It was bio time. I loved hearing what they knew about people. Were my folks unusual in their knowledge of their compatriots, or was it common among Francos to know more about their own than any other ethnic group about theirs? This happenstance because of their common faith, language, ethnic enclaves, lifestyle, and the "unwritten rule" about marrying French-Canadian, keeping everything in the family, so to speak? It's why someone said the degree of separation in the city was probably just one in the past before you met someone with a link to you? As a paper boy I wondered why so many people knew me when they learned I was a Tellier and mom a Fontaine.

But about love and marriage, all the above earmarks helped parents evaluate a would-be mate if one of their adult children showed up with a marriageable prospect: *"un(e) future,"* as mom said. When the marriage prospect departed from meeting the folks for the first time, did parents, as mom did, give you his or her genealogy all the way back to Adam and Eve? It was the closest thing to an "arranged marriage," this inquiry about family, employability, domestic virtues, character, and reputation. These two latter points were not as much a concern in first- or second-generation French-Canadian families. Were they more law-abiding or are we more informed today about those afoul of the law in a major or minor way? (As an avid newspaper reader, I'm amazed how many people of all races stopped by police for an offense already have an outstanding warrant for not showing up in court or as a parole violator! It's why many try to flee or even run the cop over or open fire. Some are wary of "that third offense." Nationally, the number of officers killed, once in the 30's, has now passed over 100 some years, even with greater use of bullet proof vests. Sadly, domestic situations are often fraught with the greatest danger. I once read outstanding warrants in RI were in the thousands. Recidivism - the same people committing crimes repeatedly - is high. One criminologist said some individuals will never live within the rule of conscience and the law. Is our judiciary too lax in not keeping repeaters locked up? Or is it the cost of incarceration with states near bankruptcy? My sociology prof in Alabama said jocularly that someday 50 percent of the population will be watching the other half! Does capitalism breed more criminality because of its have and have-not features? Or guns?)

Aunt Alice married into the Arsène *et* Marie (Lincourt) Brunelle famille. All eight children of her husband Harvey's family were talented musicians, performing at the Manville Music Hall in the Manville Brass Band, a cultural force in the village. I recall one of the sons, Emile, was the organist in our St. Ann Parish when I was a kid. He walked by our house to church eliciting this newsflash from our domestic observer on the porch: *"L'organiste sen va à l'église."* (The organist is going to church.) No, homemakers didn't have the leisure to sit and watch their world go by, but they sometimes sat on their porches in their leisure moments, and I for one loved to hear their comments about pedestrians: *"les gens qui passent par chez nous"* (people passing by us). My notes on the Piazza City (Woonsocket) enlarge on that. Surely, in a "walking culture" like theirs, people got to know a lot more about each other. I like to think it was a positive thing, since comments were almost never derogatory, just newsy like encounters at the market nowadays. For one, the 8th Commandment forbade you from undermining other peoples' reputation with lies or a truth that shouldn't be told. *Soeur Sainte Émilie* said it was one thing to admit you unjustly damaged one's character and reputation and tried to redress the wrong, but how do you undo true facts that by charity or justice should have been kept secret? There's no unringing a bell! Like their dad, the Brunelle children worked at the Manville Jenckes Mill. Erected in 1872 it was at one time the largest mill under one roof in America and was located on the Blackstone River at the foot of the town. I worked there as a 16-year-old Mount St. Charles kid, sweeping the machines. In a school research project, Lesley Brunelle discovered her great-grandfather was an expert weaver and loom fixer in town who patented "The Brunelle Let-Off" loom device preventing "the weaver from changing the tension on the cloth and causing irregular widths and injury to the fabric." Do you get the impression millwork was a common occupation in Rhode Island or throughout New England? Oh, Samuel Slater, what have you woven from a single thread? Her great grandpa also received a patent for a heating system and owned the first Chrysler in town. Not to be outdone, one of his sons owned the first Packard. Despite their overturned bathtub look (as an old magazine described them), they were considered the Rolls-Royces of their day. A mild coincidence, if you will, is that *Special Interest Autos* magazine and *Hemmings Motor News* had an editor named Dave Brownell, one of the surnames *tante* Alice thinks may have spawned the Brunelle name, this before son Robert discovered another origin. (An English engineer, Brunel, built the first underground tunnel under the Thames, a project thought impossible. People walked it until a rail line was built.) Again, a Brunelle was also believed the first to own a home radio. And another was a bugler in WWI and played in the Irving Berlin Camp Shows ("You've Got to Get Up in the Morning") at Camp Upton in Long Island.

No one doubts it now, but the ingenuity, inventiveness, and artistry of those Brunelles were not the exception among Francos and others who imported their native abilities to their new country. As *ma tante* Alice realized, the Sadwins really knew a good and talented family when they saw one and she always treasured their wedding gift.

The Daily Trek to the Mills

LIKE IN YOUR TYPICAL mill family, when the immigrant Tellier *et* Fontaine children reached their 14th (later their 16th?) birthday, they ended their limited schooling, and began to work in the mills and the family "fortune" increased! Because of new labor laws in the new century, theirs was not the lot of those 550 kids among 7,327 millworkers in 1900 who unwittingly made RI, the most illiterate Northern state with many men unfit later for military service and young women unable to conceive from too much standing. So, with their newly found "affluence," they at least forgot the limitations, if not the pastoral plusses, of farming, dairying, running a sawmill, brickmaking, cheesemaking, and other manual kinds of labor they and their forbears had done for ages in parts of cold Canada. But with little to show for it.

If you lived by the mills as we did *sa* Gaulin, about a quarter mile from *la French Worsted et Lafayette chez la Hamlet:* the French Worsted and Lafayette (mills) on Hamlet, you didn't need to be an economist to deduce factory worker or millhand was almost every worker's occupational title. Especially in the Social Corner district in which "the threads of our lives were being wound." It really simplified mom's DOT, the Directory of Occupational Titles, which I got acquainted with in guidance studies at Boston College. Our professor said the U.S. economy had something like 51,000 jobs. But it didn't seem so for most Francos, as mom said, "*Ils travaillent seulement à factorie*" (They only worked in factories). But about her gender, "*Elles sont chez eux*": homemakers.

Of course, exceptions there were, like the two ladies who lived on Kendrick, *des couseuses*: dressmakers. Mom went there a couple of times, if an alteration was "*plus fort que mwè*," beyond her ability. At other times, she went across the hallway to *madame* Beauregard, another talented *couturière* (seamstress) whose family (their dad, a professional mover and storyteller) lived where we once did before sliding over to get that afternoon sun for her Saturday reading: "*mon baim d'soleil avec mon feuilleton, le Samedi.*"[16] For her, sun and salt water cured most ills. She cherished her reading break. How many women running a home and holding down a job have that kind of *loisir* or opportunity today? Kids are very active today. But about those many Francos in the mills, French-Canadian poet Remi Tremblay, was quoted by M. Alain Briottet in an edition of "L'Union," the official publication of the fraternal insurance company L'Union Saint-Jean Baptiste, confirming that many of his compatriots were indeed millworkers. But not all, as some were also farmers, bricklayers, and factotums or do- it-alls, but poorly paid:

> Émigré canadien, dans la grande fabrique
> Je file coton, ou je tisse le drap.
> Je cultive le sol and je fais de la brique.
> Je ne marchange point le travail de mes bras.

---

[16] A feuilleton is part of a newspaper or magazine devoted to fiction, criticism, or light literature – often published as a serial.

> Je travaille souvent pour un maigre salaire,
> Je ne suis pas flaneur, je fais tous les métier.

> Canadian immigrant in the big factory
> I spin cotton or I weave the woolen fabric
> I cultivate the soil and I make bricks.
> I do not *"marchange"* the work of my arms.
> I often work for meager wages,
> I am not an idler, I do all the trades.

Dad would certainly have agreed about the often-poor pay of the French-Canadian worker (*maigre salaire*) despite his recognized work ethic (*pas flaneur*: not an idler), and his jack-of-all trade skills (*tous les métiers*) as a factory worker or into farming like his brother Napoléon especially. (*Marchange*, not found even in Larousse, seems to mean to sublet or piecemeal one's work for more pay.) We highlighted what a sight it was in summer or school holidays to see the entrance and exodus of hundreds of workers pouring in and out of those huge, multi-storied brick plants over the Hamlet Avenue Bridge. A scene replicated all over the city. Like the mass exodus of Detroit auto workers you once saw on films! In the summer, we saw our fathers, if their shift was from 2 to 10 p.m., coming down from those many tenement houses of Gaulin, Dulude, Wood, Burnside, Elm, Cass, Sweet, Hebert, Cumberland, Robinson, and others. They walked towards the mills, often carrying, like dad, a recycled brown leather bag with their lunch, a small cutting knife, and an old pair of "aerated" shoes to dispel the sweat. Few had metal boxes. But some went without lunch, dad said, *Une petite économie pour navyerre plus pour la famille"*: fasting eight to ten hours to keep more for the kids at home.

One of my first jobs ever, besides working for street vendors, Carle's Bakery, delivering papers, or coat checking at Joyland Roller Skating Rink was ordering Fish 'n Chips for millworkers. After you picked up their quarter, speeding on your bike you fetched the order at any one of those small mom-and-pop places, like Patrick Martin-Beaulieu's parents on East School Street. The city, so "Catholic" if you will, was very much "piscatorial" (the mindset of a fishing village) in pre-Vatican Renewal times. The habit of not eating meat on Friday survives today, even though Catholics have long been dispensed of the obligation, except for a few days in Lent. My folks always touted fish: *"Le pwéson (poisson) est bon pour la santé"* (Fish is good for health). Then it was a cheap, healthy alternative to meat. Overfishing now has spiked prices. The nuns told us one country in Europe was exempt from the obligation because of its defense of the Pope and his lands. At our house, dad with his dietetic bible, *You Are What You Eat*, sometimes bought fish other than haddock. (I met a person in the 1990s who knew the book.) Dad always taught us to like new stuff. No reflection on mom's cooking, but he liked to eat at other people's homes since his curious culinary mind was always looking for new recipes. One time when he brought home oysters (*des huitres*) to make soup, I was the only one to try it. When my siblings saw me scoop it up with gusto, they all came around. Upon delivering those Fish 'n Chips orders on your "meals-on-wheels bike," you got a buffalo nickel, good for a Mounds candy bar, Drake's cake, a mini-pie, or half the admission to a Saturday afternoon shoot-em-up oat-opera movie. The mill working men were so jovial and welcoming, like the men in the two saloons I delivered papers. Growing up in the city was a very nurturing, enjoyable experience for a child. Children were greatly loved. As mom editorialized, "*Un bon chez eux et une bonne nourriture*" (a good home and table) were nearly every kid's fortune, so it seemed, plus a friendly and safe community.

Going to or coming back from the mills, *les ouvriers* (workers) were so numerous, they literally covered the streets where they walked. Since *les* sidewalks around the mills were too narrow to handle the volume, the men oftentimes walked in the middle of the road astride the running Blackstone River, their "gift of the Nile!" They didn't have to dodge any fast-moving sports or luxury cars, not even those inexpensive little Fords. Their gait going off to work was brisk and vigorous. Eight or ten hours later, wearied from miles and miles of keeping up with *les* mules or other machines, they trudged back home at night (on hot, hot summer nights we were still up), stoop-shouldered, and deliberate pace. Dad and *les messieurs* Carpentier, Houle, *et* Turcotte struggled against "*la Gaulin a pic*" (steep Gaulin). He eventually got the first shift, so at night our only radio had to be shut off at 9, our bedtime anyway. Mom had once lived mid-Gaulin before she married, so as an asthmatic she never got used to the rarefied air of its peak. "*Mes poumons sont magannés un peu*," about her damaged lungs. Francos always told you about their ailments, as I tease later.

Even if medical service was cheap - $5 for a home visit, and delivery too? - many millworkers could not even afford that. Even now, a study before Obamacare revealed that yearly 20,000 people with no insurance die from conditions treatable with preventive care. Also, senior citizens spend 20 percent of their income on health issues, causing some to cut their medications in half, and eat cat or dog food! But dad, even if constrained by his meager pay, used to defend what doctors made in his day because of the cost of their education. But what accounts for the high price of medicine? "Research," says companies obscure the fact the government underwrites some (half?) of it. Theirs is one of the largest profit margins. "60 Minutes" said one fault of ObamaCare is that it didn't address the high cost of medical and hospital care and insurance? As I also say later, why is it when we Americans want or need something desperately, we're made to pay exorbitantly: health, home, heat, locomotion, education? There's no justification other than greed! Corporate greed and CEO salaries have become untenable! Will the situation, the likes of which caused riotous revolts centuries ago, like the French Revolution, again breed unrest and violence? Will people again shout, "We have nothing to lose but our chains?" (In one historical exception, I read author Vincent Cronin painted a highly favorable picture of Marie-Antoinette in his *Louis & Antoinette*. It's not true she said "Let them eat cake" before her beheading. Her only faults were gambling and being "from Austria!"

In a column by Al Lewis for "Dow Jones Newswires," he wrote, "Compared with people in other countries, Americans are more likely to find care inaccessible or unaffordable. Is it getting better? The U.S. spends more on health care per person than any other nation. Is it the curse of inflation, as dad lamented? Yet we're far from the healthiest! Do we pay ourselves too much for what we do?

About millwork, Dunwell wrote, "The close, humid, lint-filled air within the mills propagated pneumonia, tuberculosis, and other respiratory diseases." He added that in Lawrence, MA, a huge mill city complex, respiratory diseases caused nearly seventy percent of all deaths among textile workers. Allowing perhaps for some genetic predisposition in their families, their millwork aggravated their condition. Byssinosis or brown lung or "cotton death" also led to emphysema and chronic bronchitis. Because of dust, workers used plug tobacco and snuff to keep moisture in their mouths. Until dad became disabled, walking and climbing didn't bother him. Having small iceboxes meant dad and mom went to the market often. When dad bought a Thanksgiving turkey, he always hoped he could keep it in cold storage in the rear hallway, along with four or five other eatables. One year after he bought the bird, he won two more in a parish raffle. Of course, he gave them away, so again from her, "*Ça cée ton père*," (Your father was made that way) as if we didn't know.

I speak only of the men here, since I never saw or knew a woman who worked in the mills. Like her, however, most I suspect had done so before marriage. During the war, 25 million women became carbon copies of Rosie the Riveter. And recall in the early years of the textile industry, female workers, mostly of Yankee stock, in Lowell, MA, later a French-Canadian enclave, were pre-adolescents, the so-called "mill girls." They're memorialized in photos showing their youthful figures draped in cheap cottony dresses against a backdrop of the machines they worked on for over 60 hours a week. But employers maintained their virtue was carefully guarded, and time was given them during and after work to read, write for the company newspaper, and play-acting. But you have to stifle a laugh when you read that because of this creative leisure, they were variably called "poets of the loom," "spinners of verse," and "artists of factory life." Surely there was a PR man on the payroll! Most early Francos would have used more "earthy prose" about working in the mills for so many hours instead of enjoying the great outdoors. But mom spoke not about the working conditions of those girls, but about their pulchritude. More than once she said, *"Les filles de Lowell sont toutes belles"* (Lowell's girls are all beautiful). Is it because the city later became another French-Canadian bastion?

About mom's work in the mills before marriage, working conditions must have improved somewhat for young women in the early 1920s, because she never told me anything bad about the experience. But her paycheck, meager as it was, made it possible to bedeck herself in the rather stylish dresses, shoes, and hats of the day, fittingly called the Roaring Twenties. But she never rose to the level of Flapper. When you look at those photos, it's hard to believe people in Cochrane during the fire once thought *les* Fontaines, especially the women, looked like *des revenants*: ghosts. Isn't that the worst comment a woman can hear, unless of course she's into the zombie or sepulchral look like Morticia of the Addams family? Yes, the Fontaines came here with only the clothes on their backs, not fringed but singed! As guardian of the family albums, I see her when she was at the height of her physical attractiveness, with a wardrobe to match. Of course, taciturn dad never, never spoke how he was smitten. I'm sure her unquenchable gaiety, quick, retentive mind, unforgettable one-liners, and, of course, her svelte figure (never more than ll0 lb.), all helped Cupid's arrow find its mark at Oakland Beach, the boy-meet-girl Scarborough Beach of its day before the 1938 Hurricane.

But "those salad days" were a tease and precursor of those terrible times of chummage[17] or joblessness dad would face six or seven years after their 1923 marriage. Fate or the vagaries of human existence weren't through with them. However wanted and loved, we five *chilluns*, born in the 1920s and '30s, added another load of responsibility. But again, I think the poignant story, heroism, selflessness, incredible make-do, plain savvy, and will to live (*"passer en travers"*) of all those parents like mine to bring their kids through the Depression is the stuff of heroic literature, perhaps not yet written. You know, like "*The Grapes of Wrath*," from a literary giant comparable to John Steinbeck and his ability to explore the human drama of displaced people of the Dust Bowl in the Southern Plains. Brokaw's *The Greatest Generation* also recalls the heroism and endurance of poor people before

---

[17] The practice of multiple people rooming together.

the war. For example, in his notes on future senator and presidential candidate Bob Dole, he says, "It may be difficult for current generations to understand just how much poverty there was across America, even after the (1st) war and continuing with working-class families living on the margins with very little left over. They were used to it, as it had been that way, but especially in rural America." Said Dole, "After the Depression, joining the Army was a step up for many Americans. It was a good deal; you got a good pair of boots, three meals a day, new clothing, and a new rifle. It was the most many young Americans had ever had." I recalled his words when I spoke to him when cousin Gene Peloquin and I attended the dedication of the WWII Monument in Washington. He sustained a lifelong injury in the war. If a millworker got a few more hours at the mill *durant les bons temps* (in good times), especially in WWII, dad beamed, "*J'travaille extré*" (I work more), which mom called "*de l'abondance*" (the abundance).

I always enjoyed job talk between him and others who came to the house or marketing (*faire les stores*) on Thursdays. But the script never changed. Since unemployment loomed large in the 1930s, to the disheartening response, "Are you working?" was the hybrid expression *J'loaf* (I'm laid off). If the respondent worked *steadé*, the next question was *sur le coton ou la laine*? (on cotton or wool?) Everyone knew the script. Their very lives hung on those threads. It was like standing under the sword of Damocles (once a popular saying about a courtier in Greece who sat at a banquet beneath a sword hung by a single hair). Today it's "the next shoe about to fall." No one ever spoke of how their investments were doing! Women, for example, spoke about their empty *portefeuilles* (pocketbooks) and their children's health.

We said as a youngster you were pretty well preordained to work in the mills someday. In fact, around the year 1900, says Gary Gerstle in *Interpreting Woonsocket History (1875-1955)*, "French-Canadian immigrants and their children comprised fully one-half of the labor force in New England's larger industry, cotton textiles." I suspect the numbers weren't too much below that in the 1930s and '40s. Since, of course, mill working called for little education, "a middle school diploma" was sufficient. It was just a bit more than our parents had received, partly in Canada or here. Because mill working was largely unskilled, especially after England-born entrepreneurs who, in defiance of British law, copied from memory their machines or invented their own in the states, untutored immigrants had a foot in, along with their work ethic and docility.

Luckily, I dodged the proverbial bullet. Not that we showed great academic precocity, but she thought the family's supposed Achilles' heel - *des poumons faibles* or weak lungs - seemed more in the cards for me as a youngster. Like my siblings, I was the progeny of a bronchiectasis father and an asthmatic mother. So, when I contracted pneumonia twice and had a somewhat catarrhal or sinus condition as a youngster, she thought I should get an education and avoid the mills. Dad wanted that too for all of us. She argued that I didn't have "*le respire*" or breath to work in air saturated with cotton or woolen dust: "*l'endurance pour travailler dans poussière.*" So, I almost backed into it. Yes, my first-and-only mill job one summer was sending cotton dust flying off the machines twice a day at that Manville plant. Claude Fournier in "*Les Tisserands du Pouvoir*" describes it in a flight-of-fancy prose: "*Des balayeurs* (sweepers) *qui livraient à la poussière une guerre vigoureuse.*" Dust getting the heave-ho! Closest thing to hitting a ball at St. Ann's Park, until my mistake of turning 16 and telling mom I'd pay for tuition at Mount.

She hated what millwork was doing to dad with his diseased lungs. Breath by breath, he was giving up his life so we might have one. Like in most families, he was the only one earning our daily bread, *le pain quotidien* that we prayed for in the "Our Father." Every night when he retired, we heard his hacking cough, like an addicted smoker. O the poignancy of his lot! A man who as a farm boy breathed the pure air blowing over the fields of Saint Cuthbert was now trying to catch a breath in swirling dust. America gave him a job, but not clean air. Again, not demeaning his profession, he could've been so much more had he lived a generation or two later. But oftentimes one member in the family's early immigration story must make that leap of faith to elevate the family into a new economic sphere and into higher education. I, for one, needed the help of the Brothers of the Sacred Heart, the teaching Order at Mount.

An outstanding example is William E. Aubuchon, Sr., former Canadian farm boy with only a fifth-grade education and no English, who established a hardware store in Fitchburg, MA, in 1908, now grown into a New England-wide enterprise of some 130 stores or more. I'm proud the president and treasurer since 1993 has been Marcus Moran, Jr, a "Brother's boy" from Notre Dame High School and a counselee, published author, and an MBA recipient, whom I recommended to college. His brother Gregory was also an ND grad - as are brothers Kevin (podiatrist) and Peter (psychiatrist - oversees the company's real estate holdings.) I said daughter Michelle (Zide), PhD from UMass Amherst, was a pioneer in documenting the rise of the drug culture in the continental 48 states. Their mother Claire (Aubuchon) often expressed pride in her French-Canadian ancestry in letters to me. Her husband Marc, who like many in the Aubuchon hardware family served proudly in WWII, worked 72 years for the company. Generously, the company continued to pay the wages of employees in the military during the conflict. In 2008, the local American-French Genealogical Society inducted the late founder Aubuchon into its Hall of Fame for his great entrepreneurial spirit, love of his heritage, and beneficent operating values. One can't help but compare him with Irish immigrant Joseph Branigan who also, despite little money and less education, grew his Woonsocket Rubber Company and other subsidiaries into a national empire. Both never forgot their ethnic roots in providing assistance and work for so many. In my 15-year tenure at Notre Dame HS, I enjoyed conversing with Mr. Aubuchon at the family summer cottage outside Fitchburg. Like all immigrants, mom had that instinctive conviction that only through education could you advance in life: "*avancé dans la vie.*" How often she told me people criticized her for this education thing. She said she'd starve before letting that dream go. Her mother, *une maitresse d'école* or teacher in Canada, had obviously taught her well. "*Les Morvans c'ta du monde cultivé,*" she said proudly about her mother's "top-shelf" family in terms of betterment through learning. Obviously, *mémère's* family financial comfort level as rather prosperous farmers made learning an affordable option in their Saint Francois-du-lac habitat. It's sad that circumstances prevented her from educating her children to the same degree. Keeping them alive became her biggest challenge and possibly the greatest benefit of her education. What she did to save her family in 1916 is an incredible saga, one that a woman at that time rarely confronted.

Thank God, mom's diagnosis of my future health was way off target, but I'm grateful her preoccupation with my supposed weak lungs led her to monitor mine and my siblings' schoolwork closely, even if it was still early in the game for Francos. About entering the Brotherhood, I still cringe about the time she met my spiritual formation master at Harrisville, *le Frère* George-Aimé Lavallée, after I had donned the habit following ceremonies at the Academy. Sounding like the mother of the Zebedee Brothers, James and John, who asked Christ for a special place for them in His Kingdom, she told him to be sure I got a good education. Never at a loss for words, he seemed stunned for a second, his cheeks reddening as he said yes. But of course, I was treated no differently. It was *la vie en commun*, an essential note of religious life. Because of her life experiences, mom didn't exhibit the timidity and lack of aggressiveness many observers say were part of the Franco character, unlike, say, the Irish, who seemed more self-promoting and assertive: "I'm Irish and I'm proud of it." But cousin Frank spoke about a Franco who boasted he too had some Irish in him, often saying McStewaye (When I see you) and McStepogne (When I catch up with you). But on St. Pat's Day, isn't everyone Irish or wishes to be? They've left a great cultural imprint on the American psyche. We had our small differences about getting jobs at the mill, but overall, we mirrored each other well in confronting poverty, defending our religious faith, and clinging to the best of our respective ways of life. (Didn't St. Patrick study in France before going to Ireland to convert them?)

You can still see the ruins in the water of that Manville mill I worked in, later levelled by a devastating fire. But the deafening noise, the swirling dust, the dropout co-worker teens, a "sporting" pregnant girl who didn't know who the father was, and the low pay all had me scurrying back to academe in the fall. Those young hirelings tried to get me to sit with them at lunch, but they had "impure pictures." The mill did shortchange me one week but paid me fully when I beefed. Since temporary summer help was not popular, I had been vague with them about going back to school in the fall of 1946. After all, seven rejections in the city were enough. No putting a sign around my neck, "Will work to study." Facetiously, she said they only wanted me "*pour la vie*," for life, clueing me in about my job interview. I don't know how many in the city she helped find jobs by telling them who was hiring. Yes, a job counselor too!

Even though those teen workers shocked me a little, I don't mean to infer the people there or in other mills weren't good people. Hey, nearly all the people we knew, many salt-of-the-earth types, worked or survived on someone's work at the mill. The adults there, for example, were extremely encouraging, friendly, and supportive. And not because I looked like a "lifer." I noticed a girl who took the bus back to Woonsocket with me, but I had no repartee even when she invitingly (?) said she was going dancing Saturday night. But I fondly remember the mill boss, "*le soupeur*." He wanted clean machines; I was giving him that, so he cut me some slack about reading behind lockers between rounds. Like dad, I've always hated *la poussière* (dust), so I liked giving the dust the heave-ho twice on my shift. I'd wear a mask today.

My brothers Bob and Ben also worked in the mills for a spell before Bob turned to technical work, Ben into building and contracting after a stint running his father-in law's (Gene Landry) laundry business. Sisters Sue and Rachel plied office careers before marriage. In fact, when Sue, a Woonsocket HS Villa Novan, attended the now long-defunct Hill College of Business in the city, it was a quantum leap in education for the Telliers. She may have been the first ever family collegian going back to the middle of the 17th Century. Beaming mom didn't let her detractors forget that: "Suzanne *va* (goes) *à* Hill College," but people at times not only didn't buy education, but they were also judgmental about those who did. A needless expense for a future *femme de maison*, mom was told. Did they think her uppity? Thinking back on her pride about Sue, even if only from an obit nowadays, I enjoy coming across a mention of Hill. A college in the city was one small step for education and a giant leap for Francos among others. A mill city with mortarboard! In reflection, to me it was a powerful message the people of Woonsocket and environs were equally endowed with an insatiable thirst for knowledge, as is so evident now in local graduation stories. With the loss of most of our better-paying industrial jobs (as high as 92 percent, I once read), now replaced by less remunerative service and clerical-like jobs, college graduates often leave the state for their careers, the "brain drain," which, for one, deprives the state of their tax support (in the millions), and their professional skills. And because of our struggling state's declining commitment in financing its three colleges as of old, some industries wary of high taxes, untold regulations, and an inadequate workforce bypass us. I enlarge on it later but is it possible our inadequate workforce stems in part from the excessive number of kids in Special Education in the city and state: over 20 percent against a national average of 12. Boys are five times more likely to be spedded[18] (put in Special Education) One wondered if we equate boyish aggressiveness with disability or language deficiency. Would we Franco kids in the 1930s and '40s have been spedded since we didn't know English well? And do some parents forgo a more challenging curriculum in favor of smaller classes and greater attention in Sped classes? I wrote to the Commissioner of Education who told me efforts are being made to lessen those numbers. But a school committee member once told me a community attracted more state dollars with more spedded kids! But not so much now after a new funding bill was passed, which I asked for in a letter. I also wrote for a new spending plan for all schools. Of course, there is need for Special Education for the truly mentally and physically challenged, rather than obvious behavioral problems, as some teachers lamented to me in my one public school. (Didn't Alan Tenreiro, MSC grad, '92, national principal of the year, set the example at Cumberland High by upping the level of difficulty in all subjects?)

Rachel later became my secretary at the Academy when I was Director of Guidance in the 1970s. A typing and shorthand whiz and perfect speller in high school, I felt like a Fortune 500 exec dictating letters which she typed lightning quick. It was the first and only time I could "dictate" to one of my sisters. The Academy quickly regretted letting her go in June because of financial straits then. Come fall when they wanted her back, she'd found a more remunerative position. When she was a student, the nuns reduced tuition by limiting her to a restricted meal plan (hard on a teenager). My folks scraped enough funds for her to attend the Presentation of Mary academy Our Lady of the Mountains in Gorham, New Hampshire, where previously cousin Doris Peloquin was valedictorian one year. Unlike Doris, Rachel did not follow the same path of indoctrination to become a nun, a high honor of the era. Instead, Rachel would repay her parents' struggle by

---

[18] SPED is an acronym for Special Education. It's the origin of the verb: "Spedded."
– ed.

becoming valedictorian, then continuing to become the second college graduate in our family graduating summa cum laude. When Sue lost little son Guilbert, the first family grandchild, in a drowning incident in the Blackstone River, Rachel was away from the family and missed comforting support. But, like the family, she endured the loss with Christian resignation. She and a few girls from the area here formed close friendship bonds and profited well from their education. When a priest gave the commencement address, he spoke about heroic women of the Old Testament, saying the two most beautiful names for women were Suzanne and Rachel, names my mother chose for them. Are there any doubts she knew her Bible? Growing up, I never knew a homemaker who knew the Bible like mom did. She was so proud when I entered religious life.

I appreciated our novice master in the Order allowing cousin Frank and me to attend heroic *mémère* Fontaine's funeral. Recall that until Church Renewal, active religious Orders in teaching were heavily "monastic" in their public contacts. But now even contemplative Orders like the Trappists in Wrentham, MA, speak to the public in conducting their chocolate sales enterprise. In how many homes did this striving to educate their first-generation American progeny burn in the hearts of fathers and mothers, before the dying embers of the once-great mill era of the city grew cold, never to be rekindled. Old times were a-changing, being swept away to the South, as my farsighted dad had always predicted. Factors were cheap labor, more modern machines (owners almost never modernized in New England), weak or no unions at all, and proximity to natural resources. But many have now left the South and even Mexico for third world countries, as he also predicted. God, he should've been a stock market guru! But what could he have invested? It's obvious how much he talked to us, educating us about the political and economic realities of life. I'm naturally proud all five of us became prudent investors and careful spenders, mindful of mom's most basic principle: Don't spend money you don't have: *"ce que non ne pa(s)."* It's easier done when buying on credit was rare.

As the mills continued to close after the war, what would fill the vacuum? Not connected to any major highway system and with most of its land covered by huge, outdated, and inefficient structures, the city faced a bleak future. A future only an educated populace, service industries, industrial park, and a highway could reinvigorate. Despite being continually labeled one of the poorer cities of the state, the city showed some resilience in its efforts to move ahead despite 79 percent reliance on the state for its schools. Good schools always attract companies in search of skilled, educated workers. The construction of Route 99 to the Highland Corporate Parks off route 122 and the continuing expansion of the CVS mega-company were invigorating steps. I attended the first meeting to construct Route

99 to the industrial park from 146 and back. Didn't it take 20 years? Some hoped it might continue to 495, a real harbinger of growth, since trucking is the key, as I noticed in Norton, MA. Wrentham, however, was hesitant about giving up some of its land.

In connection with this new service economy, dad also reasoned our high standard of living fueled by rising wages would someday make Third World countries more attractive to manufacturers. But as noted, America, once the world's industrial giant, has become a service mogul, one also requiring education. But the caveat for RI is a lot of service jobs don't pay as well as industrial ones (steel, machine shop, tools, and the like) once did. It's left our state heavily dependent on property taxes. About that brain drain I spoke about, (over 50 percent) the college educated "are replaced" by newcomers who initially at least pay lower taxes and require more support and services in and out of school. Also, cities and state struggle to cover their generous outlays, like pensions and unrealistic COLAs considered overly generous and unsustainable.

So, because immigrants now come to us in our superheated economy where prices are so high, it rivals in some way the plight of the turn-of-the-century immigrants. But upstaging dad, mom added that because "*le coup de la vie* (standard of living) *éta pa(s) cher*, that is low, the necessities of life, - housing, food, fuel, medical services - were more within reach for them. I admitted my family was poor, but we, like others, didn't feel it as much because of our parents' inventiveness, can-do, and strict budgeting. All skills not so evident now. In the Order, they told us the measure of charity should be without measure. But more and more, I feel my pride as a conscientious and hopefully generous citizen diminished when everyday press and charitable organizations tell us we're not doing enough. Specifically, a recent survey reported Catholics aren't giving enough. Someone referred to that "15-cents in the basket at Sunday Mass habit of yesteryear." But to the contrary, one can't forget RI Catholics living in one of the highest taxing states annually donate close to $8 million for the diocesan drive. This despite the decline in parishes able to meet their quota. So fewer parishioners are asked to make up, as it were, for the so-called "Nones": those not affiliated with any religion. Payroll taxes are only the firsts of "a thousand cruel cuts," as the saying goes. But there's some relief now from the Social Security taxation and income pension freedom that has made Florida a major attraction. But sadly, you can't even save without getting taxed for your thrift. Is it because "there is no second act in American life," as a playwright said? Is our state motto HOPE because we're constantly in a state of hope, as a poet said? "Hope springs eternal / Man never is, but always to be blest," or happy.

Ceaseless Drudgery and Unremitting Toil

AS DIRECTOR OF TESTING at Norton HS, one year I administered an AP Test in Modern European History to a group of seniors in Fred Bartek's class. One of the elective questions caused me to reflect as much as they did. It was about millwork in days gone by: "Prolonged and exhausting labor, continued from day to day, and from year to year, is not calculated to develop the intellectual or moral faculties of man. The dull routine of a ceaseless drudgery, in which the same mechanical process is incessantly repeated, resembles the torment of Sisyphus—toil, like the rock, recoils perpetually on the wearied operative. The mind gathers neither store nor strength from the constant extension and retraction of the same muscles. The intellect slumbers in supine inertness. To condemn man to such severity of toil is, in some measure, to cultivate in him the habits of an animal...") So wrote James P. Kay-Shuttleworth, *The Moral and Physical Conditions of the Working Classes Employed in Cotton Manufacture in Manchester*, England, 1832."

Forgetting the obvious time warp for a minute, I wondered if any of the above resembled the thousands of immigrant workers who toiled in the mills before the turn of the century and up to WWII. The statement is one of the most severe indictments of millwork I've read. Surely, I reasoned, the passing of the years, a plethora of populist work reform laws, labor unions, and the nation's rise to industrial prominence had all improved the lot of those millhands. But by how much had the lot of the early 20th Century's millworker, like dad for one, improved wages, working conditions, clean air, health coverage, and other benefits? We can only surmise how much those workers had known the worst of it in the first half of the century.

Closer to home than the English text, consider the stark poem of Thomas Man of Manville (poems: "Picture of a Factory Village," and "A Picture of Woonsocket or the Truth in its Nudity") on the evils of factory life. Gary Kulik quotes him in the opening lines of *The New England Mill Village: 1790 – 1860*:

> "For Liberty our Fathers fought,
> Which with their blood, they dearly bought,
> The Fac'try system sets at naught,
> A slave at morn, a slave at eve,
> It doth my inmost feelings grieve;
> The blood runs chilly from my heart
> To see fair Liberty depart;
> And leave the wretches in their chains,
> To feed a vampyre from their veins.
> Great Britain's curse is now our own;
> Enough to damn a King and Throne."

Man's poem is closer to home, but it's a 19th Century posting, 1833. Even if initially by its very nature millwork remained confining (compared to the former agrarian lifestyle of many of its workers) and not particularly creative, some changes had been wrought before the 20th Century, both for the worker and his work environment. For example, far from that amoral and dull work brute described above, I remember dad for one as an intellectual giant in his own right and a classic self-made man. He was also the most moral man I ever knew. And among the thousands of millworkers he labored with, his innate capabilities and moral fiber were, I suspect, the norm and not the exception. Blessed as we are today with formal education, it's unsound to think intellect and character were missing in those who didn't have the advantage of a learning environment and did work that was once considered "ceaseless drudgery." And as we now know, we can't necessarily equate white-collar work with endowed morality. So, does the above show that even if working conditions were bad, the average worker may have had a goodly measure of dignity and self-worth, since we have no evidence to the contrary?

About the work ethic and character of French Canadians, regardless of their working conditions, Dunwell quotes William MacDonald from a 1898 ed. of the *Quarterly Journal of Economics* in his article, "The French Canadians in New England": "Provincial traditions and fervent Catholicism made the former habitants of Québec very pleasing to mill owners. He is quick to learn, active and deft in his movements…. Docility is one of his most marked traits. He is not over-energetic or ambitious. His main concern is to make a living for himself and his family, and, if that seems to have been attained, he is little troubled by restless eagerness to be doing something higher than that at which he is at present engaged. Above all, he is reluctant, as compared to the Irish, to join labor unions and is loath to strike." So in researching mill working conditions and the workers' reaction to them, it struck me how dad, regardless of working conditions, was in step with his compatriots, before and after changes. If the job was there and he could support his family, why, working conditions didn't matter much and was borne with acceptance. As if anything could have been done about them anyway, especially since they initially shunned unions. What is tragic is that workers were not aware of the health hazards to lungs and hearing loss.

But apart from my own suppositions and readings, did dad reflect some on his work and working conditions, so I can compare how he and the workplace were when he toiled, especially at the Lafayette mill? It was during his forced retirement in the late 1940s and afterwards he reflected on his career from the early 1900s to 1948. Those years were a time when the boss man pretty much held all the cards. If you didn't like it, well it was up to you to move on, becoming, if you will, *"un coureur* (chaser) *de* factorie." But Dunwell cites how the mill created a kind of dependency in their workers, generally untutored, unskilled in other ways, and not greatly mobile, like pedestrian dad. Arthur Milot in his Childhood Memories also cites in certain "English quarters" French Canadians were not overly welcomed initially, certainly not in managerial or skilled production roles. You had to prove yourself first if you got in at all. Like the Irish and other immigrants, they were not initially appreciated for their talents since they lacked "book larnin" and didn't "speak the language."

Workers of the Lafayette Worsted Mill in the 1950s
Row 1, L to R: Gene Rueland, Willy Villandre, Joseph Galipeau. Row 2: Michel Mathieu, Charles Desgrave, Narcisse Lebrun. Row 3: Camille Turcotte, Edmond Tellier – nephew of the authors father, Alphonse. The mill was demolished in 2008 for construction of Woonsocket's middle schools.
(Photo submitted by Herve Tellier, son of Edmond)

So, except for a first year at the Clinton Street Mill, dad's entire working life was at the Lafayette, just a ten-minute walk away from Gaulin Ave. A test of his mettle as a worker was that he displayed more pride and humor than disgust about initially working about 60 hours a week until 1919, then later cut to 48. Still later in 1940 came the 40-hour week. But he did overtime during the war, not because he wanted to, but for the war. So, on

Saturdays he was home at noon and first to take the weekend bath. How ironic my own trek to the Academy for education was the same Hamlet route he took to his work. But for him, as soon as he crossed the bridge, he could only bank a right to the mill, but I took a left on Davison Ave. And oh, the difference to me, as poet Robert Frost says in one of his memorable poems about the paths and decisions we do or don't make. But workers like dad only had two choices: take it or leave it.

The 58-60 hours for which he initially received $5 a week (up to $15 later) came from a 10-hour-plus day, five days a week, and eight hours on Saturday. He recalled that except for Saturdays and certain times of the year, he hardly ever saw the sun, walking to and from the mill in what is poetically "the gloamin'." Was it depressing for a man born on a farm where, as Stanley Aronson, M.D. and *Providence Journal* columnist said, the dust of life was once from natural elements rather than noxious sources, like fossil fuels and untold chemical compounds workers may have been exposed to? But mom was more depressed about his working conditions than he was. The rights of the individual, an earmark of our times, were not as well established nor insisted on. But even today, popes have decried capitalists who consider the worker simply "as an economic unit." As we now see in an emerging nation like China, the same mistakes are being made, as underdeveloped nation's rush to rapid industrialization with the usual exploitation of workers, pollution, destruction of nature, tainted goods, and starvation wages. People must wear a mask there as Profit Motive pollutes the air.

Compared to today's worker, dad said his work contract at one time provided him no vacation or sick benefits whatsoever from his employers - *les* Lepoutres - or from the state or federal government. A lot of that changed when union organizers and workers became, well, militant, leading to some bloody confrontations. He told me he was at *coin* Social, September, 1934, when the Great Textile Strike brought out the National Guard, who killed two French-Canadian men. One of them was shot across the street from where he stood! They were reacting to a loss of jobs (the Depression) and from their bosses' demands for more work: "Strechout" (more machines for each worker) and "Speedup" (machines cranked up to their highest speed). The villainous Simon Legree for the workers was Frederick Taylor, the father of time and motion studies, who showed little regard for the workers' intelligence. One strike victim was Judes Courtemanche from Burnside Avenue, near our own Gaulin Ave. Joseph Plante, a co-worker at the mill, was asked to bring one victim in his car to the hospital. Plante was certainly all over the mill landscape, doing a lot of good, as we related. But sadly, political and "armed might" were always aligned with industrialists, not the rank-and-file. After the death of his son and daughter from millwork, William Madison once wrote to the President of the American Woolen Company in

Shawsheen Village, Andover, MA about working conditions. (Incidentally, the Brothers of the Sacred Heart eventually bought his grandiose office building and grounds after he committed suicide following his son's death in a motorcycle accident. I roomed there one summer to finish my Boston College counseling degree. It became the Andover Boarding School, complete with gym, cork floors, track, and playing field. Research proved bricks to build the famed Andover Prep School up the street were made on the property hundreds of years before. I saw the Patriots hold their summer practices there.)

With his saving sense of humor, dad often joked that in his 39 years the owners gave each worker an extra $10 in 1948, his last year and 50th year of the mill's opening. Of course, there was also no permanent disability or employer pension. That's probably why families then looked to their children to take care of them in retirement. Luckily, a small Social Security check was in the offing, since dad had been paying into it at the end of his working life. When mom retired from working in a North Attleboro jewelry shop to earn her 40 Social Security quarters, it's ironic that they would live better on SS than during his millhand days of low wages and sporadic employment. Of course, with the children gone and Sue and Gil Bouffard providing a second-floor apartment in their Bellingham home, it helped them live comfortably before going to Saint Antoine Hospice. It's what she called *"prendre nos aises,"* taking things easy. But I don't know if that mollified his negativity about some of Roosevelt's New Deal programs which included Social Security in 1935, a major turning point in labor history. Roosevelt, however, wasn't in favor of Social Security initially because of the cost. Will we think him prophetic in the 21st Century, with comparatively too few workers for too many longer-living retirees? One of dad's economic principles was government programs always got out of hand, and officials couldn't leave money lying around.

About working the morning shift, his only occasional complaint was rising at 5, it's why our radio went silent at 9 p.m. I recall the only exception was on Monday nights when we boys went to scout meeting and Sue listened to Radio Lux Theater which dramatized shortened versions of well-known movies from to 9 to 10 p.m.

Despite the above concerns there were actually many times when it was as if he was having the time of his life at the mill. Every day he related the antics of workers whose speech and comedic acts busted up the place. Truly, those old-time Canucks talking in a well-larded, invective-filled patois were local humorists of the highest order. Nobody did small talk better! At one time you still heard that kind of speech at the Razor's Edge Barbershop on Front Street where tonsorial artist Ray Pelletier, a moving force in the St. Joseph Veterans Association in his time, held court with kindred folks. (I met former Providence Mayor Buddy Cianci there when he ran for governor. A wit said he'd go anywhere for an opening, even for an envelope!)

There was *un travailleur* (a worker) - Omer Bricault - whom dad mentioned often. Back home and cleaned up, he told mom what Bricault said or did that day. I tuned in. Hearing his numerous anecdotes about the guy's crazy doings, I pictured his put-on buffoonery as a kind of pseudo-Laurel or Hardy type (much later, Ralph Kramden or Ed Norton of the Honeymooners) who was easily the mill room clown. He entertained as much as he worked, and dad liked both his work ethic and humor. When he passed away in retirement, regret and nostalgia welled up in dad. Here was a man whose conscious and habitual jollity did so much to relieve "the dull routine of a ceaseless drudgery," cited in the poem, in the working life of his fellow workers. God's Jester! What he did for their spirit was immeasurable. We felt bad for dad. They were in the trenches together, always wailing the refrain of the hopeful but downtrodden day laborer of yesteryear: "We Will Overcome" or "Sixteen tons and what do you get? Another day older, and deeper in debt?"

But for the typical worker, the reader shouldn't forget because it was honest toil and supported his family, as said, dad like others took pride in his work. The greatest tragedy in life for him and people at that time was not to work. The equation was simple but devastating in its import: if you didn't work, you didn't survive or deserve to, said mom. It needs to be emphasized there was no great social welfare net out there, providing sustenance and support to the unemployed. So, unlike that Sisyphus in Greek mythology condemned to push that forever recoiling rock, he, like others, accepted both the burden and the necessity of work, no matter how menial, repetitive, or uninspiring. Besides rising early (always gone when we kids got up), his only other complaint was malingerers and incompetents who didn't improve on their work or deliver an honest day's work for a day's pay. Like at home, he wanted you to do what you had to do and do it right: *Age quod agis*, the Romans said. (But one wit retorted, "Just don't do something. Stand there, or "Don't do today what someone can do for you tomorrow.")

To quote the Bible, also indelibly etched in his work ethic was "the laborer is worthy of his hire." That is, the employer should pay employees a living wage. And for dad a living wage was a steadily growing income allowing a person, especially with a growing family, to keep pace with *le coup de la vie*,[19] an expression he said often, knowing Americans would lose

---

[19] The blow or shock of life. Like chasing something in life that can't be caught or can't happen.

that race. But as a kid I wondered what "cost of living" meant? Finally, I realized since things cost more each year, a worker needed more pay to stay even or move ahead. So, the acronym COLA. He also said "inflation" in French where the "a" was "aah" instead of "ay." With paychecks so thin, every millworker had to be part banker and part *économe*. (I recommend Michael Moore's film "Capitalism" about the growing excesses of capitalism in our country, where, as reported in papers, 80 percent of the nation's wealth is in the hands of two percent of the population. Lampooned are the pay inequality of CEOs (over 400 times more, compared to Joe Worker's pay), and the risky practices of banks giving mortgages to people with little means, which initiated the recession of 2008. The filmmaker cites how empires fell because of the disparity between the haves and have-nots.)

Perhaps unrealistic, dad's preference was for things to basically stay the same. The inflationary spiral which, says a British author, really began to stick around in the first two or three decades of the 20th Century was not a welcomed guest in our house. He thought a lot of workers didn't understand a $10 raise was no good if it cost you an additional $12 to live. One day, *tante* Marie Ange came visiting, and he couldn't make her understand how her recent raise was being eaten up *par l'inflation*. "Ti-Phonse," she said, "*J'ne comprend rien d'ça*," about not understanding any of it, only more money in her paycheck. Inflation was tasteless, odorless, and invisible, until you discovered you had less than before at the end of the week in purchasing power. Everyone's malaise today! The Bible says no man is a prophet in his own country, so his inflation theories often fell on deaf ears. But who could have done anything about it anyway? Mom was also sensitive about rising prices. Someone told me she complained once about a weekly rate increase of a penny as "*pa(s) raisonable*" (not reasonable). If we asked for anything out of the ordinary, she said, "*Tout ai (est) figuré à la cenne*" (Everything is figured to the penny.) I said even my Call customers asked me to return three to five cents, if they forgot it was a five-day week instead of the usual six. Were women "the last fickle finger of fate" in the leaky dike of home finances? The one who fed the kids. I recall the twilight of a payday when word reached us a man had lost his paycheck. The locus was the road that ran parallel to the Lafayette by the Blackstone River, now two new middle schools. Inconsolable, *le pauvre gueux* (poor man) looked feverishly with a flashlight, because his family could not do without his lost $21 pay. "*J'ai besoin d' ma paye*," he wailed, hoping to flush the little brown envelope out of the shadows. The gang searched for a while and then went home for supper, never knowing if St. Antoine de Padoue (patron of lost things) had come through for him.

So, did dad clutch his little brown envelope more tightly the next Friday? If ever he had lost his pay (like any man, he was impatient about losing things, especially tools), food wise anyway, we would've been okay. I also mention elsewhere we had preserves to sustain any modern-day family facing, say, a hurricane from having to make a run to the market. Besides wine, he had root beer, applesauce, blueberries, chicken, tomatoes, all *encannés*, or preserved in jars in the back hallway or cellar. And because he bought in bulk, we always had a bushel of apples and oranges to last us for many weeks. He saved when he could and always had a few dollars in the strong box in his bedroom closet. I saw the modest stash whenever he told me to get those rope bands he brought home from the mill to tie things or helicopter chestnuts for us kids. Because his copious readings and creativity allowed him to live both in the present and future, he always foresaw things and was always ready, as in the Latin *semper paratus*. He was my model in running my guidance office. (I've told my son Jim many times, if you wait until the last minute, something always goes wrong. And Haste Makes Waste! Another irritant is when I read and agreed that gravity is the cause of a lot of our mishaps. So, a wit blamed Newton for "inventing it" when hit on the head by an apple while under a tree!)

Born a farm boy, even the weather didn't escape his purview. He was a superb weather forecaster, rarely wrong. With that good-sized nose, he told me he could smell rain and storms. Wow! So how come he didn't tell mom to skip that whist party at St. Louis Parish the day of the 1938 Hurricane? Maybe he did, but stylish *avec son chapeau neuf* (with her new hat,) was she impervious to his Cassandra-like forebodings. (Cassandra in Virgil's "Aeneid" also predicted the impending fall of Troy, so she became "a messenger of doom," as opposed to a "Pollyana.") No less forewarned, we kids went to school as usual.

About my opening query whether workers of dad's generation were still victims of "ceaseless drudgery," I think they certainly fared better than those workers in England in 1832 or in Man's account. But perhaps only by degrees and only towards the end of their careers. The American Federation of Labor (AFL), the first large labor union in the United States (with its origins in the Knights of Labor) had been organized in 1886 and workers of his generation certainly began to enjoy some changes brought about by increasing union might and strikes, however injurious and sometimes deadly at first. Even I once passed out flyers for workers trying to unionize a mill in the city. But some kids threw their flyers into a nearby river.

A Day in the Life of a Mill Worker

WHEN I WORKED with young people as a guidance counselor, it surprised me how few kids knew what their parents really did to earn the proverbial daily bread, keep a roof over their heads, and food on the table. But perhaps you can hardly blame them. Recall there are some 51,000 occupational titles today? And don't people change jobs 12 times and their careers four or five times in their average 42-year work life? We knew our parents' jobs better in the 1930s and '40s in Woonsocket because millhand or factory worker fit most working persons. The city's travails and glories were in the main embedded in its mill town genes.

But only once in dad's 38 years at the Lafayette Mill did I have a chance to see him and co-workers at their workbench or mules. If the word "workbench" connotes immobility, it's a misnomer. I don't know what brought me there, but as I arrived on dad's floor (Bob, Ben, and I debate whether it was the third or fourth), I was immediately struck by the fast pace the men kept and the clatter or roar of the machines.

Shirtless but wearing an old sleeveless union suit (a kind of heavy, one-piece, full-body long underwear we boys hated wearing in winter) to absorb the profuse sweat, and standing on an oil-stained floor, dad operated two 60-foot spinning mules, which advanced and receded, as he and helpers saw to the drawing, twisting, and winding of fibers into yarn, as well as reattaching broken strands. (You can see his alter ego in the Museum of Work and Culture's spinning room exhibit. My siblings and I had a photo taken there after choosing our Treasury of Life box which is like a time capsule which preserves mementos of families like ours whose history revolved around the mill trade.)

Four men were assigned to those two mules: a spinner or, in French, *un fileur* or *le runneur de la chaine*," dad's job; two piecers or *rattacheurs* (from his often banged-up digits he must've done some of that too), and a bobbin boy, *un ropineur*. As *une petite économie* (a small saving), some workers chose to work with battered shoes or none, even though cud-chewing millhands splattered the floor. Union boss Joseph Plante once heard mill owner Auguste Lepoutre tell his son to walk bare feet over a glass-littered floor. Cut skin healed, but torn leather cost money to repair! In the same tightwad vein, in pre-union days he wanted workers to work Christmas and New Year's Day! (If so, how "un-Catholic" for a devout Frenchman!) One Saturday, maintenance workers were nowhere to be found. But he saw one coming down from the roof where his cronies were playing cards (*jouer aux cartes*) as usual. He fired them on the spot: "*Yéza clairés*," (He fired them!) Plante said. Plante recalled *le soupeur* of the floor treated workers harshly at times. And some never integrated themselves into the community, perpetuating a kind of capitalistic-proletariat divide. I recall he once got a poor man's job back, paying five dollars to have a lawyer write a letter to get the Simon Legree fired.

Dad just couldn't be idle if work was *slaque* (slack) at his mill. Besides calcimining ceilings, he crisscrossed the whole mill landscape in search of work: the French Worsted, *la* Masurel, the Social Mill, *la* Désurmont, Guerin, *la* Verdun, *la* Montrose, Brisbane, et al. For many, millwork seemed the only job in the city, as the Blackstone River from Worcester to Pawtucket, a span of 44 miles and 400,000 acres, gave rise to 100 mills close by, but hundreds more from Worcester on down. Historically, as far back as 1807, the Slatersville Mill, the largest of its day and the brainchild of Samuel and John Slater, was built in North Smithfield in partnership with the Providence firm of Almy and Brown. The large Slatersville reservoir was the power source. The village was first settled by British colonists as a farming community. The village green was laid out in 1838 in a traditional New England pattern. At the head of the Village Green still stands the Slatersville Congregational Church, a steepled Greek revival building, which houses the oldest continuously operated Sunday School in America. In 2000 Pat and I joined hundreds in a photo in front of it to welcome the new century. Despite England's prohibition, those founders built a replica of the Arkwright Process from memory for their water-powered mill of l00 spindles.

I said Woonsocket was mostly a one-job town. Even as early as 1844, those factories dotted the landscape of the Blackstone River, one of America's fourteen American Heritage Rivers. Hope always sprang eternal, as the poet says, but after the heyday of millwork from 1900 to 1910, unemployment always "crept with its petty pace" except in wartime. Like today, unskilled workers always got the shaft first, giving rise to the word *slaque* (slack). Yes, good health and work were slippery like eels or quicksilver. Unlike stationary spinning frames, dad said working the mules required a person to walk close to 8 or 9 miles a day. No wonder his lanky, tallish frame never matched his father's for weight, topping out at 145 pounds. I got depressed one day when petite mom said none of us would be "*du gros monde*" or big people, but she was grateful later.

But small wonder too that in forced retirement, his fierce-beating heart, to the amazement of his doctors, continued to hold out from 1949 to 1982 despite the oxygen deficiency from his bronchiectasis disease. Surviving only five years was then the norm! With dietetics as a hobby, he avoided *du gras* or fat in his diet, limited bulk, ate high protein, shunned public gatherings, and daily followed an expectoration regimen. Many people told me they couldn't have done it. He kept choosing life and his food bible: *You Are What You Eat*. About fear from any kind of contagion, he couldn't attend my wedding, April l0, 1976, in New York. When we got back, Pat and I asked for his blessing. In his usual flannel shirt, he sat in the rocker next to the stove where he read his Sunday Mass missal.

Because my visit to his factory was in late spring, the heat and the noise repelled me. Since wind from open windows wreaked havoc on the wool strands, the workers usually plied their dusty trade, said Plante, in l05-

110 degrees in summer and around 90 in winter because there was no air conditioning. But rubber king Joseph Banigan had installed it in his new Alice Mill in 1890. I think he treated his Blackstone workers - mostly Irish! - better than Franco workers were treated in Woonsocket mills. He lauded sobriety and church attendance too and made great contributions to church and nuns dealing with the elderly and orphans. One told me the Lepoutres never graced the city with any benefaction.

As dad lay dying in Fogarty Hospital in 1982 from a major stroke (he'd survived a minor one a year before), Bob and I observed how worn like a carpenter's his hands were. Growing up, we sometimes felt their endearing touch (but not demonstrably outgoing in that regard) and saw those cuts and burns on his fingers. We recalled the many times he asked us to bring him a band aid: *"Apporte-mwé un plaster* (we called them plasters then) and we'd fetch them from a tin box above the kitchen sink.

Co-worker, Gerry Lambert, whom we met at the wake of dad's life-long friend, Noé Tessier, told me how injurious the work was. Because it involved twisting and pulling yarn and tying bands on moving machinery, a moment of carelessness or clumsiness resulted in a broken, bruised, or mashed digit. Is it because of the mill he strove for quickness, thoroughness, and economy of pain and effort in everything he did?

I saw legitimate pride in his face when he visited the Slater Museum in Pawtucket with the Clarks in the 1970s, hearing "mule spinner" cited as the epitome of the millworker echelon. Since he started working in the mills before WWI, he related to some of the technology, if not the appearance, of some of the old-time machines. Like any artist or worker seeing the enshrinement of his tools and handiwork in a hall of fame, he showed great joy someone remembered and understood what his working life had been all about. In himself, did he also experience pride that the city's quality mill-work had once brought it national recognition? (Banigan's Alice Mill also brought pride to the area with its shoes, boots, rubber rollers for washing machine wringers, and U.S. Keds sneakers.) Woonsocket had indeed become the Queen of the Blackstone Valley, as Pothier envisioned.[20]

Once again, about my mill visit, dad called my attention to the work of the bobbin boy. It's how he started and possibly my destiny! The boy changed the bobbins on which the wool was wound and unwound. He said this job was done always by young males, with of course little schooling

---

[20] Preserving Pothier's memory and legacy is the Governor Aram Pothier French Heritage Award, which was given to Roger Laliberté in 2011 by the Woonsocket Richelieu Club for his long running French radio program (since 1963). The club is an international service group maintaining the values and pride of the French-Canadian culture. I was once invited to speak about my folks coming to America.

and fewer prospects. It's about them he commented at times about their lack of working ambition and skill. But with any insight, imagine the depression of any young male facing an unpromising future of low wages and hand-to-mouth existence, like his dad did! They were also called doffers, meaning "to remove" says Webster.

About dad's work drive and ethic, I liked the way mom had difficulty finding fault with him. Not a critical person, she wasn't nitpicking, but like any loving couple they teased each other about work, money, and us children. Besides chiding him for his generosity (the shirt off his back: *donner sa chemise*), she said he was like the members of his birth family, to wit, he'd work until exhausted, disabled, or dead. Obviously, she liked his family. Cousins were like brothers or sisters. Unlike today, a family's social life then was largely with your extended family, typical of an immigrant culture like us Francos. Especially if pedestrian, patois-speaking, and not too literate in English.

Since he wasn't a robust man and was "*affligé*" (afflicted), can you imagine she always wanted him to do less around the house, and not overextend himself too much for his brothers, sisters, and others? He was the total opposite of that classic lazy type, with the little woman trying to coax a little more work around the house from the sluggard. It's no wonder he liked cartoons depicting that timeless domestic scene, sometimes with the little woman with her uplifted rolling pin as proof of her own industry.

In that mule room visit, I saw some of the men with bandannas to prevent sweat from dripping onto the yarn. But not dad. He always had a rather severe haircut, common in those days. It took longer between cuts and saved you a quarter. And of course, he had his dad's curly forelock. Several times mom spoke to me about it, and I wondered if it was part of her initial attraction.

Since it was forbidden to smoke, I saw men covering for each other, as they ducked into the washroom for a few quick puffs. Because of his lungs and income, before his illness he smoked maybe a pack of Lucky Strikes a month when we were kids. (I've kept an empty pack of his.) It came from a little variety store on Wood Avenue, right across the street from Carle's Bakery. He never smoked in the house or in his illness. The storeowner loved to talk but lamented he didn't have anything in the world he hadn't worked for. Thinking what the nuns said about honesty, I thought he said something very good about himself, which mom confirmed. She told me stuff; I told her stuff.

Even though people bore their poverty well during the Depression, it was a rare person who didn't pine for a bit more: "*un peu plus*," she said. The innate quest for El Dorado (gold) or a winning lottery ticket. Like that

"Bellavance" guy ("good luck" became the family name) I did some translations for. Before the productive war years and single shift, dad sometimes came home for lunch, so I was told. However, when the mill went to two shifts, there was no longer a lunch break and the workers had little or no time off to eat, because machines couldn't be stopped. It took industrialists a long time to accept the notion a coffee or snack actually paid off in greater output after. It was named after the guy whose tests proved it, so said my Boston College Occupational Titles Book.

(About working or living conditions, he said, "We've never had a water problem," he retorted with obvious glee, about living on top of Gaulin and on the third floor. They once lived in the first-floor apartment where *les* Carpentiers lived and where we gathered for the 1938 Hurricane. They had found it cold, so needing to climb stairs was a trade-off for having a warmer apartment that cost less to heat. Dad never failed to tell you what it cost to have a ton of coal or a cord of wood brought in. When he switched to oil, he told us it was seven cents a gallon. We always knew stuff like that (the size of the national debt, the population of the United States (130 million), our share of the national debt), because he liked stats, as I later got to do. That's why mom said people flocked to him for advice on so many things.

Back from the mill and cleaned up, he rested his weary bones on the little rocker next to *mémère's*. Figuring he had a right to a modicum of comfort, he ordered you out if you were perched on it: "*Donne-mwé ma chaise.*" It wasn't like an Archie Bunker edict, but more a low-tone request tinged with a fatigued, I-deserve-it tone. Then, he started to relate the day's comical doings, especially about comedic Bricault. In his own right, dad too was a local humorist, as he imitated the mannerisms, recalled the patois lines, and acted out the antics of the Lafayette Honeymooners chafing and laughing at the day's burdensome toil: *le dur quotiden*. The Bible says God loves a cheerful giver, and the men and women I knew had that joie de vivre. No one accepted their economic situation and destiny with more toleration and good humor. When he worked that 12-hour shift, he complained about missing Old Sol. In retirement when he relived his St. Cuthbert farm days as a boy, how he loved what those rays did for his tomatoes in his garden in Bellingham. His life had come full circle. He could breathe again, even with his damaged lungs.

In the 1930s mom began to lament work was beginning to slacken considerably, and he was only going to work a little. He even did WPA (Workers Project Administration) work at Cass Park. Those Depression Years were to be the cruelest test of our family and others to survive: "*passer en travers*," she sighed. The recession of 2008 was more tolerable because of huge government help, but how about living ten years of your working life in a depressive doomsday sphere. Is that why dad "laughed" at the irony of Hitler who put him back to work? (And Hirohito!) Was it a little dig at Roosevelt since unemployment was even higher in 1939? The same debate goes on today: if you tax wealthy people and industrialists too much, do you prevent them from expanding their businesses, so they invest abroad, as they did in the 1930s? And weren't taxes as high as 90 percent on captains of industry? One said recently it's not the job of government to create jobs, but of business and industry. But competition is now international with countries like China undercutting costs by subsidizing production costs (and devaluing their currency?). But I've told my son Jim no matter who's elected president, he's soon considered a fool and ineffective. That's because our problems are so massive on a national and international level and our bicameral form of government wrangles more than legislates. It happens because the minority party wants to be back in power at all costs. Are term limits the answer? A U.S. senator must raise $5,000 a week to be re-elected, one wrote. So do legislators get beholden "to them that feed them by hand?" President Carter was amazed how much lobbyists and private interests influenced the government because he hadn't come from the Senate. About wanting to be President, is it a case of "Ambition, the last infirmity of noble minds?" Remember a President's second term in office is often ineffective, like a "lame duck."

How bad was the Depression? TIME magazine's 60th anniversary issue in 1984 cited a statistic from the Depression: "The unemployed of the nation had increased to 6,050,000 the second winter (1930-31). President Hoover's relief formula was for each community to rely on local charity and self-help with nary a penny from the Federal Treasury." Where was Roosevelt when you needed him? Hoover had helped Europe so much after WWI.

Adversity can forge virtue, and my family, like others, may have come out better because of those times. But who knows what harm occurred beyond what we know? Urie Bronfenbrenner, professor at Cornell University, cites Glen Elder's study of "Children of the Great Depression" (as reported in an article on families in the *Providence Journal* by Bert Wade: 1/87), as evidence of some of the harm that period wrought: "Not only did children in those families victimized by unemployment in the 1930s do less well in school, show less stable work histories, form less stable marriages, and exhibit more emotional and social difficulties, but the disruptive psychological effects continued to be evident in the children of the children of the Great Depression. If you are worried about how to put food on the table, you don't worry about which fork to use in getting it from plate to mouth." (Not a hopeful prognosis for us born during that time! But in a limited sample, my siblings and I went to school willingly and formed stable marriages, as did almost all the people we knew. And we kept the faith.)

Lester C. Boyd, also of the *Providence Journal*, added the following: "There was no such thing as job security or paid hospital insurance or paid sick leave or paid vacation, nor was there unemployment insurance, at least through most of the Depression. When you were out of work you hoped that the proprietor of the local grocery store would carry you until things improved." (Like *mon oncle* François who ran a small variety store from 1932 to 1960 near where Al Drew's Music Center on Front Street now stands. He gave out $1,000 worth of credit that was never repaid and our landlord, Mr. Berard, forgave us our Mailloux St. apartment rent.)

So going to his mill that day was like going back to the future. We never disdained study, but now when mom said to study, the message was impactful. Like dad, she didn't disdain manual labor in the mills or anywhere, but she had worked there herself and knew how stressful it could be and, in his case, poorly paid and sporadic. Now I really knew what he did for a living. For as long as he could put up with the heat, dust, and fatigue, his job was to bind those broken skeins, hoping the feeding bobbins and machines didn't go silent altogether, as they eventually did. The closing of the Globe and Social Mills in 1927 was said to be the canary in the coal mine. Mill owners rarely improved their concerns.

Curiously, I came across one opinion how the Depression had its plusses: "What was beautiful about the Depression, even though it's not beautiful, was that you couldn't make money. So, you had to figure out what was important in life; you had no choice but to get in touch with the things that were life-affirming, aside from money." Does it speak to the grit and faith of the French Canadians I knew? But comically, if mom had read this, would she have said: "Yah, you try and cut those 'life-affirming things' with a steak knife?" Christ told the tempter that man doesn't live by bread alone, but He has us pray to the Father for our daily bread. The church also realizes a person needs at least a modicum of the good things in life before one's spirit can soar to more heavenly things. It's probably what St. Paul meant when he wrote, "Grace builds on nature," if there's enough of it left." About our recent crisis, Americans in general, who have lived beyond their means and on borrowed credit since WWII, can learn much from the Depression era and take note of the above quote. Imagine, in 2011, American families owed $13.3 trillion in mortgage debt, home-equity loans, credit-card debts, and other revolving loans! Should we all go back to Cash-and-Carry, as some credit card casualties are now doing. I've read Credit Card companies aren't too concerned about people maxing out with huge interest payments then kicking in! Do you also get credit card offers almost daily? Having too many is a possible negative said a report. I found a wallet once on the Brown University campus with no money at all but 18 credit cards! I had a hard time finding the guy. (After one Sunday Mass, my own wallet flew out of my car without my knowledge, but a good woman brought it to the police.)

Later, I relate how my penniless and widowed *mémère*, loser of both her home and farm in a huge forest fire in Ontario, told her pastor they were going to America to have any life at all. About his "Man doesn't live by bread alone," she said, "You need some to live." But what a quandary was dad's! Besides a total lack of job security, when he did work it was killing him. If he didn't work, his family, like all others, was in peril. But he never questioned his duty or put his well-being above the family's. In the Order, religious life was called a kind of daily martyrdom, *un martyre à petit coup* ("a thousand cuts," as we now say), like his work and that of others. As my professor of Occupational Trends told us at Boston College, sometimes Joe Worker has no choice but take jobs others would turn down. (Not in the same context of poverty, but he said Lawrence Welk with his foreign accent vehemently refused at first to emcee his own show. He acquiesced when the show was threatened and it became the show's premiere attraction. Dr. Cottle also cited the much-maligned liquid garbage collector of yesteryear, but without adding the comedic line about "all you can eat." He read us a book about some of the crazy jobs people did for a living and their hilarious description of it. It would be great TV fare now!)

Un bon père de famille

IN FRENCH-CANADIAN parlance, the phrase *un bon père de famille* epitomized the best a man could be to his wife and children. Ours merited that praise by a kind of love in action, as other paterfamiliases did. Your father knows how to do everything: *"Ton père sé* (sait) *tout faire"* was how mom often described our factotum. To me, this was the second clue about who he was. The first was his lankiness and stride.

In this age of specialization or affluence in which the family buys nearly all its goods and services, it boggles my mind when I recall all the things he did for ours. I've mentioned a few already. A lack of buying power had a lot to do with the self-sufficiency of families like ours. When you didn't have "the coin of the realm," you bought things with the currency of your own initiative, inventiveness, and talent. Today's "making do." Mom said, *"S'défricher,"* like freeing oneself from the coils of want and poverty. For her, life was always a struggle. In fact, for both, even breathing came at a cost.

Having inherited his electric hair cutter, I recall he first used a small, hand-powered unit to trim us boys in one session. He had built a makeshift barber's chair out of a wooden box. But you didn't want to be last and pick up the cuttings on the floor.

But what a treat when for 15 cents we got our first professional cut in Dalpé's, corner of Kendrick and Cumberland! How that Noonan's Hair Oil smelled good when the greasy-kid look was still in vogue: "A little dab'll do 'ya'." An added treat for a sport statistician nut like me was to read every *Ring* magazine ranking of every fighter in 10 divisions. (A barber told me there are now more than 12.) Just beginning to use passable English, we had difficulty pronouncing the names of the champions in the bantam and flyweight divisions, nearly all foreigners. (Even then Americans were too big for those lighter classifications!) Except for the current issue, these magazines were kept in a back room accessible from a low-slung door. So engrossed with this hideaway reading, I'd let my turn go by. Anything written, outside of the daily paper, was like a precious manuscript. Our culture was oral, not writ large. I read the Bible was chained down in Catholic churches in the Middle Ages to prevent thievery. Critics say it's because our church forbade reading it. Not so, as I told a non-believer.

Sometimes dad sent us to his Turcotte friend on Dulude astride St. Ann Park. But we had strict orders not to talk about this "underground economy." He only took a dime for each cut. I was the middle boy, but taciturn Bob and Ben, who now love to converse more than I do, said I had to do the knocking and talking. Did it have something to do with his daughters, but I, not being your Playboy of the Western World type, didn't understand their timidity? But of course, mom had the inside story.

This furtive tonsorial artist also cultivated a kind of grape, which dad used for his wine. Another kind, *rougevin* (red wine), we picked up at his brother Napoleon's Cumberland farm on Pound Road. But like Hedda Hopper or Louella Parsons, mom told me his daughters were considered beautiful ("*ses filles sont belles*"). Imagine, they lived several streets away from us, but she knew the community's pulchritude rating on them. But that made no impression on me, but Bob and Ben? Boys then didn't usually notice girls until their very late teens, hanging out only with their gang until real serious dating. Each one of us had his own gang. But once I did notice the girls' hair was full or curled, like those heroines of the novels of Jane Austen or the Bronte sisters, as I later saw in English novels and movies of that age. They were spared or had quickly shed the usual broom cut: "*les cheveux coupés en balah(ais)*," mom said. That first permanent (*permanante* in patois) was a girl's rite of passage into young womanhood. The first thing boys picked up on. Scout's honor!

Nothing, however, surpassed the thrill of having a pair of shoes resoled in the front parlor. Dad had all the tools of the cobbler's trade of old: an all-metal shoe stand with three positions; good-smelling leather which he cut with a homemade knife; picks, awls, hammer, special scissors, nails, glue, sewing thread, and even shoelaces.

If your shoes were being done, you watched the modus operandi with the anticipation of a kid buying a new pair of shoes *chez* (in) Gagné's Shoe Store on Social Street, which he patronized because they sold quality (Bostonians?). He always looked for a good arch. And doing his Alan Greenspan thing, he said you could gauge the health of the nation's economy by how often people had shoes repaired. It's what Wall Street calls a "leading indicator" in today's "business speak." A cobbler told me the city had over 30 such shops at one time; another, over 50, with Pierannunzi's, later owned by Norm Desilets, closing out the string at the Court Street Bridge in 2008. Now Robert Dion's Lincoln shoe repair shop below Manville Hill Road is where many go.

Kids kept their shoes until the body was completely shot. Not infrequently, you saw a running kid's stockings (if wearing any outside of summer), when the now un-nailed soles of a badly deteriorating pair of shoes flapped like windblown shutters. Some even used cardboard as a makeshift sole. Were we poor or were we poor? Heels completely worn out on one side rarely justified a makeover. (I felt that same touch of poverty when I did my religious training at Harrisville with the Brothers in 1950. Only given two pairs of socks despite physical work and athletics, besides, of course, academics and prayers, we wore the heels of our socks over our toes when the front part was shot. We did some darning with very coarse thread, putting the sock over a handled wooden bulb. Were they kidding when they said our poverty was detachment, not dispossession? Did we look like recruits of the Discalced (Shoeless) Franciscans?

In the summer you started off with a pair of one-dollar Keds sneakers, maybe made at Banigan's rubber mill? But to dad's exasperation, those precursors of today's expensive Nikes, Reeboks, New Balance, et al made your feet stink and smeared linoleum floors. Parents expected you to make them last the summer. By late August most sneakers were shabby and odoriferous. Boyhood friend Phil Carpentier never could make a pair last the summer and walked practically barefooted by school time. Our "make-do" dad sometimes glued parts of our sneakers, always the high cut kind. When my son Jim was a tyke, he asked why I used glue to repair almost everything!

An amateur food purist, dad abhorred cheap store-bought goodies or pastry full of sugar and shortening, but short on nutritional value. He was big on proteins. In the same vein, he never bought soda, preferring to make his own root beer by the case. Since I sometimes bought soda with the gang on Wood Avenue, I agreed his was the real thing. No bloated, gaseous feeling. Little or no sugar! Just the real taste of root beer, his boast.

One day we thought his prediction of WWII had come true when 48 bottles of freshly made root beer in the rear corridor began to explode. Too much yeast and hot weather! When he chuckled, we laughed too. It was in keeping with his love of slapstick-like comedy where things suddenly went out of control, like in the antics of Tizoon *et* Balloon, Canadian comics at the Laurier Theater. Perhaps his love of numbers and order had something to do with these comedic flights from reality. Order is the first law of Heaven, but not always where we lived. He made another batch. Bob inherited the whole setup, but a borrower, anonymous forever more, never returned it.

    Those exploding bottles had us running to the corridor just like the time we heard dad's huge animal trap snap shut. We had finally caught the big river rat that had repeatedly come up three stories and gnawed through the wall to get at our *les* Beauregards' 50 lb. bags of Potatoes. Only dad had the stomach to release the trap and slide the varmint into the stove fire. The same fate awaited the tiny mice dad caught. For them, he used these little traps that cost pennies at the hardware store. In the evening we'd be sitting in the living room when presto we heard the trap slamming. Dad put another notch on his gun. How come there was no comment from mom? Now I catch only one or two mice a year. I have a gismo in my outlets that scares them away. Except for cleaning the soda bottles, we didn't help dad out much. But not so with Sunday dinner and homemade ice cream. Once the ingredients were mixed, it was our job to turn the crank until the creamiest ice cream ever was ready. But it always took forever, delaying our meal. And what we didn't eat in one sitting became ice-hard in the icebox because there were no fillers or air holes in his *crème de glace*, he said. Since mom never failed to put up about 40 quarts of blueberries in the summer that we picked near *le maire* (major) Ernest Dupré's *maison d'été* (summer house) at Silver Lake in Bellingham, our favorite dessert was pie à la mode. "*Des bonnes tartes aux bleuah (bleuets) de Poldine*," relatives dining with us gushed about mom's good blueberry pies. "Poldine" was dad's nickname for mom, Léopoldine (but at times just "Pol"), who missed being baptized Pauline because the Canadian pastor thought it frivolous. Had he sneaked a look at the Hollywood serial *"The Perils of Pauline?"* But I recall the crust was *mémère's* inimitable art, just like the heels of our woolen stockings. Mom beamed it was grandma alone who knew how to make the crust: "*Ta grandmère ai seule qui sé comment faire la croûte*, adding "*A l'tour*," the know-how. (In the Order, as young Brothers we rarely ate out in restaurants. When once a waitress asked a young monk if he wanted pie à la mode, he said, "No, just ice cream on it." He never heard the last of it.)

    About his "domestic brewery," I never saw dad make hard liquor, only wine, a barrel at a time. The end product of his vino craft was a dark red bittersweet wine, even we children were allowed to drink in a small glass on two occasions: company and the incipience of a chill. If not wine for that chill, he made us *une ponce* (a potion!): a small shot of brandy (naturally French brandy), milk, and honey, all slightly heated. We loved it. But it's as close as we ever got to hard liquor, served only when we entertained.

Dad had no subterranean digs for his vino. His locus was our regular cellar from where he poured out the barreled wine into bottles. Recall when he arrived somewhere, relatives said, "*C'est Ti-Phonse avec son bon vin*" – It's Ti-Phonse with his good wine. (My North Smithfield friend, Lano Ferreira, has now graced my table with wine from his own grapes.) Later, in Bellingham, MA, it was garden produce from dad. Especially tomatoes that were big and juicy enough to match today's Miracle-Gro champions. Besides the satisfaction of growing or making something, his hobbies were more to augment the family's consumables and lessen expenses. Mothers, as mine did, made homemade meals, desserts, pies, doughnuts, and cakes. They also made, altered, and downsized clothes. Self-sufficiency was our lifeline.

The Bible has a beautiful saying about wine: *Bonum vinum laetificat cor hominis*, good wine gladdens the heart of man. He didn't know the saying, but he certainly made a few hearts flutter with gratitude. But *In vino veritas* is more popular. It's about truth somehow reposing in those lovely grapes or flushing it out from someone's lips. Yes, if you saw dad "brown-bagging" when not going to work, odds are he was bringing wine to a family's house. Francos always told you when you left not to count the number of times you came: "*Compte pas les tours.*" Did they say that more tastefully when he left? Mom always visited with some of us kids, but dad more by himself. I only went a couple of times and only he carried the paper bag.

One day when in the cellar with Phil Carpentier, he suddenly took a swig from a dark glass bottle he thought was dad's wine. He quickly spewed out the reddish-looking kerosene all over the wall. He'd been too quick, and alas his legendary unquenchable thirst and bottomless stomach had again prevailed over caution. And talk about a "Father John" making his own cough syrup? Does anybody remember the bluish bottle with the benign image? While not exactly concocting his own, he picked up a recipe for that too. With all due respect, like Macbeth's witches he always had a boiler of something or other on our coal stove. Luckily, when they moved to St. Antoine Hospice, I found the formula from Canada's *La Presse*. Entitled *Tonique pour les poumons* (Tonic for the lungs; It's no surprise it caught his attention.) the thick, tawny, and tasty elixir called for the following:

1. Place 6 fresh eggs in a deep dish or pot.
2. Without breaking the shells, pierce holes in them (he used his homemade awl).

3. Cover the eggs completely with the juice of a dozen big lemons.
4. Cover the pot with a towel and leave the whole thing sitting for 48 hours in a dry, cool, and shady place.
5. After that, pulverize the whole thing and strain, throwing away what has not filtered.
6. Add a pint (*chopine*) of the best cognac.
7. Add a pint of cod liver oil (*huile de Foie de Morue*).
8. Add a pint of very pure honey.
9. Mix the whole mixture in mid-sized bottles and cover them with dark-shaded paper, blue preferably.
10. Place in a cool, dry, and shady place.

The above was good for three or four bottles. So, for a bad cold or during flu season, *les* Telliers didn't run to Savard *et* Gallant or Desrochers and Brunelle's, two well-known drug stores in Social *Coin*. The dosage was a couple of soupspoons a day, usually given by mom, our nurse in situ, until you were old enough not to spill a drop of the family's medicinal defense against the predators of our supposedly frail lungs. Yes, with both my parents always suffering from mild to serious lung conditions, we were cautioned that unless we were careful or lucky, or both, we too would be afflicted. Before tissues, we were a family that went through several dozen handkerchiefs a week in winter. If anyone went to draw one from the chiffonier and drew a blank, you heard a cry. Dad chafed about how many we used. Like our pillowcases, she made them from Carle Bakery flour bags, a dime each. In a pinch, we used toilet paper, not at all Charmin soft! Did burning wood sap the moisture out of the air and make our dry noses and throats more susceptible to colds? Even chair rungs fell off from glue drying up. A UMass prof wrote a paper about the many negatives of burning wood. He said he'd rather live downwind from a nuclear plant than a wood-burning one! Too many carcinogens and chimney fires!

Like in many families I suspect, dad was a busy domestic pharmacist with other home remedies. For example, he also crushed or pulverized bones to treat a burn. Even though we had our share of sore throats and never saw it used, he spoke about a strip of salt pork (*du lard salé*, which Francos loved with their beans) placed on a piece of flannel, with salt and sliced onions added and wrapped around the neck. Did it come from a recipe mistakenly placed in the medicine cabinet? A mudpack was for a bee sting. Non-traditional medicines and procedures like these have now come back with a vengeance in today's health-conscious world. Now, $15 billion in sales at last check! But the caution is not to abandon proven, modern medicines. When my wife Pat struggled with her cancer, I heard of a California doctor who diagnosed precisely what cancer you had (probably through gene testing) to tailor the right medicine for it. It's now the practice, like at Duke University, one of the leading cancer-research centers in the nation, where Senator Ted Kennedy was treated. David B. Agus, MD, author of *The End of Illness*, suggests people get a copy of their genetic makeup to live better and longer, and provide insight if illness strikes. Even if healthy, his revealed a susceptibility to heart disease. He altered his eating habits, especially avoiding fries. The price is about $1,000, but coming down. Eventually all will get it at birth. But will employers discriminate if one has a certain genetic trait? And of course, not all susceptibilities come to fruition. A 2012 article said we have about 10,000(?) organisms in our bodies, and the ideal is to halt the negative ones. A type of cancer is no longer unique, but one of more than 100 types. Exercise, eating well, and not sitting down more than four hours a day are factors for health and longevity. Has America become too sedentary? Perhaps it's because we're no longer an industrial or agricultural nation. Based on recent findings, I would have asked my folks if they agreed that faith and regular church practices made our people healthier and quicker to recuperate when sick. Interestingly, Bossuet, a biblical commentator or exegete, wrote a commentary on the funeral of the sick Michel le Telllier of royal times, in which he also spoke about the Gospel woman with a blood problem. In Christ she found "medicine in faith," when she'd lost "faith in medicine."

    We took dad's medicine all winter and wore camphor cubes. That was not dad's idea, but mom's. We now know they were useless. She told horror stories about victims of the Spanish influenza in The Great War. I found it unbelievably ghoulish when she said people died so quickly, hearses or wagons to remove them could not keep up. The first time she said "*l'influenza espagnol*," we thought she was "speaking in tongues." But most times she simply said, "*la grippe.*" During the epidemic, a wife buried six children and a husband in one week. Worldwide some 50 million died, including 675,000 Americans. Articles still appear about its origin, whether it transmuted from pigs or animals, like the AIDS virus from monkeys.

    We took off those camphor sacs only for the Saturday night bath. They hung on our necks next to those cloth scapulars the nuns gave us. But since we now live in an intercontinental village with worldwide travel, virologists wonder when the next flu pandemic will strike. Like the H1N1 virus or Ebola! If an unexpected one comes before we're ready, they estimate some 300,000 deaths in the U.S. alone before enough vaccine is ready. But we're the best at getting up to speed in an epidemic.

    Mom averred dad's potion sweetened our pipes, nourished our frail lungs, and cured every disease lurking in or out of our cold-water flat with its drafty windows and uninsulated walls and ceilings. Besides her encyclopedic interest and knowledge about the lives and doings of the community, mom also gave you an assessment of the health of many of the people she knew or knew about. If again she said he or she *"f'ra pas vieux os,"* (won't live long), to me that was like the grim reaper tapping someone on the shoulder. *"Y va crever"* (going to croak) was also bad. She had been through too much not to know the travails of the human condition. In an age of fewer doctors, no money for medical care (even if far more affordable), and no medical insurance plans, people worried about their health. Unlike today's privacy laws about one's condition, people's health condition was next to one's work status. So, were there many "at-home doctors" like ours? Partly. Isn't that why the lack of practical sense, domestic knowledge, and doable care have resulted in unpaid emergency care (the kind people once handled themselves) one of the runaway expenses of hospitals running in the red? Besides, of course, uncompensated care, if not on ObamaCare, for people who can't afford it or choose not to. For some it's because they haven't met their deductible, a hospital worker told me. A few years ago, the medical tab to get a single aspirin in a Boston Hospital was $700! (Less for a baby aspirin?)

When you're very young, you think your parents know everything. One day *tante* Laurence told mom a woman's grossly overweight husband daily consumed a dozen eggs and a whole loaf of bread for breakfast! They commiserated the lady's lot and said, *"Y va crever"* about his precarious longevity. He passed two weeks later. Because I had those two pneumonias as a tyke, that sinus condition as a youngster, and needed his homemade cough syrup more than my siblings, I hoped she wouldn't say that about me to dad in a concerned moment. But one day she told dad a hopeful diagnosis: *"Il va s'réchapper."* I'd make it.

No doubt, because of the Depression, lack of work, our lower middle-class status, the recurring polio epidemics, and lack of miracle drugs, our lives seemed riskier. In 1901, was longevity only 41 (?), so almost double that 100 years later? Some people have labeled the 20th Century as one of the worst ever in terms of violence and cruelty (two world wars, Vietnam and Korea for us, the Holocaust), but our living longer is an unmatched feat in medical history. The problem now is quality of life in old age, and the threatened insolvency of Social Security and the weight of Medicare and Medicaid as our population ages. In 2009, a British geneticist said a child born today may reach 102 but may have to work till eighty. Pat's oncologist said longevity could extend to 115 if medical science beats cancer! But almost 70 percent now recover. Because of success in battling heart disease (by-pass, nutrition, exercise, statins), a 2011 report said cancer may soon pass heart disease as the leading cause of death. One person dies of cancer every second; one in two men get it; one in three, women. Fascinating reading is the history of cancer in *The Emperor of All Maladies* by Siddhartha

Mukkerjee. Sidney Farber of Children's Hospital in Boston is cited as a champion in understanding and healing 90 percent of those with childhood leukemia. Ted Williams was a big donor.

In all the 20-plus years we lived *sa* Gaulin, we never had a store-bought woolen hat, sweater, mittens, or stockings. Dad got on his homemade spinning wheel to ready the wool for *mémère's* knitting and also taught us how to operate it. In fabricating his Spinning Jenny, he took an electric foot pedal and motor from her old sewing machine. Unfortunately, he got rid of the Jenny when they moved to Bellingham. Another classic example of "the sturdy oak marrying the clinging vine," that is, in courting opposites attract. She held on to everything; he, nothing. Recall in literature there are basically two "eternal" or recurring themes in works: nostalgia (the past) and transitoriness (remember Gloria Mundi in transit?): the passing of things. His mind is where he kept stuff. Mom was the collector, the chronicler. An instance of Mars versus Venus between the sexes?

With our woolen goods and union suits, we easily braved the worst New England winters because as pedestrians, we walked everywhere and stayed outside much more. But because of our ingrained fear of "old man winter" and our susceptibility to colds, we couldn't leave our house unless dressed like Byrd going to the South Pole and having taken dad's medicine. At the time, keeping warm was piling on stuff, no layering like today. And at his insistence, outside of church and home we always wore a hat, since without one (*nu tête,* bareheaded) he cited a heat loss of 90 percent. Men and sinusitis[21] he said.

Since we were city kids, baseball crazy but penniless to buy baseballs, he made us woolen ones. Since the 'hood had dubbed me Window-Breaker par excellence (so recalls Rita Ducharme, née Carpentier), he got tired of changing other peoples' windowpanes, as was expected. I recall a couple of times dad walked to Pinault-Denevers Hardware in Social for the glass and put it in himself. But with woolen baseballs, we could pound the hell out of them and the glass held. He made them by winding wool into a ball shape and threading the whole at different points. Some in different woolen colors. Since we lived next to St. Ann Park and retrieved ripped baseballs and broken bats, we kept him busy. He taped balls, if we didn't kill them by hitting or throwing them in the air, seeing them unravel to a rubber core if a good ball, but corrugated paper if Chinese. He mended bats with metal screws and glue, using clamps during the drying process. He also sewed our cheap leather gloves with a thick black thread, like the bad stich job on Frankenstein's head. A sportswriter mused a kid can now buy his way into Cooperstown by buying a huge, can't miss glove. No such luck for

---

[21] Inflammation of the nasal passages.

us. In sandlot games, some kids in the outfield had no glove. Usually the last kid chosen was the one who played no man's land: right field, because no one batted left.

Dad was truly a jack-of-all-trades and master of quite a few. The word "entrepreneur," popular today in its adjectival form, described him well. But again, rather than unique, was he typical of the devoted, inventive fathers of our neighborhood who gave their families little money and luxury, but treasure-troves of time, attention, affection, and well-honed skills. And also, his presence! They were the biblical portrait of the good paterfamilias forever surprising his family with new and old things (*nova et vetera*). Later, I also speak of dad's culinary skills. Not only an expert buyer, but he was also a masterful cook whose Sunday night soup alone could have kept us alive for a week. When I learned the meaning of "husbandry" in college in an etymology course, I knew why someone thinking about fathers in this insistence coined the word, which is "the judicious use of resources." On the maternal side, life givers and nurturers by nature, people just added "ly" to "mother" to further quantify their greatness.

"How Came He by That Knowledge?"

LIKE PEOPLE OF his calling and time, dad had little formal schooling. In fact, mom said he had one year of book larnin' in Canada and maybe five or six more at St. Ann's after 1904. Then off he went to begin his mill career in his early teens. Such was the life cycle of mill town children when industrialists capitalized on young workers. Shockingly, not illegal initially.

A Shakespearean student in my college days, I was always intrigued by the age-old controversy in literary circles about whether the Bard of Avon really wrote his own plays. After all, his contemporary Ben Jonson said, how could a man with "little Latin and less Greek" (the best education in those days) have known so much about human nature, the depths of depravity, the heights of goodness, nature's fauna, and flora (over 150 plants/flowers), and the rhythmic speech of such great poetry and drama? It got me thinking. Initially I thought knowledge or education came only through books. One of my Alabama mentors in the Order, Brother Ignatius, posed the above question in jest, whenever he met a knowledgeable person with no known formal education. The question is biblical, stemming from Christ's detractors who questioned how a carpenter's son (*filius fabri*) knew so much, did wonders (*magnalia*), and pretended to teach others: "What good (*Quid boni*?) can come out of Nazareth?" As a wit said, "A critic is one who comes along to "deride": their nation is derision, very common in newspaper articles of yesteryear. Lincoln, for one, was severely derided for his tall, emaciated look; and the Irish for their supposed simian or monkey-like look and drinking; blacks for their lack of ambition, and speech. But one critic said Southerners learned their "drawl" from their slaves. Admittedly, he showed his lack of formal education with his reluctance or inability to express his thoughts in writing. But, oh, how his reflective, predictive, and spoken knowledge was profound and undeniably learned in its own untutored way! I realized he got his education some other way: the school of nature, experience, introspection, imitation, and reading, which can educate a person mightily and powerfully. The phrase "self-made person" once described those people. In one instance, in "Tables Turned" poet Wordsworth lauds Mother Nature as a great teacher: "One impulse from vernal wood / May teach you more of man / Of moral evil and of good, / Than all the sages can." Born on a farm, then millworker, and a gardener in retirement, I guess dad learned something from nature and other experiences like all people once did, unraveling nature's secrets like ancients had to. He was indeed his father's son, since *tante* Alice said their father Joseph seemed to know a lot about natural things, from A to W: "astronomy to weather." The great Saint Francis also lauded Nature as a great teacher.

I deliberately said "used to" in referring to self-made savants when I counseled students because it's harder now to succeed in our advanced culture without formal education. As one observer put it, if we, like the British, have "a caste-like system" in this country, it's one of paper or diploma which testifies to years of classroom instruction. But satirically a successful cynic revealed his secret was not letting his schooling get in the way of his education! Like other immigrants, dad had no choice in the matter. Even though Bill Gates may have aborted his college career with no observable harm to his future mega-million success, the same can't be said for all who drop out at any level. Present stats reveal, for example, a college education generates on average a million dollars more in lifetime income compared to a high school education. But sadly, we said the cost of college is getting out of hand. Our biggest personal debt! If mom were still here, she'd say, "*pour les riches seulement*": only for the rich. President Obama has promoted two-year community colleges as a good, inexpensive start, something I always told my non-college prep students in my one public school. At one point, the whole police force in Norton was comprised of students I recommended to Massasoit CC, Brockton, for criminology. Nearly all were from our Standard Program. Again, not against Special Ed, I was convinced students would be more employable with a more challenging program if they could handle it. Almost all did. A black woman educator in Chicago was convinced we should give academically challenged kids more, not less. Their problems are not learning disabilities, but poor circumstances.

Mark Twain said that until children turn 21 they don't usually think much of their parents' learning or savvy. I hadn't thought much about dad's education until mom called my attention to it. When not needling him for his altruism and industry, she expressed wonder about his knowledge and ability to do things. She had me notice how many people, learned or otherwise, came to consult him about politics, raising children, the world of work, inflation, morality, the laws of the land, upcoming conflicts (Germany and Japan), Roosevelt's future death in office, outsourcing, the unwise decline of railroading after the war, some of the negative effects of the great welfare economy, income tax reforms, the New Deal, gardening, ailments, and, most of all, nutrition and health. Obviously, in addition to trudging to the mill every day and running a comfortable home, here was a man with an active, inquisitive mind, soaking up knowledge any way he could. Besides giving the impression he never forgot a word of last Sunday's sermon, you also thought he never forgot anything he read, revealing a kind of photographic mind. No wonder she said in perfect French, "*Écoute ton père*": listen to your father. Our admiration of him first came from her. Isn't it a wise partner who does the same for his or her better half, given the imitative nature of children? In many ways she was his equal with her copious readings, knowledge of history, past and present, insights into the human condition and health, and her fabulous culinary skills, which only a degree in that field can equal today. Daughter of a teacher in the 19th Century, she and her siblings had an edge. But because of setbacks, only her grandchildren stormed the bastions of college.

Bemoaning his lack of formal education, dad sought knowledge through books and magazine articles (loved his Reader's Digest), his 24 medical books, his little Mass booklet in his infirmity, newspapers, and his "*You Are What You Eat.*" All things learned teachers, texts, and the classroom had not shared with him. Reading about nutrition and medicine were the deepest passions of his life. With a heavy heart (closest to his crying I ever saw), he revealed to me he'd have loved to go into medicine if things had been different. It startled me, never thinking parents weren't just born what they were, in his case a millworker. So, they too harbored dreams and unfulfilled ambitions. How often does a father reveal his innermost feelings like that to his children? From a modest, self-composed and unemotional man, this was probably an unguarded moment, a nostalgic note rising deep from a cacophony of unfulfilled aspirations, such as we all have, especially in adult life. As that famous Marlon Brando line from the movie *On the Waterfront* reveals so poignantly, and which I quote several times, "I coulda' been a contenda,' I coulda' been somebody." For example, a member of the healing profession cousin Doctor Roger Fontaine, *mon oncle* François' oldest boy, admired dad's wisdom and judgment.

As children, we only went to the movies once a week, but lucky for us his love of medicine allowed us one year to go 24 weeks in a row to the

Park Theater on Main St. Customarily, the house gave out prizes - dishes and toys - between features. But this time the "freebie" was those 24 volumes on medical care. Since he wanted the series but didn't like movies (except old Charlie Chaplin flicks), we went time and again. Imagine my double thrill when I also won a big double runner sled after I found I was sitting on the winning ticket! He had another volume; I had a new sled to use on Lowland over the Kendrick Bridge. How many millworkers read medical books? As naturalist Ken Weber said of doctors and lawyers of old, you read (like Lincoln did for the law) until you knew enough to practice. ("Practice," one wit said, was the cautious word for doctors of old before medical schools.)

He often consulted those medical books in treating us. We never went to an emergency room, a doctor, or hospital, except for our tonsils. *Mon uncle* Ernest Villeneuve also picked up the series, and since, like mom, he lived to be a nonagenarian, the tomes helped him too in self-diagnosis and treatment. "Physician, heal thyself."

Fascinating how he gauged so accurately how we felt by looking at us, touching our forehead, having us put our tongue out. He looked into your eyes, the color of your tongue, the pallor of your skin while you waited for the diagnosis. No need to show him a medical card! Universal medicine at the Telliers! No appointment, no waiting! But how you hated to have him look clinically at you if the diagnosis meant you had to cancel something. "Give it to me straight, Pa, how much time have I got left?" Feverish, I never forgot the time he put me to bed. Not too sick, I frolicked a bit and rolled off Ben's empty low-slung bed onto the floor. At the thump, he rushed in at a speed of an intern doing his rounds. She also ran in. But came in second, like Peter running to Christ's grave at Easter behind the swifter and more agile John, rendered as an eagle in Christian imagery.

When it came to nutrition, he was such an authority, he could tell you the protein amount and nutritional value of anything served at home. He bought 90 percent of what we ate! For example, when I started teaching, he said I should avoid just toast and coffee for breakfast. Because a teacher's work is mostly in the morning, he or she needs proteins, like in good nutritional cereals, not the sugary kind, he warned, as he touted the cereal Total, eggs, fruit, milk, juice, and the like. This lack of a good breakfast, he cited, is a fault with many Americans who start off their day with absolutely nothing nutritionally healthy, as I saw often at Norton HS with the girls. "I need time to do my hair," I heard often, as if every day was a prom. Despite his instinctive aversion for government programs, he'd be in favor of breakfast in schools because of the importance of that first meal. Because it wasn't true then, so I don't think he ever said it, but he probably saw it coming - Americans, now are supposedly the heaviest people on earth, overfed but undernourished. The nation's individual body mass index for many is over 30. A commenting wit said middle age was when you started to grow in the middle instead of both ends. Companies have seen good results by providing fitness time, like workers walking around their place of work at lunch break. When at Norton HS, I walked around the baseball field at noon where I picked up many baseballs (like I did at St. Ann's Park as a kid), and even a catcher's mitt! In 2015, a study revealed that if you sit for more than 4 hours habitually, your chance for disease, diabetes, cancer, and a shorter life are all in the making. TV showed a business where workers stood, not sat to counter that. I had guidance aides at Norton, but often ran my own errands. Growing up in Woonsocket's tenements, I loved using the stairs.

About dad's delicious soup on Sunday, he was painstaking to make it with all fresh vegetables in season. Like most families, we only had one big meal a bit past noon due to the lateness of the after-Mass breakfast. This was because a normal-sized family like ours went to two or three different Masses in the morning. At the time, Catholics were required to fast by abstaining from food and all liquids from midnight until receiving Holy Communion Sunday morning. So, this dictated our eating schedule for the Sabbath day. Because of fasting, fainting was common during mass. Slam! as another body hit the floor. During the week, there was always some of dad's leftover soup in the icebox, covered by a saucer (*une petite assiette*) over a bowl. Kids are impressionable, and hearing my parents say warmed-up soup was even better the second time made me a believer. Not a gourmet by any means, dad just loved a good, plain, but tasteful table. He wasn't "*un bec raffiné*," a kind of choosy-palate kind of a guy, to quote mom. He was easy to cook for, as we all were, and it would've been ungrateful to "criticize the cook." Between meals, we just had graham crackers in milk or a "nut-butchup" sandwich for snacks. One never outgrows his love of peanut butter.

Yes, we always ate well since they vowed we'd always have a good table, "*une bonne table*" and a roof over our heads. Not a hollow promise when even in 2013, some 50 million Americans don't have enough to eat. They weren't sure about a lot of things, except those two basic necessities of life. We had no problem with clothing because of mom's millinery skills and *mémère's* winter creations. He didn't like federal handouts, but liberal or conservative, you must agree for someone poor like him who stood to benefit from New Deal programs (he did from SS, Relief, and WPA), it was quite unusual to have his stance. Every poor man I knew in the neighborhood always mentioned Roosevelt as "our Father in Washington," *pour ce qu'il fa pour les pauvres*": what he was doing for the poor. But he always told me never to discuss family finances (what finances!) and politics with others. The former I instinctively understood. The latter, was it because dad with his well-researched and carefully thought-out political and economic theories - right or wrong - was a neighborhood maverick? Could there be such a person as a poor, mill working Catholic Republican? Was this a contradiction in terms, an oxymoron? The dictionary gives "cruel kindness" as an example.

A columnist wrote localities, people, and states not as well off as others, tend to be Democratic because of the party's basic platform of redistribution of wealth, instead of increased productivity and jobs, as Wilkie said when he ran against Roosevelt. The writer added that when people have made "their pile" in or by their 40s, they switch parties. As the Brits say, "What we 'ave, we 'old." But Pope Leo XIII in his encyclical *Rerum Novarum* gave a great Christian dimension to the obligation of government help to the needy: "Whereas the mass of the poor have no resources of their own to fall back upon, they should be specially cared for and protected by the government." *In medio stat virtus*: virtue lying in the middle, which human nature, subject to opposite pole thinking, finds hard to find or accept. The fine line between self-sufficiency and dependency on others. Everyone must find that middle. But do some play the system?

Dad lived in an age when self-sufficiency and self-reliance were still esteemed. Now with populations so great and problems so acute, even in the pursuit of life's basic necessities, which sometimes are beyond the reach of local or state agencies, the national polity must be involved. Luckily (even if this is what he feared most) the federal government doesn't have to live with a balanced budget. But as he feared, he saw it as "an intergenerational burden" of taxes for future generations, just when investment experts say today's parents will leave more money to their children than any other generation before. Will our children say, "You never had it so quick, nor lost it so fast?" But has the national disease of spending beyond revenues filtered down to states and cities? Americans are now in hock to all three! How do you get around a national debt of $19 trillion? I like to read biographies of Presidents and until Roosevelt, most were tight-fisted, like Coolidge, Truman, Ike, and Andrew Johnson. Not incurring debt was the greatest sign of a good, prudent administration. One President thought taxes were like stealing from people? Another said the French Revolution was due to many taxes on the people.

I picked up on dad's political philosophy when he invited millhouse friend and *tante* Blanche's violin-maker brother Ernest Frappier over. Since he was a pipe smoker, my job was to put a little water in a spittoon and place it next to his rocker near the window where mom read in the afternoon. Dickens said there's nothing "deader than yesterday's paper," so I put that edition under the receptacle. Women are not fond of those barroom amenities, but she never spoke about it, probably because he was truly "a straight shooter." Unless banished, I kept an ear on their fireside chat while doing homework. Dad was voting for presidential candidate Wilkie in the 1940 elections. I missed seeing him when I heard he barnstormed through the city on Cumberland Street(?) The "poor nuns" wouldn't let us out of school. But of course, Lincoln once came, as a plaque at City Hall memorializes.

Dad took pains to know his candidates and platforms. Relatives often asked him, "*Ti-Phonse, qui penses-tu que j'dwez voter?*": who(m) to vote for. I reiterate that my admiration for his savvy increased still more when, if you recall, two predictions of his were later documented by several authors; one: that Roosevelt "knew" we'd go to war against the Japanese and Germany but not when; two: he was a dying man (intestinal cancer) when he ran for a fourth term to keep his party in the White House in 1944. Advised to choose a good vice president, he chose Henry Wallace but his Democratic chairman submitted his second choice - Harry Truman (WWI hero) - at the convention. Why? He was more acceptable to more people. Did he sense, "He could better stand the heat in the kitchen," now part of the growing Truman political legacy. His daughter's biography of him is insightful. But FDR, who hogged the spotlight, didn't share much with him. Not even the development of the atom bomb. Even Stalin knew before Truman did.

Deemed colorless (once a stigma against Midwesterners!), he grew into the job, as others have done. In that regard, I don't like the man, but I do like the line Jefferson Davis delivered when accepting the presidency of the Confederate Nation: "The man and the hour have met." Begrudgingly, he's given credit as the only man ever to try "to found a new country and wage a major war at the same time." A great line for a sad cause. In the last ranking of great presidents, Truman is fifth after Lincoln, Washington, FDR, and Theodore Roosevelt.

About some who've held that high office, I initially was putting President Jackson dead last for what he did despite the Supreme Court's decision. He stripped the Cherokees of their land in Tennessee and North Carolina and sent them west on a "trail of tears" to Oklahoma, with thousands of deaths. All to satisfy the greed of settlers and landowners wishing to extend their holdings. Imagine, Chief Sequoyah had recorded and structured their language, and in two or three years most of the tribe was literate. But a biography impressed me with Jackson's innate, military-like leadership and heroism, good writing, love of family and country, and his religious foundation. Fourth President (1809-17) James Madison reminded me of St. Augustin ("Only angels can run the affairs of men") when he said, "If men were angels, no government would be necessary." A cautionary note for RI with its history of political corruption. Does our small size breed this corruption? Fifth President James Monroe helped Jefferson with the Louisiana Purchase, and he's famed for the Monroe Doctrine which warned foreign powers not to meddle in the political affairs of the Americas or it would be seen as a hostile act towards the U.S. But we did it to ourselves in the Civil War! Politics aside, dad was very conscious of his role as a moral force in our development. I wish I had a dollar for all the times he called our attention to a point of morality or religion he knew or had recently heard, usually in church. His faith, and the moral convictions flowing from it, were like *la foi du charbonnier*: Joe Workman's unquestioning faith. It was a time when lesser-educated Catholics found it easier to be totally in line with church teaching, poetically "with nary a thorn on the rose." Without a doubt, his moral fiber revealed itself in everything he did. He personified "that the best thing a man can do for his kids is to love their mother." That's gold! Cardinal Newman once said, "A gentleman is one who never inflicts pain." Dad was a gentleman. The only pain I ever saw him inflict (and rarely) was to us boys when we were tots. But only if we gave mom a hard time. He wouldn't allow it. The old shaving strap at the end of the cupboards was the deterrent.

    A couple of times the tragedy of his forced retirement in his early 50's tested his pride and Christian sense of resignation. After working so many years for so little pay, when debility came, he said he was starting to make something with his millwork. The wages of the American worker after the war would never bottom out again, like in or before the Depression. He was making close to $100 a week, even though the mills continued going south. Unfortunately, conservative Yankee owners, if still around, and their French counterparts never modernized their plants. With us kids starting to leave the nest and finally with some disposable money, in came an oil-burning stove and a refrigerator. And out went the antediluvian (think before Noah and the Great Flood!) wood-and-coal stove and icebox. And speaking of nouveau riche, even a toaster that did both sides at once!

    In a role reversal story quite common now, dad turned to homemaking (and more gardening) in forced retirement. So, after over a 30-year hiatus, including one miscarriage and five children, mom went back to work for her SS pension. Besides his talent for buying and cooking for the family, he never disdained housekeeping. He became a great Mr. Mom. While growing up, we children saw how he helped with the heavy housework, knowing without his and *mémère's* help, mom's health would've been imperiled further. Like her sisters, she battled to stay above 100 pounds all her life. Again, as a kid you never think about your parents' mortality or what your parents running a home and earning the daily bread are costing them in strength and energy. That popular French song on the Sunday morning French program - "Your mother won't live forever, so you be good" - was just a song for us. That is, until they let their guard down and told us about their own inner struggles, health, fears, and aspirations. Most kids only find out as adults. That was good to hear because as kids, we thought they existed just for us. Infants orbiting in their own little universe is a natural feeling, a psychologist wrote. One even theorized that for the first year of life, an infant may "think" mom is an extension of himself because of being held so much.

Later, I put a Christian dimension to dad's illness. With his disability increasing, if he had continued work, he wouldn't have survived much longer. In retirement, dad lived another 33 years, happily, usefully occupied, and comfortable with his modest SS pension. At first, he didn't want to hear about any disability pension or help until he'd gone through his $300 in the bank! Only that amount for 39 years of work! Largely due to the Depression and millwork, my parents' generation left the least ever. So obviously their most precious legacy was not monetary. When they left for Hospice Saint Antoine, the five of us sat down to disperse their meager possessions, like who had the most need of this or that for his/her family. I took a fan; Bob, a refrigerator for his son Kenneth; Rachel, their antique bed; Ben, tools; and Sue, household items. Mom said breaking up one's household because of old age, sickness, or death was *"casser maison."* Even if it was their decision, it was a somber moment because for Francos, *la maison ou le foyer* (home or hearth) was such an essential part of *la vie de famille* (family life). Some lived in the same house or apartment their whole married life. But now in our mobile society, the average life of a mortgage is only seven years, one wrote. Apart from economics or jobs, is it that wanderlust gene in the American makeup? Everyone's "manifest destiny" that Frederick J. Turner speaks about in *"The Frontier in American History,"* and how it has influenced the country's political and economic styles. As actor Dick Powell said at the end of a weekly drama, "It happened that way, moving West," a favorite line of Pat and me. I believe it was poet Carl Sandburg who said, "It takes a heap of livin' to make a house a home." Francos did it so well and for so long. Once farmers in Canada, they knew the importance of deep roots, like in the biblical story of The Sower, to reap benefits a hundredfold. Speaking of their forbear peasants in France, (see Graham Robb's *"The Discovery of France"*) did their own amazing stability also come from holding on to what they had: *"ce qu'on a,"* said mom?

True to his amazing powers of prediction, dad told mom and me he was going to die within two or three days of our visit at Saint Antoine. True, some said he'd been predicting his death for years. But you had to separate the muted depression of a sick man from such a sure prediction as he made to us, however resigned he was. Does a dying person know it's their time? About the imminence of death, old Francos resigned to their fate said, *"C'est mon tour"*: It's my turn. I've never forgotten best friend Donna Tardif telling Patricia it was okay to let go when she was on her deathbed in our home, December 10, 2000. Pat did not want to go until Jimmy's subdued birthday party was done. Finishing dessert, Jim went to the master bedroom, called us, and we saw her give up her beautiful spirit. I saw it rise! "Every love story ends in tragedy!"

Providence-born poet Louise A. Nickerson captures in "Sequential" the legacy of my father, mom, Pat, and people like them, whose good deeds are not interred with their bones:

> Within my heart's circumference
> You are contained.
> My inner ear records your voice.
> Your smile, retained,
> Will be for all my years ahead
> To know and to keep.
> And always mine, your love to hold;
> I have no need to weep.

A Day on the Farm

WHEN DAD AND I in the 1970s visited his brother Napoléon at Saint Antoine in his declining years, I saw much more than a flannel-shirted old man in a rocking chair. I visualized *"oncle Napoléon chez sa terre,"* as mom spoke about him, wife Maria, and their large family on the farm. I recalled a tiller of the soil, and a long, small-faced strider like dad. His now sedentary state couldn't dim one of the treasured memories of our youth when he owned a 12-acre dairy farm on Pound Road in Cumberland, where he had a sizeable herd and sold milk retail, then wholesale. Until many years ago, according to his son Edmond, the empty farmhouse still stood in a tall grassy meadow but was later transported to the left side of a cul-de-sac further down the road. Going to the farm was only a short ride from the city, but far for us pedestrians.

Coming to America at the turn of the century, my father as a boy, like his brothers, had been taken out of the country, but not the country out of them. Nostalgia aside, dad was too well read not to know the harsh economic realities of farming, with its long day's toil, seven-day week, and meager returns. Yet in his conversations, you couldn't miss his love of the land, pride of ownership, growing your own farm-fresh veggies, working in the fields rather than in the mills, taking care of livestock, and milking cows. Yes, all chores defined by one farmer "as jobs that just don't stay done." The kind of industry Jefferson wanted for this country, instead of Hamilton's industrialism. But an author wrote Jefferson also knew we needed a strong industrial base too, a major reason we bested the South in the Civil War.

In addition to economics and the mill's effect on dad's lungs, mom was also convinced he wasn't strong enough for farming: "*Sa santé ai (est) pas assez bonne*" (His health isn't good enough.) So altruistically, he did the next best thing. When single, we said he lent money to his brothers Napoléon *et* Philibert to buy their own farms. When we were poor and almost homeless during the Depression, how she wished he had his savings to keep a roof over our heads. But if someone was needy or if a relative or friend asked him for a handout or a loan, he couldn't say no. He wasn't naïve, just generous, his "biggest fault," she said. If, as Father Bob Carpentier said in a funeral eulogy, we're judged on Judgment Day by our deeds (e.g., "I was thirsty and you gave me to drink; I was naked and you clothed me," et al) rather than by our social status, education, job in life; it dawned on me in the Order that he had nothing to fear. Charity often rebounds to the giver in some way, and we were sometimes on the receiving end. *Deus Providebit*: God will provide, as He did. Why even the Bible said He even adorned the lily more beautifully than King Solomon, one of my lines in a play. (I was on stage recovering from dental surgery, and my fellow actor didn't know his lines, which were glued to the ceiling! We got away with it, with no one wondering why he never looked at me.)

But even in the city, we had a constant reminder of the farm. Every other morning as payback for his loan, my uncle or his sons left five glass quarts of milk at our third story front door. Often in winter on sub-zero days, we saw the expanding cream of the raw milk push the bottle caps about an inch above the rim. More than once in trying to bring the bottles to our icebox, two in each hand, we jostled them too much, unleashing a torrent on the linoleum. God, how I marveled how milkmen carried as many as three in one hand, if not using a rack! As boys are wont to do, we measured our hands against dad's to see if we were growing some. Good hands, big hands were important for baseball and for carrying milk bottles to the icebox! And if quick and dexterous like his, you might be a good mule spinner, the pinnacle of the trade, and tie those broken strands lickety-split after your apprenticeship as a bobbin boy! Even when raw milk was verboten, we hung on for a while, then grimaced as pasteurized milk was mandated.

On a grape-picking day for dad's winemaking, I experienced your city boy's wild-eyed wonder when I saw my uncle and sons milk cows. Awed by the massiveness and menacing (to me) look of the herd, I declined all offers to sit on a little stool to try my hand. Bob did. But even if urbanized, we weren't as bad as some inner-city kids I later heard talking while on a bus when I was a summer camp counselor in the Order at Camp Sacred Heart, Sharon. Passing by cows grazing in the field, I heard one say, "Hey, I saw in a book that's how we get milk." And not from the Superette, on the corner of Madison and Fifth, I thought about deprived kids getting out of their macadam jungle.

Unaccustomed to the ways of the farm, I marveled at the bond between *mon oncle et ses vaches* (and his cows.) A whispered name, a gentle pat, a soft shove seemed all that was needed between man and beast. Very quickly, my uncle's practiced strokes produced a brim full of thick creamy milk, which sloshed in the pails, as he or his sons walked to the cooler, one time a cat following. I was as awed as your movie Oklahoman when I walked with dad (who loved his *blé d'Indes*: Indian wheat) across rows of golden-eared corn as high, yes, "as an elephant's eye": (Rodgers and Hammerstein). Some of it was cow corn raised for fodder. As kids, we wrapped scraps of newspapers around corn silk to make our own forbidden smokes. But not there. Before marijuana, a student at the Academy would say, "A friend with a weed is a friend indeed." But not within earshot of resident minders Brothers Michael and Elisée who, like in our westerns, "put law and order in these parts."

But what a rapturous delight Bob and I experienced when one time we romped in the haybarn. We jumped, bounced, slid, and flung the sunburnt aromatic strands that seemed to float on gossamer wings before falling to the floor. We were lucky that time, falling through an opening in the second story flooring and landing into a bed of hay some 10 feet below. What boys don't tell their moms!

Not knowing all the rigors of a farm boy's life, how we wished then to be sons of the soil, breaking away from the call of the mills which seemed our only working destiny. But only one generation removed from the pull of the soil, we felt its magnetism in our bones. It had been, after all, the work of our forebears for three hundred years on Canadian soil. And probably the same in France, except for a few tile makers (so the name LeTuillier) or, yes, weavers and the spelling of our present surname. Is that why a geneticist said every child is the product of a thousand years of generation? And for us Francos, perhaps descendants also of those Vikings who attacked and eventually settled in Normandy and Northern England, called Danelaw.

As a teacher of English, history, Latin, and then as a counselor, my life's work was in a classroom or office. But, outside of reading and writing, my most relaxing moments have always been, apart from swimming, the joys of gardening, planting flowers, and landscaping. Those predilections caused my citified Brooklyn-born Patricia to exclaim, "Rene, you love dirt." The late Ken Weber, columnist for *The Providence Journal*, captured best the nostalgia of what farming once meant to a family now urbanized: "When I went out to plow, I could enjoy the unfamiliar warmth of April sunshine on my back. I could watch the robins follow the clattering tractor, ready to pounce on uncovered earthworms. I could drink in the fragrance of newly turned soil, a rich, moist, elemental smell that is hard to describe to someone who has not been out there. It's the smell of the earth, but also the smell of promise, the smell of hope, the smell of optimism." The most we do now is plant vegetable and flower gardens. For me, there is still a measure of satisfaction in spading up a garden. Occasionally, I too reach down to pick up a clod of dirt. I slowly break it apart with my fingers, partly to test the moisture, to see if the soil is ready, as farmers say, but also because it just feels right to have ground, the good earth, in my hands again." So maybe that's why our dad made gardeners out of the five of us, to experience what he had as a boy in Saint Cuthbert, P.Q., and what novelist Pearl S. Buck called *"The Good Earth."*

Traditionally, the paterfamilias in Canada bequeathed the land or portions of it to one or more of his sons to keep it in the family. At Monticello, Jefferson, who was left vast estates, said he had no greater pleasure than gardening along with public service. His vision for America, unlike John Adams' (and Federalists Hamilton, Jay, & Madison), was, again, the soil, not the loom. Only later in life did his friendship with Adams (who also farmed before and after his presidency) resume in now-treasured correspondence which lasted to their death. Incredibly both died on July 4, 1826, fifty years to the day after the adoption of the Declaration of Independence. Charles Carroll, the only Catholic to sign it, died exactly two years later, again on July 4. Maryland was founded Catholic, but 100 years later, Catholics could not even hold office. But as the richest and the biggest landowner spanning three states, he was generous, but would not compromise his faith for elected office. And because of his superior education in England and with the Jesuits in France, his talents were sought.

I said we had a good table at home, even if our fortunes were sometimes meager. Like the Irish, we ate a lot of stews - *gibelotte* in French - as those dishes seemed bottomless. And you could always "add a potato or more water if company came." Anyway, we five children were all good eaters, compared with some of today's finicky ones, who have choice and abundance, but not always good nutrition. But oh, how we paled in comparison when we sat down to a meal with my uncle, wife Maria, and eight surviving children: Léo, Armand, George, Edmond, Ovila, Léa, Thérèse, and Marcel (deceased were Albert and Muriel). I had never seen such voracious appetites. They didn't need to be told to try this or that, as we often heard at home, where dad always touted something nutritious. Like the time he brought broccoli home for the first time and oysters instead of cod one Friday. With little social banter or ideal chatter, my cousins sought to replenish those energies spent in their never-ending chores. Recall nothing was more sacred in our culture than the family meal with *le père* (father) at the head of the table and *la mère* (mother) at the other end, like in our home. "Le *souper en famille,*" (the family dinner) mom said. It so lifted her spirits to see her loved ones *à la table ensemble* (at the table together.)

At one meal on the farm, I, like most Francos as I later discovered, started looking at salt pork (*lard salé*) as a relished delicacy. Every pot of Saturday night oven-baked beans soaked overnight and sometimes heated to perfection for a small fee at a local bakery, like Carle's for us Gaulinites, had big chunks in them. My parents always ate and extolled it to us, but we children disdained it as too squishy and funny tasting. But when I saw my cousins fight for it for their homemade bread, I figured they were onto something. Later, in training in the Order, with beans served once a week, especially from *la cuisine du* (kitchen of) *Frère Célestin* in Harrisville, RI, I got to like it a lot, until it became a no-no because of its high fat content. We called it wheel grease: "*d' la graisse de roue.*" Brother Alfred (Joe Phaneuf) could never get enough of it.

After a day on the farm "*et au grand air*" (and in the open air,) to cite mom, and quickly falling asleep despite warring cats in our yard, I felt a letdown upon rising the next morning still surrounded by a world of dirt yards, hot, cracked macadam, congested houses, and those tall, red-bricked mills we could almost touch. That's why I always looked at my uncle's farm-fresh milk and dad's wine as more than just palate pleasers. They were elixirs of a life we knew was out there, just an early morning ride away in my uncle's motorized milk wagon. It's also why I love Wright's Farm as a close neighbor, even if my Gotham-citified wife didn't like the cows' blessings in my garden for fertilizer.

From Those Agrarian Days of Yore to Urban Life

RECALLING THE DAYS we spent on my uncle's farm reminded me later that until the turn of the century many Americans lived and worked in an agrarian society where people grew their own food. This before the continued rise of industrialization and the rush to suburbia in all its good and bad outcomes, like not growing your own food.

Except perhaps in the Maritime Provinces or in parts of the remote, cold Western Provinces, the same way of life also prevailed in Québec. Therefore, we surmised that immigrants from *La Belle Province* (Québec) who came to America like my dad's family were tillers of the soil on their own or rented farms. Even though *les* Fontaines did lose a farm-like property in the Ontario fire, patriarch Louis Fontaine, however, was more the entrepreneurial type with five failed businesses to his (dis)credit. Even though these habitants freely chose to come to America to find steady work in the mills and a better life for themselves and their children, initially, like my parents' families, they found themselves without land or privacy in congested cold-water flats, and beyond the sight and smell of newly mown fields and lowing herds. They were without that sense of independence agrarian life gives you over the hundreds of artificially contrived needs of a capitalistic-consumer society. Change is pain, mom said in her cryptic manner: "*Le changement est toujours plein d'peines*." Her father, Louis Fontaine, moved often, and lo and behold mom married dad who was also in the grips of urban wanderlust. In fact, when we moved to *la* Gaulin in the mid-1930s, she told him, "*Cée tassey*: enough. Moving three times, she said often, was like a fire: "*Déménager trois fois, c'est comme un incendie*."

That closeness to the soil and living things had fostered in them qualities of unsophisticated simplicity, industry, friendliness, joie de vivre, self-reliance, and integrity. If at times the congestion of their new living conditions and the confinement of their millwork cast a pall over those pristine virtues of agrarian life, those honorable traits still shot through in everyday urban life. The unusual conviviality of the city was largely infused with their great camaraderie and *entregent* (to have connections). In Social Coin, for example, everybody seemed to know everybody.

But at times she did bemoan our lack of privacy. Like so many other families, we were renters, "*des rentiers*." Thinking of dad's loans, she had her own version of Shakespeare's lament: "Neither a borrower nor a lender be." For us in the early 1930s, renting meant putting up with a noisy bar (the Rendezvous, a former renter told me recently) under us on Cass Avenue. After moving, she had to deflect criticism from *deux vielles filles* (old maids) on the second floor *sa* Gaulin, who justifiably (?) objected to the thunderous herd (five of us chilluns) often passing overhead, as Ben recalled.

Not unneighborly, she worked hard to keep us quiet and in tow. Added reasons were dad, away from the ear-busting mill engine room, and *mémère* who hated noise like sin. However, if the noise we made was normal child's play, always a stout lioness in defense of her cubs, she railed against the nitpickers, "*Des enfants, il faut q'ça grouillent*": kids, noise, and energy were a trifecta. Expectedly, some coolness and hurt feelings developed between renters, but amity soon returned. Considering the large size of families who occupied those tenement houses with their six to eight units, could big families live so close today with so little disharmony?

Also, about tenement living and everyday decorum, I recall she told me some neighbors considered her a "plain Jane" because she rarely displayed fineries and almost never wore cosmetics. Proof she wasn't the only one observing and commenting about "her people." It's not something a child would normally know or notice (kids don't rate their parents on esthetics), so her admission made an impression on me. In the 1920s, however, working as a single young woman with some money, de rigueur she sported furs, suede-like high shoes, and plumed hats as was the fashion of the day, as family photos show. She even had an outfit with some décolletage (cleavage), pray tell! But too bad, as friend Ali Beaulieu remarked about parents aging: "When your kids grow older, so do you."

But interestingly, the relative who wrote the Fontaine-Morvan chronicles in Canada said a woman who wore cosmetics (*fardée*) was considered *une femme lachée* (loose). But once married and into the Depression, mom's plainness in cosmetics and clothes were a question of priorities rather than moral correctness. Even if they chided her for "squeezing the nickel until the Indian rode the buffalo," or for being like the tightwad woman on my *Call* beat, "A *pinça la cenne*" (a penny pincher). Offending or offended, was that like a biblical instance of "seeing a speck in someone's eye, and not the beam (of wood) in one's own?" But like other homemakers in the 'hood, she was or became courageous with her fortitude during the two world wars, the influenza epidemic, the Depression, and dad's lengthy illness. Have we given women of that critical period their due? In her own defense, she struggled with dad's uncertain health and lack of steady work, but she made do with what we had. There was no thought of a personal makeover with existing money needed for necessities. No less frugal, dad added, "I've never owned a car and probably never will."

Sharing that confidence surprised us because we really didn't know what "poor" was, since, as she said, we were all in the same boat. Not surprisingly, out of earshot like any couple with finite means, they must have strategized how to make it, always keeping our needs and development first. Yes, because of the Depression's severity, worldwide grip, and decade-long duration, it was both a testing ground and learning experience for young and old, the size of which people had never seen and perhaps never will again thanks to the immediate, towering response of the federal government.

Before coming to America in 1904, dad spent the first eight years of his life on a farm. For him, the saying, "All life began in a garden" had a joyful and nostalgic meaning. By a strange twist of irony, in retirement he spent a good part of 30 years gardening and helping maintain the Bouffard home in Bellingham. Mom helped Sue with her five children, giving them lunch, playing cards, and teaching them French songs. Obvious too was dad's joy in seeing things grow in his garden, and his neighborliness to share his harvest with others, evidence of that pristine agrarian virtue.

An incident bore this out well. Soon after they moved there, I spent my first two-week vacation ever from the Brotherhood with them in the early 1950s. He was helping an old man living in an untidy shack in a nearby field. "The man's senile," mom said, he accused your father of stealing his wheelbarrow, but he still gives him garden produce," adding "*Ça cée ton père*," that is, who he was. By now, we all knew because she always told us stuff about him, so enamored was she about this paragon of decency and humaneness she married. Of course, they had their differences at times about our infantile misbehaviors and the best use of their limited resources in each situation. But what was in their favor compared to today's struggling families was they had no debt. Like most of our neighbors, having no car, mortgage, phone, or school debt, their struggle was "limited" to little or no money for expenses. Call it *le dur quotidien*, which the King James' Bible describes as "Sufficient for the day is the evil thereof."

Because I was curious about the old codger, I went with dad to the shack, which was somewhat dirty and smelled bad. But dad told me the old man had enough sanity or stubbornness to spurn his married children's wish to move him into a rest home. That senility soon became obvious when he seemed at first not to know my father, who introduced us both five times. Finally lucid, *le vieillard* (the old man) began to rile against the local ruffians who stole from his shack. But he didn't confuse dad with those miscreants. Dad gave him tomatoes and cukes and asked him if he needed anything. So, it wasn't true that good deeds are interred with one's bones, "as the Bard said. So now completely lucid and even grateful, the old man beamed, "*Merci, monsieur Tellier.*" He had been touched by dad's generosity. Like mom, I thought he should've given up on him when he accused him of stealing. But he repeated our granddad's favorite saying, "To understand is to forgive," adding you couldn't always justify what a person did, but sometimes understand why. What a pearl of wisdom! Another never-to-be-forgotten moment. The field is fully back to nature, but I reflect on the episode every time I go to the Bouffard home. Of course, we had walked over, but unlike when I was a kid, I now could keep up with his farm-boy stride. I became "a walker" in the Order at Notre Dame HS in North Worcester County's bracing air, besides learning how to ski.

Because he was always a forgiving man, read a lot, and observed closely, he seemed to know so much about the human heart. Also, with the medical bent of his mind, like a doctor he told me how senility or dementia affected the octogenarian's behavior and judgment. As usual, she put a cap on all of it, "*Il lui en passe,*" about giving him a pass. They were both showing me in real time their Christian charity in action. Much later, reflecting on the Beatitudes during morning meditation in the Order, I thought dad was willing to suffer "for justice's sake," to do some good despite having his good name impugned by a senile old man. (A couple of times in my counseling career, I told students who were wrongfully maligned or disciplined, they too were suffering for justice's or goodness' sake. I recalled a high school senior who was not given a chance to explain before being thrown out of class one day for no homework. He told me his brother ran away to New York the night before, and his mom sent him after "the prodigal son."

I was surprised he even showed up for school. He hadn't slept a wink. I once began a diary of my counseling experiences, but gave it up, thinking about the mounting problems of kids today that "it might be banned in Boston." That's why I was pleased to write guidelines for the Academy's teacher-counselor program under Brother Paul Demers' principalship and inspiration. Wasn't it a factor later in MSC being rated a Blue Ribbon School by the White House? Before referring to counselors, teachers could now react quickly to a student's dilemma. Counselor and teacher working together as a model of student advocacy. MSC's goal is that every single student is known and supported.)

So free at last from the sweaty confinement of close to 40 years of millwork and landless tenement house living, dad poured himself into gardening, finding fulfillment and longevity. He literally reveled in his long-lost boyhood love of the soil. He wrote for his catalogs and seeds in late winter, prepared his seedbeds in the spring in makeshift *serres-chaudes* (greenhouses made of old storm windows), and planted outside only after a careful observation of the phases of the moon. His father, an unschooled man, had taught him well. Like the ancients, he, like dad, was into astronomy, the moon's phases, the seasons, and their effects on growing things.

In the summer dad boasted having the first and juiciest tomatoes in town. Like Jefferson at Monticello, he too kept records of the first fruits, the largest and the sum of his yield. He started flats[22] for us his five married children, including sons-in-law, Donald Clark and Guilbert Bouffard, relatives, and friends. And he gave away - no money please - what he and mom and *les* Bouffards couldn't use. I repeat he was like a giant of the earth, as Norwegian novelist Rolvaag called those immigrants whose roots lay in or close to the soil before and after they came to America. Willa Cather, subject of my M.A. thesis, did also. In working his garden spot, he adhered to three cardinal rules: plenty of peat moss to retain moisture; natural or store-bought fertilizer, like 5-10-5, and no early planting. That advice he epitomized with "*Ne pas montrer* (show) *tes côtes* (ribs) *avant la Pentecôte.*" That is, avoid planting (like shedding your winter duds) until the Feast of Pentecost or the Coming of the Holy Spirit to the Apostles, usually the last full moon in May or early June Sunday, the birthday of Christendom. Yes, that was late enough for planting everything. He spoke of the tomato as the most delicate produce in the garden. Too early a start and all went for naught with one cold night. He always advised us to surround the young plants with toothpicks to keep the worms out. Clothing wise, we even kept our union suits until that time, evoking poet Thomas Gray's the "simple annals of the poor." A wit used "flannels" instead of "annals."

---

[22] A shallow container in which seedlings are grown. – *ed.*

Speaking of longevity, long after he began gardening, we all noticed his off-season spirits began to soar when a new planting season came. Like in writer O. Henry's "The Last Leaf," as long as he gardened (the last leaf or hold on life), he found a reserve of strength and breath to keep on. He sapped a new vitality from the fertile soil, as if in step with nature. But when finally, he said he couldn't climb the sloped terrain to where the garden was laid out, I knew, like in the epitaph by novelist and poet Robert Louis Stevenson, "Home is the sailor, home from the sea/And the hunter home from the hill."

I used to bring him to his doctor, Dr. Richard Terrill, who knew how invigorating gardening was for him, and grateful to receive a bag of freshly picked tomatoes. But finally, dad asked mom to give up taking care of their own home, *"J'veux m'en aller"* (I want to go). The same phrase he used later when he sighed for release from his earthly bonds. It was time to leave their home and accept long-term care. Typical of his generation, he didn't want to be a burden. What was also nostalgic for us five children was that for at least twenty years, our spouses and children always met Sunday afternoon at their Bouffard second-story home. Every year, a new birth added so much joy to our get-togethers, especially at Christmas which Sue hosted for close to 50 years. As the children swam in the pool in the summer, *pepère et mémère* watched from their window. Every Sunday they beamed, "We have lived to see this day." It had not been a given in the 1930s. It was hard won. Once they had nothing but their faith to hang on to!

Born January 30, 1896, dad died on Father's Day, June 20, 1982, closing a memorable life that had touched so many people. He now rests in Precious Blood Cemetery with mom, *mémère* Emérance, *tante* Marie-Ange, my wife Patricia, *oncle* Henri *et tante* Laurence, and grandchild Guilbert Bouffard. Of course, it's where my resting place will be also. It will almost be like those family cemeteries of old when we'll all welcome Christ's return when He comes in glory on the final day. Imagine, the end of creation as we know it! Christ said those "who are asleep" will meet Him first, which should please "Speedibus Mom." We will have kept the faith of old. Like Champlain said on his deathbed: "I've kept the faith I was raised in and now die in the Apostolic, Roman Catholic Faith." My grandfather Joseph, his wife Angélina, and infant Joseph Romeo, who lie in a nearby plot shared by cousin Arthur Tellier's wife, will also join our joyous group. With so many Francos in the cemetery, will the angels chant France's La Marsellaise: *"En avant, marchons ..."* marching forward from their resting place in their new immortalized humanities, never again to know pain, suffering, disease, old age, and death. In Harrisville I loved hearing Brother Josephus, founding MSC principal, singing France's patriotic song, said by some to be the best national anthem. Ours next best!

Thinking about the earth he once knew and "the new earth" where his spirit now dwells, I like to fancy that on their farm in Canada his father told him something like what Scarlett O'Hara's father told her in *Gone with the Wind*, even if he only spoke about it here below. That is, that land is "the only thing in the world that amounts to anything ... for 'tis the only thing in the world that lasts, and don't you be forgetting it! 'Tis the only thing worth working for, worth dying for...." So prophetic of heaven for us Christians. But again, earthly wise, in a Russian story I read that a peasant wanted as much land as he could get. His Romanov czar told him he could have all he could run over in one day. When he died of exhaustion, the czar provided a six-foot plot for his burial, saying, "That's all a man really needs on this earth." Saints tell us with no restriction of space and time, our glorified bodies in heaven will transcend all horizons with a mere wish.

About *oncle* Napoléon and his farm, if ever you heard an immigrant French Canadian in Woonsocket say *chez terre* (down on the farm), he or she said it with the same nostalgia and affection as Scarlett's father for their Tara plantation home. O for those agrarian days of yore, the sigh seemed to say! Again, dad had known that life for about eight years before his exodus. But it wasn't going to be his *métier* or livelihood here. But it pleased him to keep that way of life alive in his brothers' families. It set him and us back, but like the widow in the temple so praised by Christ, he had little in life to give, so what he gave was not from excess, but from his modest savings and altruism. When he gave, he never indulged in "woulda-coulda-shoulda." And he surely knew Christ's caution that when we give, we shouldn't let the left hand know what the right one is doing?

4 - THE FONTAINE SAGA

Femmes de Maison: Homemakers

RECALL THAT UNTIL marriage and children, women in mill centers were like peacetime counterparts to wartime's Rosie the Riveter. Having come to the states usually to escape the long toil and small returns of farming, as single girls they worked in the mills in and around the city, antedating the 25 million wartime female workers of WWII.

In mom's case, except for a brief work spell in a shoe factory in Derry, NH, where her family lived momentarily after the Cochrane tragedy, mom in 1916 first worked at La Montrose Mill on East School Street. She recalled a 50-hour week for about eleven dollars! She often spoke of the women she knew as working girls. A few photos in the albums survive, like her mill girls at a Halloween party. My favorite shows her, *tante* Marie, and others at the Alsace Mill on East School St. in 1919. Like the men, they all have a bit of that humorless and overworked look about them. But I read that at one time Europeans thought Americans always smiled in photos, as if life was one happy sojourn. But since we only knew her as a homemaker, photos remind us she too once had a career outside the home and was "independently wealthy," as in "single and your pockets jingle."

Family size and the traditional culture and the church's stand on mothers primarily as homemakers were big reasons for their stay-at-home status after marriage. It's a stand, incidentally, which was lauded even as late as the 1980s by conservative Pope John Paul II and Pope Francis, especially their nurturing, God-given creative role. Farther back, a 1943 editorial in *Catholic World* minced no words about the traditional stance (at least then) of men and women in the married state. It affirmed, "Women who maintain jobs outside their homes... weaken family life, endanger their own marital happiness, rob themselves of man's protective capabilities and by consequence decrease the number of children." Even accounting for the time warp, could only a man have written that? No doubt the emergence of Rosie the Riveter in wartime, the equality of job, education, and career opportunities for men and women, the phenomenon of single parent families, and other factors undermined or completely erased whatever "validity" that pronouncement once had about gender roles. As an old cigarette commercial touted, "You've come a long way, baby."

Most women in her day had even less education than men, primarily for the reason just given. And even if their *besogne* or family duties alone didn't allow them a full turn at the mill, there was also very little else they could do except sales perhaps and housework for others. But I remember our neighbor, Madame Bernadette Beauregard, even with four kids, taking in some sewing in our tenement. The Irish or Italian washer-woman type in literature, as novelist James Farrell wrote about some of America's earliest immigrant families in New York and Chicago. They didn't have her counterparts here. God, mothers had plenty with their own wash on Mondays! ("*mon gros lavage*," mom sighed: my big wash) We have said it was an all-day affair. (Humor: A laundry man came to the door of a convent, as a comedian recorded, saying, "Do you have any 'dirty habits' this week?")

Beginning my professional career as a teacher and counselor in the early 1950s, I later heard several times from parents of my male students (only in 1973 was I in my first coed situation at the Academy), they were more concerned about educating their sons and not so much their daughters. I suspect this notion was firmly entrenched in our culture, perhaps more so than with other immigrant nationalities. But credit to my parents, I never heard that discriminating thought uttered by either of them. At a time when it wasn't done or a whole lot, I recall she did encourage Sue to attend Hill College in the city. True, the travails that beset mom's Fontaine family seriously abbreviated her own academic career, but she was proud her mother was a former teacher in Canada in the 1880s and left no doubt she was her mother's daughter in mental acuity, curiosity, and love of reading. I don't know if *mémère* wrote letters, but epistolary mom sent 1,000.

But finally, the whole preferential notion of more education for men than women died a quick death after the war. Today more women attend college than men, finish, and go into M.A. programs, so the ratio is inching towards 60-40, with "coed college" now meaning men also attend, said an admissions counselor. And they get better grades in high school, as I saw repeatedly. A study, however, said the reason boys do better on SATs is because they are more willing to guess and play the odds. One theory is girls only answer when they know and, as far as math is concerned, their growing-up toys and experiences are not as mechanistic or spatially enriching. This may have been so at one time, but no longer. I was encouraged in my years at Norton HS in the 1980s and '90s to see more girls go into calculus and even physics. Most high schools now make that claim, especially in the latter science. Wasn't a Harvard president severely criticized not long ago for postulating women lacked "certain niceties" (abilities) for science? Didn't he know about Madame Curie? Pat's niece Kathy Misovec, for example, toured local colleges with me and wound up with a PhD in engineering from M.I.T. Holy Cross, a great liberal arts college also beckoned because as a great reader, she also excelled in English. I once saw her watching television while reading Tolstoy's *War and Peace*. It's the Russian novel President Kennedy, a super-fast reader, knocked off in only three days (over

1,500 pages). I took three weeks. I was once partial to Russian Literature and I agree, as a critic wrote, their literature is so ponderous with all that life holds. When I told Pat *Doctor Zhivago* was about a man loving two women at the same time, she retorted "I better be the only one!" The movie's haunting lyrical tune "Somewhere My Love," or "Lara's Theme," was our wedding song.

    Returning to our discussion of mothers at home it was a fact that what people considered a "good life" at that time didn't require a second salary. Even if men's salaries were of the hand-to-mouth variety, "making it" was whatever the father's salary afforded. He was the breadwinner; she, the homemaker. We were all in the same boat about earthly goods. Only later did TV show the difference between rich and poor and perhaps incite legitimate ambition in some, envy in others, and larceny in the misbegotten. Is there so much thievery today because wealth is so obvious? Thieves want what others have, a NJ car-thief told the police, as if wanting makes it legal.

    But the issue of two-worker families still evokes recent comments, especially about its effect on women and children. *Providence Journal* columnist Froma Harrop weighed in on the subject citing an author named Hochschild. She wrote, "Children shouldn't be in storage. Today, working mothers put in longer hours at the job, yet few social scientists have suggested they should be devoting more of their efforts to tending the home fires - until recently." Hochschild in *The Time Bind* relates that many women devote long hours to paid work, not out of economic necessity but out of preference. Many young children are now routinely left at day care centers for 10 hours at a time, supposedly to the detriment of their mental and social health. Even babies under one year of age are found to spend an average 42 hours a week in day care. I suspect other studies refute that. I raise the issue, not to offer judgment, but for comparison to another time. Yes, the issue is complex, but most Franco women were spared making those decisions. The article went on to say fathers are helping more but hardly equal their spouse's work output. But twice I read 7 million men are now stay-at-home moms. Certainly, women's equal education renders moot the idea of their not having, if wished, a career outside the home at some point or throughout their lives. Especially with men now taking on more domestic duties. But one who worked for 25 years told me she quickly realized what she missed. My Pat insisted on staying home for Jim's first five years to teach him his letters, numbers, prayers, use of a pencil and scissors for cutouts. Because of cancer in the late 1990s, it turned out to be the only retirement she ever had. It meant three of us living on less than a $10,000 salary in the 1970s. "Want not, waste not." Our vow of poverty from our religious Orders had caught up with us. Mom pointed out it often took years for newly marrieds to fully furnish their home. Hardly anyone incurred debts of any kind. You only bought what you had money for, and like our factotum dad, repaired what you owned. Built-in obsolescence (use it and discard it when out of style or broken) was practically unknown. Mom said everything was "*pour la vie*": for life. Apart from their modest circumstances, it's no wonder their life had stability and an unhurried pace we now envy in "our acquisitive society," as Paine wrote.

So "buying on time" was not in vogue. Few young couples ever had to endure the inevitable pitfalls of the "enjoy now, pay later" risk of merchandising. In our case, a millhand's salary also precluded any borrowing. How often I heard what dad didn't have now, he wasn't going to get. Some newly wedded couples were so poor, they even had to forgo a honeymoon, returning to work the same day, like in Canada, she said.

As I said earlier, only at the grocery store did people put things on their tab as *mon oncle François* let them do during the depression. Whenever we visited him *et ma tante* Blanche on a Sunday afternoon, we loved spending time at his store. He wore a meat cutter's apron with shirt cuffs covered with long plastic covers. A born storyteller, like his father Louis, he entertained his customers as much as he served them. Did I relate one customer was a ventriloquist, and one time I heard my name called from a third-story porch from across the street? Did anybody know me two miles from home? Surprised, I rushed out of the store, only to return with my uncle and his jocular friend enjoying a "Gotcha!" at my expense.

As Bob's godparents, they once brought an ice cream cake from the store to their Ross Street apartment for his birthday bash. Dad made his own ice cream, but we'd never seen an ice cream cake. That was like Shirley Temple's house where unbelievably she had her own ice cream parlor. That was El Dorado and the Holy Grail all rolled into one! Unless dad made it on Sunday to go with mom's blueberry pies, we got ice cream only on warm, summer nights on the porch, if he sprung for a quarter for five cones, or six if she wanted one. She liked maple walnut ("warnut"), which became my lifetime favorite.

Besides their homemaking status, was there another general feature about women? Do I dare to tread? ("Fools rush in where angels fear to tread," said a poet.) One obvious physical trait was their short stature and, unlike mom, a certain amount of avoirdupois: poundage. But who says heaviness is always a negative since doctors say heavier people are or can be as healthy as others? But this latter feature we recorded was a distinct contrast with the neighborhood men who were usually thin or spare like dad. Millwork just wasn't conducive to putting meat on your bones. But I'm amazed how tall young women now are. And because of sports, a report said, they're less likely to have as many skeletal-arthritic problems later in life due to bigger bone development. Studies in the 20th Century concur that better nutrition and medical care have resulted in taller and, yes, bigger (including heavier) Americans for three generations in a row. But it's now ending. Are television, videos, physical inactivity, and certain foods, like fries, sodas, burgers major culprits? Recall an author said our work no longer provides the movement it once did, so exercise must be outside the workplace. People of means are more conscious of that, and because of better nutrition (proteins instead of fats and sugars) less likely to be overweight.

As I once saw written about the first wave of foreign-born Italian women in this country, like in spaghetti sauce commercials, French-Canadian women were somewhat heavy in their middle and later years. Was this due to excessive childbearing, a protein-poor diet, and unremitting household drudgery devoid of any recreational and body-shaping benefit? But if a woman appeared too thin and devoid of womanly contours, the label was "*sec*" or spindly, like Popeye's girlfriend Olive Oyl!

Two women discussing a third woman's appearance were sometimes heard to say, "*Elle chey laisser aller*," about a woman quickly losing her figure after marriage and children. "*Elle fa d'la graisse*" (puts on poundage) was a similar assessment from her critical gender mates. A British writer said women are more judgmental of each other than men. If mom and her sisters were exceptions, it wasn't from virtue, but from their birdlike appetite (*"elle mange comme un wéseau"*: *oiseau*: she eats like a bird, said dad about mom), and their genetic make-up. In fact, upon her golden anniversary of marriage in 1973, she boasted she still weighed like the day she married. This, after five children and one miscarriage! Her two close sisters (a third went back to Canada) weighed even less. Nutrition-conscious dad teased them for liking sweets too much: "*Les Fontaines aiment le sucrage*," he chortled. They weren't on his top-ten list of good or wise eaters! Dad sometimes harped on what was good or not good to eat. But like in eating and other human activities, "as the twig is bent, so is the tree inclined forever," so he was always pushing his dietetic bible on us kids. He knew fat cells that accumulated in young children were hard to lose. Didn't one wit say raising young children was keeping one end dry, the other wet?"

Because it was not in vogue, the 'hood's gentler sex didn't display the confining benefit of today's slack wearers. During the week, a housewife was likely dressed in a cheap, shapeless cottony dress, sometimes covered over with a homemade apron, "*un tablier fait à la maison*," said mom who made her own.

Since *aller chez la friseuse* (going to the hairdresser) was an expense and a luxury, women's hairdos sometimes had that unappealing sameness called a broom cut or *cheveux coupés en balah (balais)*. But young girls far more than women! Unlike those coiffured Turcotte girls whose father cut our hair on the sly, I was fascinated one year in grammar school, when

Soeur Sainte Émilie sat me behind a girl (Isabelle Forcier?) with long ringlets of chestnut hair. Obviously, Sister didn't heed the Lord's Prayer "not to lead us into temptation." Her tresses dangled temptingly close to my inkwell, those bluish, liquid reservoirs of mischief. I was torn between rapt wonder and deviltry. I wondered why she, like those Turcotte girls, wasn't broom-cut? Did a nice hairdo mean your family had money? Really, in all my grammar school years I only thought of girls thrice, aside from those two Poulin "drop-dead gorgeous girls" on my *Call* beat. Mom said boys and girls in our culture lived like they were in separate universes until serious dating at around 20.

But if glamorous looks, svelte figure, fancy clothes, and stylish hairdos were not their appeal, theirs was a greater kind of beauty. A kind of inner radiance, selfless devotion, and pious demeanor, all virtues literally touted in the Bible's virtuous woman. A domestic artist who made a house a home, like moms still do.

Homemaking Amid Chill Penury

IN FIRST SPEAKING about *grandpère* Joseph Tellier, I cited that in the "Elegy Written in a Country Church-Yard" poet Thomas Gray wrote how poverty stifled the innate talents of the townspeople: "Chill penury repressed their noble rage, / And froze the genial current of the soul." A very poetic way of saying education-wise, they got stymied or frozen out.

In a related manner, I just suggested poverty as well as a passel of children usually undermined Franco women of some of their youthful figures. Nothing, however, obscured their inner beauty, especially their role as mothers and homemakers: *mères de famille*.

A reading of Proverbs, Chapter 31, reveals qualities they possessed:

> Who can find a virtuous woman
> For her price is far above the rubies?
> The heart of her husband doth safely
> Trust in her, so that he shall have no
> Need of spoil. She will do him good
> And not evil all the days of her life.
> She stretched out her hand to the poor,
> Yes, she reacheth forth her hands to the
> Needy. She is not afraid of the snow
> (author: those brutal New England nor'easters?)
> For all her household
> are clothed with scarlet. Strength and
> honor are her clothing; and she shall re-

joice in time to come. She openeth her mouth
with wisdom; and in her tongue is the law
of kindness. She looketh well to the ways
of her household, and eateth not the bread
of idleness. Her children arise up, and call
her blessed; her husband also, and he praiseth her.
Favor is deceitful, and beauty is
vain; but a woman that feareth the Lord, she
shall be praised. Give her of the fruit
of her hands; and let her own works praise
her in the gates (i.e., where people gather).

Without a doubt, if the Depression years up to WWII were hard on the fathers of households, robbing them of the pride of providing, imagine how difficult it was for mothers to feed and clothe their large families, sometimes with only hope and a prayer.

Except for occasional work at the mills (dad: one day every five or six weeks), public works projects, and relief handouts of food, coal, and blankets, there was little income in the 1930s. "Just waitin', waitin' for nuthin'," said a poor man.

Mom and neighborhood women often spoke depressingly of those hard times. Since most women shopping or going to church carried their money in a black, clasping change purse inside a *portefeuille* or handbag, I once heard, "*Mon Dieu, qu'il fa nwère la-dans*": My God, there's little in there (save the black lining). Like mom, they often walked, not rode, all the way to Main Street to McCarthy's, Najarian's, Kornstein's, Woonsocket Hospital Trust Bank, Kay Jewelry Store, Mullen's Furniture Store, Woonsocket Institution for Savings, Bob's Men Store, City Hall, *The Evening Call*, Mongeau Shoe Store, and others. When Uncle Ernest Villeneuve was 95, he listed all the Main St. stores in an article. But we did postulate that free from the modern-day woman's decision of wanting or having to make it both as a career person and homemaker, their lives were in a sense less hectic, their self-esteem as homemakers perhaps easier or greater (no one had to apologize for being one), and great joie de vivre.

I think Francos were second only to the Irish in storytelling, humor, and teasing and perhaps second to none in mimicry, the latter always laced with a gentle sting. Women especially regaled themselves that way in their idle hours, however rare. Dad and his brothers, for example, were more the strong, silent types, but, oh, how their sisters could talk! Dad had me notice that during those Sunday evening get-togethers. He especially poked fun at his sister, *ma tante* Marie-Louise Peloquin, who sometimes lost her trend of thought amidst her incredible recall of events, commensurate with mom's.

When she even chided herself for forgetting her line of thought, he never failed to get a laugh, saying she spoke so much, she stopped listening to herself! What a loquacious pair they made when, to help with *ma tante's* domestic tasks in later years, mom came down from the top of Gaulin to help "*avec son ménage*" (with her household chores). If mom was going to church or market, *ma tante* lay in wait to chat with her. They were more like sisters than in-laws, just as we kids thought of our Fontaine, Trottier, *et* Peloquin cousins more like siblings than cousins. What a tremendous sense of support and belonging it was! Like today, immigrant families socialized among themselves more than with others initially. And as my psychology prof said at Boston College, the bond between relatives, especially between Francos, was incredibly tight, largely because of language, customs, proximity, and lack of mobility. Were we Francos fascinating to sociologists because we were a culture within a culture? I suspected that in my college classes at Boston College and Spring Hill in Mobile, AL.

Henri Trottier Family
Ronald, Henri, Laurence (Fontaine), Claude

But of course, many forces were at work in, about, and around our adamant culture to hold it or change it. Armand Chartier in *The Franco-Americans of New England* identified three movements or groups in the struggle to dissolve or retain our culture: 1) the assimilationists (including English-speaking bishops against national churches; and ethnic high schools) who sought to adopt fully the American culture and language; 2) the reactionists, like *les Sentinellistes et la survivance* who were adamant about holding on to our culture; and 3) the integrationists who wished to fuse Francophone life, culture, and Catholicism side by side with the American way of life. (Did they coin the phrase "side by each," for which we were often teased?)

Because they raised many children, mothers had untold stories to tell and incidents to relate about their brood. I remember, for example, the angst of Henri Houle's mother when he arrived weeping from his first day of school at St. Ann's. "*Mon Dieu* (she often started with that reverent phrase), "*Ça commence de bonheur la misère*": misery begins with happiness, the vicissitudes of learning began the first day of schooling. Her manner evoked compassion from her sympathizers. Unwittingly, mothers with large broods often played the game of "Can You Top This?" about their domestic "trials." And of course, they all had their pet expressions, which we identified with them. For *madame* Houle, it was also, "*On va dire comme on dit*": today's telling it like it is. Mom had so many, I don't know if she was identified with just one. See chapter 1 on her sayings that are now gone with the wind.

Being the third child, I got to know when Bob or Sue got lost, hurt, won a prize, got a compliment, suffered a setback, and so on. For her, like all moms, nothing we did was not worth retelling at the time-honored family dinner. Like others, she hoped you avoided what an older sibling had gone through, if painful or not good. For example, because Bob missed some schooling with tonsillitis, the rest of us, minus Sue, all had that done together before we went to first grade. Was Woonsocket Hospital running a three-for-one special one day? Dad made an extra batch of ice cream. Our apartment looked like a children's ward! Baby doctors later changed their stand on this medical procedure unless it's a source of serious throat malaise. She used the word "*amygdale*" (tonsil), which I heard so often, I thought once your tonsils were out, you'd live healthy. Some of our parents' comical or bittersweet anecdotes were drawn not only from their lives in the city, but also from their early years in Canada, adding, as the song says, an aura of "faraway places with long-sounding names" to their recitals. It was so evident when we were all gathered at *les* Carpentiers' first-story apartment the night of the terrible 1938 Hurricane. But my all-time favorite was about the very rural Fontaine kids in Canada picking up a cat-like bear cub on their way home from school. My imagination went wild when she said there was a big thump on the front door that night. They parted the curtains and, yes, it was Mama Bear! They quickly threw the nursling out. I've come to believe the story more and more with increased intrusions by coyotes, deer, wild turkeys, and even a bear in RI. We didn't have any books to read at home. Didn't need to. She was folklorist and raconteur all rolled into one. I also recall her story of the panic caused by Haley's Comet in Cochrane, Ontario, in 1910 when she was 12. People emptied out their bank accounts, wanting to blow it all. When the comet returned in the 1980s, it was nostalgic for me to show it to Jimmy. Mark Twain, born in 1835 when it appeared, died in 1910 when it returned.

(Speaking about bears, friend Patrick Beaulieu, two confrères, and I avoided a possible encounter when we heeded a Shenandoah National Park (VA) ranger's advice in the 1970s to keep foodstuffs away from our camper. He said some six bears had come up the mountain that week. In his Appalachian Trail trek that was featured in the Valley Breeze, Pat and Ali's son John scared one away from his tent by singing a patriotic song. Because the professional nurse practitioner, Bryant MBA grad, and now PhD candidate was in the band at Mount '89, but not the chorus, we joked how "the bear went down the mountain" because of his singing.)

Unlike today's busy Americans who take at least two meals in five out of the home, people then nearly always ate at home. The number of meals a homemaker prepared for her family in a lifetime was, well, gastronomical. When mom entered Saint Antoine, she was ecstatic she wouldn't have to cook anymore. Unlike today, even breakfast was a prepared meal. Because of the physicality of the work in Canada and here, breakfast was always He-man. Dad always insisted on it. But for us, cereal, which he lauded if not sugary, was eaten more as a bedtime snack than breakfast. In the morning we could never get enough crêpes, French toast and *saucisse* (sausage), which during Lent were rewards for going to Mass all forty days.

In all the years we lived on Gaulin, family-style meals really meant homemade. It was probably a nutritional plus, but ingredients took longer to get ready since nothing was pre-cooked, frozen, or semi-prepared. For example, we loved French fries, but she rarely made them because she had to peel the potatoes by hand, slice them (so they were meaty, not sticks like today), and fry them, a long grease-spattering chore. Also, since all to-be-skinned vegetables were bought fresh (at least five or six months of the year), she prepared them over newspapers in the sink. "*Va j'ter la swille*" (throw out the garbage), she said when done. It was deposited in the backyard in a buried cylindrical container teeming with a million tiny worms in the summer. I've bought two homes in my lifetime and discovered one in each, along with two-man saws in the attics.

Often helped by *mémère*, she made her own desserts, like cakes, doughnuts (a hundred at a time), apple and blueberry pies, and bread pudding from crusts and stale bread. If not for pudding, the English sparrows (*les mwéneaux*) who alighted atop an abandoned bakery in our backyard got them. Favorites also were rice pudding (*la poutine au riz*), apple turnover and walnut cakes if we kids shelled the walnuts. Brown Graham crackers were practically the sole mid-afternoon concession. Dipping them in milk made them messy but palatable. When Sue took a pastry-making course, our desserts got even better. We fought to lick the cake bowl when she was done. She often wondered who had the last turn to do it! We circled like birds of prey, hoping for a memory lapse, *lapsus mentis*. Oh, those little joys of yesteryear when our burgeoning American life was enlivened and enriched by our parents' Canadian culture.

The rare store-bought pastries for us were cream puffs (a quarter apiece) and éclairs, which on Easter Sunday and feast days dad bought after Mass. He walked from St. Ann's Church on Cumberland to Bélisle's Bakery on Rathbun and back to the top of Gaulin, a long trek. Enough time for the real cream to go sour, but he said you could only get them certain months of the year. He always used that long, quick farmer's stride, as if he were lunging or pumping, much to her chagrin for Sunday Mass. Walking some eight miles a day at the mill made him a hare rather than a turtle "in the race of life." But unlike the hare, nothing distracted him from the finish line.

But one Sunday as we gorged ourselves on our pastries, mom recounted details of a notorious and, yes, unpalatable 1916 murder case in the city. I got the full story from the victim's niece, Pauline (Casavant) Laplume, of Walpole, MA, with her husband Robert, a boyhood friend of Ben, cousin Gene Peloquin, Ted Hopkins, Ray Bacon, Jim Gillooley, Armand Poisson, Paul McGee, Rev. Roger Bacon, and Monsignor Gerry Sabourin. Mom called them "*la gang à Ben*." Bob and I also had our own gang, as was customary then. Girls had fewer but closer friends.

The story mom told is that spurned in her affections, Mrs. Hattie (Merrill) Oakley sent three cream puffs laced with arsenic to Henri Casavant, carpenter, and the city's best-known violinist. He was working on Social Street at the new Pothier Building owned by the Aram Pothier family. Thinking the delicacies were from a young domestic of his acquaintance (perhaps the other woman in this love triangle?), generous Casavant offered one cream puff to the messenger, who refused it; another to Armand Vadeboncoeur, father of four; and ate the other two. Soon violently ill, Vadeboncoeur died the same day, and Casavant, the intended victim, became severely crippled, no longer capable of performing on his violin.

Street wisdom was Casavant survived because he ate two of the delicacies, helping his more besieged system repel the poison better! But Vadeboncoeur died! After police ordered an autopsy of the decedent, they quickly arrested widow Oakley who claimed Casavant had advised her to buy poison for cockroaches. But what kind of "cockroach" did she have in mind? She pleaded nolo in Superior Court to second-degree murder and served 17 of 20 years. She left the state as a condition of her release.

Casavant never harbored any ill will against the woman who denied him his muse. A direct descendant of Jean Casavant, noted French soldier and voyageur who was one of the early settlers of North America, the artist did recover somewhat the use of his fingers to play a little. If he had a classical education, he certainly must've felt the import of that famous line: "Beware of Greeks (like who is this from?) bearing gifts," referring to that Trojan horse with its hidden combatants. One never knows when that thin, flaky crust will harbor "a love potion gone sour!" (Don't poets know how to make the mundane sound sublime?)

Despite that tragedy or her account of it, whenever cream puffs graced our table at Easter, our appetite remained unabated. I don't know about Suzanne *et* Rachel, but at that time, Bob, Ben, and I didn't know the difference between a love triangle and the geometric version. But like others, I'm a willing or unwilling subject to conditioning, and so whenever in college I came across Shakespeare's famous line - "Hell hath no fury like a woman scorned," or the French admonition, *Cherchez la femme* - then like Pavlov's dog, my mouth began to water for those tempting confectioneries, now available at Wright's farm bakery in North Smithfield. But no warning is given to beware of romantic entanglements if one receives the delicacy from a jilted *"amourachée"* (a foolishly passionate person), mom said. Mom always knew how to close a case in a word.

(To digress for a second, leave it to her to tell me, as a newspaper later confirmed in a feature about the remaining dairy farms in the state, the Wright name was once Charron, as in Wheelwright. Oh no, one less French-Canadian family, at least in name, she must've lamented!) But more seriously, did she ever reflect to herself about Casavant dating outside "his own people," a strong *survivance* (survival of French culture) no-no? But sympathetic about his malediction, mom said nothing about his not dating *"une bonne fille Franco-Américaine"* (a good Franco-American girl.) Rachel and I always smothered a smile when she had trouble pronouncing *"un nom angla"* (any American name), saying in frustration, *"C'tun nom à coucher d'hors"*: a name for the doghouse. So, Oakley became "Auclèe." The cream puff stuffer was "lucky" to do her crime in far less litigious times. Otherwise, Casavant could've taken her very last dime. Did she buy them at Bélisle's?

I said because of burdensome domesticity, women after marriage didn't have much time or money to glamorize themselves much. It wasn't an age of the cult of the body beautiful. For example, if you saw mothers on washday Monday, you'd know the truth of our comment. Without a doubt, washday was a long and laborious chore for them, like in all poor cultures. Nobody has ever looked good doing wash by hand, washboard, or primitive washing machine. I also talk about it elsewhere, but in our house, for example, preparations *pour le lavage lindi (lundi)* (for the Monday wash) began Sunday night when one or two copper tubs were placed on the stove and filled with a pourer (one of her pots) from the cold-water tap. The water was heated overnight, with no danger of spillage since the stove heat declined during the night. The tedious pouring was a job for one of us children. We naturally spilled a lot going from the kitchen sink to the stove. If the spill hit a heated ring, the steam made a sizzling noise. As told to us in the Order, "A job was when something is here, and the boss wants it there." This before the Brothers became totally academicians.

When Monday came, dad or one of us boys poured the now hot water into the washing machine, another tub (*cuvette*) on a wooden rack eventually received the rinsed-out clothes fed through dangerous rubber rollers, probably from Irish Rubber Titan Joseph Banagan's mill in the city or Millville. "Dangerous" because there was never a week when she didn't warn us about the dangers of getting our fingers caught in them. She, of course, knew a few cases. Her knowledge of the community wasn't only about vital statistics, like births, deaths, and marriages, but also included the hospital beat. Her source was *The Call*, which listed the names of people who were outpatients the previous day. So, paraphrasing it, if like poet Shelley someone "fell upon the thorns of life and bled," she knew and told you. After all, isn't news "Whatever is a departure from the norm?" That's why your headline is often "What bleeds, leads." When I was an education columnist, it's one the first things I learned when I wrote my 127 weekly columns for *The Call*. I loved the fraternity of all the staffers, and when asked, I even dispensed some college counseling for those with high school children. Tom Ward, later founder and co-owner of the weekly Valley Breeze was a young photog staffer along with George Beaubien and Tom Hunt. Drew Palmer of the owning family was also a great friend.

About my folks' English literacy, even if they never mastered the English dialect with their last syllable-accented patois-speak, I suspect their reading comprehension was large. As soon as one read something of interest, out came the French translation to the other. No wonder we children switched from one language to the next! But our "be-carefuls" were in French, like *prends soin* (take care). If reading, she told dad, "Imagine *twé*" (Can you believe this?), then we knew big news was coming over the teletype. Life for them didn't come from the screen or talking head, but from newsprint and *inter vivos* (between living persons), now almost passé. Either at Spring Lake or the malls, how often I've seen a twittering, chatterbox girl talking to someone in the distant ozone, but not to her companions. Does absence make the heart grow fonder? But when people text at the wheel, they put their life in jeopardy or in another driver's hand, too often fatally, as 2,000 deaths in 2009 attested, not to mention 600,000 injured. And yet some (the profit media moguls?) don't like the ban on all telephone speaking devices in cars. Hard to believe, but four out of five kids take their cell phones to bed. Some text sleepwalking! Psychologists and psychiatrists wonder if any permanent mental damage will occur. (Don't teachers already know?) Don't we already see a loss of attention, conversation, reading, studying, and lack of concentration on what's around them? One of my convictions in a capitalistic culture is that a problem is largely unsolvable if a profit motive is involved. Kids are influenced by media today far more than by their parents, one study said. Scary. I recall one 13-year old who was molested and killed by her on-line deceiver. How many more? Has on-line technology spawned as much evil as good? You can be robbed by just the touch of a key?

In wintertime when it came time to hang the clothes out, mom grabbed dad's old hat and coat, opened the wooden storm windows in the living room, and hung the stuff out in the bitter cold. Besides porches, no scene was more indicative of Woonsocket of yesteryear than clothes on the line, "*du linge sa corde*." You still see vestiges of it, especially if watching a softball game from Bouley Field on a summer evening and you look up and beyond. Like air conditioning, dryers were only for rich people, because they used a lot of electricity.

On those cold Mondays, the bed linen looked like marble slabs or stiff canvasses waiting for a Grandma Moses to turn them into art. But not complaining, she said the sun and air were good for the clothes. I had to take chemistry at Mount and in college to learn she was right. One year at the Academy I had a third-floor class and was blessed with a long-distance vision of mom putting clothes on the line on Gaulin Ave. As the song said, "He holds the lantern (of learning!) while she chops the wood." While my siblings and I studied during the day, she worked so hard, and looked so different from her haute couture photos of the early 1920s. What an unbelievable burden immigrant women took on when they married!

The work was backbreaking, and only less so when Suzanne et Rachel were old enough to help. Remember we boys were the pourers and the coal and ice haulers over three floors, the latter after Ben and I fetched it near a quarter mile away in our homemade wagon. Both fearless of height at the time, Bob and I also climbed the backyard three-story pole when the clothesline needed changing. "Selfishly" as I think of it now, I hated Monday since it meant Sunday's leftovers: pan-fried meat that tasted like jerky. She often asked me what to make for dinner and I often suggested Shepherd's pie, but not that day. She said once she asked me because I wasn't as fussy or demanding as my siblings. You'll recall that she had to make 20 meals a week.

The kids on the block also hated Mondays in the summer because our huge yard was off limits to our favorite backyard game: quoits,[23] so popular in the city at one time. Because bedsheets from second floor dwellers hung just three or four feet off the ground, we couldn't throw quoits or play ball. We tried once or twice, but incurred the wrath of even-tempered *madame* Carpentier, whose husband Anatole, was a star player in the city. A few errant throws had dirtied the sheets, so she confiscated the family quoit set for two weeks. An extremely hospitable person, she had warned sons Paul *et* Philippe. She was the only woman I knew as a kid who was an ardent Red Sox fan! When they played on the road, she listened for the staccato tape relay on her porch radio.

To reduce trash from the eight families, her Anatole often burned some of it in the yard. One July 4th day, she put firecrackers in the pile and watched with glee as he jumped, thinking someone was shooting at him. She always smiled and greeted you on her open porch as you went upstairs. With such a close degree of friendship among Francos, you were helloed and smiled at wherever you went. Unlike Brando in "Waterfront" we were all "somebody," even with shabby sneakers in summer, dirty hands and feet, and in need of a haircut. Like in the poem, we were a "barefoot boy with cheeks of tan", the girls, ponytails and rosy cheeks.

Again, about wash, one author wrote the three tasks of *lavage* (washing), *racommodage* (sewing or mending), and *repassage* (ironing) formed the bulk of the French-Canadian homemaker's *besogne* (work.) Before the electric iron became popular, she used a stove-heated, detachable-wood-handled flatiron, an item dating back to their 1923 wedding, I treasure it in my den today, even if it burned my forearm when I came too close to it in the living room where the ironing board (*"ma planche à r'passer"* - my ironing board) was set up. She had forewarned me, but like the proverbial moth I was drawn to the flame. Out came dad's homemade crushed bone relief. We never went to the Emergency Room. Dad was always on call!

I laughed one day when she told me which one of my 58 first cousins had the rich man's fancy (*"les manières d'un riche,"*) to change his shorts and undershirt every day. Her subtle message was not lost on Bob, Ben, and me. Wash was once a week, so there were no daily changes, at least for us boys.

Thinking of all our mothers did for us, how could we not have loved them as much as we did, even if we didn't know the half of it! Children, I suspect, cannot and never will know what mothers do for them. One young mother told me she admitted to her mom she was a slob when single but

---

[23] Quoits (pronounced: *koits*): A traditional game similar to horseshoes but played instead with metal rings.

would turn neat as a pin when she had her own home. And ditto about what fathers do for their kids. Only when it's your turn do understanding and recognition come about what yours did for you. But with protracted education today, a study said maturity only comes later with mortgage, car payments, spouse, and children. Education is not a maturing process, because it's usually a totally supported lifestyle. Risky, frivolous, or dangerous college antics too often bear that out. (Humor: One cynic said, "A college education is a four-year "loaf" made possible by the folks' "dough." A student said he was taking up space when asked about his major. And 23, when asked when he got out! Dropping out is still a problem, but mostly due to economics.)

So many people write to advice columnists, saying regretfully they didn't say thank you at all or often enough for what their folks did for them. A psychologist theorized it's because we see them almost solely in that service capacity. It also explains, along with protracted education, why kids now marry much later. It would take them years to get the comfort and amenities of home. As the wit said, "I ain't talkin' while the flavor lasts." "60 Minutes" ran a piece on that, with some nationalities - Jews and Italians - more inclined to stay home longer. (At the risk of being profane, I repeat a story I heard why Christ was certainly Jewish. He didn't leave home until He was thirty, and his mother said He walked on water!)

Lastly, none of us had ever read Proverbs. If so, we surely, would have said, "Hey, they're talking about our moms." I have a feeling many families, for all their sincere religiosity, didn't have a Bible in the house. Recall our culture (and religion too) was largely oral, not academic or written. Providentially, they wrote their own "Good Book" of deeds.

Nurturing at Mother's Knee

PERHAPS MOTHERS who want or must work today may gather some solace that it's quality time, say some writers, that counts in dealing with children, not just quantity. I realize, of course, the same is true of fathers, but I speak here largely in the context of French-Canadian women's roles in a past era. A recent study said some young children come to school two years behind others because of lack of conversation and interaction at home. How different it was at one time! Direct speech is most important. Seven-month-old infant brains function when hearing speech said a recent study.

Homemaking and its attendant (usually frequent) childbearing and child-nurturing roles were all-day jobs, practically negating any other option. You'll recall I said that mom believed a woman who died giving birth went straight to heaven. Conception was a couple's cooperative act in God's creation of an immortal soul. Unfortunately, with so many children conceived, it was more common for mothers to miscarry and sometimes die because of imperfect medical science. *Memére* lost three. Mom's opinion was that too many pregnancies in succession resulted in births *"dans faiblesse,"* in a weakened condition. Reading history, I was shocked by its unbelievable frequency, like in Elizabethan times, as related by Alison Weir in *The Six Wives of Henry VIII*.

Some progress, but not a whole lot, had been made by the start of the 20th Century. But even now, given our nation's superiority in medical science, we don't fare as well as many Western industrialized nations in babies surviving birth. Do many of the unplanned one million (now declining) children born out of wedlock each year have little or no prenatal care? In one story, a young secretly pregnant girl after delivery put the dead baby (?) in a bag and trash can and resumed watching TV with her parents. A girl athlete who didn't know she was pregnant went into labor during a basketball game. One girl delivered moments after being told she was pregnant. A *Newsweek* article - "Why their children do well in American schools" - reported mothers of Asiatic children seem to greatly prioritize their role in their children's education at home and in school. I don't think the magazine meant to cast any aspersion on mothers of other nationalities. Nor do I. "Every comparison limps," Brother Marcellus in the Order used to say, and this one was slanted towards academic achievement. My wife Patricia, who taught in Woonsocket schools, couldn't help noticing Asian children's avidity towards learning. A quieter more docile nature, she said.

Without exception, all of us learned not only our letters and numbers at our mother's and grandmother's knee, but also our prayers. In French of course! We also learned the thousand-and-one life skills a child needed to enter school and the larger arena of life successfully. That's probably why I so enjoyed *"All I Need to Know I Learned in Kindergarten"* by Robert Fulghum, read in part to us by Kathi Rogers, president of our teachers' association at a new school year faculty meeting at Norton HS, to emphasize the basics of conduct with kids. Actually, we only entered St. Ann's in first grade because our kindergarten or *"jardin d'enfance,"* was at home, mom said. We didn't need the "electronic mothering," of Mr. Rogers' as someone wrote, however a force for good he was.

I was reminded of that teaching role, at least in the faith, when I was with Jimmy years ago in the chapel of the old St. Antoine Residence for the Elderly. I was trying to explain to him the meaning of Christ's Presence in the bread and wine at Mass or in the altar's tabernacle. It was déjà vu all over again of the day when she had explained it to me at St. Ann's Church in the 1930s before I started school. He asked, "Dad, how does big Jesus fit in that little box?" Wisely, mom spoke of *"le p'tit Jésus"* (little Jesus). Her explanations probably fumbled as mine did, but the important thing is that she brought me there. Her role of transmitter included the good news of the faith as well as the language and customs of her proud French-Canadian heritage. French Canadians, Italians, Poles, Irish, Spaniards, Mexicans, Hispanics, southern Germans, and Austrians were among the church's best immigrant vanguards in maintaining and propagating the Catholic faith in America. Sadly, a legacy now lost by many of the third and fourth generations. Catholics, once 24 percent of the population are now less than 20. Biblically, those no longer responding to the call of the wedding feast (symbol of the Kingdom) are being replaced by others. The Western World, once the prominent seat of Christendom for 1,500 years, has now been displaced by the more conservative East and the lower Americas as faith wanes here. Shakespeare spoke about a tide in the affairs of men, better grasped at its crest, like the faith that passes one by, as we said in the order, rather than at its ebb. Does the election of Pope Francis of Argentina reflect where the faith is growing, even if many are only so in name and not in practice? Is the Roman Catholic faith one of the most demanding because it reflects the challenge of Christ's doctrine? One which the world has never seen its equal? Like loving your enemies for example and a fixity of doctrine against doctrinal changes.

About their Christian bearing and role, I think the best qualities of neighborhood women were their inward faith and outward devotional life. The social critics (men?) who unfairly, many say, placed the decline in American morality after WWII on the supposedly eroding goodness of its women ("the keepers of the gates," said one expression). They probably had as their ideal the women who were our grandmothers, mothers, and aunts in the 1930s and '40s. Women who were largely uneducated with their social grid largely domestic and their life more conservative in action and faith. I realize that even reporting comparisons I've read about can be tinged with unfair generalizations. Why? Because the times are so different, and we men, fathers, have possibly changed for the worse too, if unwanted change has occurred in both sexes, as many allege. But who can measure goodness in either sex? One writer said any century, for example, can be painted as the best or worst in history. The underlying fact is human nature doesn't change, only its appearance or manifestation in its new historical setting. Are you counting how many global terrorists have been suspected of late of being the expected False or Anti-Christ, with their power to destroy men's souls and bodies? (Hitler, Stalin, the Ayatollah, Saddam Hussein, Bin Laden, et al.) Some in the name of religion. But history is also full of them, like Attila the Hun, Nero, Caligula. But does criticism of women stem from their rising crime rate (now faster than men's; even in bank robberies) and their drinking, as the *Providence Journal* reported? Drugs too? Is it the pressure of competing in the marketplace, as men have for so long?

About Franco women, it was still an age of modesty and decorum in every part of the feminine form. At home or in public, most women could not have been pressured for gain, jollity, or career to bare any part of their anatomy or draw men's attention to themselves as sex objects. I'm aware of the sexual licentiousness critics say underpinned Victorian women's outward reserve. But I suspect such was not the case with the women we knew and speak about. They were what they appeared to be. Even if they had not been personally inclined to be modest, the Franco neighborhood or culture, undergirded by a rather strict public and Christian morality, would have allowed no less. If someone had been caught in any kind of act of inappropriate behavior, then words, stares, indignation, coolness, if not a mild or polite rebuke, would have replaced the stones hurled at the woman taken in adultery in the Gospel. There was a strict code of morality on dress and behavior. Besides never smoking or drinking in public (of course, not immoral), they would have blushed at the tag, "You've come a long way, baby." One of their greatest Francophone roles was preservers and transmitters of our conservative culture in which appearance and strict norms had the moral imperative of a good life. As is said at times about the children of ministers and law enforcement people, women seemed to be bound by a double standard of conduct and morality. All proportions kept, you still see that kind of moral and cultural primitivism today in Middle or Far Eastern cultures towards women. But when it also denies them equality, voting, mobility, and education, then it's shamefully and doubly repressive. Recall the young girl in her school bus who was shot. She was honored internationally in 2014. In the Franco culture until after the war, women often didn't have an equal opportunity at education. But that was largely because their role was defined so much more as life givers and nurturers and, of course poverty. In this age of small families, Pope Francis hopes women will not omit their procreative role.

Most impressive was Franco women's churchgoing. They were (still are) more devotional than men, as was evident in church on Sundays, holidays, the October and May months of Mary, Confession, and even funerals. And, of course, they all heeded St. Paul's admonition to display a Christian submissiveness of being behatted. But oh, how our sight lines improved in church when that restriction was abolished in favor of an unfettered *chevelure* or tresses! Even conservative dad approved, "*J'veux tout wyère,*" *(voire*: see): (I want to see everything.) Hat maker mom didn't comment and literally "held on to her hat," even if hats were involved in two dangerous episodes in her life: her hat maker job the day her family was routed in Canada, and the 1938 Hurricane when, besides losing her new self-made hat, she struggled to get back home from a parish function at St. Louis church.

Like ancient Greek students with pedagogues or teachers constantly at their side, we had our mothers encouraging, teaching, and reproving us the lifelong day. As touched upon elsewhere, the following anecdote bears out how well they raised us to be law-abiding citizens. At the end of our Monday night meetings, Troop founder *Père* Frederíc Moreau gave his "chaplain's minute." He always spoke on aspects of the Scout Law (12), its Christian or legal reach. Speaking of Reverence for God and the law of the land, I recall he cited juvenile court judge Jalbert, who rarely dealt with French-Canadian boys. Credit went to our moms and dads. Unfortunately, today's newspaper police logs reveal all American ethnic groups grace this "hall of shame."

Mom said the most feared epithet for a woman was *lachée*, that is, wayward, or *risquée*, with its tinge of immoral behavior. How shocked, for example, our mothers were to hear two neighborhood women swore constantly at their children! Their husbands didn't. Using, as Catholics were once inclined, the name of Christ, God, and church objects to vent their anger caused ears to turn and windows to slam shut. One little girl especially shocked the neighborhood with her verbal precocity in imitating her elders. The word for a profaning woman was "*A sacre*." The nuns taught us the Second Commandment forbade taking the Lord's name in vain.

Besides our mothers, school also taught us swearing or foul mouthing was a sinful thing to do. And of course, priests in their sermons also weighed in. (They were much more prohibitive in admonitions than today's priests with their emphasis on love and service.) Bishop Tobin in 2015 also weighed in on the harm malicious speech can do. But monkey-see, monkey-do, we kids learned quickly to express our anger in the same watered-down fashion adults did. If an expression was considered sinful, we circumvented the prohibition by slightly altering their sound or spelling. For example, since *maudit* (damn) was considered bad, we sandwiched the syllable "ta" to make *mautadit*, a harmless substitute. If *ciboire*, a vessel for the hosts in church, was verboten, we changed it to *niboire*. As Lady Macbeth said, a little water (for us, a slight word exorcism) cleared us of any wrongdoing. Francos knew the Ten Commandments. A latter-day Moses didn't need to throw stone tablets at us, as he did at his idolatrous people at Mt. Sinai! Mothers all "had a set" in raising large broods.

You heard heavy swearing if you walked by the poolroom (see my notes on WWII) across the street from the Laurier Theater on Cumberland St. Young men uttered tabernacle, the repository of the Real Presence in church; *calvaire*, site of the crucifixion; *calice*, another Communion vessel, and others. What they said and how they did it seemed serious to us impressionable kids. Neighborhood men playing quoits said *viarge* (virgin), but it wasn't considered serious, either in jest or anger. Dad used it. *Monsieur* Carpentier often said *caltor*, a harmless derivative I think of *calvaire* (Cavalry). With the overactive but innocent antics of his son Phil, he needed a verbal release valve.

    I read the comment that Christian cultures (for example, the southern part of Germany, which remained deeply Catholic as did Austria after the Protestant Reformation) are more prone to take the Lord's name and sacred things in vain, so close to the heart and mouth does Christianity lie. In today's neo-pagan, secular, humanistic, or religiously neuter era, swearing (accepting the still liberal use of Christ's name) is more likely to be sexually derived, a measure of the nation's sophomoric infatuation with Biology 101. Not to mention its plethora of so-called one-joke comedians or TV actors in family comedies who use the sex joke or storyline ad nauseam, instead of the once, time-honored but innocuous mother-in-law target. When local women got angry at their children, they got "their Irish up." and crafted their words mostly towards their behavior because talking back to your parents in our culture was almost unheard of. Popular invectives from parents were *polisson* (impolite), *verreux* (disobedient; origin?), *mon p'tit torrieux* (uncontrollable; origin?) and rarely, *batârd* (bastard). Notice the word was often prefaced by *mon p'tit*, that is, "my little...." Men used it too. Mothers rarely used sacred words and vessels in anger.

    But if initially we deified mothers of that era, a more balancing picture of their earthiness emerges when I recall "window fights" in the backyard. These imbroglios happened when their maternal instinct propelled them to jump in before ferreting out the good from the bad guys in the Gaulin Colosseum. Blood always thicker than water.

    The most vociferous women were unflatteringly (uncharitably!) called *la queule à...* (their name included here), meaning "the jaw of Mrs...." *Bouche* (mouth) was too kind! Since the Carle tenement houses side by side rose four stories high in the rear, the third and fourth floor women had the high ground to scream down vituperations against those brats who dared inflict injury or cast aspersions against their offspring. In their eyes, these "innocent victims" were *"les enfants de ma chaire"*: their own flesh and blood. A ruffian was saddled with *"Yé plein de mauva coups"*: full of mischief. But bless 'em, girls rarely misbehaved, save hair-pulling and name-calling. Girls outnumber boys today, but *la grosse* (big) Gaulin was easily Boyz of the Hood, numbers-wise. Mother Nature is compensatory with more boys being born in wartime especially. But also, were the vagaries or mysteries of genetics at work in mill towns where men's shorter longevity resulted somehow in more male children being born? Women's lifespan ascended due largely to medical advancements and safer (and fewer?) births, and not puffing "on the noxious weed," as smoking was first demeaned in Virginia. Elsewhere we report smoking shortens your life by 9 minutes per smoke, 10 years of your life overall; marijuana, 5 minutes per joint.

Pity the women who were lower floor dwellers. It was no mean trick to screw your neck up like a rubber hose and hit your verbal target some 20 feet straight up. It was strictly *une femme de maison* (a housewife) thing. I never saw or heard two fathers in a verbal clash! Hey, they were always at the mill, and if at home too tired to bother with boyish behaviors they once indulged in growing up. A boy had to show the gang he could hold his own and not be a mama's boy. But once dad did come down from our eagle's nest and took my BB gun away, fearing our quarrelling might turn dangerous. In an age when almost every kid had one, mom worried about our eyes: "*le danger de perdre un oeil*" (the danger of losing an eye.) (When Jim was a tyke here in town and a young teen came through our neighborhood shooting birds, I called the police, fearing some kid might get hurt. Angry at losing his gun, he came towards me menacingly, but he cooled down when I explained why. He eventually got his gun back.)

No one ever won or lost those shouting matches. The final judgment of any embattled backyard matriarch in this mid-Depression People's Court was again the slamming of windows. Always, the "life-and-death" struggle of the kids in front of them soon became the usual fun-and-games, once the gallery goddesses retired to their domestic pursuits. Sometimes a little coolness developed for a few days between them, as they walked past each other on their way to market or, yes, church. (Did they know the Gospel admonition "of forgiving your enemy before bringing your gifts to the altar?") At times you were told to avoid playing with this or that *mal élevé*: ill-brought-up kid. But the joys of youthful friendships and short memories quickly loosed us from those binding admonitions. We were learning toleration and forgiveness, all of us first generation Americans living in a tight, urbanized ring, so far removed from the wide-open, untroubled Canadian farmlands of our parents. Our behavior and control then have much to teach today's violence-prone dwellers of large inner-city housing projects where guns, drugs, larceny, and shootings are frequent and sadly, convicted teens lose their liberty for life for one stupid act. I will elaborate about my thoughts on guns later, but I must point out that I don't remember any kid then who was so abject, alone, or harassed, to be inclined towards serious criminal mayhem, either in school or public place. You never, never saw a gun except on a policeman's belt and the few millworkers who hunted or collected guns as a hobby! Trying "to bag" a job was the target. (Once, I even had the boldness to suggest to the Providence Police Chief that areas where gangs are should be mandated "gun-free zones" to save lives of shooters and intended victims. I'm sure the ACLU would object.)

To use a Walter Cronkite-like expression,[24] even the casual observer would conclude that "that's the way it is" or was in this closely-knit world of tenement living. People jammed "a heap of livin'," to use poet Carl Sandburg's felicitous phrase in those high-rises of the poor. Each one was a microcosm of mill town French-Canadian life, somewhat poor, populous, and *paysan* in its rugged simplicity and down-to-earth goodness. All before America's postwar middle-class prosperity of cars, white picket fences, larger single-family homes, fewer kids, drugs, guns in inner cities, and electronic marvels replaced the good outcomes of the hoods of yesteryear.

Cochrane Inferno Routs the Fontaines

WORKING IN THE FIELD with his brothers and sisters, *mon oncle* François kept looking up at the billowing black and white clouds of smoke rising ominously in the sky. It was Saturday morning, July 29, 1916, and for days one question persisted in the minds of the people of Cochrane, Ontario, and surrounding towns. Would this forest fire, like the one in 1911 that scorched the whole area, again wreak unimaginable devastation in its wake? Literally, was lightning going to strike twice?

François et Auray and the rest of the family knew all too well the crippling power of fire. Three years after the 1911 fire and not long after their father Louis died of a heart attack, the family saw its sawmill destroyed by arson, "*notre moulin à bois*" (our wood mill,) said mom. They suspected someone but couldn't prove it. (*Oncle* François still remembered the name but took it to his grave) There was no CSI: Canadian Sleuthing Investigation!

The motive? After their father's death in 1914, Auray, Urgel, Edmour, et François, the latter teaming up with mom to pile up the crusts from the planks into four-foot stacks, continued to run the mill. Remembering, however, their father's poor managerial skills (too generous like my dad, mom said), people now had to bring their wood in before *les* Fontaines cut it. It caused some grumbling among their clientele, and the boys thought an angry one resorted to *une incendie* (a fire). It was a classic reversal of the maxim *Caveat Emptor*: let the buyer beware. *Les* Fontaines are the ones who got torched: *Caveat Vendor*.

Even if the sawmill was now gone, the family continued to summer on the property some six miles out of town. It was a long walk, but François

---

[24] A popular TV news anchorman in the 1960s and 70s often referred to as "the most trusted man in America."

liked doing it, but not his sisters. On that little farm, *tante* Laurence said they had a cow and chickens, but they grew hardly anything because Cochrane was just too far north and cold for much vegetable farming. Besides, their dad Louis was the entrepreneurial type, "*pa(s) un fermier*," (not a farmer) mom said. But as it turned out, on the fateful incendiary day, no one was left to watch the house in downtown Cochrane. My mom wasn't at the farm or at the house either, helping and babysitting for *madame* Gendreau, a hat maker: "*une faiseuse de chapeau*," she said, where she learned the art. Would *les* Fontaines have avoided a double tragedy that day if they weren't all scattered? Probably not, given "*la malchance des Fontaines*" (the bad luck of the Fontaines,) a frequent lament when the family met in Woonsocket. They couldn't win for losing. Without bad luck, they had no luck at all!

As François and villagers looked at the rim of the trees, everything looked all right for the moment. But then the wind shifted, and swooshing and crackling embers jettisoned towards the sky, falling like huge, spent fireworks. In fact, if you stood in just the right place, you saw the flames jumping from tree to tree like flying squirrels. My uncles hoped the winds wouldn't now turn in an easterly direction towards them. But they knew the wind changed direction with lightning speed in Ontario's northern latitudes.

But as the Cochrane newspaper *Northland Post* said, suddenly the wind-whipped fire did turn and unleashed a two-pronged Panzer-like attack towards Cochrane and towns like Porquis Junction, Kelso, Monteith, Nushka, Matheson, and Bourkes. As the fire sped through and over the trees, it also ran underground, igniting a peat-like substance called muskeg. *Ma marraine* (my godmother) told me if you stayed too long in one spot and tried to dodge airborne embers, your feet were encircled by a ring of fire.

Embers falling on their summer retreat quickly enveloped the wooden house, reducing it to charred timbers and ashes, and killing the cow and chickens in an adjoining barn. Salvaging a few possessions, the family immediately started going back to their home in downtown Cochrane, like people had done from their outlying farms in 1911. But unknowingly, that was going to be the hardest six miles they ever walked. And the last time they would ever do it.

As they marched back, Auray *et* François kept members of the family covered with wet blankets against the falling embers. Despite the fear of suffocating due to the acrid air and getting her reddish tresses (a trait from her father) singed, aunt Laurence like Lot's wife in the biblical story of Gomorrah dared to look back to satisfy her curiosity. She said people were running *à la rivière* (to the river) Abitibi, a mile away from town, seeking the safety of the waters. But many were being turned back because some part of the river itself was broiling. As they approached downtown, the fire was now near the southwest corner of town. Valiantly, the firemen had been battling it for days, hoping to keep its advancing fury south of the railroad tracks. But just when it seemed it was almost extinguished, a tremendous wind again came out of nowhere and rekindled dying embers into a roaring flame. Rumford's Lumber Yard became a towering inferno with planks, logs, railroad ties, sawdust, and shavings all engulfed in the flames. At that moment, what every resident feared but didn't dare whisper, happened. The inferno jumped over the railroad tracks to a depot where barrels of gas and oil were kept. Downtown Cochrane, like Civil War Atlanta, was now under a fiery siege. One after the other, gas and oil containers exploded, hurtling dangerous debris towards citizens who had rushed forward to fight the fire with ditches and barriers.

Undefended, the Fontaine home - "*la maison paternelle*," (the paternal house) as she nostalgically recalled - was consumed, but unknowingly to them. The swath of destruction didn't spare a supposedly fireproof Taylor hardware store, a Methodist church, and most businesses. A hospital, however, was spared as a later northern rain extinguished flames that had reached the lower windows. As happens often when death occurs, a new sign of life, a baby, was born there that morning. Did *mémère* Emérance, a former teacher, also find solace the public school was spared, even though the local pastor forbade Catholics from attending under pain of sin? (He also thought the states were "heathen America.")

In a scene reminiscent of the 1912 sinking of the Titanic, people like *les* Fontaines reacted to ward off disaster or live with its aftermath. Some donned extra clothing and one even a fur coat despite the sizzling July weather. Others, like Scarlett O'Hara and Civil War victims fleeing burning Atlanta, fled out of town in wagons, drays, and tumbrels, with whatever worldly goods they could carry. But being on the edge of town and away from home, it left the family with only the clothes on their backs, the same they would come to America with.

Laurence, barely eleven, still held on to her furry cat tightly. But frightened, it slipped out and was never seen again. People told her they saw dead bodies by a little bridge that led to downtown. A later report said that no fewer than 300 people in the 600 square-mile fire had perished in and around Cochrane: the population just thousands.

Like Lazarus returning to life, *les* Fontaines stunned people who were surprised to see them alive. They were dirty, disheveled, ashen, and their clothing singed by fire. People called them "*des revenants*" (ghosts) or resurrected from the dead. Did they feel they had the cat's proverbial nine lives, survivors already of their father's death, his five failed businesses, arson, and the previous forest fire? It's why the family moved often and why mom said moving three times in Woonsocket was like going through a fire. No other lost or unaccounted family made it back to town.

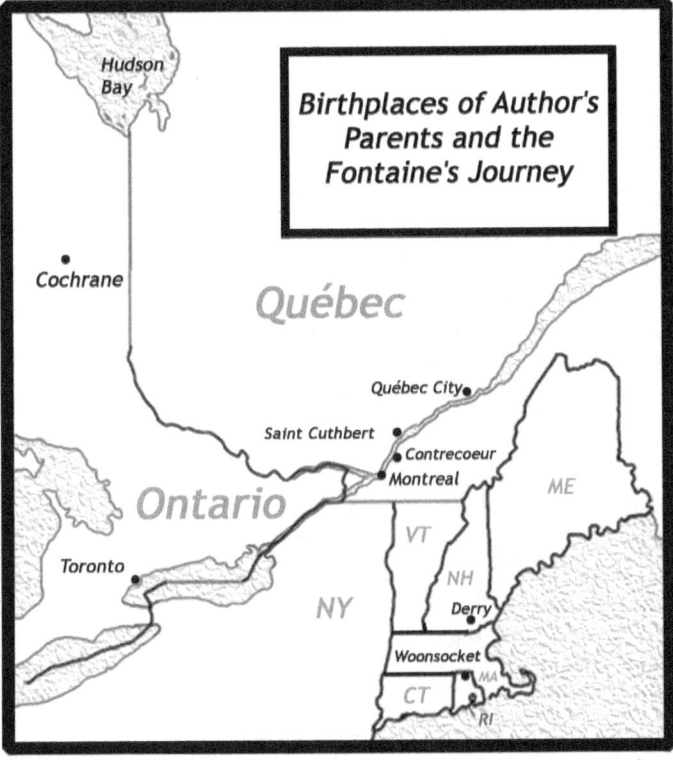

The author's mother, Léopoldine, was born in Contrecoeur in 1898 about 20 miles south of her future husband Alphonse's birthplace in St. Cuthbert in 1896. The Fontaines eventually moved to Cochrane in northern Ontario and following the fire that destroyed their homes, gradually journeyed by train to Woonsocket, RI, an odyssey estimated to be about 1,000 miles. – ed.

Les Fontaines had lost their farm and home, as they soon found out, but at least they were alive, prompting their friends to thank God for their return. They again left town that night (no one could put them up) but came back the next day for provisions from the government and free passage out. But they faced another painful situation. Without a father, shelter, livelihood, and only the clothes on their backs, how could they stay in the country of their forebears and rebuild their fortunes? Was time running out on them in Canada? Was the 251st year of the Fontaine Chronicle in Canada going to be their last? Or like the fabled phoenix, would they rise from the ashes and start over as they had done so many times? Weren't they already on their ninth life? Should they go to the golden Canadian West, a land like America of "purple mountain majesties above the fruited plains," or stay close to their native soil? Or should they crash land in America in one of New England's many French-Canadian enclaves where steady millwork put money in your pockets, despite crowding you into an ethnic corner of a city with all its urban woes? Poor people caught up in tragedies usually have only two choices: slim and none!

Coins of Despair in Cochrane Ashes

SHAKESPEARE HAS A PASSAGE about the wheel of fortune bringing tragedy in numbers, like in the Kennedy family, a magazine said. Even if an educated person by Canada's standards for women before and up to 1916, *mémère* Emérance probably didn't know the Bard's line but felt its truth in the deepest recesses of her beleaguered soul and faith.

True, people thought they were lucky to be alive, but tragically upon the family's return the next day from the ashes of their burnt-out summer retreat, they saw the smoldering ruins of their downtown Cochrane home. Was any other family so completely dispossessed? Did it make sense that one family lost two homes, six miles apart in the same fire? If trouble came in threes, what was next? Was *le bon Dieu* (the good God) merciless? Was God trying them like his servant Job, having given them everything to take it all away? If they moved again, as they did time and again after their dad's failures, would they just back up into more trouble for the sixth time? But imagine if they had any premonition of what awaited them in America: WWI, like in Canada, *La Grosse Depression* (the Great Depression), a worldwide influenza epidemic of American origin, unemployment, near homelessness, then WWII, the death of two kin soldiers, and, for mom, a chilling moment when Bob told her a Japanese kamikaze just missed his ship.

My mom, not with the family when the fire struck, learned how her mother tried vainly to salvage whatever she could from the ashes. But despairingly, the only things were three daguerreotype prints (photos on silver-colored photo plates) of herself and her husband Louis and a single of him at the time of their engagement, and two coins worth *cinquante sous*: fifty cents. One of the photos mom gave me displays *mémère's* very comely hourglass figure in a lovely dress. Another displays *pepère* Louis in a rather stiff sitting position. The sum of the Fontaine album! To mom, the collector, that was probably the most material lasting effect of the fire. "*Mon Dieu, les photos perdues,*" (My God, the lost photos) she told me one day. Unlike Scarlett O'Hara who saw tomorrow as the harbinger of better things, *mémère* rolled the coins she had found in her sooty hand, wailed, and threw them into the ashes. She never wore a ring in America because incredibly, she threw that in too. One more scar on her widowhood!

In mom's collection of photos taken later in America, I did discover another picture of *pepère* drinking beer with a friend way back in 1903. How had it escaped the fire and gotten out of Canada? Like one of my professors said about poet Robert Burns, *pepère* Louis was very "convivial." But not intemperate. Like in Ben Franklin's advice, he knew, "Not to eat to satiety nor drink to elevation." In the 1990s after discovering the photo, I had an artist superimpose it onto the Fontaine family photo taken in Woonsocket, *sans la bière* (without the beer). In a similar circumstance, dad's Tellier family photo lacks his mother who died in 1907. Not one photo of her survives, but I hope to find one among the Durands in the Family Association in Canada. Tragedy so beset both families, even getting together for a family photo was beyond the realm of good fortune.

Fire scorched wedding photos of Emérance and Louis Fontaine salvaged from the 1916 Cochrane, Ontario fire.

Resuming our story, *mémère*, thinking of all her husband's failed businesses, widowhood, the burden of raising eight children without a helpmate, the suspected arson of their sawmill, and now the loss of both their homes and all their worldly possessions except the clothes on their back, uttered this cry of despair when she flung the coins into the ashes, "*Mon Dieu, vous avez tout pris. Prenez-ça aussi!*" "My God, you took everything else, take that, too!" she wailed in the depths of her despair. How could He do this to a devout Christian woman? How did her kids, already orphaned of their father, deserve this? Like a sainted, persecuted woman said, did she too wonder "If He treats His friends like this, will He have any left?"

Always the notion God had sorely tried mom's family was a recurrent theme with *les* Fontaines in their get-togethers. It forged in them a kind of why-us mentality. "On a *mangé de la misère nwère" (noire)*, (We survived so much misery,) she said. At first light, it seemed irreverent, a kind of slippage from their unshakable belief He didn't fill your bucket of woe more than you could carry. Mom added, "*Cée comme-ci le bon Dieu nous en voula*," meaning He was out to get them! She had hundreds of expressions and opinions, but Rachel thinks it's her most heart-wrenching or poignant. Was God really after a family whose members were all, yes, like the salt of the earth, the little people Christ so loved in the Gospels? The ones about whom He said, "Not one hair falls from their head without the Father knowing it." Unlike those who left Christ for good one day, when what He said was too hard (about the Eucharist, one wrote). *Les* Fontaines were not Catholics *à gros grain*, (not just on the surface but to their core) or as mom put it, "*à Roger bon temps*," that is, staying on only when the good times rolled. Their faith was always, "Lord, thy will be done, and not ours."

About the tragedy, *mémère's* Canadian niece in her book "*Florentine Raconte*" related that because of the fire and other misfortunes, *mémère* always seemed bewildered or disoriented: "*Ma tante en est restée un peu perdue.*" But in our Tellier or Trottier home in Woonsocket she was pious, helpful, happy, and quiet, if not exuberant. Thus, we children never noticed anything nor suspected the depths of despair she had known until mom told us after she died in 1949 at 84. *Oncle* François recalled it took a long time for the family to get back on its feet, "*pour se relever.*" Almost like vagabonds the rest of the summer, they returned to their native Québec landscape and went from relative to relative before embarking for America. Both he and mom told me how much the fire damaged them, not only materially, but emotionally and, yes, spiritually. Even if conservative in their faith, did their grief nevertheless obscure the notion that "bad things happen even to good people," as an author later wrote. Misfortune, like the young man in the Gospels born blind, was not a sign of His displeasure towards him or his parents.

Deeply Christian, however, and with an unshakable belief in Divine Providence (Whatever happens, happens for the best), mom later always concluded the family's tale of woe with a reaffirmation of the rock-bound faith of a true believer: "*On a passé à travers.*" (We got through it.) Also like the Apostle Paul who boasted he held on to the faith despite all his sufferings, calamities, and shipwrecks, they too tried to rejoice in prosperity and bear up under adversity. It's without exaggeration (at least hearing it from her) that the Fontaines did come to see the whole catastrophe in a Christian perspective, despite some very natural malingering. In the bosom of that family, I marveled hearing how in Canada and here their whole life was God and church-centered, their actions firmly anchored in the Decalogue (Ten Commandments), their conversations and actions directed by a strict sense of morality, and their faith and philosophy of life anchored in the belief of ultimate salvation. Again, how had the church ever succeeded so well with them? Is that why they seemed to take so many punches and still got up from the canvas to finish the fight? It did occur to me once, if the whole family had died, we of course would have been deprived of the gift of life, the greatest gift of God and parents.

(Entering the Order where the pursuit of Christian perfection was the ideal, I found, excepting for our vows of poverty, chastity, and obedience, that theirs was the same Christ or God-centeredness in their lives. But one must lament this weakening of the faith in our rather secular, humanistic culture. And especially its shocking decline in *la belle Province de Québec* where its initial flowering occurred in the New World. Yes, because I'm French-Canadian, I feel it even more deeply. This loss of Christian orientation and religion has claimed more and more of my heritage because their fall from grace, so to speak, is from such a lofty niche in Christian history. The first nation in Europe called to Christianity, even if by royal edict. But as we were told in the Order, "Lilies that fester smell far worse in decay." That is, the bigger, the higher, the more renowned you are, the harder you fall, as media reminds us daily. Of course, the ultimate example in Christian thought is the fall of the bad angels from heaven itself. Lucifer - his name means light-bearer or most intelligent - let his pride foment a rebellion, so he and his minions were cast out of heaven by Michael and the good angels, as Nincheri's magnum opus fresco at St. Ann's depicts so graphically.)

Cousin Gene Peloquin, retired principal of Halliwell School, North Smithfield, always saw that resiliency and perseverance as the wellspring of my mother's reputation as a person who could face up to any person and any situation without anxiety or tremor. Only an irritating finger-tapping habit unmasked possible tension, we children noticed. "She'd been through everything. What more could happen to her?" is how he put it. Thinking of the Fontaine saga, Rachel always thought she was a perfect example of the don't worry, don't fret, don't sweat it philosophy. Christ said you couldn't add a cubit to your height if you tried. Maybe so, but the Fontaines, short like most Canadians, seemed with all their problems to have been taken down one of those cubits. (A cubit is the length of the forearm from the elbow to the tip of the middle finger, usually from 18 to 21 inches. I needed to know that when I taught novices in religious formation one year.)

Like Californians, Floridians, or Tornado Alley victims on television who have lost everything to forest fire, flood, earthquake, hurricane, or tornado, *les* Fontaines were at least grateful their lives had been spared. Many had lost theirs. *Oncle* François still remembered the plight of the

Proulx family who had all perished near their home, close to the cemetery where *grandpère* Louis is buried. (His stone is shown in Florentine's book.) In their footrace to reach *la rivière* (the river) Abitibi the five children were not swift or fortunate enough to avoid being burnt alive, leaving them hardly recognizable in death. Probably they had not been able to draw a breath without searing their lungs. As many did, another friend of the family sought safety in a well but suffocated. When they found the parents' bodies in a field, the toll came to eight who had known each other. In their dying moment, did the parents also agonize about the fate of their five children from whom they had become separated? Another parent who also lost five went mad.

Equally tragic was the loss of the Morella baby. As Mrs. Morella was shopping in a furniture store with her newborn, she left it in good hands to rush back to her endangered frame house. Thank God, it wasn't in peril, but suddenly the fire crossed the street. It cut off her frantic return and engulfed the store and baby in minutes. Almost like the Bible's Rachel, she was inconsolable because the child of her womb was no more. (The organization helping women who later lament their abortion bears her name. They're four times more likely to commit suicide and experience sadness on birthdays.)

Throughout the whole day and night, people sought refuge, food and water, even scavenging icebox dripping pans to assuage their parched throats. Hundreds like them were homeless and sought shelter in surviving houses and barns. François recalled the family asking one weary habitant for shelter after they got back to town, but he had none to give. You couldn't lie down anywhere in Cochrane. He too had striven all day to save his house and shed but failed. "I can only offer you an open field," he said.

Where to turn to? With darkness approaching, their guiding biblical column of light, like in the Old Testament, came from friends whose house on the outskirts of town had been spared. They offered them food and a place to sleep. *Les* Fontaines were instant celebrities of a sort because they were "*des revenants*," back from the dead. Nobody could have gone through what they did and live to tell about it. So briefly, they thought more about what they had gained than lost. Mom knew a lot about the New Testament, but did she know the passage "about the final days, the days of desolation": *Priez que votre fuite ne soit pas en hiver et que vous ne soyez pas enceinte?* (Pray that your escape is not in winter and that you are not pregnant.) Yes, providentially it wasn't winter (September 29) and the four girls were not pregnant (*enceinte*). The natural progression of marriage, home, and children was still pro forma then.

What a day it had been for them! Never since the arrival of the family's forebear Nicolas Pion dit LaFontaine to the New World in the 1670's had the family been so sorely tried. But mercifully for them and everyone, a second thunderstorm at midnight brought an end to the fire, deaths, and damage. But what kind of day would tomorrow be, so that like the heroine of *Gone with the Wind* they too could hope against hope for better days and never be hungry again? Because still ahead lay the long train ride to America in singed clothing without food, money, and luggage.

Like survivors from Civil War Atlanta and other tragedies, upon rising the next morning the stricken family looked about and cried silently at the blackened ruins of all that was left from their many years of toil, sacrifice, and wanderings. Like them, townspeople everywhere echoed their despair, especially those who lost loved ones. Mom said nobody else survived among those reported missing. So, they were blessed if you will, thanks to Auray, Urgel, François, *et* Edmour, God's ministering angels to their own family. No wonder mom and their sisters loved them. So *mémère*, however understandably distraught, had been "wrong." God hadn't taken everything. Because how many in Cochrane had a Lazarus-like incident like theirs, escaping Death's unremitting scythe? Later Saint Brother André worked two miracles for our related families in America. I like to think their narrow escape in Canada was the first.

What a story if *mémère*, as her children have passed it on, had decided to break *avec* (with) *le Canada* for America at the very moment she flung those coins. Her action was rife with symbolism, but she had thought about it after her husband died in 1914. We've mentioned how business was unkind to him, and as fate would have it, he died *d'une attaque du coeur* (of a heart attack), yes, while doing business downtown. She knew her sisters - Julienne Duguay *et* Sédulie Girard - were already residing in Woonsocket on Cumberland Street. Their respective families occupied each side of the third floor of a four-story, eight-tenement house where the Fournier Funeral Home parking lot and flood control wall are now located. Bob told me there were two other huge tenement houses next to it. Families were more likely to come if relatives were here and served as *pied-à-terre* or steppingstones. Since history records 1,800,000 Canadians came from 1814 on, those steppingstones paved "the Canuck Highway." Of that total, we said 800,000 came to New England, establishing almost unassailable ethnic communities, because of the deep encircling moat of faith, language, and customs. *Ici on parle le français. Seulement.* (Here we speak French. Only.)

But if *mémère* had been weighing her options, including America, she now had but one course of action. Instead of coming here to make a better life, it was to have any kind of life at all. Quick-witted mom said it best, "*On éta sa paille. On nava rien,*": down to sackcloth and ashes like Job. Forgetting for a minute her womanly decorum, earthy mom also used a little bathroom humor, "*On nava pas même un pot pour pisser*": not even a pot to pee in. Fortunately, from her sisters' letters or a recruiting agent, *mémère* knew there was steady work in those city mills. (Romeo Berthiaume portrayed recruiting agent Jean Boisvert so well at the Museum of Work & Culture during the American-French Genealogical Society induction ceremonies.) She also knew that thousands had already come, making the city *le Canada en-bas*. It would almost be like going back to Québec. Facetiously, was it foreshadowing, as seen in literature (hints of bad things to come), those recruiters who went from New England to Canada were called "slavers." They got a dollar for every person they got into the mills, including young boys and girls. In defense of the move, mom said, "*Il falla se débrouiller*" (We had to manage) since they only had two options: one, stand there and die; or two, do something, as if they had a fire in their posterior: "*le feu dans le derrière*." I suspect any Franco mother with, say, five or more kids had some "earthiness" in her speech that belied her decorum and modest ways.

Shortly after the fire, some 700 boisterous harvesters came through by train, headed for the grain fields in the West. At the sight of the town's devastation, their he-man guffaws and shouts became an awed silence. How many looking at mom's family and other survivors said to themselves, "There but for the grace of God, goeth I"? Growing up, we loved our *mémère*, but what if we had known that without a helpmate, she moved to a new country and brought her family over all by herself, just like a modern liberated woman pulling off a tremendous undertaking. Yes, this was the old lady by the stove that we cherished, dressed in black, praying and knitting, if not helping mom with the cooking and baking. Truly a pioneer woman of the highest order, unknown, unsung, but all proportions kept, no less memorable to her family than those biblical heroines who rose to save their people. How fortunate she was given an education enabling her to move so bravely in what was strictly a man's world at the time. Again, how I wish mom had told us the story before *memére* passed away! Was it too painful? You sometimes know a person's triumphs, as we did from mom, but not the despair before it.

In retrospect, anyone knowing Malachi's lines (3: 19-20) was prophetic on the fateful morning of July 29, 1916, when the fiery scourge had finally come: "Lo, the day is coming, blazing like an oven. And the day that is coming will set them on fire, leaving them neither root nor branch. But for you who fear my name, there will arise the sun of justice with its healthy rays." *Les* Fontaines, of course, had no premonition about finding "the sun of justice with its healthy rays in America." But they would identify experientially with "neither root nor branch," that is, neither money nor wardrobe.

I shudder to think what it feels like to wake up one day, devoid of all you've worked for and saved in your life. They say every individual or family eventually plants roots somewhere, but luckily not everyone gets totally uprooted. For sure, it's a life-altering experience, and it explains why they always spoke about "the days of their lives" when they gathered. Always tuned in, I enjoyed hearing their saga - like reality TV - because someone always added a detail unknown to others or forgotten. Like some 50 years later, *tante* Laurence told me about the train conductor on their trip here, as we soon relate. Imagine, a detail mom left out! And yet *ma tante* didn't make the initial trip, staying in Canada with *tante* Marie-Ange for their schooling.

As it turned out, America and Woonsocket would indeed heal wounds for these displaced habitants. But as is always the immigrant's lot, dark clouds both economic and racial would sometimes obscure the hopeful parts of the prophet's message. Could they ever have imagined that even in America, the modern-day Promised Land "flowing with milk and honey" (biblical symbols of plenty), an economic tidal wave like *La Grosse Depression* would hit? But of course, it was a worldwide downturn, which would again re-acquaint them with a poverty as searing as the one they had known after the fire. Poet Francis Thompson's poem, "The Hound of Heaven," (the symbol of a pursuing, purifying God) conjures up the continuing difficulties dogging the pathways of these soon-to-be émigrés. Even if unlike the sinful fugitive in the poem, they were, she thought, "*du bon monde*" (good people.) Faith-wise, I can only imagine how He must have loved them to try them so much to strengthen their already strong belief in His goodness and the afterlife. Didn't Christ challenge His disciples to carry their cross? A writer reminds us a cross has two pieces, symbolic of the pluralism of earthly problems. The Fontaines had "enough wood" for a lot of crosses! Mom always wanted to know why things happened, why the bullseye always seemed to be on their backs. But in the worst of their recollections, their soul-searching was never without some joy and thanksgiving. As I listened to them at *mon oncle* François *et ma tante* Blanche's house on Ross Street, I saw the elation of survivors basking in a second chance at life. "*On éta content de s'échapper,*" (We were glad to escape) she said, like Scarlett O'Hara with more tomorrows to start over. Like that famous line in "The Aeneid" where Aeneas says someday, they'll forget losing Troy, remembering only the good times they once had: "*jucunda olim meminisse.*" The soothing selectivity of memory when it's not Post Traumatic Stress.

Can You Spare a Dime for the Fontaines?

WITH NO CESSATION in their tragedy, the forest fire would now usher in the searing pain of separation. A separation that would last forever for most of them. With so many survivors made homeless by the fire, government officials only provided ten dollars, food, and a tent. As insensitive and strange as this laissez-faire policy seems to us today, didn't President Hoover's administration react basically the same way when the Depression hit? Help would have to come from family, neighbors, and local government. Far from me to justify its response, but remember it was still a time when community and family resources were our good Samaritans, not "Our Father Who Art in Washington," a wit said.

Out of several thousands, some 300 *sans demeures* (homeless) decided, like them, to leave for good. Like refugees from a war-torn country, their choice was to move towards jobs and a more hospitable climate if possible. Much like the American Dust Bowl victims of the late 1930s. For the Fontaines, who reflected on all that happened to them since 1914, it was natural to put some distance between them and the country of their birth. It's as if they were misbegotten Canadians or "children of a lesser god." I thought of the church hymn "You shall wander far in safety, though you do not know the way / You shall speak your words in foreign lands (USA) and all will understand! / If you walk amid the burning flames, you shall not be harmed." I've seen photos of incoming people at Ellis Island with their little boxes and musty satchels. But I'm moved when I think mom's family came barely with their lives, some hope, and faith in His mercy. I learned "the rest of the story" when I recorded mom every week at Saint Antoine. As a genealogist said, when you talk to your folks about your family history, you're on a timeline of 50 to 100 years because of the knowledge of their parents and even grandparents. A treasure trove of one's history worthy of remembrance and record! As someone said, "The past is not gone; it's still with us." None of us could have imagined our mom's family had a story like theirs.

Initially they left Cochrane to seek temporary relief with relatives in places like St. Majorique, St. Hughes twice, St. Francois du Lac (*mémère* Morvan's ancestral home), and finally St. Hyacinthe, where they embarked for the states. I don't know if a displaced person is more aware of their troubled itinerary, but mom recalled all the stops. This some 60 or 70 years later! But how come they still had their singed clothing on the train? And no money? Mom told me most people lived on the margin.

Always with some emotion, she related how her mother chose who was coming or staying. There was no money to bring the whole family, so as not to overly burden her two sisters' families in Woonsocket. The two older boys - Auray *et* Urgel - were staying because they had or could find jobs in a paper mill after joining the Canadian Expeditionary Force. Their WWI enlistment, as I relate later, embroiled both, but especially Auray, in horrific trench warfare, exposure to gassing, rats, disease, and several life-saving exploits in France.

A college professor said one of the Protestant reformers, including Puritans, in the 16th Century espoused the notion that God rewarded good people on earth and punished the bad with misfortune and failure. Despite her family's woes, mom, if she knew about John Calvin (a Frenchman named Lefevre) never subscribed to that thinking, never doubting they were "du bon monde" (good people) and what happened was Divine Providence. She was convinced God thought a lot about them, but not as mercifully as she would have liked. I beg the reader's indulgence in stressing this point, but nothing revealed more to me the depth of their faith, Christian resignation, and unshakable tenacity. Mom often spoke about Job of the Old Testament. Not verbatim, but the family lived by what he said: "For I know my Redeemer liveth and in the last day I shall rise out of the earth. And I shall be clothed again with my skin, and in my flesh I shall see my God; the life of man upon earth is a warfare, and his days are like the days of a hireling." But from *Inside Heaven and Hell* by Thomas W. Petrisko and the 16th Century Council of Trent, as it were, mom's family knew that after the travails of life was the enjoyment of heaven and the vision of God. Petrisko relates saints and mystics in their visions relate happiness in heaven will be according to one's merits on earth; a restored perfect body not bound by space; an immaterial body, and the community of the blessed.

Also like in the Parable of the Sower, their faith had been planted in deep soil, not to be swept away like seeds with shallow roots, choked by thorns, or wasted in hard gravel. In the autobiography of John Gerard, S.J. – *The Autobiography of a Hunted Priest* - he often reiterates his thinking that Divine Providence allowed, if you will, torture at the hands of Queen Elizabeth I's ministers because of his faith to make him turn towards God even more. To avoid capture, he escaped detection in hideaways crafted by an expert.

In *mémère* Emerance's post fire plans, the two youngest girls, Marie Ange *et* Laurence, who were in a Presentation of Mary convent school at St. Hughes, were staying till the end of the school year. Even though *l'école en pension* (boarding school) was relatively inexpensive in those days, only *mémère's* passion for education explains how she made plans for it, even if penniless. As I saw several times in my Order, the Presentation of Mary nuns, who taught thousands of us in Woonsocket for so little, let them stay without payment. Cousin Claude Trottier found a picture of the St. Hughes school. My grandmother even promised to send *tante* Laurence back a second year if their fortunes in America improved with millwork. She did. The family album shows Urgel in his Canadian army uniform with my two aunts in their outfits in front of the school. (When I taught at Notre Dame HS in Fitchburg, 1955-70, the city's most prominent doctor was unbelievably generous towards the Brothers. Why? When he and his brother, a lawyer, were youngsters and the family couldn't afford the tuition at Sacred Heart School, Sharon, the Brothers took them in anyway. Again, who's the wiseacre who said no good deed goes unpunished? One year, he gifted a new station wagon car to the school.)

As for the Fontaine story, the dispossessed group consisted of *mémère, oncles* François *et* Edmour, mom, *et* Yvonne. When Yvonne went back, she married the brother of Edmour's wife, and she and her husband Edez Villemure raised a large family in Cochrane.

Going back a bit, imagine the absolute shock mom experienced when she returned from babysitting from *la chapelière* (the hatter), madame Gendreau. Her *chez eux* (home) was in ashes and the family out of town. Speak about a sudden reversal of fortune and cries of disbelief! But such was the art (or lack of it) of communication in those days. Especially after the fire. She was vague about the details, but somehow, she caught up with the family in one of those temporary stays. Was that why she always seemed in a hurry-up mode? Did she never want to be left behind again? But I also know that trying to keep a step ahead of those Four Horsemen of the Apocalypse (War, Death, Famine, and Pestilence) from WWI on is what made her that way.

When she was confused, behind schedule, or just plain lost in thought, she often said, "*J'cré baim q'suis perdue*": I think I'm lost. I can only imagine with what anguish she uttered the same words when her beloved Tara, *la maison paternelle*, (her paternal home) and family were suddenly gone from the scene. Humor me once more and color in a Canadian Scarlett O'Hara here, as her will to survive, find her family, and start again at that moment helped forge that indomitable will and utter fearlessness people said were personal characteristics of her life. It's why I like the felicitous comparison with the literary heroine of Margaret Mitchell's Civil War saga. Her real counterpart has existed how many times in the course of history and human disasters? We recognize them more now.

But in what must be one of the most grief-wrenching scenes possible, *cousine* Clémence (Fontaine) Paulhus, *oncle* François' youngest daughter, related how her father described the scene at the station when the family entrained for the states forever. *Oncle* Urgel, whom I remember from his visits to America as a high-strung, emotional man simply did not want to be separated from his mother and family. (After the war he lived a bit in America, but Washington declared him persona non grata, said mom in muted tones.) He pleaded, wailed, and flung his arms towards his boarding family.

As the train began to roll, he clung to a station post in disconsolate grief, creating quite a heart-wrenching scene. True, he was 19, but young in character and needy, and Canadian families were tightly knit. And of course, this was one more devastating blow on top of so many others, all happening in his early and late teenage years. Auray, Laurence, and Marie-Ange tried to comfort him, but to no avail. Like Auray he was to remain Canadian.

Edez and Yvonne (Fontaine) Villemure Family
Cochrane, Ontario, Canada

What we now might consider just a long trip, or a short airplane hop was immeasurably farther then, and not just in miles. The boys did come down three or four times for one or two-week stays. But because of penury, *mémère* returned to Canada only once. Of course, residual bitterness probably held her away, causing mom to say, "*C'ta trop pour elle.*" (It's too much for her.) When mom went to Canada, she never failed to visit *l'Oratoire de Saint Joseph à Montréal* to pay homage to now sainted Frère André.

Mom kept letters she got from her brothers and sister in Canada. Some, with their joyful or sorrowful news, are in the family albums, along with photos of their Canadian children. Our Villemure cousins obviously inherited our grandmother's thirst for learning. Many still living in and around or beyond Cochrane, Ontario, possess advanced academic degrees. François did return to Cochrane once, but it was an unsettling experience, remembering what he saw: the family that lost seven the day of the fire's holocaust. Was it as novelist Thomas Wolfe said, "You can't go home again"?

Immigrants had once come in wagons, horses, or partly on foot, but not the Fontaines. With *les p'tits chars* (the train) chugging ahead and people settling in their seats, their bedraggled appearance immediately drew the conductor's attention. You can imagine fellow travelers registering shock at their appearance. *Tante* Laurence, who in retirement lived at Chateau Clare in the city, was told how the "sainted conductor" (*un monsieur* Picard) was moved by the plight of *mémère* and her gallant, battered band. He turned out to be a Good Samaritan and St. Christopher (patron of travelers) all in one person.

I mentioned that just this once someone outdid mom's steel-trap and voluminous memory. Not as competitors of course, but as oral historians of their Francophone world, she and *tante* Laurence complemented each other perfectly. The news reporter savants of oral transmission in the family, with *tante* Marie-Louise Peloquin on the Tellier side completing the triumvirate. One time, my wife Patricia, who only knew English, and I chauffeured mom and Laurence to a nephew's wedding, some 30 miles out. I marveled how the two sisters in the back seat talking patois knew so many people and so many incidents of their family's immigration story. My understanding wife must have felt left out! Unknowingly, I was storing it all up. Usually, only historians after much learning and research attain such a detailed grasp of a people's history. Incidentally, research seems to show Francos were the only worldwide immigrant group to arrive here solely by train. But how could it be otherwise at the time? The trip from Montreal to Rhode Island was about 22 hours for a $10 ticket. Imagine, that's all it took to buy you another country and a whole new way of life! As the presence of *monsieur* Picard on the "Fontaine-makeover" train makes clear, the railroad obviously supplied French-speaking conductors. Said mom, "*Pour aider aux voyageurs à s'défricher*," - to help travelers get orientated.

Besides taking in their impoverished look, *le conducteur* had noticed *mémère's* singed dress. Approaching them, he said, "With the way you people look, you won't get through customs." "*Passer aux lignes*" (Pass through border customs), mom said. "Do two things," he advised. "Tell custom agents you have rich relatives there (he said everyone believed that fiction about Americans) and show them some money." So, he "gave" them *des piastres* (dollars) and told *mémère* to give them back after the crossing. How often had he done this for others? Was Saint Christopher a Canadian?

Cousin Clémence said her dad also related how Picard took pity on their famished look. No, he didn't send them to the dining car, if any, to eat *pour rien* (for nothing). But he asked other riders to share their lunch with them: "*Vouley-vous partagez votre goutée avec ce monde-ici?*" (Will you share your snacks with these people here?) in perfect French. Whatever they got, I picture the family feeling like Dickens' deprived Oliver Twist in the orphanage, devouring their handouts, while the more fortunate ate copiously. Grandma was so religious; did she thank *le bon Dieu* (good God) for this daily bread? - "I was hungry and you fed me." But I wonder if she ate at all. With all that grief on her plate, was there room left for food?

Notwithstanding this angel of mercy and the family's gratitude, one senses how deeply mortifying the whole scene must have been. Since *les voyageurs* (the travelers) shared their lunch, it underscores they joined in the conductor's neighborliness. And to answer my own question, no one in the family ever spoke of muted sneering remarks or condescending stares either. Just normal curiosity. But this total dependence or bottom of-the-barrel status must have really hurt. *Mémère* knew it's better to give than receive, but her family since September 29 had been put by God at the mercy of the more fortunate, a humbling experience. Did she feel as a parent she should have been able to protect her children from harm and want? But it didn't happen, and now she had to thrust her proud hand out for her children to eat. She who had been born in a comfortable, land-owning family that sent their children to higher learning before the turn of the century! She was now bringing her family *aux états* (to the states) with perhaps less than anyone ever before! Also, *mémère* surely knew how many who came to New England were criticized as a serious defection in the body politic and integrity of the Québec populace. One slur was *"canailles"*: scum, rabble, riff-raff. They were now immigrants who at times were demeaned by those who remained and then by some non-Franco nativists upon arrival!

The late and eloquent Bishop Fulton J. Sheen (proclaimed "Venerable" by Pope Benedict XVI; the first step towards sanctity) in his famed *Life is Worth Living* TV talks once spoke how we're born with nothing (*tabula rasa*: like an empty blackboard) but acquire a part of our self-worth through having or getting, unlike God who is Being. If so, what was *memére's* self-worth at that point as a person and provider? How do you start over again past mid-life when you're a widow (*une veuve*), penniless, with eight children, and going to a country where most don't speak your language, worship the same God, and don't know your customs? But upon arrival, how her heart must've beaten fast to see her two sisters in the city and share the warmth and comfort of family! Did Julienne *et* Sédulie and families know they were coming? Were they shocked at their appearance? Did their welcoming well up copious tears and ecstatic joys, the kind people experience when a loved one has literally come back from the portals of death, like Mary and Martha felt about Lazarus out of the tomb? In one of my favorite stories, I see a link between *mémère's* mild criticism for His not being there for them in the worst moments of their tragedy, with Mary chiding Christ for letting her brother die: "If you'd been here, it would not have happened." But God works on a "timeless schedule." He was touched by the sister's sorrow, as he surely was for the Fontaines. And at every turn, there was a ministering angel, called conductor Picard or caring passengers. And again, they were the only lost, missing family to come out alive from the fire. They didn't know how close God was to them.

Again, before embarking, *oncle* François told me he helped with the haying at one of the farm shelters the relatives provided them. No matter how sympathetic their Canadian relatives may have been, they couldn't stay too long anywhere. It wasn't like Ben Franklin's observation "that fish and visitors stinketh after three days," but again it was because of the limited means of those hardscrabble farmers, related or not. At any time, did *mémère* regret in her utter despair as she searched through the embers of her home she had told God He could keep the coins she found? But the family is so grateful she kept those daguerreotype photos with their splotchy sooty stains, which never cease to fascinate me with the full and horrific story they hold. But do those jettisoned coins remain buried with all the hopes and dreams they once had in Canada? Yes, *mémère* had rendered "to Caesar what was Caesar's," and despite her anger and frustration gave God what was God's: the family's resignation. She had nothing more to give; she had lost everything. Mom said, "*On é (est) venu avec nos guenilles*": We came in rags.

The refugees made it through customs with their "newly-found wealth," which they returned to Picard. In the history of the family, he's in the hall of fame, along with the Berard landlord who carried my family for a couple of years during the Depression. About those two, I'm reminded what Christ said of the centurion, "Greater faith (aka love), I haven't found in all of Israel." I said God sent a ministering angel each time, who even spoke their language. "I've not lost any of those you've given me," Christ once told His Father with tearful affection. About *les* Fontaines, did He also say, "I knew they would bend, but not break?"

They initially arrived without further incident "*à la maison de mon grand-oncle Médéric*," (to the house of my great uncle Médéric) she said, in Derry, NH. She always fondly recalled, "*Y ma servi de père*," (He served as my father) about giving her away in marriage in Woonsocket in 1923. Photos in the album show their Gaulin Ave. home after the wedding. About that short stop in the Granite State, they stayed long enough to assuage the pain of their tragedy and deprived passage, even taking a temporary job in a local shoe factory for quick money. (A present Derry resident told me the shoe mill is still there.) And so, they undid their Cochrane holocaust look, that ghoulish Morticia or undertaker appearance. About being told in Canada they looked like they were back from the dead, I've wondered who had the greater shock? Townspeople who thought they were dead or *les* Fontaines being told that? I heard no word whether, like Mark Twain, they saw some humor in the report of their supposed demise. Twain, you remember, was once reported dead by the press. So, he retorted, "The news of my death has been greatly exaggerated." Imagine, after having lost all your possessions, someone also tells you, you look as if you've also lost the only thing you came to this earth with, your life.

In the Order, the late Brother Ronald Dion told me a Brother stunned a returning missionary confrère with the "grave" revelation that he thought he was dead. Abetting the confusion is missionaries from Africa at one time only came home every seven years. When I studied at Spring Hill College in Mobile, I returned home unannounced for my first vacation after more than two years in the South. Five inches taller and 40 pounds heavier, I knocked at the door to see mom's reaction. Never having seen me in a black suit, but only in a cassock, she very courteously said, *"Bonjour monsieur l'abbé* (Hello reverend), to which I replied *"Cée mwé, René"* (It's me, Rene). Her hands went to her face and tears flowed down her cheeks.

After about a month in Derry, NH, the Fontaines finally journeyed to Woonsocket - *Québec Retrouvé* (Québec rediscovered) - where if you could imagine farms where mills and tenements were, everything else felt the same and everyone talked and lived like the places they once knew before in Ontario and Québec: *"le pays de mes amours"* (the country of my loves), she remembered. By virtually bringing their "home" with them, no other immigrant people would work harder to disprove "that you can't go home again," at least in memory. They would see compatriots battle assimilation with the force of *la Résistance* and the militant Sentinellist Movement.

Brother Alphonse, SC (Rene Tellier) visits his parents Léopoldine and Alphonse in 1952.

Mon oncle François did stay a little longer in Derry. But when he finally arrived in the city (variously spelled "Woonsokette," "Winsock-et," and "Wind Socket" on his brothers' Canadian war records), it didn't take him long to discover *le Coin Social* (Social Corner) was just as lively a place at night like the downtown Cochrane he once knew. Or at any of the other places they lived following their ebullient, creative, but managerially poor father. Quickly he noticed there was good French conversation; good humor (obviously he enlarged his vast repertoire of French jokes); hearty companions (he remembered Ernest Dupré, later mayor); and even a little gambling, *du jeu* (and gaming.) "The action," he confessed, was in a hall near or above *le théatre* Laurier. I later delivered *The Call* there as a kid, when it was, I think, the ITU (the Independent Textile Union; later the broader Industrial Trade Union Hall). Like the two saloons I also delivered to, when I opened the door I saw a long bar, obviously to encourage and sustain camaraderie in its thirsty members.

You had to learn a few English words to get by, he related. The time, 1916, when you could live your whole life without hearing a word of English in sections of the city was beginning to crack just a tiny bit. He said he asked a lot of questions, struggled through whatever English materials he could get his hands on, and, when all else failed, looked sheepish and uncomprehending. Everyone knows the vacuous, bland look of the earnest, lately arrived, but confused immigrant whose English, as mom often said of her own, "*est pa(s) trop fort*" (Was not too strong.) Why, even in the 1930s and early 1940s, many Francos still had to assume that look in social situations or in public school! I repeat my contention that WWII was the global cataclysm that brought about our total assimilation into the American culture and language. But also add a media boost from telephone and television. When *les* Fontaines *et les* Telliers arrived, those marvels were still embryonic.

But sounding a lot like the song, "How ya gonna keep 'em down on the farm after they've seen Paree?" he said he liked it here from the start. The Fontaines were on the Americanization track. Except for one brother and sister we said, they weren't going back, as some prejudiced Anglo-Americans may have wanted them to. But as mom often said during the 10 years of the Depression when the light at the end of the tunnel was just one more oncoming train, God wasn't finished with them: "*Les mauva(is) temps sont pas finis.*" (The bad times aren't over.) I do find it unbelievable that roughly from 1914 (patriarch Louis Fontaine's heart attack) to 1945, *les* Fontaines lived with the threat of one disaster after another, save for *du bon temps* (the good times) in the 1920s. Someone had taken out the last two words in the greeting: "Welcome to the Land of Opportunity." Opportunity never knocked twice; it didn't knock at all. Because they came from Canada, did it seem the Statue of Liberty fudged a bit when she beckoned "Give me your tired, your poor" to a better life? And cruelly, the statue was a donation from France, the land where their forebears came from!

Misfortune a Constant Traveler

IN PAST CHAPTERS I've related in broad strokes the Fontaine story as it related to some facet of their life in the city. But Franco families were large and their experiences and travails, past and present, spread over a wide area, adding more amusing and tragic details to the Fontaine saga. In all the years my family lived at 309 Gaulin Avenue (1935 to 1952), you couldn't forget mom's people were *les* Fontaines. There was too much history about them, and she, for one, wasn't going to let anybody forget their saga. It wasn't self-aggrandizement or their misfortune unique and therefore unforgettable, but more their pride in their survival. As if to say, you too can do what we did to get here and eventually prosper.

Since she was the acknowledged chronicler of her family with *tante* Laurence *et mon oncle* François, she never ceased to recall this or that event in Canada and in America. Tenacious; she didn't know it but once she described herself: "*Une memwère a tout casser*," meaning "a memory to break everything."

Even though no direct link to the Fontaines was found (contrary to what mom told us), it's interesting to note many Francos supposedly trace their roots to Louis Hébert. He arrived in Québec for good from Paris in 1617 with his wife Marie Rollet and three children. He had initially sailed to Acadia in 1604 but returned to France. Though an apothecary by profession, he came back and chose to make a living from the land and is considered *le premier colon* (the first settler) in Canada who stayed through thick and thin. The fur traders tried to prevent his settling in viewing colonists like him a threat to their fur-trading monopoly. But surprisingly, he had the support and friendship of Samuel de Champlain, even if an officer in that fur-trading company, *La Compagnie des Cents Associés*. As mentioned, Champlain warred against the five tribes of the Iroquois - Mohawk, Oneida, Onondaga, Cayuga, and Seneca - the most warlike among the 500 nations in North America. Except for them, many of those nations (the Hurons, Montagnais, Algonquins) helped the French and were called "the French Normans." One of Hébert's children was Guillemette, and mom once thought we were from her line. She married a Couillard, another great family name in Québec. But cousins Claude Trottier *et* François Fontaine both found our lineage from the already mentioned Nicolas Pion dit LaFontaine.

Going back even further, cousin François traced his mother Blanche's family (*les* Frappiers) way back to Charlemagne and his forebears, 602 A.D., through Catherine Baillon, one of the King's Daughters, *Les Filles du Roi*. Patrick Beaulieu also found a link. With the promise of a dowry, these Daughters came to Canada, married a colonist and received provisions to set up housekeeping. It required women capable of hard work, endurance, and courage to brave Indian attacks and a harsh climate. About one of these daughters (among the first of the Daughters of the King) the *Providence Journal* printed my notes about Jeanne Amiot, 22, an ancestor of ours, who left St. Pierre de Losne in Burgundy and quickly upon her arrival married Nicolas in 1673, 12 years her senior. She became *une veuve* (a widow) at fifty-two in 1703. She then married François Chicoine, the son of another King's Daughter. But it gets better as Jeanne's son Maurice was married to her new husband François' sister Thérèse Chicoine, which made Jeanne her daughter-in-law's sister-in-law! (See: American French Genealogical Society to sort it out!)

An important part of our social life was our close association with *mon oncle François;* his wife Blanche, and their four children: Roger, who maintained the tradition of doctors among the Fontaines; Lucille (Langlois); Clémence (Paulhus), and Brother Francois of the Brothers of the Sacred Heart, with whom I trained, attended college, and taught at Sacred Heart School in Sharon and the Academy. Matchmaker mom was proud she told her favorite and courting brother what a good wife and mother Blanche would make: "*A va faire une bonne femme de famille.*" Yes, matchmaking was important, as long as you married French-Canadian: "*du monde comme nous autres.*" (People like us.) Add also to the visiting or visited clan *tante* Laurence Trottier's family, husband Henri, sons Claude *et* Ronald, *mémère* Emérance, and spinster (*vieille fille*), *tante* Marie-Ange. Our link with mom's brothers and sister in Canada was strictly through correspondence and rare visits from Auray *et* Urgel, who remained bachelors: *des vieux garcons*. So, none of us children ever saw Yvonne *et* Edmour or their children. In how many other poor families separated by immigration did this happen? Immigration, forced or initiated for a better life, caused tearful, lasting pangs of separation, like the dramatic departure of the Fontaines at the railroad station. But I was impressed in Chartier's *The Franco-Americans of New England* that besides economics or jobs, the clergy and some immigrants also wanted to bring the Catholic faith to Americans and seek conversions, like the priests did, an apostolic thrust called *messianisme* or evangelization.

The Moment! Long before the ravages of the 1938 Hurricane, mom said a relative had a cottage at Oakland Beach, Warwick, RI. The Scarborough Beach of its day. There she met my dad at a beach party. Album photos show the conservative bathing suits were strictly 1920ish, when public decorum was still de rigueur, as it still was when I joined the Order in 1947 and went swimming with my group at Sucker Pond in Harrisville. They were married at St. Ann's in Woonsocket, November 19, 1923, and the five of us, Robert, Suzanne, I, Bernard, *et* Rachel, were born between 1925 and 1937, years of increasing financial challenge. Mom miscarried once before Bob came.

When the folks celebrated their 50th wedding anniversary November 26, 1973 and my *Call* press release said the "deceased" Reverend Normand Meunier married them, he quickly let the family know his death had been greatly exaggerated, à la Mark Twain. She enjoyed the whole incident and gave a comical rendition of what he said over the phone: "*Je ne suis pas fort, mais je ne suis pas mort,*" (I'm not strong, but I'm not dead,) a comment I heard in the Order from older Brothers who still had their hands to the plow, even if their output was diminished. My folks celebrated their anniversary with Mass at Assumption Church in Bellingham, dinner at Ma Glockners restaurant, and a reception at home. As teacher, guidance counselor, athletic director, admissions, and publicist, I wrote thousands of press releases, but because of that snafu (*mea culpa*), I never forgot the first and second law of journalism: Get the name right and don't assume anything.

I often mention *les* Telliers, Fontaines, Trottiers, Peloquins in the same breath because whenever those families met, the adults spoke of the "good old days": *les bons vieux temps*. I narrated *les* Fontaines had literally been tried by fire and couldn't forget the pain. So, every time they met, I picked up one more thread in the rich tapestry of their incredibly adventurous life that led them here, thanks to Divine Providence and a stand-in St. Christopher, patron of travelers. Eventually I realized theirs was a rich oral tradition, fascinating as any other immigrant family. But memory's selective, said poet Virgil, and their reminiscences drew more laughter than gloom.

Wedding of Alphonse Tellier and Léopoldine Fontaine, St. Ann Church, November 19, 1923
Back l to r: Great-uncle Médéric Fontaine and Joseph Tellier.

Another constant, visual reminder of the Fontaine heritage was mom's family portrait, a large oval-shaped picture mounted in a dark-stained wooden frame. It occupied a prominent place in our salon. Four things stand out in my mind from all the years and times I looked at that picture; one, *pepère* Louis is not in the photo; two, my godmother, *tante* Laurence, the youngest and a pretty teen with a white beau in her hair;

three, a later fused insert of *mon oncle* Edmour in Canada when the photo was taken; and fourth, mom, who never said "cheese" to a photographer. That was a standing joke in the family because she was really *une ricaneuse*, one who laughed easily. The original photo of my parents with my siblings and me is now in my possession and is on the cover of this book. I also have a retouched photo of my purse-lipped mother when she was engaged to dad and their wedding photo. But too-frugal dad nearly ruined several of these by removing them from their rich wooden frames causing a tear in our family photo. Was he trying to downsize when they joined *les* Bouffards in Bellingham? Or is it just a man thing of not thinking how important nostalgic photos are to women?

Author Rene Tellier's godmother aunt Laurence (Fontaine) Trottier at the Presentation of Mary school, St. Hughes, Québec, Canada in 1916.

Sharing her gender's preoccupation about appearance, when mom told us a woman was beautiful, she said, "*A passé pour belle*." When all five of us were at home and living through the Depression, we might not have thought she was *belle* (beautiful) without cosmetics or fancy clothes. But looking at her engagement photo, her regal neck, creamy complexion, striking brown tresses (not as light or reddish blond as the other Fontaines), and clear doe-shaped eyes were all highlights. In French, *des beaux traits* (beautiful features), but she never touted her own. How difficult it was for these *femmes de maison* (housewives) with a lot of kids and little money to maintain their youthful look! One writer said Franco women always looked their age, with no obsession to look younger than what they were.

Mom related how her mother Emérance and father Louis were a happily married couple. But like others, they encountered a lot of personal and economic misfortunes in raising their family. Born in St. Germain de Brandon, P.Q., 1861, *pepère* Louis, named after his father, was three years older than *mémère* when they married in the 1880s. His first name was popular in French history with 19 kings bearing it. Of course, mom knew it was royalty. I'm surprised one of us boys weren't so named! I believe the name morphed from Clovis, an earlier great Frankish king, instrumental in making France Catholic, like Constantine did. One writer called him "Connie."

Besides being a family *"de moyen"* (of means), *mémère's* family had one member with an adventuresome streak. Along with 160,000 prospectors, our granduncle Émile spent some 20 years in the Alaskan Yukon in his quest for gold. He went twice and "ashamed to beg and unable to dig," he became *un hotelier*, innkeeper. Life was rough there and one day 60 were killed, including the vilest of them all. And a good and a bad guy both shot themselves dead.

Speaking about timing, twenty years later, gold seeker Émile Morvan returned one night during *une soirée de famille*, (a family get-together,) but to everyone's chagrin he had practically lost all his French. *"Yava perdu son frança,"* (He lost his French,) mom related, as if now a persona non grata. Was he the first forebear ever to speak English? Given their belief French and faith were inseparable, did they fear for his immortal soul *à la perte de son langage*? (to the loss of his language)? I must confess when she told me the story, my own concern was not for his soul but rather I wondered if we finally had "a rich uncle." One whose last will, if discovered, (*"son testament,"* she said) would lift us out of our millhand's living standard and give us a place of our own, *un chez-nous*? But alas, he never found the mother lode. I've seen footage of those turn-of-the-century Alaskan miners slogging up snow-covered peaks in search of gold. Life was raw and expensive. A documentary said an egg cost fifty cents and like in California, only those who sold goods or provided services made money. Pies sold for $5 - $80 in today's money. (Was there gold in "dem dar crusts?")

In 2000 I inquired whether an Yvonne Fontaine with an unclaimed $3,000 insurance policy in RI, was maybe mom's sister, who returned to Canada before 1920. Documentation from her son Paul, who told me so much about the Cochrane inferno, said no. I was hoping to send them a nice *boni*, (bonus) as we said in the Order. Later when Bob told me I was listed in the state's unclaimed money, I got about $70. Like most parents did at the birth of a child, mom opened an account in my name. A big saver, she knew bad times were never far away. How did she know that?

Further genealogy research by cousins François *et* Claude reveal the spelling variations of the family name, like Pion dit La Fontaine, Jean dit Fontaine. Louis Fontaine Pion, some with dit Lafortune, others not. A speaker who gave a genealogical talk at Harris Hall said problems in research occur because some records are erroneous, falsified, misspelled, or transcribed wrong. Our great-grandfather, another Louis, married in 1860, was just Fontaine. I've read that the invention of the Gutenberg printing press in the 15th Century helped give some fixity to names and words, but universal education was still centuries away, and our culture was oral. Recall dad's reason for our slow trek to academia: our farming roots in Canada and our mill working culture in New England. So, members of the same family, all untutored, spelled their names differently at baptisms and weddings when challenged by the unfamiliar pen. American writer Ralph Waldo Emerson said, "A foolish consistency (sameness) is the hobgoblin (like a bad habit) of small minds." Our forebears had no such consistency when life (and spelling) had more originals than copies. That's why I love to read about Elizabethan times and the unbelievable spelling variations among the players, this when French (from the Norman conquest of 1066 and the influx of 90,000 words) was still a big influence. It's obvious too in *The Canterbury Tales* of Chaucer in the 14th Century. It's half English, half French.

How did family names originate? Did the Fontaine name come from forebears living near a fountain, a spring, or a church steeple, which she called "*un pion*?" (Elsewhere I list French names that were anglicized.) My friend Patrick Beaulieu-Martin, already mentioned, discovered his family name was simply Martin and at other times Martin *dit* Beaulieu or simply hyphenated. The Beaulieu portion was derived from an ancestor living near a beautiful site: *un beau lieu*. The name was also known in the South during the Civil War era. One Canadian ancestor of his - Abraham Martin - lived on land near Québec City that was eventually named after him: The Plains of Abraham. Site of a seminal battle in Canadian history between the French and British for control of the area. Martin was an admired friend of Champlain and his chief inheritor.

Not really into farming like most, we said mom's family moved a lot in Canada in search of economic stability. We did too here since all five of us children were born at different residences (all home births). So, our dad was like his father-in-law in Canada. Without a car, he was always looking for *un logis* (a home) within walking distance to work (for him), school (children), and church (family). In Canada, her family lived in spurts in places like St. Gabriel de Brandon; Contrecoeur, her birthplace; St. Maurice; Shawinigan Falls; and finally, Cochrane, Ontario, their Waterloo. A reader of history, mom, alluding to the "little corporal's Waterloo," told me about his sacrilegious God-defying boast that even God couldn't stop his armies in Russia in 1811-1812. He did take Moscow initially, but after a lull was thrown all the way back to France a year or so later. Like for Hitler in WWII, the bitter cold of Russia's "General Winter" was the victor. Mom was a so-called "Renaissance woman" ("the whole world is my oyster") with interests and knowledge far beyond her insular French-Canadian world. Impressive for someone with only a grammar school education. Like dad, she had no choice but to be a self-made person.

She often spoke of her father as a reddish-blond man whose incurable optimism was matched only by his love of people, infectious humor, and gifted storytelling. Because his farming father did not bequeath him the land, *la terre paternelle*, he had to get into something else. On mom's baptism certificate, October 28, 1898, his profession was listed as *un fromagier*: cheesemaker. When he bought that sawmill that was torched after his death, wood sales were only fair. When he bought a brick-making concern, he couldn't get the right ingredients or straw, and the bricks - symbolically like the captive Jews in Moses' Egypt - crumbled like his luck. When he made his Camembert,[25] or the like, it didn't sell due to the mineral content in the cow's milk. Incidentally, in a dairy province like Québec, cheesemaking even warranted military exemption for producers, as author Florentine's husband, Upton Maher, got in WWI. When Patricia and I visited Contrecoeur in 1977, the pastor, an avid local historian, showed us the little meat market - *un marché à viande* - that *pepère* ran before 1900. But he failed too as *un épicier* (a grocer). And then the irony of his death while doing business in Cochrane in 1914. He never gave up, but his heart did.

Besides failed enterprises, deaths also stalked the family. We said with families so large and births occurring almost yearly during the mother's childbearing years, infant mortality was common due to weakened mothers. In fact, so terrified was I by that revelation, I feared it might happen to us. Another infant mortality cause was limited medical knowledge about the source of infection that was often abetted by unhygienic midwives and suturing thread.

Mom lost her first pregnancy, so we were "only" five children, not an overly large French-Canadian family like *les* Carpentiers, *les* Turcottes, *et les* Bérubes, all with seven or more kids. Childless or single-child couples were as rare as multiple births. Even if I don't think it ever happened *aux états*, (in the states,) *curé* (priest) Normand Demers in his book about Québec's faith and culture at one time related how a couple was castigated from the pulpit for limiting the size of their family. Among *mémère's* children, death claimed Edmour's twin brother Ernest at birth; Emile, 3, of respiratory causes; and Robert, 4, of diphtheria. In Emile's case, mom spoke of respiratory ills as a genetic weakness. Marrying dad whose whole family save one, we said, was to die of bronchiectasis or related causes, created her mindset we children might be afflicted the same way unless careful or lucky. Outside of heart disease and cancer, I thought in our house only respiratory diseases were fatal. I've already related how committed our parents were to protect us from these health threats.

---

[25] A rich, soft, creamy cheese with a white rind that originated near Camembert in Normandy, France. – *ed.*

But for her, also getting caught in a *courant d'air* (a draft) was about one of the worst health hazards you could run into. Wet shoes were not far behind. "*Aller nu tête*" or hatless was dad's concern for us boys, since women were always behatted. She said the air in Canada was dry, but after their flight to America, *les poumons* (the lungs) *des* Fontaines struggled in the damp New England climate. *Tante* Marie-Ange was the worst but was cured by Brother Saint Andrè. A bit on the frail side like all Fontaine women, did millwork before marriage undermine mom's genetically weak lungs? Beverly York, director of the Windham Textile and History Museum in Willimantic, CT, urged visitors "to imagine working conditions, long hours, the danger of flying shuttles, lung disease from exposure to airborne fibers, and the din of the massive machines. Owners controlled everything – wages, prices, and working conditions, reinforcing a kind of paternalism."

If all mom's family had survived, there would have been eleven children, not an unusual number for Canadian families. But again, in Demers' book, *Revolution in Quebec: A Past Rejected, A Future in Doubt* about the moral, educational, and family concerns there, how things have changed, since theirs is now one of the lowest birthrates in the Western World. But either with a good start in Canada or continuity in the states, not surprisingly many of the early-come families were large. Was it partly the strategy of trying "to out-generate" their English conquerors and thus gain a measure of control by the sheer force of numbers - *la revanche du berceau*, (revenge of the cradle,) as encouraged by the clergy? Or was it simply God's "Be fruitful and multiply." In 1966 some 8 million of French Québeckian ancestry living in North America were descendants from 1,425 women and 1,800 men from the years 1608-1680. But historically, a chief reason given for the fall of French Canada and its vast territories in North America was its low population density. I speak of how the loss of Québec to England doomed another ascendance of the French language and culture in at least all the vast lands France and colonizers possessed. The most crushing blow for Francos then was the sale of the so-called Louisiana Purchase, which practically doubled our nation, a great happenstance. Before that Jefferson thought it would take hundreds of years before the West was settled. I once saw a thousand years.

But I found fascinating the reading of "When the United States Spoke French" by François Furstenberg. Five wealthy families and others who fled the French Revolution and Santo Domingo (now Haiti after the blacks revolted and gained control) all gathered in Philadelphia, once our capital, infusing the city with French art, music, dance, language, cuisine, manners, dress, culture, furniture, and architecture. But it went into decline later when in the tug of war between England and France, we "sided" with the former, much to the dismay of France after what she had done to help us in the American Revolution. I say elsewhere our country's genetic links were strongly with England, not to mention her world-best maritime forces. And according to Champlain, those early French investors were in for the money, not colonization, as Champlain had encouraged. And except for the outbreaks and ouster of Protestant Huguenots, France with its greater standard of living had no equal convulsive religious crises of so long a duration as that which roiled Britannia for more than a century. Religious oppression in Britain sparked immigration, starting with the Puritans. Roger Howell's biography, Cromwell, (an archenemy of Catholics, priests, and Ireland) records the mass killings in the religious-political wars in England, Scotland, Wales, and Ireland in the mid-17th Century. Cromwell was, however, a gifted, self-taught military leader.

I reported earlier that the two largest families I knew were *les* Etienne *et* Annette (dad's sister) Lebels, 14, and *les* Bérards, more than 15, as cited. Four of the boys joined the Order, and Fernand *et* Jules were at Notre Dame HS with me. If God gives the call to religious life, he must have liked us peddlers of the Fourth Estate, as newspaper people (carriers too?) were called. God couldn't find too many fishermen angling in the murky Blackstone River.

Finally, I return to discussing how mom was always a fount of French phrases describing the pathos or folly of the human condition. One comment revealing hers and *les* Fontaines' heroic Christian optimism in all their trials was "*Tout finit par s'passer enfin*," that is, even bad times came to an end; day followed night; night was darkest just before dawn; the calm returned after the storm; and, in their great religious sensibility, the Resurrection of Easter came only after the First Friday Crucifixion. It all meant *Finis Coronat Opus*: The End Crowns the Work. She was never without that great Christian buoyancy. Or, in the cinematic realism I like so much, without the gutsy hope of a Scarlett O'Hara, that one day she wouldn't be hungry again. She did have a lot of good days, dying in her 90th year in 1988, having beaten incredible odds to live that long. Because the Fontaine women were so tiny, did Death's sickle miss them time and again? Perhaps too the Hound of Heaven's "uplifted stroke" never found them because they were never in one place too long.

Is it ironic or providential they settled in a state whose motto is HOPE? Like all immigrants, did they help "capitalize" the motto? But thinking of the Fontaine saga, one of my fantasies is to have been present for some events in history, like Lazarus rising from the dead, Peter walking on water, and the Transfiguration on Mt. Tabor, all suspensions of the laws of nature, which I find fascinating. But even if not of a miraculous nature, when thinking of mom's family going through Customs, how I would've liked to see their faces when, as she said with bemused incredulity, the agent asked if they had anything to declare: "*Avez-vous quelque chose à déclarer?*" I can only think of Jack Benny's face registering a composite of disbelief, wounded dignity, and humor at the improbable question. Today's "Did he just say what I think he said?" I don't know if there's a phrase in French for "What you see is what you get," but it may have crossed their minds. No search was done. You'll recall that the money in *mémère's portefeuille* (wallet) was not even hers, but Mr. Picard's. What they crossed with was courage, hope, and indomitable faith, and *leur belle vie de famille*, (their beautiful family lives,) their greatest contributions to their new country.

5 - NEIGHBORHOOOD AS EXTENDED FAMILY

Tenement House: High-Rise of the Poor

IN THE WAVE of immigrants to America, it's a sociological fact that nothing's been so predictable as the gathering of the same nationalities into certain areas of a city or town. The phrase "ethnic neighborhood" speaks to that phenomenon. It's the *chez nous* (family home) *les* Fontaines *et les* Telliers certainly lived in, like most of the 800,000 New England Francos.

This phenomenon in the city was also identifiable not only with Francos living closely together, but nearly always it seemed in three-to-four story tenement houses: the "high-rises of the poor" or as we called them: *tennemans*. They came in three designs: classical, gambrel, and functional: the latter like ours on 309 Gaulin Ave. My college sociology professor explained how nationalities, largely depending on their economic pecking order, replace one another in a given sequence in city neighborhoods. He cited the brownstones of Boston as an example, citing the three or four nationalities that followed the Anglos.

Front of 309 Gaulin Ave. where my parents raised five children. (3rd floor, left) It was demolished in 1972 the day after Dr. Roger Fontaine took this photo.

Locally, recent immigrants have given new residential life to those tenement houses in the city. Once thought outmoded, these houses, built for $5,000 were later selling for around $150,000. They've held up well despite families with large broods. Milltown Woonsocket saturated most of its acreage, as well as 30 to 40 feet above it. Hence the label "high rise," which so endeared mom who loved that afternoon sun emblazoning our kitchen windows. It was also the best seat for the 1938 Hurricane, dad's mill on Hamlet, and Mt. St. Charles Academy. And of course, St. Ann's Church.

I recall these wooden structures nearly always featured front porches, a big living room and parlor, three or four bedrooms, front and back hallways with inner staircases, a bathroom (not all had a bathtub) with a pull-chain toilet, and cold-water amenities. There were no attached or detached garages, but a cellar space to store wood, coal, and oil. In our master bedroom a capped pipe protruded from the ceiling next to the light. Mom told me tenement houses around the turn of the century featured gas lights rather than electric.

For Québec émigrés, sheer economic necessity dictated they find refuge initially with already-come relatives. These had achieved a moderate subsistence from their mill jobs and offered shelter and food until newcomers got on their feet. Welfare then was truly private with people helping their own so well. The key was strong, intact families, as President Coolidge alluded to when the Depression hit.

For that first job there was no need of a job agency. "*Y va parler pour mwé*" (put in a good word for me) is how she described a millworker's effort to help a family member, relative, or friend get a job. It involved talking to the *soupair*: not "soup for two," but the boss. A worker rarely forgot the person who spoke for him. That first job for the first wave of immigrants was literally the difference between life and death or going back to Canada. There was no unemployment net to catch the jobless, especially a recent immigrant. Initially, they didn't know enough English or possess any occupational skill to do much else (carpentry a notable exception and light clerical work), unless they were like dad's brothers who went back to farming like they did in Canada. But even though mom marveled at all dad knew and did, "occupationally" she said, "*Ton père a seulement son métier*": You father only has millwork.

About employment and his brother, cousin Gene Peloquin told me how my dad's job recommendation for his nephew Normand at the Lafayette mill *chez la* (on) Hamlet became a humorous story at family gatherings. After his first day on the job, neither Normand nor the super seemed to know who the other was despite dad's good word. It soon became apparent Normand mistook *la* French Worsted mill across the street for dad's mill and got hired on the spot. Normand, who spent his last years in the city after a decorated Army career in the Pacific Theatre (Hawaii especially) and Europe, also enjoyed telling me the story. It revealed how young adolescents were very home-based before looking for a job. His father Armand had a car and a phone for his union agent work, but most families didn't. A teen at the wheel was a rare sight, so fatalities were rare.

Even if only with anecdotal evidence, it's safe to conclude Francos who came here usually clustered in the same cities and towns, like our own Woonsocket. Similar enclaves were Manville, Central Falls, West Warwick, Lewiston and Biddeford, ME., Nashua and Manchester, NH; Lowell and Lawrence, MA, and Putnam, CT, to name but a few. In our own 'hood, absolutely everyone was of the same Canadian national origin, except one Italian-named family whose mother, however, was French-Canadian. Also, exceptions were those Belgians and Frenchmen who lived on Lower Gaulin, and two red-headed Irish-American boys who lived on parallel Wood Avenue. I loved talking with them whenever I cut across properties on Wood and Dulude to get to St. Ann's Park bordering on Cass and Dulude.

In Providence's Trinity Repertory Company Playbill of "*Joe Turner's Come and Gone*," Maury Klein speaks about the sense of belonging ethnic neighborhoods and boardinghouses (think of "tenement houses") gave new arrivals. "The city," he says, "was also a cluster of ethnic neighborhoods, tight islands of homogeneity in a sea of diversity." (I love that phrase.) "In every ethnic enclave the boardinghouse offered strangers to the city a curious mixture of the familiar and the exotic. Since most of the newcomers were from the country or at least much smaller towns, the city was for them a jarring dislocation, filled with strange sights, sounds, and smells, where everything moved in mysterious ways and at much faster speeds. For country folk, little if anything connected with their past experience. To find a haven in this alien place where people at least spoke your language or knew your customs was a godsend for the immigrant. In the ethnic neighborhoods and their boardinghouses could be found people who were strangers but not strange to each other." Mom's take was "*On aime baim être avec notre monde*," about liking those who were kin or like you, especially in language and faith. Her farming roots were evident when she said, "*La vache aime son veau*," about an animal, like a cow, loving its offspring.

La rue (the street) Gaulin, for one, was a microcosm of Canada or *le Canada en bas*. Outside the Belgians Bultot, Hermal, Schneider, and, yes, Fontaine, and a French family Vandeville, the other Gaulinites all came out of villages in Québec: Laplume, Lavergne, Lemire, Cournoyer, Blondin, Bourget, Blanchette, Béssette, St. Germain, Beauregard, Tellier (twice, no relation), Choquette, Lafond, Larochelle, Lanoie, Carpentier, Turcotte, Charron, Carle, Houle, Bérubé, Courtemanche, Jacob, Dubois, Jolicoeur, Archambault, Desrochers, Gosselin, Laferriere, Frappier, *et* Champagne. Our Peloquin cousins lived on lower Gaulin near the Kendrick corner and school. Good friend Maurice Vandal, whose mother was a close friend of the Fontaine sisters before marriage, also lived on lower Kendrick and scouted and schooled with us.

Luckily, Francos loved camaderie and conviviality, evident in their joie de vivre. Having left the open stretches of land in Canada and the fields of its farming towns, they were forced by economics to rent an apartment in a tenement house and stacked *comme des sardines* (like sardines). A mill town offered little zoning for privacy and greenery. Every available inch of land was covered with those high-rises and mills near the Blackstone River or tributaries. The river was the only power source before coal, electricity, and oil. For kids, neighbors were like your extended family, since they lived so close and were in and out of your life. I always found it funny to come out of our apartment at the same time a neighbor also did. If it was another kid, you lunged to hit the stairs first. And if dad was around, I didn't slide down the banisters. Our corduroys, jeans, and soiled hands made varnish disappear. Going upstairs it was how many steps you could take in one leap. For our first leap, we got a running start from the outside porch, hard by the Carpentier digs. If you did any of the landings in only two leaps, you qualified for the Olympics. Boys lived with bruised shins all the time. One time, dad was shocked by my eight bruises. With few sports available (only softball at St. Ann's), girls usually displayed the same decorum as their mothers, save some hair pulling. (It's hard to believe, but a recent study said one-fourth of all girls from 14 to 17 now engage in fighting. Is it because there's a shortage of boys?) To mom's peeve and asthmatic distress, climbing stairs was another essential note of our life, unless you were the landlord, *le propriétaire*, who "possessively," always chose the first floor. I doubt those early French settlers in Canada climbed too many stairs, other than in the barn.

The mill economy from its beginning and progress was supportive for the city and its people, but not greatly remunerative or education promising. So later when the mills declined and left, the city's tightly packed neighborhoods and outdated mills left very little land for diversified industrial expansion within its limits. And with the ascendancy of highway trucking after the war and the decline of the railway transportation of goods (also denounced by my clairvoyant dad after the war), the city's lack of highway access also made retooling and recovery difficult. Even if dad never drove, did he foresee bigger and bigger rigs crushing roads never built to handle them? In 2015 Governor Raimondo said they cause 90 percent of road wear and tear. After President Reagan deregulated the industry, one wondered if the driver alongside you had been on the road too many hours. Like the one who killed Pat's college freshman niece, Peggy Misovec, in Virginia. He'd been driving 18 hours. Until bad driver data was nationally computerized, they simply moved on to other states. Of course, I'm not indicting the whole profession with its many good drivers but the pressure to get goods faster to markets has chipped away at the notion we had as kids that they were the best drivers in the world and knew the best places to eat!

With the exodus of mills, family members, relatives, and neighbors who had once worked in local mills began to seek jobs out of town. After WWII, some of my relatives went to Connecticut to work in aircraft or related industries. Other cousins to Springfield, MA. My brother Ben and others like him were partial commuters, returning on weekends. They were the second wave of job migration to America. Later, educated grads went all over American for jobs. The brain-drain is now fifty percent or more of our grads! But as more Northerners and mills went south, there was initially a kind of reverse displacement when, said a college professor, a lot of Southerners, especially African Americans, sold lands and small farms that had been theirs since after the Civil War and moved to Detroit and environs to work in the expanding auto industry. But eventually, unsustainable salaries and benefits spelled disaster when Japan made cars cheaper and better. The trend is now reversed, as prosperity has now come to the Southeast and Southwest where jobs and the sun are magnets. As a result, our growth in RI has been largely in service-related jobs that aren't as remunerative as industrial jobs once were. Will biotech, computers, financial services, arts, and tourism be saviors? We're one of three states losing population. Woonsocket has dropped from 49,816 people to 41,195.

But unlike factory work that didn't encourage or require education, today's jobs usually do. This puts dropouts, always numerous in the city and state, in an unenviable situation. The *Providence Journal* recently stated there are good jobs out there, but many 20-25-year-olds don't have the education for them. As it was for people like my folks, the state has always been a target for newcomers, who most times don't arrive with diploma or degree in hand. But we spoke of our reputation as basically unfriendly to business due to high taxes, licensing delays, bureaucracy, some bad schools, and corruption. Added to that are our state and city financial woes due to unsustainable largess to its retirees, now being mended. Ramifications are Central Falls, once a Franco bastion, had to be rescued from bankruptcy and Woonsocket's finances were monitored by the state for a while. A survey revealed our two top attractions are our beaches and colleges. But state aid to our colleges has declined (URI once covered 75 percent of student tuition; now 25 percent). Luckily, out-of-state students, who pay more, help some. We noted the high number of RI kids who are in special education (state: 29,000 or 20 percent; Woonsocket, 22 percent; the nation, 12 percent) has hurt our job readiness image. Especially when many jobs now require post high school education. But academe has not helped since college costs have risen faster (400 percent) than almost any other "business." Some have blamed the federal government's loan and scholarship "generosity," which colleges, with their questionable administrative costs and McMansion facilities have used to raise their prices, knowing the government will up its help. But no more. How do you tell a young college graduate who's jobless that she was perhaps imprudent in amassing over $100,000 in school debts? (The average debt, however, is a third of that!)

It's almost like the housing crisis of 2008 and on. It was a dream so cherished. Did some spend too much to get something they didn't have the money for? It makes one wonder how other nations keep education so affordable? I repeat my own theory that whatever Americans desperately want – like education, health, private housing - manipulative forces put them out of reach for a lot of people because of the greed for high profits of Wall Street and mega banks. "*Seulement pour les riches*," (only for the rich), to cite mom. Yes, capitalism may be one of the best economic systems possible but only if regulated as Presidents T. Roosevelt and Wilson both deduced and tried to rein in. With so many now in poverty across the land, one report said one-third of the federal budget goes to meet peoples' needs. I'm not wishing to be alarmist, but it isn't as bad (yet) as the French Revolution where *les citoyens* (the citizens) said, "We have nothing to lose but our chains." But today's Americans are not known for their patience. From the study of the history of nations, is it almost a given that in time there comes a catastrophic divide between the have and have nots?

Once again, the recent migration was more of an intellectual vector than job relocation. With mills and other jobs gone and distant commuter jobs limited by the exigencies of time and travel, Francos, often chided by dad for not pursuing higher education as avidly as other nationalities, finally turned to education for knowledge and training. At one time, detractors called us "Canariens," as in: know-nothing Canadians. These attainments now took them all over the country in a kind of ultimate melting pot odyssey. As my Boston College professor noted about early come French Canadians, no longer would newly-marrieds bound for the mills "live across the street from their parents." Initially, many just wanted a mill job and naturalization, but not assimilation and education. Now that has changed.

As a result, it also meant that by the end of the 1980s decade, Francos constituted less than 50 percent of the city's ethnic stock. Wasn't it 25 or 30 percent higher at one time? Of course, not all the city's Francos spread out wide. Many went to the burbs of North Smithfield, Lincoln, Cumberland, Smithfield, Blackstone, and Bellingham while continuing to shop and sometimes school in the city. This migration caused, said a report, a building boom in those towns, gobbling up a lot of pastures and farmlands (including *oncle* Napoléon's farm on Pound Rd. in Cumberland), and a disparity of income levels between former urban mill centers like Woonsocket, Central

Falls, Pawtucket, Providence, West Warwick, and the more prosperous suburbs and exurbs. Mobility was always ingrained in Americans. One report said in a four or five-year period, 40 percent of Americans move. Another said the average life of a mortgage is only seven years! The South, somewhat poor for over a hundred years after the Civil War, saw tremendous growth with lower costs and taxes, sun, tourism, auto industry, and no Social Security or pension taxes.

Since my career was education, I've followed closely the court-contested battle of the state's school money distribution system. Not generally "a wealthy state," especially now, it's too bad RI can't satisfy the needs of both cities and towns. The situation has created an unhealthy disparity in statewide assessment scores. Limited means has also created a mindset of dependency that is necessary or expected in the poorer cities mentioned. Thus, it doesn't project the importance education should have with voters who should be willing to pay a greater share for the education they want. Because the state has money problems of its own, what will those cities do now when the state can no longer give them what they want or need? In those urban communities, what will be the fate of enrichment programs, AP classes, sports, music, the arts, and smaller class sizes? How do we help achieving school systems continue prospering, while also helping the underachieving ones reach New England and national standards and parity with the suburbs and exurbs, even if an MIT prof said that couldn't be done? Unschooled parents, single parent families, weak English skills, poverty, lack of academic models, poor neighborhoods are causes not easily cured.

Touching again on privacy, there was almost no single-family residence on our street, except for our Carle landlord whose house and bakery were across our street and the Lavergne Market people near Kendrick Avenue. Most proprietors lived in one of their own houses and absentee landlords were somewhat rare. They watched over their holdings with a very close eye, assessing damage when they came around to collect the rent. Mom, perhaps envisioning a black-clad, unfeeling property owner (see movies of that era) casting us out into the cold, warned us not to cause damage to his property. With the Cochrane tragedy and a close call during the Depression, homelessness in her mind probably ranked close to the devil and sin. Aren't mothers the tenacious guardians of the amenities of life: nutrition, hygiene, comfortable housing, warm clothing, besides an unbounded affection for their families?

Respecting the neighbor's property was the stuff of the 7th Commandment, which we learned in school. The Age of Rip-off or Vandalism it was not. As I noted, in our community there was no wealth disparity to excite envy and thievery. Now, because wealth is displayed everywhere, we have house break-ins, murders, car thefts, and store robberies, to name a few.

That's why in some cities even leaving your car running while shopping is a violation, because it's juvenile jailbait. It happened when I worked at Norton High School. A work-study counselee of mine not only stole a running car near school, but also killed the owner's mother-in-law who was in the back seat by setting the car on fire. She was the police chief's mother! My now deceased good friend and faculty colleague Paul Mongeon picked up "one of our students" as he hiked back to Norton High, not knowing the student had just done the deed near the Paul Dever School in Taunton. He was caught that night and got 20 years.

I find it strange criminals when interrogated on television can't cite moral slippage for what they've done. Then we hear social theorists cite the effects of poverty, broken families, lack of supervision, depression, bullying, et al. Each may have a kernel of truth, but for us, we at least always knew the moral law, because everything we did or didn't do was measured on that innate and biblical ten-point scale, the Decalogue (Commandments). Recently an author wrote that fear of social embarrassment rather than fear of the law, human and divine, is now the prevailing restraint in many people's minds. Because I believe the Founding Founders meant to insure us "freedom of religion" and not "freedom from religion," I'm not against posting Moses' Commandments from God in school or in courts if it helps. "How will they know, if no one teaches them," as was written, and is now too common. And we're talking about human decency, neighborliness, and the golden rule, underwriting almost every Commandment, as Christ said, and the judiciary.

If more is needed, add character formation, safeguarding one's reputation, and maintaining integrity, as is now being taught and emphasized at the Naval Academy after a spate of immoral behavior by young Middies a while back. Recruits in all three Academies now reflect the moral slippage of society, including sexual misbehavior. When as a counselor I visited all three academies, two were still reeling from cheating scandals, now epidemic in all walks of life. An opportunist explained you must succeed at all costs, like the steroidal use argument now affecting professional and Olympic athletes. What's the answer? Are we worse than ever before or just better informed about each other's failings? I repeat later, "Character is what you stand for; reputation is what you fall for."

Tenement living made it convenient to report damage to our apartment and get money for improvements. But landlords were tight by today's standards. They only gave out small sums for ameliorations after several requests and if we did the work ourselves, like painting, wallpapering (bought usually from the Pinault *de* Nevers hardware store in Social) and repairs in and out of the apartment. It gave us a sense of ownership and made us good renters. One year *les* Carpentiers, Houles, *et* Telliers painted the hallway from top to bottom, with fathers and sons working side by side. Another time, dad and Bob insulated the attic. For mom, it was a *chez nous* (our home) moment, as if our own home, the one she wanted so much: "For all sad words of tongue or pen, the saddest are these, "It might have been." Who hasn't experienced its veracity and poignancy umpteenth times in life? Doesn't it also resonate with poet Robert Frost's *"The Road Not Taken"*? Or mom's *"The House Not Bought"*? And "if,": A small word, but it holds so much water.

Since there were children of your age in your tenement, you were like family in their homes. The neighbor's kid was like one of theirs, with any number of surrogate-like parents seeing him or her grow from infancy to adolescence, given the high degree of permanence in the 'hood. Besides welcoming you, families shared their fare, gave good advice, and always inquired about your parents' well-being, your success in school, scouting, altar boys, and church choir if a girl. Because you weren't some distant neighbor's kid, there was very little they didn't know about you. So, you forged a reputation either as *un bon garçon* (a good boy) or, God forbid, *un mal élevé*: a badly brought-up kid, reflecting badly on your parents. But never said to a kid's face. Long before Hilary's book, it was understood it took a village to raise a kid, beginning of course with *une bonne famille* (a good family). Those immigrant families did it superbly, a tradition from the country of their birth. Once our culture's most cohesive force, now tottering.

Psychologists now say it's the absence of that nuclear family linkage that is the source of alienation and rootlessness at the heart of many teenage suicides and violence. With no extended support system except a tenuous one at home, and perhaps already stressed by internal family disruptions or dysfunctions, they suffer disproportionately from poor grades, loss of boyfriend/girlfriend, or the inability to fit in at school or neighborhood. Suicide or a violent rampage, as seen in the Columbine and Newtown bloodbaths are, in their confused minds, an escape, relief, or justification that often ends with their own suicide! At a conference given by a child psychologist, my wife Patricia and I heard him say every article he collected over 20 years about juvenile criminal behavior always mentioned the word "loner." I was shocked when one article he read was about that Norton workstudy student of mine. He feared the military wouldn't take him because he'd been arrested before. Aren't most "smash-and-grab" thieves chronic looters?

So, because neighbors knew you and your parents, there was a strong neighborhood ethic of expected behavior. The fear of having your parents told by a neighbor of misbehavior, like fighting, cursing, and damaging property, usually made "cowards of us all," as Shakespeare describes a fear-shaped conscience. Generally, parents weren't as threatened being told something negative about you, since they all enforced the same rules. One model was madame Carpentier who, if she mildly chided you, did it with a smile and tenderness. At one time or another we all stood "before the bar of the neighborhood court." So, this was one of the moral buttresses of our life where church, school, family, neighborhood, and the community-at-large spoke and reinforced the same message. Who had the wisdom to put it all together? Who broke it up?

In our 'hood, the serious misbehaviors of some of today's teens - binge drinking, drugs, driving to endanger, breaking and entering, physical abuse of elders, lewd behavior, and even murder were unknown. It was almost like the biblical reminder "that evil should not even be mentioned among you." Any quick perusal of today's newspapers about juvenile misdoings reveals how all that's changed now among young people of all ethnic groups. True, human nature doesn't change, so perhaps there's some validity that juvenile crimes today, like all crimes for that matter, are much better reported, thus the illusion (?) of greater occurrence. That notwithstanding, it is hard to argue against the severity and numbers of today's youth crimes compared to the old days. Society has been so shocked by teens committing so-called adult crimes, they are now being punished with long sentences. The law's "tough love." I shudder at a teen gone for life, a loss of human capital. (I am, however, opposed to a life sentence without parole for teenagers.)

If those repeaters commit 60-70 percent of all crimes – "recidivism" is the term - I'm partial to more jail time to keep them away from the public. But all told, we're talking about two or more million incarcerated people, each costing some $40,000 a year while in jail; at least three times more than what we spend on a child's education. Crime doesn't pay, but it's damn expensive. People are shocked the incarcerated may get heart transplants and a sex change. A poor man who needed a new heart considered crime and jail to get one. One criminal psychologist said we must accept some individuals will never want to live according to the laws of God and society. If they couldn't make it before in polite society with their meager education, weak moral character, and dysfunctional upbringing, how can they succeed when out again? Repeat offenders are as high as 80 percent in our state! Again, have you noticed almost everyone trying to avoid arrest has an outstanding warrant? It's why more cops are injured and killed each year. Some with two offenses fear the "three strikes-you're-out" law in some states.

Causes abound, but you must think the vanished neighborhoods of yesteryear are also causative. Are those vicious urban gangs a truncated attempt to give their followers a sense of turf and friendly support those long-ago neighborhoods of immigrant America once did so well? The kind of places which the military's former Chairman of the Joint Chiefs of Staff, Colin Powell, says kept him on the straight and narrow. And speaking about the role of family, wasn't the late NY Senator Patrick Moynihan prophetic when he predicted in the early 1980s the growing dissolution of the American family would have tremendous repercussions in 2000 and beyond? The cry wasn't heeded "to circle the wagons" or "stop the bleeding," so more and more kids now go to school from splintered homes. The challenge for the single and often overburdened, impoverished, and valiant parent is tremendous, because these children are more prone to delinquency and dropout. At a convention, we counselors were told to look out for "fatherless kids." But not all of them as many single mothers are to be commended for their valiant efforts.

The Piazza or Porch Culture

"THE FRONT PORCH has always been a brand of Americana. It is definitely an American institution, and the nostalgia continues to live on. Few front porches are found in countries outside of our shores. Like in the movie *Oklahoma!*, it was ingrained in our lifestyle." So wrote Grover Brinkman, a freelance Illinois journalist. His thoughts on the subject would have received a resounding chorus of approval from Francos of yesteryear because the porch or *galerie* played a vital social and familial role in their lives.

Fortunately, the nostalgia lives on in the city and elsewhere since hundreds upon hundreds of tenement houses are still bedecked with them. (Even if the Depression dealt a final blow to their construction.) In the past, like the marketplace of old, they were *la mise en scène* or daily stage for many sounds and sights of francophonie. In a case of déjà vu, even modern homes are now bringing back so-called farmers' porches, even if you rarely see people sitting or conversing there.

But like the passing of much of our culture, many porches have sagged under the relentless weight of time and elements. In some tenements, they're like the decaying features of a former beauty. But in remodeling their tenements, many homeowners, absentee or residing, have restored them to their former pride, sometimes replacing their rotting wood columns with more enduring aluminum ones that look, dare we say, like French wrought iron! Why the enduring fascination? Many aver that to eliminate those porches altogether would mar the customary facades of those creations of a bygone industrial mill town era.

The functions of those porches were almost too numerous to count. Like a Mohammedan muezzin in his minaret, your cry went out to say hi to a passing friend; bid the ragman, iceman, or fruit peddler to stop his horse or wagon; display bunting and flags on patriotic days; talk to other porch dwellers on levels below or above you. And for us, sip homemade root beer on a summer's eve or lick a five-cent cone; string a small clothesline for small items like diapers, stockings, undershirt; call kids for the evening meal or day's end; and escape the stifling summer heat.

Our own tenement house had three long porches for the six families living on one side or the other of the three floors in front. Two more families without a porch lived in the sunless rear. Mom who often spoke about the recuperative powers of bathing in salt water and the sun's rays felt sorry for them. When she read her feuilleton while absorbing *"notre baim du soleil"* (our sun bath), in that moment "God's in His heaven," as poet Robert Browning wrote, and "All's right with the world."

For five or six months a year, families like ours made almost daily use of the porch. In the summer, we, including diapered infants, were out there since air conditioning was unknown. How often she repeated, *"L'air conditioné cée (c'est) pour les riches."* (Air conditioning is for the rich.) But accepting your status in life was a Franco trait, reflecting the paraphrased line of poet Tennyson: "Ours is not to reason why / Ours is but to do and die." For the poor, always the double play choice of slim and none.

But what a grownup privilege to sleep on the couch-like swing on the porch! Families on the first floor, like les Capentiers et Bérubés, had a smaller swing hanging from the ceiling by chain links, but because their porch was a public access, it forbade any sleeping convenience. Theirs was used for outdoor parlor games when it was too hot or rainy to play on the street or backyard.

Speak about being under the watchful eyes of your parents! Because many of our neighborhood games (excepting quoits) were played in the street after supper, we were always subject to their instant praise or reproof. Any boisterous, reckless, or *pas-beau* (not nice) conduct, like fights, name-calling, or hair pulling always drew instant reprimands from our parental Moses atop their Mount Sinais. A belligerent child who did not heed the initial warning was ejected from the playing field: *hors du jeu*, as in "You're outta here." Armageddon was an angry parent dislodging himself and hauling the renegade in by the collar or with a little "moral uplift" (persuasion in the posterior, a writer quipped about kids being "brought up by hand"). How mortifying it was for parent and child! But the Greek chorus or porch jury always approved. It might be their turn the next day!

But parents didn't care what the scene looked like in public if on top of misbehavior you added the unforgivable sin of disobeying your parents in front of others. You paid the price, because parents were intensely proud or *fiers* about the behavior of their children. Present child psychologist John Rosemond's lament about declining parental authority would not have included them: "We are in the throes of a national emergency, one that could spell more serious consequences for the future than the water shortage, the energy deficit, inflation, unemployment, or the national debt. America is suffering a shortage of authority figures." Granted, it might have been easier for our parents, because authority then was considered inviolable throughout society in general. The dreaded curse of "doing my own thing" had not yet dawned. Nor the mantra "this is a free country, and nobody can tell me what to do." No doubt today's clashes between parental authority and teenage rebelliousness underlie the million "throwaway kids" who are thrown out, or leave on their own, not infrequently from small towns to the big cities. In the 1920s, author Sherwood Anderson debunked the notion that small-town America was all peaches and cream.

In his reflections on the porches of yesteryear, Brinkman also relates young romance bloomed on those porch swings. But I never saw any evidence of it in our neighborhood. Francos were very discreet in this matter, but I saw a variation of "passing through the (dating) gauntlet." In those days, dating was a newsworthy item on the neighborhood grapevine circuit. Young lovers walking hand in hand below those porches were stared at, talked about, and verbally teased. If two young people could go through that, they had something going. "Nary a thorn among the roses," a poet said. Going to Mass together on Sunday, the Laurier Theater on Friday night, and downtown Main Street Saturday night for a cabinet or milkshake at Brown's drugstore were like pre-society page highlights.[26] Shades of Thornton Wilder's *Our Town* about how little things have lifelong histories. If mom saw a young couple in these stages, like gossip columnists Hedda Hopper and Louella Parsons, she said, "*Cée sérieux.*" (It's serious.) There's no way a new couple with possible marital intentions could keep their romantic musings under wraps if they came up or down Gaulin and passed by either hers or *tante* Marie-Louise's porch. With 13 kids between them, they qualified as "incurable romantics" in their insatiable curiosity to know the warp and weft (the two directions of thread in cloth; a fitting mill city figure of speech!) of our life.

But there were other commentators. Again, like a Greek chorus, other gallery gods chimed in with their comments about the lovebirds.

---

[26] A coffee cabinet is a type of milkshake popular in Rhode Island and southeastern MA made with coffee ice cream, coffee milk and coffee syrup blended together.

"Earl's Pearls" (a term for society writings of a Boston columnist) were their families' reputation or character ("*du bon monde*" – good people); place of the parents' origin *au* Canada (mom, the Atlas); the young lovers' looks and behavioral traits; and his or her overall suitability as a marriage mate: *un ou une future* (his or her future). A good young man was *un bon garçon*; a good girl, *une bonne fille* ("the girl next door" in American parlance). It was like the community elders passing judgment on the worthiness of an impending union. If you passed all those evaluations, it was like premarital classes, with the assurance yours would be a good marriage. Recall my chapter on mom's patois about what the community said if you didn't choose a mate wisely. People couldn't spell "indissolubility," but lived it, since marriages were "until death do us part." You had to get it right the first and only time.

Dating as we now know it, that is, going out with whom you like best at the present time, was generally unknown. It's only when you separated yourself from the guys or gals you socialized with in your late teens and started dating seriously that steps to engagement and matrimony occurred. But above all else in the dating game, there were two vital elements in the continuation of our life and culture. One, of course, was marrying French-Canadian; two, marrying Catholic, almost a corollary of the first. True as that was for us, I was surprised how vehemently the strict choice of nationality by many could be expressed at one time, as one writer reported: "Intermarriages with outside nationalities was considered a crime against God and a natural abomination." Wow! But for Catholics, any irregularity, like another religion, or none, usually meant the wedding was private (no Mass) and in the rectory and with a promise from the non-Catholic to raise children in our faith; now no longer. But I could tell from her hushed tone to dad that a Catholic marrying in front of a Justice of the Peace was eye-raising. It was because it wasn't sacramental or Catholic and often resulted in severance from the faith, a most shocking aftermath at the time, however infrequent. My *Boston College* magazine reported 46 percent of Catholics in such marriages initially no longer practice. But about half return, especially for Baptism and sometimes Confirmation for their children who otherwise can't marry Catholic. Pope Francis is easing the cost and process of those who seek dispensation from their vows. The local parish priest is now a counselor-confessor.

The time Rachel brought her future husband to meet my parents became another humorous family story. When he left and we turned to our matriarch for her appraisal, she declared, "*Ya d'lair smatte mais yé t'irlanda*": nice but Irish (she used that nationality interchangeably at times for English, Scottish or non-Franco). Because of or despite that assessment, she did become Mrs. Donald Clark, and he affectionately called her "Mem." And when minding their kids, she delighted teaching some French words to either Donald Jr., or David, or Christopher. They also reveled in dad's applesauce. Professionally, the family was in the vanguard of New Englanders leaving for the South for career reasons. The locus of Don's career was with Texas Instruments in So. Attleboro until promoted to direct a new plant in Johnson City, TN., then a move to Plano, TX, before retiring to Williamsburg, VA.

For kids like us, porches were literally good jumping-off points. In wintertime, the second story porch *de la famille Houle* (of the Houle family) provided us with a good 12-to-15 foot jump into snow piles below. One day after work, dad saw our foolhardy bravado and put a stop to it. We never tried jumping from our third-floor porch but thought about it. On a previous jump from the second floor, I'd gone clear through the snow to the ground, so I took his advice. Otherwise, I might be known as "Shorty" today!

Since tiny tots could slip through the balusters of the porch rails, dad put a protective screen cover over them and a three-inch high wire over the railing. *Madame* Bernadette Beauregard, who later shared our porch with her family (husband Alfred, sons Robert *et* René, daughters Violette *et* Rina), told mom and me about a near tragedy at a previous tenement. Heeding one of her children's entreaties, she ran out to the porch and grabbed her child as he was about to fall. An expert seamstress, she had mom's admiration for her sewing skills and quick manner. Obviously thinking of the rescue, she said: "*C'tune couseuse qui va vite.*" (She's a seamstress who is fast.) Mom was also a good seamstress if she had a pattern: *un patron,* often a gift from *tante* Laurence.

Since the porch was one continuous length from one family to the other with an access door in the middle, you shared the middle section. The porch provided a place for small talk and friendly banter. We said *monsieur* Beauregard was a mover (*un déménageur*) who traveled all over the country for Bourcier Movers. He held us spellbound with stories about traversing states we only knew from our beat-up geography books. Once he told us how he and his partner slept under their truck in open desert (no travel allowance for Joe's Dry Gulch Motel?) only to discover in the morning a snake lying on one of them. After that slithery serpentine surprise (my English prof would've loved my "sibilant" or "s" alliteration), they put up a mover's rope around the four tires to form a protective ring. Later, a television story confirmed the trick about snakes not crawling over ropes! For the snake's role in the Garden of Eden fall from grace, weren't they condemned to crawl in the dirt?

Since cars were almost non-existent in our neighborhood, we thought of ourselves as traveling the highways and byways of America on the fanciful wings of *monsieur* Beauregard's stories. He was our Charles Kuralt on the road or Steinbeck's *Travels with Charlie,* since we had neither books nor *National Geographic* magazines. To us, whose fathers always returned home from work every day, it blew our minds he could be gone for a whole week. How did you get from here to there? What vistas lay beyond our circumscribed city world where everyone and everything near and dear to us was within walking distance? Almost like a microcosm of our state! America was bound "from sea to shining sea," but until scouting, many of us had never been beyond the Blackstone River! Kids like me in those days dreamed of being a fireman or policeman: visible public figures. But a mover also seemed: "a moveable feast." He said he mastered the art of getting the most out of his truck space. Not surprisingly, dad praised that since he too worshiped order and economy in all things. Kinda' like Ben Franklin's "Waste not, want not," saying applied to a truck space.

Even though mule-spinner dad was respected in the mill trade, but at times unemployed, he spoke out loud once about being a mover. (I chuckled in college when my theology prof called God "The Prime Mover"; I wondered what He displaced!). Probably because of us five high-energy kids and not wanting him to be away from the house more than eight hours a day, mom told him he didn't have "*une forte constitution*" or robust health, like our neighbor did. Like dad's father, *monsieur* Beauregard was Paul Bunyaneske, a physique you didn't often see in male Francos. But gentle.

But before *les* Beauregards became our next-door neighbor, we shared the porch with a family whose father was a maniacal, demented tyrant. He was subject to fits of rage, which reduced his piteous wife to a quivering mass. We related his daughter, whose boyfriend he objected to, ran away one day and was never heard from again. One day she endeared herself to my impecunious state by giving me a nickel tip for the morning *Boston Daily Record*. Did she want the train schedule for her getaway?

What a battle royal ensued between him and fearless mom when he tore into diapered Rachel for wetting the neutral terrain. At her best if we were attacked unjustly, our *coeur-de-lion* (lion-hearted) mom stood her ground, repulsed his angry outbursts with well-timed zingers, and saw him slink back into his apartment. And dad, always a stickler for cleanliness and hygiene (he hated germs, the devil, and inflation in that order) asked me to fetch the sailor mop "to swab the deck." At first, cowed by our neighbor's tirade, irrepressible Rachel (Coucou) looked on the scene with wide-eyed wonderment, unaware she had touched off a Gallery War in one of the city's tenement galaxies. Ah! Privacy, the last bastion of true wealth, have we lamented already? The poor need not apply. Their nation is congestion!

As with so many other pieces of Americana passing from the scene, perhaps we're the poorer for the gradual disappearance or disuse of those skyline niches (or eagle's aeries) we called *les galleries*. Poorer perhaps because they bound us to family, domestic felicity, and neighbors, at one time this country's most cohesive forces before the auto separated us, as a writer said.

Michael Walsh, Universal Press Syndicate writer, also blamed a big part of urban malaise on their disappearance, since many people hardly know their neighbors now. In an article in the *Providence Journal*, he pined for their return. "In many ways, a front porch is a metaphor for domestic life. Wide and open, a porch is to a house what a smile is to a face. It gives a home or farmhouse a friendly countenance. And reaching out as it does, a porch is also something of an architectural handshake extended to visitors long before they reach the door." Hearing Walsh's tribute, Francos would've said, "Hey, we've got that!" Yes, it's how Francos on their porches greeted you. Of their conviviality, mom said, "*Ils sont du monde recevant*" they greet the world, or like the Motel 6 commercial, "They always left the light on for ya."

That Wonderful Gang of Mine

Despite an enormous amount of socializing opportunities today, the fear of raising "the loner child" exists more than it once did, since one-child families are common with women having only 1.9 children, said one report; another said 1.1 children. How different the situation was from the turn of the century to the 1930s, '40s, and postwar! Even though most Canadian-born parents like mine raised fewer children than in their own families, good-sized families were the rule and not the exception. It was commonplace in any tenement block of six to eight families that almost every child had an alter ego of his or her own age and sex.

But now, single-parent or smaller families, private ownership of homes thinning out kids over a wider area, and the mobility of the American family, all make childhood friendships today harder to find and cultivate near one's own home. Commonly, a youth's associations and friendships are now formed around school, church, civic, cultural, sports groups and activities. Certainly, all good outcomes, but a caveat concerns bullying. Some 20 percent of the kids don't find acceptance and are subject to physical and social rejection in these environments. Schools are now addressing the problem. Also, these distant groupings require a tremendous amount of chauffeuring by parents, solicitous to see their child achieve connection, communication, and participation with peers. It's why minivans and SUVs are crucial for "soccer moms!" Kids have 70 percent of their play regulated or scheduled, unlike ours was. But now would its absence mean more TV and video game time instead of outdoor play like we enjoyed? Girls usually play outside far less than boys. Twenty minutes a day, the latest stat.

A child psychologist lamented this regulated play has caused the virtual disappearance of youngsters' free time and creative play. Excessive programmed play with its league practices, schedules, and travel outside home all bring attending pressures on kids as well as parents. And far more knee and arm injuries or strains, a physician recently reported, since kids go from sport to sport, or play the same sport all year, using the same muscles. Some episodes of practice or game confrontations between parents and coaches or their child's opponents have produced melees of criminal dimensions, even homicide. Hey, we're talking potential college scholarships or even pro sports here, even if a very small percentage achieve that. (Less than 5 percent in Division I scholarship schools.) A letter from a Southern school teacher-friend in an urban school told me it's what her kids dream about, "not studying or a 9-to-5 job or any career outside the stadium, court, or arena." A black educator said over 90 percent would achieve their goals with studies, but only 5 percent in sports. No doubt many are unduly influenced by newspaper and television sports reporting those mega-million salaries. Fewer now, but how many pro athletes still have no clue how to handle their earnings, or think their career will last forever? Athletes in one pro sport are notorious for having children out of wedlock. The reality is that a pro's career usually ends at an age when other professions are ascending into high gear. Did I hear right that 70 percent of cut/retired NFL players face bankruptcy two years after? Was their education worthy of the name? Or just eligibility!

Parents watched us play in the yard or in the street, especially on long summer evenings, but in all my 17 years at home I never saw a parent at our daylong sandlot games at St. Ann's Park, Cass Park, or behind Bell Spinning across the Kendrick Street Bridge. By and large, we made our own rules, and in disagreements, the people's court was us. But once I did play softball against dad at St. Ann's Park in a game organized by Mr. Jannell, our scoutmaster. I was crushed when I dropped a flyball with dad nearby. An excellent judge of talent, did he think I was going to the mills instead of the Red Sox, our fantasy in those days? Perhaps that's why *mémère* never knitted red stockings. Not oblivious of more primal urges, religion and economics were some of the causes of large Franco families and a plethora of friends in childhood. Catholic doctrine emphasized procreation as well as mutuality of affection. As it still intends today, but with less emphasis it seems, at least from couples, as is often evident in "richer, better-educated cultures." The marriage vow was sealed with the promise of begetting and raising children into God-fearing, God-loving people. And as many as God sent, since any kind of artificial interruption of conception was virtually unknown. (The first book ever published on the subject was during the presidency of Andrew Jackson in the 1820s, said one bio.) Only abstention agreed upon by both husband and wife could limit the size of a family, apart from any natural preventive condition. Otherwise, the sole refraining partner could be guilty of serious sin, which incredibly, mom said once with some difficulty. A lot of stuff she said went over my head at the time but came back when I recorded her weekly over the years. About the size of families now, is the cost of raising a child - near a million, not counting education - a weighty consideration? It's noteworthy that there were fewer births in the 2008 recession.

As mentioned by local historian Alton P. Thomas in Woonsocket, the mill economy also encouraged large families. Said the author: "This is how the French working class survived and how French parents were able to support such large families. When all those pay checks came in from their grown children, many could buy their own homes or set aside a nice nest egg for their retirement--if they were lucky." Older children at home, as I witnessed, only kept a small allowance from their own wages. But bless 'em, what parents often did was to spend only what was needed for room and board, often surprising their marrying children with a nice *boni* (bonus) to help them get a start: "*Commencer leur chez eux*" (start their home) mom said tenderly.

I don't know a single facet of our life she didn't comment on. With her bristling, curious life beat, we often got an instant commentary on the whole modus operandi of our way of life, whose memory these writings will hopefully preserve. With only one radio, an occasional movie, elementary education, and a lower middle-class mill culture, fortunately parents like mine were daily pedagogues teaching, instructing, shaping our whole persona. But I related a disturbing report that television, electronic information, and forces outside the home, friends especially, and other factors, now exercise a greater influence on kids' upbringing than parents! Scary, but better than none.

Faith-wise, for example, it's probably why (with the help of a vast Catholic school system) parents were so successful in transmitting the faith whole and inviolate, unlike one or two future generations removed where 40 percent of all Americans have left "the faith of their fathers." Another 25-30 million "in the mist" don't practice their faith. The increase in "Nones" – people who claim no religious affiliation – has caused seven thousand churches of all denominations to close every year. Father John A. Kiley in the *Rhode Island Catholic* wrote "The individual Catholic was not prepared for post-1960s individualism, pluralism (author: hundreds of different sects and beliefs), and faithless secularism. The novelty within the church's liturgical and religious life, plus premarital sex, drugs, homosexuality and abortion, aided by the intrusive entertainment industry, along with the move to affluent suburbia were the several loose cards which shook the

20th century Catholic Church. And the disintegration of the Catholic family through divorce, through inattention to authentic gender roles, through Sabbath disregard and through the embrace of rights over duties will be the fatal card to collapse America's Catholic Church." A recent report said Americans still believe in God, but not as much in church itself as a means to salvation. Pope Benedict hoped to bring back faith in Christ and His church. Hans Küng in *The Church* says worshipping together along with belief in Christ and Communion are the foundations of Catholicism and all Christian religions, all of whom owe their start in some way, however fraught with dissension, to Mother Church. He uses the word "daughters" for other churches, not to stress our superiority, but faith linkage. For too long we swiped at each other instead of looking for common faith elements.

With the indictment today against teen workers keeping all their earnings but saving very little in favor of here-and-now consumables, you must agree the old-time system had some merit to it. We already gave stats, but research also says young people often outspend their parents with fast foods, cars, cosmetics, clothing, concerts, videos, and phones quickly separating them from their specie. Digest again that "America's 33 million teenagers spend $100 billion (yes, not millions) annually and have a say in how their parents spend another $50 billion?" Involved in college placement for a great part of my 42-year career, I also read that collegians, once considered one of the "poorest segments" of our population, have a per capita credit card bill of around $3,000. One Ivy League girl, fearing her parents would be crushed, committed suicide over her $10,000 bill. Credit card companies on college opening day are now forbidden to give out credit cards like candy.

As I saw in one talented counselee, I tried to sell higher education to, he said he couldn't even afford community college, less than $2000 a year in MA at the time, because he had dropped $8,000 "on a set of wheels." He forgot all about oil and blew the engine. But I did succeed with his sister who was almost thrown out as an ill-disciplined and failing frosh. She pulled herself up to high honors when she became amazed, as she told me, her boyfriend played football, ate dirt, got dinged, and was pushed around three hours a day, and still got top grades. The incident was not unique, since as an earlier athletic director at Notre Dame HS, I often saw student-athletes finding direction and motivation from their sports, often with the encouragement and scrutiny of their concerned coaches. Notre Dame University often boasts athletes have a higher GPA than the rest of the school, an outcome not true, however, with some Division I basketball schools, which are notorious for very low graduation rates among their athletes. A former hoop star and grad couldn't get a job because he couldn't read and fill out a job application!

I expand on it later, but I mention here for reasons of custom, prudence in the matter of boy-girl relationships, and religious mores, boys at one time usually socialized with boys only, girls with girls. When I asked mom just once why that was, she simply said: *"Cée d'même qu'ça ya,"* meaning, that's the way it was. We related dating near young adulthood (21) was the acceptable prelude to marriage. Small wonder then in the wake of millions of adolescents having children out of wedlock, social critics again begrudgingly laud "the ancients" for being a little bit wiser about human nature and relationships than today's so-called experts. For one, the late Dominican Friar Joseph Lennon of Providence College wrote about the folly of our culture in this regard, promoting as it does the sexuality of our young people but hopefully not its activity. A case in point: teen pop music phenoms, even with obvious talents, quickly project themselves as desirable sex objects instead of their artistry. It probably accounts for their short shelf life, as rivals crowd the stage in turn with more outlandish lyrics, dress, and choreography. Some speak of the legacy of Janis Joplin, the first famous performer to die of a drug overdose. One report said musicians helped spread the drug culture.

But of course, our 'hood wasn't all like the Garden of Eden before the fall. One day, forgetting this was the same kid who in church took money from the poor box, I went downtown with him on a shopping spree. At day's end, I learned "his stash" was stolen from family guests whose coats and purses were on the master bedroom bed the night before - An inside job. He had called up to my third-floor bedroom window one Saturday morning, flashing a wad of bills "he earned." Walking downtown, we drank sodas, ate ice cream at Beaupré's, and bought a $6 baseball glove at Jack and Harry's. Besides a bike, a baseball glove then was about the best thing you could give a kid. We used both all day five or six months a year. He got nabbed, and for the second time I had to return something I wanted badly. (The first was the stolen bike Bob and I bought unawares.) So, I had to wait for Bob to join the navy and bring me back a real, professional glove. *La Gaulin*'s matriarchal Moses chided my judgment, if not my integrity: *"Comment penses-tu quia trouver c'targent-là?"*: How in my right mind did I think he got all that money? (About $25 in all.) A week's pay for a bobbin boy or doffer.

But it was a good neighborhood because of its people, permanence, numbers, and moral values. In it were new Americans born in the 20th century, more aware each day of its ideals, rich history, language, and culture. Our Canadian-born parents also grew fonder of their newly adopted country while remaining nostalgically bound to their roots. Every year another neighbor became a citizen after learning enough English and taking night classes. No doubt the motto *La Belle Province de Québec: Je Me Souviens*[27] (seen on Québec license plates: I remember) continued to stir fond memories. Many then, like mom, still had family there. But because of poverty, family bonds were kept alive only by sporadic letters. But the motorized Houle *famille* made many trips *au* Canada. About one excursion, mom told me *monsieur* Houle had eight flat tires with those rubber doughnuts of yesteryear. (Did our neighbors submit a travel log to our "Triple A" mom?)

To use baseball parlance, for my brothers Bob, Ben, and I, the boys of summer were at various times the Carpentier brothers: Paul André, Philippe, Marcel, Robert, *et* Lucien, the latter a Vietnam War casualty; cousins Roger and Eugène Peloquin; Maurice Vandal, Richard Bérubé, Roger *et* Robert Charron, Robert *et* Bernard Lanoie, Lucien *et* Normand Laferriere, Robert *et* Réne Beauregard, *l' autre* (the other) Robert Tellier, Henri et Maurice Houle, Robert Laplume, Robert Bourget, Roger Courtemanche, and future cartoonist Larry Champagne, who could draw anything (later an architect from RISD) and teach you to walk on your hands. Greg Bouley, lifelong friend, fellow Mountie, and future Brother of the Sacred Heart with me, and later African missionary, was also a close friend from *"la Cumberline"* street. I wrote for him when in civilian life he became Director of Welfare. He was incredibly successful in finding jobs for people (some at Mount).

Unlike now, girls were not as numerous as the boys, but with their lack of gregariousness in favor of fewer but deeper friendships, they also formed close bonds. Sue *et* Rachel had friends like Pierrette *et* Ghislaine Bérubé; cousines Doris *et* Connie Peloquin; Rina *et* Violette Beauregard; Rita *et* Solange Carpentier; Madeleine Carle, Lucille Laferriere, *et* Annette Tellier, from the other Tellier family. We kids were the neighborhood glue. One of the reasons why your folks got to know other parents well, in contrast to school, organized sports, and clubs like today. With the high price of energy, I've read about a desired trend to bring back the neighborhoods of yesteryear, with family needs and services all within walking distance, as they once were. The same reason a German bride in our North Smithfield neighborhood said her former American soldier who was once posted there, initiated a move to return. Six weeks of vacation! Because of its central location in Europe and multifaceted talents, Germany is always prosperous. The brightest exchange students I counseled at Norton HS were from Germany and Scandinavia.

Surely, it was a good feeling to belong, to know and be known, to share and enjoy with others, secure in your own family; and also part of a neighborhood that enveloped and nurtured you with its warmth, friendship,

---

[27] The Beautiful Province of Quebec: I Remember. (*Je Me Souviens* is Quebec's motto.)

values, and caring. None of us knew it wasn't like that for everybody. And sadly, that kind of societal lifestyle would one day see a lot of its pristine elements evaporate in that all-consuming melting pot.

Our gang! I could have sworn the word was French because mom who loved the 'hood and its people used it often. "*Toute la gang ensemble*," (The whole gang together) when, with dad at the mill, she saw us playing in our two-tenement yard. She didn't know that was a pretty good translation of the country's motto: E Pluribus Unum: "Out of many, one." And an extension of *chez nous* or home she and dad made for us, as other parents did for their kids. With also the friendship of other ethnics, no wonder the city was a happy, nurturing city where la joie de vivre could've been its motto.

It bears repeating that immigrants brought a lot of cultural richness to their new land, but none more important for national integrity, solidarity, and, yes, morality, than family and neighborhood. Their absence and longing for their return now fuel the preaching and moral urgings of the nation's religious leaders and family supporters. Especially as the "loner child" (not to be confused with "single child") sometimes threatens even the very lives of kids in their neighborhoods or, shockingly, the once peaceful and hallowed halls of learning in schools and college.

The Playing Fields of Eton They Were Not

A DENSELY POPULATED mill city like the Woonsocket of yesteryear offered us very few manicured playing fields like those of the renowned playgrounds of England's famous Eton School, which I visited with the Smokey and Maryanne Cerrone family and the Andover Prep hockey team in the early 1970s. But with typical youthful Yankee or Gallic ingenuity, we tenement dwellers whose yards were just hardscrabble strips of shin-scraping gravel between houses managed quite well.

With families running large, we were never without the first necessary element of play: playmates. We high-rise kids were close friends, not just acquaintances or seasonal teammates who went their separate ways after a game or season. In fact, I said if parents like mine were typical, you were sometimes reminded about too many friends. We mined our tenement and neighborhood friendships to the fullest because outside of scouting and school acquaintances, we children were each other's whole social life. Like our parents too, our social circuitry had a narrow grid but it was full and rich. We had relatives all over the city, but in general, no friends across town.

Street names were at one time an identifying trait of who you were. You'll recall we were the kids from *La Grosse* (Big) Gaulin, a turf name we took pride in. Some other kids we played against were the Independent Juniors of Diamond Hill, with Italian names like Richard Caselli, Chuck Dinunngio, Armando, and Rodney Delasanta. But they had some French-Canadian kids playing for them - Conrad Hamel, Mike Miclette, Normand Auclair, which kind of surprised us. And they did entice a kid named Charlie Gould to catch for them. He was later a state representative. He lived close to the cutting edge of both our neighborhoods in a house we once lived in off Mailloux and Cass.

We loved being active and pitied the girls who sat on porch swings and stoops, if not playing hopscotch, jumping rope, or running errands. With the implementation of Title 9 (equality of sports opportunity for girls) still 50 years away, few sports outside of a little parish softball and skating (roller and ice) were available to them. I cited a study about less osteoarthritis expected in later years in today's young women because of larger bone development from intense activity and exercise as seen especially in soccer, basketball, and track. But a caveat about playing sports forever, a study said women over 55 still playing tennis and golf, for example, are now getting 60 percent of knee operations. Does it run counter to "With proper care, our bodies could last us a lifetime?" A coach said women's wider hips mean less support for the knees. A special exercise is needed. In our play, the separation of the sexes was an extension of the same segregation we practiced in school and church

Fostered by Canadian tradition and the strict teaching of the Church, the diocese, for one, boasted all its high schools were single sex until the Academy, after boarding ceased, was the very first to go coed in the early 1970s under the direction of principal Brother Paul Demers. But this constant separation perpetuated a sexual innocence considered naïve or unnatural today. As we grew up, knowledge of procreation and of the male and female forms was arcane knowledge. Any sign of precocious curiosity or interest in those areas was considered well-nigh sinful or reprehensible. (In *Catherine the Great* (1729--1796) by Henri Troyat, he relates her angst at her total ignorance of the connubial arts and her mother Johanna rebuked her for asking. Luckily, when her marriage for royal accession was arranged, her husband Peter II got drunk and didn't show. He was ugly, uncouth, and unlearned with war games his only interest.)

Several times in my pre-teen years, for example, I inquired from mom how babies were born only to hear the usual "from the reservation" story: *chez les Indiens*. Of German Irish descent from New York, my wife Pat said her mother used the common stork story. Since there was no talk of human propagation from any individual or institution in our lives, how did elders think that knowledge transmitted? I don't mean today's sophomoric obsession with its supermarket tabloid physical aspects, but the procreative powers and duties of husband and wife. In my Canadian relative's book about the Fontaine/Morvan families, she too cites her premarital ignorance of procreation. Being a farm girl, she knew from animals there was a necessary physical chemistry. Marrying a more traveled and "knowing husband" (this without any elaboration), Upton Maher, she appreciated his patience before she learned the connubial arts. She obviously learned well, since they had just two fewer children than *Cheaper by the Dozen*, to borrow the comedy film title which starred one of my favorites, Clifton Webb.

As said, this silence or reticence about sexual matters represented a clear-cut moral stance on the subject. A stance they thought would also foster sexual integrity (the new Catholic Catechism speaks about this goal), a deep Christian respect for the sexes, and marriage and children usually only in adulthood. Almost the total reversal of our culture's infantile preoccupation with the matter (check out those comedies in prime time). Our parent's code, even if restrictive by today's standards, precluded the excesses of today's sexual revolution: teen marriages often doomed to failure; near a million teen pregnancies a year; 56 million abortions thus far (4,000 a year in RI); rampant immorality in word, action, and dress; deviant lifestyles; and unwed mothers as struggling heads of households, the new poverty class in America. As a guidance counselor whose work was largely college placement, I became convinced early motherhood and fatherhood, with or without marriage, were often a major cause of limited education and blighted careers. I was so pleased one year at Norton HS when I convinced a pregnant top honor girl not to forego her four-year nursing degree ambitions. Her mom offered to babysit, help that's unfortunately not often available today because of single and/or working mothers. But as hinted, a study said the extension of young people's education beyond their 20s may be a cause of delayed maturity today, so evident on college campuses. I've already discussed how college is not a true maturing experience because it's usually funded by parents, scholarships, or grants. But even if Professor Cottle at Boston College said few of us would ever work strictly in our collegiate field, he believed a college education gave you four more years to mature and the tools to learn the job a company hires you for. Graduation is proof you had the discipline to see it through, "stick-to-itive-ness," is not usually a young person's greatest asset. Too many, however, still drop out with finances more and more a factor. When I started counseling, I never would have believed college would cost what it does now. But the country seems to be waking up to the scandal of its outrageous costs that burden grads for 20 or more years. Is it why young people aren't marrying? I spoke to a couple, both professionals, who owed $87,000. But a report cited that not going even to a 2-year college is a $500,000 hit in lifetime earnings. Unskilled jobs are often the first to go in a downturn economy.

Coming back to my neighborhood discussion, a typical play day for us began by rounding up the gang. Any early riser came a-calling in the hallway or from the backyard. Soon a gang of six or seven would sit on the front steps to plan our course of action. The ability to improvise served us well when the Gaulin gang joined Troop 4. Invariably, if Scoutmaster Jannell asked the Patrols (ours was Daniel Boone) to put on an original skit, comical or serious (we once put on the Birth of Christ, with Magi and all), we always walked away with the prize. One time it was a whole bag of pennies, good for treats after the Monday night meeting! Not everyone in the gang knew the names of the three Magi (as mom told us in our home), but they carried their "gifts" well. But like our parents, we could only fantasize about gifts of gold, myrrh, and frankincense. Just spelling the last two was a challenge. In French "myrrh" has a final "e"; "frankincense" is *encens*; gold is *or*.

Because we loved baseball so much, we looked for an open field if we couldn't get St. Ann's Park. We played in the backyard (except on Washday Monday), using a cupped hand to hit a soft rubber ball or one of dad's woolen balls. After supper our game was in the street. One time as we played, I watched Philippe Turcotte, a young adult in our tenement, change a tire. Obviously in a hurry, he bolted out without putting the lugs back on. I ran to tell him the wheel was falling off. He later opened a junk car lot in Blackstone. We also played in a little open field next to the hospital superintendent's house (Mr. Leroy T. Cox) on Cass where Dunkin Donuts is today. And in a little patch of green near Bell Spinning Mill over the Kendrick Street Bridge, the same mill we saw flattened from our house by the 1938 Hurricane. The doors flew out, the roof heaved, and crashed. Playing there, we often had to retrieve foul balls from the Blackstone River behind home plate and the dirt road to the right of the bridge. Finally, we played at the bottom of the sandbanks (behind the Woonsocket Hospital laundry room) which sloped towards Sylvestre Pond. When tired of playing ball, we leaped over the top of those banks to land as far as we could below, never thinking about a landslide. Like at the beach, we buried ourselves up to our waist with our jump. It's why a child psychologist wondered how so many kids survive to adulthood! But didn't he know we had a guardian angel assigned to us at baptism, as seen in a holy card, hovering over a child at river's edge?

But with the Blackstone River zigzagging unfettered and accessible in parts of the city at one time, those celestial watchers were kept busy. But sadly, it's how my three-year-old nephew, Guilbert Bouffard, drowned after he threw his hat in and tried to recover it, so a playmate said. I never told anyone but officiating a soccer game at Sacred Heart School in Sharon, I felt a sense of dread about him at the very hour he drowned, as I learned the next day. Sue and Guil also raised Patricia, Julie, Denis, Claude, and Christine, encouraging them all to higher education, all largely paid for with their mom-and-pop upholstery and curtain business in Bellingham.

I never told mom about the kid packin' a gun at the sandbanks who wanted me to stop a bullet at 20 feet, like he said he had done. His was a real gambler's pistol, like the ones card sharks hid up their sleeve in our westerns or riverboat flicks. Gosh, how would mom have reacted if she knew what we did on a given day? But lucky for us, she was a legendary non-worrier and typical of boys, as I saw in my counseling career, we told her little about what we did and where we went. Just the opposite of the girls! As one Norton HS mother told me, her son's principal could be shot and he'd tell her nothing out of the ordinary happened that day. But her daughter told her everything. Like in the military, boys keep their mouths shut and don't volunteer.

Case in point. Both Bob and cousin Ray Peloquin increased their chance of surviving the war by not volunteering. Sailor Bob remembered as we watched a recent Iwo Jima film that he could've been involved in that embattled marine landing operation if he had said yes to fleet marine duty as a pharmacist's mate. Ray, a top test scorer and fluent in French, wished to stay with his 83rd Division for the Normandy landing. So, he said no to training to parachute into France to set up radio communication before June 6. In training in the states, he even refused to be discharged home when his knee acted up in boot training. He barely survived the Battle of the Bulge which caused him nightmarish dreams for years. He saw his close buddy die inches away in a foxhole when they were told to fire a bazooka they never trained for. It's so true that after a battle starts, all plans go bust, like they did on D-Day, said a tactician. And the fight is largely between opposing combatants. Soldiers say they don't fight for their country, but for the buddy next to them. Understandable.

Talking one day about *tante* Marie Louise Peloquin, who was solicitous about her children, but whose daughter Doris had been hit by a car, mom said the more you worried, the more happened to you. Life should be so simple for parents and their children's welfare! But everything was simple cause and effect for her forebears in France, so we read. But like all mothers, she was prudent, judging by her thousand-and-one you-be-carefuls: "*Prends soin.*"

Without a doubt, baseball was our great consuming sport, with only the adulation given to Brother Adelard's Mount Saint Charles's Flying Frenchmen hockey teams competing for most of our attention. And some great Woonsocket HS grid teams led by famed coach Gus Savaria. Most men and even some women were diehard baseball fans. Dad, for example, was quite knowledgeable about the game and had seen some of the greats play: Ruth (in Providence as well as Boston?), Gherig, Foxx, and Greenberg. Even mom said she saw major leaguers barnstorm at the Academy's field when it was one of the best diamonds in the 1920s until the 1938 Hurricane. Red Sox fans, mostly men, swore at Yankee luck, but dad said they won because of better players: "*des bons joueurs.*" I certainly agreed with him when I became a baseball buff and knew their stars, especially the '27 team (even if it was three years before I was born). To describe Yankee luck in the last innings, fans in the city used a little bathroom humor: "*Ils sont mardeux*" (They are shitty).

During the season, you had to know whether the Sox had won or lost the previous day, especially if on the road. Sources were the radio, *The Daily Record*, and in the afternoon, *The Woonsocket Call*. As all adult sports fans did, we kids too knew the Sox had last won the World Series in 1918. Dad said he was 22 at the time, never thinking he would die an old man (86) without another championship. About that unspeakable transaction, that is, the sale of Babe Ruth to the Yankees by a show-investing owner, he sighed, "*Ils l'ont vendu.*" (They sold him.) How many times I heard the owner's name, Harry Frazee, when "the Curse of the Bambino" surfaced again after another late-season collapse. He could have borrowed the money to finance a show, but thought Ruth was more saleable in 1919 after a down year. But the Sox finally became world champs in 2004. Some fans went to the cemetery to tell departed ones the Sox had risen from the dead! The gang was into card collecting and buying bubble gum in packages with one or two cards. From the newspaper, we knew about present and past stars of local vintage, as mentioned later.

Most kids also knew the players of all the teams (there were far fewer teams then), because before Curt Flood and free agency, they often played for the same team their whole career (like Musial and Williams), unless involved in occasional blockbuster trades. Their stats to fuel our backyard exchanges about our favorites came from the Sunday paper with pitching and batting records. I vied with Bob and Ben to get the sports page first after Mass. If you held it too long, a parent was called in "to arbitrate." Even the funnies were second choice. During the war, Bob brought home a buddy and the gob was amazed I knew every player of every team and their stats. Bob had not told him not to ask Abbott and Costello's "Who's on first?" An author said people in oral cultures often develop a good memory by necessity. Where else did you store or retrieve stuff, like my folks did?

What a thrill in the late 1930s when I saw my first Fenway Park Sox game and players Doc Cramer, Jimmy Foxx, shortstop Joe Cronin, and third sacker Jim Tabor. We sat in right field. Accompanied by Bob's older and rougher friends, even the 50-mile ride in an open truck with bad-shocks didn't dampen my enthusiasm. You didn't have to sell the family jewels to buy a ticket and park back them. It was my first time out of state!

When not in a pickup game, we kids spent hours playing Pitch and Catch. This we did from sidewalk to sidewalk, in the road, or in our yard from the base of a little retaining wall to an abandoned bakery whose brick wall bounded *notre cour* (our yard) on one side. You made your bones as a catcher if you could handle the fastball of the older kids, like Bob and Paul Carpentier. If you couldn't handle a pitch or if thrown too high, you had to duck to avoid the punishing ricochet. We also enjoyed Grounders. Two players vied to commit fewer errors over nine innings by cleanly handling a rubber ball thrown against the cement wall foundation of the Lanoie apartment. A grounder fielded cleanly was an out. A miscue was a run. Paul and I were the best, dueling often in 1-0 or 2-1 games. He married Georgette Bastien, the only girl we knew who could really play softball. One marvels today at the skills of the girls who play fast pitch softball now. Sue Tessier, who, after Brother Leo Labbe, eventually replaced me as director of guidance at the Academy, was the driving force in the state for fast-pitch softball, making college scholarships possible. As a result, MSC greatly upgraded the softball and the baseball fields. Before I started the initial Alumni Association, which widened the driveway and redressed and fenced the field, it was in terrible shape since anyone in the city could use it.

If not playing ball in the summer, we were swimming, walking, or biking. Sometimes over five miles to find a swimmin' hole like Silver Lake. Our favorite spot was Harris Pond behind Precious Blood Cemetery on the Blackstone, MA, state line. A little sandy beach, fairly deep water, and even diving possibilities at one end made it attractive to us for the merit badge in scouting. Maybe a good mile or more from home, we cut across Privilege Street where it intersects with Rathbun, trespassing at the corner house with a tempting apple tree. But again, thwack! For the second time in my life, an apple tree was my undoing.

When I studied Milton's *Paradise Lost* in college about our First Parents, I enjoyed my prof's witty observation about Eve listening to God chastising Adam for his transgression. He deadpanned that it was the first ever instance of "Eve-sdropping." But Adam soon did too. Again, picking on her, he said she blamed the serpent ("passing the buck") for what happened. But his worst anti-feminist faux pas was hinting Eve was merely "a side issue" out of Adam's rib or side. His tongue-in-cheek comments did provide some relief from memorizing long passages from that magnum opus: "Of man's first disobedience and the fruit of that forbidden tree...." But he evened the score for "the weaker sex" when he suggested woman was superior since, unlike Adam, she was created from bone, not earth. Therefore, she's "made of better stuff," he theorized.

Back at Harris Pond, some rough house kids cavorted at both ends of the beach, one, a spillway, the other, maybe a foundation. We heard older kids dove in that area, but twice rumors swirled about drownings, possibly from material beneath the surface! At the spillway over to our left, we were leery of a mannish girl with long, stringy hair and stooped corpus, who looked aggressive. She lived on Cumberland Street where I saw her as I delivered papers. Then the gang saw her no more and wondered why.

We also found our way to Spring Lake in Glendale, and, like Silver Lake in Bellingham, MA, good distances and hard on our cheap sneakers and balloon bike tires. In the city, we sought sprinkling relief at Social Park from an old broken-down swimming pool.

In wintertime we were euphoric when the city barred some city streets (like Villa Nova Street across the Kendrick Bridge) to vehicular traffic for sledding. After supper, young and older kids stayed out till 9 p.m., even on school nights. We Gaulin kids also had an empty hillside lot behind *Docteur* Auray Fontaine's home on Wood Avenue. We pretended we were a rescue squad for kids who had overturned or who came too close to a four-foot retaining wall on the Gaulin side. In summer, we also played "Swords" in that field, with slats culled from construction debris in the neighborhood. So, like our own Clem Labine, Gil Hodges, Pete Reiser, Don Newcome, Pee Wee Reese, Carl Furillo et al, we were like "the Boys of Summer" ... and Winter.

With no ice rinks in the area, in winter we also hunted for frozen ponds in the city and North Smithfield. On a Sunday afternoon, Cass Pond was mobbed with hundreds of skaters of all ages. For some, it was also a date night ... "by the light of the silvery moon!" On Sylvestre Pond on lower Cumberland Hill, players had to shovel to skate or play hockey. Some had real sticks, but you saw homemade sticks or suitable tree limbs, as famed Brother Adelard, *le père d'Hockey* (the father of hockey) in RI, used when he initiated the sport in Central Falls in 1912.

The shoe portion of our skates was weak and non-supportive, a bane to weak-ankled skaters like me. The blades were no better. Bauers or CCMs, top-of-the-line skates, they were not! It was a time when Americans, none in the NHL I believe, were considered poor skaters. And rarely did you sport new skates if you had older siblings. If hand-me-down skates were too big, we put on two pairs of those woolen stockings *mémère* knit. With clothes, sports equipment, bike, and what-else all coming down to you from older siblings, immigrant kids made do with a "second-hand Rose" wardrobe. It was that or go without. Nobody spent money they didn't have. We were in a Reagan-like trickle-down economy, but in a mill town like ours "the wealth of nations" rarely trickled down to us.

My worst crash happened in my first teaching assignment at Sacred Heart School, Sharon, in the early 1950s. Brother Clarence, now Gerard Proulx, lost his stick on the pond behind the school. Being lighter, I volunteered to retrieve it but quickly broke through 10 feet from shore. Putting my elbows on the nearest rim of ice, I went down again. Luckily, the ice held when I did it again, and lying flat on the ice he pulled me out with his stick. I didn't tell my first-ever principal, Brother Jean Rosaire, he almost lost one of his new fifth grade teachers and, as he later said, his best recruiter when inquiring parents came to visit with their boys. (It was great training for one of my future roles at MSC!) I listened to what they wanted for their son and, if we had it, I sold them on it. A business principle I had read in a magazine. I planned a route and a spiel. Every kid the school took in went up ten or more points in his work. Perfect attendance (of course), structured study halls, small classes, no distractions, and regular hours were the key. I liked playing softball with my students at recess. Like a baseball announcer, I narrated the game as I pitched for both teams, with the kids going wild hearing their highlights at bat or in the field. Back in class, they were energized, like after the proverbial coffee break. If a kid transferred in, they didn't like to take him in on their team. But I insisted "there was always room in the in(n)."

Also, since my religious group was the first American class to get a full college degree before teaching, he asked me to do some of his correspondence because I was both a French Canadian and an English major. He told me his brother, who shipped produce out of Boston, had sent 500 pounds of unsold bananas for the students. Could I write a thank you note? I did, using "bonanza" (like the popular TV show) as the name of this so-named "bounty." Canadian by birth, bilingual, but more fluent in French, he corrected me, saying his brother had sent bananas over, not bonanzas! The younger Brothers roared when I told the story. A very caring principal for us young teachers, he came into your class unexpectedly and told you to take the afternoon off. He loved teaching the kids in a go-get-em manner. And even if fiftyish, he dripped *Montréal Canadien* rouge, putting on skates, getting up a game between staffers, and making *une monter* or a dash up the ice on our pond. Teachers never forget their first class; I, my first principal too. He even allowed us two picnics a year, usually to Hampton and Salisbury beaches, even if the Provincial in the house frowned upon it. One time an older "ingratiating" night-watchman monk squealed on us. A "Canonical Divide!" That hurt. But every Monday night, the staff got together for a soirée and *Gaulois Frère Jean's bon vin*, (Gallic Brother Jean's fine wine,) good for esprit de corps.

In late winter at Cass Park there were days when the whole sheet of slushy ice, already ringed with water, heaved from end to end as skaters refused to accept the coming of the vernal equinox. A wild thing was to join other skaters in those human whips that were always formed by thrill-seekers. Like that last Ice Follies' girl skating long and hard to catch up with the end of the whip, you felt great when you did. You took off like a speeding iceboat when you let go, covering almost half the surface. Young tots and creaky adults often came in for some jostling and bruised derrières when they stood in the way or crossed the whip's speeding scythe.

Oh, those sports of youth when we boys in summer were, as in the poem, "like barefoot boys with cheeks of tan." And in winter we, like the girls, sported ruby-red cheeks from being outdoors, sledding or skating all afternoon. When home, mom often burst out, "*Vous avez les joues roses.*" (You have rosy cheeks.) Red cheeks were always a sign of health for her. She always looked for that in a baby. We were spared the pallor of today's young, addicted video watchers who rarely play outside. About rosy cheeks, when baby Rachel took her first formal photo, she liked that the best about babyhood. Don't the first and last child get the most pictures in the family albums, as I once heard a middle child character say in a play at the St. Michael College Playhouse, who sarcastically felt everyone, even her parents, looked past her? "I live here too," she shouted. Catholic University's John Voight, whose daughter is Angelina Jolie, was a thespian in training. He said 90 percent of actors are unemployed at any one time. He was a great character actor. While counseling, I only had two or three students who wanted to go into acting. I always told them Voight's caution.

One time when we lived on Mailloux St. off Cass, I said mom was criticized because even in winter she put us out on the porch, all bundled up in one of those domed wicker carriages of yesteryear. In some way, we were deprived of most of the enrichments enjoyed by today's young people, but wisely mom had that covered too: "*One manque pas ce qu'on n'a pas,*" (We don't miss what we don't have). In the Order, it was, "*On s'en passe avec avantage,*" about the less we have the better. Franklin himself touted some 12 virtues, but told his readers, "Simplify." And didn't Christ simplify the whole law as loving God and neighbor as oneself?

Babes in Toyland

A POET ONCE CALLED April the cruelest month, at least in England. For us kids, the problem was what to do between winter and summer when skating, swimming, and baseball were not in season. We didn't know basketball. No one on the street owned one, and I saw my first one at the Academy. Woonsocket was not "Hoopdom" unless you read about Woonsocket HS's Moe Enright whom I saw play once, or when the Mount Brothers went for a change of pace from hockey and had an intramural league after lunch. About hockey, some 20 years before the Arena was built, Brother Michael and faculty members sometimes got up in the early morning hours to make ice for an outdoor rink near the old gym. And at Christmas, they framed the whole building with lights, visible from the surrounding city. And in the summer, the front was a floral paradise. There were over 40 Brothers on the staff through the 1970s when I roomed above the chapel. Now Brothers live in smaller, family-sized communities, one outcome from Renewal that no one should live like a stranger in a large community.

Can you imagine hydrant jumping was a Gaulin Gang favorite? The contest was who could jump over the highest one or post, like the pipe preventing vehicles from entering our backyard. You hurdled a hydrant from a standing position, pivoting with two hands. Then you tried one hand; then two hands again, but from the road and not from the edge of the sidewalk. We did it for the usual classic reason: they were there. Like the fanciful character Holden Caulfield, we were just "catchers in the rye," doing a carefree, innocent thing. (A controversial novel of that name when it came out - the young man is foul-mouthed - I was the first one to teach it at Notre Dame HS. I was armed with a priest-critic's review that his "dirty tongue" was simply a lack of vocabulary, and he was basically good and decent in his encounter with the nuns and a prostitute at the hotel. Later, however, I made the mistake of expurgating another novel I was about to teach juniors. ("Bowdlerizing" is the literary term for eliminating racy parts of a book.) The librarian told me it caused the biggest rush to the Fitchburg library ever. But anyway, recalling Shakespeare's words about vaulted ambition (leaping over a horse), if your hydrant jump was more than your bold intent, you tore a good pair of overalls in the crotch and bruised your incipient manhood.

In our wanderings throughout the city, we picked up empty cigarette packages (Camels, Chesterfields, Old Golds, Lucky Strikes) with numbers under the bottom flap for some. If you guessed right, you hit the loser with as many taps as the number. If you lost, you took the hit. A small number meant two or three 'hard' blows; a big number, a hundred love taps. Hey, we looked into other people's barrels, so we weren't above picking up an empty pack with a cigarette or two in it. Imagine, we even emptied Coke bottles from delivery trucks in front of Lavergne's Market! Because we had no money, and mothers insisted you eat only at meals, we couldn't satisfy the mini-cravings kids get throughout the day. Mine wanted us to drink water, not soda between meals, except dad's own root beer sparingly. (About infection, we heard poor kids were more resistant to germs because of greater immunity buildup from conditions in their 'hoods, like the seemingly poorer "Cumberline' kids," who lived next to the Blackstone River.)

"Buck, Buck, How Many Fingers Up?" was the horseplay boys liked so much. After selecting teams, the leader of one team bent from the waist against a wall with "his horses" behind him bending and holding on to the front guy's waist. Then the other team's "men" jumped on them at running speed, each pivoting on the last horse to land as far forward as possible. The first jumper then asked the first pack horse how many fingers he had up. A right guess and the nags became the leapers. We developed strong backs, as if we were Pennsylvania kids destined for the mines instead of the mills.

We also played a similar game called "Horsie." A team duo of horse and rider took on all comers until one team was left standing, like shore swimmers once did. So strong and enduring was Henri Houle, he was nicknamed after the game. But it was tough on our clothes. Was it English medieval jousting in Frenchville? "Êtes-vous fous?" (Are you crazy?) mom would've said about this horseplay, but we were unseen on a blind side of the house. Our Saturday afternoon oat operas at the Laurier endeared us to games with equine creatures. In those days we knew the horse names of our cowboy favorites: The Lone Ranger (Silver), Roy Rogers (Trigger), and Gene Autry (Champion). For us city kids, even with hardly a blade around, the fantasy of owning a horse was like owning a sports car today. The closest you got was a photo by a roaming photographer with a horse. But pinchpenny mom said we couldn't afford it. So, there's only one such photo in the albums: our Fontaine cousins on Ross Street. Mom probably figured she already had seven bipeds to feed, so adding a four-legged hay burner to our home's feed bag wasn't an option.

"Follow the Leader" appealed to our copycat instinct and desire to maintain status with the gang. It was a good test of the leader's creativity to come up with feats of derring-do others could try matching or die trying. At the end of our yard, for example, you scaled a fence with a pivoting hand, falling 6 or 7 feet into a neighbor's gravel yard, right next to a rhubarb patch, our only summer afternoon snack. Or walking the top of a picket fence across the street, even if a fall might cause a ruptured spleen, deep gash, or piercing those one-dollar Keds meant to last the summer. Dad ordered me off one time, ending my high-flying Wallenda pretensions. (Twenty-five years later in the Order, I unknowingly cracked a vertebra while challenging seniors to match my diving moves at a cottage. I hardly could put on my cassock at the residence. Dr. Stanley Balon reminded me when I returned to RI how relieved I was the pain wasn't a heart attack.)

We also played a game that's long a victim of today's heavily trafficked streets. Our French word was *pays*, but *Providence Journal*'s Bob Kerr called it Peggy Ball: "a highly polished wood" peg and a broomstick. In our version, the batter used a broom handle to send the peg airborne, one of the other players retrieved it and threw it back, trying to hit the upright stick held by the batter or landing it in a circle drawn around it. If you did, you became the hitter. Because it was a dead-end street, we played it when we lived on Mailloux across from the hospital. I wondered if the game had any influence in the development of baseball, but the game "Peggy" isn't mentioned in histories of baseball.

Besides "Hopscotch" (the front sidewalk was always chalked for play), the only other outdoor game the girls joined us in was "Hide-and-Go-Seek." With the way city builders put up houses on every available inch of land, it was hardly a challenge to find a nook, porch, or dark unlighted first floor hallway to avoid detection and race to the starting point while the searcher looked vainly. Is it the first game little tykes learn to play?

If we couldn't play outdoors because of rain or washday Monday, *les* Carpentiers had a popular horserace game with moving parts we bet pennies on. Also, their "Beechnut Game" (directing little wooden rings to their target) we never tired of. At our house it was "Parcheesi" or "Home" on the reverse side of an oil cloth dad used. He also made us a wooden foot-and-a-half bridge-like span with numbered holes in it. You won more marbles by rolling them in certain holes. And he cut a block of wood with rounded nails placed in a cruciform manner. If you jumped the nails right, you were left with only one in the middle hole. Bob made and gave me one a few years ago. When expert but bored, we did it over and over to see how fast we could do it. It gave us future mule spinners incredible hand speed!

We also liked "Chopsticks," which sharpened our manual dexterity. You tried to pick each lying colored stick without moving any other. And like every kid, I had several board games good for quiet time. I favored Chinese checkers where I tried to move marbles from one side of a triangle to another in as few moves as possible. I worked on that for a long time until I couldn't lower my score anymore. Also, if perhaps irksome to the folks, I kept count how many times I kept a ball in motion on a rubber string tied to a paddle. I got into the hundreds. But I wasn't so good with a cheap Yo-Yo. How did those vaudevillians at the Park Theatre make them "sleep?"

It was the Canadian-born family of *les* Berubés, however, who really introduced us to the pleasure of parlor games. Ghislaine, one of the older girls with a Canadian name we had never heard before, taught us how to play *Monopoly* (definitely high finance in our low-rent neighborhood) and *Authors*. Since we didn't want to carry over a game, we played a shortened version of our own. After all the properties were bought, we then had a buying and selling period. If you had two pieces of a real estate or utility, someone had to sell you the third. If you had equal parts (railroads, for example), you rolled the dice. Then the game proceeded to its usual appointed hour or so on the porch they shared with *les* Carpentiers.

In *Authors* you identified a writer or work to win cards. What a boon for my future major in college to learn all my American authors and works by heart! They were mostly of the American Romantic Period, like Thoreau, Bryant, Emerson, Longfellow, and the like. It was a "learning is fun" approach long before that became an educational aide. But can you believe even we Francos had a joke about Longfellow? Like who was the only poet who sat on the Brooklyn Bridge and soaked his feet in the river below? This anti-Sentinellist intrusion into our comic spirit was from a page of jokes in our Boy Scout magazine. Printed in English, of course.

We were playing on the porch one morning when a kid ran in with the *Boston Record*. Evocative of the Nazis' Stuka dive-bomber, its big, bold headlines screeched that Germany attacked Poland. It was September 1, 1939, and little did we know "that shot fired in anger in a foreign field" would claim in the next six years some of its 60 million victims from our very neighborhood, one in the next house. As is one of the themes of our narrative, it also heralded the end of our almost inclusive Franco way of life in an America whose language and culture we didn't know too well. Just as WWI, so we read, helped Francos Americanize some. War unites and divides.

In one edition of *The Woonsocket Call* in 1946, the *Monopoly* gang also saw the headline about the murder of a prominent North End city man, Jack Letendre, whose death remains a mystery. One theory was that "he ran afoul of some gambling operators at racetracks and night clubs in RI." But the family was upset recently by an article suggesting so. Dad shrugged his shoulders when I asked him. Clueless mom admitted "*Ça nous dépasse*," meaning like the mysteries of our faith, it was beyond our grasp and we shouldn't ask too many questions about it. Nothing ever bothered her too long.

But if the season didn't allow us our favorite sports and we disdained indoor games for the moment, we often went down to Cumberland Street where two attractions lured us. On the Blackstone River side of Cumberland Street was the Larochelle Garage owned by a comfortable family with a big cream-colored car who lived on our Gaulin Ave. You could hear their daughter sing and play the piano in the summer. Later, was she in the reputed St. Joseph Parish choir? With scores of junk cars littering the banks of the river, what a thrill to go through a door, busted trunk, rumble seat, or car flooring to find a good hiding place to smoke with no fear of sibling (sisters) detection! Because cars were piled on top of one another some 15-20 feet, we were secure in "our depths of iniquity." If not smoking behind the hospital laundry room, we were there. After all, we sandlot urchins couldn't play ball all the time, even though we tried when shoveling snow in early spring and playing with mittens on! But I can't believe the attraction smoking had on us! Was it copycat behavior? An author surmised recently why thousands begin smoking every day, largely because the nicotine was chemically hyped tenfold in the 1970s, so young smokers are hooked in a matter of days. A doctor said the evil is not how much you've smoked, but how long. We really attacked the problem in my one public school, but no school could afford a staffer in the lavatories. But it's now against the law, including on school property. We called the cops, so kids got the message: "Book 'em, Dano."[28] It's a leading cause of gene mutation leading to oncogene and cancer, an oncologist wrote. Recall that on average, a study said a cigarette costs you nine minutes of longevity and ten years of life! But a European nation was deemed insensitive for lauding it as a good outcome because of smokers dying sooner and ending pensions! Fewer than 20 million now?

We always bought *Wings* cigarettes. The brand never won any T-Zone honors (a popular commercial point then) like the best-selling brands, but they were the Benson and Hedges of the day, that is, the longest and the cheapest, and that's all our trickle-down allowance afforded us. (Even today, price is the biggest deterrent for teens.) No matter how enterprising, we were sometimes short of money, even to buy *Wings*. The closest we came to getting caught was the time we tried cigars at noon on a school day. We went to class in the afternoon, looking to throw up. "The wages of sin," or as the Bible says: *speculum peccati*!

Even though at Notre Dame HS I sometimes smoked one cigarette as I walked with one monk or another for 15 years after supper, I never touched a cigar again. Even if allowed a carton of cigarettes every 15 days (if you ran out, you rolled your own with a little contraption in the community room), I never took nor carried them. Mom would've threatened me with excommunication after what she and dad did to keep our lungs healthy growing up. One confrère I walked with said I smoked O.P.'s: Other People's! But "Vengeance is mine," saith the Lord. With two or more hours of prayers in chapel every day, an addicted, hacking smoker bedeviled me constantly with his cough into the back of my neck. I was relieved when he left to become a priest. In his ministry, I mused he could now inhale "incense in His sight," (*sicut incensum in conspectu tuo*) during the Benediction of the Blessed Sacrament. After successor Brother Robert was transferred to another school, I became the Athletic Director for The Crusaders. We all wore "many hats" as religious teachers. Up to 12 for me one year! I never could gain weight, but because of my daily evening walk in North Worcester County's cold and bracing air, I didn't have a cold for ten years. When Brother Robert Breault, later Provincial, walked with me, we had so much fun, suggesting we'd write to this or that owner suggesting changes he

---

[28] A popular quote from the original *Hawaii Five-O* television police drama series which ran from 1968 – 1980. – *ed.*

should make to his property. One year when food buyer Brother Adelard, who roamed meat stores on Saturdays for bargains, unknowingly bought tainted meat, four of us got sick. My only sick days in 42 years in education! Unfortunately, unlike lucky, retiring friends Pat Beaulieu and Marcel Tardif of Bellingham HS, Norton didn't compensate you for unused sick days. I had close to 200. My wife Pat chided me for going in even if I wasn't tip top. I loved the work. And student problems piled up after just one day, besides all that mail from colleges. I wrote all my college recommendations in early fall before guidance became Grand Central Station. I worked with great counselors John Kieser, Susan McLaughlin, and Claire Ford, all expert in one counseling aspect or other. And a great staff.

As in society in general, smoking is now banned everywhere like in the Order's residences. At one time, the rule book banned you from smoking until you had made final vows after six years of temporary profession. In my first year in Sharon, I enrolled a kid whose father told me he was thrown out of our Order because he got caught smoking! We had an expression for a monk who bummed cigarettes when his carton was empty and didn't like rolling his own: "*un grand fumeur dans le Seigneur.*" (A great smoker in the Lord.) You could pick out a heavy smoker because of tiny burn holes in his cassock. One confrère especially drew everyone's attention. He always had ashes about an inch long, which, if no one was looking, he flicked hither and yon. Community living was like family life with all its joys and small irritations. Brother Clarence, who dismembered a bell I was supposed to ring during the first Mass I ever served, also found a big hole in his cassock, but not from smoking. He always secretly kept a pet chipmunk in his room and one burrowed into a pocket and gnawed its way out. The cassock was new, and you didn't get one every year. Like him, I do love the little guy on my property in the summer. A poet said caterpillars do the will of God slowly; chipmunks do it quickly. I keep an eye out for "Bunky" who lives in my backwall where I sometimes put food around his hole. I think he's wise to hibernate in winter. I don't know "their religious sensitivities," but he and a squirrel at times perch on my statue of St. Theresa, part of a flower memorial shrine in Pat's memory, next to a birdbath. I'm fascinated by bird flights and animal movements. I was quite saddened over losing our cat Brooklyn years ago, but Jim convinced me to give little Bruin a home in 2014. He was a hit. He too wakes me up at 8. Unbelievably athletic and affectionate. Is it true "If you don't like cats, it's because you're independent like them?"

When we kids weren't at Ratte's Variety Store next to the bridge on Cumberland (we bought our dime comics and model airplane kits there), we played under the bridge, sliding to the water's edge. A no-no challenge for the gang was to walk the huge pipe spanning a second and much smaller body of water that was a remnant of the Blackstone Canal as you neared the

Bell Mill side on the right. We often talked about it, but we sensed, "prudence the better part of valor." A slip would've meant a dunking in the dirtiest, murkiest, and mono-threatening water you ever saw. A waste pit for mill discharges. (Museum of Work & Culture volunteer and popular thespian Irene Blais' father, who ran a store nearby, was commended for his attempt to rescue a child who fell in and drowned.)

We said mothers had no idea we ever went there. More tractable now, but how do you stop students from speeding? Cell phones help if they answer when they know parents are calling. But other technologies are catching up! Our own fantasy was having those two-way wrist radios seen in the Dick Tracy cartoon strip. Even as a kid I believed we'd all have one someday. Today's smart phones? But on our wrist, not in our ear. (One came out in 2013, but wasn't practical, say techies.) Mom who seemed to know what was going on everywhere, but not our stuff, would have shrieked knowing we killed rats on the hospital grounds, drowned cats in the river, played on the river's edge, and climbed people's trees for apples or nuts. Mill town Tom Sawyers! Kids' antics today are not so Cro-Magnon, but far more life threatening at times. The curiosity to know and experience, said my Adolescent Psych teacher at Boston College. We weren't bad kids and most turned out well.

About drowning a litter of cats, the gang did, but only when parents said no to keeping them. More than once, a cat dropped a litter under the wooden stoop of the Laferriere family in the rear of the Carle tenement. Definitely a no-no by today's ASPCA standards, we placed the kitties in an open paper bag and threw it into the Blackstone from the Kendrick bridge. Mercifully, if the kitties were old enough, they swam ashore to begin their feral existence. We never heard of a place for unwanted animals, and we would never have killed them with physical force. But without some action, the backyard would've been "a bedlam" of warring cats. (Interestingly, in an etymology course at St. Michael's College, Prof Doc Fairbanks said the word bedlam came from a loud and cruel insane asylum in England named St Mary's of Bethlehem, aka, bedlam. Brits slur the ending of words, like "milit'ry" and "diction'ry.")

Fantasy is the stuff of childhood, and our favorite creative play was full of it. On practically the only patch of grass in the neighborhood (the fenced-in area between our house and *les* Jolicoeurs next door), we played "Superman." Always, the smallest kid, Lucien Laferrière, became Clark Kent who was "ulped"[29] (how we loved that push in Kent's face by his tormentors in our comic books) since he was as defenseless as the bespectacled

---

[29] "ulped": One of many words created by cartoon artists to represent nonverbal sounds or actions. (e.g. – "Pow," "Bam") – *ed.*

reporter. But after taking his lumps, Gaulin's Clark Kent, sans telephone booth, suddenly changed into Superman (symbolically a neck kerchief served as a cape) and wreaked his pretended fury on the tormentors of his alter ego. At his airy, Herculean blows, we fell backwards, rolling and collapsing like blasted villains. At times, we also played "Batman and Robin," with one of us playing to Lucien as Robin. Being little was a plus in our neighborhood and showed the gang had a good heart and liked the underdog who, like in our Saturday afternoon matinees, always won in the end and got the girl, but not so for Lucien in our strictly male kingdom arena.

But unlike today, however, our playful imitation of cinematic or comic book "violence" never carried over into our daily societal and family life, as some studies say media mayhem now does for some: desensitization. A study said your average kindergartner has seen 5000 murders on TV before he comes to school. One mused if we think good television does good, how come we don't think "bad" TV has a negative influence? Now add violent videos, games, and movies, where like in some Shakespearean plays, no one is left standing at the end, a prof had us notice. Another wondered if every kid realizes in real life, the much-mauled Road Runner often doesn't survive? When they told a first grader a classmate had died, he asked, "Who shot him?"

I lost sight of Lucien for over 45 years, only to have nostalgic memories wash over me when he died fairly young in 1985. His funeral was at the St. Ann's Convent Chapel on Elm Street where we worshipped a couple of times as grammar school kids. I relate later how he and I - both lightweights - were swept up Gaulin in the '38 Hurricane.

We were so endeared to those neighborhood games, that long after we left for the Order, college, and teaching, we often thought of "that old gang of mine." How wonderful it all was! With complete absorption of youth in fantasy play, we easily reverted to *Babes in Toyland*, whenever fancy or boredom hit us and we wanted to get away from the dull confines of our mill town world. Play has a kind of escapist magic about it, and even when the gang was nowhere to be seen by parents, we proved the adage, "Never less alone than when left alone." And so, like the adventurers of *Alice in Wonderland, Tom Sawyer, Huckleberry Finn,* and *The Wizard of Oz*, we were propelled on the wings of fancy and imagination. The gang slipped unnoticed into a mythical dimension of reality our parents and teachers had left a long time ago. The song said you couldn't go back to Toyland, but we did often. We knew the way, but never told anybody.

Peddler for the Fourth Estate

MY OWN PERSONAL economy consisting of a weekly nickel allowance and those bottle discard refunds really turned bullish when I went into business for myself. I became a carrier as a member of the Fourth Estate: *The Woonsocket Call*. The three other estates were once nobility, clergy, and the common man, at least in France.

Our Peloquin cousins, who delivered the newspaper to our house were looking to reduce their route, especially along the streets of Cumberland, Locust, Brook, Clinton, and Social. I bought off some 30 customers, but soon developed another 20. My new customers came by word-of-mouth when word got out I did not back down for dogs. There were no leash laws in those days and I certainly wasn't less scared than most when the canines growled and threatened to bite. But because I loved making and counting money, to pick up new customers I stood my ground until the menacing mastiffs knew I wasn't going to back off. Self-preservation may be man's first instinct, but making money is a close second in our capitalistic society. Yes, that elusive stuff like quicksilver that my folks could never get their hands on. What most French-Canadian immigrants had never known, or had little of on their farms in Canada, said one historian. Their wealth was their land and animals. Even a farmer friend in Lebanon, New Hampshire, Howard Patch, told me that on his Civil War-era Walhowdon spread. Equipment is expensive.

I especially recall one family that lived on the second floor of a house next to St. Ann's on lower Gaulin. They harbored a small, mean-looking bulldog that had already chewed up and spat out two carriers. The family was at a crossroad: Do we get rid of the dog or go without the paper? Since they heard about me ("He'll even stare down a pit bull for money") or seen me go by bedecked in railroad jeans and Bob's navy hat at a jaunty angle, they offered to pay extra. Could I stand up to their pugnacious Winston Churchill, as the breed was compared to? "*On veut notre papier,*" (We want our paper) the man pleaded. (Remember the Winston cigarette commercial about it tasting good? During the war, the joke went around that the bulldog, symbol of English tenacity, bit a look-alike of the Prime Minister and exclaimed, "Winston tastes good like a Prime Minister should.")

What a tense little drama unfolded during the first delivery! Come *High Noon*, I opened and closed the door, and stood there firmly with paper in hand. I swear they sold tickets to see the winner in this Coliseum-like battle between "the lion and the Christian (me representing St. Ann's?). I saw not just the man and woman of the house, but five adults, like moviegoers wondering if King Kong was going to grab me like the cinematic Fay Wray. They stared with fixed eyes and bated breath as the dog darted noisily across the linoleum floor, circling around me since I had left about a foot in case I needed to step back fast. But I felt no tug on the back of my overalls. When the little intimidator had completed his appointed round, he went back near the stove. The place exploded. The family cheered, shook my hand,

and the man repeated his offer to tip me "handsomely" (a quarter), a rarity with poor Francos. The stagecoach, like cinematic John Wayne and Claire Trevor, had gotten through. They could again "Read All About It" about life in Social *Coin* and beyond. Incidentally, Sue said it's the same house single dad once thought of buying before helping his brothers buy their farms. Mom never told me that. Going to church, was it painful for her walking by there?

They say dogs can sense your fear. My poker face (I was "playing" for money here) may have fooled him because he didn't read me well. What price fortune? I obviously didn't know Christ's words then about the foolishness of gaining the whole world (more money to buy War Bonds) and losing one's life or limb. But he never interfered with my right "to earn a living." Did he sense if I didn't win the standoff, his carrier-chasing days might have ended post-abortively?

I recall now how much my route became like a conduit to the inner and outer world of our life and culture in Social *Coin*. I met new people, learned to transact with them (on my first payday, a Cumberland Street hairdresser helped me make change), and saw first-hand situations worse than my family's. But remember my family's lot was never one of severe deprivation, but one of simple means. Mom always reminded us we were "*à peu près toute la même chose*": pretty much all the same. Later I realized how cleverly she aborted any tendency, especially at Christmas, towards our "me-too-isms,": that is, getting what we thought others had.

I always used my treasured Schwinn bike I inherited from Bob with its heralded front post spring to absorb the shock of the city's roads. To help with the steep hills of Kendrick and Gaulin, I bought and installed a large rear sprocket wheel that made pedaling as easy as a rare ten-speed bike. We bought all our parts from a friendly old man with a bike shop on Rathbun near East School Street.

At first, like most carriers, I slung my *Call* bag over the front handlebars. But I found it hard to balance the bag perfectly, since it listed to and fro. I then tried rear twin wire baskets but switched to canvas saddlebags to avoid shredding the paper. But what a fright when I saw a young girl careening down Kendrick with bad brakes, as she raced towards Cumberland Street where miraculously she sped across without hitting a car or smacking into the bridge railing! It reminded me to check mine often, something we kids did frequently in the days when fixing your bike was a backyard skill. I quickly learned why mechanics had dirty hands.

Whenever I saw a movie where a carrier simply flung the paper from his moving bike onto a one-story home, I thought how much tougher my route was. Oh, those three- and four-story tenement houses! My toughest climb for a little more than a penny a day was the Brouillard Bar tenement house, corner of Cumberland and Brook. The bar owner, a Peloquin related to our first cousins, sometimes took the paper downstairs at the bar. Good! But at other times, his wife wanted it upstairs, some thirty steps up. If a kid was around, I subcontracted the delivery for a little less than a penny a day. Unknowingly, I was learning about outsourcing. Being at street level, I had to walk some 10 feet in to put the paper on a polished bar shrouded in heavy, stale smoke. The vinegary eggs in a dirty multi-gallon jar on the bar always fascinated me. Slightly tipsy but convivial imbibers kidded me about having one for the road. "*Un p'tit coup*," (a little snort), they said, like I often heard on New Year's Day.

The smell of stale beer, dim lights, and murky air made me hurry the delivery. Although I suspect the regulars were just good but thirsty *après*-mill (after-mill) 'working stiffs,' I always felt a bit uneasy because priests, nuns, and parents were negative about saloons, especially about bibulous regulars who had four or five nickel-quaffs at one sitting. Drunkenness (*se souler*) was a matter for confession, because like overeating (*gourmandise*) it was a form of excess with bad outcomes. One of the Seven Capital Sins.

After visiting a watering hole, stumbling drunks were public spectacles as they weaved from sidewalk to gutter on their way home. If one was sighted, the news got around fast. The gang teased this John Barleycorn (a literary name for a drunkard) to see if he got mad at you in sloshed anger or gave you money. One time the gang followed an inebriate all the way to the sandbanks by Sylvestre Pond. He was recently married to a nice, young woman, someone said, proving life in Social was known to all by *viva voce* (orally rather than written). The town drunk du jour! He lay at the base of the bank. Avoiding the drama of today's drunk driver, the mill economy and large families precluded drunkards from having a car. Naturally, mom spoke critically about *les ivrognes* (drunks). Abstemious Dad, who still made wine (beer and hard liquor only during Prohibition and the start of the Depression) always took a more bemused look at an inebriant: "*La mer est haute*," (The sea is high/rough) about someone staggering, he chuckled. But she had known the horror men inflicted on their wives and families by washing down their already meager pay: "*bwère (buver) sa paye*." (To drink his pay.) A domestic sin.

At his mother's request, I went once with a kid to haul his dad from a saloon on Cumberland St. ("*Va chercher ton père*" – Go get your father.) It was payday at the mill! My last customer was also a bar, about 100 feet from the Cumberland-Social Street corner. Not as well patronized nor as dimly lit, I was never hesitant about the bar that had not pickled eggs. But they were victimized if I was a paper short on some days! I just shrugged my shoulders the next day or blamed the delivery guy.

The Laurier Theater was a favorite customer of mine on Cumberland Street. After my route on Saturday, I had a free pass, but I wondered my first time if they recognized me as "the mix-and-mingle kid" who was caught twice sneaking in at intermission when inveterate smokers were let out the side door between features. Did I look like a little stunted fellow amidst grownups? It's amusing that one of my all-time favorite movies, "Gone with the Wind," with that hauntingly nostalgic musical theme "*Tara*," is the only picture I ever passed up seeing there. I had no foreshadowing its aura of the past was to fit so well with my future narrative. Was it one of those mushy love stories the Gaulin Gang shunned with, yes, a passion? Our favorites were cops-and-robbers and western movies. These were Buck Jones (a Boston Coconut Grove fire victim in 1941); Wild Bill Hickock with his fringed vest; The Cisco Kid, Lash Larue (loved the name and the alliteration of the two "l's" sounding like a cracking whip); Roy Rogers, and Gene Autry; and all-time favorite The Lone Ranger and his faithful companion Tonto, Jay Silverheels, a real Indian. We loved his "Kemo Sabe," but had no idea how it was spelled. Hey, we were already struggling to learn three languages (if you count our patois as one), never mind a Native American dialect, even if a lot of us Francos have Indian blood or genes from those *coureurs de bois* (fur traders) who were among the first to come to Canada. Over 40 percent of Canadians do. *Métis* is the term. The gang roared when a comic said The Lone Ranger split from Tonto, because someone finally told the masked one what "Kemo Sabe" meant!!! In what today is an ethnic slur, misbehaving kids in class or the 'hood were called "*une bande d'Indiens*" (a band of Indians). Years ago, many sports teams dropped their Indian name because of demeaning reactions from fans.

    I lamented that newspaper customers who tipped were rare, but I had those three good ones at St. Ann's rectory - *Pères* Moreau, Massicotte, *et* Fournier - who paid me monthly and handsomely. No one else ever did that. The "problem" for Francos was usually having enough money to pay weekly bills, so paying monthly or generously was risky since other necessities might intervene. It was one of the constants of the hand-to-mouth mill economy. *Les trois prêtres* (The three priests) also gave me a Christmas bonus. And I only had two steps to climb. When I returned to the city in 1970 after an absence of almost 25 years, I enjoyed going back to the rectory to inquire about the nuns who once staffed it. Some Sacred Heart Brothers later lived there until it was sold after the church closed and became an Arts and Culture Center.

    About those devoted nuns, one absolute of our parish was that two pews from the side door on the rectory side were reserved for those three (or four?) religious who ran the daily routine of the rectory. Members of the Order of *Les Servantes de Notre Dame - Reine du Clergé* - founded in 1929 to assist priests, *les paroissiens* (the parishioners) appreciated them for their quiet, unassuming ways, perfect French in answering the phone or door, and cordiality in receiving you. When I rang the bell, I saw them up close and licked my chops over the succulent smells of the rectory supper. But I hurried to get back to hear mom and her inexhaustible and interesting stories of who we were and how we got here. She never suspected she passed on a valuable legacy, along with those good, healthy meals she served every day of the week, save dad's famous Sunday night soup. Only one nun remained for two priests when I visited to offer parish and school research materials to former MSC counselee and pastor Reverend Roger Houle and author Paul A. Bourget and staffers of the parish's centennial book *Towers of Faith and Family*. It's hard to believe the whole complex of St. Ann's Parish - convent, gymnasium, school, rectory, and finally the church - are now, yes, gone with the wind, despite their unbelievable vibrancy and importance for a century in Social *Coin* life and faith.

Was it flight to suburbia or a severe diminution of faith? Or the inevitability of assimilation, as more children born in America turned away from their parents' faith and into the country's liberal American culture of individualism, materialism, and weak church membership, especially in mid-20th Century? For St. Ann's, the detonating cap was the destruction of our Big Gaulin neighborhood, a priest told me, affecting 800 families going back 100 years. But as is the theme of my narrative, those elements, while they lasted, formed an incredible synthesis shaping untold thousands of French Canadians into strong faith practitioners and proud, loyal citizens of the country. No one thought it would ever end. No prediction from dad whose own family worshipped there from 1904; mom and the Fontaines from 1916. It closed in 2000. Our family name and others are mentioned in its history, as they were on banners at a centennial anniversary Mass. Even if faith in God is relatively strong in America, many churches, as I saw in France, bear witness by their silent, cavern-like space to the low, if not total disappearance of communal worship, now below 20 percent, who now have the challenge of keeping their churches afloat. At one time, one of the glories of our life in Social *Coin* on Sundays was to see thousands marching towards their common faith and worship center. Nothing else attracted crowds like that except Sentinellist rallies in the 1920s to keep local schools French.

Because tipping was honored more in the breach than in the practice, I recall a small dilemma occurred during a five-day week. During the three years I had the route, I recall paying about 18 cents for each paper weekly and collecting 24 or 25 cents from customers. If customers gave you the same amount for a short week, did they mean for me to have the extra or had they forgotten? This quandary came because some people left money under mats, lamps, doilies, etc. and some worked second-shift at the mills. So, I often presumed "in the bank's favor." But some customers always came to grief about their unintended "largess" and asked for a refund on "Blue Monday."

One such customer lived on the third floor of a tenement house behind where the Marquette Credit Union once was on Cumberland. Walking through their yard, I saw a truck mounted with a bench and a huge, unshielded rotary blade powered by an old Ford engine. Yes, Murphy's Law had cost him. Missing from one hand were three of his middle fingers. A good man, as I soon found out, but *misère nwère* (gloom and doom), if his "Mrs. Pennypacker" overpaid me, she wanted the pennies back. The first time it happened, he felt bad for me, while it seemed to her I had absconded with the family jewels. He protested a bit, but her cold, impecunious air (having little or no money) made him withdraw his good heart and one good hand from this domestic tug-of-war over a domestic "excess."

Perhaps because five-day weeks were the exception, she never seemed to remember, and blithely I always took the full amount. A bit fiendishly, I did have cold satisfaction returning a few pennies into an adult's hand, as if to say she needed them more than I did. I didn't know poet Pope's line about "hope springing eternal," but I never despaired her helpmate might "win one for the Gipper." (I'm talking about me, not the cinematic Reagan.) But not to undermine his domestic felicity, he only put up the good fight once. He didn't want to lose more fingers or his *chez eux* (home). But I never forgot him.

My brother Ben replaced me as a *Woonsocket Call* newspaper carrier in the greater Social District

Mom dismissed her out of hand: "*C'tune femme qui serre la cenne*," that is, a pinchpenny, which, in truth, mom herself told me some people said that of her for how she carefully watched over dad's $44 paycheck (when he was working). But she didn't mind that kind of "criticism!" When that miserly lady passed on, did

Saint Pete chide her for lacking generosity to a peddler for the Fourth Estate? "Didn't you ever read the Beatitudes about helping the needy," the Keeper of the Keys of the Kingdom grilled her, especially for a kid delivering in the high Woonsocket tenements?

Newspaper Carrier Days: A Blessed Seedtime

ONE OF THE HARD THINGS about being a *Call* carrier, besides all those tenement stairs, was walking all the way to downtown on Saturdays to pay your bill. Carriers and customers were cash-and-carry consumers.

Once you arrived, a young man emptied your coin bag and counted the money by hand with great speed. Because he was swamped, sometimes his tally didn't equal yours. He didn't like to recount, but sometimes the mistake was his. If mine, having to cough up that extra dime or so cost me a soda for the walk back from Main Street to *la* Gaulin, or a wiener or two across the street. They were a nickel apiece; six for a quarter! I never bought that many as I was afraid to look like a dachshund. Because cousin Gene and I knew a shortcut, we often walked instead of biking it. We cut across the Kendrick Street Bridge, veered right onto a dirt road and crossed an old, covered railroad bridge balancing ourselves on the tracks. It took us across the river and almost behind St. James Episcopal Church. I'm reminded how scared I was the first time mom walked me over the nearby Court Street bridge with its see-through surface! Reassuringly, she dismissed my fears: "*René, ta rien avwerre peur*" (Rene, you have nothing to be afraid of). I never saw it happen, but about those railroad tracks, Bob told me some kids actually stayed on the end of the railroad ties outside the rails when trains came chugging through. Wisely, the shortcut is no longer a venue!

When Ben, four years younger than me, did accompany us downtown, he sometimes experienced weariness. The inspirational saying, "He's ain't heavy, he's my brother" did nothing to alleviate carrying him on my shoulders, sometimes with cousin Gene's help.

Delivery boys and girls don't seem to last too long nowadays with competing jobs and sports. Now adults often deliver by car. But as a kid I liked comparing their delivery style. Unlike most whose style was deliberate and conversational, mine, to use football parlance, was a kind of bump-and-run modus operandi. It was not without domestic perils vis-à-vis the canons of Franco prudishness or modesty. Always a guy who finished things quickly, I knocked, opened the door, and shovel-passed the paper onto a table.

But a few times I caught the lady of the house or an older daughter in near or totally *dishabille* (undressed). I heard a shriek, as if I was an intruder or robber. Embarrassed myself, I didn't apologize, but ran like the women did. But because it was the fastest way, I never changed my style. After all, that's the way our Saturday afternoon insurance collector and bread man entered our apartment. Was there in large families less sense of privacy among members, due primarily to lack of space? (Comically, a married counselor friend of mine once told me if you're "sitting on the throne" and the wife, or the reverse, nonchalantly walks in for whatever reason without any reaction from either of you - you know you've been married for a while!)

I never thought my *Call* carrier look - railroad overalls and navy hat - was alluring. But at least two families on Cumberland St., each with three young females (predatory as on the prowl, but not "raptorial," like falcons or hawks) made me wonder. Close to the Kendrick Street Bridge, a lot of giggles and bashful glances were directed my way when parents of the girls were not around to hasten them back to a more nubile modesty. Worse, further down the street across from St. Ann's were the other three girls whom I heard plotting one day on the second floor, as I opened the front door downstairs. "Make believe he has to come into the living room," said one of the coquettish co-conspirators. "We'll get him there." Since it wasn't payday, I just threw the paper up the stairs and ran, aborting their tender trap. From that time on, I no longer knocked there, content to roll up the paper in the doorknob, like in the movies.

The only romantic flutter I experienced was across the street from the bridge. The mother, Mrs. Poulin, had two of the loveliest girls I had ever seen. (I never saw the father, perhaps he worked second shift.) Lucille had red hair, Germaine, darker tresses? That boyish delirium about their hair stemmed from all the girls on our street and school usually having those broom cuts, which for us was "plain Jane." If they were different, they didn't have the "St. Ann's look!" Boys instinctively knew what the Old Testament line says, "A woman's hair is her crowning glory."

Timid as hell, I remained a distant admirer, since I never spoke except to say, "Here's the paper." As I climbed the three flights, my daily fantasy was wondering who would open the door after I knocked, I scrapped my speed-delivery routine to make it last. A typical Franco family, if you will, I later learned they also had an older sister and three brothers. I did wonder at first if they were full-blooded sisters, which cousin Gene confirmed. Two or three years ago, one brother, Armand, was in a military photo in *The Call* with Ben, Gene, and a Norm Holcomb.

My route also let me see what other people had or didn't, a situation more obvious today because of television and movies. But didn't I say the poverty of Francos and others of the 1930s and early '40s was not as wrenching (save perhaps during the Depression) as nowadays, when it often coexists near luxury and affluence. My parents and others didn't think they were poor in the sense a poor family is today. Family stability, a warm comfortable apartment, tasty, homecooked meals, and suitable clothing belied real poverty because life then was more affordable. Families could afford the basics of renting *un logis* (an apartment), food, clothing, with no mortgage, car, or education debt for most. Also, no medical insurance, which has increased astronomically the last century, unlike in Europe. But how did they live so long without any? Was it healthier nutrition and a walking lifestyle?

I dreaded those rear apartments that bordered the Blackstone River side on Cumberland. I encountered rats up from the littered river's edge where we sometimes played. Whenever I made my way inside those apartments on payday, I saw real poverty. It was so evident in the lack of furnishings, the shabby clothes, their hollow, despairing looks. One day I saw a little boy, dirty, dressed in rags, flies buzzing, as he sat on the floor. But they subscribed to the paper. Poverty of the body, but not of the mind! Once, a big rat crossed my path, so I just flung the paper and ran, not to be bitten. I also saw rats around the hospital refuse barrels, like tenement families had.

I especially felt compassion for a young mother of two. She said her husband had joined the service because he could make more money ($21 a month!). I wasn't an overly perceptive youngster, but I knew loneliness and heartache when I saw it. Mom's almost daily observations on the human condition had taught me in subconscious ways to be an observer like her. On paydays when I lingered to make change, I inquired about his welfare. She often had news because he wrote often, as mom and Bob did during the war. She liked to talk about him. And I knew you didn't have to do something big to do your scouting good deed every day. Just listening and showing a little compassion was enough to lift someone's spirit. Ah, the genius of our culture in raising kids! Everyone was taught the Golden Rule.

Even though mine wasn't a "moneyed route," I said people usually paid me regularly, no matter their means. Mom told me your typical family never lived on borrowed credit because the breadwinner in a mill town never knew when times would go bad or worse. I recall she used the word "*slague*" (rhyming with "ark") to mean unemployment, temporary or lasting. And so, it was with my customers. They paid me on time, conscious a missed payment was more than twice as hard to pay later.

Because most people walked then, I met a lot of folks, especially on Cumberland, Brook, Clinton, and Social Streets with their many stores and services. I was thrilled if I met a priest customer. If he didn't return a greeting, except for a slight nod of the head, I knew he was carrying the Viaticum (Holy Communion "for the journey") to a parishioner at home, where often very sick people stayed until death, or recovery. Young priests walked a beat. The Presentation of Mary nuns always walked in pairs, the time-honored "Rule of Two," of safety in numbers for women especially. Male religious orders like the Brothers had long abandoned the practice. One wit said they couldn't find two monks who got along!

It was a rare delivery day when I didn't also meet a relative (58 cousins), fellow scout, acquaintance, or school chum. French Canadians loved to connect and communicate, and their delight was obvious if upon seeing you, you shared news about your family. I liked the comment that Woonsocket, a city of over forty thousand, felt like a small town because of its Shakespearean hail-fellow-well-met friendliness. And many knowing I was *un* Tellier asked me the first time if I was the son of *le* policeman Tellier with a beat on Social Corner. (Even in the 1990s, someone asked me that!) When more familiar with me, I was the son of "that tall, thin guy who walks everywhere." It was as if their world was a perfectly ordered little cosmos with everyone linked to someone and some place in it. There was a small degree of separation between Francos, especially in the city before you found a spouse. "The unwritten rule" of marrying French-Canadian and Catholic a reason I thought.

But I swear no societal custom has changed more due to myriad causes, like mobility, job relocation, motorization, urban crime, family disintegration, and now the Internet and iPhones. Mom, who spent her whole life making or recognizing those linkages, almost never spoke of anyone without telling you his or her parentage, place of origin, and residence (tenement and street). I think a lot of women were like her. Homemaking, children, and societal relationships were their trifecta.

But not content with her recall of everyone and everything this side of the hereafter, mom was also at her best when going *pierre à pierre*, that is, monument to monument, in Precious Blood Cemetery with her mother Emérance and sister Laurence who lived across the street on Rathbun. The veil of time was very transparent for her. Even if departed, if she had known them, she still could retrace to some degree the threads of their lives. "*C'ta notre monde*," about their being part of our world even in death because, as the liturgy of the Mass of the Dead proclaimed, their lives were, yes, changed, but not obliterated. I think only someone like her, so involved in the immigration experience herself and our people's faith in the hereafter, could have maintained those storylines. It was a continuing chapter for her and other domestic historians, while for us it's now a storied past. People in history uprooted by violence, war, injustice, territorial greed, religious persecution, homelessness, or just better prospects forge a bond unequal in the human condition, especially if life-altering like for *les* Fontaines. I can't count how many times I heard them talk about it, adding another detail. It's why, like a broken record, if you will, I often come back to it in this book. An unbelievable story!

Largely because of the influence of my parents who went through the Depression with little work and practically no savings, I was typical of youngsters whose parents droned into them the notion of saving for a rainy day. When my parents made mention an expense of theirs had reduced their "savings" ("*manger du vieux*," dad said about "old money"), an air of concern came over them, as if they had lost part of their rear guard and stood near a sinkhole that could get larger. There was now less to fall back on in hard times in *le fi(u)ture*, (the future) like the constants of death and taxes. They were always battling just to make it, never mind prosper! I still wonder how their joie de vivre masked it so well. Was it their faith? Or God loving "the joyful giver?"

I said dad often spoke about the national debt always getting bigger and laying a heavier financial burden on all Francos (he spoke for the people he knew). He said no President would ever be seriously concerned about reducing it, a prediction our ten years of prosperity in the 1990s negated. (A nod to President Clinton; one critic said, "He turned Republican" to do it and cut spending). It's another reason why even as a poor man who stood to gain, he was generally against ruinous federal programs per se. He didn't want to saddle future generations with overspending. Every now and then when he had finished reading the paper about the nation's economic climate, he told us where we stood, especially our part of the federal debt. One time when he said the population was 130 million, he told us we owed the government $8,000 each. We gasped with disbelief, since the amount was astronomical for a 1940s child who hadn't done anything to incur it.

Someone wrote kids have an instinctive sense of fairness and justice, so all of us said it wasn't fair. I for one vowed the money I had (my black purse cash, Woonsocket Institute of Savings account, and war bonds) wasn't going to pay that debt. No sir! But I didn't join the Order to avoid paying taxes! It was dad who encouraged me to funnel my carrier earnings into war bonds during the war. Every $18.75 was worth $25 down the line. He made savers of the five of us. It got me a private education and a home.

The whole newspaper delivery experience, as Wordsworth said of his youth, was a blessed seedtime. Minus a few, some fifty years later I tried to recall almost every stop and face, especially the woodcutter's stingy wife whose relative I met in 2004. Except for the ticket lady at the Laurier Theater and men at the Industrial Trade Union headquarters, I don't recall I ever heard any English from my customers. It's ironic a kid like me, who learned French before English, was probably one of the few daily conduits (save the radio) my *Call* customers had with the English language. It was just past the time when a kid like me would have been hawking those French papers that still found their way to our house, like *La Presse, Le Samedi, L'Almanach du Peuple*, along with *The Call. Prie Dieu* (God forbid!) Did I help undermine *la Survivance* to keep French and the faith unified? Chartier in *The Franco-Americans of New England* wrote it was fast disappearing, but still discernible with orators, writers, organizations, or publications desperately battling to keep it so. Like Sisyphus with that forever recoiling rock coming downhill.

Yes, unwittingly was I a messenger and herald of Anglo-Americanism, helping people read and learn English, as I did myself from its pages? That was like God sending Moses, a stutterer he whined, to deliver His people! But the Bible says, "He works in mysterious ways His wonders to perform." But lest you think I was afflicted with the so-called Messianic Complex; I didn't have a sense of mission to Americanize Social *Coin*. And certainly not to convert Anglos, if any, or those who had left the faith. I know Christ said you couldn't serve two masters, but I did want Mammon (the god of riches) to send me a few shekels for climbing all those stairs in the nosebleed bastions of my customers. Dad said you saved heat on the higher floors and on Gaulin we could see a fraction of the city at our feet. Our own video of the 1938 Hurricane would've earned an Emmy, complete with a running commentary from mom, with English subtitles of course, and flashbacks to the Ontario conflagration.

St. Ann's Park: Wake Up the Echoes of Yesteryear

HEARING IN THE LATE 1940s that St. Ann's Park, corner of Cass and Dulude, was doomed to join the ash heap of local sports history, Paul Ducharme, St. Ann and Mount classmate, '48, and Troop 4 fellow scout, captured it for the ages with a masterful pen-and-ink drawing.

Later, a highly successful artist and architect whose earliest creative fantasy was to be a cartoonist, as he was during his earlier Air Force sojourn, Paul signed the 6-by-16 inch work with his professional handle of Duche, 17, in 1947. Another prized possession of ours, incidentally, is a letter and cartoon entitled "Rene, Terror of the Test Tube," which he sent me after we joined the Order and studied chemistry. Naturally I blow up the whole lab in the last comic box. Expectedly, Duche was inducted into the first Mount Saint Charles Arts and Music Hall of Fame in 2013 by staffers Marc Blanchette and John Guevremont.

Just a glance at Duche's "*Le Parc Sainte Anne*" is enough to well up a flood of nostalgia-tinged memories. Like the Newport rich at the turn of the century with their summer playgrounds in those fabulous mansions by the sea, we kids also had our play resort for those long, sun-filled carefree months. It was still a time, as evoked in Ken Burns' epic baseball documentaries, when kids, young and old, and working adults especially, enthroned sandlot baseball as king of the hill. At one time Burns says it seemed every town and city, club and society, business and industry, fielded a team. Some ethnic groups too, especially blacks and Jews. As I expand on it later, for a lot of immigrant Americans working the livelong day in enclosed, somber, and dusty worksites, baseball in the great outdoors was God's remedy for a young, gasping industrial nation, whose many laborers had been born on farms and had enjoyed "*le grand air*" (the great outdoors).

Built in 1924 by the Rev. Camille Villiard, Pastor of St. Ann's Parish, the wood-planked park provided us with a chance to play baseball all day in its cavernous spaces. And if we weren't playing, we were watching amateur, semi-professional, industrial league, schoolboy, and even "professional sports" on a Sunday afternoon or summer's eve under portable lights. During fall and spring, the schoolboy sports of football and baseball, chiefly between the city's Villa Novans and Mounties, were the draw, as they competed in the now RI Interscholastic League. Except for games, the park was nearly always closed, but to us kids, the unwritten rule was you could use the field if you could get in. They had no security. The front door was strictly for games. But there was never an inclination to wreak vandalism on what we considered "our park." After all, possession is nine-tenths of the law, and nobody used it as much as we did. Imagine, kids of mill working parents with their own baseball park! It was a homerun.

Since the wooden facility was aging rapidly (the planking was weather-beaten like barn boards), it was hardly a challenge for our Knot Hole Gang to find an opening to slip through. Thin like my folks, I could slither through anything if I could get a leg in. Why, I even walked on crusted snow in winter! When older and heavier, you simply leaned your bike like a stepladder against the fence, or a friend boosted you up. When you grasped the top framing board, you then shimmied up like a telephone lineman. Once on top, you either jumped onto the banks scalloping the field or came down the crosspieces on the interior side of the fence. But even the front door could be pushed back, so we could get in. In fact, so easy was it to get in, it was beneath our dignity as streetwise urchins to spend money to pay for games, especially money we didn't have! If ever you did, you saved a dime or quarter to get a hot dog and soda or candy bars at the stand run by policeman George Lessard and wife, customers on my Cumberland Street *Call* beat. The parents of Ray Bacon of the Museum of Work and Culture, Harry and Laurentia, were also concessionaires.

The diamond was mostly off limits, especially if groundskeepers Rostant Bouchard *et* Joe Mandeville were around. So, we set home plate up on the outer edge of the infield grass to give us a chance to reach the leftfield fence. Unless we played a simulated game with four or five kids on each side, we mostly played "One Strike You're Out" and "Rotation," (you hit and ran until out). These were all resourceful adaptations, because even with a ton of kids, we couldn't always fulfill the biblical question: "Where are the other nine?" (An irreverent wit opined that that question by Christ to the one-and-only returning leper He healed foreshadowed the invention of the game.)

Groundskeeper Mandeville, a good club pitcher like his brother Roger who with brothers Antonio, Raoul, *et* Gaston were later all in WWII, was usually on hand. Not only did he like us kids, but he was also one hell of a worker. Imagine, with only a push mower he prepared the field for a Sunday game by starting to cut the grass three days before! On the other hand, Joseph Plante, cited about millwork, told me *le* policeman Courchesne on Sunday drove kids out of the park in the 1920s because of the Sunday Blue Laws. So even Catholic Woonsocket was not beyond the restrictive reach of earlier-come Puritans, who I read spent nearly all their worship day in church whether it was sweltering or freezing. Poet Frost later wondered which is the worse hell. (The cold! More ways of beating the heat).

Before I ever went to the park with the gang (about an eighth of a mile from *la* Gaulin), I tagged along with dad. Imagine my pride, walking with him, topped as he was with his straw hat (de rigueur after Memorial Day) and dressed in a long-sleeved shirt banded at the elbows. I tried gamely, as did Bob and Ben, to keep step with his long trademark stride. I loved his insights on the game and players. He knew the game well, as most Americans in small towns and cities did in those days. Like an oddsmaker, he always predicted game and series outcomes and assessed the present stage of a player's career. If a player was past his prime, he said, "*Yé pi bon*," patois for "*Il n'est plus bon*." (He is no longer good.) Like a talent scout, he had a sharp eye and told you who could make it past St. Ann's teams. He especially looked for quickness in a hitter, using the expression "*du naire*," patois for *nerf*, meaning nerve or sinew in its anatomical sense.

As much as he enjoyed the games, there was a crusty old man named Sweeney whose vocal and bodily antics in the stands delighted him and fans. For example, if a foul ball landed on the roof behind the batter, he yelled: "Foul ball, Cass Avenue." (Incidentally, the sound of the ball hitting the roof with a thud is what I miss at McCoy in Pawtucket (former home of the PawSox). The old diehard's voice carried quite a bit with the help of a small sheepherder's horn. The gravelly-voiced, white-haired senior fan believed certain numbers were more productive than others. When a local player wearing a lucky one came to bat, especially in crucial situations, Sweeney reminded him and the fans that his number "always went to town," hoping to raise the batter's confidence and coax a hit out of his Louisville Slugger ... with that engraved "Powerized" center.

A benevolent gallery god, the old codger needled and kidded players from both teams. He sat in the roofed and screened stands next to the bubbler[30] on the third base side, like dad did too. If a player came to drink, he assuaged his thirst, but not without getting a little jibe if he erred. But a fair man, he doled out merited praise, home team or not.

And speaking of that bubbler, how often I heard in the stands that somewhere "in Mudville or across the land," to cite a line from "*Casey at the Bat*," an overheated player went into shock and died from drinking cold water after an extra base hit or running catch. Every time we played there, we reminded ourselves if the bubbler was left on. Later as athletic director, I learned there was no truth to the dire medical prediction, except in one

---

[30] A "bubbler" is a commonly used name for a water or drinking fountain in southeastern New England. – *ed.*

incident. The greatest harm is when coaches deny water to athletes "to toughen them up," a practice soon abandoned. The Taft-Peirce American Wringer Combine of the Industrial League played some of the best baseball at the park, as did my brother Bob's Woonsocket Independent Club (WIC), headquartered *sur la p'tite* Gaulin (on little Gaulin).

Since radio and press were the only media available about the Sox, local players were our luminaries. To a degree, they almost rivaled the likes of Ted Williams, Jimmy Foxx (the Double X was to distinguish him from another Fox), Joe Cronin, Bob Feller, Johnny Pesky, Doc Cramer, Jim Tabor, Dom and Joe Dimaggio (not brother Vin in the NL), Babe Ruth (on his last legs), and many others. These local favorites were Greg Greene, infielder and later sports editor of *The Call*; Bill Tracy, a lefthanded outfielder with homerun power to rightfield; Lou Lepine, Jr., a former all stater at MSC and hurler for the Providence Grays of the Eastern Baseball League whose 250-pound bulk seemed to cover the whole mound; and Lou Lussier who later went to the bigs. Dad told me he had seen Lepine's father pitch and thought he was better. A team from Franklin featured mostly Italian-Americans who were great batsmen.

An added treat during the war was a few major leaguers who, stationed at Fort Devens, Ayer, MA, came down with service teams. There was no mainland reserve duty or deferments for professional athletes like Ted Williams, Hank Greenberg, and many others, a rule modified later. One Sunday, one of those players, supposedly a Yankee catcher playing under an assumed name (Aaron Robinson?), hit two homers in a game, something we had never seen. Another pro (Pete Appleton of the Chisox?) tantalized local hitters with his so-called butterfly (knuckler?) pitch. The assumed names hid so-called "ringers." It's why I said we saw professional athletes.

Since I never missed a Sunday baseball game, I was there October 5, 1941, when, with the press box giving occasional updates, the Brooklyn Dodgers were about to tie the World Series at 2-2 with the hated Yankees. In what's been called by Sports Illustrated one of the classic miscues in baseball history (antedating the Buckner error in the '86 Sox-Mets Series), Flatbush catcher Mickey Owen let a Hugh Casey third-strike pitch to Tommy Heinrich get by him, allowing the Bronx Bombers a chance to tie and win the game with one of their patented late-inning rallies.

Elated fans thought the Yankees might lose and - who knows? - weaken their grip on the Series. I heard about the miscue from the announcer as I was leaving the park for the time-honored family supper. When I arrived, the radio said the inevitable had happened again, and the Pin Stripes eventually won the World Series. Some attributed these late-inning heroics to holding-a-tiger-by-the-tail syndrome, with teams self-destructing by "snatching defeat from the jaws of victory," a wit said. The Red Sox had outstanding teams in those days, but always succumbed to the Curse of the Bambino finishing second in a late-season swoon. Built for power in Fenway Park, the Sox often won at home, but with no speed and just fair pitching, they did poorly on the road. The secret to a championship, one manager said, was winning three-fourths of your games at home and splitting on the road. (Obviously the Sox didn't know that!)

Whenever I felt brave or foolish, instead of the safety of the screened stands, I sat on a low open bleacher parallel to the right field line behind first base. If either shortstop or third baseman was an errant thrower, you ducked to avoid harm. But the angry baseball gods still found me. One Sunday I was hit on my left lower arm by a curving line shot from a lefthanded hitter. As I wailed at the pain and possible damage, I was immediately surrounded by bleacherites who rubbed my arm. Now wise, I moved to the Sweeney side where dad probably knew the odds of getting hit if you sat where I'd been.

Two of the best high school hurlers I saw were future Dodger relief ace Clem Labine (one of The Boys of Summer) of the Villa Novans and Mount's Nell Andrews, later police traffic division chief. Because it would have been forty years ago, neither, when contacted, could remember what I thought had been a masterful 1-0 duel between them, with Labine the winner. Regardless, I enjoyed seeing them pitch, against each other or not. Once, when Labine pitched in the National League and went to bat, I heard an announcer say he didn't connect often, but when he did, he went deep. Wow! It's what I remembered about him at St. Ann's Park, as I had seen him hit the top of the leftfield fence. One of the best relievers of his day (and a good spot starter), he humbly pooh-poohed my opinion the Hall of Fame Old Timers Committee should consider him for admission. No, he didn't save 300 games or more, as can happen today, but I felt he deserved consideration for his record in limited opportunities, the norm then. He helped usher in the Age of the Reliever. He twice led the National League in saves, recording 98 in his 13-year career while compiling a 77-56 record. With Brother Adelard at Notre Dame HS, I listened to his 1-0 win against the Yankees in 1956, the day after Don Larsen's perfect no-hitter. Of course, today's starters are not usually expected to go more than six innings, giving way to everyday "firemen," or "arsonists," as one witty writer said about fanning the fire instead of putting it out.

A great draw was the classic grid Thanksgiving match-up between the two high schools. Luckily, most people walked to the park because there was no parking for the five to ten thousand who came when both teams were good. MSC, more famous for its state and national hockey championships under legendary Brother Adelard, never had much of a football tradition, except in '42. The Novans often walloped them. But in one game, a talented trio of Jimmy Sinatro, Tommy Perkins, and Charlie Lamoureux won one for the Hilltoppers. I was there. A couple of Gus Savaria teams featured the bruising fullback running of future Third Team All American Herb Rowey. Garrett Coyne, inducted into MSC's Athletic Hall of Fame, starred for the Hilltopers. Sue telling me Rowey talked to her at school increased her status with me, a sports nut. Mom always told everyone her Quiver yearbook called her "Pretty Sue." So, for her, all yearbooks were "Quivers," not Mount's "Excelsior" or Notre Dame HS's "The Crusader." Ah, what's in a name? Didn't the Bard say, "A rose by any other name would smell as sweet?"

When some enterprising promoters brought in night boxing matches under those portable lights, we were there too. I boasted I was quite knowledgeable about all the top fighters in each weight class from those *Ring* magazines at the barbershop. But the park didn't usually card those ranked fighters. The purse just wasn't big enough. They were local or area pugilists, and maybe "a ringer," or two, as I relate.

I stayed outside the park until fight time, hoping to catch sight of the boxers coming in. We followed closely the fortunes of local pugilist greats, Al and Tony Costa who fought, respectively, in the welterweight and featherweight classes, with Tony once ranked in the top ten. Later, we got to know Al well when I was guidance director at the Academy and he was a juvenile division officer in the city. When I told him I saw him fight often, he said he was the last boxer ever to fight at the park. I regretted the Costa's passing in the 1980s.

We also saw the future Providence College athletic trainer Pete Louthis fight as a heavyweight. Powerfully built, quick for a big man, and with a solid punch, I understood why that weight class and its champions always captured the imagination of fightdom and got the biggest purses. They were Joe Louis, Billy Conn, Max Bear, Primo Carnera, Max Schmelling (the embodiment, said Hitler, of Aryan racial superiority), beefy Tony Galento, Jack Dempsey, and Gene Tunney. A heavyweight fight was like the Super Bowl, a must on the radio if your parents let you stay up past 9 p.m.

The ring was set up across the infield near the mound area. Special folding chairs around the four sides required a more expensive ducat. Because of the glaring lights and attire of those who could afford to sit there, we couldn't crack the security and watched with the *hoi polloi* (Greek for common people like us) in the grandstands.

1939 photos of St. Ann Park which was located at the intersection of Cass and Dulude Avenues directly across from Woonsocket Hospital (Now Landmark Medical Center). The tenements in the distance in the top photo are on Dulude and some are still standing. The bottom photo looks towards Cass Ave.
(Courtesy of Woonsocket Historical Society)

It's funny how you remember little things sometimes. One night I heard a boxer introduced as Coley Welch. I immediately felt a Coley Welch (his ancestors hard-boiled miners in a dirt-poor Welsh town?) should be a boxer. It had a tough ring (no pun intended) to it. He had spiDerry arms that allowed him to reach his foe. If he's the same, I was amazed to read in his obit some 50 years later that he fought champion Jake LaMotta and was boxing's third-ranked middleweight. He was a body puncher who wore down opponents, compiling a record of l00-22-2, with 35 knockouts. In the 1940s, he was the New England middleweight champion for six years. Did his handlers hide his "Real McCoy" talent (a true fighter substitution story; in Maine?) to pick up a few bucks against a local stiff. But I've forgotten the name of a fighter who fought often, always coming in as a zoot-suiter, with baggy pants, a long chain, multi-colored tie, wide-brimmed hat, rings and bling, pointed shoes, and colored socks. It was Barnum and Bailey come to town! I didn't want to miss his grand *entrée*. But what a sight to behold in a mill town where cheap cotton dresses, railroad jeans, open shirt, and stovepipe pants were the getup, save Sunday Mass and functions like weddings and funerals.

I don't ever remember a French-Canadian name on the card. I guess mom's people didn't fight for a living; they did a daily shift at the mill for it, unlike other poor ethnic individuals who saw pugilism as a ladder to fame and fortune, a writer said. He said no successful fighter ever encouraged his children to follow in his footsteps. But Ali's daughter became one. In my first year of teaching in Sharon in the early 1950s, I met and spoke to Brockton's unbeaten heavyweight champ, Rocky Marciano, who spoke to the kids. He later died in a plane crash, like Roberto Clemente. I also remember wrestling matches in the red-bricked St. Ann's Gymnasium on Cumberland St, the historical structure whose demolition city preservationists Larry Poitras and Phyllis Thomas tried to prevent. The management (Mr. Gingras?) let kids fill empty seats after the bouts started. A lot of us kids were familiar with the bowling alleys downstairs where you set up pins for a nickel a string. It was a first job (besides shining shoes and selling for vendors) for us kids, but you got hurt easily because you had no cover as you sat atop the back or on the sidewalls. A string cost a quarter. Self-preservation being primo, I lasted a day when a kid showed me his battle scars. "Cannon fodder," he was out of action for two weeks.

Until my paper route and hawking for a street vendor, the park, besides providing me thousands of hours of active and passive recreation, was, I said, my first source of income. Occasionally I hawked soda and stuff in the stands but recall that wasn't my biggest revenue there. Soon I started imitating kids who probed the dirt for dropped money that slipped through the bleacher flooring spaces and soda bottles. The Bacon family concessionaires had their sons pick up empty soda bottles, but they missed some. An after-Sunday search could generate from a quarter to a dollar, no mean sum for us kids. People carried a lot of loose change then. My parents droned the importance of saving into us constantly, but some of my "pickup money" went for soda pop, Eskimo pies, Drake's cakes, five cent pies, and an occasional movie apart from my Saturday afternoon freebie at the Laurier. Besides dime comic books, airplane model kits, and bicycle parts, it's what the gang spent money on. Things didn't cost a fortune, money was worth more, and we made our own smokes.

Because of all the sodas and pastries we bought, you might think we were starving waifs. Some was the lure of forbidden fruit because our parents served us nothing but nutritional homemade foods, scorning store-bought confectioneries loaded with sugar, sodium, and fats. They were all rated low in dad's dietetic bible: *You Are What You Eat*. If we wanted to snack between meals at our house, it had to be an apple (a lifelong habit with me), oranges, or figs. He always feared constipation for himself or us, so he had mail-ordered purgatives in the icebox. If we wanted a drink, mom showed us the tap or dad's root beer. Of course, dad knew you should have at least six glasses of water a day, but said most foods had a high-water content.

I never failed after a game or next day to check the playing field and under the players' benches. Over the years, I retrieved dozens of bats, broken but fixable by dad, an occasional hat, and baseballs especially. If the threads were broken, we tore the cover off and taped the ball. Good baseballs were either left behind by mistake or not retrieved immediately and forgotten after a foul ball. Joe Mandeville didn't always cut the grass on the banks enveloping leftfield and centerfield, so balls lay hidden there. Like old man Sweeney, I followed the trajectory of every thrown and batted foul ball to see if ball "shackers" recovered it. If they were not swift or eagle-eyed, we got the booty later. If you competed for a game ball with a shacker (a paid job) and got it, you had to continue running home or give it back. Like Little League teams today, teams then were not rich enough to kiss foul balls goodbye. And no player ever threw a ball in the stands. About competition in sports or life itself, reporter Grantland Rice (1880-1954) wrote the classic, "For when the One Great Scorer comes / To mark against your name, / He writes - not that you won or lost - / But how you played the Game." I like to believe games, players, and fans were not as heated like today.

One Monday my biggest thrill was finding a whole dozen new baseballs in a box under the visitors' bench. A manager must've gone mad! To a kid like me, it was a Megabucks feeling! When I became athletic director at Notre Dame HS in Fitchburg, I of course had student managers to help with equipment at games. But I never trusted them completely and found items overlooked, including home plate one time. "Trust but vigilance," Brother Edgar at Sharon had told me my first day of teaching

After I left the city in 1947, not to return until my guidance job at MSC in 1970, I felt part of my youth was gone forever when mom wrote the park had been demolished for stores in the 1950s. Had "the Wal-Marting of America" begun? Many times now as a silent passer-by, I still wax nostalgic, waking the echoes of so many sports moments of yesteryear. As kids, we always saw the community at market, Sunday Mass, or marching to the mills. But at the park, you saw workaday people in a rare moment of relaxation, a sporting leisure that baseball especially brought to a young industrial America. And I still hear old man Sweeney's voice and see dad with his banded long-sleeved shirt and straw hat. A precious moment to remember him by in his prime. But sadly, I also get that classic Thomas Wolfe feeling: *You Can't Go Home Again.* Time never goes backward, because, as quoted, "It's a river I go a-swimmin' in."

Quoits: Pursuit of the Perfect 35

FOR A LONG TIME, Woonsocket was a hotbed of quoits [*koits*], the other "horseshoe game." In fact, before the surge of adult softball leagues, the city had some 35 clubs playing the sport mostly under the lights. In everyday parlance, it was *jouer aux fers* (to play the iron).

Our perspective here is the past, but the game survives in the city, like His Honor Charles Baldelli's Senior League. A quoit, from which the game is named, is round, weighs about three or four pounds, has a six-inch diameter, a three-inch hole, is flat on one side, and beveled on the other. The object of the game is to score 21 points by ringing the pin, getting leaners, or coming closer to it more often than your opponent.

In imitation of our fathers, we learned the game, grew to love it, and played it often. After the art of catching, throwing, and hitting a baseball, learning to throw quoits was the second most important rite of passage for us boys. The girls didn't play, not because it was a boy-man thing, but largely the weight of the irons. Riding a bike was innate. When I got his bike, Bob taught me in five minutes, but he had to remind me to signal if crossing lanes.

So prevalent was the game, I never threw a horseshoe until my late teens in the Order. Never liking it very much, like quoits, I threw them in a rotating saucer way, rather than flipping the irons end over end as good players do. My unorthodox style got me near the pin, but very few ringers.

In our backyard, the Carpentier boys, whose father Anatole, we said, was one of the best players in the city like his brothers, taught older sons Paul André and Philippe who in turn taught us on the hand-me-down set he gave them. Besides Par-X off Cass Ave., other clubs of note were Bolduc, the I.W.C,[31] and later the St. Joseph Vets Post.

Since our backyard was about 30 yards long and served two tenement houses and 16 families, we found two locations where the pins could be set at 35 feet or less. Unless it was Washday Monday and Mrs. Carpentier's bedsheets hung low, we set up below the rear apartment windows from where our cheering moms sometimes watched us. Our other playing site was under a partly sheltered rear outdoor staircase in the adjoining Carle tenement house. It wasn't 35 feet, but it gave us an out on Monday. The men who played there made a tally wheel, which made us feel grownup when we used it. Learning how to throw was no easy task, with some of the trajectories falling short or slicing one way or the other like in golf. The art was to heave the iron in a tightly controlled, ascending-descending saucer-like-flight to best your opponent who played singly or as someone's partner against you and your teammate.

Monsieur Carpentier was an especially good role model in teaching us how to hold a quoit balanced in hand, sight the pin through the middle of the iron, and deliver it in a smooth, arm-swinging manner. Your power, he showed us, came from a moderate push from the foot on the throwing side, while the other foot provided anchor and balance. A gentle, patient man, he taught you how to lay down "ice" (*d'la glace*) or cover if you played first. This so your foe's irons might clang against yours and careen out of sight, or for the men, the half-encircling wood base in the lighted pit across the street. Like a surfer in search of that perfect wave, the ultimate was *un trente-cinq* (a 35-foot throw) or ringer directly from the air without bounce or anything. It didn't count more, but it was the *ne plus ultra* (ultimate) in shooting accuracy. Like a hole in one! Leaners against the pin were three points and irons nearer the pin than your opponent's were single points.

The yard also rang with cheers whenever a player hit a ringer that bounced in off the dirt or another quoit. (You learned where the ground's "springs" were.) In patois, players like monsieur Carpentier called those springs *"mon spotte"* (my spot). Those cheers went an octave higher if you topped your own ringer or your opponent's. Once, my partner and I got ringers with each of our two quoits so that all four were stacked up. Everyone looked on in disbelief. All mothers were called to the window, and we couldn't wait to tell our dads when they got home from the mill. I don't know if it was "According to Hoyle," but the way we played, four ringers at one time was 20 points for the guy who topped the other quoits. A game was 21 points. We definitely had that "You Asked for It" feeling when the yard

---

[31] I.W.C. – Italian Workingmen's Club. Located on Diamond Hill Rd. which was the Italian section of Woonsocket.

turned out for that blast. You must remember that besides the improbability of four consecutive ringers from the same side, you had to overcome the probability of the third or fourth ringer bouncing out when it hit the other rings already on the pin. After three, it seemed like there was no room left in the "in." But sometimes because we used closer pits (20-25 ft,) and taller pins than usual, ringers, well, were like chip shots. That's why it may have happened. I've never forgotten it. A player I spoke to later doubted we ever did it. But we played for hours on end. Men on the first shift could only play after supper.

A whole industry developed around the game to keep the pits leveled, tapped, and somewhat moist. While you waited to replace the loser(s), you raked the soil back to the pit, sprinkled a little water, and smoothed the whole area with the back of a rake or small roller. Meanwhile in their kitchens, our moms must've thanked the household gods, the Roman Lares and Penates, as my Latin prof said, because the game captivated and freed us from backyard squabbles. Of course, our playing locales weren't as good as the men's who had two game sites across the street. Coal ash was recommended for a good surface along with loam and sand for firmness and drainage, but I don't know if they had it.

As kids, we traveled all over the city by bike or on foot looking for swimming holes, playing fields, and quoits sites. They could be found even in a mill city overbuilt with tenement houses and crowded with millworker families. At these quoits sites, we stayed on the fringes and watched the men play bathed in white light from overhead spotlights. It must have been so relaxing for them after their grueling day at the mill, what with the camaraderie, friendly competition, humorous exchanges in patois, and the great outdoors. A welcome respite from the dust and deafening noise of their worksite and those bells that clocked their movements.

In those days, there was no such thing as taking a day off to play golf (not in the city anyway), work on the lawn (?), a game of quoits, a Fenway jaunt, or a few beers at a saloon. Their already puny paycheck would've been even smaller, so I never heard dad speak about personal or sick days. Hey, not even a cup of coffee! Sick or bored of *le dur quotidien* (the typical day's unremitting toil), the laborer still went in. But dad told me several times even President Roosevelt took the day off if he didn't feel well. Dad was very conscious about the spread of germs, and never wanted to inflict others, a frequent situation today, because irreplaceable workers also don't want to lose a day's pay. (But about this workforce of old, I read these men and women fashioned what was once the world's greatest work ethic in a rating among nations. Are we now 12th? But "Made in America" is coming back, as Chinese salaries, for example, are rising and our industry is better. Their working conditions are atrocious like ours in the early days of the Industrial Revolution in England and here. Like in all cultures, if Profit Motive is involved, change is agonizingly slow. Always St. Paul's *Cupidas radix malorum*, as in greed the root of all evils in humankind.)

Quite noticeably then, during quoits games there was a warm *entre nous* (feeling between us) and an almost English-like sporting code among the players, with competitors, as Olympics announcer Jim McKay used to say, "humble in victory and gracious in defeat." Except for a few inquiries about the larger business of life and work (*"Travailles-tu steadey?"* – Do you have steady work?) and family, the conversation was the dialect of quoits, peppered with mild invectives when the god of sport devilishly misguided a throw. Lamentations were *calvaire*: Calvary, where Christ died; *caltor*: the same derivation(?); *misère; tonnerre* (thunder); *viarge* (the Virgin Mary); *malchance* (bad luck); *maudit* (damn); and (my favorite) *J'* give up.

If a guy was on his game and got ringers off the same location, the men said, "Ya son spotte," (he has his spot) like golf's "putt." Unknowingly, with their friendly and even demeanor, the men gave their sons an understated but strong example of the self-control and true sportsmanship our backyard games sometimes lacked. I reported that recent research says much of the youthful violence in all areas of life today, by boys especially, stems from a lack of fathers, real or virtual, in their lives as examples of restraint and moderation. Yes, not so much one's neighborhood or poverty, but the absence of a male figure in the teenage years is often the behavioral gene in violence. Like in the Renaissance city gangs!

Two scenes are unforgettable. I remember a lower Gaulin player, who later lost a leg to disease, I was told. He was seeking advice from an onlooker because he faced his first skunking (he said *beigne* - donut - for not scoring a single point in a match ever in his life.) From his look, you could tell his pride as a man and player would be diminished if it happened. It did. His shoulders sank, as he accepted the consoling words of the men around him. "*Ça 'rive à tout l'monde*," (It happens to everybody) was the biblical "balm in Gilead." It was good for us kids to hear that too. There wasn't much the gang missed, because our "boots" were made for walking (or biking) all over the city. We knew our dads and neighbors, and they knew us. Another 11th commandment was your parents must never be told you strayed from the straight and narrow. Just as politics is local today, as Speaker O'Neil said during the Reagan administration, so in our young life was good conduct, home-based and in public.

Also remembered is a young man, name forgotten, who played both with us and with the men. When the war came, he was soon drafted after he married a neighborhood girl. But we learned his outfit was being sent to Europe before his coming home even once. But here he was one weekend, having snuck out to see his bride. He played his last game of quoits with us because he was soon killed in combat. Quite honest about his escapade, he told the clueless gang what AWOL meant: Absent Without Leave. Had he come in from Ft. Devens in Ayer, MA? With 16 million in the service, the Military Police, like the unit cousin Gerald Peloquin served in, couldn't catch everybody.

The tenor of our games was peaceful, but with kids of all ages throwing irons, moms thought the backyard at times had become a bloody crash scene. Young players who hadn't mastered Mr. Carpentier's classic delivery usually grasped the iron, hand on top, not under, flinging it sideways instead of up and forward. Spectating children ran for cover, with some across the path of delivery with the iron in suborbital flight. What a scene when a kid got hit! There was blood, children's dirty handkerchiefs pressed against the cut, wails of pain, and yells in the direction of the window where his mom had been before Armageddon. Because this was not to be resolved from the window, "*par la fenêtre*," as mine said, I remember *madame* Houle coming down one day, wailing and using many of the stock expressions our domestic divas had when these mini tragedies hit, like "*Mon Doux*" (from Mon Dieu: My God). As reporters say, "If it bleeds, it leads," so mine was more verbose with her usual editorial spin, "*Avec des enfants, il ya toujours queque chose quia 'rive.*" (With children, there's always something going on.) Children and accidents went hand in hand, as any hospital emergency attendant will tell you. But how much more when families had four, five or more kids? It's no wonder *The Call* ran that daily injury log that everybody read. "The fickle finger of fate!" With 42 kids in the hood, there was often a new victim.

The game was a wonderful pastime. It bound us to each other, boys and men and our mothers and sisters who watched us. As we played, we too, like our dads, learned the gentle art of conversation, quiet humor, and the notion that competing, not winning, is the ultimate goal of sports, the gentle ones anyway.

With the popular conviction, however, of the late Green Bay Packers Coach Vince Lombardi that "winning isn't everything, it's the only thing," it isn't easy today to view contests as just fun and games, especially if your child is competing. Organized sports somehow have taken on a more serious note than those at-home games and contests we kids organized. College admissions and maybe scholarships, we said, have intensified parental involvement. But to be fair, we kids too showed our bias and impatience at times, because we also liked to win too much. As I learned later, didn't the great St. Paul say we should run the race to win, even if he spoke about the sprint to salvation?

How much, for example, did we want to win at quoits? If we couldn't agree on whose iron was closest to the pin by using our fingers, Paul Carpentier (deceased in June 2011), the oldest kid in the yard, said, "*J'va aller crire (chercher) la mésure à mon père*," he would get a measuring device that was like a homemade protractor the men used. Yesterday's replay! For us and them too it was "a game of inches," If you thought you were right and the device proved it, you boasted you knew all along, "*J'te lava dit*" (I told you).

Comment ça va? - What Ails You?

BECAUSE IT'S THE American way or it was during the Depression, I said I noticed adult French Canadians when they met usually asked each other about work. Even though the question is still asked today among adults, but more about the kind of work one does, the difference unmasked an edge of fear and desperation if the answer was negative. Lack of work, mom called "*la misère nwère*," (Black Death or misery?) or "*sa paille*," the biblical image of sackcloth and ashes. Both terms evoked fears of hunger, deprivation, and eviction in both speakers. It wasn't just social banter because about halfway through the Depression in 1934, some 12 million Americans were out of work - some say a third of the workforce - with no means of support initially. Some Gothamites sold apples. My Old Testament teacher in college said a stranger will ask you what you do before who you are? As if work is your identity or persona in our vast capitalistic complex. Sadly, is that why workplaces have been the scene of shooting rampages from terminated workers who think despairingly they've lost their identity, self-worth, and reason for living?

But if the question of work was first, equally predictable was the second query: *Comment ça file? File* (pronounced like fill) was an Anglicism: "How are you feeling?" I understood why adults like my parents always mentioned working and health in the same breath, because to live (*pour vivre*), you had to work. Psychologists, like Maslow who've studied people's felt needs later said the equation of work and health (or life itself) was no longer as valid as it once was. The "once was" occurred before a whole plethora of social programs came into being during the New Deal (FDR) or the Great Society (Johnson) to take care of the needy, jobless, and destitute segments of the population. Life now, said Maslow, was not solely work and survival, but more self-actualization through education and a fulfilling career. So generally, people now living longer enjoy a quality of life not solely defined by the rigors of work and a do-or-die mentality, but one enriched by relaxation, reading, travel, sports, repose, gardening, flowers, and hobbies.

In fact, didn't some in the 1960s generation disdain work as too capitalistic, Big Brother, bourgeois, or beneath their dignity? But even if there came a time when work was available for everybody, insightful dad told me one day we'd never get unemployment below three or four percent. Deep down, some just didn't want to work, he postulated, like slackers at the mill: "*des flaneurs.*" It reflected his strong immigrant work ethic. His worst-case scenario was the lazy guy who asked the boss to put his weekly pay in his pocket at the mill. He let out a chuckle when he told me that. Humor?

Psychologists might've had a field day analyzing whether Francos internalized their poverty or stress with real or just imagined pain or sickness. But it always seemed to me that few ever answered the concern about health with, "*Ca va baim*": okay. Most often it was "*Ca va mal,*": not good. As a kid I got the impression not feeling well or good was more natural than *la bonne santé* (good health). With close to 320 million people and longevity into the octogenarian and nonagenarian years, is it true again?

I reasoned dad's bronchiectasis and mom's asthma were reasons they often spoke about health or infirmities. But theirs was not malingering, but real medical situations. But leave it to her, who knew so much about her compatriots' immigration and economic struggles, to often know what ailment, if any, people she knew were laboring with or under. People talked to people a lot and sickness was big news. If someone was suffering big time, she said, "*Yé t'éprouvé*" (He was stricken). If not for her pipeline, we would've thought she had office hours like her relative on Wood Avenue, *Docteur* Auray Fontaine, who treated dad. It took me a long time to understand those French medical terms that spiced their interchanges. In a bilingual world, you must learn twice as much about everybody and everything. Europeans often do, but not Americans who are somewhat "insular," a prof said, because they're isolated between two oceans. Oceans which have also sheltered us from the last two world wars. But no longer in this nuclear age, said one, if some third rate, rogue nation wants to play with the big boys, while people starve, like in North Korea. And of course, our electronic age where someone in Europe or Africa can raise your blood pressure, say, and abscond with your investments with a few strokes. Ours is a sinful world, says Hans Küng, so I sometimes wonder whether new things are producing bad more than good? In one instance, a punk kid induced an innocent teen to commit suicide after undermining her self-worth by media. And stores like Target, Home Depot, and Benny's have had customer accounts raided. Electronic thievery has even infiltrated the personnel records of government workers.

As a youngster I noticed this health-history obsession, but especially after I joined the Order. Perhaps as sharp an observer of the human scene as anyone, fellow trainee, *le Frère* (Brother) Morel, called my attention to it when parents and relatives came to visit us in training at Harrisville, RI. Our mothers especially always seemed to be battling some discomfort in one part of their anatomy or other. Or somebody they knew did. Since the language of the Order was a more proper Canadian French in the early 1950s, we were also bemused with the older Brothers' jargon, medical or otherwise. We readily recognized it from our respective childhoods in Woonsocket, Central Falls, Nashua, Lewiston, and other Canuck centers we were from. Brother Ronald Dupuis, a member of my religious group who later served as Provincial and eventually ordained like Morel, also showed a fine-tuned ear for the often-hilarious amalgam of French and English used by our parents and those Brothers not trained to teach. He recalled the immortal lines, once heard in the city, of the struggling Francophone who wondered how people knew he hadn't come over on the Mayflower: "How could you told I'm French? By my spoke?"; "driving around the 'rosary' [rotary] in a car."; "sanitizing a room with three jerks from a can." Our laugh was tempered because we'd been there at one time. But we were getting an education to get past it, an attainment denied the generation before us.

Before collegiate studies in the French language, we never knew the meaning of *rognon* (kidney), but certainly recognized it from the numerous times we heard it in the city. Had I known, I'd have wondered why most internal ills seemed localized there! Again, Brother Morel was inimitable with his put-on mannerisms and patois in recreating the oft-heard complaint: *Le mal ché j'ter dans mes rognons* (The sickness jumped to my kidneys). Like the would-be malingerer, he contorted his face in pain, looked suppliant-like, and put his hand where those mischievous kidneys were. We also laughed at our colorful idiom, and like the Irish, at our propensity for our long-suffering mentality in our history in North America.

My own fascination with this constant reference to bodily pain or discomfort was this *mal* (ache, sickness) was a real thing, almost a person. It had a mind of its own, struck at will, invaded any part of the body, and always had people begging for mercy or relief. It wasn't just the absence of something, like health or well-being, but something real. It had the same devilish connotation when the nuns spoke to us about moral evil - *Le mal*.

When company came to our house, Biology 101 was on the docket. This *mal* respected neither age, station in life, nor sex. Sample topics from an evening were of course *le mal aux rognons*; *mal au dos* (my aching back); *mal aux jambes* (legs); *mal à tête* (headache); *mal à mon fessier* (posterior); *mal aux poumons* (mom lamenting the weak Fontaine-Tellier lungs); *mal à grosse orteille* (big toe, the only one on the lamentation list); and in patois, the ubiquitous: *mal queuque (quelque)* part. This last usage came about only when the last whiner saw nothing left on the anatomy chart. Any discomfort,

I noticed, evoked a sympathetic air from *la visite* (visitors) and a can-you-top-this look from *la raconteuse* (the storyteller). Yes, mostly woman talk. The men, on the other hand, spoke about *"Roseville"* (Roosevelt), *l'infla(w)tion* (inflation), *le travail à factorie:* factory work, *et les gages*: and wages. Never investments.

For all their real or imaginary ills, however, I don't think the people I knew were generally less healthy or long-lived as others. On the contrary, old people like *pepère* Tellier and *mémère* Fontaine were fixtures in our lives and Canadian folklore. After their own brood was settled, they lived out many more years, often with a married daughter, and many departed to their reward as older senior citizens, a decade or more above the average lifespan at the time. Given the displacement and the labor-intensive aspect of their lives - most as millworkers or *femmes de maison* with *une grosse besogne* (a big job) - they were proof that hard work, pedestrian life, as touted by modern studies, frugal living, home cooking, and, as reported recently, their churchgoing and faith, all somehow contributed to *une bonne vieillesse* (a good old-age). About the benefit of moving and exercising, a researcher said 20th and 21st century people are the first ever who need to do it outside of work. Excessive sitting, like four hours a day, besides lack of good nutrition and exercise, are factors in obesity, David B. Agus, MD, writes in *The End of Illness*. He cites an English researcher who first correlated one's longevity with work. He said drivers at the wheel in England's two-story buses lived ten years less because of immobility compared to their stair-climbing co-workers of the upper deck. The body is in a negative stance, as it were when one is sitting, he said. Harder work for the pumping heart. One study in 2015 said after so many sitting hours, the body is like 90 percent-plus shut down. Affluent people are more likely to exercise, as well as eat better.

But you couldn't miss the sadness of mom's voice if someone died young: *"Yé mort jeune,"* as happened when a relative in Canada died in a scaffolding accident. His widow came to see us and mom commiserated in her loss: *"Ya pa(s) faite vieux os,"* dying "before his bones were aged." In one instance, I saw longevity in *mémère's* family. Even though they weren't all from Woonsocket of course, the local or visiting members of her Morvan clan (RI and Canada) had their picture taken for a June 15, 1939, edition of *The Call*. The seven in the picture totaled 568 years! They spoke not a word of English but talked about the good old days: *les bons vieux temps* they had known in 19th Century Canada when it was still very rural, very French, and so very Catholic.

Also, I think the observation about Woonsocket nowadays having a good elderly population living in those high-rises stems in large part from long-lived French Canadians. Again, sturdy, frugal, and hard-working people of simple means, those city forebears thrived on adversity with unbelievable true grit. Despite their *dur quotidien* or burdensome daily toil, theirs, however, was not a life of quiet desperation. True, mom often thought what *les* Fontaines and other families went through getting here and staying alive during the Depression should've killed them off. But her proudest boast was always, "*On a passé à travers*," about going through thick and thin, unbowed if not unscathed. Like a good NFL rubber-band defense, they could bend or stretch against the onslaught of the vicissitudes of life - want and setbacks - but not break. What's amazing too is this longevity often came without what is now essential for it, like personal family physicians, annual checkups, medical insurance, ready hospitalization, retirement benefits in old age, and of course, today's miracle drugs: "*les remèdes d'aujourd'hui*," (remedies of today) she said. She lamented people once died of a burst appendix or during childbirth. But strangely, for all the good of our present medical situation, we're not the healthiest people, and a report said one-third of all interventions are not necessary, a $7 billion loss. Many countries who spend far less are healthier. A thorough doctor's visit in France is only $31. There's massive scamming in Medicare. Phony clinics haul in healthy people and send "bills" to be paid without any check on their validity. But progress is being made. Because of our generous systems, corruption thrives. (Recently in RI, people on food allotments were selling them to some 20 stores for far less than their worth, presumably to buy drugs and alcohol. Stores got the full value of the card from the government. No more patronage for them.)

    I also noticed if people were quick to claim this *mal* or pain for emotional sympathy from others, their tone took on a lugubrious tone if something was serious or *mortel*. Perhaps she didn't want us to hear, but if she whispered, "*Il est atteint du coeur*," (heart disease), her voice was barely a whisper. The other person, often my *tante* Laurence, flung her head back, eyes registering shock or terror. This was a real illness and life threatening, and not malingering. Because medicine then had no effective response against the disease, its incipience meant his days were numbered: "*Ses jours sont finis*." Of course, women were equally afflicted; their leading cause of death. In fact, first cousin Doris (Tellier) Garçeau, daughter of *mon oncle* Philibert *et tante* Jeanne, was one of the first ever to undergo open-heart surgery in Boston. It prolonged her life allowing she and her husband to raise their son Roger, an MSC grad, '52. I once spoke to her coming out of St. Ann's Church. Mom told me about her heroic struggle.

    Besides heart disease, *le cancer* also registered 8 or 9 on their health Richter scale. Once, mom told *tante* Laurence someone had it and my loquacious aunt was again speechless. The disease was considered the ultimate ravager, like AIDS when it first hit. What was frightening, especially when loved ones often died at home, was the tremendous burden it placed on the family and the unbearable pain the victim suffered because of limited medical knowledge about it and the absence of today's pain-blocking drugs and lifesaving treatments. Sadly, she said of an emaciated victim, "*Yé réduit aux os*": bare bones. But legendary in their caregiving, I noticed how sympathetic and helpful women folk and especially nurses were to people in pain. Dad, for one, was no less helpful but his first instinct was what he was going to do if called upon. What advice he could give or his knowledge of professional medical help available. Besides his cough syrup and potion for an incoming cold, he once devised a special support for my godchild, Ronald Trottier, with a hernia as an infant. An article recently said that because of our success against heart disease (exercise, nutrition, statins, bypass surgery), there's been a 20 percent drop; and cancer, even if more than 70 percent recover, will soon be the number one killer. Patricia's oncologist told us if we ever beat cancer people may live to 115. One person in 10,000 used to live to be 100: now it's one in 5,000 and soon to be 1,000 less than that. I cited the unintended consequence on the public of the cost of our healthcare system. If only the cost of our Middle East wars went to health care! Again, wait to be amazed by Einsenhower's reflection how military costs limit spending on health and progress. Yes, one of the greatest warriors of the century.

Unlike dad, who read from his treasured medical books, mom had a very specific (simplistic?) folklore cause-and-effect approach to sickness and disease. Did it stem from a lack of formal education or from an accumulated trove of wisdom from the ages? What we call folk or alternative medicine, now again very much a part of our health delivery system to the tune of $15 to 20 billion and climbing.

So, in her oral medical compendium on the causes of ill health, there was no gray area in her diagnostic causes for ailments. For example, if you ate "*trop riche comme les rois*," (too rich like kings) you got gout (*la goutte*); if you went out in winter without hat or storm footwear, you could catch pneumonia: *la pneumonie* or a cold: *un rhume*; too many sweets: *du sucrage*, you got diabetes: *la diabète*. And if you pushed yourself too hard, *s'pousser trop fort*, you risked heart disease. If your diet was devoid of *vitamines*, you became weak: *faible*, an opinion shared by dad; ate "heavy" foods: *chargeant*, at supper, like pork, bananas, creamy desserts, then you'd have trouble digesting and sleeping. Dad said it was better to eat smaller amounts more often than big meals. I read that too.

Did the pre-modern regimentation of their faith lead her people to believe in a well-ordered world where nothing happened by chance, like their forebears in France at one time, some 300 years ago? Recall they attributed a lot to Divine Providence, that celestial ordering of all things in history by God for His own inscrutable end and the final happiness, hopefully, of his human creatures. But did they believe too much, and we too little? Webster defines "nihilism" "as a viewpoint that traditional values and beliefs are unfounded, and that existence is senseless and useless." Nihilists they were not. A book about the faith of the Founding Fathers, for example, revealed nearly all of them believed in good works and life after death, as we cited. For one, 11th President James Knox Polk (1845-1849) on his deathbed echoed their belief: "I have filled the highest station on earth, but I will soon go the way of all the earth. I pray God to prepare me to meet the great event." God, it makes you wonder about that great moment! I recall when Pat died at home, it's as if I saw her spirit leave her body. And I wondered what she saw at that moment. In the Order, it was, "Eye hath not seen; ear hath not heard; nor the heart understood what God has readied for us." Grandiose and naturally hard to grasp, so it's no wonder Christ said of some, "O ye of little faith." Like doubting Thomas after the Resurrection, no matter where we live, we all have a little bit of the "Show Me State" in us. A theologian said Thomas by his disbelief and Christ's second visit later helped us believe even more in the Resurrection. The whole faith panorama is so grandiose and beyond belief. So it's little wonder that some say "It can't happen here." And yet we recorded more and more people are becoming non-believers. Recall that Reagan advised to be on the right side if one is not sure. There's no second chance once you've crossed the Great Divide.

Whoever said, "Order is the first law of the universe" had his legions in the city. The beauty of it all is their life also had meaning, never losing sight of "the grand design," like people in Morris Bishop's *The Middle Ages*. Many were untutored, but not clueless of life's meaning and destiny. The lowly and the poor in history confounding the high and the mighty! St. John Vianney (*Curé d'Ars*) versus Voltaire, who dismissed the church: "*Écraser l'infâme.*" (Wipe out the infamous.) My professor said he took all his arguments against the Catholic Church by simply restating them in the negative from what St. Thomas wrote in his *Summa Theologica*, a massive defense of the faith. Considered the most brilliant mind of the Middle Ages and maybe ever, Thomas was, however, considered too trusting and gullible. When a monk told him it was "raining cats and dogs," he went to the window to see, never thinking a fellow religious would mislead him. I liked hearing about the little foibles or weaknesses of great saints, making them more human like us sinners. Like St. Dominic not liking to eat with a wooden spoon; Saint Bernard never looking at his mother's eyes; Peter's denials; Thomas' disbelief about the risen Christ, Saint Ambrose of the early church not liking people who weren't good looking, the nose especially.

I enjoyed mom's version of humanity and science, medical and otherwise: *la théologie selon Léopoldine* (theology according to Léopoldine)? She thought God could have told Adam and Eve everything they and the world needed to know from the very beginning. But in His wisdom, He decided not to make them lazy, allowing their minds - "*leur génie*" (their genius) to uncover things gradually throughout the course of history. Fascinating theory of human progress! She never told me how she evolved it but living her life in a century marked by unequalled advancements in science, technology, and medicine, it was obvious to her the 20th Century was the century of progress. What a mind - girded by apron strings!

But humbly, whenever a new medicine, procedure, or invention came on the scene beyond her understanding, she said, "*Ca cé(e) trop fort pour mwé*," It's too hard for me, but grateful to God anyway: "*J'remercie le bon Dieu pour ça.*" (I thank the good lord for that.) She was especially thankful for breakthroughs in medicine which alleviated suffering and prolonged life. Children dying in childbirth, common in Canada with large families, tore at her heart. What's admirable in this person of little formal education is she didn't have that mistrust towards science and professionals you once saw in people not favored with learning. In the medical profession, for example, she often lauded Dr. Walter Rocheleau and the visiting Irish nurse who taught her how to take care of us babies, whom she feared might be beset with respiratory problems. Hard to believe she said she once knew little about the whole birthing and nursing process.

A people's beliefs are often reflected in their written language, conversation, and practices. If mill working Francos and others had been people of formal education, material means, and worldly achievement, these laudable attainments might have been the everyday stuff of their conversations and aspirations. But because in the main they were poor by today's standards, filled with some pain and sadness, their conversations and thoughts, like the people of the Middle Ages, never wavered far from the eternal verities. That is, God created you; life was a temporary seven-step stage (not dogma of course, but poetically by Shakespeare); acts were good or bad; pain and suffering were conditions of life; and death finally sealed your salvation or damnation. For example, when ailing dad said he wanted to go ("*J'veux m'en aller*"), he knew he was going into another life, as his funeral Mass emphasized. Life was changed, but not ended. If indeed the above belief was once true for most, is today's moral and faith slippage in young people, as reported in a Gallup poll, cause for alarm, since more than half think their faith and belief in God are less important than for their parents and grandparents? Again, did Francos of old have too much simple faith, a defector might ask, and their progeny too little? And as a college teacher of mine was fond of repeating, "Faith is the belief in things the evidence of which appears not." And Christ said, "Blessed are they who have not seen but who have believed." But I guess we all have a bit of that "show-me" mentality in us and like Thomas, we sometimes want to put our hand in Christ's side before we believe. That's why He lauded those who believed without seeing Him. (My own fantasy is that Christ would've come back every century to make sure His doctrine was still as He first laid it down. When I told a teacher, he said every century would've killed Him again, so unnatural, as in otherworldly, is His message. It's why the church needs constant reform, says Küng. Its founder is divine, but its adherents are human, fallible, and prone to erroneous changes by "wolves in sheep's clothing." But would his coming again and again prevent a glut of religions with contrary doctrines or non-believers, some with shocking moral accommodations. When one of the Oxford Movement converts of the late 19th Century was told another religion was coming aboard, he replied, "We don't need another; we haven't tried the one we have." Touché.

Undoubtedly their station in life, whether as homemakers or millworkers or unskilled service jobbers for the most part, belied the great theater their life's play was being played on. Literary critics, I've read, who lament the disappearance of truly evil characters in literature in terms of moral standards, such as you see otherwise in the works of Chaucer, Shakespeare, and Milton, blame the situation on the loss of this grand vision of good and evil that people in the Ages of Faith and the period of mass migrations had. The thinking is that there is no saint without the notion of virtue; no sinner without sin, even if a negative in itself. I've read that not only the Catholic ethos, but also the Protestant ethic, the bedrock of our Founding Fathers' thinking and our constitutional freedoms, also eroded at the same time from our national fabric. The Perfect Storm! What some have described as America losing her innocence sometime between the end of WWII up to the Vietnam Era and beyond just as Europe had long done (excepting a few countries), with now Spain and Ireland also starting to forget "the faith of our fathers." Devotees of the Fatima apparitions in Portugal in the 19th Century even included the world's economic mess, as one result of our present faithlessness. Pope Francis is a devotee. The three children - Jacinta, Francisco, and Lucy - cite moral turpitude especially for condemnation after death. Isn't sexual slavery still prevalent in some countries? The children said they didn't like looking at hell. Mentioned 20 times in the Bible!

French Canadians like mom and those oracles of our moral education - our catechism teachers in school and the curates in the pulpit on Sunday - would have made short shrift of the notion of sin being no more than uncontrollable urges, complexes, honest mistakes, or near justifiable weaknesses. There were no situational ethicists or anti-heroes in our catechism books or church history texts. If she had ever encountered determinists and behaviorists, mom would have deflected their arguments with one of her oft-repeated moral reminders: *"Il faut être responsable,"* meaning "you were the captain of your own ship," as poet Walt Whitman said. True, it did make them and the church look absolutist at times, like the paterfamilias banishing an adolescent child for not going to church, or a suicide not being allowed a Christian burial. But having a clear-cut sense of right and wrong gave them and us a sense of certainty and stability now missing in modern life. Pilate asked Christ "What is the truth?" But didn't wait for an answer. I like to think a lot of our immigrant ancestors didn't need to ask that question.

I recall how Sister Saint Émilie often told us how God's hand was ready to come down on sinful man but was held back by His mother. I'm glad no one uses that imagery now, even if the Bible says, "Fear is the beginning of wisdom." But now it's the finger on the nuclear button we fear more. I recall a professor said somewhat fancifully, "Adam and Eve began the world; Atom and Evil will end it." I again beg the reader's patience for dwelling so much on the faith of Francos, but it was their essence, their life, their hoped-for destiny. If we indict them for too much faith, do we have too little?

Leslie Y. Gutterman, Rabbi of Temple Beth-el, Providence, RI, wrote an insightful poem about the grand design people once lived by more intensely than we do now:

> Isn't it strange that princes and kings
> And clowns that caper in sawdust nights,
> And common people like you and me,
> Are builders for all eternity?
> To each is given a bag of tools
> A piece of clay and a book of rules.
> And each must fashion ere life has flown
> A stumbling block or a stepping-stone.

Hearing the above, again my challenged *madre* might have said of his erudite King's English: *"Son angla est trop fort pour mwé,"* meaning too hard to understand. But if I told her its message of personal responsibility and stewardship towards salvation, she would've blurted out, *"Ça cé(e) vra"*: it's the honest truth.

The Unnamed Hurricane of 1938

UNTIL ADULTHOOD, when I read the biblical account of Doomsday with its preceding wars, tidal waves, and falling celestial bodies, nothing was more graphically seared in my mind than 9/21/1938, the Year of the Hurricane: "*l'année de l'ouragan*," said mom.

Without a doubt one of the worst devastating events ever to occur in Rhode Island, the calamity, so stealthy and so deadly, claimed 262 lives and caused property damage near $100 million. Winds roared close to 125 miles per hour and created 20-foot waves, flooding downtown Providence to a depth of 10 feet or more. In Woonsocket, the Alice Mill roof was blown off and the downtown Najarian store was practically shredded. Mrs. Timothy J. McKee and her children from the city perished when their car overturned at Charlestown beach. Others also.

In our 309 Gaulin home, outside of dad's medical books, our most prized possession in "the family library" was a 1938 commemorative book of the storm. Sadly, it fell apart from too much handling. Because we experienced the horror of the hurricane, we never ceased to look at storm photos, while scrounging up reminiscences of that first unforgettable day in our young lives. Cousin Gene lent me his copy of *Hurricane Havoc - As the Call Camera Saw the Big Blow*.

The hurricane became so unforgettable, it even replaced the oft-mentioned Depression before and after which it seemed - like the birth of Christ in the Christian calendar - all events and time were referred to by my parents. So instead of *Avant ou Après la Depression* (Before or After the Depression), it was now *Avant ou Après l'Ouragan* (…Hurricane) I guess calamities, like all mortal flesh, have their shelf life because after the 59-inch snowstorm of '78, I noticed people often used that as a reference point. But not so much for 9/11/01 and its horror.

Because on Gaulin we lived on the third floor of an area of the city with a panoramic view of a section of it, like the Hamlet mill area, we viewed damage firsthand. With dad at the mill, before we eventually gathered in our living room in late afternoon with each one fighting fears of impending doom, the day had proceeded just a bit off the ordinary. The U.S. Weather Bureau had not been putting out any undue storm warnings. So, until mid-afternoon of September 21, there was no indication it was going to hit here. Unfortunately, hurricane forecasting and naming were not the sophisticated art or science they are today. Complacency or blissful oversight was the counterpoint to today's massive media coverage. So, there was no rush for milk and bread - it was home delivered anyway!

I had gone to school as usual with Lucien Laferrière and was out of school around 3 p.m. Like two kids reveling in their first roller coaster ride, we began to laugh and shout with joy as the mounting winds literally pushed us up Gaulin to our homes. Both lightweights and with no idea what a hurricane was, we thought we were dealing only with a strong wind, the strongest ever. I was 8; he, 7.

Arriving home, we intended to play in the backyard as usual, until we noticed something strange. The lashing, driving wind was making water falling from the roof above somehow jet out down below from the corner of his house just above the foundation. But the falling jet of water was being flung into the air instead of splashing on our graveled yard. Puzzled about it, we scooted for the safety of our homes.

As a full-time homemaker mom was always home when we arrived from school. But this day she had walked to a whist party at St. Louis Parish on Rathbun Street (her sister Laurence's parish), a good walk. Wet, wind-whipped and *sans le chapeau* (without the hat) she had made the day before, she described how she barely managed to climb our street one fence picket or wall stone at a time. She blurted out, "*Le diable s'en mêle*," as in the devil's hell and damnation.

In the living room we were quickly shrouded by the loss of power. But she found a blessed candle - *une chandelle bénite* - which she put on the dining room table. Families like us had holy water from Holy Week services, as well as a special crucifix that contained a blessed candle in its shaft. That's in case the priest came to administer Extreme Unction, now the Sacrament of the Anointing of the Sick, to a grievously ill member of the family. Terminally ill people, especially with cancer, lung, or heart disease, often died *à la maison* (at home). You bought the crucifix, but one year I won one at St. Ann's. Fortunately, it wasn't a case of foreshadowing: "*un signe avant coureur*" (a warning sign), as we said in the Order.

I sneaked a look at the candle when I lifted my head from under the tablecloth. I also listened to the sound and the fury of the increasing storm. The nuns told us the wax was a symbol of Christ's body; the wick, his humanity; the flame, his divinity. Hopefully three times divine insurance or assurance!

As usual, pious *mémère* sat by the stove, her wrinkled fingers racing over her shiny brown beads, worn smooth by a million *avés*. Was she remembering perhaps the terrible Cochrane, Ontario fire of 1916 that wiped out everything her family had? Mom, Bob, Sue, and I kept watching dad's mill. Ben and Rachel, 4 and 2, respectively, had a clinging foreboding of danger: "Mom, when will it be over?": *Comment longtemps?*

Mom was worried because dad had not yet arrived "*d'la factorie*" (from the mill) and it was way past 2. From our windows, we could always see the mill and floors where he worked. Imagine our collective terror when as we looked, the corner of his mill facing *la* Hamlet was being sheared off by the wind. Bricks were being propelled like from a bazooka. But finally, he arrived, saying the workers had been rebuffed by the wind: "*par le vent*." He spoke of flying debris, uprooted trees, blown-off roofs, and overturned cars. Our marketer, dad was a man who was always two weeks ahead of everybody when it came to planning. If things got worse, he knew we could hold out for quite a while because of his habit of always buying *en gros* (in bulk).

With him home, we were bolder to observe the storm, keeping however a safe distance from the windows in case bricks from spitting chimneys and ripped roofing materials came crashing through. Since it was early fall, the storm windows were not in yet. Living on the third floor, we feared the wind would rip our roof right off, as it did to some homes. But there was an amazing oddity in my parents' bedroom some twenty feet away from the other Carle tenement house. The windowpane was broken in a perfectly cylindrical manner, probably from small roof pebbles picked up by the wind and hurled rotary-wise at the glass. He made a ball-like cloth plug for the hole and asked for "*la petite brosse et porte-ordure*" (the small brush and dustpan in the closet behind the stove) to pick up the scattered glass. We closed the door.

After supper was eaten with the same foreboding as a condemned man having his last meal, we got word everyone in the house was going down *chez les* Carpentiers on the first floor. It was the safe thing to do for us especially, living *au troisième étage* (on the third floor), even if it meant giving up our unequalled view of the storm. I don't know who thought of the move first, but it was typical of the togetherness and community of the eight apartment residents whose lives were so intertwined daily. Isn't it still America's finest trait, this incredible neighborliness in emergencies, here or in other countries? America's saving grace! Didn't Christ say even a glass of water given in His name will not go unrewarded?

The first floor did give us a ground-zero view of the storm raging in front on our street. It was littered with debris, a fallen tree across the street where the Dubois lived and where dachshunds were bred, and incredibly, a man battling the fury of the wind on his way home around 6 p.m. With his shirt or jacket almost ripped off his back, like a billowing parachute, he made stumbling advances, fence picket by picket. Finally, he disappeared from our collective view. Since in our neighborhood no one was or remained anonymous for long, sure enough someone knew his name. But to me, it was one of the few times she, our roving reporter, didn't tell her entourage "His life and times." She was too preoccupied spinning tales to her captive audience about her family's Cochrane catastrophe. It was the first time I ever heard it, with the full story evolving over the years. You'll recall it was even mentioned in the book *Florentine Raconte* when the Fontaines and the Morvans lived in Canada. She related the story and no one could top it. The best "survivor" story they had ever heard! But we kids at the Carpentiers felt dwarfed by all the adults. No way could we run around the rooms, as we loved to do. It's why I tuned in, as I often did when she spoke.

If you keep in mind that over 45 people lived in our eight-tenement house, you get an idea what a gathering it was. It never happened again. This was one of those one-hundred-year events, the so-called perfect storm. So gathered there were young and old, frightened, and brave, mute and talkative, timid and bold, raconteurs like mom and listeners, the tragedy-tested and the unwary. We were mostly all in the large front parlor, a nice feature of our high-rise. It was usually reserved for company. And company *les* Carpentiers had that night! This was not like adding one more potato to *la gibelotte* (the stew), because someone dropped in!

What I remember most was the camaraderie, like in the Blizzard of '78, and the narratives in French about the tragedies the storytellers had lived through in Canada and in the states. Because it was still the Depression and war rumors had not yet stimulated the U.S. economy much, mom wisecracked the storm might take the last of their meager belongings: "*le restant de nos quenilles*" (rags). Adults all knew the expression. It was small comfort to think you couldn't lose much because you didn't have much! Did she think that once again, like 22 years before in 1916, she'd have to start all over, like the Fontaines entraining for America with nothing but the singed clothing on their backs! Like anyone who's afflicted more than once, she thought the Lord of Calamities visited them too often. "*Cé(e) comme- ci le bon Dieu nous en voula*," is how she dared say God wanted His pound of flesh from them. In modern lingo: the "Why Us?" lament so often heard now with disasters occurring more often and devastatingly. (Once three or four major catastrophes occurred worldwide, now it's more like 15 said a recent report. One televangelist said it was a sign of God's retribution for the sins of mankind, a notion once quite popular or biblical-like in the Old Testament.)

In those pre-TV days, people retired early. But it was late evening when we returned to our apartments. The wind had subsided enough to ease the fear of the house losing its cover, exposing "*notre ameublement*" (our furniture), she said. How like a procession it was, with people leaving the Carpentier apartment with lighted candles and flashlights to chase away the gloom of the unlit hallway. Later, Dr. Jeremiah Durick, one of my English professors at St. Michael's College, Vermont, was fond of saying when exasperated or tired: "O, how I wish I were in my bed again." That's how we children felt after the worst day of our lives. But like our heroes in those Saturday afternoon movies at the Laurier Theater, we had a Gary Cooper *High Noon* challenge and came away unscathed. We slept the sleep of the just, as we said in the Order: *l'oreiller du juste*: the pillow of the righteous person. Mom, a Fontaine, had dodged one more bullet: her 9th.

When we woke up in the morning, the rear-guard wind still teased in the street and between the houses, refusing to admit it had already blown its stack. Like in the biblical story about the often-unsettled Lake Galilee, or "the troubled Tiber chafing with her shores," as the Bard said, September 22 was the calm after the storm.

Being a schoolboy, we naturally wondered if there was school Thursday. In those days, I don't remember radio cancellations for Catholic schools, and so we always had to guess, if word of mouth (or school bell?) didn't reach you. Hearing conflicting reports, Bob and I told mom there wasn't any and took off to tour the city.

On our damage tour, I remember a huge tree fallen in the downstreet yard of our Peloquin cousins where we sometimes played ball, using it as home plate. The rest of the city we saw was like our own street magnified to the nth degree: roofs gone, trees uprooted, chimney bricks flung everywhere, doors blown open, house pieces and whole dwellings wrenched from their foundations, fences and lines downed, cars overturned, and people turned outdoors. In Social *Coin* and other places, the swollen Blackstone River had again jumped its bank to wreak its all too frequent waterborne misery, especially in the most low-lying sections.

Only after hurricanes of the 1950s, would the river finally be hemmed in, thanks largely to the efforts of Mayor Kevin Coleman, who, they say, had an encounter with the raging waters caused by Hurricane Diane (1955). But now, everywhere in the city men with axes and two-man saws (loved seeing those in action as a kid) were busy clearing trees. They were "the power saws" of the day. Dad called it *un gadendar*, but Claire Quintal, former head of *L'Institut Français du collège de l'Assomption*, told me *le vrai mot est "godendard"* (the real word is "*godendard*"). On our way home, we met a Morin friend of mine whose family lived on Kendrick near the bridge. He was bursting to tell me something. "Would you believe it," he whined like a man who had missed Powerball by one number, "My younger sister found a big wad of bills ("*un gros montant d'argent*,") during the storm and gave it to the first man she asked if he lost it?" Was it the naïveté of a child or what happens in a tragedy when pillage and thievery run rampant, as insensitive louts add to people's misery? Many homeowners in New Orleans ravaged by Katrina were scammed by pseudo repairers: Eighty percent!

When we finally got home, dad told us his theory about wars and hurricanes occurring every 20 to 25 years, give or take a few. I thought of his tempest theory when Hurricane Diane hit, causing the Great Flood which demolished Horseshoe Falls and flooded Social *Coin*. It wasn't even respectful of the dearly departed, as I said, "this nice name for a terrible storm," as a report called it, deposited caskets from Precious Blood Cemetery on the steps of St. Ann's Church and elsewhere. Nearly 10.5 inches of rain fell on the city, washing away the earthen banks of Harris Pond, wiping out the falls, and sending a 20-foot wall of water cascading towards the Social District. It caused $31 million in damage, a phenomenal amount in a working-class city like Woonsocket. Cousin Gene, and scouts Gerry Baillargeon, Paul Lauzon, Milton Wilbur and Mr. Walter Lauzon helped retrieve bodies.

Dad died in 1982, some three years before Hurricane Gloria touched us and just a bit late for his quarter century hurricane theory. We've been visited by a few minor hurricanes in the 1990s, but no significant damage. Now with dad's prognosticating days over, I hope where he sits in the New Jerusalem he intercedes with the Lord of Fair Skies "who can turn the tide and calm the angry seas," as He did on Lake Galilee.

Le guy des vues in the Theaters of Yesteryear
[The guy(s) who make movies]

WHEN IN 1984 I read about the impending demolition of the remaining charred skeleton of the old Olympia Block on Main Street, it reminded me how important the city's six movie houses had been in the life of first- and second-generation Francos.

The six venues - the Park, Stadium, Bijou, Rialto, Laurier, and Olympia - had been, well, like Hollywood's Theater of the Poor for immigrants and their children. In those houses' heavily draped decor, they could glimpse for a dime or a quarter the so-called Hollywood Mystique. That is, a world different from the one they lived in. One where usually there was no searing poverty, good and evil were clearly demarcated, romance was young and seemingly lasting. It was also where hard work and honesty prevailed, crooks got caught in the end, and the good guy got the girl, as the sun at the end set gloriously in the West. It was a time, a critic said, when you felt better about life and yourself when you left the theater. The age of exaggerated, hard-boiled realism and the depiction of the worst elements of human cruelty, violence, and depravity came mostly after the despair and disillusionment of the Vietnam Conflict and other global events when America lost its innocence. When any kind of public decency in film and print was severely battered on the shoals of a libertine or licentious interpretation of the right of free expression, like even cyberspace eroticism.

Both mom and dad spoke nostalgically of the early silent or first talking movie greats, like Fairbanks Sr., Valentino, Chaplin, et al. We said dad, whose taste in comedy ran a bit into buffoonery, liked the antics of the little English comedian. After all, who wouldn't want a bit of madcap antics after those long, tedious hours at the mill? I never asked him if he liked The Keystone Cops. His favorite live Canadian comics at the Laurier were Tizoon *et* Balloon, physical comedians of the highest order, like precursors or contemporaries of America's The Three Stooges, Laurel and Hardy, and Abbot and Costello. All the best ever, some say.

As a youngster I was amused by a movie expression Francos used to explain why or how a happy event came to be. Like most people of yesteryear of deep faith but little opportunity for advanced education, they often ascribed natural events to the will of God - *la volonté du bon Dieu* - or the devil, as we related. But for nice, make-believe endings, such as Hollywood shaped them to expect, they said, tongue in cheek, "*Ça c'tarrangé avec le guy des vues,*" that is, only movie producers did that.

When I entered the Order in the late 1940s, movies were somewhat frowned upon, because, as old Brother Anselm told me, they featured actors like Tyrone Power and Errol Flynn whose romantic antics were considered risqué. But there was a story about an older monk who was asked why he liked movies so much, he replied, "*Le bon Dieu a ses vues; moi, j'ai mes movins*" (The good Lord has his "*vues,*" me, I have my movies). The subtlety is that in French the word "vues" means both God's Divine Providence as well as movies ("*movins*"). So, if God had His, why couldn't a monk have his also?

One of my confreres, Brother Anthony, was a keyboard impresario during silent film days. He was fond of retelling how when asked if he knew the tune "Napoleon's Last Charge," he said, "No, I don't know it. How much was it?" He's the same witty *Frère* who when told by a doctor he needed a local anesthesia, said he was glad he didn't have to go out of town for it.

Movies, radio, and newspapers taught my parents a lot of English words. At home, mom always sang in French during her domestic chores. (I was once asked to read a doctoral thesis where the writer quoted a Greek philosopher who said every man has a song in his heart at work. He researched whether music helped or hindered kids studying. The results – classical music: neutral; modern music, a bit negative.) But with mom, occasionally you heard a musical note from one of the movies of Nelson Eddy (a Rhode Islander) and Jeannette MacDonald. Especially from "*Maytime,*" her all-time favorite, along with the song "Indian Love Call" from the film *Rose Marie.*" Other favorites were "Beyond the Blue Horizon," "Ah! Sweet Mystery of Life," "Stouthearted Men" (which I loved in the Order), and the "The Sweetheart Waltz." Then, as if she felt a twang of remorse about this cultural slippage, she'd revert back to French. Her favorite was a French ballad she taught all of us: "*Au clair de la lune, mon ami Pierrot. Prêtes-moi ta plume pour écrire un mot.*" Pierrot is asked to lend a pen, by the light of the silvery moon. Josée Vachon, composer and popular chanteuse who has performed many times at Autumnfest and the Museum of Work and Culture sang it, when I requested it.

Long after we children were far more comfortable and adept with English than our parents would ever be, she cracked us up with her opinion of a movie she saw or book she tried to read: *"Son angla éta trop fort pour mwé,"* meaning she ran smack-dab into English dialogue that was over her head. But she never stopped trying. Like Scarlett O'Hara, she said it with her usual grittiness and laissez-faire, confident that tomorrow would come anyway. She had come to America too late (at 18) and too insulated in an all-French milieu to learn English well. As nearly all did, she lived, as my Mobile college prof lyricized, "in a kind of isolated, cultural island in a sea of Americanism." I didn't tell her that, fearing she might say, *"Lache mwé avec ça"*: Who cares!

Of all six movie houses, the Olympia was last in the pecking order. Before going there, you saw what was playing at the other five theaters. We also went there if we couldn't raise the price of admission to the better theaters, a frequent happenstance in the Depression before we became nouveaux riche during and after the war. Like when I paid my *Call* bill on Saturdays, we walked all the way to the Olympia on Main Street to save a few pennies. The local namesake for the once Grecian site of Olympian games was cheaper to get in. It had to be.

Fueling the theater's reputation was the unsavory epithet it bore like a second name. I was told it was called "The Scratch House," a revelation that those famed miniscule biting insects inhabited its stained carpets, faded tapestries, and torn seats. The same popularized by the shortest poem of them all, so said Father Murray in Mobile: "Adam had 'em," that is: fleas."

Its dilapidated appearance, however, never tempted owners to weaken its moralistic stance (by showing X-rated movies to perk up sagging attendance). No, its Republic movies were actually old morality plays where, like our westerns, good and evil characters were in sharp contrast. (Flicks from Warner Brothers, Columbia, Twentieth Century Fox, and MGM played at the more upscale theaters.) Of course, we were strictly enjoined by our parents, priests, nuns, and the diocesan paper, *The Providence Visitor* in its weekly movie ratings, from watching bad ones. Going in to see one would've been like going into a house of ill repute, as they once called a whorehouse in polite literature. Is it a so-called cultural barometer of our times that to increase their drawing power, producers now seek the very R rating that once would've kept people away? Poet Pope wrote the most insightful lines about the attraction of evil: "Vice is a monster of so frightful mien, / As, to be hated, needs but to be seen; / Yet seen too oft, familiar with her face, / We first endure, then pity, then embrace." No wonder nuns often spoke about avoiding the occasion of sin. "Out of sight, out of mind."

In our westerns, dress, language, and manners separated the good from the bad guys. Those flicks were cowboys chasing outlaws, often featuring one daring stop of a riderless stagecoach. The hero jumped from his horse onto one of the wildly galloping horses in the team, one near the coach, working his way underneath or sideways to one of the leading horses. Inside the coach was the damsel in distress, along with an accompanying doughty (not a Miss America hopeful!) lady-in-waiting dressed in very subdued browns. The contrast with the heroine's white dress and colorful bonnet was obvious. Sorta' like Grace Kelly in *High Noon*.

Always the chief villain abandoned the last shootout, repairing to the office safe to abscond with the loot. But our hero always spotted his move and withdrew from the six-shooter exchange with the bad 'uns to intercept him. Since producers cranked out a western in four days, we never sat through a repeat. The rest of the card comprised a serial (The Lone Ranger, the Green Hornet, Batman and Robin, etc.), a cartoon (often Bugs Bunny with Mel Blanc's famous last line: "That's all, folks!"), coming attractions, and a raffle, all for eleven cents. But along with candy, it was a lot to give up for Lent because we went to Mass every morning, a popular penitential resolution. After Easter, we loved hearing The Lone Ranger's intro: "A fiery horse with a speed of light, a cloud of dust, and a hearty Hi-Yo, Silver!" It meant the bad 'uns were again on the run.

Our full-time homemakers never needed babysitters, but those movies on Saturdays would've been cheap alternatives. We were literally blinded as we emerged from close to four hours of viewing on Saturday afternoons. *Le* Laurier was packed top to bottom. The Gaulin gang - we innocent "Boyz of the Hood" - all sat together. Creatures of habit, we perched our boyhood fantasies on the ground floor about a dozen rows up on the left side aisle. We had a good view of the clock to egg it on towards the one o'clock starting time! And later, a quick exit through the side door. The silence must've been heavenly in our Gaulin digs, as if only adults lived there. We were in our own fantasy world, like in our comic books. We heard more English in four hours than all week in our Canuck-speaking 'hood!

The Rialto, also downtown, was more expensive, and we spurned the luxury of the seven-cent bus. When mom, with one of us children along, occasionally shopped downtown ("*magaziner en ville*," she said), I, a couple of times, rode the bus with her back to Cass Avenue if she had "*beaucoup d'achats*" (lots of shopping). Once I rode my bike while she walked. Having bought drinking glasses at Kresge's, she put them in my rear cloth newspaper saddlebags. The city's roads weren't too smooth, so all the glasses were broken when we got back. Not mad, she said I should be more careful next time: "*prendre plus de précaution la prochaine fois*." Thank God, our lifestyle didn't make her angry, envious, or exasperated. Recall her mantra was nobody had any more than any other: *"pas plus que les autres."* We've already discussed Dad's affection for the Jews because of their mutual trust, something my parents thought was lacking in French Canadians. More in the minority than us in the national psyche, they displayed great cohesiveness. I was surprised mom even reminded us once Jesus Christ was a Jew: *un juif.* She liked shopping in their store(s) in Social because they spoke passable French.

The other theater palaces - the Bijou, artistic Stadium and the Park, were more "top shelf" or adult theaters. Young adolescents frequented *le* Laurier on Social, especially on Friday nights, a kind of group date night. But price aside, the kinds of movies also dictated our choice. The Stadium and Bijou adult cinemas charged a quarter and often featured love stories. But one Sunday afternoon I saw vaudeville at the Park on North Main because boyhood friend Maurice Vandal's dad paid the quarter. Since at home I enjoyed radio comedians Jack Benny and Fred Allen, I liked the glib, fast-talking comic who made us feel good when he said our city was one of the friendliest cities he'd been in. The deflating punch line was the moment he put his hand in his back pocket, someone else had his hand there to shake it! Also, a super-quick prestidigitator, he took a wristwatch off a volunteer without his realizing it. A doubting Thomas thought he was "a plant."

My folks liked to go to the Laurier if those Canadian comics and cast appeared live. They were talking my parents' language and they swapped their jokes and re-mouthed their lines for weeks. Canadian humor was hilarious, racy, buffoon-like, and jokingly biting, and immigrants ate it up. As entertainment critic mom said, *"On riait d'bon coeur,"* about laughing heartily. I'm not sure if a Rosanne-type singer of risqué verses I saw (recall her massacre of the National Anthem, compared to Whitney Houston's) was a Madame Bolduc, who was later reprimanded (excommunicated?) by our church in Canada.

Speaking of our six-shooter favorites, we were lukewarm about the likes of Roy Rogers and Gene Autry, whose horses we loved, but who did too much guitar plunking and singing. But they didn't romance and that was good. Their crotchety or folksy sidekicks like Gabby Hayes, Fuzzy Knight, Andy Devine, Smiley Burnette provided hee-haw comic relief. But I said our real favorites were those rip-roarin', snip-snortin', six-shootin' action types, like Wild Bill Hickock, the Cisco Kid, aging Buck Jones, Lash Larue, the Durango Kid, and a bunkhouse of others. They were all straight arrows, morality figures really, fighting for law and order in the old West. We mouthed some of their lines in our games. The best one-liner: "I'm gonna' put law and order in 'dese' parts," (pronounced: "pots" in Rhode Islandese), whenever a kid felt antsy and disruptive. "Trying to head 'em off at the pass" was another. If someone said, "There's a herd of cattle at the pass," the reply was "How many heads?" "One per cattle" was the joke.

Built by local industrialist Arthur I. Darman in 1926, only the ornate Stadium now remains with great civic efforts to restore this architectural gem (a mute classical oracle of what moviedom once was in the city) under the leadership of the late Honorable Francis Lanctot and other devotees. During its heyday, stars like Charlie Chaplin, Al Jolson, and Will Rogers graced its stage. That is, before shopping mall theaters and outdoor movies (one left in RI) and playhouses turned time and tide against them. When few if any homes had AC, drive-ins were the only relief. The Stadium's Executive Director/CEO, Cathy Levesque, has been indefatigable in advertising and attracting talented performers and productions. I shook hands with Andy Rooney a few years ago. I knew I might meet him at a side door. Local talent with annual plays or musicals, like John Guevremont's MSC productions, have all displayed great talent in Northern RI and beyond.

But even if Francos went to movies for enjoyment and a form of escapism, the great unifying influence that media culturist Marshall Mcluhan wrote about helped them see how Americans, real or fictional, now or yesterday, lived or wished to live in this country. So, films helped Americanize them in a profound manner. Foreigners now react the same way to our films, as their perceptions of America, naturally laden with their own cultural bias and sometimes dogmatic faith, skewer what we really are. Simply, they sometimes think life and people in America are what they appear to be in the movies, but with sophistication, less and less is America seen as an El Dorado where streets are paved with gold. It was 1916, but the conductor who helped *les* Fontaines to America had a bit of American pixie dust in his psyche. Remember how he advised the refugees to tell customs about rich relatives in America, a common belief about those living below the 49th parallel.

So, it was a kind of cinematic false reality that took on a life of its own the world over. Why, with their extravagant lifestyles, numerous romantic entanglements, palatial homes, unusual attire, and lavish weddings, even now actors often blur the difference between their pristine celluloid image and their real selves in the mind of their fans, perpetuating a kind of voyeuristic cult among their devotees. I recall when in real life Jennifer Jones divorced soon after she played the holy nun Bernadette Soubirous to whom Mary appeared in Lourdes, France. I heard people question how she could fall from grace so fast! The movie was "*The Song of Bernadette*" from a best-selling book by Jewish author, Franz Werfel, whose family was helped by Catholics to escape the Nazis.

So even in simpler times and simpler movies, for a few hours it was good to be transfixed and transported. Almost like the effect you get from reading a good book that enfolds you completely. But today, as we exit the theater, we may repair to our comfortable cars and maybe go out for a bite. But in working class mill cities, exiting patrons immediately touched down on the cold macadam of reality. A reality, yes, of good people like themselves, with solid urban anchors of homes, churches, schools, and marketplace, but also of surrounding mills, low wages, and the everyday struggle to make ends meet. What mom called, "*s'tenir en avant,*" trying to stay ahead and "*nos efforts pour garder notre chez-nous,*" the struggle to keep a roof over our heads. Imagine having the wolf at the door every waking hour of the day. Shockingly, a situation again becoming more and more common in our times as the divide between rich and poor widens. Again, is it the inevitability of unbridled capitalism (especially if not closely regulated, as Teddy Roosevelt and Wilson tried to do), even if it's supposedly the best economic "ism" out there? Throwing several of the great philanthropic families of the 1920s under the bus, one of my professors said if unchecked, they would have eventually owned everything. Once despised by many, only with philanthropy did those families restore their good name. Absolution by contribution. I once read that "with all their so-called faults," unlike today's wealthy, they gave and established many enduring monuments, museums, and philanthropies.

So, movies were a good escape valve, a temporary flight from reality, and a kind of fantasy fix. And, as mom said, a chance "*pour apprendre notre angla,*" to learn the King's English. After all, Scoutmaster Jannell told us scouts it was the language of America, and not French or our patois. How in the world did he get an idea like that in *Sochelle Coin*? Didn't he know about the dogmatic link between French and the faith, as King Louis XIV and first Canadian Bishop Laval ordered affirmed?

6 - WORLD WAR II AND THE AMERICANIZATION OF FRENCH-CANADIAN WOONSOCKET

The Nazi Peril

"GERMANY ATTACKS POLAND." Yes, it was September 1, 1939, a date burned into my memory. Its import, I said, would affect us, our life, and culture in the city like nothing else before or after. Young men we knew would die, like the young quoits player, the next-door submariner in the Pacific, and two soldiers from across the street. And in my entire related family, 20 would answer the call during or soon after the war with two making the ultimate sacrifice, one in France, the other in Italy. Mom was so proud of our related families' call to arms. She told me the first Tellier and Fontaine ancestors here were soldiers of the king, with some adding *dit Lafortune* to both our family names, as seen in our genealogies.

In 1939-40, I enjoyed the war story between Russia and Finland, picturing the Finnish soldier-skiers swooshing down against the vast Red Army hordes and defeating five of their armies. They enticed their attackers to doomed pursuits over snowy terrains concealing deep crevices or thin ice. Says Richard Overy in *Russia's War*, "Frostbite and hunger added to the casualties inflicted by fast-moving Finnish troops and snipers." With their all-white hooded uniforms and bravado, they were winning the world's admiration, but not its support. The U.S. only gave $30 million for non-military purposes. I wondered what chance they had, since dad said they'd lose. I felt bad the Russian Bear was swallowing Latvia, Estonia, Lithuania, and finally Finland. The famed Nazi Wehrmacht soldiers and elite Panzer divisions considered the Finns their equal or superior. Only years later would they regain their freedom, with Pope John Paul II having a moral and diplomatic influence in communism's fall there and his country Poland.

Because it lasted so long and involved so many millions here and abroad, WWII affected our neighborhood and life in Woonsocket more dramatically than anything else ever did. But is that why the century's greatest event fashioned the greatest generation and events in all their good outreaches. And highlighted leaders, combatants, and everyday citizens more prominently than in ordinary times? Was it like in church histories, the blood of martyrs revealed great faith and heroism, so said Tertullian?

Not to retell the war, as already done in thousands of books, I want to highlight events and strategies not known until war's end, as well as the role of our local combatants who fought with their national counterparts in this global war, and at home: the workers who created the miracle of "The

Arsenal of Democracy," assuring us of victory. And as one of the theses of this book, these Francos speeded up our Americanization from our quasi-Quebéckian way of life, especially with respect to language, education, and advancement in the higher realms of the nation's economy.

The war was a totally popular one against enemies inimical to our freedoms. Thus, from 1939, but especially from 1941 until the cessation of all hostilities in 1945, our own God's little acre labored, prayed, and spilled some of its young blood to defeat the Hitlerian menace and restore peace. A peace not only over "the white cliffs of Dover," but over the whole world. Again, a world war, just like the one from 1914-1918 my folks often spoke about: "The war to end all wars!" But not in dad's mind! Even if our entry into WWII occurred with the attack on Pearl Harbor in 1941, and Hitler's declaration of war against us days later, it was revealing to read how we were "sooner and secretly in a war mode" before the attack, as seen in Wild Bill Donovan: *The Spy Who Created The OSS, Modern and Modern American Espionage* by Douglas Waller, and also *A Man Called Intrepid* by Canadian William Stevenson, whose preemptive spy work led Churchill to send him to America to run British Intelligence here in the U.S.A. They all convinced Roosevelt through Enigma intercepts that Germany was plotting against us long before our entry into the war. Imagine, long before its hostilities, Germany had over 280 espionage centers all over the world.

But providentially their aggrandized self-esteem led them to believe their transmissions were safe, as reported in David Khan's *Hitler's Spies*. Because of that, "enlightened FDR secretly dared to go against the nation's strong pacific leaning prompting him through clever political maneuvers to give 50 destroyers to England when she neared collapse. His foresight literally saved England and us because intercepts revealed we were next. We learned a lot from the English, expert at espionage from their many European wars, compared to us. FDR admitted he could've been impeached "to get us ready." In peace and war, aren't we often unaware or unbelieving of the inner workings of our nation or others? I read, for example, that President Lyndon Johnson for the longest time hid much from the American people about the Vietnam War, its questionable war status, financial sinkhole, and defeat after defeat. Finally, is that why collegians especially said, "Hell no, we won't go." One critic said America "had made the mistake of educating its young people (so unlike WWI) who weren't going to die in a war so Americans at home could have both" guns (war) and butter (prosperity)" at their expense. Hadn't the French who failed there told us not to go? We know now it's risky to invade a country that's divided. Who are the good guys?

Eisenhower's memorable message to the troops before D-Day, June 6, 1944, encapsulated the titanic struggle and hopefully the results their efforts would achieve. Soldiers would bring about "the destruction of the German war machine, the elimination of Nazi tyranny over the oppressed peoples of Europe, and security for ourselves in a free world. Your task will not be an easy one. Your enemy is well trained, well-equipped, and battle-hardened. He will fight savagely." That was one big mandate! No wonder on that day he carried a message in his jacket, taking full responsibility if our initial invasion of Europe failed. Imagine, it eventually involved 1.8 million combatants of many friendly nations. No wonder he smoked all three days before the invasion, as he labored to make a crucial decision about the finicky English Channel weather a day after June 5, much to the surprise of the Nazis.

After our actual entry after Pearl Harbor, we were riveted by daily newspaper reports, radio broadcasts, and Movietone News.[32] At first, unchallenged German submarines preyed mercilessly on shipping vessels along the Eastern Coast. Finally, our admiralty, including Admiral King who initially was concerned only with the Pacific, acted, ending what Nazi submariners called "the happy times." The United States protected the mid-Atlantic with our codebreaking, superior radar, better use of convoys and interceptor planes, making sure England wouldn't starve. Later this became a staging area for the Overlord invasion. Although grateful for U.S. support, the British Tommies groaned about our soldiers "being over here, over paid, and oversexed."

Popular radio broadcasts were Walter Winchell's staccato blasts and Doug Heater's somber notes, adding to the news in *The Woonsocket Call*, *The Providence Journal*, and *The Boston Daily Record*. Initially every report warned of the mounting British futility on land and sea, their bold headlines shrank the intervening safety barrier of the Atlantic Ocean. And after that December Day of Infamy, even the mightier Pacific no longer seemed to gird us with its immense watery bastion. In the East, fearful of the U-boat menace, coastal cities went into a defensive, low-light posture. Even to this day our own Atlantic seaboard remains the watery grave of several *Das Boots* (German boats). Read the fascinating discovery of a sunken marauder off the New Jersey Coast in Robert Kurson's *Shadow Divers*, and why even German records didn't know it was there during and after the war. There's also one off Point Judith, the watery grave of its submariners.

---

[32] *Movietone News* were newsreels that ran in the US from 1928 – 1963. They were shown in theaters along with full length movies. – *ed*.

Since we had practically cut our reading teeth on the exploits of the heroic Finnish and Baltic nations' skiing troops in their battles against Russia in the late 1930s, we now read the daily reports of both theaters of war with the same curiosity. They were our history book. No dull recitation of dusty historical facts, but blood and guts scenarios, written on the scene by heroic reporters like Ernie Pyle, Andy Rooney, and others. Eventually over 3,000 young men in the city, like my brother Bob, his 12 or more buddies, 19 other family relatives during or just after the war, and another 16 million heard "A Call to Arms!"

Imagine my heightened interest some 15 years later when as a faculty member at Notre Dame in Fitchburg, MA, a private high school run by the Brothers of the Sacred Heart and attended by the sons of officers at Fort Devens in nearby Ayer, we saw all our own military films and captured footage of both theaters of war. Included were the ghastly death camp horrors long before people ever saw all or part of them in documentaries on television or in movie adaptations. That's when I realized how sugar-coated those Saturday matinee Movietone newsreels - "The Eyes of the World" - had been when "edited" by the Office of War Information (OWI). We never seemed to lose a battle or a man. Like in our westerns, white men, the "supposed good guys", always won. But to the faithful, it was comforting to know clergy of all faiths also served, including 8,000 chaplains, four of whom were POWs, 200 wounded, and they built 1,500 places of worship.

Since dad was a student of political and military history, I listened whenever he discussed the war with mom, relatives, and his Lafayette millpal Ernest Frappier, the spittoon user. But long before school and American History, I had also learned a bit from my folks about WWI and our fight against the Kaiser's forces. Mom spoke about famous battle sites like the Marne, Verdun, Somme, Flanders, Chateau-Thierry, but not about the Battle of Vimy Ridge, as I later read, where a French-Canadian regiment distinguished itself but suffered 10,600 casualties, nearly 3,600 of which were fatal. John Keegan in *The First World War* is in disbelief that European nations let the conflict happen. He describes "a cataclysm that left ten million dead and created the modern world. It was a struggle of unprecedented ferocity that ended the rational, liberal culture that had prevailed in Europe since the Enlightenment, swept away the great European empires, and unleashed the demons including mechanized warfare, mass death, and totalitarian politics that have made the twentieth century the bloodiest in history."

Future Prime Minister Anthony Eden while in the trenches wrote in *Another World 1897-1917:* "The stench, the mud, the corpses, the destruction everywhere, the torn and twisted guns and limbers, the shattered wagons, the mutilated horses and mules created a scene of desolation beyond description." Like mom's brother Auray in that war, he tried to find comfort,

"If a bullet didn't have your name on it, you'd survive." Eden feared mutilation for life more than death. Fortunately, both mom's Canadian brothers Urgel and Auray survived the war, and dad's lungs exempted him, but author Keegan says that between the ages of 19 and 22, some 35-37 percent of combat warriors perished, thus "The Lost Generation" tag, which spawned its own literature. A course I took at Spring Hill College in Mobile, Alabama in the early 1950's exposed me to these stories. World War 1 was like a repeat of the Civil War, which decimated a whole generation, *"la chair du canon,"* my professor told me: soldiers as cannon fodder. You can't underestimate the heroism of soldiers who, as President Obama said "answer the call" or MacArthur's thought about the gift of one's life for the country. Like us, did other Franco families in Woonsocket also have relatives in the Canadian army in WWI? I was naturally disappointed to read that we, like the Germans, used gas at one time, but briefly.

Born in Québec Canada in 1896 and here in the U.S. since 1904, Dad was willing to fight but never told me he was turned down in the draft. When out of Dad's earshot, Mom shared with me several times that Dad had serious respiratory problems that plagued him. With no medical insurance, she regretted the loss of veteran medical help to arrest or cure his bronchiectasis disease in its early stages. Since it didn't happen, she never mentioned he might never have come back! Or, as Eden wrote, talk much about those "filthy, rain-drenched, gas-filled, rat-infested trenches" her brothers in the Canadian Army survived during the stalemated warfare that became its most prominent feature from hell. A surviving veteran was our next-door neighbor on Gaulin Avenue, *Monsieur* Charron, who couldn't work in the mills as a result. We grew up with his two sons, Robert and Roger. Around 4,000,000 American soldiers were mobilized during World War 1 with over 116,000 dying and a little more than 204,000 wounded. Of those deaths, the Spanish Influenza killed more men than weaponry.

Frank Buckles, the last WWI survivor who died in 2011 at 110 years; recalls his experiences as one of a dozen interviewed as centenarians by Richard Rubin in *The Last of the Doughboys.* In John Milton Cooper, Jr.'s *Woodrow Wilson - A Biography*, he relates how for two tortuous years and unceasing criticism from warlike Theodore D. Roosevelt, the President sought to keep us out of the conflict, asking Germany to stop killing Americans with their submarines. The nation, like in 1941, was basically noninterventionist until the sinking of the Lusitania when more than 100 Americans died. Americans did not want to get involved with Europe's problems. Aren't we still debating the wisdom of our involvement in Vietnam and now the Middle East? When you are the world's greatest power, does it also oblige you to be the world's policeman and mediator? The answer is not simple, because even from a religious or humanitarian dimension, nations like individuals have obligations to help the oppressed, the downtrodden, the besieged. In that one sense America has been heroic.

When Mom spoke about *La Première Guerre et le Kaiser* (The First War and the Kaiser), she especially dealt with the exploits of her brother Auray, who escaped death several times in France. Information I received from Canadian military archives indicate he and Urgel entered February 16, 1918, and were discharged March 19, 1919, having both sailed to England to fight with the Canadian Expeditionary Force. Photos of their ships are in the family albums and one missed being torpedoed. She related how Auray once disarmed a concealed Kraut (derogatory term for a German soldier) who lunged at him with his bayonet in the trenches. It lodged between his hip and shirt. Auray disarmed him but shockingly, and without any remorse, his commanding officer shot the German dead. When Auray asked why, the officer said matter-of-factly, "He tried to kill you." Once Auray and three other men went to reconnoiter an enemy position across a stretch of No Man's Land. Spotted and fired upon, his three companions jumped into a foxhole, telling him there was "no more room in the inn," so he ran to find his own cover. When the shelling ceased an hour later, he returned and found his buddies all dead. I found it touching when he told me he found honey on a dead Kraut with a photo of his *fräulein* (Germain for young woman).

Auray and Urgel Fontaine fought in the Depot Battalion, 2nd Regiment of the Canadian Army in WWI.

Gen. John Pershing saved thousands of lives by insisting his soldiers "fight as Americans", in an aggressive fashion, instead of the unhealthy, murderous "Over the Top" trench war. The Germans with their superior weaponry, especially their machine guns, killed thousands who advanced in open fields. The French were the first to introduce steel helmets as one defense in this brutal war.

The war ended the day before Auray would've met almost certain death if his 3rd Division had gone over a hill into a virtual trap. And in one major battle with thousands upon thousands of casualties, - Mom thought it was Chateau-Thierry, birthplace of writer Jean de La Fontaine – Auray, the medic, was amazed he only had a thumb scratch, while everyone in his outfit had been hit and the carnage was everywhere. But typical of veterans who have seen death and destruction, he never spoke about it much when he visited a few times and took us to Harris Pond for a swim. If he didn't come out from the war the most decorated, he was certainly the luckiest. If our *Mémère* Fontaine prayed for him and Urgel like our mom prayed the rosary for Bob, no power on earth could've touched them both. It's understandable *Mémère* never shared her maternal war fears, no more than her incredible firestorm ordeal of 1916. Outside of Mom, I've never known a more spiritual woman on this earth to suffer so much affliction without loss of faith.

I've wondered how in the world Mom and Dad, with their little formal education, knew so much? Later in college, I learned about these so-called "Renaissance people" for whom "the whole world was their oyster." They tried to know everything knowable. In their own limited ethnic world I think my folks were plebeian (poor), self-taught reincarnations of these inquisitive minds. I so liked the term "Pavement Platos," as one of my favorite columnists used to say, as he gleaned nuggets of wisdom from "the little people," whom the Bible says God favors. Typical of oral culture, their memory was phenomenal. Is that why now in our educated, book-and-electronic-saturated culture, generally we seem to know or remember so little? Or need to! A college professor said knowledge was knowing or knowing where to get it. No doubt, the emphasis now is on the latter. One psychologist said we don't use more than 50 percent of our intellectual gifts. Is that why savants amaze us?

Auray, I should add, was the physical specimen among the spare Fontaine men. He overcame, we said, the fear of dying "in a foreign field" when without foolish bravado he told himself, "If a bullet didn't have your name on it, it wasn't going to find you." Less heroically, Urgel's discharge papers revealed he received a sanction for losing a pair of socks, a table knife, and some identity discs worth a pound in English money. Not a rich man's army! Another WWI vet never worried, knowing he'd never know the moment of his obliteration. Germans shelled constantly. France was the one wrecked by war since the Germans stayed where they had first dug in.

I noticed when the Fontaines met at *oncle* François' or *tante* Laurence's house, Urgel, spare, high-strung, and chain-smoking, was always the one they worried about living *au Canada* (in Canada). Only once mom whispered that Urgel lived in our nation's capital, becoming persona non grata, in his case a "knight of the road" or "rider of the rails." But he finally settled down in his native Canada and worked in newspaper printing like Auray. But even in his discharge from the service, he couldn't escape another indignity of sorts. His papers said his mother was Emerouse instead of Emérance and lived in Wind Socket, as bad as Woonsokette (a little dig at French's emphasis on the last syllable) on his brother Auray's papers. Like at Ellis Island, the name became what the English-speaking bureaucrat heard. Smarting from the indignity of their mangled names, these French Canadians, always quick with a repartee like mom, called an offending scribe *"un maudit angla"* (a damn Anglo). One of my Notre Dame HS students said his immigrant ancestors came as Chartrands but became Shatraws at the stroke of a pen. "Give me your tired, your poor," and your Canuck name.

Unfortunately, their cousin, *mémère* Fontaine's nephew Hervey Morvan, age 25, gave the full measure of devotion in Flanders, Belgium on October 2, 1915. Looking at his mortuary card in the photo album reminded me of his sacrifice. Mom was hardly a year in America when she got the news from Canada. She said, *"Yé mort pour sa patrie"* (He died for his homeland). I thought of him in college when I read Col. John McCrae's poem: "In Flanders fields the poppies blow / Between the crosses, row on row, / That mark our place; and in the sky / The larks, still bravely singing, fly / Scarce heard amid the guns below. We are the Dead. Short days ago / We lived, felt dawn, saw sunset flow, / Loved, and were loved, and now we lie in Flanders fields. Take up our quarrel with the foe: / To you from failing hands we throw / The torch; be yours to hold it high, / If ye break faith with us who die / We shall not sleep, though poppies grow / In Flanders Field."

Returning to WWII, just as Dad predicted in the late 1930s that we would fight the Japanese, he was also convinced Hitler wouldn't be appeased with anything less than world conquest and domination. Dad knew what every tinhorn dictator or megalomaniac knows: the best way to pick up a devastated country's slumping or moribund economy is to go on war alert and rev up the munitions factories. On par with what Christopher Chant later said in *Warfare and The Third Reich*, Dad reasoned Germany was also thirsting for revenge after WWI. The Treaty of Versailles destabilized Germany's economy and militarism, imposed all war costs on them, and stripped her of territories. Hitler, crushed by Germany's defeat in the First War, had found a cause. Germany, he thought, should not have surrendered. But remembering that war, the German people and military leaders did not want another. Sadly, efforts to curb his rise and even kill him came to naught. The difference or consequence: the war's 60 million bloodbath. One assassin had him in his line of fire. "Of all the saddest things of words and pen, the saddest are these, it might have been." But one author said WWI (the number not spaced, as often seen in books) was caused by militaristic Austria-Hungary, not Germany per se. The war destroyed their empire. Didn't Christ say, "those who live by the sword, die by the sword?"

Dad also thought the English Prime Minister's "peace-in-our-times" assessment was too optimistic. Chamberlain, who lamented the million Englishmen killed in the first war, hoped Hitler would be appeased if

England and France didn't interfere with his annexation of Austria and the Sudetenland of Czechoslovakia. But eventually Hitler misfired with Poland and the Corridor. During the war I laughed when I heard a comedian at the Park Theater say Hitler wanted "peace": a piece of Poland; a piece of Austria; a piece of Czechoslovakia! Maybe not for Dad who loved to predict, but it all seemed too distant for most of us to be wary. But there was a bullet headed our way, and by the mysterious weave of cause and effect, towards our French-Canadian way of life.

Geopolitically, Dad also figured out Japan's expansion into Manchuria, China, and the whole Pacific basin was to procure more raw materials for its expanding markets. The U.S. cut off our oil exports when they didn't get out of China. Unwisely, Japan chose militarism over diplomacy. (Officers were really in charge of the country for over 800 years, one wrote.) One author opined they lost the war the day they attacked Pearl Harbor, since they shook America from its laissez faire, deep-seated, non-intervention mindset. Roosevelt's speech, "Let's Remember Pearl Harbor" was on everyone's lips. They had attacked first, which is what analysts said he wanted and needed to overcome our pacifism. We had broken the Japanese JN-25 code, but we didn't know when and where they would strike. All agree Hitler lost his European War when he declared war against us. Overextended, he now had to contend with us, England, and Russia, and many small nations, over 20. His maniacal, singlemindedness to capture more living space for Germany obscured any notion of caution and preparedness. For one, he vastly underestimated Russia's manpower.

Leading American historian David McCullough (I spoke to him in Newport) in the biography *John Adams* cited how contemporaries thought the "colossus of independence" (as Jefferson called Adams) always saw the long view, the ultimate consequences of here-and-now actions. In his own small sphere, Dad too seemed clairvoyant. Imagine I, a neighborhood kid, who because his dad told him, clued the gang we'd fight the Germans and the Japanese. I'll never forgot Phil Carpentier's question, "Do we know those guys? Do they have a team?" Phil later served in the military; his brother Lucien died in Vietnam.

I emphasized Dad didn't want us to tell anyone he was Republican, perhaps because of a self-sufficiency born of the old school of self-reliance and self-initiative, common in those immigrants. But his predictions weren't classified. His only other restriction was family finances. Hey, he had his pride! Would anybody believe a guy who knew so much had so little? In the city, most made their money at the mills, not in boardrooms or in war games enclaves like the War College in Newport.

But about Japan's militarism! It's only when I read *At War, At Seas* by Ronald Spector did I find out that since the Washington Conferences of

1922 and 1930, it was almost a given in Washington that Japan would resort to war in the Pacific. But again, how in the world did Dad know that living atop *la Gaulin* (Avenue) where the Secretary of Defense never called? Was he perhaps that guy who quietly, furtively, went to the library and emptied out the history section unnoticed in some dusty, unlit corner? Oh, the poet was so right about his kind when he said, "Ocean depths (the mill culture!) often hid gems of purest ray serene," or "some flowers were born to blush unseen and waste their sweetness on the desert air." Those immigrants are convincing evidence never to look at a man or woman, immigrant or not, and judge his or her worth only by their modest appearance, lack of education, earning power and station in life.

But wars, hurricanes and economics weren't his only predictions. In a lighter vein, if ever I wanted to know who'd win an upcoming heavyweight fight or other sports event, I consulted Dad, the oracle. Predictions became a hobby of mine too. But unlike Roman priests, he didn't check if sacrificial animals had spotted entrails, the divining custom in those classical days. Ditto about the weather, a predictive source for us baseball-crazy kids, long before television and weather forecasting. How often he predicted rain when Troop 4 went camping, but the troop didn't know that. I never told our scoutmaster.

I was in awe of his insights, and as boys will do ("My dad can lick your dad!"), I did flaunt at times these predictions to gain prestige with the gang. To paraphrase the line in "The Deserted Village," I too wondered, "How one small head (especially after a severe haircut chez Dalpé's) could hold all he knew." But in truth, he was an analyst, not a diviner. He figured things out from what he read. As cousin Frank said about the Indian who amazed everyone with his uncanny weather predictions: "he read the paper!" He also knew the human heart. Without formal education, he had to develop his store of knowledge in a more instinctive, natural way, the way people do in oral cultures where formal education is barely elementary and reading is from the book of life.

With the war on, the St. Ann nuns shared with us the fear of Germany's world conquest, including America. But in both world wars, say historians, Germany hoped to win the European conflict by submarine warfare before a somnolent America intervened. Churchill worked very hard on Roosevelt, who feared for his re-election, to break down this hesitancy because England could not make it alone. Neither would an "ungrateful" Russia make it until the U.S.'s lend-lease programs which sent them 28,000 jeeps; 218,000 guns; 4,000 tanks; and thousands of planes to help turn the tide against Hitler. The erstwhile paperhanger (Hitler) had snookered Russia into a deal to carve up Poland, but then attacked the Bear (Russia). Because of the intercepted Enigma messages from the Germans, the U.S. knew Hitler was going to attack Russia, but couldn't tell and expose how we knew. But later in the biggest tank battle ever at Kursk, Russia, a turning point in the war in the East, we told the Russians the Nazi strategy. Experts believe all our intercepts shortened the war by two years! Despite multiple warnings by his own sources, Stalin remained unconvinced of the Fuhrer's would-be treachery, proving even crooks can't tell themselves apart. Stalin remained in a funk for a whole week.

By 1941, Hitler had 70 million people and 11 countries under control. When he declared war on the U.S. after Pearl Harbor, it was the first time he had done so since 1939 against anyone. So, in only 20 days, some 134,000 "mad-as-hell" young U.S. men enlisted. The first draft was only for men between 21-30. Two-thirds had never held a gun and our army was only the 17th largest in the word, smaller than Romania's or Portugal's! Who knew about "Vigilance, the Eternal Price of Freedom?" Or did Americans believe what Croesus, the King of Lydia in 546 B.C., said about war? "Peace is better than war, because in peace sons bury their fathers, but in war the fathers bury their sons." And now we must acknowledge mothers burying their daughters too. Incidentally, Croesus, fabulously rich, later gave rise to the phrase "creasing one's palm," with money or gold.

The only "praise" I ever read about Hitler is that he was one of the first after the pope to recognize the European menace of Russia's Communism, a happenstance we saw after the war, the Russians so ungrateful for our help. America was really caught between a rock and a hard place before the war, trying to decide which was the greater evil, Nazism or Communism. We destroyed one and the other collapsed from within, but 50 years later. Churchill is given credit for divining Stalin's post-war reach, an ailing Roosevelt not.

Often as fourth graders in 1940, we were led by our teacher, who feared the invasion, the fall of Britain and eventually the U.S, Atlantic or no Atlantic, and who like Moses prayed with outstretched arms. Luckily, refueling in mid-ocean was a problem the Nazis couldn't solve by plane, ship, or sub, and their rockets were not transatlantic. If Hitler had waited for more subs and listened to his generals who said the nation wasn't ready for a long war, our victory would've been delayed two years, militarists say. I found it unbelievable that if they had bombed us, Hitler's primary target was where most Jews lived, God's own chosen people! An absolute megalomaniac! Someone who tried to eliminate an entire ethnic group? His place in hell? Later I report six million were slaughtered in hellish work camps, along with millions of other ethnic and religious groups, 15 million in all. Reinhard Heydrich and Himler, the worst killers, as revealed on the History Channel. When Heydrich was assassinated, Hitler wiped out an entire town. On the third floor of our residence at Notre Dame HS, we young monks had a huge Hitler photo we threw darts at, even if it was the 1950's.

Our prayers then were somewhat self-serving. We knelt on those rough, ink-stained wooden floors, with a few nail heads visible where planks were gouged with pen points or grooved with cracks. With our short pants we feared for our bony knees, but since self-preservation is man's first instinct, we hated the Krauts more. Our prayers would've been even more intense if we had known, as revealed after the war, that Admiral Karl Dönitz's submariners came close enough to be amazed at the brilliance of the New York skyline at night. I recall Dad had gone to the New York World's Fair in 1939 and bought a souvenir book, which he added to our collection of one other, the 1938 Hurricane tome. Gotham City was closer than we realized!

Six saboteurs were eventually caught and executed. Dönitz wrote in his *Memoirs: Ten Years and Twenty Days* about his U-boats against our Atlantic attack carriers, planes, and superior radar. Even in postwar, he still didn't believe the Allies had cracked the Enigma secret code machine with its million combinations!

Dönitz insisted on almost daily reports from his subs, helping to sink many. William T.Y. Blood in *Hunter-Killer* says 785 out of 1,162 were sunk, with near 30,000 submariners killed. Despite differences on how best to defeat the menace, we and the English were on the same page. We were better because our carrier personnel also knew aviation tactics. In charge when Goering, Himmler, and Goebbels were dead or on the loose, he took the helm for a short time after Hitler's death and sued for peace. Nuremberg sentenced Dönitz to ten years in prison.

Before we got serious about protecting shipping from the Eastern Seaboard to the Gulf of Mexico, German U-boats in Operation Drumbeat in 1942 sank more than 600 ships totaling 3.1 million tons. In the entire war, their subs killed 30,000 seamen (3,628 in subs), sank thousands of merchant ships (60 in one day) killing many merchant mariners, 175 warships, and 58 subs. (Operation Drumbeat by Michael Gannon.)

Wartime flicks showed German U-boats as perilous, stealthy, and seemingly invincible. But in the 1990's, the movie *"Das Boot"* showed the often-fatal outcome of the men and machines of that naval arm. As war progressed, Germany resorted to drafting younger men in all branches of the military. But facetiously, how young was the crew that landed at an amusement park in Jacksonville, Florida? ("Gruber, I hope you didn't forget the tickets!") For us Gaulinites, undersea warfare was personal because our neighbor was a submariner in the Pacific. Every day going to school, church, or market, we looked at the star in the window of his Gaulin Avenue home, which unfortunately he was never to return. Imagine, initially our subs were our only attacking naval weapon after Pearl Harbor. Educated in America and privy to our size and might, Japanese Admiral Yamamoto initially told his country not to take us on. He did us a favor when he nixed a second run at Pearl Harbor the same day against oil dumps and repair facilities. If they did, our navy could not have moved for another 18 months. Later in 1943 the U.S. debated "the legality," but decided to shoot down his plane when Enigma intercepted his itinerary for inspecting bases in the South Pacific. "All's fair in love and war.

England tried valiantly to keep its shipping lanes open for food and arms. I loved reading about the war in the paper (I was learning English) and listening to radiocasts. When I read much later that Britain lost thousands of ships, I realized I missed a few. With the advent of sophisticated radar, fast destroyer ships, control of the skies, and cracking the Enigma code, England's losses diminished, and German Admiral Dönitz eventually withdrew his boats from the Atlantic. A model of the Enigma (the machine's name; the decodes are called Ultra) was captured by the Poles before WWI, then given to the French, who gave it to England just weeks before the war. It practically let Churchill (and America) know every German flight, sea, and land movement, except for the surprise Battle of the Bulge, also known as the Ardennes Offensive. It took place in the densely forested Ardennes region between Belgium and Luxemborg from December 16, 1944, to January 25, 1945. Some think Hitler, suspecting leakage, used only secure interior lines of communication and nearly succeeded in a final breakthrough to the coast, but ran out of gas! His generals were against the battle. Casualties, dead, wounded and missing for the unsuspecting Allies, whose stories appear in Tom Brokaw's *The Greatest Generation Speaks*, were around 89,500 wounded and 19,000 killed. Initially only Eisenhower thought the Ardennes Forest breakthrough was a major German push.

Said later, relatives Raymond Peloquin and in-law Eugène Godin were in that battle. Normand Malo was wounded. Even if unwanted, it was the so-called "million-dollar wound" soldiers credited for sparing their lives if serious enough to end their soldiering for good or for a while. But a few wounds were even self-inflicted by soldiers driven out of their minds by the cold (worst in a century) and the deaths and savagery of the wintry campaign of 1944-5. Our boots were not as good as theirs. Trench foot disabled more soldiers than the enemy did. Roger Mandeville, one of five brothers in the service, told me in 2010 his trench foot still bothered him, and cannonading damaged his hearing. Recovering from his wounds, Roger was told to join another outfit. No way, he thought, so on his own he went back to his unit buddies. Roger died in 2012. Of the 16 million who fought in WWII only a few million are left and about 1,000 pass on each day. My brother Bob's friend Rene Hemond, who signed up for the Navy on the same day, passed away in June 2013. His dad, a grocer, who often drove his younger son to Mount Saint Charles Academy, frequently picked me up too.

The decoder was so important we continued listening to postwar doings (especially about sly, devious Russia) and didn't disclose Enigma's existence until 50 years later. Even Russia wasn't telling us everything in the war, but we learned a lot from German interceptors, also expert at code breaking. In fact, they also knew our naval code until we changed it in '43. Even in WWI, France had broken our code before we entered the war on her side with England. Studies of peacetime espionage, an aspect of the war many don't know about, are great reads. Even the Bible advises knowing your enemy's strength before engaging him and perhaps suing for peace.

Germans began spying in 1920. Alan Turing of England, a math genius, was the first to break the multi-million complicity of the German machine, which they thought could never be broken. A homosexual, then considered a crime in Britain, he had to submit to an operation. Like author Oscar Wilde, he was exiled to France. He committed suicide after the war. The movie *"The Imitation Game"* about Turing won honors.

Bernard Montgomery in *The Memoirs* reveals the often-wide rift in strategy between him and Ike. The British general, a great tactician even if conceited and self-promoting, believed in a concentrated push on one strong point towards Germany rather than Ike's wide-front strategy. The Brit believed his way would've ended the war before the cruel winter of 1944-5, saving thousands of lives. Fighting a war alongside another nation is very difficult, and only Ike had the savoir-faire and temperament to put up with good, obstinate, too-cautious Montgomery, who deflected every criticism. Like Lincoln said of one of his Civil War generals, he had a case "of the slows." One should read *Eisenhower* (Ike) by Michael Korda for the whole story. Not to mention also loose-cannon General George Patton whom the Germans feared most. Charles De Gaulle (*le grand Charles*) was also recalcitrant, (a kicking horse.) He aggrandized his importance and showed up in Paris on the day of its liberation, even when told not to.

Who knew some 400,000 Nazi prisoners were detained in 500 U.S. stateside camps away from the coast, including three admirals and 40 generals? All were sent home in 1946 but only after de-Nazification programs. We followed the Geneva Convention of 1929, so the Krauts were amazed how well they were fed and treated. Some local citizens complained they had it worse than the German prisoners. We executed some half dozen hardcore Nazis who killed an English-speaking comrade who was soft on Hitler. I once read just one escaped all the way to Germany by way of South America, but no corroboration. Camps were surrounded by deserts and trackless lands, so escapees came back voluntarily.

The German Air Force also suffered from our eavesdropping, so wrote Cajus Baekker in *The Luftwaffe War Diaries*. But Dad told me not to worry too much about their huge successes in 1940 and '41. With his passion for stats and numbers, did he have a notion of the size of England's (small at first) and our growing military might after 1941?

After Pearl Harbor, our amazing productivity, as seen in our own city of Woonsocket, and unmatched in history for rapidity and volume, quickly made us the Arsenal of Democracy. Historians agree it practically guaranteed us victory. The History Channel quoted Hitler saying he couldn't win when told we built a Liberty ship in less than five days, some built in Rhode Island. He said the same when the Russians built their famous tank (the T-34) faster than their Panzers could destroy them. What was a dictator to do? His generals had also told him not to fight on two fronts. But Hitler thought Russia would fold "like a deck of cards in six weeks." He had become intoxicated with the rapidity and totality of his first acquisitions over Austria, Czechoslovakia, Poland and France. Lucky for us, he took control of the war when he sacked a lot of his generals near the end. If they gave up an inch of ground, he ousted them. How prophetic his words: "Whoever lights the torch of war can wish for nothing but chaos." I rejoiced when "General Winter" again won the frozen war in Russia, like against Napoleon in 1812. The "little corporal" did capture Moscow but the Russians burned it and the weather forced him to retreat. A few years ago, they found the skeletal remains of retreating French who froze to death.

Imagine, Hitler slept when we invaded Normandy. He gave orders not to wake him before eleven. Didn't he know there was a war on? And Rommel (a Catholic) was at his wife's birthday in Berlin! The weather too foul for an invasion, he thought. The Latin proverb of *aliquando bonus dormitat Homerus* speaks to the fact that even the great, like Homer, are sometimes (*aliquando*) asleep (*dormitat*) at the switch. In earlier history, even King George III was said to be asleep during a crucial moment about the Revolutionary War requiring his attention, even if an ocean away. German speaking, he hardly knew a word of English. The U.S. also made historical blunders like the attack on Pearl Harbor, for despite 100 or more intercepts, including one picked up on radar, they were not passed on. Tragedies often come from many small missteps.

Besides some 92,000 Rhode Island combatants, winning the war was also due to the sweat and toil of Joe Worker and Rosie the Riveter. In 2012 the *Valley Breeze* (a weekly newspaper in northern RI) detailed that effort: "In 1941 the Guerin mills received contracts worth more than $1.25 million for production of woolen Army cloth. The Alice Mill of the U. S. Rubber Company in Fairmount (a neighborhood in Woonsocket, RI) reopened to fill a secret government contract for inflatable rubber decoys of military equipment like tanks, jeeps, boats and wading suits. In 2013 the Stadium showed Rick Beyer's "Ghost Army" film, highlighting how 1,100 men of the 23rd Headquarters Special Troop used truckloads of inflatable tanks, a massive collection of sound effects to trick the Germans about the strength and location of American units in France in the summer of 1944. Footage by Beyer and his wife Marilyn Rea also documented the city's role in "the Ghost Army." Many like me went on stage to see and touch a replica of an inflatable tank, designed by Fred Patten for the U.S. Rubber Company and built-in part at the Alice Mill in the city. A display also ran at the museum on Veteran's Day where ceremonies were held outdoors and dedicated to Julien Mitchell, former Mount Saint Charles teacher and administrator, veteran, and one of the driving forces behind the Georges Dubois Veterans Museum in Woonsocket. Other companies like Jacob Finkelstein & Sons pioneered in the manufacture of raincoats from rubberless but rain-proof materials and specialized in making thousands of the popular and functional Army field jackets. The Taft-Peirce Company of Michigan was the first to manufacture the breech casing and hand grip for the 20mm anti-aircraft Oerlikon machine gun and fulfill government contracts for barrage balloons to protect convoys and cities. The decoys were to deceive the Germans about the Allied invasion plans for D-Day on June 6, 1944. Dad thought he worked on Army uniform material at the Lafayette Mill. So critical was our workforce, the Alice Mill had a Student Shift, 2 to 6 p.m., 49 cents an hour, for high school students like Thérèse Ricard who painted camouflage on decoy tanks.

Again, Germans believed Gen. Patton was readying an invasion force in Dover, England, where "you could almost touch Calais," a mere 18 miles away. Thinking it was the D-Day target, the Germans took the bait and heavily defended Calais with many guns and crack Panzer divisions. With the Normandy invasion, they woke Hitler from his beauty sleep, but he thought it was a feint for Calais, and held his best Panzer units back. Rommel had told him if the Allies landed, it was kaput. Meanwhile, blood-and-guts Patton chafed as the would-be general of this pseudo-attack force. We made sure they intercepted messages about this "real army." He finally made it to France and relieved encircled Bastogne in the Battle of the Bulge. In the Mediterranean theater of war, the Allies floated the body of a "well-documented" officer with invasion plans on him. Our intercepts revealed "they now bought" the invasion of Crete, not Sicily. The 1956 movie *The Man Who Never Was* dramatized this plot. In 2015 I learned of a failed invasion practice at Slapton Sands, England, where 800 soldiers were killed, including an incautious officer whose body was used in the deception. The Nazis recovered the Normandy invasion plans on this officer. Luckily the foul weather June 6 also helped us.

Besides Rosie the Riveter, nurses, entertainers, clerical workers, women flyers, and fireside moms all contributed magnificently. Sadly, many nurses lost their lives in Bataan, as recorded by Emily Yellin in *Our Mother's War*. Shocking to read the prejudice women were subjected to, especially black and Jewish women. Was this the evilest incident of the war when some men, who were so prejudiced against women pilots testing and flying planes out to airfields, that they put sugar into one tank, causing two women pilots to die in a crash? No mention whether they got the firing squad! Is there a deeper section of hell than Italian poet Dante's nine levels for scumbags like them? Was the travesty hushed up because it was "a man's war" or because women warriors would have demanded justice? "Hell hath no fury …."

But on a more positive note, the USO (United Service Organizations) entertained military here and abroad. Even German-born Marlene Dietrich, who infuriated Hitler. The USO even provided women escorts for men to go to church: "If you want to go to heaven, go to church with an angel."

Unlike the English who were masters of the art, "intelligence" was not our strong suit initially. Can you believe we first thought it was somewhat ungentlemanly to do that! But the U.S. quickly redeemed itself in the intercept business, as is told in *The Secret in Building 26* by Jim DeBrosse and Colin Burke. This was done by greatly perfecting machines called bombes to decode more quickly those Enigma intercepts. A University of Dayton graduate, Joe Desch, was the man of the hour. The work was so secret, even co-workers, his wife and family were kept out of the loop the whole war. Imagine the Desch family dinner: "How was your day at the office, Joe?" "The usual. What's for dinner, Annabelle?" "Dad, our scout troop is picking up tin cans for the war effort. What about where you work?" The college recruited at Notre Dame High School every year when I counseled there.

We also wondered how England could survive the almost daily aerial pounding of Air Marshal Göring's Luftwaffe planes in "The Battle of Britain." Incidentally, we kids knew our warplanes, theirs and ours, as kids do cars today. To cite Churchill, "Never in the field of human conflict was so much owed by so many to so few", the 2,000 courageous RAF pilots who won that air war. Abiding by Hitler's wish, pompous Göring made the fatal mistake of stopping strategic bombing when England was close to the breaking point in retaliatory power. Instead, he tried to break the British spirit by bombing cities like London and Coventry. So, Hitler cancelled the invasion of Britain, called the Sea Lion operation. Then, like Napoleon, he attacked Russia, putting Germany between two major fronts. Even Mom, a closet historian of royalty and not a strategist like Dad, told me Hitler was making the same mistake as "the little corporal," who boasted not even God, or the cold couldn't stop him. So, she reveled in the blasphemer's prideful downfall. Korda cites him, "In war men are nothing; one man is everything. An Army is nothing without the head." Proud Napoleon was unequalled in sizing up a battle situation and inspiring his men, but ambition crushed him. Shakespeare compares ambition to a man overjumping his horse and landing on the other side.

Even edited as they were, our weekly Saturday afternoon Movietone Newsreels at the Laurier Theater gave the Nazi horde an aura of invincibility. Their blitzkrieg tank movements developed by General Heinz Guderian, (who was later sacked by Hitler in Russia; I found his book in a Seekonk bookstore), the ever-stalking U-boats, screeching Messerschmitt fighters, superior weaponry (the Teutonic genius!), seeming impotence of the European opposition, and, to us schoolboys, that terrific German helmet, all seemed an unstoppable juggernaut. I was fascinated to read Ernst Udet, Germany's air supply chief during the war, came up with the screeching, terrorizing dive-bomber after witnessing and buying a Curtis Hawk barnstorming plane here. An alcoholic, he committed suicide with defeat at hand. Our other foe, the Japanese, also showed a genius for copying us, a trend that continued after the war, as addicted young video devotees can attest. Learning in other countries always seems more intense, but an article in 2011 said no one equals our creativity. Like the Romans who copied the Greeks, nations copy us. It's why the Russians got the atom bomb ten years before we thought they would – the Rosenberg couple betrayed us and were executed.

The British in WWII thought we were the best in massing war materials, but not using it well, as we preferred (thank God!) to expend weaponry to save lives. It spoke of our culture's respect for life, a writer said. The Russians, on the other hand, had a shocking disrespect for the lives of their soldiers. On the Eastern Front they forced released convicts to walk over uncleared minefields. In their defense of Stalingrad, if you retreated you were shot by death squads. Russia lost the most people, 20 million, in the war. But Stalin, the worst homicidal maniac ever, had already killed some 30 million before hostilities, sacking most of the military leadership, except General Zhukov, the future savior of Stalingrad and liberator of Berlin, who made Stalin uncomfortable with his popularity after the war. Was Stalin or Hitler the Anti-Christ? They expanded our notion of man's depth of iniquity!

For soldiers, the war was the greatest event in their lives, the greatest global event ever, and yet many in our city had never left it before its start. A mechanized war, and yet most families never had a car. Even if two oceans insulated us from the violence and horrors of war itself, so often the dramatic personae of military events involved our men, relatives, neighbors, other city residents, all part of the 3,000 plus who served from the city, with 151 (another figure: over 160) deaths, 34 POWs, and 23 missing at war's end. The war brought unparalleled changes to American life, including our own Franco way of life. As I emphasized, it was happening before the war, but wartime hastened it with the speed of a bullet. Authors of Francocentric history agree with that.

So, people prayed the Lord of Hosts favored our side. (Churchill's "May God prosper our arms.") When a freshman at the Academy in 1944, I was incredulous when I heard a war chaplain say he spoke to many Catholic German soldiers (or Lutheran?) on the Western Front, who thought God was with the Fatherland. How could that be? In Citizen Soldiers, Stephen Ambrose reveals a greater percentage of our G.I.s in Europe were of German descent, and some even used the Teutonic language to trick the enemy. Once on a lark, four of them drove a German vehicle into their lines. In *The Frontier in American History*, Frederick Jackson Turner speaks of the great number of German immigrant-farmers who migrated to the U.S. Shades of our hold on our own Franco life, those in Pennsylvania and the Northern Plains even thought of establishing a country of their own, complete with their own language, beliefs, manners, and government.

In speaking about the religious factor and trying to guess whose side God was on, reflect what Hitler said: "But then all those will be called before the judgment seat who today, in possession of power, trample on laws and rights who have led our people into destitution and ruin, and who, when their Fatherland was suffering, valued themselves above the life of the community." Yes, "Thine own words have condemned thee."

Incidentally, it's only after the war many of us realized the myth of this Nazi invincibility stemmed largely from the success of the German war machine against third-rate (in terms of size and preparedness) countries. Also, that this onslaught had been made possible initially by France's oversimplistic reliance on the static Maginot Line and the leadership of old WWI leaders, as David Schoenbrun relates in *Soldiers of the Night*. And on England's military somnolence, as described in President Kennedy's graduation thesis *Why England Slept*. Recall Prime Minister Chamberlain's disarming assessment of the war hysteria at the time. He didn't want more Englishmen to die, like in WWI. Dad was right on about his colossal appeasement mistake, but in his defense, Hitler lied to him. One commentator thinks Churchill, a Navy man who favored a ten-year moratorium on airplane development and expansion, emboldened Hitler to think England was weak. Recall Hitler's insistence on fighter planes rather than bombers eventually doomed his invasion of Russia since Stalin removed all factories to Siberia, beyond the reach of Nazi bombers. Korda also adds because England had lost so many men in the Great War, with a million wounded, like us it became pacifist and demilitarized. We don't make the same mistake now, but isn't military readiness costly?

Mom expanded on the saying, *la chair du canon*, (the cannon pulpit) about how nations sacrifice many of its young people to fight a war. But we said the Vietnam generation didn't buy into that. Because we were now educating our young people, a writer said protesters of that war were the first ever to understand that and say, "Hell no, we won't go." But in his so-correct divining of another world war, could dad have imagined his own son, a godchild, in-laws, and so many nephews would one day be involved in another conflict? Books and novels have been written about the dread in combatants' minds before combat. But have authors been too silent about people on the home front? How I remember WWII parents fearing that fateful knock on the door! In her dementia, mom jumped at a knock on the door at St. Antoine. But it happened to the Carpentier family during the Vietnam Conflict for their son Lucien, they were vacationing in California when given the devastating news.

Yes, Roosevelt hoped we didn't strike first. But by a strange coincidence, we actually fired the first shot against one of those six mini subs launched from Japanese ships at Pearl Harbor. Was the one shown in Woonsocket the same that attacked us? I think not, but Troop 4 scouts were on duty at the Social site. What a torrent of literature and debates there are about whether top officials, including FDR, knew or didn't know about the attack and its time and place. I now delve into this event.

Harry Hopkins, Secretary of Defense, confirmed that in 1938 Roosevelt confided we would go to war and needed to increase our air power. And *The Chicago Tribune* had once published FDR's "war plans." But some writers questioned how much Roosevelt knew. For one, on Dec. 4, naval radio operator Ralph Briggs had intercepted a Japanese signal revealing a severance of relations with us. Also, someone with a good French name, Joseph Rochefort, chief of the Navy's Combat Intelligence Unit, detected the first faint signals indicating Japan was about to strike. Further, a Japanese plane was mistaken for a B-17 by a military named Tyler, but it was not passed on. Another intercept the night before by Captain George Linn was told to the President. "This means war," he's quoted as saying. But were all these messages cold-stone certain? Eventually, a Congressional Inquiry on Pearl Harbor declared, "Beyond serious question Army and Navy officials back in Hawaii and in Washington were beset by a lassitude ("What me worry?") born of 23 years of peace." So, the fault, if so, lay in a kind of somnolence (sleeping on the job) and a "can't-happen-here" mentality. Some even thought Japanese, with their small stature and squinting eyes, couldn't hit the side a barn! As we hear in Shakespeare's *Julius Caesar* "The fault is not in our stars but in ourselves." In our wide-open culture, I personally don't think vigilance has ever been one of our strong suits as several disasters have proven the last 10-15 years. But tremendous progress has now been made. Now Americans worry if too much electronic and airborne spying (drones) is sapping our right to privacy from illegal search. Isn't it better to be safe than sorry?

In the President's defense, Gordon Prange in *At Dawn We Slept* wrote that there is "not one iota of evidence Roosevelt knew of the attack beforehand." But if known, were General Kimmel and Admiral Short back at Pearl Harbor told soon enough to avoid being scapegoated? There are books on both sides of the question. In his *Day of Deceit,* Robert Stennett claims FDR knew three hours before the attack. Sadly, the toll for our laissez-faire or delay, if not our minimal vigilance, was 2,403 dead (more than 20 sets of brothers). Sunday is a day Confederate Stonewall Jackson would not fight on, but the Japanese knew it was well chosen due to shore leaves, reduced readiness, and, yes, church services on ship decks shaded by sun-obstructing tarps. And our tied-up planes to prevent sabotage were sitting ducks.

For one final opinion among this scattering of opinions for and against, a reading of Stanley Weintraub's *Long Day's Journey into War* presents convincing arguments that once again FDR knew eventually, we'd have to fight Germany and Japan, but not "when." In 1934, Japan had renounced the Washington Naval Treaty of 1922. So the fault, if any, was not reacting to imminent warnings and sightings. When destroyer Captain Outerbridge in his first ship command sent a report about sighting and attacking a mini sub, the message wasn't passed on, yes, because it was his rookie command! Unbelievable! Before appearing before a joint session of Congress and uttering his famous "Day of Infamy" line, Roosevelt had expressed it was a "terrible disappointment to be President in time of war," especially when circumstances came so unexpectedly. I believe he loved his country, its people, and combatants too much not to have been surprised as we all were by Japan's treachery. The reader must decide for himself. "True history," one wrote, only comes 100 years later when all the players are deceased. It hasn't been 100 years since WWII, but in *If the Allies Had Fallen*, edited by Dennis E. Showaler and Harold C. Deutch is a compilation of some "Sixty Alternate Scenarios of WWII, which reveals so much of the thinking, plans, and actions of our military, which were or were not put into action, with good or not-so-good outcomes, some with millions of lives affected.

At Pearl Harbor, besides all those deaths, some 1,738 were wounded and 23 ships sunk or damaged, only after the attack did the Japanese in their final embassy communiqué to us (the last two pages, which came later) declare a state of war. So even if we had exercised some vigilance, that still left room for treachery on their part and blame on us for "sleeping at the switch." Revisionist books have largely exculpated the blame laid on Kimmel (Navy) and Short (Army) in some nine investigations. Some have blamed a few muckamucks in Washington. There must've been other Woonsocketers at Pearl but for us with a Lebel first cousin there, it made it even more relevant. The ships we lost were not on par with the Japanese fleet.

News about Pearl Harbor reached the nation that same Sunday, December 7, 1941. Thousands of parishioners flocked to Sunday Mass as always, and I thought initially I had heard the news when all Social *Coin*, as usual, walked, talked, and exchanged news after Mass at St. Ann's. Had *Monsieur* Albert Foisy's French music program, a must for every family then, announced it? But lately I've read that here in the East we didn't find out until later. Imagine, even the President found out by radio! Simpler times!

Every Sunday after that, we prayed for our military, a ritual virtually unbroken until August 14, 1945, when the war came to an end. General MacArthur said, "There are no atheists in foxholes" and there were none in parishes either as prayers wafted up to heaven in ardent supplication for combatants in harm's way. Unlike today when devotees in all religions are declining, the war had the opposite effect. Praying in those days was something the "faith-full" did naturally, like eating, working, sleeping. Women always had beads in their purses. A child going to bed heard "Make sure to say your prayers": *"Fa ta priere."* to cite mom. Even in scout camp. You could hardly get a seat in church and ushers showed you where to sit. Like Jews in the Old Testament, does it take disasters for us get in touch with eternal verities as well as man's propensity for evil? But didn't Christ say there'll be wars till the end of time?

So, for me it was my second reckoning about "Where were you when you heard...?" It was on the sidewalk in front of the Bérubé apartment on 309 Gaulin. My third was in the Order when Kennedy died at the same time I was teaching ancient Roman Cicero's orations about people of affluence needing public service and acclaim for a sense of fulfillment! The first I said was Sept 1, 1939, the start of WWII, as we kids played Monopoly on Ghislaine Bérubé's first floor porch. Trouble in threes!

After the president's speech and our declaration of war against Japan on December 8 (only one opposing vote), and against the Axis Powers on December 11, day by day, we began to feel the stateside effects of war. The stirring of national pride, the will to fight, war songs, the bold cries of patriotism, and war bond rallies were all tremendous highs that overnight replaced the usual talk about the Depression. But we kids who knew little about World War I didn't really grasp the undercurrent of fear gripping our parents. Nor know, as General Sherman said, "War is hell," even if it brought employment, one of the elusive will-of-the-wisps of millwork. But millworkers and others couldn't buy a break. They now had buying power, but loved ones were in peril and there was rationing and shortages.

Back to WWI and before the armistice was signed in 1918 on the eleventh month, day, and hour (the often-asked 11-11-11 question), a reporter wrote: "Last night, for the first time since August in the first year of the war, there was no light of gunfire in the sky; no sudden stabs of flames through darkness; no spreading glow above black trees where for four years of nights human beings were smashed to death. The fires of hell had been put out." But twenty-one years later, 1939, it was Deja vu all over again, with monstrous increments. Dad could've added we don't learn anything from history, but only know when it happens again.

Is there really a war to end all wars? Or does the last one generate the next? MacArthur was asleep at the switch in WWII in the Philippines after Pearl Harbor had been bombed and again bears, some say, much of the blame for predicting China would surely not cross the Yalu River to attack us in North Korea in 1950. It's the Korean war my 1948 class at the Academy later served in, with some alumni deaths occurring. We walked into the biggest trap ever at the Chosin Reservoir. Cousin Brunelle also served in Korea. Imagine, the author of *The Coldest Winter*, David Halberstam, was killed by a car while bringing his superlative manuscript to the printer; Margaret Mitchell of *Gone with the Wind* was also killed by a vehicle in Atlanta?)

With the nation fully engaged in the war, popular songs tugged at our heartstrings, flagged our drooping spirits, and stirred our hopes for the future. These were "When The Lights Go On Again," "I'll Be Seeing You" "I'll Be Home For Christmas," "I've Got A Girl In Kalamazoo," "I Left My Heart At The Stage Door Canteen," "Sentimental Journey," "Don't Sit Under The Apple Tree," "I'll Walk Alone," "The White Cliffs Of Dover," "Boogie Woogie Bugle Boy" by the Andrews sisters, "Night and Day," "Don't Fence Me In," "We'll Meet Again," and others. Overseas, soldiers loved hearing Bob Hope's USO show entertainers perform those melodies. It was a time when lyrics were sentimental and music soothing and uplifting, not raucous or jarring like today. No one lost hearing listening to the music. A critic said singers now sound like the instrument they play. Maybe it's why many come and go?

The branches of the military vied for our hearts and ears with "Anchors Away," "The Marines' Hymn," "Army Air Corps,"[33] "The Caissons

---

[33] In 1947, the Air Force separated from the army and the song became "The U.S.

Go Rolling Along,"[34] Also "When Johnny Comes Marching Home Again," and Irving Berlin's "You're In The Army Now."

Pharmacist's Mate Third Class (PhM3) Robert J. P. Tellier served in WWII on the ammunition supply ship U.S.S. Firedrake (AE-14) from 1944 – 1946.

Why, we knew the lyrics of those songs as well as those French hymns and songs we sang in school and church. Like the popular one to Our Lady: "*J'irai la voir un jour*," about seeing her in heaven someday, which cousin Gene requested for his veteran brother Raymond at his funeral in 1996. Their sister Connie said it lyricizes our faith and Franco-Canadianism, besides displaying our great devotion towards Mary. Many are now requesting it for their farewell, including my sisters Suzanne, Rachel, *et moi* (and me). Of late, it was also sung at the burial site of a religious *confrère* (colleague) at the Brothers' cemetery in Harrisville. But for my deceased and very German-Irish Patricia, who never learned French in our 25 years together, the moving recessional was the soaring "How Great Thou Art."

Other daily realities were higher prices, growing shortages, and, for parents, siblings, and wives, the inevitable compulsory or voluntary response of young men (some volunteer women too eventually: WACS, WAVES, MARINES, SPAR, WASP to serve in the war. About this will to serve, in how many homes like mine did parents try to cool the ardor of their would-be warriors, pleading with them to wait for the draft, as I heard mom tell Bob, but to no avail. Was she thinking of a Canadian cousin who died in Flanders in WWI? Two cousins would die in WWII, one from "little Gaulin."

Air Force song" keeping its familiar lyric: "Off we go into the wild blue yonder..."
[34] The title and lyrics of this song have been updated to "The Army Goes Rolling Along" and is also commonly called "The Army Song." – *ed.*

Knowledgeable about history, mom never cared much for her ancestral France's long history and glorification of war on the European Continent, epitomized in its rallying cry of *la gloire des armées francaises* (the proud tradition of French militarism and conquest). Elsewhere I cite the three justifiable reasons St. Augustin gave to justify war. All moms feared losing their sons; our mom her first born: the first to break the womb, as I once heard. Born in 1925, Bob would soon come of age after 1941 when the world conflict drew us in, requiring older and younger combatants. That's why he's always been five years younger than the average veteran GI.

Whenever I watch the James Stewart movie, *It's a Wonderful Life*, in which his character sees the tremendous loss his missing life will make in the people he loves, I especially think of Bob and cousin Raymond. In their respective service in the navy and army, both had near misses: Bob from a suicide flyer; Raymond from a German sniper who killed his buddy inches away. Ray's gone now, but I reflect how both survived to be examples of service, work ethic, love of family, faith, integrity, involvement in military causes, and for Bob additionally, love and devotion to his wife Millie and four children. I shudder to think of the vacuum in the families of the hundreds of thousands, and for us locally, the loss of cousin Gérard Vincent in the invasion of Italy and Sgt. Armand Lapierre in the battle for St. Lo in France. And the 60 million worldwide to the countries of their birth? Of those two predictions of Christ we cited, I lament there will be wars until the end of time. Is it that "tooth and claw" gene anthropologists say was embedded from early man's violent struggle to survive in a cruel world? A gene that is still with us, a writer opined, under a veneer of gentility, education, and expected manners. Or, as the faithful believe, again, is it the Original Sin, our fallen nature, as Cain ("Am I my brother's keeper?") soon exhibited when he slew his brother Abel. Imagine, a murder in the very first family ever! And we're all descended from them? Not wishing to be heavily theological, I pass along a revealing and insightful notion from one of my religious teachers. As said elsewhere, the first sin, he said, caused a triple rebellion: we from God; our lower from our higher self as St. Paul and Franklin both lamented; and nature from us. A struggle three times over! He added that of the five orders of creation: mineral, vegetative, animal, human, and angelic, only we are flesh and spirit, a volatile, combustible mix. It's why God forgives, a preacher added, and why His Son was so patient with His own chosen disciples, as He is with us. Didn't he tell Peter: "to forgive seventy times seven," when Peter thought he was being magnanimous with seven?

Very quickly the military uniform became commonplace and a badge of honor. Everywhere you went - market, church, other private and public places, you saw the uniform of the services and learned the stripes.

Those who wore the uniform wore it with pride. Those of fighting age not drafted or enlisted were consumed with envy. Younger guys like me wore military hats (navy especially) and scarves sent home. Young men in slacks or "railroad overalls" seemed to disappear overnight, enough perhaps to undercut sales perhaps at clothiers like McCarthy's, Najarian's and Eisenberg and Tickton, three popular stores. Girls even sported V for Victory hairdos, but I never saw one.

A gnawing fear was to be 4-F, medically unfit, especially for flat feet, a sobriquet or label that stuck to you. Why get turned down for that? Did recruiters think inductees were all going to serve under the likes of the Civil War's Stonewall Jackson, unequalled in marching his "foot cavalry?" The cruelest derision was to call someone that. If you did, with or without cause, your own war was at hand. It made a guy feel he didn't measure up. Unlike the divisive Vietnam War, only later did I learn only a few tried to dodge the draft in what was a popular, officially declared war, the last so-called in the 20th Century before Desert Storm, one writer said. Unfortunately for those who served, Korea became "the forgotten war." And Vietnam returnees were sometimes despised or forgotten, instead of honored for their service. I read the French had failed there and told us not to go in. Hard to tell who the good and bad guys were. And sadly, President Kennedy, for one, knew the plot to kill the Catholic South Vietnamese leader while his wife was here! He had organized hamlets well for defense. After his demise, the situation there got worse. But one history pans him. His religion a factor?

But apart from patriotism, joining the military in WWII, says Brokaw, was a step up for most recruits, as former Senator and presidential hopeful Bob Dole verified. True, Woonsocket men had worn shoes and eaten, I presume, three squares in peacetime, but not all Americans. But for many here in the city, their minds had been deprived of learning due to poverty, as they marched off to the mills at the "ripe age" of 16 to help their families. No wonder a near-record number (over 140) received their high school diploma at Woonsocket HS some 50-plus years later in a ceremony organized by cousin Gene who has devoted time and effort to make sure vets aren't forgotten. Before Pearl Harbor, nationally 79 percent had never finished high school and 40 percent had never been. Some couldn't read. So, the city's mill culture wasn't alone or solely blameworthy for its educational lack. Poverty and low salaries were across the land.

Those "Uncle Sam Wants You" posters, recruiting drives, newspaper accounts, radio broadcasts, war movies, military on furlough, and war newsreels all helped gather up the 16 million who served in the conflict. The city responded in a magnificent way with draftees and volunteers. God, every family we knew with grown sons had somebody in the service, like on our street. Once during the war, *The Call* showed the photo of those five Lebel cousins in the service all at one time: Lucien (the Pearl Harbor survivor), Albert, Laurent, Edgar, *et* Armand, a member of the Seabees, those builder-warriors about whom an interesting movie was made and a museum built. Sons of dad's brothers: Napoleon (unable to verify whom) and Philibert (Romeo, George, Arthur) also served, as did sons of his sister Alice Brunelle: Normand in WWII and Robert in Korea. Not to be outdone, my five Peloquin cousins also answered the call: Gerard, Normand, (career), Raymond, Roger, and Eugène, the last two post-war. Brother Ben also served in Germany after the war, as did Rachel's husband, Donald Clark. Armand (killed in France), Lucien, Leo, Ernest, et René were those five Burrillville Lapierres in the conflict. Two other brothers, Albert et Raymond, served in Korea, as did some members of my MSC 1948 class, including Robert Hiney and Daniel Turgeon (he sat next to me in class) who were killed, and other Mounties before and after my class, like outstanding athlete Garrett Coyne, '47, arguably the best athlete ever to attend Mount, who we said killed ten Chinese. That war's toll: 33,629 killed in action; 103,284 wounded; 7,000 captured. I mention elsewhere that Sue's husband, Gil Bouffard, was a sailor in WWII in the dangerous run on the USS Edmonds to Russia from England in the Lafayette North Sea. His ship got stuck once in Russia for months. Gil joked he had to swab the deck every day.

With surely the gratitude of the nation, I once thought the Lebels *et* Lapierres were some of the "servingest" families of WWII, at least locally. But I later discovered that Mr. and Mrs. Joseph E. Coté of Diamond Hill Road had eight (a 9th at war's end) sons in the military, all highlighted once in the Labor Museum's military annex. And there were 10 Fredette brothers from East Braintree, MA, and, unbelievably, 16 Gauthier Brothers from Fort Worth, Texas. (Aren't things always bigger in Texas?)

What excitement when Bob enlisted in the Navy with lifelong friend René Hémond, December 15, 1943, reporting to Sampson Navy Base, Lake Seneca, NY, along with 400,000 others all told. He later trained as a corpsman and served as pharmacist mate in Memphis, Tennessee; New Orleans, Louisiana; and Portsmouth, Virginia. He eventually saw action in the Pacific around Okinawa and the Philippines on the ammo ship, the USS Firedrake AE-14 in Admiral Halsey's Third Fleet. Mom kept some of his letters. For example, that kamikaze attack really unnerved her. It seems his ship was the only one not hidden by a smoke screen. Besides killing several thousand seamen, kamikazes also sank 57 warships, seriously damaged 100, and reduced the effectiveness of 300 more. A self-defeating if effective strategy, feared more than anything else by Nimitz, it cost the Japanese some 1,900 planes and irreplaceable pilots.

For his service Bob received the American Campaign Medal, the Asiatic-Pacific Campaign Medal, the World War II Victory Medal, and the Philippine Campaign Medal. He brought home a lot of Philippine money and photos of natives. In its lifetime, his ship had 18 skippers and served with distinction again in the Korean and Vietnam conflicts. She was decommissioned in 1970 after 26 years of service. In a Baton Rouge, LA reunion in 2011, Bob reconnected with three sailors who served with him in the war. He wrote he lost six pounds as a pharmacist mate assisting his first operation.

Didn't I say that because of dad and his 24 medical volumes and mom's daily health tips, the family was medicine and health oriented. Providentially, Bob married into the Savoie family, which now boasts twelve health care professionals. Eleven of them are active or retired nurses starting with his wife Mildred (a Cadet Nurse Corps of WWII), her daughters Janine (Tellier) Reale, Anne-Marie (Tellier) Bibeault and her daughter Melissa; Mildred's sister Patricia (Savoie) Benoit and her granddaughter Brianna Benoit; Mildred's other sister Jacqueline (Savoie-Brodeur) Cournoyer and daughters Debra (Brodeur) Allard, Catherine (Brodeur) Nowak, and Donna (Brodeur) Leclair, a radiology technologist; Debra's daughter-in-law Christina Rose Allard and Mildred's brother Albert Savoie's granddaughter, Meagan (Marchand) Goodier are also nurses. I was thrilled to do a photo and feature story of nine of them in 2007 and again in 2014 when Mildred passed on. At the time, they totaled over 225 years of service in every field of nursing. Their greatest pride was seeing their work finally achieving its own professional status in the nation's health delivery system. At one time five served at Landmark Hospital in Woonsocket, and the family's pride was that many patients during their stay benefited from their care. Elderly patients were glad to hear French from Millie, Pat and Jackie.

A Japanese officer said he and better-educated militants scorned suicide missions. Our Navy officials admitted those pilots had a 32 percent success rate overall, almost ten times more than the usual strafing, dive-bombing tactics. It's one more reason why we didn't invade Japan, opting to drop the atom bomb since they were readying to throw everything they had left at the invading fleet. Recall because of the sneak attack on Pearl Harbor, we thought they were backhanded fighters. In Hollywood flicks, they always snuck up behind our soldiers, like one about Bataan and Corregidor we saw. When would MacArthur fulfill his famous vow, "I shall return?" The rescue of the Bataan Death March survivors in 1945 *Ghost Soldiers* made fascinating reading. The Japanese had started killing their POWs.

But getting back to Bob's enlistment for a second, it looked like that scene from Scarlett's party at Tara when war broke out and the men rushed out to join, with their Southern belles sighing and swooning. But it wasn't so romantic in conservative Woonsocket, what with watchful mothers keeping predatory Scarlett O'Haras at bay! Two years after Pearl Harbor, he had

Three Generations of Nurses and Counting
Seven of the twelve nurses in the Savoie extended family.
Front (l to r): sisters Patricia (Savoie) Benoit, Mildred (Savoie) Tellier, and Jacqueline (Savoie-Brodeur) Cournoyer. Back : Janine (Tellier) Reale, Anne-Marie (Tellier) Bibeault, Melissa Bibeault, and Debra (Brodeur) Allard.

come home one day, saying nearly his whole gang (members of The Woonsocket Independent Club on Little Gaulin Avenue and others) was being drafted or enlisting. They were Edgar Demers, Norm St. George, Maurice Brunelle, Robert Bastien, René Hémond, Omer Gaudet, Lionel Dion, Aurélien Lamoureux, Raymond Dussault, Norm Martel, and Bob Kuster. All survived and gathered for a postwar military photo I christened "Young America at War." What captain and future Supreme Court Justice Oliver Wendell Holmes said in the Civil War about young men also prefigured them, "It was given to us in youth to be touched with fire. We really knew what passion was." Not discounting the sufferings and deaths war brought, you envied them for being called by the gods to embrace a moment of greatness, far above the ordinariness of their lives, pre- or post-war. They were in the greatest event of the 20th Century! Or perhaps since the dawn of history! Now in the 21st Century our men and women have been embroiled in wars in Iraq and Afghanistan.

    Younger by four years, I had enjoyed watching Bob's gang play ball at St. Ann's Park. I even worked out with them once, until one of the beefier guys separated me from the ball in an attempted double play. So, I was shipped "to the minors" - my own Gaulin gang. No one ever did that to me again because I knew how hard the hit was going to be. But do baseball buffs remember the All-Star game when Hot Dog Pete Rose curtailed a catcher's career with a battering-ram collision at the plate? New rules now.

Twelve neighborhood WWII vets commemorate surviving the war.
Front (l to r): Edgar Demers, Lionel Dion, Rene Hemond, Maurice Brunelle, Norm St. George, Robert Bastien, Aurelien Lamoureux
Back: Robert Tellier, Ray Dussault, Robert Kuster, Omer Gaudet, Norm Martel.

    Bob and his friends hoped some of them would serve in the same unit, but wound up in different companies, except Hémond and him, at least in boot camp. The death of the five Sullivan brothers all on one ship (the USS Juneau; I saw the movie at the Stadium) caused the Navy to tighten up, if not eliminate, the policy of allowing brothers to serve in the same unit. A Civil War buff, I've read how devastating it was for a town or city to lose so many men at once, since military units were often formed in the same locale. Like proud families with someone serving in the military, we in turn displayed his Company photo (506--Unit G) in the parlor. And had a blue star in a window. A wartime photo of my cousin Rita Godin's son Robert and her brother Gerald Peloquin's daughter Muriel at a window beneath the stars of Muriel's dad and his two Peloquin brothers was poignantly touching. If a soldier was killed, the star became gold. Thus, the tradition of Gold Star mothers, who were often recognized in parades. One such mother related when she went to New York to receive the body of her son, she saw there were thousands of coffins on the boat. Such was the cruelty of war, as FDR, then Secretary of the Navy, said when he visited the front in WWI.

Later, if only to prove how close the war was to our neighborhood, I list some of the known 151 city casualties who lived not only in the city, but in or close to our neighborhood. Of course, the scythe of death and injury in the war cut a wide swath, with no distinction between the sons and daughters of the Mayflower, recent arrivals, rich enclaves, or poverty pockets. Neighborhoods were so close and tight; I suspect they too like our Gaulin neighbors felt the death sting of war more acutely when the paper or War Department announced the sad news of those they knew in their neighborhood.

The excitement over Bob's enlistment was only surpassed by news of his coming home on furlough the first time. We coulda' been that Norm Rockwell magazine cover about such a homecoming. I waited on our third story porch to be the bearer of good news when the car arrived. I can only imagine how hard my mother's heart was beating, she who did so much praying for his safe return, even from basic training.

"Furlough," unknown to old-time Francos before and during the war, spawned some humor. When *une bonne femme de maison* (a good housewife) read in a letter her son was coming home on furlough, she immediately wrote to come home on a train (*en char*) instead! "*Yé tan en furlo*" was the way a family radiated its news. They were our celebrities, and the newspaper often reported their homecoming. With her pipeline, mom often knew first

Besides the magnetism of the uniform and the pride of a brother home from the military, we children were also awed one of our own had gone somewhere far out of Woonsocket and returned. One who had left our small, provincial world to fight for his country, "*pour la patrie*," she said. We felt a common cause, a feeling good for us who sometimes felt or were made to feel not as "native American" as earlier-come immigrants with a better command of the language and more education and means. You didn't have to tell us there were no Francos on the Mayflower passenger list! Or so I thought until Chartier in his book mentions Guillaume Molines, a Frenchman on board. Chauvinistically, did he insist, "*Ici on parle le français*," (Here we speak French) and for him was the ship *la Fleur de Mai* (May flower)? Was he short like his English mates? In the story "The Courtship of Myles Standish," his two children were "characterized" by John and Priscilla Alden.

In a somewhat corollary, if you will, to be seen like full-blooded Americans, historian James M. McPherson in his superb Civil War book *Drawn With the Sword* says blacks finally felt great pride and acceptance when Lincoln allowed them to fight for the Union. Of course, no such problem for us Francos, but so many other ethnics like us had, were or had been in a long struggle for full acceptance in society like blacks, who at first had it worst and were paid less. Quickly whites saw their courage and willingness to fight and die as many did at the battle of Fort Wagner near Charleston in 1863 and other battles. The movie "Glory" was a good depiction of their sacrifice. Yet the initial intent of Lincoln's Emancipation Proclamation was to free only Southern slaves who did a lot of defensive work for their masters, since his intent was first to save the Union and not alienate two or three border states with slaves. Little wonder the Rebs didn't treat captured black soldiers with "pre-Geneva Convention-like" decency. About atrocities in war, I was disgusted at Japanese barbarities when they captured Nanking, China in 1937. Estimates range from 100,000 to 300,000 butchered. Author Irish Chang in *The Rape of Nanking* said Japan denied it for years. Also, their Bataan Death March during WWII. The Vietcong also mistreated our downed airmen.

About our part in the country's virtual or real isolationism before the war, the conflict made things happen more quickly, as if one is racing against time or death itself. In fact, for all Americans, the war ushered in great changes in the country's way of life and economy. The average yearly income before the war was less than $1,000, prompting one writer to say that Americans were poor and generally victims of a cruel industrial economy long before the Depression. In their letters home, Bob and cousins wrote about other ethnic soldiers they trained and fought with. Some were of Italian, English, German, Austrian, Indian, Scandinavian, Irish, Polish, Jewish descent, et al. To us, a veritable league of nations with names not generally heard in our home. "*Du monde pa(s) comme nous autres*," (of a world not like ours) said mom, but not as an ethnic slur. Since we practically lived only with Francos in our Social District, I remember how curious we were when Bob on short leave brought home that English-speaking navy buddy. I think the only other non-Franco to enter our home was a would-be boyfriend of Sue's.

Talk with relatives at the market, church, or family gatherings fed mom's wartime hotline. Besides our own, these soldiers, so highly praised in Ambrose's book, lived in cities, towns, and farms, big and small from all over America. When cousin Raymond died some 50 years later, many of the condolences sent Gene were from buddies of all nationalities. I was moved reading them. He had kept in touch at reunions, some of them in France. Woonsocket soldiers had really gone cosmopolitan to save Western democracy from Hitler's dream of a thousand-year Reich – it lasted only 12 years!

Oh, the irony of helping England and France retain their sovereignties! Twice, one had fought bitterly to deny or undermine our independence in 1776 and 1812; and the other had helped us win by neutralizing Britannia's naval superiority. Something Founding Father John Adams said was necessary also for us as a nation to protect us from future European interference, as was expressed in the Monroe Doctrine in 1823. So, when *les matelots français* (French sailors) bottled up the English at Yorktown, we finally became a free nation having bested Europe's most powerful armed nation. The odds against it were astronomical. To use sports jargon, one of the greatest upsets of all times! Washington's army was incredibly ragtag. What did you expect from poor farmers, poorly fed, dressed in rags and barely equipped? Imagine how their families were faring at home, since their men weren't being paid on time or at all! Desertions were common. Washington's genius was "not to win," but to avoid losing badly while England with its 3,000-mile supply line petered itself out. He often retreated until he pounced at Yorktown, Va., catching the Brits in a vise. Pat, Jim, and I visited the battleground.

Besides the usual war reports in papers, radio, and Movietone News, Bob's frequent letters were the family's own eyes and ears on the Pacific Theater. On the other hand, most of my Peloquin, Tellier, Vincent, Morvan, Lebel, *et* Fontaine first cousins served mostly in Europe, as did most of the Lapierres from Burrillville. I found it funny as we looked through Bob's letters where Uncle Sam had cut sensitive information out. Soldiers tried to tell you where they were or going by altering their first or middle names. Bob said he only did it once or twice. I don't think mom caught it. Post office posters screamed "Loose lips sink ships." Another showed a dog at the top. of a chair draped with a dead sailor's uniform: "Because someone talked." And "Don't Kill Her Daddy with Careless Talk." God, how many spies were there among us? Recall the Germans landed spies in Maine, N.Y., and Florida, but were quickly caught. Poorly trained, they were basically on their own after landing. So unlike their passion for efficiency.

We said those songs and slogans raised our spirit up. For example, our Army Lebel cousin and his Pearl Harbor mates were proud of that stirring "Let's Remember Pearl Harbor" song. And his Seabee brother's Construction Battalion had a feisty, combative one too: "We're the Seabees of the Navy, / We can build and we can fight. / We'll pave the way to victory / And guard it day and night." To us kids, it seemed life had taken on a patriotic, combative tone, which fit our go-get-'em nature. We were no longer in a city prosperity had bypassed; the embers of its once textile greatness seemingly cooled forever during the Depression. The ghostly specter of unemployment, long our worst enemy, had now been replaced with flesh-and-blood villains like Hitler, Il Duce, and Hirohito. As one said, "I'd rather fight the devil I know than the one I don't."

I don't know if the European Theater was considered more dangerous than the Pacific, but mom breathed a sigh of relief when shipping-out orders to Europe for a Robert Tellier turned out to be a namesake. The guy didn't have J.P. (Jean Paul) as his middle name. (She probably didn't understand one of his letters.) If true, Bob is amused by the story, and the irony is that he never liked his middle name and cringed every time she told him it nearly was his first name. Equally, he was also relieved when she told him he might have been Noêl (Christmas in French), if born December 25th instead of the 26th. Did he think that beautiful, sonorous feast name too Catholic or too French? It's also a surname. Her mother had lost *un* Robert in infancy. At supper once she told me why she chose it.

Like Catholics at one time, every French-Canadian child was given a saint's name at Baptism for protection and imitation. There are thousands of saints, but French-Canadian parents pretty much adhered to the same names, definitely non-English. That's why in our house and street, for example, Robert *et* René were common. I guess with such large families, they ran out of desired names, like in my Order. The Brothers then got into compound names before restoring our family names, long after the specter of France's turn-of-the century anticlericalism was gone. I was told religious there were singled out for longer military service. Overnight I was again Rene Tellier after years of being Brother Alphonse, having missed out on January 22's Vincent, the saint for my birthday. Clothing labels had to be changed, so the Brother in charge of the laundry (me once) could return them to their owner. Like in any family we all had a household job, even latrine duty. Nostalgically, I cherish my old devotional books and the Order's Rule of Life with my adopted name. And when in 2009 I went to Notre Dame HS's 50th reunion, some grads, now 67-68, asked if they could still call me *Frère* or Brother Alphonse. Great time, but saddened 17 had passed on. Parent or teacher, you think children and students are going to outlive you. Rene Cormier, M.D., was one of the great organizers with help from St. Bernard HS graduates of Fitchburg for their grads. I was the longest tenured staffer from 1955 to 1970. Loved the cold, bracing North Worcester County air. With daily walks, I was immune from colds all that time. Record snow, so many skied. I shouldn't have tried the highest slope my first run on Mt. Wachusett!

Like the guardian angel given you at birth, the nuns said your patron saint prayed or watched over you. It's why with so many heavenly beings guarding us, we felt safe. Add to that, when I entered the Order there were those big letters over the sink in the dormitory: *Dieu Me Voit*: God Sees Me. The good nuns told us He didn't delegate all the watching. He too always knew what we were doing and thinking. We were conscious of that. Like the beat cop or later the patrol car on the highway! And, yes, mom hurled a

Commandment (luckily not on a stone tablet like Moses threw at his idolatrous people) if a misdeed matched it. Or tell us this or that was matter for Confession. If one thinks all this was overbearing, recall the juvenile judge said he never saw a Franco kid in court!

Seriously, one day the gang tried to figure ways we could do something, anything, without God knowing about it first! Like changing our minds at the last minute before doing something, catching God off stride! But we got deflated when Phil Carpentier said God knew we were going to change our minds! Not bad for a pavement theologian from *la Gaulin*! When I returned from Mobile for my first teaching assignment at Sacred Heart School, Sharon, MA and resident kids now slept in that same dorm I once did, an Irish kid asked me what "Dew Me Voight" meant.

How heartwarming it was to see young school kids love someone wishing them a good night's sleep. Brother-minder as surrogate mom! Later when I proctored the Order's novices (pre-college) in Harrisville at lights out, they were even more effusive in their joy. Did it bring back all the tenderness and affection from their moms and dads, when they were young tykes? But unlike mom, I didn't suggest prayer, which they did each day, like the professed faculty. And in school, kids, as is/was customary in Catholic schools, started the day and every subject in high school with a prayer.

Brother Morel told the kids at Notre Dame, "If you're late for prayer, you're late for class." Prayer was like the Alpha and Omega of our life: the first and last letters of the Greek alphabet. Our distant relative, Saint Brother André Bessette, CSC, slept only a few hours compared to his time in prayer, saying "When you pray, God is on your lips." Mom knew so much about him; she could have written his bio. Like us in the Order, she read about saints and the faith. Publications from the *Montreal Oratory* were of course in French. Louise Barba, a relative of his who works at the rectory of St. Theresa's in Nasonville, Burrillville, gave me more literature on his life and attended his canonization in Rome. As an aunt did too. A simple porter with little education and frail health, he was a saintly monk who did so much to sustain and enlarge the vibrant faith of Montreal and beyond with the Oratory of Saint Joseph which is visited each year by two million. Elsewhere I related he levitated in prayer. Saint Joseph is the patron of Québec and carpenters, a common profession with Francophones at one time, like my brother Ben and my cousin namesake, Rene Tellier, also of North Smithfield. If I submit an op-ed piece for *The Valley Breeze* or *The Call*, people congratulate him, he told me. As Paul Demers and I often said, "As long as good is being done, it matters not by whom."

The family was shocked when Bob told us a larcenous gob (a lousy thief!) stole his unattended going-away gift watch worth about $20. (It also happened in the Civil War's Gettysburg!) In our rather strict code of morality, we always placed a dollar value on a serious transgression (that is, a mortal sin, so hell if not told in Confession) against the 7th Commandment. In French, the little Baltimore catechism said, *"Le bien d'autrui tu ne prendras, / Ni retiendras à ton escient"* - beautiful French about not stealing or knowingly keeping what isn't yours. In the 1940s, war or no war, twenty dollars was way over the limit. She called the guy heartless (*"Ya pa d'coeur"*), a lost soul. Generally, in the city, you didn't have to tie, bolt, and weld something down to the earth's iron core to prevent thievery, not discounting the stolen bike story and the shopping spree downtown with a friend's stolen money. Yes, the same kid *avec les doights longs* (with long thieving fingers) who also stole from St. Ann's poor box. A common expression was *L'occasion fait le larron*: opportunity bringing thieves out, like in disasters. Wow! Three times as a kid I was present at a theft! Mom called me up once on *"mes amitiés"*: my friends. But 42 kids lived in our 'hood. One writer stressed even Christ had one bad apple out of 12 apostles!

Why, in my 42-year school career, I was shocked by several deaths (one, an innocent target; still unsolved) and two suicides (once considered a failing, until better understood: a love-stricken freshman at Notre Dame HS; the other at Norton HS, possibly from depression.) And in the Order, two murders and a near-fatal stabbing. I enlarge on it later, but even if we're (the USA) only 5 percent of the world's population, we're 25 percent of its jailbirds. That's one in every 33 American adults in correctional control; gun homicide rate 10 to 20 percent higher than comparable nations with 4.7 percent of murders and non-negligent manslaughter per 100,000 people. (2015, totaled about 32,000 victims.) Don't we seem "to be at war" here all the time? I especially deplore the number of women, five, killed every day in this country, usually by someone known, as if maliciously "might is right." When will we "take back the night" on that issue, like they've done for sexual assault? Can it be true that one in five coeds is a victim of assault on college campuses, who are silent for fear of negative publicity? Victims should be encouraged to tell the police. But not all do.

During the war, we said every military family had souvenirs, like pennants and silken pillows (with embroidered unit insignias) displayed on parlor walls or sofas. But much to my chagrin, Bob in the navy said you didn't get to pick up helmets, flags, and rifles from the fallen enemy on the battlefield. We'd have to settle for the usual touristy thing made in some part of China not yet occupied by the Japanese. But cousin Raymond with the 83rd Division (329th Infantry) picked up a rifle, bayonet, and coveted Luger, which nicked him in the finger when it discharged. Later after his death, his brother Gene asked the State Department - with senior Senator

Chafee's help - to ship those spoils of war to a French town Ray's outfit had fought near. The curator promised to display the booty in a special vitrine or showcase. Philippe Jutras, an American from Maine who landed at Omaha Beach, later married a French widow and founded that museum.

Raymond, Godin, and Malo, as mentioned, fought in five major campaigns with their outfit. Their toughest challenge was relieving the 101st Airborne and battling two crack Panzer divisions after D-Day when Hitler finally woke up and allowed them to come from Calais. No less than 4,000 from their outfit made the supreme sacrifice the first day; 900 the next. Korda in *Ike* said if they had been at Normandy on June 6, their immense firepower would've mowed down our men. Twice buddies of Ray, just a few feet away, were severely wounded or killed. And as related, when he and a Foote buddy were asked to use an unfamiliar bazooka weapon against an incoming German tank, they were spotted and his comrade killed. A near miss from a German grenade tossed into his foxhole also troubled his sleep the last few years of his life. Single and a consummate world traveler, Gene said he often returned to France with some of his buddies. And he had the honor of reading the names of his division comrades receiving medals from a grateful French town on the 50th anniversary of 1944. *Qui sait deux langues, vaut deux hommes"*: knowing two languages doubles your worth,

Ray developed a bond of affection with the family that befriended him in one of his visits. Members of the Louis *et* Marguerite Leprelle family have come to America at the behest of Gene. He showed me a letter still infused with gratitude for their liberation from the Nazis. In an irony of war, his division helped liberate a town near Coutances, Normandie, where an ancestor of his mother, my father, and the family, Jean Baptiste Letellier dit Lafortune, departed for America in 1665. A soldier of the king, like mom's first ancestor, he too initiated a proud history of military service in the extended Tellier et Fontaine families in Canada and here. Proudly, mom said, *"On a faite notre part,"* about doing their bit, as the Brits say. Continuing a family tradition of service, United States Air Force Major Michael E. (Spike) Tellier, my brother Ben and Gloria's son, concluded a 26-year military career in 2011. During his time in service, he flew strategic bombers including the B-52 Stratofortress (BUFF) and B-1B Lancer (BONE). He also flew the E-4B, a version of the Boeing 747-200 called the National Airborne Operations Center (NAOC). While assigned to the E-4B, he often flew international missions with United States secretaries of state, secretaries of defense and other civilian and military leaders. He is a 1979 graduate of Mount Saint Charles Academy and a 1983 graduate of the University of Lowell, now UMASS (Lowell). Mike's flying career continues as a pilot for NASA flying a Boeing 747SP known as SOFIA, the Strategic Observation for Infrared Astronomy. His brother Alan, now a railroad engineer for CSX, served our country in the Marines. Cousin and author Claude Trottier, PhD. also earned his captain bars in the Army Material Command in the mid-1960s. I believe he's the first PhD in the clan.

And speaking of our own indebtedness to the French, I read we never repaid *La Belle France* for all her monetary and military help (in the $millions) in the Revolutionary War. If so, the interest would be enormous now! The movie "Jefferson in Paris" talked about it. Melanie Randolph Miller in her book *Envoy to the Terror* about Gouverneur Morris narrates the whole confusing scenario, since King Louis XVI was beheaded when payments were about to start. As our envoy, he saw five or six murderous regimes during the chaotic French Revolution in the 1790s. As the poet said, "Oh, what a tangled web we weave when first we practice to deceive." But about our debt, what about the cost in terms of blood and materiel to liberate them twice in 25 years in WW I and II? But of course, one can't forget France lost thousands of men here during the Revolutionary War. Like in all human endeavors, war does make for strange bedfellows. Several states in the Civil War had divided loyalties, creating in one instance two Virginias. And what blows my mind is President Lincoln's wife had brothers fighting for the Confederacy: in-laws as out-laws! Certainly, off-limits in their conversations, but not her spending sprees, all on his bare-bones salary. She became unsettled after the loss of two sons and his death. I had a chance to see the room and bed where he died in a house across the street from Ford's Theater where Booth shot him, as retold grippingly in Bill O'Reilly's and Matin Dugard's *Killing Lincoln*. He had a premonition he'd be killed. Hard to believe a security guard didn't show up at the theater.

A final thought about those war souvenirs. While with Gene at a ceremony on the U.S.S. Kennedy in Fall River, a Pearl Harbor survivor told me he later picked up a Japanese-scripted cloth from a dead soldier at Iwo Jima. The island was the scene of that famous flag-raising photo. The survivor told me he had the cloth translated and returned to the Japanese family whose son had written poignant thoughts "just before the battle, mother," as the song says. He also gave to a museum a bandanna he picked up from another battle scene. It all reminded me of a poem in high school where a soldier laments the death of a soldier he killed. If not for the war, he might have shared a drink (a nipperkin!) in a tavern.

Also, who can forget one of the city's outstanding police officers, business owner, state senator, and champion of veterans' causes - Alphonse Auclair - who also fought at Iwo Jima with the 3rd Marine Corps. I was honored when he asked me to serve on the committee and submit a grant for funds (even if not successful) to erect the Aram Pothier monument in front of the Museum of Work and Culture. Auclair helped found the St. Joseph

Veterans Association (I'm an honorary member on the scholarship committee which Bob served, and Ben one of the building factotums); organized the local 50th anniversary remembrance of Pearl Harbor, and with Jacques Staelen, found and returned the lost Merci Boxcar (a gift from France after WWI) to Woonsocket where it is exhibited in the Lt. George Dubois Veterans Museum adjoining the Museum of Work and Culture. And what surely was also dear to him, the renaming of Route 99 the Iwo-Jima Memorial Highway. He passed away in October of 2007. In my Order, we were taught "To serve is to rule" (*Servire est regnare*), and without a doubt he who served his community and country so well also wore the mantle of leadership with humility and great devotion. *Requiescat in pace* – Rest in Peace.

When I told that vet in Fall River he should write his memoirs before it's too late, he said he didn't have any family to leave them to. That's why I think the efforts of Gene Peloquin, Roger Petit, Cumberland artist Ann Jalette, and others to help some Connecticut and Cumberland school children record the exploits of the vanishing veterans of WWII was important. Lest we forget. Didn't Christ want children to be heard? "If they be silent, the stones will speak." In this case for the vets.

If, as Milton said, books are "the precious lifeblood of great minds," what about the often-untold stories of soldiers who literally saved Western civilization from tyrannies, the scope and savagery of which the world had not seen up to that time. One must read *Interrogations: The Nazi Elite in Allied Hands*, 1945, by Richard Overy to grasp the Nazi dimension of evil. Like us, Germans still wonder how a few nondescript men could have created a government whose thirst for evil, destruction, and annihilation shocked the world. Both FDR and Churchill were aghast even before Hitler set things in motion. Most nations have a grievous stain in their history, but none to equal "The Final Solution." Could it happen again? For all of Germany's great engineering marvels, technical genius, and great philosophical, musical, and intellectual élan, the wonder is how in the space of 30 years the people sheepishly fell to the inducements of first, the Kaiser, and then Hitler. Unlike the saying, "Like sheep led to the slaughter," Hitler led them to slaughtering.

One of Bob's navy accoutrements actually made me a little richer. One day as I examined a money belt he sent home to me I found a twenty-dollar bill flattened out against the interior pocket lining. He was heeding mom's advice to safeguard his money: "*Prends pa(s) d' chance*" (Don't take a chance). Obviously, he'd forgotten all about the "Andrew Jackson," and in a bureau we shared I found it on a rainy day. In those days, if you couldn't play outside and alone and bored with indoor games, days were dreary. I didn't get to keep the whole 'score,' just a few bucks. Despite his meager military pay, Bob was self-sufficient, unlike some buddies whose monthly income needed boosting by their folks. Mom often reminded us that millworkers couldn't count on having much tomorrow, so if any today, you should save *"pour le mauva(is) temps"* (for the bad times). Like many parents, mom wrote Bob every time he did and more. It was the same when Ben was serving in Germany; I in the Order for 25 years; and Rachel at Our Lady of the Mountains Academy, Gorham, NH, run by the same Presentation of Mary nuns of the parish. Meanwhile, Sue helped them keep the home fires burning.

Since we never had a phone and a stamp only cost three cents, mom reached out to touch us all with her letters. Her collected letters would fill volumes if still extant. In them, she crammed the stuff of everyday life, which soldiers and faraway students crave to read about home and loved ones. Because she was *une femme de maison* (a housewife), you swore her letters were like a photographic or Rockwellian rendition of the "noiseless tenor" of daily Woonsocket life in peace and war. Bryant College Professor Judy Barrett Litoff edited a book with Professor David Smith about those wartime correspondences. It's entitled *Miss You: The World War II Letters of Barbara Woodall and Charles Taylor*. If I had known, I would've contributed one from mom (in patois!) and Bob from the albums.

In one of his *Greatest Generation* books, Brokaw also reprints many such letters. When I was Assistant Director at Notre Dame HS and fellow religious Brother Gabe Couture and I worked together to develop our athletic field on South Street in the early 1960s, I found a whole treasure trove of war letters all neatly stacked in a box in a pit being filled in for a parking lot across our Crusader Athletic Field. Reading only one, I found the soldier's longing so touching and personal. For one, he regretted she cut her long tresses. But I felt I was invading their privacy somehow and reburied the box before the bulldozer arrived. Why thrown away? Had death or disaffection blighted their wartime love? Will they be unearthed generations hence, like Civil War letters and diaries in attics and trunks, and old books? The athletic field on South Street later became condos when the school became a layman-run fifth year prep school for Division One hoopsters. Lack of religious faculty was a reason for the closure. It had been a great source of vocations for the Brotherhood and Priesthood. When we put in a football field complete with lights from a Whitinsville, MA, plant, we used extra beams left over from construction of Brother Adelard Arena at Mount Saint Charles Academy for our bleachers.

I share the wonder of the high degree of literacy of Civil War soldiers. Outside of speech, diaries and letters were the only way to communicate. Many were well written. I read one such book of collected letters and expectedly, it was from someone in the trenches. War was violent, inhuman, and, yes, often immoral. That's why surviving families cleaned up ("bowdlerized," named after the first to sanitize writing) the more crude and sexual passages before passing it on to posterity. But the most touching is that memorable and foreboding letter from a RI Civil War combatant Ballou to his young wife.

When mom and dad moved to Hospice Saint Antoine, I enjoyed reading her wartime letter Bob brought back from the war. Dated August 24, 1944, the flourishing Spenserian-styled letter (think of John Hancock's signature on the Declaration of Independence) says butter is going to be scarce but hopes the Kennedy Store on Main Street will have some. Meat even rarer, garden tomatoes won't grow (*"les tomates ne veulent pas murir"*), but *mon oncle* Henri Trottier on Rathbun has a green thumb with his Victory Garden. Mom, Sue, and friend Madeleine Carle went to a Kiwanis-sponsored circus at St. Ann's Park. And Auray, her WW I hero-brother, whom she hadn't seen for 21 years, came to visit from Ontario. Her closing was like Walter Cronkite's "And that's the way it is" but in a more motherly tone: *"Bonne chance, ta maman (Good Luck, your Mom)."* Is there a more beautiful closing in the French language? I loved it in the Order. It made me feel I was still at home, no matter what state, religious house, or school I was in. I realized what letters meant to soldiers away from home and hearth. Cronkite's other signature ending also resonated with me: "What sort of a day was it? A day like all days, filled with those events that alter and illuminate our times. And you were there." That's because I felt I was still sitting next to her and listening to her stories at the dinner table.

So her letters were the glue that kept us all together, as education, war, and religious life took us far away from the city. Hopefully e-mailing or i-phoning moms and dads can be as personal and homey with an electronic medium. Some authors once thought a cold, metallic typewriter could never punch out a human-interest novel like a handwritten script. Shelby Foote, famous for his folksy comments in Ken Burn's *Civil War* series and author of a superb three-volume epic on the fratricidal conflict, wrote it all by hand. It took me all summer to read, courtesy of a sympathetic Wheaton College librarian in Norton. She mused it wasn't your usual book-at-the-beach choice. The Civil War was so unlike the sights and sounds of the cool, peaceful waters of Spring Lake, the ecstatic cries of tots swooshing down the water slide, the 1920s Arcade with kids coaxing more specie from mom to win carnival prizes.

But President Wilson, who initially wrote all his speeches by hand, gradually warmed up to the typewriter. He also developed his own shorthand before fleshing out his thoughts in print or speech. No ghost writer. He loved being alone to decide what he was going to do in a crucial situation, like going to war with Germany, even if he worked hard to restore peace in

Europe. This despite bellicose Teddy Roosevelt who still wanted to lead a company into battle in France, like his Rough Riders at San Juan Hill, Cuba in the Spanish-American War. When he died, I thought of Thomas Gray's "The boast of heraldry, the pomp of power, / And all that Beauty, all that wealth e'er gave, / Awaits alike the inevitable hour. / The paths of glory lead but to the grave." He was once shot campaigning, but still finished his speech when pocket material blunted the missile.

    Like all soldier mothers, mom kept the home fires burning and without being a Rosie the Riveter, helped win the war in ways she never dreamed of. That's why I've contributed to have hers and dad's name recorded in Washington's new WWII monument records along with Bob's. How many millions of moms, dads, wives, and older children were our goal-line defense at home or in the workplace? But what fears and what dread wrung her maternal heart, thinking daily about her oldest son in perilous combat away from home? She knew too well the ways of instant tragedy. What a tell-all book it would have been - Hers to sound the emotional depth of mothers' worrisome hearts.

    Not surprisingly, we know mothers even worry about their older children out late at night. Perhaps if we'd been older, we could've gauged the slight tremor of her voice when suddenly in the evening she said, "*Il faut qu'jécrive à Robert*": I have to write to Robert/Bob. Did it mean those tinges of fear, caring, and love had welled up into an imperative too poignant to be kept to herself? Her correspondences became a family thing, an act of togetherness. She asked about our schooling, scouting, and friends. For example, she wrote about my Second-Class scouting badge project of pouring a cement flag stand which crumbled because my mix was too watery. Bob, a former scout leader, jabbed me in his reply. He liked to hear about how the few remaining young men (not drafted yet or physically unfit) were faring. Dad, taciturn like his brothers Napoléon *et* Philippe, kept his fears to himself. His predictions were so unbelievably correct, was it better not to share his thoughts or feelings with us about Bob's chances for survival? Like men of his time, his feelings, piety, and faith were deep, not demonstrative.

    About piety and men, I never saw a man "razzing" his rosary against the backside of the front pew in church. That was a pious woman thing, always more visible about their prayers in contrast to their modesty in dress and appearance. The men's three-point stance kneeling in the pews was an observable decorum slip. But I said unlike novelist Frank McCourt's buddies, they didn't leave services early "for the thirst." Early exits were common at one time, and some priests weren't shy about calling them back if before *Ita missa est*: Mass is over. I spoke to one priest about it some fifty years later when he retired. A courageous move on his part. Surely mom prayed "a bullet (or salvo) with his name on it," like the one her brother Auray spoke about in France, would never find Bob on his ship. The War Department never came knocking at our door as it did for some families on our street. But with one war after another, the miasma of Vietnam's jungles covered our 309 Gaulin house with the stench of death in the Carpentier home for their son Lucien. The Beauregards, (he, the mover; she, a gifted seamstress) who had moved, lost their grandson Robert there also. Cousin Ronald Ouellette, MSC grad Class of 1961, formerly a local radio announcer, deceased in 2013, received the Purple Heart in that war.

Since radio was our only entertainment before, during, and after the war, the family enjoyed its own company most evenings - a beautiful Franco tradition. Dad often read, obviously the wellspring of his wisdom and encyclopedic knowledge. *Mémère* prayed the rosary, thus assuring the family a constant intercessor *avec la Sainte Vierge* (with the Blessed Virgin). I remember in the Order an infirm Brother in our Andover (MA) school was considered a *paratonnere* or lightning rod for his ability to draw graces on the rest of us with his constant prayers. We recited the rosary on our knees around the dinner table. I'm convinced He heard our cry. God knew mom - *une* Fontaine - had borne enough.

It's always a mystery whose prayers are answered! In the Fatima apparition chronicle, Mary tells the three children some of their prayers will be answered, others not. She told the older Lucia (10) she'd live a long life (died in her 90s), while her cousins Jacinta (7) and Francisco (9) would die young. I've written several eulogies at the death of students, citing God in the Old Testament about their having lived a full life in a few short years. Also quoted poet Alfred Housman's "To an Athlete Dying Young" about finding comfort that it comes before the hurrahs of fame have ceased like it did for Bosox rookie first baseman Harry Agganis of Boston University. He was batting 313. Ted Williams visited him on his deathbed. "Now you will not swell the rout of those who wore their honors out," the poet added.

After help from Suzanne *et* Rachel with the dishes, mom sat at the dinner table to write. Homework done and our catechism learned or recited to her if needed (the Baltimore Catechism was always on the best seller list, and in every schoolbag), we generally entertained ourselves with parlor-like games, some made by dad. Even in those pre-TV days, we played the radio very little because he retired at 9. Sue liked a station that played music all day. Quite naively I asked her once how come they didn't run out of tunes! The same about movie titles! I thought people knew as little English as I did.

I remember mom's letter-writing so clearly because it had an auditory dimension to it. With pen and paper, she wrote in a bold, sweeping style, typical of her quick, nervous manner, her pen strokes like an ancient stylus over dry parchment. She always wanted one of those dipping pens from our school bag: "*Apporte mwé ta plume* (Bring me your pen)"

I wouldn't be surprised if during WWI, even if she was now in America, she wrote to her brothers in France. She kept their soldier pictures in a box before I urged her to identify them for me, along with almost 500 other collected photos taken in America. *Les* Fontaines - not *les* Telliers - loved to pose and surely helped make Kodak rich! Like those famed Peabody girls at the turn of the century, dad's sisters were unbelievably gorgeous (*belle chevelure* - beautiful hair - no broom cuts) and photogenic in their prime, so it's a pity only one family and two single photos survive of their first years in America. One singlet is of Diana, dead at 20, yes, of respiratory causes. Another in poor condition is *pepère* Joseph with his delivery wagon. The family photo was taken only after grandmother Angélina (Durand) died of complications from bronchiectasis, an affliction to all to some extent, except for *tante* Alice who moved to N.Y. with her Brunelle family.

Only in 2001 did I learn *mémère* Angèlina also gave birth here to Joseph Roméo (JR), who died at 18 months but whose name is not on my grandparents' Precious Blood gravestone, as it was on a previous one. City hall records confirmed JR too died of respiratory causes. Again, it's why mom was so concerned about the health of our lungs! I've read that in poor cultures, lung problems are more common and virulent, what with less prevention.

Despite the loss of home and other comforts, it doesn't surprise me when hurricane, flood, fire, and tornado victims, as seen on TV, lament the loss of irreplaceable family heirlooms, like photos. You can imagine what that loss meant to her, the collector, one of the self-appointed historians of her own family and proud people. Like Biblical Job's possessions reduced to ashes, she whined. "*On éta sa paille. Nos photos ont passé au feu.*" (We were his straw. Our photos were destroyed in the fire.) Fire, sackcloth, and ashes! The trifecta of the Fontaine saga!

Cousin Claude Trottier showed me a circa 1870s photo, which I believe is my grandfather Louis Fontaine, born in the 1860s. So did the family come out of Canada with four, not three photos? The find highlights the importance of family research, especially in boxes of photos people inherit from elders. You know those photos someone was going to put in an album someday! Like mom with all those photos in their Bellingham apartment's spare room. She and I took two years to identify people in them to create a comprehensive family album. If one waits until parents and grandparents are gone, you create a void of almost a hundred years, said a genealogist. For us, it's back to the Civil War, but of course in Canada. But with or without my interest in the Civil War, I found that epochal when mom first told me. It put that time into perspective and within reach, so to speak. It means three grandparents were born at a time when a future country of theirs was almost torn in two. Immigrants in the family would have been like "Damn Yankees."

In prose, isn't the most touching and nostalgic literature those written thoughts of fighting men and women on the verge of battle, like the Japanese story I related? In my Civil War readings, I've often felt the poignancy of those men, who in the face of almost certain death, (like the night before Pickett's charge at Gettysburg) asked surviving comrades to send last thoughts home. I said the most famous and poignant is undoubtedly RI's combatant Sullivan Ballou's letter to his wife Sarah, with its loving message and intimation of death before an upcoming first Civil War battle. Ken Burns featured it in his television epic. Born in Smithfield, RI and educated at Brown, he became a lawyer and was elected to the RI House of Representatives in 1854. Just as much as Bob said he anxiously waited for mail call every day, so too did we rush to the mailbox when the postman came. We carried the letter upstairs to our apartment like a gold bar or precious missive from the Pope or the President himself. Only she should read it first. Our mailbox was on the first-floor porch and entrance where all others were too. No security or lock ever needed. No checks or refunds ever came in the mail. I've given thanks that our honest-to-goodness neighbors, the 309 Gaulin tenement dwellers, were spared at the time from the ravages of Hurricane 1938, WWII, Korea, and later a polio epidemic. But yes, sadly, not Vietnam for the Carpentiers and Beauregards.

Touching were the words of a French official at a Utah Beach memorial celebration, attended among others by Tom Hanks of *Saving Private Ryan* fame. The Gallois said in impeccable French: "*Laissons pour un moment les discours et lesparades, en mémoire de ces mères qui n'ont jamais revu leur fils, de ces femmes qui on attendu en vain le retour du fiancé ou du mari, de ces enfants si jeunes orphelins.*" Translation: 'The exhortation is to look beyond the festivities of the moment to all mothers, sweethearts, and children for whom a loved one, spouse, or a parent never returned.' An admiral added France remained free because of them: "*grâce à eux* (thanks to them)." Some 199 RI soldiers are buried at Colleville sur Mer, Normandie, interring a bit of Rhode Island in French soil, to use a poignant phrase by English war poet Rupert Brooke about Tommies who died in WWI.

Since infamous Cain slew Abel, haven't mothers especially from time immemorial been shaken by the death of a child, especially in wartime? Now with women in the military, the scythe of death causes mothers to weep for their daughters too, conjuring up the poet saying when she died, "Underneath this stone doth lie / As much beauty as could die." Of course, not demeaning their patriotism and desire to also serve and defend their country more actively, their passing brings another dimension of grief to hearth and home. Great heroines, as seen in the Old Testament - Judith, Esther, Rachel, the mother of the seven Maccabees, et al, and in modern times *Jeanne d'Arc* (Joan of Arc) in France - also arose to save their people or uphold their faith. Now at least 100 have made the ultimate sacrifice in the Middle East? When I was in France, I asked *deux petits garçons* (two little boys) to pose in front of a column where the Maid of Orleans was burnt to death. I gave them *des sous* (money).

James Tellier with daughter Mackenzie, 4, and *pepère* Rene Tellier

I'm proud a Norton High School counselee became a jet pilot fighter. In school, she was no less an honor student, all-star softball player, and prom queen to boot. I felt good about helping her mom return twice to school for nursing degrees. I didn't want to hear she hadn't done well in high school. Anyone who was a spouse, ran a home, had children, (three in her case), was employed, but wanted to attend college, was recommendable in my book. She aced her programs. Word had gotten out that with principal Dan Wheeler's blessing, I counseled adults, Norton High School grads or not. Told them that counting all collegiate students, part- time, full-time, daytime, nighttime, degree or non-degree programs, the average age was now over 30. Learning is now cradle to grave, especially since Americans have a 42-year working career, four employment vectors, and twelve job changes. Son Jim who went back at 33 and always on the dean's list, garnered his Associate's in Information Technology – He did networking at N.E. Institute of Technology in 2013 at the new East Greenwich campus before his insurance work. Kareem Abdul Jabbar, basketball's greatest scorer, spoke to 1,100 graduates at the Providence Convention Center, "Learning is lifetime," he said eloquently and, of course, "elongatingly," another Tom Swiftie.

Woonsocket in the Depths of War

AS THE WAR PROGRESSED, even if 309 Gaulin was always spared, the pride we felt in and for our country's soldiers was alloyed by a chronic foreboding sense of grief as daily reports of the city's wartime injuries and deaths appeared in the paper. Of the 96,000 who served from the Ocean State, we recorded 2,340 in one figure who made the ultimate sacrifice with some city families touched "by fire and blood." Hitting close to home was the September 29, 1944 edition reporting the death (with photo) of cousin Sgt. Gerard Vincent. The family lived *chez la petite Gaulin* behind the church. A former Mountie and student of St. Joseph School, Berthierville, Québec, he was killed in Sicily. He was a member of the famed First Division, which so distinguished itself in Africa, then Italy, and later in Germany. In a letter were the comforting words of the Mass celebrant: "A cross has been placed on your shoulders. Your son has lost his life. He left the service of his country to render a greater service, to serve his God." In operation TORCH in North Africa, our forces eventually became a tested, combative force.

But from the tragic to the mundane, the same edition reported a new mandate from the Director of the Office of Rubber, a division of Price Administration. "From now on, only those who drive more than 601 miles a month qualify for new tires. Few were affected on our pedestrian street. But you were also forbidden to buy more than three pairs of shoes a year? Was this a slight against us *"marche-à-pied Francos* (walking Francos)?"

Also reported was the wounding of Corporal Pelletier, the only son of Mr. and Mrs. Joseph A. Pelletier of 266 Knight Street. He sustained an injury to his left side in the hot fighting that raged in Salerno, Italy September 13. "I am O.K.," he reassures them, "and it is nothing serious." His Purple Heart medal came in the mail from the American Red Cross. Before that, he saw action with the Fifth Army in Tunisia, North Africa.

Even though the most telling battles of the war were fought in France and Germany, we can't forget the struggle in Italy for Monte Cassino, Anzio, and Sicily; "the under belly of Europe," said Churchill who insisted on the unpopular strategy. Catholics all over the world worried about the safety of the pope and Rome's treasures. Yes, a recent book revealed Hitler's plan to kidnap the pope and steal those Vatican's treasures. Both Hitler and Goering tried to outdo the other in seizing art treasures, some taken from Jewish owners sent to concentration camps. Families to this day are seeking the court's help to have their collections returned. The movie "Monument Men," highlighted many recoveries at war's end.

Because of our slow advance in Italy, I recall the Germans "forcing" us to bomb the lofty Benedictine monastery itself, a questionable move because the ruins in and around the buildings quickly provided them with excellent shooting cover. Initially, in our Movietone news we saw Germans scurrying around like rats, but not from within because their commander, a Benedictine Tertiary lay member, had not allowed it. So, like the Army chaplain told us at Mount, they had some "good guys" too! In fact, many southern Germans and of course Austrians were Catholic or Lutheran. Later, the German general in charge mercifully left Rome an open city, preferring to build three lines of defense beyond the Eternal City and up to the Alps and Southern France. Here too, General Montgomery laments that we allowed them to do this by our spread-out attack policy instead of a unified thrust, his chosen method of warfare like in Africa. It's the reason for his tug-of-war with Ike. Military theory favored Monty, as the Germans did to us, despite their ultimate defeat due to lack of gasoline and the return of good weather for our planes in the Battle of the Bulge, December '44. Self-serving General Mark Clark was criticized for wanting to be first to seize Rome, fouling strategy to contain fleeing Nazis.

The History Channel acknowledged the German generally fought an honorable war in the West, usually abiding by the Geneva Convention except for atrocities in the Battle of the Bulge, especially the Malmedy (Belgium) massacre for which one general was condemned at the Nuremberg Trials. But in their dealings with Russia, tales abound of mass executions of prisoners, the intelligentsia, Jews, and authority figures. It reflected Hitler's maniacal hatred of Communism and the Slavs whom he considered subhuman. As they did against Napoleon, the Russians used the same Scorched Earth tactic, which left the Germans without shelter when winter set in early and ferociously. Germany lost six million people in the war, Russia, 20 million, and 417,000 U.S. soldiers. Some 18,000 in the Battle of the Bulge alone, at a time when we thought the Germans were kaput. Again, Hitler's decision, against the advice of his generals. "He who counts only on himself for direction is a fool."

My formation master in the Order who spent four years as a prisoner in Stalag XB - *Frére* George Aimé Lavallée - told me Russian POWs didn't survive long in captivity. He, fellow Brothers and Oblates, survivors of the ship Zamzam, fared better, since Red Cross packages usually got through. A total of 1,472 days in captivity. A tall, well-built man, he barely weighed 100 pounds when released. But oh, the drag of nicotine! Germans practically gave you "state secrets" for smokes, he said. Photos show him in a home-made baseball uniform in camp, since the Germans allowed sports, plays, and correspondence courses from Oxford and Cambridge Universities. He must've loved the sport, since every Sunday in season during training we had a game in Harrisville on a field we laid out. In French only, *s'il vous plait* (please), during Speak Only French week.

Unbelievably, some commandants allowed "known escape digs" until breakout to keep prisoners busy! Ingenious how prisoners made Nazi uniforms, forged passports and money, built tunnels with ventilation, and cleverly released sand hidden in their pant legs as they walked outside. In one camp, they built a glider in a chateau's third floor room the Germans didn't know existed until the war's end! It had been paneled over.

In Brother Lavallée's stalag, the inventive POWs, but not the monks, also used a makeshift theater as a good cache for contraband and a ruse for breakout. Another Brother also wrote about his imprisonment titled: *Au Fond du Gouffre*: Bottom of the Pit. Brother Lavallée's is called *Marking Time Behind Barbed Wire*. Brother Lavallée was a Mount Saint Charles librarian assistant in the 1990s, and Brother Andre a staffer too at one time. The Oblates and the Brothers were bound for Basutoland, South Africa, when their ship was sunk. It was before we entered the war, but because they possessed American and Canadian citizenships, they were imprisoned after plucked from the Atlantic. But an American mother and missionary wishing to join her husband with her five children were allowed to return to the states. The survivors met at times after the war.

Authors Frank and Rogge's, book *The German Raider Atlantis* and *Miracle at Sea* by Anderson tell the story of the April 17, 1941 sinking of the Zamzam. The raider thought the innocent ship was really in disguise, a ruse they themselves often used. *Frére* Lavallée did make it to the Order's South African missions after the war. Along with his book, he also gave me copies of works of his foundations during his years as Provincial of the New England Province, like Cor Jesu Terrace and Motherhouse in Harrisville, Bishop Guertin High School in Nashua, and a school in Hertfordshire, England, which I visited. At first, English authorities were incredulous about Americans wanting to build a school in England. Weren't they innovators in establishing schools? And weren't their schools outstanding? He was thrilled one year when the Brothers' school surpassed a centuries-old school in merit. I loved seeing the Roman aqueduct and coins found on the property at St. Albans.

Cousin Sgt. Armand Lapierre of Burrillville was killed in France, June 19, 1944, and his parents sent his mortuary card. Lapierre, who with his outfit stormed Normandy, June 7, 1944, was at St. Lo trying to rescue a buddy. So posthumously he was awarded the Silver Star and Purple Heart for his bravery and sacrifice. A half-century later, his family received his *Médaille du Jubilée* (Jubilee Medal) on the 50th anniversary. His last letter home, now framed and treasured, had reassured the family: "I'll be home soon." It arrived after his death had been announced.

Their grandmother Julienne Morvan, *mémère* Emérance's sister, married Arsène Duguay and sheltered *les* Fontaines, as did her sister Sédulie Girard when they arrived in 1916. Unlike *La Belle* France, their long-ago ancestral country whose declining birthrate after WWI presaged dire consequences, families here continued to be fruitful and saw many sons answer the call. That's why, said cousin Gene, the city and the Blackstone Valley seemed to have so many casualties. Not to be outdone so to speak by their five patriotic brothers, we said the two Lapierre sisters married soldiers: Florence to Raymond Cahill, later the Oakland postmaster, and Irène to Lt. Commander Russell Proulx.

As other communities and churches did, St. Theresa's Church, Nasonville, RI, honored its veterans with an imposing memorial at its entrance. One day as the parish bells of St. Ann's tolled the death and burial of another soldier, I recall *Soeur* Sainte Emilie reminded us about the three most meritorious deaths: the faith, another person, and one's country. A nice feminine touch if you will, when I told mom she added a woman dying in childbirth went to heaven. I realized later how it spoke volumes for her reverence for life as a life-giver, which so defined the lives of immigrant women and their large broods.

When in late afternoon the paper arrived, mom burst out with a plaintive and resigned "*Ca ya*" (It's happened) when another soldier died. She used the same expression when I told her at St. Antoine dad had died at Fogarty Hospital in 1982. She had such a sense of community, especially about her compatriots. Her sorrow and pain were as if she'd lost a near and dear one. Like in English poet John Donne's line about the European continent being lessened even if just a clod of dirt broke off, she felt diminished by a soldier's passing. In her own way, the famous line, "Ask not for whom the bell tolls, it tolls for thee" came out as "*Ça peu arrivé à tout l'monde* (it can happen to anyone), adding, "*C'est de valeur*," a great loss. Like other life givers, she was "the mother of a thousand soldiers," so great is the affection and compassion for all living things mothers have.

The news of military casualties was like Churchill's "ring of terror" waiting to encircle us within its crushing vise. If you had a family member in the military, you worried about that knock at your door. Keeping a sense of proportion, the only comparable thing in my young mind was later, before the Salk vaccine, when polio was coming up our Gaulin street one house after another. Even though Roosevelt and the press carefully hid his crippling polio condition, dad had startled me with that revelation. I had a polio victim in my class at St. Ann's, adding another layer of fear when we saw those Movietone clips at the Laurier of people in an iron lung. Luckily, it passed over our house, but struck Sue's best friend, Madeleine (Carle) Ethier and one of her children. Tragedies often coming in multiples, as the Bard wrote, her older brother Armand was also a victim years before. Hobbled, he was later an accident victim. And sadly, her youngest brother Leopold was severely crippled by a car on our very street.

About the polio scare, parents advised us not to get overheated or overtired, because Roosevelt had come down with it after a swim. One time in the summer when I ran back home and was flushed and excited from play, dad grabbed my tiny wrist and told me to slow down and not get "*échauffé*.": overheated. A home medic, he had remedies for some ills, but for polio they hoped "*la paralysie enfantine nous dépasse*": the infantile paralysis got by us.

Besides my Vincent *et* Lapierre cousins, the paper reported all those 151 deaths, 23 MIAs, and 34 POWs. Proximity wise, I wondered how many she knew or knew about whose families lived so close to our pedestrian world. As a limited example, the obits of Pfc. Albert J. Aubin, 206 Cumberland St., killed in France; Ensign Walter Bacon, 89 Hamlet, killed in a plane crash in Florida; Normand P. Belhumeur, fireman 1C, 578 Elm, killed in action at sea; Staff Sgt. Eugene Bélisle, 67 Brook, killed in Leyte, Philippines; Pfc. Aram Blanchette, 233 Dulude, killed in France; next-door neighbor Walter A. Blanchette, torpedoman, 3C, 293 Gaulin, lost in the Pacific; Alcide Brouillard, 296 Gaulin, killed in Italy; Emile J. Chamberland, 215 Dulude, of bullet wounds in Maine.

Because in 'Sochelle *Coin*' practically everyone walked, went to the same church, had children at St. Ann's (over 1,000), and worked in the same mills, parents like mine knew so many people and their homes. That's why moms like her may have reacted and grieved even more about "neighborhood soldiers" who died in the war. Long after, I found myself wondering when I read *Pig Boats* by Theodore Roscoe about the U.S. submarine war against Japan, which of the 52 subs lost was Walter Blanchette in? We could touch his house from ours; he was like kin. In the Pacific, submarine fatalities totaled 3,131 sailors and 374 officers, almost one in five. But they sank 1,113 Japanese merchant ships, 201 naval vessels, and 65 others. After Pearl, they were our only war arm in that ocean. A Vice Admiral "on loan" after the war from Germany cited the crushing job our subs did on those merchant ships, so vital to Japan's scarce island resources. Even if the Pacific war to us seemed as intense as Europe, historians say the first strategy was to defeat the Nazi machine, much to MacArthur's frustration and his island strategy.

Every time we went to Mass, school, or market, we looked at peoples' window star, hoping their blue star hadn't turned to gold. So even without Bob, the war would have been personal, because of her instant eulogies. Theirs was not an obsession, because after all they were in their second world war in less than 25 years. And in many ways, both wars were very personal. Not diminishing the sacrifice of other nationalities, the fact that Francos were such a large part of the city's population with its tremendous social intimacy magnified and personalized those losses. They were known or known about. Of course, no one death was more tragic than any other, but we continue to record here some war deaths in our neighborhood, Social *Coin*, and a bit beyond, confirming, as it were, that war, injury, and death were at peoples' doorsteps. We young people had never lived with the fear and imminence of death.

Other close neighbors were: Alfred J. Charpentier, 178 Gaulin, killed in France; Pfc. Roland O. Desrosiers, 123 Brook, France; Normand A. Galipeau, seaman IC, 378 Cumberland Hill, dead of wounds in a hospital; Pfc. Lionel Gravel, 1082 Social, dead of wounds in Italy; Sylvio O. Glaude, 234 Gaulin, France; Pvt. Robert E. Hémond, 228 Dulude, France; Sgt. Walter D. Lambert, 576 Wood, crash victim in RI.

Also: Hector A. Lefèbvre, 296 Gaulin (same house as Pfc. Brouillard), killed in France; Pfc. Gustave E. Ménard, 115 Brook, France; Cpl. Gustave Nadeau, 16 Lowland, in the Pacific; Pvt. Alfred Pecori, 409 Wood, drowned in Italy; Pfc. Arthur R. Salois, 587 Social, France; Staff Sgt. Lionel A. St. Gelais, 267 Burnside, the Philippines; Pvt. Reginald R. Tessier, 67 Brook, Italy; Pfc. Thomas R. Turcotte, 566 Clinton, Sicily; and Pvt. Arthur A. Favreau, 279 Bernon, at Pearl Harbor.

Sadly, one family lost two sons: 1st Lt. Fred J. Bedford, a B-29 pilot, killed on Guam, and his brother Pfc. William T. Bedford, in Italy, but I doubt mom knew them or of them. As I saw in a guided tour through Precious Blood Cemetery with Mount Saint Charles counselee Robert Bellerose, a commemorative-like shrine lists many of the city's war dead who, in Lincoln's famous words, "gave the last full measure of devotion." Women of course also served in the military and 400 died, but no one I believe from the city. How fitting the Museum of Work and Culture has dedicated the Lt. George Dubois Veterans Museum to all our combatants. Docent and military veteran Julian Mitchell, a faculty member with me at the Academy, gathered some of the service memorabilia. He and chairman

Jacques Staelen, Chevalier of the French Legion of Honor, were the driving forces. Solemn remembrance ceremonies are held on Veterans Day at the museum, with uniformed volunteers of all wars in formation and Woonsocket High School's ROTC unit. Lest we forget!

But with the Vietnam War in the late 1960s, sadly the War Department found our 309 Gaulin address. The first floor Carpentier family received word their son Lucien was killed there. And *les* Beauregards, once our third-floor neighbors, lost their grandson Richard. His father, Robert, and uncle René were boyhood friends, along with sisters Violette and Rina who both married servicemen. I said Robert *et* Lucien are memorialized on the Vietnam Memorial Monument near the post office and police station in the city. A Wall of Remembrance has been established at Hendricken High School in Warwick, honoring Rhode Islanders who died in that war.

Because the Vietnam War was so unpopular and unheralded, I think fitting here to recall and honor those other city men who also fought and died there: Pfc. Ronald J. Brissette; 2nd Lt. Dennis E. Burke; Cpl. Rene R. Coutu; A1/C Alan D. Curtis; SPfc. Paul L. Durand; Sgt. Robert J. Frisk; Cpl. Craig B. Holt; S. Sgt. Henry R. Lambert; Sp/4 Richard L. Lanctot; Sp/4 Robert W. Lauzon; Cpl. Gerald H. Lavoie; Sp/4 Robert N. Lebrun; S. Sgt. James M. Ray; and Sp/5 Anthony Silba. So even if Roman poet Cicero said, "It is sweet and fitting to die for your country," how tragic for families and community. General MacArthur also spoke about the sublimity of all military deaths: "The soldier who is called upon to offer and give his life for his country is the noblest development of mankind.

But mom received some good news (and always kept the article and photo) about our Lowell cousin, Staff Sgt. Joseph Morvan. Fighting in General Patton's (old Blood and Guts himself with the pearl-handled sidearm!) Army in 1945, he met with an improbable, life-altering experience. Nearing Berchtesgaden (Hitler's summer residence called the Berghof), he found a young woman, Jeannine Serer, cowering in an abandoned schoolhouse cellar. She was a displaced and escaped slave laborer from La Rochelle - "proud city of the waters" - near Cherbourg, a Lowell newspaper article reported. When American armies started shelling and bombing Munich, she fled to near the Fuhrer's lair, thinking it would be safer. But she didn't know the Russians were in hot pursuit and the Germans in retreat.

But Cupid was on her side. Since my cousin, of course, spoke French, there was an immediate attraction between them. She asked to be returned to Munich and eventually her hometown. But *au contraire* (on the contrary), not wishing to leave this hopefully love-of-his-life ("*son amour*," mom said), he with wartime haste successfully professed his affection, put a GI uniform on her, and slipped her into camp. And incredibly she rode and fought in his tank for the last few weeks of the war? Wasn't theirs the amorous truism of Shakespeare's line: "He loved not who loved not at first sight."

The disguise lasted till war's end when he hoped to bring her home on the same ship. But when boarding, the ruse became known with no mention if her cover was blown by a physical or her accent! Disconsolate but hopeful, he sailed home and waited for her to come to Lowell where they were married and raised four children. Their daughter Suzanne, a faculty member at the former Daniel Webster College, Nashua, NH, told me her parents still live in Melbourne, Florida, and touted her mother as a linguist with four languages. The three other Morvan children are Linda, Paul, and Rich who live in our area. I wanted to enlarge on their parents' wartime experiences in his tank, but perhaps because of age or health, they've not responded. An unbelievable story! But in truth, how many women fought in disguise in previous wars? And can you believe one million foreign women married servicemen? How many waiting women at home were left sighing? Commercially, an article revealed other countries, again like German guards, were so crazy about U.S. smokes servicemen sent home $11 million in sales.

Another "high" was Woonsocket's own John Godfrey, a pilot initially with the Royal Canadian Air Force, and later the U.S. Air Corps Fourth Fighter Group. He was credited with 36 enemy aircraft kills, a record at the time. A Villa Novan class president, Class of 1940, I read his obit in 1958 when he died of Lou Gehrig's disease (ALS – amyotrophic lateral sclerosis). I learned he parlayed his wartime exploits into a political career, serving in the state senate in '52, but said no to the GOP's invitation to run for governor. A true native close by the Blackstone River, he turned his attention to manufacturing. How contrary are the pursuits of peace in contrast to the fabrication and use of killing machines! I was also edified at the heroics of Woonsocketer and Navy Ensign Paul Farley who was on the Oklahoma "when a tremendous explosion shook the ship. My first emotion was cold fear." As a pilot he went on to win two Distinguished Flying Crosses and five air medals while flying 600 combat hours in the Pacific. Promoted to the rank of commander of Torpedo Squadron 37, he attacked Japanese bases in the Pacific; met President Harry Truman and retired in 1954. In 2012 he was enshrined in the RI Aviation Hall of Fame. Why is he unknown? Is my research incorrect?

There's a picture in the family album of a tall, single, and handsome lad, recalcitrant forelock, in front of the poolroom across the street from the old Laurier Theater on Cumberland St. in the 1920s with friends. Our future dad! One day in the same doorway, I heard a player uttering a string of profanities. Had he lost a game, his pride? I, of course, had been taught that kind of "dirty talk" was sinful. His face burned into my memory. Well, some time later, I saw his picture in the paper and read the story of his death in Germany. Possessing, like so many others, that sometimes-overwrought Catholic grammar school conscience, I didn't know what to think. It was the one time my never wanting to forget a face (something mom who always described someone's appearance had taught me to do) caused me confusion. Gee! There was that theft of Bob's watch, a sure mortal sin, so mom thought ($20), and now this. Did Moses need to go back to Mt. Sinai for more tablets?

I was also stunned by the story told to mom and me one day about a young wife just streets away. Receiving news of her soldier-husband's death, she raised a fist in anger against God. At first blush, *un sacrilège*. But sympathetic mom understood her great loss, saying poignantly: "*A perdu son gros morceau*," about losing the biggest, most important part of one's life (as I later experienced). The fate of a widow or widower. She understood her anger, her despair, as God did too! She had not forgotten her saintly mom muttered God's name in crushed hope when she threw the 50 cents from her incinerated Cochrane home into the ashes. Did mémére stay "mad" at God? This was the same pious woman in our home who never failed to say her rosary daily, recite her morning and evening prayers, and read spiritual books en masse! A giant of the faith, she may have grumbled at times as we all do, but her center held. And neither would our parents fold despite so many misfortunes: wars, poverty, ill health, joblessness. Sounding like the guy who is wearily pursued in Francis Thompson's poem, "The Hound of Heaven" (a figure of Christ chasing a sinner), she always stayed in the race. For His own inscrutable designs, He was after the Fontaines and wanted them in the crucible of suffering. I recall Rachel laughed, thinking it was a reach for mom to think God had a bull's-eye on their backs: "*Cée comme-ci le bon Dieu nous en voula* (This is how the good Lord resented us)."

As a religious Brother, I later wondered if mom's Christian resignation stemmed from Christ's word that not a single hair or sparrow falls without His Father's permission? When in training, my bald but bewigged novice teacher, *Frère* Théodore, bemusedly related God had allowed all his hair to go at once, not just one strand at a time. What we called in the Order, "a general permission."

Nuns in school and priests in their sermons often dealt with the notion we Catholics call Divine Providence. Or, as St. Paul puts it, that all things happen for the best. A hard thing to understand or accept sometimes, peacetime or wartime! Men and women dying in Flanders Fields all over the world during the war undoubtedly tested the faith of their loved ones at home. A video of the 50th anniversary ceremonies of the Normandy invasion sweeps across the cemetery containing those 10,000 crosses of fallen comrades at Colleville-sur-Mer near Omaha Beach, which we visited.

But I liked someone's retort when challenged by a crestfallen person who, in the face of unspeakable tragedy and crime, cried out, "Where was God?" Simply, he said, "Where was man?" In reading biographies of our Founding Fathers, I was edified by their intrinsic belief in God and His mercy. As columnist Dale O'Leary said in a Journal article: "Our founding fathers believed that religion was the foundation of virtue and that without virtue the republic would perish." We've lamented that in the name of political correctness or the misunderstood concept of separation of church and state, liberal courts and justices are forever trying to tear away the religious fabric and wellspring of our democracy, "the last best hope of mankind." Do they know Jefferson, not a greatly religious man, had no doubt whatsoever about the inalienable rights he wrote about, fearing if the basis of those liberties were removed: "A conviction in the minds of the people that their liberties are the gift of God?" Remembering their travails with England, our Founding Fathers did not want a state-sponsored religion, but not the government abolition of one's private, chosen religion from the daily fabric of their lives. It's the reason why Roger Williams fled from the MA colony.

Sadly, we're no longer "the Christian nation" we once were, like so many European nations. Ultraliberal groups and courts have helped create a neo-pagan culture. If something is doable, they're for it, masking a civil rights aura around it, or falsely citing a Constitutional right, not to mention secular politicians wearing down the opposition by gnawing on the same bone time and again. Like same sex marriage on the docket in RI for a decade or more. About "the right to bear arms," what would the Founding Fathers say about many thousands of people dying of gunshot wounds every year? Hasn't the legacy of our Founding Fathers' "right to bear arms" directly or indirectly resulted in the deaths of countless Americans since the 1770s? It's why I'm anti-gun or for severe gun control because I believe the Founding Fathers overreacted to their wartime travails with the British. To me the culprit is availability. Our culture is saturated with guns, so they're the first resort, not only for adults but also teens in situations of violence. The abundance of guns propels them to settle even little disagreements with them. Sadly, convicted teens lose their liberty for life for one stupid act. At one time young and older people simply duked it out. But I said I'm against life sentences without parole for teens. Justice should be tempered by mercy. I read it's very expensive to keep a prisoner till death. The Constitution can be changed. President Wilson said it and it has been, but the National Rifle Association is a stumbling block convinced "the right to bear arms" was given to Moses by God on Mt. Sinai like an 11th Commandment. Too many

Americans are killed by guns every year as it is now a daily occurrence. For ten years I predicted to my son Jim a mass shooting like the one in Newtown, CT that would finally trigger a serious revamping of our loose gun-buying policies, gun size, kinds of ammo, and lack of background checks for purchases at gun shows. But alas, it didn't happen. Europeans can't believe how many guns we have and how easily available they are here. Additionally, homicides by guns occur 20 times more often here than in other wealthy nations; gun suicides 20,000 out of 30,000; and two out of five robberies. Should we Northeasterners gloat our crime rate is "only" 16.2 percent compared with 44.3 in the South; 22.9 in the West; and 19.5 in the Midwest? Sadly, because of America's liberal mindset, we look for solutions to problems only after the barn door has been left open; like millions of guns in circulation, making control almost impossible.

One time *Soeur Sainte* Émilie told us God seemed to let you know why this or that tragedy occurred. When 12, I read in the *Boston Daily Record* the devastating Coconut Grove fire in Boston, Nov. 28, 1942, killing 498 people, including cowboy favorite, Buck Jones. Boston College, later one of my Alma Maters, was to celebrate an unbeaten football season there that very night. But that afternoon a decidedly underdog Holy Cross team annihilated them. The crestfallen Eagles cancelled a planned nightclub frolic, averting possible tragedy for some or all 52 players. The hand of Divine Providence in the football loss? When some drew that conclusion, it made an impression on me, thinking what she said. Blocked exits, overcrowding, and flammable decor all helped spawn the tragedy. (We don't learn from history, as we experienced again with the Station nightclub fire in 2003 in RI.)

In our school, we prayed in class for the defeat of the enemy and the return of our soldiers. In church, young and old thronged to special liturgies and prayed the rosary. Politicians, military leaders, and soldiers shared our common faith and hope for God's blessing. As Omar N. Bradley cites in his biography *A Soldier's Story*, the Nazis had us on the ropes initially, so all our prayers helped.

His later troubles with Truman notwithstanding, I like what someone said of MacArthur: "He was as good as a man can be without virtue; as wise as a man could be without modesty." Third-best student ever, he went through West Point with very few demerits and only bested by General Robert E. Lee, the epitome of Southern manhood, and another forgotten cadet. But shockingly, he did use gas on those WWI vets who marched on Washington for benefits! At Lee's former home in Arlington Cemetery, I saw the chair he sat in all night, finally foregoing the leadership of Union forces from Lincoln, to not fight against his own Virginia countrymen. If he had led the Union, strategists think the Civil War would've ended two years sooner. His only possible fault as a general was his reliance on officers to handle the details. Was he oblivious "the devil is in the details?" Lee became an educator after the war, and his name was later affixed to the college he led - Washington and Lee, Lexington, VA.

Gettysburg - "the high tide of the Confederacy" - and the victory at The Little Round Top redounds a lot to the brilliant leadership of Bowdoin College professor and future Maine governor, Joshua Lawrence Chamberlain, who, without ammunition, led a winning charge down that hill. Victory for the South at Gettysburg meant the probable fall of Baltimore and Washington D.C. and would have likely resulted in a divided country. It's fortunate for the North that Chamberlain took a secretive Bowdoin academic leave of absence, "supposedly" for studies abroad. He mastered battle manuals in just a few days. A gentleman, Grant gave him the responsibility of treating the beaten rebels with the utmost respect at Appomattox.

Some humor: When at Spring Hill College in Mobile Alabama with my religious group, cousin Frank had a funny story about Lee. A Southern police officer tried to dissuade a would-be suicide on a bridge, telling him about his country, wife, children, friends. Nothing worked. Finally, the officer said, "Think of Robert E. Lee." When the depressed man said he didn't know any Lee, the "Johnny Reb" officer said, "Jump, you damn Yankee."

If old enough, people today who lament the decline of formal religion and church attendance tell you how wars and other global tragedies (all "foxholes" of a sort) bring back a sense of reverence and church attendance very quickly. By Francophone standards my family wasn't more religious than others. But in the evening, we prayed the rosary on our knees around the family table for Bob and cousins. American boys learn very quickly not to be emotional or devotional in public, and I felt bashful when we first did it. I sat on those wooden, much-mended table chairs a thousand times, but I had never prayed with my hands and beads on the seat. The beads made the same razzing noise like on church pews. Thinking of one more way of helping Bob return safely was mom's idea, like an edict from the Vatican: "*On va dire le chapla* (le *chapelet*) pour *Robert* (We are going to say the rosary for Bob)." She left no stone unturned to bring him back "*en vie et en santé* (alive and healthy)," telling God He only had two choices. Can God say no to a woman with beads in her hands?

O those fireside mothers! Are they the ones God finally hears to avoid wars or restore peace? In history, didn't they once carry their men on their backs out of town to avoid conflict? Or threaten to banish them from the marriage bed if they made war instead of peace? Also, not unfittingly I hope, I compare's mom's persistence to Christ's story about the sleeping shopkeeper who, to get rid of a late customer, finally got up to wait on him despite "the ungodly hour." Fancifully, did God say to Himself, "I'm giving her this one; she won't give me any rest?" I've always been fond of Christ's promise that anything we ask the Father in His name, He will grant. Incredible promise. I can't think of anything more hopeful. The anchor in my own medical setback, along with St. Theresa of the Child Jesus whose relic was put on my neck, the one given to the Nasonville parish by my Order after theirs was stolen. I told the story to pastor Father Gerard Caron, now at St. John's in Slatersville. He noticed I was losing my hair. Does he know the first Mass ever said in the U.S. was by a Father Caron, a Franciscan, as was once the pastor?

Tennyson has a line about more things on earth being wrought by prayer than this world dreams of. Yes, who knows that she, who supported Bob emotionally with so many letters, didn't also save him with one of those after-dinner prayers. Did she remind God that no matter what He had thrown at the Fontaines, they were resigned and never, never lost the faith? Did she tell Him He owed her one, her oldest son? Did He bring her to America penniless and homeless to sacrifice her son, like Abraham was asked by God until He realized his great faith? She had Bob girded in His armor. She gave him life; she made sure he came back from the war with it, to give life, as he did, with his wife Millie (Savoie) to their four children, Janine, R. Kenneth, Bruce, and Anne-Marie, sparing her the grief of those gold star mothers, as He did for *mémère's* two sons in WWI.

A teacher said we'll be amazed what is revealed on that final day: prayers answered, deathbed repentances known only to Him, as mom said reading the life of the *Curé d'Ars* (Priest of Ars - St. John Vianney). One day time will be no more, and the Last Judgment, painted so majestically in Nincheri's magnum opus in St. Ann's dome, will appear on the world's stage, fresco-fresh live as he laid it down in the 1940s. Will God give credit to all the Michelangelos who throughout history gave the world a magnificent preview of what will be the greatest scene of all times? Only eternity will remain after that where, as it is written, ten thousand years will seem like a day, and a day like ten thousand, so perfect our happiness, with our transformed bodies and the sight of God. More Humor: A first grader was told that in Heaven we'd marvel at God's infinite beauty, majesty, and power. But that didn't seem like fun to him. At home he whined to his mom, "Do we have to go there?"

For people considered generally peaceful and home loving, French Canadians, including namesakes of the Fontaines and Telliers, have cropped up in my war readings. In the fratricidal war between the states, three of them served of local vintage. They are Siméon Fontaine *et* Robert *et* Peter *dit* LaFontaine, but mom never spoke about that war, the time of her parents' birth. But Frenchmen and French Canadians are writ large in the discovery, exploration, and conquests of North America. So, it's not surprising Albert Aubin in *The French in Rhode Island* says French explorers mapped or colonized 31 percent of the present United States and most of Canada. And so, I suspect most French-Canadian researchers will find genealogical kin or namesakes almost everywhere as explorers, soldiers, colonizers. I don't know which word in French translates best our word "wanderlust," but our forebears had it. So many place names in America are of French origin. As an avid Lewis and Clark reader of the exploration of the Louisiana Purchase, I'm proud several Canadian-Frenchmen were indispensable to the Corps of Discovery: Toussaint Charboneau (wife Sacagawea and son Jean Baptiste), Pierre Cruzatte, George Drouillard, *et* François Labiche. and others mentioned elsewhere. One wit even placed Francos in the Garden of Eden: Adam "*Terre-rien*" (Therrien: Lackland in English) *et* Eve "*Coté*" (from Adam's side), a felicitous reference to their creation.

Catholics are also mindful that their forbears (the French) brought the faith during their stay in Newport in the Revolutionary War. From that time on, bigotry or opposition to our faith and its practice relaxed there and other places. Initially, the Anglos who had come to RI to escape religious intolerance had not always extended that choice to Catholics and others, including Roger Williams. In fact, the notion "of a state religion," if you will, had a lot to do with colonial fixation on it. The Puritans still wanted some vestiges of the state-based religions of England. But Canadian Francos didn't come here for religious freedom, but more in fear of losing it, so priests and compatriots in Québec cautioned them. That tragedy for some came later when they lost their ethnic churches and the safeguarding bastions of church, school, rectory, and convent. One wrote they had received Catholicism too easily, almost by osmosis. In announcing 2013 a year of faith, Pope Benedict admitted people still have faith, but not so much in their church, as people once did. But without that support or membership, faith waters down and beliefs becomes a mishmash of what the prevailing culture says or does. The church of Christ, says Küng, is or should be all of creation and humanity worshipping as an entity. *Ut Unum Sunt* (they're like one). The very meaning of "Catholic" is "universal." I like to think, not only in doctrine, but in worldwide worship.

St. Ann's Church was at times the scene of military funerals, with or without the corpus of the fallen hero. As a kid I thought all fallen soldiers were returned home for burial. But later I learned that at a family's request - like *les* Lapierres *et les* Vincents for their respective sons - burial was in the land they fought to liberate. From our seat in school across the street during the war, we heard the church bells lolling their deep, mournful sounds in the morning. I related if you craned your neck from the second-floor window row, you saw people gathering below for a military funeral service on Gaulin.

One day when our nun caught a few of us looking, she very wisely turned it to a teaching moment. Perhaps a few years before, a fallen soldier being buried this day had sat in our very seat. The point was not maudlin. The thought of life as a fleeting, transitory state was a very popular Medieval Catholic thought.

In fact, the afterlife was one of the earliest truths in our small *Baltimore Catechism*. Of the three so-called most crucial questions in a person's life: Who is God? How do I serve Him? Why did He create me? the latter was definitely the most accented. As heard in the Order, a medieval (not "middle evil," as a kid wrote) monk, Thomas à Kempis, wrote *The Imitation of Christ*, which promoted the afterlife as the "only" purpose of our creation. In the 1960s, however, a more "Life is worth living" credo began to coexist, if you will, with Pope John XXIII's *Aggiornamento*, Church Renewal or Opening up the Windows. It stressed building up the so-called Earthly Kingdom, instead of just putting up resignedly with the "bad" one as it is.

Again, in the Order, a wizened old monk in a mixture of *patois* and French admitted life was rough, but with good portions or parts: "*La vie est rough, mais ya des bons petits bouts* (boo) (Life is rough but there are good little parts/bits)." Not only Christianity, but also some of the greatest cultures and civilizations the world has known have been anchored in the belief of a deity or deities and life after death. It was the wellspring of French-Canadian life. Recall St. Paul said if Christ hadn't risen, we wouldn't either and our faith was vain. It's the joy of Easter, however obscured today by the growing secularization of nearly all our holy days.

It may be the rose-colored failing of hindsight, but the Black Market and other home front mayhem notwithstanding, the criminality, material indulgence, and moral vacuum experienced by the nation, especially during the Vietnam War, was not as prevalent during WWII. Of course, the latter was a totally popular war, morally defensible, and officially declared and supported. At the time, Roosevelt's words, now on his monument, seemed achievable: "More than an end to war, we want an end to the beginnings of all wars." But Christ said we'll have wars till the end of time.

Again, like Moses whose forces kept on winning when he prayed, we never doubted we'd win if we were good. But the war seemed endless at times, as if that's how life was always going to be, like a visible reminder of the never-ending struggles between good and evil, like in the Middle East now. But with hope springing eternal, as poet Alexander Pope wrote, we never lost sight of the uplifting tune of the wartime song, "There'll be peace over the white cliffs of Dover, just you wait and see." But would our own shores, stalked by those U-boats, be invaded? Would we kids, not even teens when it started, eventually march off to war as our older brothers had? And again, paraphrasing poet John Donne's famous line, would those church bells toll for us one day, with baby-faced school kids craning for a look at the gathering mourners?

Woonsocket as a Homefront in the War

WHEN I TALKED with former teacher and Nazi POW Brother Lavallée, SC, and read about his Stalag IX internment, I sensed a begrudging respect for the Germany and her soldiers he was forced to know as a captive. Their leaders, mechanized war machine, and military were a fist of steel and a will of iron to conquer the world and establish the Third Reich of a thousand years. But we in America were all *Unum* (all One) There was no question this was a war to preserve Roosevelt's Four Freedoms: "the freedom of speech, the freedom of worship, the freedom from want, and the freedom from fear!" Even if for us the war was fought across the seas, it was a titanic struggle to remain "the best last hope of mankind."

In an industrial mill city like Woonsocket, people worked feverishly on the cotton and wool military materiel needed by our fighting men and women. But aged 45 in 1941, dad said he was too old to be drafted (patriotically unmindful of his frail lungs and rejection in World War I) and his war bit was mule spinning. Even though the money was the best ever, he was not a physical specimen and wanted to work only 40 hours a week. Walking 8-9 miles or more a day at the mules in the mill did that to you! Perhaps too, he had started to feel the incipient effects of the dreaded, breath-sapping bronchiectasis disease, his family's Achilles' heel? He never told us. Recall mom once told me what his hacking cough meant when he retired. Also, consider there wasn't that feverish workaholic drive for the male breadwinner to define his role, consciously or not, as a provider not only of necessities, but also of wished-for comforts and luxuries. It's why Europeans think we're the most workaholic people! But today it isn't just for luxuries, but the steep price of everyday necessities.

In 2013, economists said America is creating a dangerous divide between the haves and the have-nots, which we repeat often. No angry marches yet, but as we try to scale back our $19 trillion debt with cutbacks like Sequester, SNAP (nutrition for the poor), Medicaid, SS Disability, will handout receivers get into a foul mood? The income of the middle class and the poor in terms of buying power has been decreasing, unlike for the rich. As good as capitalism is, isn't it inevitable? In other countries with other kinds of "isms," isn't the divide the same? But, again, it's crueler now because of the high cost of modern living.

Dad never worked towards a home, car, or family vacations; however laudable those are. The sly comment made recently that Americans don't take time to smell the flowers, but only buy them, could not have been made of most workers then. Of course, before the war, often there wasn't even one job, never mind overtime. What would his commentary be now that 15 million Americans work two jobs (if not victims of the recession), some out of necessity, yes, but how many just for luxuries? Yet, as recently reported and as I also comment elsewhere, many Americans save nothing, spending, one said, one percent more than what they make. Would-be retirees are now forced to work longer or come out of retirement because of living longer. Their retirement is vastly underfunded for 46 percent, said a 2015 study. Are we all victims of "you 'auto-buy now'?" Dad laughed at the idea of saving by buying. We said Americans had a credit bill near $8,000 when the recession hit in 2007-8. Now it's $14,000, but does that include all debts? So, for the war effort, dad and others worked another six hours (6 to noon) on Saturdays, like in his early mill career. But that left them only Saturday afternoon and Sunday to escape the burden of their physically draining jobs, especially as they got older. Is that why the Sunday afternoon nap was once almost *de rigueur* (strictly) for men?

In a special I saw about another hardworking immigrant Catholic group of men; it attributed their absence at Mass on Sunday to a desire to get the rest their long workweek denied them. I'm edified this was not the case, at least at St. Ann. Even if they looked out of character in their Sunday suit and indulged in "the three-point landing" in the pews, they were always there with their wives, *leur bonnes* (their good), a tender expression. Hey, if at one time the paterfamilias cast out an adolescent child for missing Mass, theirs wasn't "Do as I say, but not as I do."

Veritably Sunday Mass was Family Day, again as depicted in that backwall painting at the city's Kay's Restaurant, where a family is shown going to church. Were truer words ever spoken by "Rosary Priest" Father Patrick Payton?: "A family that prays together, stays together." Saw him in Mobile. Because of his boyish, active nature, his schoolteacher predicted he was the only boy in class who wouldn't be a priest or teaching brother. "Gotcha!" I suspect she never became her Order's Vocation Director! Boston College professor Cottle told us many high school boys seem so unpromising initially yet turn out exceptionally well. Many times, their missteps were simply a desire to know, to experiment, to do like others. Scary, we said, but the overall influence on a child's moral development is now from outside the home! He didn't comment on the girls, whose crime rate is now surging faster than the boys. Unisex!

I learned "mule" in mule spinning didn't mean the guys at the mill worked like that beast of burden. The textile industry borrowed it because making yarn combined two spinning techniques. The so-called warp and woof (or weft) of the trade where a lengthwise yarn is traversed sideways by a filling thread. Since a mule is the hybrid of a donkey and a horse, they borrowed the term. So workers everywhere strove mightily to win Efficiency honors and fly banners announcing their huge productivity during the war. In contrast, German slave laborers (foolishly underfed and overworked, a historian wrote) couldn't compete with our "Arsenal-for-Democracy" workers, especially since Hitler wanted frau women to stay at home and make babies. Many slave laborers, like the French girl from La Rochelle, Jeannine Serer, whom our cousin married, often sabotaged weapons they made.

In college, I chuckled at both Napoleon's and Russia's Frederick the Great's tongue-in-cheek observation that God is usually on the side of the heaviest (that is, best equipped or well-armed) battalions! Whether they knew or not about that snide observation, local workers were convinced their output and quality had to be the best for our soldiers. Woonsocket workers instinctively knew the importance of rapid response and readiness, as they joined Roosevelt's call to arm and clothe our soldiers in unequalled time. Like Wilson wanted when he declared war on Germany in 1917. In the Civil War, the Union overcame the Confederacy with more armament, food, and equipment. But also, with more men. The agrarian South had only one armament factory (Richmond) and little rolling stock. And immigration was mostly in the North, like the Irish.

This increased wartime national productivity in the 1940s remains an almost unparalleled miracle, says T.H. Watkins in *The Great Depression*. Historian John Geegan agreed. It reminded me of dad's economic belief that nothing turns around a nation's working fortune like war. That's why he knew Hitler would. As Speer, Hitler's architect, quotes him in *Interrogations: The Nazi Elite in Allied Hands*, 1945, by Richard Overy.

But despite our massive bombing, Armament Chief Speer is given credit for keeping the materiel-making efforts of Germany at a very high level till their surrender. There were unseen factories in caves. But their unsolvable problem was lack of fuel like in the Battle of the Bulge. He was nearly absolved at the Nuremberg Trials, but the Russians insisted on a sentence because he helped destroy most of their country. But after initially losing several million men, I was shocked to read the Soviets in 1943 thought of approaching the Nazis for peace. Churchill nearly had a heart attack. Were they giving up on "General Winter" winning the war? As they did in early 1945 and before that, some German officials also sent out feelers to us about keeping the Russians out of Europe. As Churchill thought, did our leaders suspect they would become a bigger problem than the Nazis after the war, a problem that lasted over 50 years, now seemingly rearing its head with scheming, duplicitous Putin? He hates our global influence. But a 2013 editorial said Russia has a lot of problems: corruption, smoking, drinking, and unequal incomes much greater than ours. And in 2014 declining oil prices, their chief export, along with gas, and our sanctions for seizing the Chechnya and Crimea.

Overnight it seems, the problem was finding workers, not jobs. But what irony! Now dad finally had a steady job and the family had more than survival money and more purchasing power. But food and amenities were scarce. And of course, Bob's welfare. Because of those German U-boats spotted off the coasts of RI and MA, after some reluctance the whole Eastern seaboard observed the rules of wartime curfew. One, we said, was sunk in RI waters, south of Point Judith. Now the submarine U-853, nicknamed *der Seiltänzer* (The Tightrope Walker), because of its numerous escapes until May 5, 1945, remains, at Germany's request, the undisturbed grave of 55 submariners. Yes, our fears weren't groundless, when we learned in 1942 the FBI captured eight Nazi saboteurs on Long Island. Two divers lost their lives exploring the sub.

For fear of coastal sightings, motorists dimmed the top of their headlights at night. One day, the gang was amazed to learn a lighted cigarette could be seen thousands of feet in the air! Why warn us? Had anyone seen us smoking when we should've been studying our catechism at dusk? Or was it just another trick to have us give up our smokes for fear of stunting our growth, a fear then. At the time, there was no known causality between smoking and cancer.

No less patriotic than others, we never smoked our forbidden cigarettes at sundown. In my youthful naivete, if bombed I couldn't imagine telling mom the Luftwaffe found Woonsocket because of the fiery tips of our cigarettes! If dad was on the afternoon shift, menacingly would she have said, "*Attend qu'ton père arrive d'la factorie* (Wait for your father to arrive from the factory)" about hell and damnation at 10 p.m., when we were asleep. Just as he begged relief from her moneyed kings and queens, recall our bone-weary provider back from the mill, and wanting sedentary relief, told her to let him be with some Archie Bunker annoyance: "*Lâche-mwé avec ça.* (Let that go)" He dealt with recalcitrant threads all day; he didn't want more errant skeins from us boys, domestic mules!

But not knowing about the uses of propaganda before dad told me about those sanitized war news, I thought those threats were real cloak-and-dagger stuff. Were eavesdroppers in those two saloons where I delivered papers with their atmosphere so smoky and conspiratorial like the café in

"*Casablanca*?" But wasn't our patois, like the Navaho language, understood only by us "French-Canadian codebreakers?"

Books like *The Red Badge of Courage* and others have been written about the fears of combatants before and during the battle. What about the gnawing fear we touched upon that gripped parents' hearts and minds in WWII, as it has since humanity turned to aggression to settle differences? My parents hid it well, but what tremors did every letter or knock on the door stir in them, like once for mom in her last years at hospice with her dementia?

In case the city was blitzed like London, Scoutmaster Jannell had us participate in a First Aid readiness program in front of Woonsocket Hospital, captured in one of the album photos. Besides those submarines, recall Hitler was working on a transatlantic bomber and rockets towards the end of the war. But not so much on the atom bomb, as Einstein thought. Christopher Chant in *Warfare and the Third Reich* wrote, "Hitler envisaged a second phase of expansion when a German dominated continent would wrestle with America (after Britain) for western world mastery." Frightening! Hitler looked too far ahead!

At war's end, we, like the Russians, were so enamored by Nazi scientific ingenuity we created the disputed Odessa File "to clean up" the dossier of many German scientists and engineers. Some of the best were brought here to show us their advanced research in weaponry, jet propulsion, and rockets. It's ironic they helped us defeat the Japanese, part of the Axis Pact. War makes strange bedfellows! Humorists were quick to see comedic material in this "marriage of opportunity" between Germany and us after the war (absolution for contribution). But when the Russians first beat us in the space race with Sputnik, comically Bob Hope wondered if their German scientists were better than ours.

Catholic school children all over the country sold over $1 million in war bonds and stamps. My own *Call* carrier profits nearly all went to buy bonds. But war or no war, mom, twice penniless in her life (Canada and the Depression), said, "*Il faut toujours en garder pour le fi(u)ture*," that is, save for a rainy day. Too many of those!

A classroom teacher before my counseling career, I was amused by a "wartime school story" still going around. When a student was asked to give an example of a collective noun like army, navy, squad he said paper, bottles, clothing, and stuff. When told they weren't collective nouns, he replied, "My parents said they got collected every week at my house during the war." Our state still has one of the best recycling records in the nation. Since generally we've never been a great moneyed polity, conservation is genetic in the Ocean State psyche. Mom repeated, "What we didn't have, we weren't going to get." No wonder we never asked the folks for money.

I read that Ted Williams used to slip 100-dollar bills into his children's pockets. Extremely gross and discourteous at times, he was nevertheless a great, secret supporter of poor and sickly children, like for The Jimmy Fund. I didn't know he and his brother practically raised themselves since their father ran off and their mother was out all day collecting for a benevolent association. As a tyke he became fascinated with hitting and brought his bat to school which he put under his desk. How you get to bat over 400? He respected Catholicism.

Our priests held services where flags were blessed and displayed, and they read or posted the names of parishioners serving in the military. Franco-American fraternal and charitable societies in New England also headed bond drives to build several Liberty ships, some, we said, at the Rheem Shipyard at Field's Point in Providence. Some 29 diocesan or religious priests also served as war chaplains and several were decorated for valor. One of two priests killed in the war was French-Canadian, *Père* Valmore Savignac. But no less heroic was Father Anthony Czubak, killed in the Battle of the Bulge. Their names are on the wall of the Veterans' Memorial Oratory in Providence. Chaplains, rabbis, and ministers served side by side. In faculty meetings at the Academy during the critical 1970s when we met often to save the Academy during that challenging time, I suggested their famous line: "We agree to disagree agreeably."

But by far, I said the closest impact of the war on those on the home front was rationing. Since the city was not overly motorized, especially in our 'hood where only a couple of families owned a car, the rationing of food, not the lack of gas and tires, hurt most. Joe Ferreira, a former garage owner, once told me you could only get four gallons at one time, with police conducting spot checks. But some had a second tank which didn't register when filled. A toy, lawn windmill, and miniature railroad car builder, Joe had the most meticulous mind and total recall I've ever encountered. I enjoyed his story of running the switchboard at the Wallum Lake Sanitarium after his recovery from TB. He was told to inform a wife her husband died one night. The following morning staffers realized with two patients having the same name, the wrong wife had been notified.

Since food stamps or coupons were allotted to families according to size, ours had about the same as before the war. But dad knew the plight of childless families, like *mon* uncle Ernest *et tante* Marie-Rose Villeneuve, his sister. No matter if their childless family (rare in those days) bespoke greater means, if they played it straight, stamps only got them bare necessities. Stamps were worth their weight in gold and coveted by hook or by crook.

One wonders how gigantic the problem would be today if rationing ever came around again. We're so numerous and more morally challenged now. Again, providing mom with needling fodder, once she chided dad for wanting to give away "our surplus." Of course, with canning and volume purchasing, he practically ran his own store! He who didn't want any government assistance when he became disabled until he spent the $300 in the bank after nearly 40 years in the mills! And one who, in a futuristic concept that is gaining some believers today, thought generous COLAs (cost-of-living increases) to his annual Social Security check hurt the young, struggling workers with family who at the federal level now support longer-living retirees. He saw the ratio of workers to retirees getting lower each year, from 5 to 1 on down.

Dad lived to see raises sometimes adjusted to the inflation rate, but can you imagine anyone now uncomfortable with a raise? Self-effacing, the other guy always came first. Did we appreciate enough his great soul as we did his great mind? Someone did ask me, "Did God break the mold after He made him?" But I think his kind was legion in those immigrant times, as of course now too, if not so evident. But haven't we learned now how in both city and state, unrealistic COLAS and pensions for retirees from public service have caused severe indebtedness? Dad right again. But since people quickly learn to live at the level of their resources, how painful to financially strapped Central Falls, Providence, Woonsocket, Pawtucket, West Warwick et al. Court battles ensued. As I quoted a hillbilly who said to a collector, "You ain't takin' nuttin' of 'en' this prop'ty." Americans are only used to accretion, no reduction.

About conservatism, at one time a kind of pilgrim or pioneer spirit still prevailed, like old Yankee Ralph Waldo Emerson's famous creed of Self-Reliance: "Trust thyself; every heart beats to that iron string," which in literature and movies we identified with those firsters and Westerners. The quasi-Socialist State, for which rightfully or wrongly dad-blamed Roosevelt, had not yet fully arrived before the Depression. Dad didn't want "redistributed money" from the government. He just wanted a job to earn his own. I say elsewhere he voted for Wilkie with his 1940 campaign message: "I say that we must substitute for the philosophy of distributed scarcity, the philosophy of unlimited productivity." So quotes Robert McElvane in *The Great Depression - America 1929-41*. But dad's life and Christian altruism are proof he wasn't without Roosevelt's compassion for the really deserving poor, but he always feared losing the earmarks of his character: self-control and self-sufficiency. He too benefited from Relief during the Depression, and later he and mom lived on their Social Security pensions which were never meant to be a sole retirement, but many had no other. They couldn't save what they never had. FDR himself said people hated being on the dole with their hand out and just receiving, which sapped their pride. That's why some of his programs, like the CCC (Civilian Conservation Corps: 3 million young men; $30 a month of which $25 sent home) and WPA (Works Progress Administration) involved pride-building work for wages. But mom said the word for those who abused something good, like government largess, was *ambitioner sur le pain bénit,* with its religious overtone of wasting or abusing a good thing, like blessed bread. A hard call, but some say extending unemployment today saps in some the will to find work. Lower paying jobs, like in fast foods, provide less than government assistance.

    Unfortunately, isn't it necessary for the government to respond to tragedy in our country or elsewhere? – Hurricane Katrina, for example, over 80 percent of repairers were scammers. Disasters are usually a chronic setting for waste, inefficiency, and downright thievery by those involved in rebuilding and incompetent bureaucrats(?) With several philanthropists recently pledging fortunes to help the needy, I've seen articles about how hard it is to give away money. No wonder Christ said we'll have the poor with us until the end of time. Yet we mustn't be "weary of well-doing," the Bible says. Dad, near poor himself, urged caution about taking it from the rich to give it to the poor rather than having them earn it if they could. Like Lincoln, he thought investments from those with capital created industries and jobs, his wish. An article said the wealthy pay 40 percent of all taxes, but another said that's inaccurate because of our system's many loopholes that allow them to avoid taxes on much of their wealth increase every year. So at election time politicos foment class warfare by blaming them for not doing enough. Who's right? FDR's philosophy of redistribution naturally attracts immigrants, the poor, the have-nots (But in one recent instance, more Mexicans are leaving us than coming.) Is the big problem in life not so much doing good, but what is the good? Is there any doubt we've lapsed into a handout mentality, necessary for some, but abused by others? But history records the lot of the poor was once inhuman. About "gaming the system," I heard a collegian about the merit system at his college: the teachers soon have the merit, but students quickly the system!

    Dad chafed his mill owners only gave him a $10 bonus during his 39 years there. And recall his story about some co-workers eating nothing but bread and water at the mill so their families could eat. He tried to achieve a political balance between the need for public assistance and self-initiative. All of the above shows dad was a fascinating political creature, a man who knew the times and economy he lived in, and wrestled with the thorny issues of the day. He never just went along, unthinking, unconcerned, uninvolved. He was never a one-lever, one-ticket man in the voting booth, unlike some who always voted the same way, their decision based on one little kernel of political wisdom, if any ("color of hair" said one voter).

Not a professional political strategist, he nevertheless knew the danger of single-party government, which, yes, largely afflicts our state and invites corruption. (The "I know-a-guy state.) As a wit said, Jesus Christ himself could run on the minority party ticket in Rhody and not get in. On the national scene, FDR's re-electability, as people in the 'hood said it, was "*ce qui'il fa pour les pauvres*": what he was doing for the poor. Putting his hand out may have dented dad's pride a bit, but I remember dad laughed when we walked back home from the Relief center. Did he see the humor and disconnect of getting something from Roosevelt, whom he was never to vote for? But Pope Leo XIII in his encyclical *Rerum Novarum* (About New Things) sounded a note Roosevelt would have liked: "When there is question of defending the rights of individuals, the poor and badly off have a claim to special consideration. The richer classes have many ways of shielding themselves and stand less in need of help from the State; whereas the mass of the poor have no resources of their own to fall back upon." All the above reveals how difficult the problem is. How much help to accept without compromising honesty and self-sufficiency, especially in a Have and Have-Not nation!

About rationing, because a lot of people didn't want to play the game straight, there arose a vast underground Black Market: "*Le Marché Noire*," she said. Whenever you heard men speaking about the war, soon it was about the shortage of food and supplies. Like people adrift on a raft or dying of thirst in the desert, it's as if people could think of nothing else. Inevitably, someone mentioned how a neighbor, acquaintance, relative, or co-worker had a food source or was raising, say, chickens or livestock somewhere. Or had a deal for something not in stores.

It replaced the usual exchanges about work and health, those two eternal verities of every *tête-à-tête* (face to face). Did they speak low because they thought no matter how small the transgression, offenders could be punished for an illegality? I became privy to one such conversation one day when an adult told dad and me, he and a friend were about to slaughter an "incognito" cow. The guy's eyes lit up with gustatory anticipation. If above board, why was he being so secretive? Maybe like the inventor of a better mousetrap, he didn't want a stampede to his door from the rationing board!

Bob told me *oncle* Napoléon on his farm on Pound Road in Cumberland did some bovine slaughtering to shore up his and our sometimes-meatless fare. He was grateful to dad for his farm. So this was on top of those five free quarts of milk every other day. A form of bartering obvious in dire economic times when money or goods are rare.

Nothing in all of Woonsocket dramatized more the shortage of everyday staples than long lines at the Kennedy Butter Store on Main Street. On a Saturday morning especially, the line extended from near the end of Main Street up to the Court Street Bridge next to McCarthy's Department Store. I remembered that when it later moved to Walnut Hill Plaza and eventually closing its doors in 1989, its 100th year. Saturday at breakfast we decided whose turn it was to do picket duty, excepting mom, Ben, and Rachel with "a youth exemption." Most moved stoically with the line, chatting with fellow standees, but some read or sat hunched on a stool, almost like Rodin's "Thinker," cursing the war.

Feigning conversation with those online, some tried to slip into the march as it moved. I found it hard to tell an adult who did that to me. An old lady fainted one day. In her bag, they found several cuts of butter. Obviously, she had returned to the end of the line once or twice, giving "the full measure of devotion" for her family. Or she wanted to make a killing by scalping the buttery gold! Mom saw the humor in it, capping it with that abuse of "blessed bread" judgment: (*ambitioner sur le pain bénit*), about being greedy.

When once I compared notes with dad about the Kennedy butter rush, he asked, "Did I notice how deadpan the salesgirls were?" No. He reasoned that with such a crush of humanity for so many hours (like the registry nowadays?), no *commis* (clerk) could stand it, if she moved at the same feverish pace or surge of the thundering herd. A self-made efficiency expert, dad despised wasted effort, telling you how to do a thing better if he saw something wasteful in your *modus operandi*. Bob picked it up from him. One day when dad saw Sue go from her bedroom to the living room mirror six or seven times for a date, he suggested how to economize her steps by thinking ahead. His millwork shaped him. He never pretended to any overt leadership quality, but the owners missed a damn good *soupeur*: boss man. Like any good theologian or scientist, he believed order was the first law of the universe, but he was not a meddler in people's affairs, unless asked. If he was out of the loop about a situation, he said, "*J'm'en fou baim*," like Clark Cable's line in the *Gone with the Wind* epic: "I don't give a damn." Or today's "No skin off my nose" or "I could care less" (not grammatical; should be "I couldn't"). About pet expressions, Pat liked what teacher-friend Mrs. Lanoie, at the Grove Street school told her hyperkinetic kids if too pushy: "Cool your jets."

But standing in line at Kennedy's wasn't a do-or-die situation for us "privileged Telliers." We had our own butter connection during the conflict. No, it wasn't Black Market! Faithful customers of Belhumeur's Market on Cumberland, we received a pound a week on Thursdays. Margarine wasn't allowed in the house. Dad praised him for his generosity to the very poor. He or sons secretly put the "gold bar" in our shopping bag. Recall you read your shopping one item at a time, and the clerk went and got it, using a grabbing mechanism for the top shelf. What a conspiratorial feeling of privilege when dad nodded his head or blinked an eye (this item not read) and an odd-shaped package was quietly put into our bag. But not like crestfallen Pharaoh's wife, trying "to bag" an unsuspecting Moses with royal gold in his basket for spurning her advances. I put on that "I'm-with-him look," my lips pursing tighter than Stone Philips' on "Dateline," as I saw later.

Other favored customers may have played out that little scenario too, but we were concerned only with our business, don't talk about it: "*avec notre affaire"; parles-en pas*," said mom. Our "minivan" was a wooden wagon a neighbor made when we lived on Mailloux. Recall a weekly marketing bill for our family of seven was around $8! But "*Le coup d' la vie est monté* (the cost of life is mounting/climbing)" he later moaned about *l'inflation* (inflation)" when prices rose during and after the war. It's a word he used several times a day, because I suspect it was his biggest hurdle in keeping us afloat on his meager salary before the war. Has any worker (the immigrant jobber of yesteryear!) ever had so many kids and threadbare ("mill speak") paycheck? Luckily, money was worth more than twice what is today. A family's two salaries today doesn't buy what one salary did fifty years ago.

Before the war, what a delight to have butter cut from one of the half-tubs behind the counter in a cooler. Called *beurre en tinette* (butter in a barrel) in French. To me, the smell of freshly cut butter and the savory aroma of freshly-ground coffee made going to the market - *aller au marché* - tolerable. *Le jeudi* (Thursday) marketing day. I don't know if it was payday, because only a few times did I ever see his little pay envelope. Finances were a carefully guarded secret, even if little to hide. If there was more one week ("*un peu plus*," she gushed), families didn't attract attention or stir up any jealous feelings in neighbors. Besides, it would have been demeaning, and I never saw my parents purposefully harm others. Especially dad who was so extraordinary.

As only a man fascinated with numbers knew, he enlightened me one day when he threw some of our "daily bread" out of our third story backyard window: "Don't forget the birds, they eat two or three times their weight in one day." As said, befitting our "low rent district," I never saw any other species but English sparrows. My parents called them "*mwénaux*," patois for *moineaux*. Robins, hummingbirds, cardinals, chickadees, goldfinches, and Baltimore orioles, all with an attractive plumage didn't come into our drab, colorless yard. So, ours was not poet Chaucer's "The Parliament of Fowls," where on Valentine Day many birds gathered to discuss how to choose a mate, with the lower-class birds (our sparrows?) showing little patience.

But too bad about the absent robins, because *Soeur Sainte Émilie* told us their red breast came from the bleeding Christ on the cross! I thought of them when in the South I heard the Negro spiritual for the first time: "Were you there when they crucified my Lord?" In my present North Smithfield yard, I always called Pat to the window when cardinals appeared, especially on a snowy day, contrasting with their plumage. I've counted 21 species. Best way to cut down on mosquitoes I read. Along with cat and dog food, birdfeed is a big grocery seller, especially in the Northeast, since with global warming many no longer winter in Florida or lower Americas. And they no longer smack against my picture window, since I installed a kind of treated appliqué they can see. Birds flying into windows happened often at our college scholasticate in Mobile with its many windows.

When Pat and I saw young Jim bypass the top crust in a loaf, I remembered we children did the same. When the two crusts met at the bottom, not spurning I guess God's gift of *notre pain quotidien* (our daily bread), dad made himself a sandwich. Or made those sparrows happy! In her bread pudding, mom put a lot of raisins for dad's regularity.

Like most kids, we took it for granted our folks liked and loved each other. But every time she had us notice some quality he had, she passed that affection on to us. As he did too with his praises, but more privately, not wanting her to hear. No doubt their two greatest triumphs as parents and homemakers (besides character formation and the gift of faith) were taking us through the Depression and World War II, battered but upright at the helm of the USS Tellier, like other parents.

Even if Americans then weren't the meat eaters they later became, the absence of meat, both choice and quantity, caused human carnivores to groan during the war. In a grocery store across the street from Belhumeur's (Roger Petit, advocate for veterans and city humanitarian, says it was his family's market), my dad cracked up the store one day. Seeing the showcase with only pigs' feet, loudly and facetiously he whined, "Where the rest of that pig?" (*le restant du cochon*). Remember when the little old lady got her 15 minutes of fame with "Where's the beef?" My folks made a tasty dish called *pattes de cochons* with those pigs' feet. Canadian-like, a restaurant on Providence Street in the city now serves it Tuesdays where relative Gerry Blais loved to eat it. We liked it like black pudding or blood sausage called *boudin*, also from pigs. Two of us married spouses of English or English-German ancestry, so we never saw it on our tables. You noticed their disdain at the mere mention of it, as if a cannibalistic food. Humorously, speaking about cannibalism, I was told never to ask a practitioner how he 'liked' his fellow man!

The secret, of course, to culinary survival and wise husbandry of coupons during the war was baking and cooking family-style. Since poor families like ours were said in French to be *élevées à la gibelotte*," that is, raised or fed like the Irish on stews and boiled dinners, my folks had no problem with rationing. Fortunately, dad found a man, a mill buddy I think, who slaughtered a lot of chickens and so we canned some 40 jars one year along with 40 quarts of blueberries and summer produce from Gardella's. No wonder our rear hallway was always jammed with canning paraphernalia: glass jars, red rubber rings, huge pots. And of course, his own root beer. Our house was like a domestic Farmer's Market. Poor people knew how to feed themselves, especially when agriculture had once been a way of life whose values lingered in dire urban life.

If we ate well, had a roof over our heads, and dressed warmly with *mémère's* knitting, were we really poor? Like for many "inventive families," the Depression had alighted on some can-do people who thumbed their nose at that awful decade. I guess the difference with today is, as Brokaw says, we were so close to the poverty line to begin with, we adjusted better than today's struggling families accustomed to amenities and luxuries not existing or within reach of people of little means at one time.

To alleviate shortages, people during the war were encouraged to grow their own food (still America's biggest pastime) with Victory Gardens. For as long as the family lived on Gaulin, he, of course, didn't. Perhaps thinking of those lush green fields of the family's farm in St. Cuthbert, he moaned all we had *sa Gaulin* was *"de la poussière,"* that is, dust. Later he enjoyed the pleasure of gardening when they moved. "The kiss of the sun for pardon, / The song of the birds for mirth; You are nearer God's heart in a garden / Than any place on earth." Adam and Eve's first mortgage and garden?

When they moved to Bellingham to Sue and Guil Bouffard's house on Freeman St, he finally had a garden and made gardeners of us all and prolonged his life to boot. All life began in a garden, said a naturalist, so like Jefferson he enjoyed the fruits of the land. It was the symbolism of life ever reinventing itself in new growth. It meant his life had come full circle from his farming youth. No greater blessing in his golden years! He went back to nature, which the four walls of his mill obscured in a swirl of woolen dust and noisy machinery for 40 years. Shouldn't have lived to be 86 with his disease, but Mother Nature showed him the restorative power of clean air, rich soil, and outdoor work. A study in 2014 confirmed that, as did my dad's doctor (Dr Terrill) who loved dad's tomatoes.

Before canning all those blueberries (*encanner*), we picked as a family, either on a friend's farm (monsieur Mathurin) or near *le maire* (Mayor) Ernest Dupré's summer home outside the city. It made you proud to show your parents your haul. But she chided me once for picking too fast, having too many berries "*pas muris*," not ripe. Those glorious days in the patch meant Sunday's dessert: blueberry pie and his own ice cream. During the week, it was cupcakes and blueberry turnover cake. It's why cousin Doctor Roger Fontaine liked to come on Sunday to "*mon oncle Alphonse et ma tante Léopoldine.*"

Like other families, recall we also collected recyclables for the war effort. Rubber, metal, newspaper, grease, all were hoarded to be sold or brought to a center. It must have been a bit of a sacrifice in some families to part with that cooking grease. But it blows my cholesterol-conscious mind that after it congealed in the icebox, some families used it as a toast spread, along with their beans. In the Order, it was a table delight jokingly called "*de la graisse de roue*": wheel grease. What harm it may have caused? In my religious group, class of 1949, Brother Alfred (Joseph Phaneuf) from the city couldn't get enough of it, all the more to supplement our meager fare to tackle a heavy schedule of prayers, studies, sports, and landscaping the property. In my second stage of training, 1949-50 in the Novitiate, mom wanted me to come home. I looked like *les Fontaines* did when they entrained to America without morsel or currency. To this day, *confrères* (colleagues) and I chuckle when we look at a group photo after the annual retreat at the Academy. To put it charitably, we looked ascetic (like monks in the desert). No Friar Tuck among us. Like in the army, we didn't like getting up early and the food. But those are two healthy outlets to complain about, a psychiatrist said about the human experience. Later, "a good table" became the norm in training and in our schools when school tuitions began to rise.

But a Woonsocket barely recovered from the throes of the Depression didn't think the specter of want and deprivation an unusual visitor. Picture a wizened Depression-weary Franco learning about the war's coming deprivation: "*Mon doux (Dieu), il faut manger d'la misère nwère encore*": hard times and black misery here again. Dad simply said to mom, "*Je t'lava dit, Poldine,*" about forewarning us. With undeniable pride because she saw him right so often, she, who always put a terse verbal cap on events, again said, "*Ton père sé (sait) toute*, (Your father knows all)" about his omniscience. She was always boosting our pride in him, telling us things we hadn't noticed. I can't say it enough, she really liked and loved "the guy," and we caught it from her. In his little mill town sphere, was he like a Renaissance man of the 16th Century, a guy who wanted to know everything? Of course, mom's already mentioned knowledge of who was who in our world amazed him as much as it did us. So, he was into WHAT; she into WHO. With their ingenuity, they provided us with a lot of things they didn't really have the money for. And that included curiosity about the world we lived in and "a home-based education." How blessed we were to be enriched by two cultures, a vibrant ethnic enclave, strong nuclear family, all rooted in the faith, manners, and even language of their proud France-to-Canada history. Only the upper reaches of education were missing for many until after the war.

Even though like most couples they had the usual spousal loggerheads about our sibling rivalries, theirs was the typical good French-Canadian marriage destined to endure and flourish until death did them part. ("Every love story ends in tragedy," as we cited C.S. Lewis about the separation of death). Like his taciturn brothers, dad wasn't bombastic or a soapbox box orator: the weight of his opinions was their substance, his manner not "Trumpish". He typified a line I like: "Hollow drums beat loudly; deep rivers flow silently." Or mom's "*Un bon homme, ton père* (A good man, your father)." A mutual admiration story!

If the three families - Telliers, Trottiers, *et* Fontaines - didn't buy the same lot and tombstone, and he and mom were buried there alone, the above French phrase would be a great epitaph to his memory. For her, *C'est une bonne femme*, (She's a good woman)" one of the sublime praises of French-Canadian womanhood. He loved her, with "nary a thorn ever on the rose" of their friendship and mutual admiration. Of course, the Fontaine *et* Trottier children could also have eulogized their parents equally, if on their own stone or monument.

As Brokaw wrote, their generation produced the greatest generation ever, the men and women who won WWII and ushered in today's material, economic, and academic achievements. Since Brother Ignatius, our formation master in Mobile, loved to say, "No river rises above its source," going back further, what does that tell you also about the generation that fought, worked and lived through WWI? Steeled in the cauldron of immigration and hardened by the Depression, many saw their strength, sinews, and sacrifice course through the bloodstream of their progeny. The same that won the war and went on to build the most powerful nation on earth from 1945 on. It's why the nation is so grateful today to these veterans, men and women, and also our home front heroes who worked and prayed for them.

But for their own chance at the brass ring, educationally and financially, it's as if my parents and others were born a generation too soon. The seed of greatness was there, but not the opportunity. Savor again the line, "Many a flower is born to blush unseen / And waste its sweetness on the desert air," or "Full many a gem of purest ray serene, the dark unfathomed caves of ocean bear." Their children would enjoy the bloom of success and sow the desert with the marvels of science, technology, medicine, and education in the latter half of the 20th Century. Timing! As the Bible says, "One worker sows, another waters, and a third reaps." Yes, they got to the field too early, even though the celestial reward (the Parable of the Workers) is the same, but not here below. But humble, if praise had come their way, would they have cited the Good Book, as I once heard MSC Principal, Br. Paul Demers say, he who did so much to save the Academy in the 1970s. "As long as good is being done, it matters not who does it?"

War-Weary Woonsocket Longs for Peace

THINKING OF YOUTH'S fanciful imagination, as victory over the Nazis became more certain, we kids switched to the Japanese theater in our war games. So less and less did we imitate Hitler by combing our hair sideways and feigning a mustache with a black comb. Gone too were goose-stepping and throwing Heil Hitlers all over the place! Kaput!

As a result of the "surprise" Japanese attack on Pearl Harbor, Americans were quickly propagandized to consider them as sneaky, back-stabbing foes. So, in our war games, one kid played "Jap" (the derogatory term we all used at the time) and attacked us good guys from the rear with a pretended knife: a stick. Then WWII, now the Pacific Theater, ensued, complete with banzai charges, unintelligible sounds, and falling bodies. In my own case, with Bob serving in the Pacific and sending letters home, my imagination had fertile ground. And of course, we saw all those war movies where our guys, like actor Robert Walker, were manning their overheated machine guns as the fanatical Japanese made their suicidal charges. Only when I saw the movie "Bridge on the River Kwai," did I get a cinematic notion of their human dimension and ordinariness, despite their cruelty.

Of course, if the war had gone on, we too would've come of age and fantasy would have turned to reality. Or else, as one of my friends did across the street upon turning 16, drop out of school to work in the Kaiser Shipbuilding Plant in Providence. Since dad's wartime wages were still below $100 a week at the mill, I had visions of a nouveau riche when the adolescent tempter told me he was making more with overtime. But mom said Providence was too far, war or no war. Taking the bus was expensive. When Sue did for work, she wasn't too pleased, especially when her foot got run over. Her heliocentric concept of the world was Woonsocket at the epicenter. You should radiate towards it, not out of it, so you didn't meet strangers, "*du monde étrange,*" she said with Francophone insularity, born of living only with her own, like nearly all did.

When 15 years old in 1945, I was old enough to sense a war-weariness among people, coupled with a prayerful longing for its end. It had been over five years since Hitler had attacked Poland; close to four since Pearl. Like in our family, we hoped peace came before we got bad news of combat injury or death to Bob, relatives, and friends. For example, David Schoenbrun's *Soldiers of the Night,* about the French Resistance touches upon the irony of 582 civilians killed (another report, 1,000), August 25, 1944, the Liberation Day of Paris, a day they waited four years for. Much earlier, were you touched by the short, aging Frenchman with a round, robust face, weeping as French flags and remaining French troops marched past through the streets of Marseilles as they departed defeated France for exile in Africa?[35] He looked so Woonsocket Franco!

If you could forget for a minute war's horrors and tragedies, the war years had been momentous for us: great Allied victories, the absence of war from our own shores, a national outpouring of patriotism, dozens of unforgettable songs and movies, war bond rallies from the cinematic greats. Also, the thrilling sight of men and women in uniform, the unmistakable religious fervor of the people, the moral certitude that God was on our side. What also fascinated me were predictions of air, auto, science, and architecture coming after the war; letters from combatants from places we only knew in geography class; comforting Rooseveltian fireside chats; snippets from those stirring blood-and-guts speeches from Churchill; and riding pickup trucks as Scouts for recyclables.

But beneath it all, there was a deeply felt sorrow at so much death, suffering, and deprivation for so long. Imagine everyone knew about the unspeakable horror of Germany's Final Solution (*Endlösung der Judenfrage*) and their extermination of six million Jews, and a total of 15 million of all faiths and nationalities! America would've been less reluctant to deny ships of Jewish refugees from coming here. Historians largely agree Churchill and FDR knew the Nazis came close to victory and the destruction of Western civilization of some 1,500 years: the fall of Rome in 476 AD to 1939.

When August 1945 came, the hoped-for surrender of the Japanese was the only conversation in town, especially after the "Enola Gay" dropped the first atom bomb on Hiroshima, August 6, killing or scarring 250,000 people. A second bomb, even more powerful, pummeled Nagasaki, killing another 80,000. Unbelievably, the country had gone from the depths of the Depression to the Atomic Age in 15 short years! Paul Tibbet named the first

---

[35] Search "The Weeping Frenchman" on the internet to see this historical WWII picture. – *ed.*

plane after his mom, thinking no one else could duplicate it. I visited the Mobile (Ala.) Hiroshima Museum while in the South in the early 1950s. Later I taught John Hersey's *Hiroshima* to seniors at Notre Dame HS. The author interviewed six survivors a day or two later, one a Jesuit. However desirable the outcome of the bomb, the Pope denounced the bomb as immoral. My ethics professor, *le Frère* Allyre, nixed it too, citing the morality of an action with both a good and bad effect. The rule is that the good should not come from the bad, as it did with the bomb: the slaughter (bad) which ushered peace (good). A well-known example is "Robin Hood morality," where you steal from the rich and give it to the poor. Of course, the pope weighing in on it made our perspective easier, but many years later, veterans and others still aren't concerned or convinced about that moral dilemma. They cite what they did to us at Pearl, the Bataan Death March, their hellish prison camps, and the killing and raping of the Chinese in "the Rape of Nanking." God said, "Vengeance is mine," but many wanted their pound of flesh too. In legal practice, Robin Hood morality is "the fruit from a poisoned tree," as seen in TV crime shows.

Truman was told it would shorten the war and save a million men. And in war logic, our incendiary bombs had already wiped out 61 cities and killed as many as the bomb would, just more quickly! And in their fanaticism, the whole Japanese nation - every man, woman, and child - was ready to perish for their homeland.

A Japanese surrender, as we found out in our island-hopping campaigns, was a Bushido warrior no-no since it prevented them from being enshrined in a special memorial at home, so as not to disgrace the Emperor who enjoyed a deistic cult. Truman was also concerned with Russia, barely six days in the war. Would they relinquish conquests against the Japanese in the Northern Pacific, or make Japan half communist, half democratic? So, does war have a morality of its own? About the Civil War, some have also cited Gen. Sherman's march to the sea in the South as immoral, with his "bummers" laying waste to everything, evoking the total war concept. General Phil Sheridan did the same thing in the Shenandoah Valley generating the comment that a bird flying over needed to carry its own provisions! And perhaps our own greatest stain of wiping out thousands of Native Americans and their 600 tribes for their lands. Our rationale: our Manifest Destiny or the Alexander the Great complex, one said.

In my war readings for these chapters, for relief I also read *The True Story of Fatima* by John de Marchi. He cites our Lady's apparitions from 1913 on to three Portuguese children (Lucia, Jacinta, Francisco), who were told wars are God's punishments for a sinful world. She asked for Russia's consecration to her Immaculate Heart to bring world peace after its conversion. Critics say that because of some confusion and delays by popes and one Curia bishop especially, the world was consecrated, but not Russia solely, as she asked. So, she then said WWII would end a bit sooner, but no world peace. Later, can you believe Churchill said that after the partial consecration of Russia we won all our battles, whereas we had lost all of them before? Our Lady also told the children about the coming war in Spain in the mid- 1930's. In her last apparition at Fatima, 100,000 saw the sun wobble out of its orbit "in a mighty zigzag motion... an unheard-of movement beyond all cosmic laws." The viewers, soaked by rain, saw their clothes dry instantly. So the debate rages whether God uses the elements to punish sinful man. He does control the elements, as you read in King David's Psalms. Musically, recall the song years ago about His stilling the waters and calming the seas, as He did on Lake Galilee? Another cited His wrath for the grievous sin of millions of abortions! Destroying our own species.

More and more as the nature and weaponry of war evolve, our leaders are led to take preemptive rather than reactive measures, a course of action which some say doesn't square with St. Augustine's rules for a "good war," like a just cause, legitimate authority, proportional response, reasonable hope of success, and the right intention. Preemption was not a factor then. A Jesuit theologian and expert on the Catholic Teaching on Peace and War spoke at Pastor Father Finnegan's St. Charles Parish. He stressed peace and non-violence should always be the first principles, with war allowable only when inevitable. "Intelligence" and electronic eavesdropping, which made Churchill and Roosevelt certain about WWII, will now be crucial, says the author of *A Man Called Intrepid*. We said FDR is lauded now for getting us ready a whole year ahead of time because of intercepts. We'd be amazed what the federal government knows now or at any one time, raising the larger question of how much privacy must be sacrificed for security.

For example, in the 1950s English war hero General Bernard Law Montgomery in *The Memoirs* considered the thorny problem of when to strike when Communist Russia also had nuclear weapons. Suppose the Axis Alliance of 1938 - Germany, Russia, Italy, Japan - had advanced weapon technology, like unmanned rockets, jet propulsion, and uranium-based bombs, could Pearl Harbor attack have been a hundred times more destructive? Could we have gone down with one sucker punch? And if we possessed any sure knowledge of their possible intentions, would we have been justified to strike first? That's why Montgomery says he was such a force in developing multinational NATO forces with Eisenhower in the 1950s. Readiness has not always been the strong suit of the good, us especially. Recall we didn't believe or respond to all those intercepts before Pearl. I read just recently that a European spy told FBI's Hoover that Japan was going to attack us. He all but threw him out of his office. The result? 2,403 victims. Later, didn't President Kennedy face a similar dilemma with Cuba armed with nuclear missiles sighted at our mainland? Some feared a nuclear catastrophe and end of life as we knew it that very night. It's never been that close for us. The President at his best.

I mentioned Woonsocket born pilot Godfrey got 36 kills, but some German pilots flying since 1939 compiled bigger records: 103 pilots with 100 or more kills; 13 over 200 kills; and two over 300. But many of their kills against Poles and Russians were with their planes on the ground, as ours were at Pearl Harbor and the Philippines. Hard to believe, but Russia secretly helped reestablish the German Air Force during the 1930's when still forbidden by the Treaty of Versailles. They paid for it later! Brother Reginald Casavant, later a LaSalette priest, was convinced industrialists favored war and financed it.

On a personal note, we never read for enjoyment in school, and so I learned to read English in *The Call's* wartime reports. My first history book! A story went round that a voracious reader was given a telephone book to read when there was nothing else. He admitted the list of characters was impressive, but the plot thin! One guy read Victor Hugo's *Les Miserabl(es)* but found no Portuguese character with that name in the book!

I touch upon it later, but traditionally Troop 4 always went to Camp Yawgoog, Hopkinton, RI, the second week of August. But scouts like myself hesitated about going wanting to be home for the war's end. In the morning, August 14, 1945, Mr. Jannell told us at breakfast if the Japanese capitulated that day, a horn would herald the good news. It was mid-afternoon and I was rowing with Phil Carpentier on Yawgoog Pond when the sweetest sound I ever heard signaled the end of almost six long years of global madness. Just a little less than half of our young lives! Jubilant, I yelled and stroked my right oar at the same moment, sending a cascade of water over him. My brother Bob had survived the war, evading, again, English war poet Rupert Brooks' line of dead soldiers burying a bit of their country in a foreign field.

When they received word of the Japanese surrender, my brother Bob's ship, the Firedrake, was part of a convoy sailing to join the invasion fleet off the coast of Japan. Some 67 years later in 2012, he attended a reunion of former crew members in New Orleans with granddaughters Cathy and Chris Reale. Two shipmates reminisced with him about that critical time in 1945 when 15 to 30 percent of the invasion fleet of 5,000 ships might be put out of action before soldiers even hit the beach. He also visited the WWII Museum there when it was bracing for a Mississippi flood. Author Stephen Ambrose, who spoke at Bryant College, was one of the first to champion the museum. I asked him which was better military policy: the English who replaced whole units at a time after a serious depletion, or, like us, replacing individual soldiers? He favored the British way. Some U.S. solders still on the line said they wouldn't even speak to young replacement novices thinking many would soon be dead. It hurt less that way. But one vet said he took them under his wing anyway. Patton was for whole unit replacements.

I invite you to share my astonishment at war's end when I heard dad's final thoughts about the war and peace afterwards. By now, you know my folks had opinions about everything, since they loved discussion, reading, and conversation. Their curiosity was global. What he said amazed me, like his predictions before the war!

"There were no winners in war," he said, as my face contortioned into a question mark! How could that be? Wasn't that what the fighting and the praying and the dying had been all about? After all, even in our backyard war games, we always had a winner. "But wars," he went on, "severely halted human progress in peaceful arts and sciences; caused a substantial loss of a nation's generation (mom's *"la chaire du canon* - the canon pulpit"); made shambles of nations' economies; piled up debts for future generations; destroyed cities and countries needing to be rebuilt, and caused a shaky peace to ensue, broken within 25 years, give or take." The most profound, unexpected revelation I heard in my life up to that time! If our 309 Gaulin home was still standing, I could tell you exactly where I stood when he said it. All I could do was go out and play, awestruck by what he said. In my Boston College course on I.Q. testing, I had to select some 70 subjects, ranging from the mentally challenged to the brilliant. How I wished I could have done him! A good I.Q. test, said Professor Cottle at BC, can test people without much formal education, since it's not about book learning per se, but understanding, reasoning, experiential knowledge.

Where did he learn all that? How come I didn't hear it from anyone else? Was there ever a truer pacifist in the best sense of that term? He should have been in President Wilson's corner after WWI to voice his dissent to the Senate for "dissing" his League of Nations and 14 Points and the one who said, "God gave us the Ten Commandments, Wilson, 14." Every day he taught us something we didn't learn in school. But this wasn't just knowledge, but Wisdom, yes, with a capital W, the higher ground, the farthest reach of the human spirit. The way things ought to be, if our nature had not been vitiated by our First Parents, as Cardinal Newman said. That same Wisdom, the most noble of all virtues the Bible speaks about so glowingly, when it was with God as He built his purpose and mind into the world at creation. But sadly, it turned to "warring nations that clash by night," as we cited Victorian poet Matthew Arnold.

Dad's philosophy on war and peace helped me understand later why he was such a non-confrontational man; one willing to go to all justifiable lengths not to embroil himself in an argument or dispute that could be resolved with a little understanding. Like his own dad! As I mentioned earlier, I liked the distinction he made about people's actions, as cited: You couldn't always justify someone's motives or actions, but sometimes you could understand why. As someone said, "Behind every argument lies someone's ignorance." He lived by that, but he was also wise enough to think the ignorance just might be his.

America's comedian, Will Rogers, also spoke about the futility of war: "War is a game where everybody loses. I don't know why they keep playing it." We Catholics don't believe in reincarnation, but if so, with finally a chance at book larnin', fancifully I picture dad lecturing at the War College in Newport or the Pentagon, if mom didn't think it was too far! But realism an integral part of his pacifism, there'd be no more unsuspecting Pearl Harbors on his watch! Because he knew human nature so well and the progression of human events, dad lived by "Eternal Vigilance, the Price of Freedom." He left little to chance, because for people like him with a hand-to-mouth salary and survival at stake, there was no margin for error or second chance. So even though we had a luckless dad always looking for work during the Depression, with no car or home, once living with his family in a cold water flat, the loss of his mother as a child and one sibling, how blessed to have him who knew the past, present, and incredibly, with his predictions, some of the future.

The Sermon on the Mount speaks of peacemakers like him inheriting the earth. Where he now rests in the Precious Blood Cemetery, he awaits the New Jerusalem of Heaven. He left no enemies. No mean feat in our contentious, get-out-of-my face world! Imagine, by the age of 47, he faced two world wars sandwiched around the Great Depression and joblessness, the latter while supporting a family of seven. My God, he must have thought, why is it so hard for a family man to raise a family and live in peace? Christ said we'd have wars till the end of time, but why on the heels of one another?

We missed the city's victory celebration, but around a 75-foot bonfire, we rejoiced with scouts spared the fighting and dying in the greatest of all wars. Recall historian Ambrose said the Allies suffered more casualties in January 1945 than in any month of the war. And many soldiers who faced one of Europe's worst winters and braved Germans armed with superior high-tech weaponry were just teenagers, many not even high school graduates. Months before at their prom, were they crooning "Moonlight and Roses" to their dates, as one wrote?

As is one of the themes of our narrative, with the return of our soldiers Woonsocket would never be the same. A statement perhaps true of every town and city in America, but more so in ethnic enclaves like in our "Little Canada." Our city's military had been part of this national will to save the world from enslavement; had crossed both oceans; fought alongside soldiers from all walks of life, race, nationality, and creed; heard only their country's native tongue, while training, traveling, and fighting in places their sheltered youth didn't know existed. And most importantly, they returned with the support of the G.I. Bill to acquire an education in high school and even college for some. The WWI lyric said it best: "How ya' gonna keep 'em down on the farm after they've seen Paree?" The same for Rosie the Riveter.

With mills closing or leaving, the city discovered that in diversification and education, the quality of life and the economy could be better. And even with lingering urban woes, the city's brightest and most motivated began to bring more glory than ever in academics, professions, service careers, and skilled trades, as mortarboards replaced helmets.

The "Quebéckian grip" on the city and elsewhere had lasted one hundred years, an historian wrote, but America had finally "won." We said Chartier in his book detailed so magnificently the efforts of many to prevent that, but it was not to be. French Canadians had explored a great part of America before it was a nation, but when Montcalm lost Québec to Wolfe in 1759, we were destined to become at least patriotically and linguistically "Anglophone-Americans" instead of Canadian-Francophones. François Furstenberg in *When the United States Spoke French* (in certain states and locales) chronicled the efforts of French *émigrés* (emigrants) to make that happen in some states.

But a saving grace, if we had remained a possession of France and not become the arsenal of democracy and a world power, who would've been there to twice rescue and save the great European Continent and thwart the Greater Pacific expansion of Japan? And negatively, would the French Revolution of the 1790s with its bloodletting and unbridled atheistic liberalism have also infected us here? Even liberal Jefferson changed his mind about them. At this hour, I like to think even the European Union is always threatened because Europe lost its great Christian orientation and belief in God's Providence.

Again, about the wars, like so many Abrahams willing to sacrifice their Isaacs because the country beckoned, parents had sent their sons into the jaws of hell, wondering if they would return to hearth and home? Six hundred thousand of all nationalities didn't in WWII. Wilson, we said, had warned us after the Great War, but like St. John the Baptist, he was *Vox clemantis in deserto*: a voice crying in the desert, unheard. Amazing how one person was the only one right against millions!

For anyone who survived, the poignant question was "Why me?" Recall my uncle Auray's take on it. But more providentially, I especially like that God still had something special, however cloaked in ordinariness, for survivors to do in their life. People come from God, said a priest at a funeral Mass, and pass like a comet through other people's lives, adding we should be grateful for their stay among us, however short.

I'll let Dwight Eisenhower, Supreme Commander and President, speak of the terrible price war exacts on us all: "Every gun that is made, every warship launched, every rocket fired signifies, in the final sense, a theft from those who hunger and are not fed, those who are cold and are not clothed. The world in arms is not spending money alone. It is spending the sweat of its laborers, the genius of its scientists, the hope of its children. This is not a way of life at all, in a true sense. Under the cloud of threatening war, it is humanity hanging from a cross of iron." Amazing insight and words from one of the great warriors of the 20th Century! In his own small mill town world, dad's postwar thoughts said the same in a more non-West Point, plebian prose. Ike's words should be emblazoned on the wall of the U.N. and in the halls of diplomacy of every nation.

Imagine if the world was not always in the grip of "tooth and claw" or warfare, how much pain, physical deformity, destruction, annihilation, ill health, deprivation, hopelessness, poverty, and homelessness we could eradicate with the unspent currency of "the wealth of arms." God's question to Cain resonates throughout history: "Oh, Cain, where is thy brother?" Is God still asking nations today "What are you doing with the wealth I've given you? Why the slaughter in the battlefield ... and the womb?"

1956 photo of cousin Gene Peloquin, Navy, and my brother Ben Tellier, Army, taken on Gaulin Ave. near the Peloquin home

St. Ann Church is now St. Ann Arts and Cultural Center

7 - CATHEDRAL OF THE SPIRIT

<u>Church Wasn't Just a Building</u>

IN CISTERCIAN MONK Thomas Merton's *Seven Storey Mountain*, he describes a typical Medieval Catholic town of dwellings encircling one prominent and eminent edifice: the church or cathedral. This architecturally centrist arrangement was symbolic of the church's place and influence in the spiritual life of the villagers in the Christian Western world. But even if St. Ann's Church was not topographically a visible locus for some of the 3,000 families in the parish, the lives of the faithful were still centered on its twin symbolic towers of faith and family, as highlighted in the centennial book.

And as it still does today in another guise, the magnificently Romanesque and Nincheri-frescoed edifice between Gaulin and Cumberland streets was also with its two spires or fingers of God a link between heaven and earth. Like in ages of faith, for near 100 years it was a sermon in stone. An unforgettable scene, we said, for a Social *Coin* youth of the 1930s and 1940s, was the sight of over 6,000 churchgoers walking to Mass on Sunday. Since the church lay at the bottom of our neighborhood valley, down came the faithful from the streets and avenues of Wood, Burnside, Elm, Mailloux, Cumberland Hill, Cass, *la grosse et petite Gaulin (the big and small Gaulin Avenue)*, and others from the Flatlands or Social *Coin* (corner). For most workers, it was a small redirection from their usual weekday trek to the mills, especially if on Hamlet or Clinton or Social. Order founder St. Benedict's motto of *Laborare et Orare*: (*To Work and To Pray*) was their living and marching orders.

Not to the manner born and more accustomed to the habiliments and dresses of their daily toil, husbands and wives, however, glowed in their best finery. Walking together on Sundays, they displayed a powerful example of parental piety and devotion now lacking, a recent diocesan study said. Never a man to display affection publicly, dad generally didn't escort mom, as some men did their wives, where the woman tucked her gloved hand under his arm. In winter, women draped in a fur coat sometimes used a fur-lined muff. But not mom. For us Tellier, Trottier, *et* Fontaine adults and children, *Mémère* Fontaine provided us with everyday woolen mittens, gloves, *et tuques* (and hats).

Mom had a fur coat in her maiden days, but it dried up due to inadequate storage. Knowing its sentimental value, I disposed of it only after her death. What memories it must've held for her! But sometimes dad did walk alongside of her, modifying his long Lincolnesque gait, probably honed as a boy on his family's Saint Cuthbert farm in Québec. "*Attends-mwé (wait for me),*" she pleaded to mitigate his rabbit pace, especially if in winter she feared falling despite *des crampons,* gripping devices under her overshoes. Falls were more prevalent because everyone walked, and snow and ice lingered for days.

School children attended Mass in a body on Sunday, so we ran to the school playground to form ranks with our class. And since teenage dating was a rare public thing, young adolescents like Bob and Sue often went with the boys and girls they socialized with during the week. When an adolescent couple started coming to church together, mom heralded, "*C'est sérieux* (it's serious)" Lovebirds went to church together even before the banns of their engagement and marriage were announced in church.

The presence of these adolescents with or without their betrothed, now a somewhat rare occurrence (college is one reason and the "brain drain" out of RI), was proof of the success of Catholic education and parents in inculcating the continuing practice of the faith and Sunday Mass in America. Despite the above, older or late-middle-aged people in the pews now are proof our generation has not been as successful in passing the faith along to our children, breaking a 1,700-year-old tradition in people of Frankish descent. Recall 40 percent of young people have left the church (all denominations) their parents brought them up in. Only the advent of Hispanic and Portuguese immigrants has stabilized and even increased Catholic numbers. One in three Americans were once Catholic, now one in four. In a word of caution symbolic of heaven, the Gospel speaks of absentee wedding guests replaced by others at the wedding feast. Those on the fence about their spiritual destiny, consider what President Reagan said, "Err on the side of caution." When you've crossed the divide, it's too late, as the once rich, miserly Dives (Biblical term for rich man) in the lower regions was told. He wanted to come back to tell his brother to change his ways.

Jesuit Father William J. Byron of *Catholic News Service* thinks "the virus of individualism dulls the desire to be with others at Mass on Sunday. We should worship as a community," he adds, because "we were redeemed as a people, as a community, and are obliged to share with and care about the others with whom we form the 'one body' of Christ." Apart from the obligation, it was almost un-neighborly not to attend like everyone did. You saw your whole street, neighborhood, and Social *Coin* (corner) it seemed. *De rigueur* (required), you met at the Lord's Table, a foretaste of the Heavenly Banquet. "Unless you eat my flesh..." Christ said, you'll not go where He went at His Ascension.

As in the Negro spiritual, the faithful wanted "to be in that number" when God called. With their rock-solid belief in the afterlife, most had this tune in their heart, "When Christ shall come with shouts of acclamation...." Without fear of being fanciful or ethnically myopic, with all of creation assembled, I swear no one will rejoice more in the great spectacle of the Last Judgment than convivial Francos. Their special earmark, along with Italians, Irish, Poles especially! For parishioners, it'll be Nincheri's masterpiece in real time. "On stage," as emcee Ed Sullivan often intoned about a coming spectacle. (One time a comic mocked him, saying he was having the entire Civil War cast on stage the following week!)

But pity the student who missed Mass with his class! Of course, the teacher recorded it in a little black book. On Monday morning, "the prodigal child" received a stern lecture on the consequences of not attending with the school group. Or worse, but rarely, of bypassing the Church's most serious commandment at the time, one with salvation overtones. Because of schoolmates, your nun knew why you missed. The court convened Monday: "Here come da' judge."

Is there a better word to convey "togetherness" than the word "Com (cum in Latin meaning with or together) Union?" And in the former Latin Mass, the priest often intoned *Dominus (the Lord) Vobiscum (is with you)*, emphasizing the whole congregation since Vobis is strictly plural in Latin. Tecum is singular, as Gabriel used in addressing Mary. I recall a few funny "interpretations" of Latin: A student said in a history test that the Romans' greatest achievement was learning Latin! And a young woman, a first timer, who heard the priest say it so often at Mass she thought he meant the collection: "Dominic, go frisk 'em." Another, as it appeared in the *Valley Breeze* in a follow-up to my article on the old-time Mass, thought *Ora Pro Nobis* (*Pray for Us*) meant Hurrah for Nobis, whom she deduced must be quite a guy since the priest said it 7 or 8 times. Former Pastor Michael Wooley of St. Joseph's Parish celebrates the Latin Mass occasionally, the so-called Tridentine Mass: solemn, longer, but not as interactive.

Of course, in my childhood talking and laughing were all forbidden. And the nuns hoped you put in the penny parents gave you for the collection basket. A friend once cracked up our pew when he told the collector, "Here you are, my good man."

Our nuns were the Presentation of Mary Order of French origin (there is also an Irish-based Community; in my 15-year stay in Fitchburg, a French-Canadian, Woonsocket girl was in their Order). Locally not the first but more numerous than others, their congregation responded to help immigrants preserve their language, culture, and faith, as did priests and teaching Brothers. That apostolic synergism, a recurring theme with us, was epitomized in *Qui perd sa langue, perd sa foi* – Who loses his language, loses his faith. But because St. Paul said faith came from the Jews (*fides ex Judeis*), Pope John Paul called them "our oldest brothers in the faith," but Francos thought it came from the *Le Verbe* (the verb): French! Did they think Moses' Commandments from God on Mt. Sinai was also in the Gallic tongue? And in French couplet style for us. In reading about the Council of Trent (1545-1563) to cure abuses and refute Luther's 98 theses (gripes), France wished to be the center of Christendom instead of Rome. Protestants were also invited to discuss their differences, but they disagreed over the agenda and left.

No matter her size or age, each nun projected a rather formidable pre-Vatican renewal look. A sea of black serge and a white rimmed bonnet crowned a pallid face, adding to her religious aura! Besides beads dangling from her cinctured waist, a pectoral cross also defined her modest corpus. Ranks were not required for non-obligatory everyday Lenten Mass or devotions to Mary in October and May at night, so at a side entrance you saw their long black line like West Point cadets. They were over 40 strong in our day, walking in twos with heads slightly bowed, *les yeux modestement* *baissés (*eyes modestly lowered*)*, as I later did in my Brothers of the Sacred Heart Order.

The thrust of religion by Nuns, Brothers, and Priests has always borne fruit, said a recent study, citing that religious faith was strengthened by education. University of Virginia sociologist W. Bradford Wilcox revealed that the least-educated Americans are more likely to turn their backs on religion, "whereas forty-six percent of college-educated whites are frequent churchgoers. But encouragingly churchgoing among blacks and Latinos has been more consistent regardless of education levels." One severe indictment, however, revealed American Christians give away a miserly 3 percent of their income to church or charity, and that "every day, the church is becoming more like the world it allegedly seeks to change," said an article. But on the contrary, RI Catholics despite fewer parishes annually donate close to $8 million dollars to the annual Providence diocesan drive which helps a vast number of people, education, faith action groups, and non-Catholics too. Keeps the Heat On in winter too.

On a personal note, "eyes modestly lowered" was the only compliment I received when I pursued my religious training. Like the fallen angels in Milton's *Paradise Lost* who looked for treasures on Heaven's floor before ejected, recall as a kid I had the habit of looking down for dropped money at St. Ann's Park. So, a friend mistook my "venality" for modesty at my profession at Mount Saint Charles Academy. I said my biggest finds in life: a $75 check, which resolved a wrangle between a parent and the school treasurer in Sharon; that 1803 coin at the now Crystal Lake golf course; an arrow point at Spring Lake; in Fitchburg, a real safe; a pair of official handcuffs; two rings (handed in) at the beach; a dozen new baseballs, a fossilized butterfly, a piece of a Spanish galleon, and those wartime love letters I reburied. Didn't a Californian find $11million in the dirt two years ago. But taxable-like income!

Since *les bonnes soeurs* (the good Sisters) rewarded attendance at Mass, Benediction of the Blessed Sacrament, and May and October devotions, what pride you felt if you picked out your teacher in line, and she relaxed her studied modesty and saw you. If so, we chanced a *"Bonjour, ma Soeur"* (even in the evening), but she didn't overly acknowledge it. Her eyes said it though. If the next day, outside the pale of her strict rule and Mother Superior, she brought it up, you felt like the elect will at the Last Judgment when called. It was the same good feeling if I met them shopping in Social during my paper route. They never had a car, so sometimes they begged for a ride. But that didn't sit well with some. If the same family was often the lender, tongues wagged about favoritism for their children in school. "Saintly mom" was not beyond reproach in this regard. Several times she told me she was denied a first-place prize because the eventual winner's family had supplied *"une machine pour les bonnes Soeurs* (a machine/car for the good sisters)." How come she didn't know the make, model, year?

Dad said our people were not beyond nitpicking, besides lacking fraternal support at times, a universal failing I suspect. A teachers' convention speaker in Worcester said there didn't exist a student (and parent?) without *une crotte sur le coeur* (a gripe) about some teacher and supposed injustice. Hey, with millions of students in school for 12-16 years today, those perceived slights are understandable. Notes on my Academy education and the worst encounter I ever got bear that out. An article said some parents are quick to complain if, say, a "degrading B+" isn't morphed into a "deserved A." But we've seen parental malingering in sports too. As Assistant Director at Notre Dame HS, I blunted criticism of my yearly selection of the school's best senior athlete by using a strict mathematical formula. But a wiseacre snapped, "Yes, figures don't lie, but liars figure."

If within earshot, it must've been embarrassing when we signaled a nun out with an unflattering name. By today's standards nothing derogatory, but the usually perceptive student's remarks about a teacher's height, weight, looks, pet expression or peeve, mannerisms, temper, teaching manner, and the like. Or one of those religious names! Later in the Order, our usual party comedian with a way of embellishing the already long, sanctimonious names of some women religious entertained us once with the moniker of "Sister Esmeralda of the Purple Tabernacle Door Half-Opened." Exaggeration the basis of humor! Or like in journalism, "What is contrary to the norm."

At Mount too, classmates jabbed the Brothers with nicknames. For example, a baldish Brother Theodoric was "The Skull." Brother Honorius' name was metamorphosed into an unflattering fish name. Why, when we ourselves started teaching, we too had them, outrageous or realistic, for each other. I guess it's the American way! It ended when religious were finally allowed to use their Christian and family names. They only resurfaced with latter-day stage comedies of the "Nunsense" and "Late Night Catechism" variety and the comedy routine of "Father Misgivings." As in any family, communal living in religious life was an inexhaustible source of humor and teasing. Joining, no one left his idiosyncrasies or foibles at the door.

Previously too we spoke how in some families missing Mass on Sundays was also a serious domestic breach. But more in Canada, mom said. Parents didn't tolerate it and gave the recalcitrant son or daughter a bend-or-break option. Not original with her, mom called this loose-practicing kind of Catholic *"un Catholique à gros grain,"* the pick-and-choose Cafeteria Catholic of today. Also, because unity in doctrine is one of the four marks of the Catholic Church throughout the world, our faith is seen by some as the most intransigent, with no-take-it or leave-it margin, an almost constitutional right in the American psyche. But on the other hand, the greatest pitfall of other faiths, said a writer, stems from self-interpretation of the Bible only. With so many contrasting beliefs, some opt for no belief at all. In Leonie Frieda's *Catherine de Medici - Renaissance Queen of France* - 16th Century Calvinists (Huguenots) chafed especially at papal authority and the Real Presence in the Eucharist. "Huguenot" came from dissidents meeting in that town.

I enlarge on it later, but if at death someone was not brought to church for burial, she said, "*Ya pa(s) entré dans l'église.*" Denial of a Catholic burial was the ultimate shame or sorrow for a Catholic deceased person's family. It's as if there was no resurrection or salvation with the elect. Judgment is now relaxed, perhaps for consideration of the bereaved family and the fallacy of human judgment. So, again, how can anyone dwell on the ordinariness of the lives of the faithful, when they lived with that grand design, now missing, said a convert. The faithful didn't feel oppressed with the expectations of their faith. If truth sets a person free, freedom rang in their inner being.

A sad situation has now arisen with cremation an accepted and far less expensive practice. Ashes in some cases are not deposited in holy ground in keeping with the body having been the temple of the Holy Spirit. Stories abound of ashes incorporated into jewelry, left behind by moving families, improperly buried with bones protruding in the backyard, or just scattered willy-nilly. How does it all relate to the belief you can always judge a culture by how it honors its dead? Hopefully, those practices are more from ignorance and disregard of consequences than disrespect of loved ones. But a paper reported that to pocket the money, incredibly children have gone against their deceased parents' written or spoken wishes about a church burial and proper internment. Grave robbers! A case of "We have met the enemy and they are us."

It sounds so cruel today, but the expression *enterré comme un chien* (buried like a dog) was how the faithful said no church burial. Unlike that character in "Macbeth," their leaving life was not the best thing he or she had done if they weren't in God's graces. People were so attuned "to dying right," you always heard talk whether death was accidental or unexpected: "Did he do the nine First Friday Masses of the month to the Sacred Heart, or five First Saturdays (Mary) in his life?" Both promise a good death. "Didn't I see her at Mass last Sunday?" "O yes, she went to confession every month." And so, it went. Always you should live in a state of grace and readiness because death came quietly *avec ses bas d'laines*, like with woolen socks.

When nuclear annihilation became a threat after WWII, it spawned a survival joke with a religious reminder. When someone asked the safest state to live in, Father Theodore Hesburgh of Notre Dame University (he died in 2015 at the age of 97) said, "The state of grace." At the end of the cold war, records revealed Russia had a warhead aimed at every city of 50,000 plus. Four or five thousand shy, did Woonsocket luckily not make the list, "safe" between Providence and Worcester? Or doomed to be a nuclear sandwich if those cities hit? Who knew?

Of course, if death had been expected, the decedent probably died in God's graces, since the priest was called for the Last Rites. Because young priests walked, you knew if one was going to perform that rite somewhere if he didn't return your greeting. Unless he was bringing Communion to a recovering shut-in, he was carrying the sacred viaticum or host for the ritual. "*Viaticum*" means "for the journey." Now the ritual is nearly always done in a hospital or rest home (now called a nursing home or long-term care facility), if not prevented or omitted by those over-the-top privacy issues! The sacrament is now the Anointing of the Sick. The previous name was too predictive, and didn't reflect Christ and the church's compassion, concern, and entreaties to God the Father for solace and even healing, like Christ healing many including Apostle Peter's mother. She was so motherly; a writer noted she began to serve as soon as she got on her feet!

About dying at home, when friend Patrick Beaulieu and I discovered ex-Brother and teacher-friend, Edmond Patenaude dead in his home in the 1970s, the Medical Examiner initially called for an autopsy, since "Hardly anyone dies at home now". He changed his mind when I told him the deceased told me at table in the Order that men in his family died fairly young. I became suspicious when he didn't answer my call to see *The French Connection* the day, I believe, after the wedding of Marcel and Donna Tardif in NY in 1975. Beaulieu, I, and the police broke into his locked house to get to his body slumped in a chair, the radio playing. Out of gratitude for my call to the family, they made it possible for me to buy his home with my War Bond savings and dad's help, who returned a loan I made to him when I was in training and he became disabled. Mom always preached, "*En sauver (save) pour le lendemain.*" - Save for tomorrow.

But some conservative pastors still held a very tight rein who could be brought into church for Mass and burial. As happened in 1987 with a Connecticut pastor, a donnybrook erupted between *le curé* (the priest) and family of a decedent reputed "to have lived in sin," as was the label. Pastors generally didn't tolerate abandonment of religious practices like non-attendance at Sunday Mass, public scandal, cohabitation without marriage, also a legal no-no at one time. I wrote to the bishop to fully clarify the status of Catholics who, without a dispensation, marry again in front of a Justice of the Peace. They are still Catholic, of course, but denied Communion. One frustrated teacher told me she now felt like a second-class Catholic. It's sad if the aggrieved Catholic spouse dealt with abuse, alcoholism, drugs, infidelity, or abandonment from his/her partner. Unfortunately, too many non-practicing Catholics are "in the mist" because of marital malaises: 70 percent I once heard. My Boston College magazine said Catholics now divorce and cohabit almost like the general population. Other figures vary. Pope Francis in 2015 made getting a dispensation from a bad marriage much easier, including forgiveness by local priests in Confession.

Before civil law was changed about cohabitation, a Catholic priest in Fitchburg on call by police, as was customary, made me laugh when he told me an arrested cohabiter told him he was only helping her say the rosary in bed. "Too much emphasis on the "Glory Be," the padre joked. Catholics who only entered church three times in their lives to be baptized, married, and buried ("hatched," "matched," and "dispatched,") came under critical review. The church is much more tolerant or forgiving today. But again, membership is the critical factor for a Catholic burial. Gotham Don John Gotti was denied, not because of his lifestyle, but non-membership. As in Christ's story of the wedding feast, the nattily dressed Mafioso wasn't "wearing the white robe," symbolic of membership and attendance.

Deathbed conversions have always been the stuff of high drama. Recall the Good Thief (St. Dismas), Al Capone, Timothy McVeigh (the Oklahoma bomber), and England's notorious Oscar Wilde ("Wild Oscar") all made it under the wire. No matter what their life had been, a final penance or conversion was like *Finis Coronat Opus:* The End Crowns the Work. Thomas W. Petrisko in *Inside Purgatory* cites saints and mystics who saw Purgatory where "near misses" have a longer stay and more intense suffering until purification; some until the end of the world.

The church still adhered to the beliefs of St. Thomas Aquinas, a great theologian of the Middle Ages, who wrote in the *Summa Theologica*, that reason and faith were not contradictory, a person possessed free will, and is responsible for all his acts. Determinists like Watson and Skinner who say we're supposedly programmed like Pavlov's dog to do what we do strictly by nature, instinct, training, or circumstances, rather than conscience and free will, didn't sit on any Vatican tribunal in those days! To cite literary lines, everyone was the arbiter of his soul and the captain of his ship, so poetized Walt Whitman.

There was no shifting blame, an earmark of our times. But recall Mother Eve did it first, blaming the serpent. And Adam too, it's probably why the confessional was mobbed when I was a kid, rather than the psychiatrist's couch, as TV orator Bishop Sheen lamented. We went every month from school, and parents like mine, one Saturday a month. Sitting in a hot, airless confessional box for hours and hearing the peccadilloes of Adam and Eve's progeny was once considered the priesthood's most onerous duty. (Read *The Edge of Sadness* by Woonsocket's Edwin O'Connor about a depressed priest who has heard too many confessions.) Second was asking for money from strapped mill workers to build and maintain those big churches, like St. Charles, Precious Blood, and St. Ann's. But even tithing - one-tenth of your income - is still honored in some parishes. My parish, Our Lady Queen of Martyrs – Holy Trinity, tithes its carnival revenues to a worthy organization. Pastor Maurice Brindamour said giving involves a trifecta of time, talent, and treasury, but so many demands are now made on people in our state with its high taxes, fees, and unemployment. But about giving up one's time, women, God bless 'em, are 70 percent of all church volunteers.

But what may also inhibit giving is that not only in socialist Sweden but also here, said a tax preparer, we eventually pay 50 percent of all we make in taxes. Your pay is just the start of an endless line of taxes, always being expanded. Didn't someone in the city even suggest taxing "the air above what you own?" And another even your mileage? This flow of money to state and federal governments, which greatly irked dad, has led to uncontrolled spending and need for more taxes. Rhody's reputation is a bane for businesses and new jobs and why we lose graduates and have an inadequate workforce. But new state politicos in 2015 aim to reverse the trend. A boon to some seniors: no more taxing Social Security pensions.

Besides Sunday Mass, you observed holy days of obligation. These were Christmas, New Year's (its religious significance; now the Solemnity of Mary, Mother of God), Christ's Ascension into Heaven, the Assumption of Mary, her Immaculate Conception, and All Saints. In the Middle Ages, 40 holy days dispensed serfs from work on feudal lands. For us school serfs, it meant no school. Why we felt umbrage about Catholic public-school kids who - God forbid! - had school on feast days. How come someone didn't know about Ascension Thursday and stuff and did the ABCs on the day Christ rose to Heaven? No wonder at one time Catholics thought they were practically alone on the "got-it-made list!" And of course, for us Francos, with French and Faith being one practically "saved you a seat" in the Kingdom if you lived a good life. From what I understand of the French character, I get a sense of their supposed superiority, especially on the European Continent, what with their great art, culture, literature, haute couture, and manners. Catherine the Great of Russia, for one, copied France wholesale, including *toujours l'amour* (love forever) with her paramours. Gallicanism[36]

---

[36] A complex of French ecclesiastical and political doctrines and practices advocating restriction of papal power, it characterized the life of the Roman Catholic Church in France at certain periods. – *ed.*

sums it all well.

But did we Francos look too much to the past and not enough to the future, as the English thought of *les Québécois* (Quebec natives)? But I was edified the first French stressed conversion rather than colonization, unlike the English for control and economization in Canada. Said Champlain, "The salvation of a soul is more important than the conquest of an empire; and Kings must not think of extending their dominion over countries in which idolatry reigns, except to submit them to Jesus Christ." I found wonderful insights about him in *Champlain, the Life of Fortitude*. Apart from religion (but some abuses too), the new thinking today is that many conquerors and colonizers undermined with weapons, greed, ideology, and, yes, viruses' intact cultures of great achievements and noble beliefs. Every year now, Columbus Day, for example, is no longer a welcomed feast for some, locally at Brown University, much to the anger of Italo-American people. Jared Diamond in *Guns, Germs, and Steel* makes a convincing case about what determines the winners (guns, steel, viruses) and losers from time immemorial. Along with writing, these led to the rise of empires for some, or a continuing primitive culture, or the dust of history.

Recall one of the proofs of this grand design of life was a New Year's Day wish among Francos. After health - *bonne sante* - and happiness - *le bonheur* - the hoped-for blessing was *le paradis à la fin de vos jours*: eternal salvation at death. I still use it when I meet someone who still remembers. A lady's face lit up. Along with other Catholic nations, the French-Canadian faith in the province of Québec and mill enclaves of New England, upstate New York, the Midwest, and beyond was nothing short of admirable in all of Christendom. We noted much stemmed from French Canadians exploring two-thirds (figures vary) of America. And the Spaniards the South and West. Also, the Dominicans established many missions in California, a day's trip from each other, like San Juan Capistrano, where birds return faithfully on the first day in spring.

God forbid, I admitted our motives for attending Mass, including Lent, were alloyed with mundane reasons. Since the start of school was delayed, mom promised us our favorite breakfasts: *du pain doré* (French toast) or *crêpes* (pancakes), especially on First Fridays. Add the small gifts of rosaries and holy pictures the nuns gave us. A lot of us kids went all 40 days in Lent, besides giving up candy and movies. R-E-L-I-E-F was when St. Ann's Church bells rang at noon on Holy Saturday, signaling the end of the penitential season. I don't know if churches still ring them today (I live too far), but because of less emphasis on those mortifications, I don't get the same feeling of relief or closure when *le carême* (Lent) ends. It felt good again to go *au théatre Laurier* (to the Laurier Theater) on Saturday to see our cowboy heroes battle the lawless West. Had the bad 'uns gotten the upper hand in Lent? And of course, eat our Almond Joys and Babe Ruths and sleep late. Rising was always tough for me, so how did I ever join a religious order and get up at 5:30 am! and why mom pooh-poohed my being an altar boy. Bad enough getting me up for school. She even doused me one time (education by aspersion!). A study found high school kids don't get enough sleep, coming to school "with their head still on the pillow". One private school in RI delayed its start and scores went up. Trouble is that as kids grow older, they go to bed later, a report said. Sleepiness at the wheel a dangerous threat!

With the practice of formal religion and regular weekly church attendance taking a steady decline after WWII and Vietnam, we children of that prewar era are perhaps the last ones with that habit so deeply ingrained. I cite a figure elsewhere but suffice to mention here in the Northeast (even if once settled by religious zealots), single and young people, and political liberals (with print and TV people at the head) have the poorest church attendance record. True, it was in the 1950s, but when some of us young Brothers studied in Mobile (like Woonsocket, "the City of Churches,") we were impressed by the many places of worship and people attending Sunday services in their best finery. The Bible Belt! For us Thundermisters, like cousin Francois *et* Joseph Phaneuf, it was *déjà vu* all over again. A CW (CBS and Warner Brothers) network story said the faith was 40 percent stronger in the South at the time. So, it wasn't just Robert E. Lee! Agriculture has deeper religious roots than industry. Crowded urban centers at times a breeding ground for idleness, broken families, unemployment, drugs, homelessness, and crime from sheer boredom and cupidity to get what others have. England during the Industrial Revolution is a classic example! Over 100 laws for capital punishment, one for stealing a loaf of bread.

Growing as they do today in an affluent and permissive era, a mounting loss of respect for all forms of authority, sexual license, drug dependency, and random violence, some young people have weak formal church affiliations if any at all. Music idols, media stars (many famous for only being famous), and feet-of-clay athletes occupy those niches in their minds we once reserved for saints, national heroes of the moment, and historical figures. A biography of Pope John Paul II revealed his concern about this Western decadence. Fortunately, the Roman Catholic church is growing in more conservative parts of the world, as the West, once the bastion of Christianity, yields to the East. In writing the EURO Constitution, the premiere of France, for one, didn't recognize at all the two-thousand-year legacy of the church in the continent's faith, learning, civilization, and culture. The great Oxford Movement converts of England at the turn of the 20th Century

(Belloc, Chesterton, Eliot, Newman, Knox, Edith Sitwell, et al) blamed the 16th Century Reformation for secularly undermining objective truth for private interpretation; spouting the belief in the unbounded perfectibility of man; and the enthronement of science as the only reality. It greatly doomed Christ's wish, *Ut unum sint*: Oneness network.

About young people, John Paul sought to strengthen their faith with World Youth Day gatherings and other appeals. His concern for the West, an author wrote, was just a little less than his struggle with communism whose fall he helped precipitate. Did he fear the outcome of that literary line? "Ill fares the land / To hastening ills a prey / Where wealth accumulates and men decay." What is it about affluence that corrupts? Is it like the famous line about power corrupting and absolute power even more so? Notice what's happened to our biggest corporations and their ravenous CEOs and banks! Money is of course not intrinsically evil unless its acquisition is at the expense of the have-nots and not accessible to the needy. The struggle is between God and Mammon, the latter the debasing influence of (ill-gotten?) wealth, says Webster.

But everything is cyclical, which tempers any pessimistic view. How often I've read Socrates' lament about the waywardness of youth in 400 BC! I hope because today's young people will have lived only in our now changed culture (we parents, didn't) they may do a better job with their own children, products of this period. But all the above is not to disparage today's youth by any means. Even though we've been shocked by some of their violence and criminality, we've marveled at their greater opportunities and unequalled influence for good, as I saw in my 42-year career. They excel in many meaningful areas, one writer said. I'm not a Manichean about an equal God of Good and of Evil, but I think that the more evil seems to abound, the more good there is to equal and surpass it. Let's hope the frequent war cataclysms of the 20th Century won't be necessary to bring back "the faith of old" in the 21st Century.

Some 30 minor wars are going on in the world. It's scary, but WWI was started by an assassination, and precipitated from longstanding and festering nationalistic shortsightedness, like in the Middle East now. Because, we said, of our unique role as the world's policeman and superpower, trouble ricochets to our shores. "Vigilance, the eternal price of freedom." St. Paul said the same thing: "Let him who stands take heed lest he fall." Historian Gibbon said all nations on earth go through five cycles: birth, rise, apex, decline, and dissolution. Are we in the fourth or declining mode, as some think? Like Nineveh, do we need a messenger from God like Jonah to have a rebirth of faith and "righteousness," a word, a prof said, that was once the driving force of this nation's Protestant ethic, which meshed beautifully with Catholic, Jewish, and other faiths?

Sermon in Stone

THERE'S NO DOUBT today's Christian is much more freethinking or laissez-faire in faith and morals than his counterpart in almost any century in Christendom. The reason of course isn't all moral dissolution or rejection of authority, even though it's an earmark of our times. A more enlightened and better-educated brethren has given rise to differences of opinions and practices that for centuries the Church would have thought too liberal. For example, not too long ago, an article in my Boston College magazine reported how "enlightened" Catholics were asking either for pastors and priests of their own liberal or conservative way of thinking and imparting the faith. Since Catholics are now among the best educated in the nation, does it explain why Rome considers American Catholicism, despite its unequalled generosity, a concern? Noise from pro-choice Catholics, including Catholic politicians, and women's rights groups for the priesthood (recall the nun who "challenged" the Pope in one of his visits here) are two cases in point.

French-Canadian faith and morality, as we knew and saw it in action at St. Ann's and in the city, were, however, generally unquestioning and piously submissive. *La foi du charbonnier*, that is, the workingman's simple, unquestioning faith. In more satirical terms, a Jesuit prof said, "Rome has spoken; let no dog bark." It was a facetious translation of the Vatican's rule: *Roma locuta, causa finita est* - Case closed!

But their submissiveness stemmed not so much from fear and ignorance, but from a childlike - not childish - acquiescence to God's word, as given them by the Pope, the teaching Magisterium of the Church, Tradition, the Bible, with bishops, priests, catechists, religious teachers, and parents as everyday transmitters. But there's no doubt the little formal religious and academic education the faithful once received made their kind of faith easier and almost unquestionable. And they lived in a cocoon of faith.

A corollary of that simple faith was that priests and teachers in our parish - like the cleric and schoolteacher in English poet Oliver Goldsmith's "The Deserted Village" -were looked upon in awe for all they knew, taught, and preached. For the most part, they were the only educated people the immigrant faithful knew on a daily basis, outside of sporadic contacts with doctors, dentists, and lawyers. About those other few academically endowed, like college professors and teachers, my folks uttered the ultimate compliment: "*Ils ont faites des études poussées*": they have degrees far beyond the ordinary. Later in the Order, Brother Morel, who knew the expression as a youth, and I chuckled whenever we heard it used by our visiting parents and relatives, as we advanced in our religious and collegiate studies.

A case in point! Should I have laughed or felt honored when I returned home with my B.A. degree for my first two-week vacation in the Order after five years. Watching one of my first telecasts ever in 1951 at a cousin's home, I answered four questions (one was about Hemingway) in a quiz show about American and English Literature, my collegiate major. Quick as a flash, she used the expression, and I sensed her admiration. For teachers at St. Ann's, I now had *"de la lumière,"* that is, I was among "the enlightened." But I speak humbly and sincerely, when I vouch the wisdom and native intelligence - if not academic degrees denied them - of my parents and other Francos were also admirable, sometimes surpassing our bookish learning. They had no choice, but facetiously "they never let schooling get in the way of their education!" Someone wrote recently that people in the Middle Ages, for example, may have known more about their way of life than we do ours with its unbelievable complexity and technological challenges. But a negative about education, said one, is that it holds a book between the learner and real life. An article recently questioned whether technology-based learning is better than interaction between teachers and students.

Because of their education, celebration of the Mass, the Sacraments, the spoken word, and the moral tenor of their lives, priests exerted a tremendous influence on the faith of parishioners. The reverence our parents had for them was so obvious, as it was one time in Canada, but now greatly diminished since the early 1970s after a series of critical articles by Marist Brother Jean-Paul Desbiens in *Les insolences du Frère Untel* (The Impertinences of Brother Anonymous), which became a clear-cut case of throwing the baby out with the bath water. Parents like mine maintained a "close working relationship" with priests because, if heaven was the goal of life, priests were the conveyors through the Sacraments from which grace, resolution, and forgiveness were to be had. Nuns and our parents taught us to greet them with respect, doff our hat with a *"Bonjour, mon père* (hello, my Father)"

This faith of our parents was at the core of their role in our moral upbringing and character formation. Today, people shudder at mounting juvenile crime statistics and perhaps unfairly blame parents for failing in their duty. Strangely, families were larger then and poorer, a dual situation which should have made this parental duty more difficult. But times were different. Their children didn't contend with a lot of questionable peer influences, now the surpassing influence in a child's upbringing. How often it's mentioned in true crime stories on TV. Recall, a frightening lack of family cohesiveness, especially absent fathers, is seen as the most critical factor in male teenage crimes and dropout. A writer added a five-year stretch of dead-end jobs by dropouts creates a seedbed for drugs and crime to get what other people have achieved through education. They once wanted it "now"; but "now" is no more. So, they want it from others.

If mom had seen our present dilemma, would she have said, "*Ou est la bonne vie de famille?* (Where is the good family life?)" How would we have turned out if we didn't hear her say a thousand times dad was coming home from the mill? Or any kind of work! After all, doesn't the Bible say, "Fear is the beginning of wisdom?" In many instances now, dad isn't coming home from work, if he ever did. Over 40 percent of households are now run by women alone. My formation teacher in the Order taught us many reasons to be good, way up to the love of God, but the most basic was *la crainte de Dieu* or fear of the Lord. About submission to parents, a 19th Century writer chortled kids should always "respect them as brought them up by hand!" Literally by hand. What one wit called "the moral uplift," applied where the sun doesn't shine. But seriously, we now know physical punishment breeds resistance, rebellion, and imitation.

Like in "the formation of conscience" in the Order, not only were we exposed to hours of religious instruction at school, but also what happened at home was I think typical with dad making references to Sunday's sermon if it had relevance to our behavior. Home, church-school, and neighborhood were the triune structure of our rather strict, but not oppressive, Franco way of life. I don't know who put all those elements together, but it's unlikely we'll ever see this kind of interaction or synergism again, at least as perfectly. Fragmentation is now more the order of the day. Instead of one voice, we now have a lot of false prophets, "wolves in sheep's clothing," Christ called them in His day. *Survivance* (survival) of the Francophone faith of yesteryear was severely diminished when those elements were no longer there as completely and forcefully for the grandchildren of Canadian-born immigrants, who had it by sheer osmosis, as in built-in.

With the serious decline in priestly vocations today, there's a dire prediction of more parishes without priests in the coming decades. Consider St. Ann's back then had no less than four or five priests ministering to its 1,600 families. They were the nobility of our caste system, well known and often spoken about. Necessity now forces some to be almost like itinerant ministers or "circuit riders," servicing more than one parish. Will centers of combined parishes, now being set up in Boston, stave off extinction of cherished churches, or claim more magnificent temples like St. Ann.

Where have all the flowers gone? When in Alabama I met clerics from the Bay State whose Boston Archdiocese had so many priests, their only option was to minister in Southern small-town parishes. But are there exceptions to this shortage today? Poland, always so Catholic despite centuries of oppression from Germany and Russia, is awash with priestly vocations. Is adversity, like WWII, fertile soil for devotion and vocations? But overall fewer Catholic schools, smaller families, and diminished faith have hurt.

Conversational tidbits about priests were their priestly style, mannerisms, quirks, sermons, length of time saying Mass (30 minutes the fault line), and, yes, severity of penance in the confessional. For mom, their education and family. Their training was either in Canada, Baltimore, or sometimes Rome, the latter an inkling of future clerical ascendancy in diocesan governance, so she thought. (A pipeline to the chancery too?) In our home, if she found out, she told us who their parents were. Unknowingly she highlighted the interrelationships of all the players in our world. Unlike the so-called 400 families of New York or Newport with their great wealth and opulent mansions, you didn't need "to have," but "to be French Canadian" for inclusion in her ethnic register.

Everyone had his favorite - *embarrass du choix* - as in too many to choose from. My parents liked *Père* (Father) Frédéric Moreau because he spoke loud and clear. Why, he could be heard clearly despite the church's vaulted echoing ceiling and poor sound system. But to us "speedibus kids," *Père* Moreau's Mass lasted beyond 30 minutes! He probed in confession and didn't like garbling; and even gave a whole decade of the rosary for penance. And asked if you were working to correct a transgression you confessed every month? He remembered. Knowing you might have him for Confession kept you "pure and holy in His sight," as the Bible says. But older curates Arthur Fournier *et* André Massicotte were somewhat frog-voiced (smokers?) and inaudible in the pulpit. That was okay with us, but annoying to my parents, who didn't want to miss a word. But their Masses were quicker and their movements faster and less stylish than *Père* Moreau, who, a tall French Canadian, cut a nice, imposing figure at the altar despite the heavy, stiff (Romanesque?) ornaments of the day. Also, the speedy duo never asked any questions in the confessional and only gave you three Hail Mary's for penance. We school children loved them.

About the length of Mass, a parishioner complained to a priest – perhaps Father Moreau? - his Mass went beyond 30 minutes. The perfect squelch? "My Masses aren't too long, it's your piety that's too short." Another chided a priest for being late for Mass one day. He retorted, "Oh, has Mass started?"

Pastors *Père* Ernest Morin and later *Père* Adrien Forest were administrators and not as visible as the curates. Mom kept *Père* Morin's obit card in her missal, entitled *Guide de la Jeune Fille* - "Guide for Young

Girls." *Père* Morin was born in Manville, RI (like Albion, even more French than Woonsocket at one time) in 1888, he was ordained in 1914 and became our pastor October, 1929. He died in August, 1941.

She mixed the prosaic with the divine when before marriage, she inserted an article in her missal about the astrology of Léopoldine. She must have glowed. It said, "She possesses a nice imagination (*belle imagination*), loves money (*aime l'argent*), and is ambitious (*ambitieuse*)." Marrying a millworker who was incredibly ethical, encyclopedic, multi-talented, industrious, but often out of work during the Depression and always poorly paid, mistakenly the astrologer predicted some good luck: *un bon succès*. Financially no, but in other respects, yes. So much for divination, instead of the divine! Apart from material wealth, their marriage of almost sixty years was a fulfilling, fruitful sacramental union, as we five siblings attest.

In the picture album, I loved seeing a handsome, happy couple departing for their honeymoon (*les noces*). The world like them was young and promising in 1923, but they were oblivious of the upcoming tragedies of the Depression and WWII. Better they didn't know they would struggle to raise a family in the world's greatest economic upheaval ever. As novelist Dickens said in part about the French Revolution, "It was the worst of times," and made more dire with little education between them, no money, no medical coverage, sluggish mill employment, and later only small handouts at the birth of a child in the 1930's. As in the English marriage vows version, had "for better" been erased?" Someone wrote that the eighth year of a marriage is a critical time: sameness? routine? trials? children? The Depression began near 1930, yes, close to the eighth year of their connubial bliss, but those problems were not of their own making.

So then came a ten-year sinkhole; what an English novelist called "a slough of despond," as in a deep pit. Even with today's government largess, would anyone have the fortitude to be stuck in the mud and mire of joblessness and want for ten years? Like in the French Revolution of 1790, if our economy lingers on in some degree, especially the great disparity of wealth between rich and poor, specifically about jobs, will governmental, banking, and retail "Bastilles" be stormed figuratively or actually at the gates by people looking for breadcrumbs? What doesn't look good now is that even the middle class (60 million more are now "poor," we recorded) as the cost of housing, food, education, energy, health care, and wars have become boiling points, all exacerbated by uncontrolled federal spending, corruption, and constant bickering between parties instead of action. I cited dad's prediction we would never catch up with rising prices with more pay.

But whenever my parents talked about the pastor, it was about his ability to run the parish: *"ce qu'il fa pour la parwaist"* (*paroisse*) (what he does for the parish). Besides lauding a devout pastor who spoke loud and clear, French Canadians in the mill trade, who knew how hard it was to stay afloat financially, liked *un bon administrateur* (a good administrator) who kept his little piece of St. Peter's bark (symbol of the church in a tempest-tossed world) on an even keel despite threatening swells and tides of economic ruin. God, what did the collection look like in the 1930's? Did 15 cents become just a nickel or pennies? Or nothing? One Sunday my folks looked at each other before heading off to church. Were there any coins in that old shaving mug in the cupboard, the same I once filched a nickel for my Saturday afternoon movie? Is that when "Give till it hurts" was born in our hood?

In fact, look at any majestic church like St. Ann's, Precious Blood, or St. Charles and wonder how a pastor could have coaxed enough money from millhands, rubber boot workers, tracklayers, and canal builders, small shopkeepers, and homemakers to erect such magnificent temples. I know money was worth more then, but there was so little of it. People scrounged to give because, as mom said, it was *"pour l'église (for the church)."* Historically, that's why constructions in Europe sometimes took 100 years or more, but generations got them built. They were building for the ages, never thinking future centuries of lesser faith or avaricious rulers like King Henry VIII and one king of France would close them. Friend Donald Pelletier, who taught in England while in the Brotherhood, wrote about the dissolution of a Catholic a nunnery like Sopwell, as all over England Henry VIII ingratiated himself with his friends with the gift of those Catholic lands and church vessels. Monks and nuns were reduced to begging. But Queen Mary, daughter of Henry and Catharine of Aragon tried, we said, to reclaim those illegal pilferings from the unwilling gentry, refuseniks, who remained Protestant after her father's death.

Did this happen at St. Ann's during its construction in the early 1900s? *Trois travailleurs* (three workers) were asked by a passerby about their work. "I'm doing my job," said one; "earning a living," said another; the third, "building a church." The latter obviously shared the vision of the faithful.

Unlike today's single collector, they often worked in pairs, one holding a coin exchange box. Never saw paper money. No envelopes. Oblivious of the great military line, "I shall not ask any quarter (terms from the enemy) nor give any," *les paroissiens* (the parishioners) gave a quarter and got a dime back! Now fewer and fewer use the weekly envelope because they are no-shows, creating a support burden for the devout.

About housekeeping, because we didn't buy a whole lot, we generated little trash, unlike Americans who now produce five pounds (a lot!) of trash a day! Consumerism and obsolescence weren't housemates until after the war. So, like in the universe I guess, matter - domestic goods in this case - rarely vanished, but turned into something. I spoke about siblings having a wardrobe (not forgetting skates, bikes, sports equipment) that was mostly hand-me-downs. Despite the usual sibling rivalry, we never entertained the fantasy of being an only child. But later I did read a Portland Maine family had 27 children; another, 31, in *Trois Rivieres* (Three Rivers, Province of Québec), reminding me that generally French-Canadian one-child families were as rare as "blue lobstahs in Roe Dyelin." (blue lobsters in Rhode Island).

Because of necessity and poverty, make-do French Canadians were recyclers. Between them, Mom was the conservator by a wide margin. Every now and then, with a fetish for order and cleanliness to keep *les germes (the germs)* away, Dad uncluttered a corner and threw things out. One day, the wooden icebox with metal hinges, the one in the rear hallway for his famed root beer and canning stuff that Bob said would command $150 after the war. He also removed those rich dark frames around family heirloom photos (nothing personal, he loved her family), her engagement portrait, even their wedding photo. Without frames, they took a beating, with *ma marraine* (my Godmother), *tante* Laurence almost split in two in the Fontaine family photo, now restored.

Curiously I saw the same dichotomy in the Order: pack rats and neat freaks. I guess *The Odd Couple* is a genetically universal phenomenon. I'm a saver like mom was. But some people, I've read, need psychological help to keep their surroundings clean, like adolescents and college kids until maturity and marriage. But with mom "the picker-upper," as most are, I wasn't good either until I joined the Order. In training, the weekly Chapter of Faults where you stood up and *confrères (*colleagues*)* zeroed in on your disregard of house rules changed me. The practice spawned some humor. The community guffawed in Mobile, AL when a Brother "accused" another of not having his orange juice for breakfast. Told by Brother Ignatius it wasn't an obligation, the accuser protested, "It would be good for him." Other things like putting a hand to your face (an affectation), climbing two stairs at a time (as I did even in a cassock), crossing your legs while sitting, and not holding the door as you entered chapel were all gotcha no-nos. The practice soon discontinued. Early recruits in 1821 were all "from the turnip truck," so their lives were heavily regimented. And after the French Revolution, people's manners were almost bestial, said a writer. But earlier, King Louis XIV (1638-1715) became so disgusted with the manners of his courtiers at banquets, he asked everyone to pick up a ticket at a meal and observe its recommendation, the origin of the word "et-i-quette."

About Sunday Mass and our faith, so imbued were we with *le Dimanche* (Sunday) as the Lord's Day, there were even afternoon devotions.

Though not obligatory, the Benediction of the Blessed Sacrament was strongly recommended by priests and parents. Special hymns, the wafting of incense, and the exposition of the Real Presence in the monstrance (like a sunburst) made the practice popular with the faithful. It's ironic that Sunday football is now called "America's electronic religion," with viewing *de rigueur* (required), like Sunday Mass "once was" for the faithful, the competing fare for us living in the Social District was again *le* Laurier's one o'clock movie if you didn't go Friday night or Saturday afternoon. Otherwise, before TV, it was a dull Sunday afternoon, if there wasn't a game at St. Ann's Park in the summer or skating at Cass Park in winter. But occasionally, *oncle* Henri Trottier *et tante* Laurence took us for a ride to see "how the other half lived." Remember when impatient drivers were somewhat spiteful of slow-going, sightseeing "Sunday drivers?" Guilty! Imagine, a car ride was a treat.

One family we knew allowed their kids to go to movies more than once a week. Penurious mom thought that was *"d'la luxure,* (a luxury)" above a millhand's salary. But their father was that nationwide mover. Dad, the practical economist who absolutely knew the price of everything, rarely begrudged us the cost of anything within the parameters of his pay. But mom often did. They had both known deprivation, but she had been penniless when her family was touched by fire before immigration. But she was tough on herself, causing some to whisper she could've used a little makeup! Was she a tightwad at times because he was too philanthropic (*généreux*)? Was he distancing himself from a comic's take of an egotist? "One who thinks more of himself than me?"

I wondered how anyone got to be like dad was. Did he possess a rare altruistic gene, or was it truly great virtue? I said in the Order we had a goal of moral perfection. But in my 25 years, I think I only saw one who by genetics or virtue had the altruism or charity to the degree Dad had. Of course, none of us with a vow of poverty had little to give of a material nature. But Brother Cyril, whom I replaced in guidance at the Academy, was similarly teased for his extraordinary goodness, equanimity, and charity. We called him *"le bon frère Cyril* (the good Brother Cyril)." The standing joke was God would rib him about being too good. His reply, "What about you, Lord?" He should've had the name of a Canadian Brother with a truly great handle: *Sauveur* (savior) *Labonté* (goodness).

About names, in my tenure at Norton High School, I had a girl named Diana Huntress, twice invoking the classical goddess of the hunt. If she married, I advised her not to give up her name! I got her a college scholarship but not for that reason. Also, as Assistant Director at Notre Dame HS, I marveled at a Ken Letellier with lightning speed as a halfback. The QB faked to John Lambert, a 250-pound fullback, and when the defense gunned for him, Letellier sped around the corner.

Recall mom said what dad didn't have, he wasn't going to get: "*Ça quia pa(s), y va pa avyerre.*" Realism 101 in a mill town. That line burned into my memory. Aren't most spousal conversations about kids and finances? Partition of household chores third as I discovered about the laws of marital tranquility. Dad was also truly exemplary in helping her at home, worried about her asthma and slight Fontaine frame. But with those good Fontaine-Morvan genes she lived to be a nonagenarian. But I didn't use that jawbreaker when she turned 90 and we feted her in a North Smithfield Rest Home, her great memory of family and people lost in a confusing web of present and past. She would have laughed at "dementia" or "Alzheimer's," words not brought into the house: "*des noms à coucher dehors.*" The best *tante* Laurence came up with was "*Alpima*" when I visited her at Chateau Clare. Unfortunately, the cure is proving to be as difficult. Amyloid deposits on the nerve endings of the brain! One out of five a victim the longer we live, the more "obscure" illnesses come to the fore. Didn't I say about cancer that an author said it was once little known because people died young? We now know cancer is not a single illness. So, no one magic bullet. Over 100 kinds, one article said, better identified and treated after genetic testing for the right medicine, like at Duke University. The environment a major cause? Fruits and veggies recommended, and not sitting down more than four hours a day to avoid obesity and other outcomes. We're now a sedentary nation.

I enlarge on it later, but I vouch parishioners of St. Ann always had a love affair with their church, a magnificent symbol of their transported faith from Canada and France. I also share the pride of all who worshiped there. Described as "a beautiful temple and a glory of the Catholic Church in all New England," the church was an outgrowth of the too small or too distant Precious Blood Church. Woonsocket's Franco population was doubling every 30 years, so St. Ann parish was formed in 1890. Construction of the church was begun at its present site in 1914 and blessed at its completion, August 11, 1918.

Until the church's construction (photos show workers plying their wheelbarrows in the depths of the foundation) and completion, parishioners used the first floor of St. Ann's School as a Sunday chapel. For almost a hundred years, the church's façade, columns, vast inner space, and famed twin steeples defined *le Coin Sochelle*. Its centennial was celebrated in 1990 with a book commemorating its long history of French-Canadian faith and family: *Towers of Faith and Family*. A lot of families like the Telliers, Fontaines, Peloquins, Frappiers, Carpentiers, Vandals, Turcottes, Carles, Houles, and others on or near Gaulin Avenue were like founding families of the parish, hence the demolition of our neighborhood caused its closure. Cousin Dr. Roger Fontaine took a photo of our eight-family tenement house the day before the headache ball crushed "a heap of livin'," as poet Sandburg said about what makes a house a home. In this instance it was "a heap of praying." So church, St. Ann's Park, auditorium, neighborhood, and school all vanished one by one into "Franco-Americana Land." Buildings like people "have no lasting dwelling here." When I visited London, they showed us the one remaining building from the Bard's Day, fire the ravager.

With its high vaulted ceiling, massive walls, large nave, huge stained-glass windows, and cavernous seating capacity, what an awesome feeling of loftiness and grandeur filled youngsters taken there by their mothers for the first time. The appellation "Sermon in Stone" for churches like St. Ann's was not simply a felicitous architectural or pious phrase. Because Catholics at one time were largely uneducated, the church's interior and exterior masonry, images, statues, paintings, altars, candles, and liturgical celebrations were visual concretization of divine and biblical events, sacred mysteries, Mary, the saints, angels, Major and Minor Prophets, and the triune God. As forcefully as the spoken word from the pulpit, but with the eloquence of art often surpassing speech, they all spoke to you from the dawn of creation history through the unfolding of the faith across the ages. If the real spoken word was at times lost in the church's vast inner space, the pageantry of the faith was always there, like a teacher fleshing out a mental concept. A *Bible* in marble and fresco, which *Merriam-Webster* defines as "the art of painting on freshly spread moist lime plaster with pigments suspended in a water vehicle." To which artist Nincheri, who popularized it in America, brushed on his own genius. What a masterpiece he brought to Woonsocket. Shouldn't there be a memorial statue of him even now?

Mom often spoke of the fierce attachment parishioners had for their church. Before moving to Bellingham in the 1950s, my family's life was within sight and shadow of St. Ann's, their faith anchor: *a l'ombre du clocher* (in the shadow of the steeple*)*. When restless dad thought of moving - *"le feu dans l'derrière"* (a fire in his back) - a hot brand where the sun doesn't shine, she whined. Moving to a new location would distance the family from Dad's work, school for the children but most of all the church. For us the realty mantra of location, location, location was thrice St. Ann's. We could only afford a cold-water apartment, yet magnificent, towering St. Ann's was our church next door, below Rome-like Palatine Hill of Gaulin. Hey, if possession is nine-tenths of the law, we really "owned" it since we were often there in those decades of the faith prior to the 1960s. The *Bible* shouts, "I shall dwell in the house of the Lord forever," a foretaste for us.

Always walking to school, marketing, visiting, the theater, or *The Call* deliveries, it was a rare day when we didn't pass by and doff our hat. It was like our Ark of the Covenant, its presence, radiance, and God's living space easily the biggest and most impressive structure in Social *Coin*.

Yes, like pious women (*"des femmes de pieté,"* said mom), even we kids sometimes dropped in during the week. Why I said a friend once rifled the poor box. Apart from Nincheri's artistic treasures, lighted candles for a quarter, and that poor box, Chaucer's expression of "poor as a church mouse" described his pickings, which I didn't touch. For my friend, was it like baby-faced Nelson who said he robbed banks "because that's where the money was?" Imagine, stealing when with a friend!

So fierce was that attachment, mom related people were ready to defy their bishop trying to wrest control of the parish, as it were, from Franco-blooded priests. What aggravated the problem, said dad, was the episcopacy was rarely if ever French-Canadian, a divisive element for those first fiercely chauvinists (from a Napoléon diehard, Nicholas Chauvin) *citoyens* (citizens) from Canada. When I asked him why that was (that is, lack of Francos at the episcopate level), he reiterated our people didn't care (or couldn't) about education like other immigrants. Chartier wrote the Irish episcopacy felt the time for national churches should come to an end in favor of territorial churches "with the King's English." Recall some parents even complained when catechism in school was no longer in French. A difficult transitional period, because eventually not all priests knew French, like Latin later in the liturgy. Americans, unlike Europeans, became monolingual.

I speak about it in other parts of the book, but *les paroissiens* (the parishioners) showed their *survivance* doggedness in 1914 when Révérend Napoléon Leclerc, founding pastor, died, and Bishop Matthew Harkins called the Marists in. They spoke French, but *sacré bleu (*dam it*)*, they were Belgian priests, not close enough, and adding insult to injury, in Maine some favored assimilation into the American culture. Only here in 1916, someone told her a Vigilance Committee, headed by future *Sentinelliste* prime mover Elphège Daignault, blocked the rectory entrance to *Père* Raymond Plasmans and four assistants. Akin to "Katie, Bar the Door," the purists hired watchmen to convince the Marists "they were being cast into the darkness." When it came to the faith, they tolerated no miscegenation or mélange in their clergy. Faith was French, French, Faith. How different the picture today: 17 percent of the nation's 18,000 parishes have no priest and 44 percent share a priest; 27 or more of these parishes are in RI. Given its size, were they unwise even then to refuse five priests? Did a frustrated Fr. Plasmans think of Christ's advice to His disciples "about shaking the dust from their feet if not welcomed?" The whole scene presaged a greater cataclysm in the 1920s. But also earlier, when Fall River and Notre Dame de Lourdes parish were part of the RI diocese under Bishop Hendricken, parishioners in 1874 also refused two French-speaking pastors. One was of Irish ancestry; the other, half-French, half-Irish. A cultural mix that shouldn't vivify the parish corpus, they thought.

A mediating Governor Aram Pothier helped convince "the usurpers" the faithful would never give them the time of day (aka pew money) or *la bienvenue (*welcome*)*. The bishop licked his wounds and backed off, appointing *Père* Camille Villiard second pastor. He was still there when Mom started her love affair with all things Francocentric in the city, secular or divine. About this clerical tug-of-war, out came a frequent comment: *"on voula du monde comme nous autres" (*wanting people like us). Or *prie Dieu* (pray God) like that film title, *Children of a Lesser God.* In their extreme nativism, did they sometimes forget the first mark of our church, its Oneness? Or the Pentecost story when the assembled spoke in so many tongues, but understood each other? Did Francos unknowingly reflect a growth of extreme nationalism in the late 19th Century and early 20th Century, which Edmund Morris in *Colonel Roosevelt* said that Theodore, Spanish-American War hero, feared? He wanted to establish a kind of United Nations, as did Wilson later, but one with some military might to address problems. President Taft and later the Senate, controlled by MA Senator Henry Cabot Lodge, opposed. In his book, Morris mentions Joseph Bucklin Bishop, Roosevelt's journalist confidant and great granduncle of Chip Bishop, formerly of the city, who spoke at the Museum about his beautifully written and meticulously researched book, *The Lion and the Journalist.* His kin greatly helped inform readers and Washington about the need for the Panama Canal after the French failed for lack of machinery, funds, and control of disease-causing mosquitoes, which Americans greatly abated by eliminating all standing water! Even today we gardeners are advised about not leaving standing water. Today I have pellets to kill the pests, ticks included.

To whom is "the greater sin": the fierce attachment to their French-Canadian kind of church, or the indifference of so many today for any formalized religion? Entering the Order, I was shocked at God's words, "If you're tepid (as in lukewarm about your faith), I will vomit on you." Ugh! Savingly, the parishioners were obstinate and defiant, but not lukewarm. More like overheated! Like Christ who threw out moneychangers from the Temple, St. Ann parishioners were ready to cast out anyone not French Canadian. What an irony some 75 years later, when their sons and daughters, some through laxity, loss of faith, and indifference, have undermined the walls of their church, the same one their parents or grandparents "defended" fiercely at one time. "We have met the enemy, and they are us?"

Imagine, *survivance* (survival) zealots actually wanted Rome to appoint their own French-Canadian priests (and bishop?) in RI. And in the 1870s, ultranationalists at Precious Blood had clearly set this example of ecclesiastical defiance, if not total inclusiveness. Bishop Hendricken assigned a French-speaking priest - another Belgian, Rev. James Berkins - to run the parish after *curé* (priest) Antoine Bernard realized the founding and building task too burdensome. With *un nom angla* (an English name), he didn't stand a chance! But in reading friend Bob Lafrenaye's copy of the parish centennial book, I'm reminded how the non-ethnically minded Irish of St. Charles Parish welcomed Franco parishioners during construction of their churches.

About two dioceses, can you imagine two parallel ones built on fault lines over shifting and colliding ethnically tectonic plates? For sure, a holy war (they're the bloodiest, historians say) of words and mistrust might have erupted. So back to Berkins, the faithful organized a pew strike in protest, like St. Ann's did later, until the bishop sent Canadian-born priest Charles Dauray by way of Central Falls (*Saintrell in patois*)

We repeat, the mother of all breakups happened from 1924-1928 when parishioners didn't take too kindly to the bishop taking money out of the parish to establish English-speaking schools where English, not French, would be prime. The donnybrook gave rise to the worst canonical rift ever between parishioners of Franco descent and the Irish bishop Hickey of the Diocese of Providence, named the Sentinelle Affair. Some were even excommunicated, that is, *ex cathedra* or out of the pale of the church, like "shunning" for the Amish. An historian speaking about the movement at the Woonsocket Work and Culture Museum said St. Ann's was the seedbed of defiance. Mom and dad's countrymen had brought everything here from Québec except the farm (*la terre*) itself! And their faith and language (especially in church and schools) were, mom said, like two drops of water: *"deux gouttes d'eau."* But defying the episcopacy, well, that was like moving the Rock of St. Peter, the Church itself. And Christ said even the gates of hell couldn't do that! The speaker said the bishop should've been less adamant.

Musing about this cultural dimension of their beliefs, if St. Ann's twin towers of faith and family had been built in triune form, would the third architectural "finger of God" have symbolized French? If they were the first European mainland people to convert en masse to Christianity, shouldn't "the firstest get the mostest?" And hadn't the papacy one time resided in France (Avignon: 1378-1417) until Doctor of the Church St. Catherine of Siena convinced Pope Gregory XI to return to Rome?

Does it lessen their culpability if we keep in mind these first-come French Canadians had a common origin, limited education, farming or mill working, narrow fortunes, simple faith, and lack of mobility, thus making them all carbon copies of themselves, which stifled a more outgoing spirit of accommodation? Since I've read we're all descended from the three sons of Noah: Sem, Cham, and Japheth, should we be grateful he wasn't more fruitful? Their descendants are the three major racial stocks!

The Cult of the Living Dead

LEON URIS' BOOK *Trinity* is about Irish life in the 19th Century, but I didn't agree with his satiric perception of the value of suffering. Like Karl Marx labeling religion "the opium of the people," Uris pokes fun at the persecuted peasants, belittling them for their belief in saints and the Blessed Mother, who they think will someday help them obtain the peace and joy their present life lacks. But contrarily, it was enlightened wisdom on their part, since, as Paul Johnson says in *The Renaissance*, "The general effect of the Last Judgment is to make most people think seriously about what is likely to happen to them when they die," adding "it's also why some don't want to think about it." Like the Poles, Spanish, Irish, Germans, Austrians, French and others, we can't overemphasize that Francos had at the very root of their belief system the Gentile Apostle's conviction that Christ's and their own resurrection was the central mystery of their faith. St. Paul affirmed, "If the dead do not rise, then vain is my preaching and vain too is your faith." With no risen Christ, suffering, duty, morality had no meaning. English poet John Donne of the 16th and 17th Century had no doubt about the afterlife and the obliteration of death itself: "Death be not proud // For those whom thou think'st thou dost overthrow / Die not, poor Death, nor yet canst thou kill me // One short sleep past, we wake eternally, / And Death shall be no more; Death, thou shalt die." Strong and convincing words from "a man about town."

Like in the history of Greeks and Egyptians, this afterlife inspired a lot of what they did in life and afterlife. It established in their mind that life was not a lasting abode, but a journey like John Bunyan's *The Pilgrim's Progress* of the 17th Century. And that Christ, besides being the Truth and the Life, was also the Way. Unlike Robert Frost's poem, theirs was not the road not taken. There was only one road to heaven, and you had better be on it. Or, if lucky or blessed, at the end forgiven like the Good Thief at the Crucifixion.

Our very first precepts of morality learned at our mother's or grandmother's knee, like purity of body and soul; respecting other people's property, reputation, and person; obedience to lawful authority; belief in God, respect for His name; and observance of His day, abhorring violence, and other faith observances were all anchored in the belief that good and bad works were recorded on a "heavenly ledger." So, you couldn't be found lacking good works, like the Gospel's unwise administrator who buried his one talent.

The Church had long reaffirmed this linkage between faith and good works since Reformation times, when some reformers erroneously thought belief alone in Christ or His grace was sufficient. It's a theological gap rooted in a differing interpretation of the Scriptures. But Pope John Paul and Lutheran leaders announced a rapprochement in resolving the five-century misunderstanding on the subject. The result, as Catholics have always thought, man must cooperate with God's salvific graces. Call it the reaffirmation of St. James, "Faith without good works is dead." *"S'faire aller"* (get going) mom called it. Mom knew Luther had 'dissed' Indulgences, "the remission through good works or prayer of part or all the temporal (purgatorial) punishment due for sins," this after the elimination of eternal punishment for serious failures, if any, through the Sacrament of Confession." Franco women like her were so profoundly devout. Küng in *The Church* speaks of individuals like them whom the Spirit gives a charism, character or calling to spread the faith with no title. Aren't they all around us?

It seemed there was never a day in school, church, and home when you didn't hear about indulgences for prayers and pious or charitable acts. In school we kept a scorecard, *un trésor spirituel* (a spiritual treasure), of our good works for the beatification of Presentation of Mary (PM) foundress Anne-Marie Rivier. In the Middle Ages indulgences for forgiveness of sins were greatly sought by the faithful for almsgiving, pilgrimages, and the Crusades to liberate Jerusalem. Their popularity, however, gave rise to venality and corruption when they were "sold" rather than earned. Even for the building of St. Peter's in Rome! The Council of Trent (1545-1563) corrected abuses.

Recall that because mom thought her pious family *"du bon monde"* (good people), she wondered why *les* Fontaines were so sorely tried. But a prof of mine could've told her, unlike a 16th Century breakaway heretic, success and prosperity weren't necessarily signs of God's kindly favor, nor of His disfavor when tragedy struck! A graphic example of course is the blind man in the New Testament, whom Christ healed, while admonishing those who wondered if his or his parents' sins caused his malediction.

In a strange contradiction only faith can explain, like the Irish mom believed in heaven the more she and her people suffered and were deprived. Believing obviously that adversity is good for the soul, their faith was therapy ("terrapee" in her mouth) against depression in the face of searing loss and want. She didn't know chapter and verse, but in her own way she knew about St. Paul's advice that God doesn't allow more than one can bear: "My grace is sufficient for you; for strength is made perfect in weakness." I loved it in her patois: *"Le bon Dieu nous envyeye (envoie: send) pas plus qu'onta capable."*

As you grew up and went to school, it was important in this effort to avoid hell and go to heaven, to learn the difference between mortal and venial sin. Teachers taught you a lot about the former, because if you died with a conscience so burdened, it could strip you of your eternal reward. For something to be "mortal," the act or matter was serious, like murder - you knew it and you still did it. A capital offense in civil law! It was so often repeated, you thought it was easy to transgress mightily. Now, with a modern-day morality in which the notion of sin has all but disappeared, at least outside the pale of religion, and replaced by so-called uncontrollable psychological urges, social tolerances ("everyone does it") and genetic weaknesses or predispositions ("I'm only human, you know"), is mortal sin passé? Didn't John XXIII say the greatest sin of our times is no sense of sin at all?

On the other hand, venial or minor sins, if not atoned for on earth, only diminished your reward and delayed your celestial entry at death until the cleansing fires of Purgatory had done their job. If in Christian art, Heaven was thought imaginatively to be above and Hell below (artistically, see the dome above St. Ann's nave), Purgatory was said by some, but without theological foundation, to be between Heaven and Earth (Middle Earth?). Why, a teacher of mine even said some theologians thought in death "you cooled your heels" where you had mildly transgressed on earth. My wife Pat, a theology major, also heard that. Regardless, citing Old Testament passages about even "the good deed" of gold being purified from dross or impurities, the good nuns said those fires were painful, but not as lasting as hell's, said close to 20 times in the *Bible*. Some have difficulty reconciling a merciful God with eternal damnation. But even human justice has capital punishment or a lifetime sentence. Some saints had visions of people going to Hell, especially for moral turpitude, which the Fatima children attested to. But I read the feasts of Mary's Assumption and Christmas are days when many souls are released. And that we should never stop praying for the deliverance of loved ones not yet purified. Again, the drama of salvation is so grand, yet some dismiss it as fiction.

But isn't it John Paul II who said hell after death is really the absence of God and His love, a worse affliction than fire? In Maccabees in the Old Testament, there is a strong encouragement not to forget the departed, "It is a holy and a wholesome thought to pray for the dead that they may be loosed from their sins." The Church Councils of Florence and Trent formulated the doctrine of faith about Purgatory. Despite indulgences, most souls spend some time there. My parish laments that fewer Masses being requested by families for their departed reveals a lack of connection with the hereafter?

Canonized saints with or without Purgatory are thought to have made it to heaven and act as intercessors for favors needed. Thinking speed (*"la vitesse"*) was crucial, mom believed a decedent's (*"un disparu"*) first favor from heaven was yours if you were first to pray for that soul's blessedness. I liked when she theologized. Because of what she said, I've always prayed to and for a deceased, like I did for my wife Pat who died in 2000 and Paul Mongeon who died 2013 and many others. (Brother) Paul, a devout person who often prayed the rosary with others, was my traveling companion to Norton High School for 18 years. For Catholics, the feast of All Souls, November 2, is like a spiritual Memorial Day! Many visit cemeteries that day.

In the Order, our formation master in Harrisville, Rhode Island, asked us to visit the Province's cemetery (my novice class of 1949, helped build it) at morning break. Like the faithful for their departed, the Order celebrated numerous Masses for deceased confrères. Brothers who had positions of leadership had more Masses said. But one wit said that was because anybody who had been in charge of others (parents too?) needed more Masses to get past St. Peter at the gates! Even St. Theresa of Avila, doctor of the church, said that too because of their increased responsibility. In authority or not, it was quite a challenge to live monastically where the goal was perfection. Before church renewal, I thought our life was somewhat strict for an active, teaching Order (as opposed to a praying, contemplative life like the Trappists), until I read that St. Columba, 600 A.D., ordered six lashes for a monk who didn't say "Amen"; ten if he notched a table with his knife; and six if he sang out of tune. Considered a pre-Columbian discoverer of America, did monks hope he didn't come back? But before church renewal, our Rule book also said we too couldn't have a knife. St. Columba's trenchant influence!?

A wit said there were three kinds of monks or religious: the Confessors who knew all the rules and didn't let you forget; the Saints, who obeyed them all; and, finally, the Martyrs, the rest of us, who lived with those two groups! No wonder someone said religious life was a slow burn or daily martyrdom: *"un martyre à gros grain"* or *"le dur quotidien."* The daily grind which also recalls the great line, "Our lives are ones of quiet desperation." Very wisely, St. Augustin felt this unrest we have is a kind of hidden yearning for God Himself, the full satisfaction of all our aspirations. A professor offered that as another "proof" of God's existence, more satisfying than the cold, rational First Cause (or Uncaused Cause) about someone (God) having to be there with no beginning. In Latin, it's *nihil ex nihilno* about "nothing coming from nothing." Another prof quoted God's word to Moses at the burning bush. Asked who He was, God said, "I am that I am," so since existence cannot but exist, it revealed His eternal nature. But the prof said God didn't speak "grammatically" since it should've been "who is," which, however, is not as existential as "am." Finally, about religious life, I also liked the monk who advised us to put all our disappointments at the foot of the cross: *"Il faut mettre ça au pied de la croix."* A confrère (colleague) told him there would be quite a load there.

This notion of sin, part of the overall formation of one's conscience, may seem psychologically depressing by today's freethinking standards. But actually, the typical, jovial, fun-loving Franco developed very few scruples or moral dilemmas because of it. Unlike the Old Testament, the overall emphasis of the New Testament was love and forgiveness. But in explaining to us in catechism class why seven of our Ten Commandments said, "Don't," *Soeur Sainte* Émilie told us that was about right for our human nature undermined by Original Sin. In other words, *notre* (our) nature was, if you will, three parts good and seven parts in need of control in the aftermath of Adam and Eve's fall.

I noted *ma Soeur* (my Sister) said Francos always stressed God's goodness as in *le bon Dieu*. English-speaking people see His power as in "Almighty God"; so, another point for us of the Gallo-Canadian heritage. With the way she touted our culture and faith, you didn't feel like a depressed or picked-upon member of a minority group. That only happened on scouting trips or at the Academy: "Hey, you're French, aren't you?" It did sound like we had some communicable disease! Why didn't we have a good comeback line like the sons of Erin?: "Yes, I'm Irish, and proud of it."

As Uris says of the Irish, sins of the flesh, so Francos thought, were considered most serious, along with us not attending Mass on Sunday, and mistakenly eating meat on Friday. But at that time, there was not the Vatican Renewal emphasis that sins of the flesh pale in comparison with failings against racial, social, and economic justice. That is, victims like *"les outriders,"* as mom called them, who never really got a decent wage at the mill, a paid vacation, sickness and unemployment benefits, or even healthy working conditions until late in the 19th Century or later. Even long after the start of the Industrial Revolution, everything was stacked against the Bible's admonition "that the laborer is worthy of his hire." Yes, emerging nations are now going through the same inhuman cycle. Great wealth for the few; poverty for the masses. One economist said it means inexpensive clothing for us in the West, but at what price for those workers who, like dad as a young worker, never saw the sun coming up or going down.

We said our priests at one time spoke mostly to immigrants or first-generation Catholics with rudimentary grasp of the faith, so Sunday sermons often had an inkling of the "fire and brimstone," or hellish fear. But nowhere near the unabashed horror of a preacher like Colonial American theologian Jonathan Edwards (1703-1758) with his pulpit blaster: "Sinners in the Hands of an Angry God." If you think a warning from a priest or traffic cop is a moral deterrent, read that sermon in American Literature when you feel "the spirit is willing, but the flesh is weak." The puritanical preacher has people hanging by a thread over the yawning abyss of hell. Like medicine, it was an age when anything to be good had to be painful. No Julie Andrews in sight with "A spoonful of sugar makes the medicine go down".

The closest we ever got to that kind of pulpit blast occurred when visiting priests - Oblates, Dominicans, Franciscans, Redemptorists - gave parish retreats. They were Lenten weeklong exercises of powerful sermons and moral spring cleaning, like Christ's invitation to the Apostles "to come and rest awhile." That is, to fall back and regroup morally after a time of activity, apostolic or otherwise, like the yearly retreat while in the Order, once 30-days long! A benevolent director in Andover gave us a break after 20 days with a swim at Plum Island, MA, where one young beachy lass, sensing bachelors *en masse*, asked us who we were. Couldn't figure us out since we weren't priests, married, or bachelors per se!) When I taught Latin, I discovered that Cicero in one of his Orations in the Roman Senate gave the same advice: back off and regroup. Called a sabbatical today, like Michael Jordan took in his playing days.

Men and women, young and old, single and married, all were encouraged to attend the evening retreat during their special week. No matter if dad was weary after a day at the mill or mom from domestic chores, they never missed. During their week, each said, "*J'va faire ma r'traite (I'm going to retreat)*." Clever! It wasn't only to tell us where each was going and reachable (not by phone!), but a reminder when done with school we would have our own week. In her prayer book, I found two retreat mementoes: *Souvenir de la Mission* (Remembrance of the Mission). One, by the Redemptorists during the pastorate of *le curé* (the priest) Villiard in 1924, with advice from the founder, St. Alphonse (the name I chose in the Order to honor dad): "*Priez le matin et le soir, avant et après vos travaux, vos repas. Celui qui prie se sauve. Celui qui ne prie pas se damne*" (Pray always, day and night, before and after work and at meals to be saved).

The saintly bilocator was, yes, seen in two places at once at times. Wouldn't mothers like a celestial dispensation from the laws of physics like that? Her other holy card strengthened the conviction central to her people's faith: the greatest tragedy was to lose your soul and not go to heaven. It reads (from Matthew actually): "*Que sert à l'homme de gagner le monde entier, s'il a le malheur de perdre son âme?*" ("What is the use of man gaining the whole world, if he has the misfortune to lose his soul?")

Recall Dives, a rich man in the Gospel, who omitted Christian charity to beggars and found himself in Gehenna or hell after death. He pleaded for a second chance, but Francos could've told him you were past match point when you died. Mom's version of the situation was "*Quand c'est fini, c'est fini* (When it's over, it's over)" in impeccable French. So, like him, if on earth you didn't listen to your faith givers, even a message "from the Twilight Zone" wouldn't reach your cell!

I also found a dried boutonnière (flower placed in a buttonhole, usually on the lapel) in her book. I pictured her when she was young, glowing, and scented like the bloom. As poet Keats said about a maiden, "A thing of beauty is a joy forever." Like in the "Ode to a Grecian Urn," the little flower gained some immortality by morphing itself (as the running maiden did on the enduring vase) into a more lasting keepsake in a young maiden's book. How art can be at times more enduring than life itself, as Nincheri knew! Mom didn't know the line of Hippocrates and Seneca about *Ars longa, sed vita brevis* (Life is short, but art enduring), but she made it happen, as we all do, when we store things away from the wear and tear of life.

Those visiting priests were expert preachers with booming voices heard anywhere in church and "speaking with authority," as Christ told His disciples, they thundered and fulminated against the abominations of the flesh especially. Little wonder most of us got the impression that sexual purity of body and mind (6th and 9th Commandments) was most imperative and their violation serious. After all, we did worship God, at least on Sunday (1st Commandment); didn't swear or curse grievously (2nd); never missed Sunday Mass (3rd); didn't disobey our parents seriously (4th); didn't kill, "despite having siblings!" (5th); didn't steal big (just fruits and ice from peddlers and empty Coke bottles to finance a movie); didn't covet the neighbor's property or mate (7th and 10th); or hurt anyone's reputation with truth or lies (8th). So, I guess that left the 6th and the 9th. The confessional was jammed in those days. Like checkout lines at the market, you often had to wait in line "to fess up."

Recall in defense of our lower nature, a prof said we're the only creation made up of flesh and spirit, two diametrical forces always warring against each other, as St. Paul lamented, and Franklin and Saint Francis de Sales too, as I saw in a painting in a rectory. Overall, original sin caused the triple rebellions rising from it in us between our higher and lower nature, nature itself, and God. For one, recall Adam and Eve quickly became uncomfortable with their unadorned state. Yes, schooled heavily as we were into religion by nuns, Brothers, and priests, man's original sin (*le péché originel*) has always intrigued me how so much evil and misery entered the world because of our first parents. Naturally they're not popular with afflicted mankind. But one mystic nun saw a depressed Adam in a vision. How blissful life would've been without that primal fall! But would any of us have done any better, one wrote? And without the Redemption, would we have been elevated anyway to the supernatural life we now have, a prof wondered? In Holy Saturday services, the primal fall is called *felix culpa*, a happy fault, because of that redemption and elevation to God's own life. How can anyone call any of it menial or humdrum, when we're all central figures in that drama? Again, doubters should heed President Reagan's caution: If you doubt, err on the side of caution. Because as mom said, *"Quand cée fini, cée fini.* (When it's over, it's over.)"

One is almost tempted to be surprised by this extreme negativity and pessimism about this special failing in our times. Yet, when you look at the prevalence of AIDS, venereal disease, rape, abortion as a casual means of birth control, murder, euthanasia, the assault on the nature of marriage, no wonder we again need to hear the message. Supposedly, no less the wisest man ever, Solomon said only with God's grace can we combat and win against what that prof said was one of those three rebellions from Original Sin and against our "better angels," as Lincoln said. But Solomon wasn't good all his life, so doubts about his salvation.

Because it was almost forbidden knowledge, how we struggled in lower grades to understand words like *adultère, impudique* and *luxurye* *(*adultery indecent and lust*)*. Those words with their immoral import cropped up in our recitation of catechism and Ten Commandments. Their meaning of immorality, adultery, or fornication was quickly skipped over by our modest teachers. You were told the shame you would feel if you did whatever it meant to do those things! Was it St. Paul's "Let evil not even be mentioned among you?" It was easier to do in those days without TV, salacious literature, electronic devices with their perversion potential, X-rated movies, and scandal rags! But most movies at one time, said a critic, left you with a good feeling and a better sense of humanity, like *Going My Way, The Fighting Sullivans, How Green Was My Valley, et al.*

It was a time obviously when innocence, not knowledge, was bliss. So, the nuns in their teaching kept a respectful line. In her patois, mom rendered what Paul meant above, *"On é (est) mieux d'sen passé,"* meaning we were better off without some knowledge, a thought prevalent in the Middle Ages. In our Order, Brother Bartholome also advised us to steer clear of allurements or foolishness: *"On s'en passe avec advantage."* (It's to our advantage to let it go.)

But because retreat masters also spoke to adolescent boys and girls apart during their given week, you finally understood what transgressing the 6th and 9th Commandments entailed. A friend told me I'd learn more in a week "about those things" than in my whole life. Like Adam, we always wanted to know about the tree of good and evil, but unlike him we didn't bite the apple! Precocious in this matter, he's the same kid who shocked me one day, when over the Kendrick Street Bridge, he showed me a condom (it had a different name then) in his wallet. Remember, this was in the 1940's when I was a strait-laced kid.

Forwarding for a moment to the 1960s, after I became a counselor at Notre Dame Prep School in Fitchburg, MA, my first case was advising a student store clerk who thought it was immoral for him to sell condoms. A good kid obviously - later a priest and a school administrator in a nearby diocese - I told him to let the boss make the sale. But as a cartoon joked about it, today it's more "sinful" to sell cigarettes to minors! The latter negated one of the first "English maxims" I learned from a boarder at the Academy: "A friend with weed is a friend indeed," when it was just nicotine. The dare at the Academy was not about smoking in the lavatory (once a major curse in high schools), but during the backyard recess with mountainous *Frère* Elisée doing guard duty. If he grabbed you with his bear-claw hands, it was like the Jaws of Life, squeezing the nicotine out of violators. As literary adviser to our *All-American Notre Dame Prep Life* paper, I "anonymously" submitted an article about the ill effects of smoking, with the byline of "Nick O'Tine, 62," but no one asked who the 'the kid' was.

About timing and repentance, Augustin's mother Monica prayed 24 years for his conversion. Certainly, the patroness of mothers with sons, wayward or not! The future bishop kept saying, "Yes, I want to, but not yet?" Our prof made us read his Confessions. His mother was Catholic, his father, not. So, they delayed his Baptism, his choice when older, like the thinking of the 16th Century Anabaptists, said a teacher. But he theorized he missed a new birth in Christ to help him grow with the grace of God to resist temptation. Good, or even lax Catholic parents want baptism for their children, but sometimes a prohibition.

We truly lived in an age of faith, and we were fortunate to be spared a kind of secularism for two or three generations, unlike today's immigrants and their children who have no national churches and ethnic schools. But about those deathbed conversions, mom told me it was unwise to call it that close: *"Il faut faire sartain" (certain) et pa(s) attendre (not wait) à dernière minute"* (Do it now and not at the last minute). "Maxims by Léopoldine," if published, would've been required reading in religion or CCD classes. Mom, a domestic CCD teacher!

About food and nutrition in and out of the Depression, our *Father Knows Best*[37] had us play a game I liked. Often when home from the market, he asked how much a bag of foodstuff weighed. Out came the scale we kept

---

[37] A popular 1950's TV sitcom that centered around an idealized family with a sage-like father.

in the back hallway to see who won. Did Dad want us to be curious like him, or just a good parent: teaching, advising, inspiring? Was his intellectual curiosity genetic? Or did the little schooling he received awaken a curiosity never to be dulled his whole life, not even by the roar or monotonous clickety-clack of the mules at the mill? Like many who fondly recall the influence of one mentor, was it an inspiring teacher, as a sticker on a rear bumper said, "If you can read this, thank a teacher." Incidentally, about our teachers at St. Ann's, unlike mom, Dad only spoke about *Soeur Sainte* Apolline, a redoubtable third grade teacher of arithmetic with zero tolerance for error. A bit of humor, true or fictional to share: A student did a long arithmetic problem, only to get zero as an answer. "Gee, all that work for nothing!" he sighed.

Death Ushers in New Life

LIKE FOR THE IRISH, Franco wakes and funerals were like domestic dramas, if not as dramatic. But despite the hope of the resurrection if a death was in the faith, funerals were somewhat somber. For people of means, our church was draped with black or purplish banners: *Aujourd'hui, c'est mon tour, demain le vôtre*: today my turn; tomorrow yours. Priests wore somber vestments, not white like today where the decedent's new life in the hereafter is emphasized.

An epistle tells us we shouldn't weep or despair over the death of a beloved, as if there is no hope or afterlife. "Life is changed, but not ended, and when the body of our earthly dwelling lies in death, we gain an everlasting dwelling place in heaven." And at the end of the service: "May the angels lead you into paradise," as the final hymn echoes amid sobs and tears. We sang it in Latin in the Order: "*Deducant te Angeli*", as I again heard it the last day of 2011 at the funeral of Madeleine (Carle) Ethier, my sister Sue's friend.

When the New England. Province had over 300 Brothers and some 40 sang a funeral Mass (either Gregorian or Pietro Yon's more modern version) for a departed confrère, it was so moving, you 'kinda' wished you were the one the angels had come for! Can you believe I lamented forsaking that future sendoff when I laicized! Now living not far from the Motherhouse in Harrisville, I attend many funerals of Brothers I trained, lived, and taught with. Even if fewer in numbers, the liturgy and music are, if more subdued, no less devotional and soulful, especially with the traditional hymn of the Order: "*Animé de l'amour dont on s'aime entre frère*": Infused with love for our Brothers. It's sung in chapel or at the Province's cemetery. Cousin Frank of Mount Saint Charles and Shawn McAneny and Willie Morin of the Motherhouse also lead the Brothers and guests.

Besides the immediate family, relatives, and friends at funerals, pious women were always in attendance, causing mom to say, *"Cée (C'est) des femmes de dévotion."* A biblical tradition of sorts, as I discovered later when I taught novices (aspirants) the New Testament, pious women ministered to Christ when alive and dead or found wailing at wakes, some in a professional capacity. One time Christ told some crying women the daughter of Jairus, whom they thought dead, was not moribund to His merciful intervention. He would do what he did for his friend Lazarus. Brother Clarence (Gerry Proulx) and I loved to repeat the phrase said when He raised her: *"Talitha cumi" (or koom)*: Young girl, arise". I've long lost that little thumbnail Latin Bible, my first reading ever of the sacred book, no bigger than my First Communion missal. It came from discarded books from Merrimack College, North Andover, MA, when I was librarian at Notre Dame HS. One of my student helpers, Paul Loiselle, was such a bibliophile, if I asked him to move a book from one shelf to another, he began reading it. Got a PhD at USC (University of Southern California). The school found him so incredibly brilliant and well-read, they asked if I had others like him. He went into the Peace Corps. Also at Notre Dame, Brother Harold Greer was also my devoted librarian aide. He went on to teach religion at Mount where he taught my son Jim. He celebrated his 50 years of religious life in 2014. He not only embraced the faith, I said, but also became one of my recruits (went to Zambia in 2015); along with the Marcotte brothers: Roger (laicized) and Robert. Notre Dame in Fitchburg MA was a very fertile ground for priestly and religious vocations. The *Fitchburg Sentinel* once highlighted my record of recommending 100 percent of the seniors to college, like the famed Boston Latin High School. Eight one year in highly selective Holy Cross. And eight from the class of 1960 became lawyers, all were in Brother Casavant's outstanding debate society. Notre Dame HS is, unfortunately, now closed.

Gospel miracles fascinate and make me wonder which ones I wish I'd been there for! Because of the finality of death, the restoration to life of Mary and Martha's brother Lazarus is the one. The wonder or commotion must've been unbelievable: *magnalia* (great works) says the New Testament. Peter walking on water until his lack of faith brought Newton's "suspended law of gravity" back into play is a close second. In a lighter vein about miracles - for which I was once admonished for my lack of gravity in training - I mused with Fr. Paul Grenon, former Our Lady Queen of Martyrs' pastor, after he spoke about the Transfiguration of Christ on Mt. Tabor. I told him Christ dismissed TV to all when He told the three disciples as they came down the mountain: "Tell-the-vision to no one." Another was Christ inventing baseball when He asked the one returning, healed leper, "Where are the other nine?" Humor in religious life. "God loves the cheerful giver," St. Paul wrote.

Returning to our funeral discussion, the bereaved family and relatives were all dressed in black or somber colors: "*des habits d'enterrement*," (funeral clothes), mom said. Like the hearse, cars too were nearly always black. When dad bought a dark suit in his old age, he reminded us it would be his burial suit. A grieving wife wore her "widow's weeds" for a year; a widower, a cloth symbol or other on the lapel of his conservative suit, like President Wilson did. The bereaved was largely incommunicado to any kind of festive gathering, no matter how innocent. Of a widower mom said, "*Yé tan deuille pour sa femme* (he's in mourning for his wife)".

She told me once about a family flap when to remarry. In hushed tones, she described the flap among the Tellier clan when our widowed uncle, Ernest Villeneuve, didn't wait a whole year to remarry. Like courting before marriage, a kind of French-Canadian unwritten rule. With her predilection for underdogs, she said, "*Ya souffert avec sa première femme*," that is, he endured much with his long, ailing wife, Marie Rose (Tellier), who had the family's bronchiectasis curse worse. Dad even showed me her autopsy report from the Zambarano facility, the only one I've seen. He understood full well what the medical examiner wrote. Because mom, dad, or others in the Tellier or Fontaine families had some kind of lung problem, they were sympathetic about respiratory diseases. Mom had asthma, which was not greatly debilitating but sometimes caused labored breathing. One time Mom doubled over, rasping and looking for her next breath. Because Bob and Sue were out, she asked me to pound her back. I was more scared than she was. Another time, I heard her whine to *tante* Laurence: "*J'ai d'la misère avec mon respire* (I have trouble with my breathing)". She blamed the damp New England climate.

Later I ran across a saying about a healthy respiratory system the secret to a long life: "*Une bonne haleine (breath) est le secret d'une longue vie.*" Sadly, aren't people of lower means more subject to respiratory diseases: crowded living conditions, pollution, little medical care, less protection against the vagaries of heat and cold, poor nutrition, unhealthy working conditions and unhealthy personal habits? But about infirmity and mortality, her pearl of wisdom was if you had a disease and took care of it, it would take care of you. As it is, she lived to be 90, he, 86, despite their lung problems, a misfortune all five of us escaped. This, largely through their prudence, his medical books, homemade cough syrup, *mémère's* woolens, new antibiotics, and common sense, like not smoking (me in adult life), proper rest, and good nutrition. But mom felt bad for people in Canada who died at one time of *appendicitis*.

Customarily, the deceased were laid out at home. True their wakes never attained the social and political crescendo of Irish ones (see the city's Edwin O'Connor's award-winning author of *The Last Hurrah*) but were attended by three days of paying respect to the departed, comforting the bereaved, catching up on the lives of the families gathered, and eating and drinking from the stores brought by the mourners. Some who came from afar, like Canada or New England enclaves, often lodged with the bereaving family or relatives. Thank God for those four-bedroom apartments of yesteryear! As people over 40 once did faithfully, my parents scanned the obits every night. Whoever read it first conveyed the death of anyone known to both. If she knew enough about the decedent, her raspy throat cleared, she gave us chapter and verse about his or her life, family and immigration story to America, marriage and children, mill jobs, sickness and health.

Knowing what she did about people, she was an instant eulogist. I liked hearing her. It again reminded us that everyone out there, especially if Franco, was a part of us, and we of them. If she learned it in citizenship class, is it fanciful to think *E Pluribus Unum* for her also meant All of Us French Canadians? Because of the proximity of families to each other, my parents' revelations of someone's death must've been repeated in homes. Births, marriages, and even deaths were the lifeblood of survivance, "*la révolution tranquille* (the quiet revolution)," to surpass Anglos.

No matter where the wake was, my folks set off on foot after supper "*pour prier au corps*": to pray for the deceased. As mom filled us in more on the decedent's life after their return, our wonder grew. Where did you learn stuff about people who never made news or were written about? Unlike the line about "little-known things about well-known people," hers was about little-known people whose importance was almost solely in our culture: "*parmi notre people* (among our people)." That made them her beat, not as a busybody as it may seem, but as someone interconnected *avec leur travail, leur famille, et leur foi* (with their work, their family and their faith), almost like 16th Century France's cry of unity:"*un roi, une loi, une foi (*one king, one law, one faith)" Hers was an earlier-time response, as it turns out, against the fractionalism and disconnectedness that came to characterize the latter half of the 20th century, even among people of the same culture and origin. This largely because of population growth, gentrification ("you can't live here if you need to know the price"), homelessness, suburbanization, locked-door caution against crime in cities and suburbs, motorized culture, and moving often, sometimes due to job relocation.

And now electronic media where you interact more with strangers in the ozone than your own people! How often do you see people talking on their cell phone and not with the person they're with! And what about that "helicoptering" fixation where people must check on their own by the hour, like mothers with collegians? "How was your 10:20 class, dear?" Students tell parents to let them call home! Columnist Bill O'Reilly said in part that "we're becoming a nation of cyberspace zombies: Facebooking, googling, blogging, flaming, spamming, and downloading, addicted to machines that shut out real life." Theorists wonder if our mental abilities will shrink, like eye contact has. Latin speaks of our mind *as tabula rasa* (blank). Now the Tablet is in our hands, not between the ears!

After we moved from above that noisome bar on Cass and Mailloux, one day I was drawn back there from *la* Gaulin. One of Charlie Gould's brothers had died and was being brought out from the family's second story (third if you count the bar) after his wake. Much later, George - "the computer cop" with the fabulous memory for license plates of stolen autos - told me their brother James had died. They waked him close to six days to give the whole family a chance to gather. Did they know what Mary and Martha told Christ about their odoriferous brother entombed for three whole days? But thank God for embalmers, which George later became, besides his police work.

What a funeral director's nightmare to bring a casket in and out after the usual three days. I watched as the movers gingerly lowered the casket. Because I was very young, if I remember correctly, they had previously removed part of the window casing, installed a pulley on the roof edge and leaned planks against the house. What a traffic stopper! This removal scene (not always as dramatic of course) was enacted whenever you saw a black funeral wreath on the front door and the decedent's family was gathered: "*rassemblées,*" said mom. The staircase at times was too narrow for the coffin.

Someone asked if there's a feeling now the whole ritual of mourning and burying has been somehow desensitized because of modern funeral methods and efficiency? Everything is done for you. A mixed blessing? If true, it certainly wasn't so when time-honored practices and rituals, such as the Irish and French Canadians had, seemed to touch the family and friends more intimately. Good or bad, did suffering, death, and mourning at home evoke a more emotional response from the family because of memories and associations? Like in movies or books, deathbed scenes with the family gathered round, like Lincoln's, were the stuff of profound family dramas. Canadian religious art often dealt with that scene with *le prêtre* (the priest) and his uplifted crucifix.

But practically and fortunately today's greater number of deaths all argue for our modern methods. So even the Roman Catholic church has relaxed its reluctance in America (never a moral issue!) on cremation. And now, wakes are only one day, if any. For the growing number of unchurched, no church ritual at all. With people living much longer and dying more of "wasting diseases," as niece Jan Reale, a hospice nurse and Rivier University nursing teacher, told me, some families opt for a closed casket, if any. And urns are now allowed in church. But some even rent caskets before cremation is done after the services.

Mom made me laugh when once she said a casket and body were so heavy, the flooring gave way, showering plaster and debris on the renters below. Since we mostly lived on the second or third floor of those tenement houses, no wonder my parents welcomed wakes "*chez* Fournier *ou Ménard* (at Fournier or Menard)," to cite two local funeral homes. Efficient dad emphasized that when I related the Gould wake to him.

For Francos, someone laid out was "*Yé chez planches*" (laid out on boards). Was it a vestige meaning of an ancient Viking or Indian custom or simply a practice of the poor of long ago because even Francos were usually laid out in caskets? But planks, Miss Fournier told me, were only used until the casket was brought into the home. If an expensive casket, mom said, "*Ils l'yont acheté une belle tombe* (they bought him a beautiful casket) *"cée du monde de moyen"*, a family of means. Another "rich-poor comparison" of hers, but without envy. It was a truth in the Middle Ages that there was a certain fixity in people's station in life and goods, when "knowing your place" and "your betters" was almost like a law of nature.

So, there was a pecking order in buying a casket. Ditto with your cemetery stone! Who could afford a *Gouverneur* (Governor) Pothier monument? How she loved his classical and majestic burial edifice, the centerpiece of the Precious Blood Cemetery! Again, is there any coincidence *les* Telliers, Fontaines, *et* Trottiers bought their plot nearby? Not proud in that sense, did they think a little name-dropping at the pearly gates might impress St. Pete: "*Nous autres, on t'avec le gouverneur.*(we're with the governor)" In one humorous story, some unmeritorious ne'er-do-well - "*d'la rapace,*" Rachel liked to say - wasn't going to get in Heaven. But since in life he took in wash at the chancery, he hoped to get in with the bishop's laundry! "Tide in, dirt out," did he boast? And a baseball card collector wondered why he was being held up there. St. Pete told him God wanted his Honus Wagner for a Joe Dimaggio and a Ted Williams. Only a few Hall of Fame Wagner cards (2B) exist, because he pulled out when the cards were sponsored by a tobacco company in the early 1900s.

No matter how poor, people like my parents purchased a small burial life insurance for two or three hundred dollars, paying them off in dimes. Like the Egyptians and especially the Greeks who feared they'd never cross the river Styx (Charon, almost French, the boatman) or be with the gods if they weren't properly buried, Catholic Francos scrounged to have enough to be buried: "*Pour navyerre (avoir) assez pour m'enterrer* (to have enough to bury me)," she repeated. It was one of two economic convictions people had: work to support yourself (*gagner sa vie*) and be buried properly. No grief over the content of The High Price of Dying. They could not have afforded it.

About our extended family plot and monument, when I buried my wife Patricia, December 14, 2000, I discovered the three families paid $300 for the monument in the 1940's; now $4,000. But as said elsewhere, most of the deceased Fontaines are buried in Roger and Janice's plot in Blackstone's St. Paul Cemetery. I'm grateful my lower middle-class family lived when food, transportation, heating, housing, clothing, education, insurance, and even dying were all affordable. Now nothing is.

"How quickly are the dead forgotten" was a topic of meditation in the Order. But it reminded us *les disparus* (the deceased) were not out of mind, if out of sight. In parishes, besides Masses for the dead, people often paid their respect to the departed, especially in November, in Precious Blood Cemetery (but now full) where many Francos were buried, Saint Jean-Baptiste Cemetery in Bellingham and Resurrection Cemetery in Cumberland. Parish cemeteries now inter most local Catholics. But regrettably for some "Catholics," burial in consecrated grounds is no longer a concern! Two "Catholics" said they could be thrown anywhere.

One Sunday mom and I visited with *tante* Laurence who lived across the cemetery at 520 Rathbun Street. It was my first glimpse of mom's steel-trap memory of the lives and times of those buried there. Even my aunt, a good chronicler herself, was stunned at her recall. "Poldine," she gasped, *"Tu t'rappellle (*recall*) de toute* (you remember everything!)," as if her sister could be an assistant to the Almighty on Judgment Day.

What *mémoires* (memoirs) hers would have been if she had inscribed them herself! But her culture was an oral one, where the spoken transmission of known history, culture, medicine, faith, family lore, and accumulated wisdom was nothing short of stupendous at times. As in other poor cultures, not so much by pen (even if she did write maybe close to 1,000 letters in her lifetime), but by word of mouth, did she "writ large" about everyday history. In our war notes, we said her bit, or "literature" was epistolary: letter writing. Those letters to family (three brothers and a sister) in Canada; Rachel in boarding school; me the Order; and Bob and Ben in the military would've been, if preserved, a treasure trove to regional historians studying Francophone life from 1916 on. Two of Bob's wartime letters survive and several from her siblings in Canada. But I did record her a lot. That's why this book is largely hers. Humbly she said, *"Tu m'donne trop d'crédit* (You give me too much credit)." Self-effacing - a common French-Canadian trait!

Mel B. Yoken said this about writing letters: "Spoken words grow dim with time; written words last forever. Letters are truly literary monuments that show deep feelings, emotions, and character. They delineate how people felt, lived and acted; they celebrate friendships, progress, love affairs, admiration, and also turmoil and heartbreaks." "Don't say it, write it," I read on brother-in-law Donald Clark's desk at Texas Instruments in Attleboro, MA. Hey, even Shakespeare said to write: "Words to the heat of deeds, too cold a breath give."

About Precious Blood cemetery, I recall the first time I saw the plot of Marie Rose Ferron, a stigmatist in life with the five wounds of Christ (two hands, feet, and side) on her body and also a crown of thorns on her forehead at times. Many French-Canadian homes had her biography (in French in our home; my copy now in English, thanks to Our Lady Queen of Martyrs – Holy Trinity and the caretaking Smith family) with its photos of a homemade altar, Marie Rose lying in a bed of pain and sorrow for the conversion of sinners, and even for a resolution of the Sentinellist crisis. Reacting to a desire from the faithful to initiate her cause for sainthood, Bishop Russell McVinney, not impressed with her after a visit, announced tersely it would not go forward. Was the source of her raptures or ecstasies questioned? No one supposedly allowed to be alone with her was one comment I read? Morphine a factor? Woonsocket thought she'd be the city's first saint. Besides the related family whom I met at the site, dwindling devotees (one priest at St. Antoine?) are left, hoping she will eventually be honored for her saintly life, great piety, and extraordinary favors, often with a scent of roses. In 2012, an article said stigmatism is the most difficult saintliness to authenticate. Recall a teacher said nine times out of ten, it's only "misty-cism." But I'm a devotee and pray to her, as surely mom did. I often visit her grave, along with Pat's.

Her cause reminded me of another reputed stigmatist, Theresa Newman of Germany, whom mom read about. In the Order, I was shocked by a book debunking her stigmata and her living solely on Communion! Sneaking food at night was the suspicion if I recall correctly. Her name is never mentioned now.

In Catholic hagiography (lives of the saints), stigmatists are revered, such as Saint Paul, Saint Francis of Assisi, and the recently sainted Padre Pio of Italy, who cured an American. His wounds disappeared only after death. In life, doctors even covered his wounds for a couple of weeks, thinking they would dry up, but no. One day when I was at Pat's grave in Precious Blood Cemetery, a Worcester family asked me to show them Marie Rose's resting place. Their hope was for their young, beautiful and blind daughter. I've admitted a great interest in Christ's miracles, and I thought of the time He put spittle and dirt on the blind man's eyes to restore his sight. How I wish He'd been there! I wanted her to see the magnificent day it was and the adoring faces of her loved ones. For reasons only known to Him, "Sometimes the miracle we get is the one we don't."

This cult of the "living dead" among the faithful was fueled by a beautiful Church doctrine, the Communion of Saints. Catholics are taught the faithful belong in successive stages to one of three groups. On earth, the Church Militant fighting to win salvation; in death, the Church Suffering in Purgatory for most; and finally, the Church Triumphant in Heaven for saints and the finally purified. You couldn't miss the optimism we'd eventually make it to step three because Beelzebub was not in that trilogy. As a Militant, you prayed for the souls in Purgatory to mitigate their suffering, so they prayed for you when they got out and joined the Triumphants in prayer. In school we especially prayed for the most desperate in purgatory. I found this belief unbelievably comforting, because it gathered up the whole human family into the same aspiring celestial destiny.

Presentation nuns still pray for the canonization of their founder, Blessed *Soeur* Anne-Marie Rivier.[38] Her cause is still before Rome, so said my now deceased cousin Doris Peloquin, who taught at the Order's Rivier College (renamed Rivier University in July, 2012), Nashua, NH, before laicizing. She obtained for me a plastic-encased piece of linen, which has touched the bones of the saintly nun, the object of many school prayers. The Brothers of the Sacred Heart are also advancing the cause of first Superior General, Brother Polycarp, who died in the 19th Century.

About those purgatorial fires, teachers said they purified, but didn't consume. The gang didn't understand that because at times we burnt our fingertips when we lit our forbidden corn silk cigarettes and it hurt! We 'sort a' took it on faith there was a kind of fire that didn't burn! About this dispensation from the laws of science, we told our parents, *"La soeur la dit,"* dogma! (The Sisters said it's dogma) Mom's only comment was *"Ça nous dépasse* (It's beyond us)."

The night before dad's second stroke, I sat with him and mom at St. Antoine. Seemingly okay for an 86-year-old man with bronchiectasis for 30 years (reportedly a medical record), dad said, *"Cée mon tour. J'veux m'en aller"*: "It's my turn to leave" to his eternal home and end of pain and debility. It wasn't fatalism or depression, but a great act of faith the trials of this life would usher in a better one. He had so loved activity, yes, even unremitting, tiring millwork, walking, tinkering, cutting hair, shoe repairing,

---

[38] Anne-Marie Rivier was canonized by Pope Frances on May 15, 2022. The youngest daughter of the author's brother, Bob, was named after her by his wife Millie in thanks for her being born healthy. - *ed.*

making and repairing toys, cooking, canning, winemaking, reading, and gardening. And of course, predicting, fireside politicking, and diagnosing. Fancifully, he would have tarried, if the Lord had seen fit to restore him to the joys and springtime of his youth, especially those first seven years in the verdant pastures of their farm in Saint Cuthbert, Province of Québec, Canada. Oh, how on a late spring morn scented with tall, aromatic hay, the sound of whirring birds, the lark on the wing, and a lush, green garden, it was so good to be alive.

How symbolic he got his wish on Father's Day, June 20, 1982, when I got the call - the most dreaded one of all, the death either of a parent, spouse, sibling, or child. He shared the faith of 1,800,000 French Canadians who by choice or necessity chose a different homeland for that titanic struggle between heaven and earth they believed they were involved in. The stuff of high drama, not to be dismissed by the ordinariness of their lives! Faithwise, he and others lived at a time when giants walked the earth, so near heaven were they in belief and action. Will we see their equal again in the 21st Century? As God often does, will He again confound the mighty and the proud with humble, salt-of-the-earth people whose "noiseless tenor" will mask their grandeur?

I said a priest friend moved me when he preached that at the Last Judgment our corporal and spiritual works of mercy will be the measure of our everlasting destiny, as the Gospel says. And not our attainments in life - education, wealth, position, acclaim - however lofty and good these were! I thought it was a validation of those immigrant peoples of all races before, during, and after the turn of the century, whose lives the English poet said were just "the short and simple annals of the poor." A touching line which self-taught Lincoln knew. He said it was the measure of his boyhood, pure and simple. Greatness comes in many disguises and a thousand faces. Hard to believe, but Lincoln only had a single year of formal schooling, but luckily he had a book-loving mom.

Joyeux noël
[Merry Christmas]

FOR FRENCH CANADIANS, Christmas or *Noël* in its full religious significance was a joyous and solemn feast, almost unsurpassed in the church's panorama of liturgical seasons of the birth, life, death, and resurrection of Christ. Perhaps only Easter because of its validation of their faith and their own resurrection at the Last Judgment equaled it.

New beginnings in the spirit are always occasions of hope and joy. So, the start of the whole redemptive cycle buoyed the faithful with great expectation. But for us mundane kids, the festivity was more the gift-giving or receiving, as it still is today as this holy day, however, now struggles to maintain its once solely Christian significance.

About gifts, in how many homes like mine did the hand-to-mouth constrictions of a millhand's salary preclude quantity and quality of giving and receiving? Another restraint on the breadwinner's salary (the two-worker family was rare) was its size, so much larger than today's 3.1, said one report. Another says 1.9. When counseling at Norton High School, a teacher complained to me about having "a 0.9 kid" in class! Because priests and nuns told us the four weeks of Advent was a December time of spiritual readiness second only to Lent, expectations of the young for gifts was less, but just as intense as today's kids who, God bless 'em, often get what they wish for.

How I remember being disappointed one year what *le bonhomme* (good man) "*Sainta Claus*" or *le petit Jésus* (the baby Jesus) put under our tree. It didn't seem much for all their shared potential to fulfill your material requests upon a mere wish and a prayer. Even though we young children had two gift-givers, one spiritual (yes, we thought Jesus delivered gifts somehow), the other one mundane (parents in the role of St. Nicholas), our gifts didn't equal Santa's today. One year I stared disappointingly at my gift, a hand-sized, black leather coin holder with four value slots. Yes, we didn't have much. But so often your best lasting gift is an inexpensive one. I used it for a decade., counting my newspaper carrier or coat checking money earned at the Joyland Roller Skating Ring on Cumberland Hill Road in Woonsocket, owned by the funeral Fournier family.

Since the culture didn't make us young consumers, it was easier to save. We instinctively knew, "You've gotta know when to hold or fold 'em." With mom it was always tomorrow, *le lendemain* (the next day), always creeping with its petty pace, as the Bard says.

Before my counseling career, I taught Dickens' *A Christmas Carol*, telling sophomores the critic's comment about Scrooge's miserliness, to wit, that for some who've been poor, they sometimes can't put enough money between them and the dreaded poverty they once knew. At times you read about *nouveau riche* people hoarding or dying of self-neglect and malnutrition, if not because of senescence or mental illness. Our own personal hoarding was not that Scroogian, and besides, we never had enough money for that dilemma! Not the way my customers tipped in those days! The notion of saving was an ingrained cultural and family thing, a reflection of the times we lived in. There was fixity about people's economic status in our mill town. That's why people lived frugally and rarely borrowed. No buying on credit, a bane for many now. I saw a young lady on TV who was shocked her credit card came with a bill!

When we grew older, we understood better how economics played a part in what we didn't receive. Even though dad was the financial wizard who expounded on inflation, the nation's economy, debt, tax laws, the income tax, and the New Deal, mom, like a latter-day Alan Greenspan, is the one who gave us a periodic assessment of the family's finances. If around Christmas time she intoned with calculated good timing, "*Ton père a trouvé ça dull à factorie,*" (dad's sporadic work in the factory), we downsized our expectations. And also not to be bothered about what would be under the tree, she said, "*Lâche mwé avec ça*": take a powder. Author and columnist John Rosemond said parents were once less concerned about "displeasing their children," since the culture was less child driven.

When Advent season dwindled down to its final weekend, Bob, Ben, and I trekked behind long-striding dad to a gas station (monsieur Tessier's?) for a *un bon arbre de Noël (a good Christmas tree)*. We looked for freshness, fullness, and low price. The same judicious deliberation when buying a cut of meat, always knowing what part of an animal it came from because it affected its chewability. Never bought a cut from "between the horns" or from "a steer that walked all the way from Texas!" He never wanted to spend $5 for a big tree, only $2.

If working full time, he had a salary just above $40. And we were seven, all wanting to be fed three times a day since families always ate at home then! Once we asked about getting a car, but nothing else. It was a time when children should be seen, not heard, not about finances anyway. But like mom, he got us through the Depression, and we never saw him angry, hurt, or depressed about it. He was too savvy to be beaten. Because people were all poor to begin with, they were better able to handle hard times. Does today's level of comfort and dispensable income invite more imprudence in money management, our "buy-now, pay-later" economy? One biographer said people who have, feel entitled, and want more. We said it's shocking to read about athletes, cinematic stars, financiers, and Powerball winners (40 percent broke after four years) who reverse the rags to riches scenario.

Picture the scene in Shakespeare's *Macbeth* where the camouflaging trees from Birnam Wood hid the army advancing on the murderous usurper king, and you visualize us hauling a tree home. Holding the trunk, dad was the pathfinder, while his shielded sons placed the prickly branches on their young Herculean shoulders. "Are we there yet, dad?": "*On tu arrivés?* (Have we arrived)" We trudged up steep Gaulin, littering a bit the three flights of stairs with needles. But recall he said rising heat was a small economy, an insight into "the managed poverty" of their lives. In winter he told us how much a cord of wood or a ton of coal cost that year. Perhaps he was getting us ready to run our own home someday, a happenstance some forty years later when he beamed we five all had *"notre propre demeure* (our own home)." Even though owners can of course lose their homes, as millions now have, owning one gave you a little more security than renting, like our family on Cass Avenue when we couldn't pay the rent. It's said you could buy a home during the Depression for around $10,000, but he didn't have it. Not even a home-building kit from Sears and Roebucks! It was never his choice, but he told me the one thing you couldn't lose on was an education. A pensive insight into what he was denied because he lent money to his brothers for farms. With his great mind, little schooling was the tragedy of his life. Homo sapiens, meaning he was a wise man who knew what he knew, and what he didn't because of his elementary education.

No wonder *tante* Alice said they missed him terribly when their widowed father remarried unwisely, as it turned out, and dad went to live with friend Noél Tessier. They lost their accountant-in-residence. Calculators, computers, and adding machines didn't exist then but he didn't need them anyway. He just wrote on scraps of paper, often torn from one of those brown shopping bags. On them, I saw everything except Einstein's famous equation. O the pity he wasn't born fifty years later! That's why I empathize with Gray's "Elegy Written in A Country Churchyard," where the cemetery is filled with people "who coulda' been somebody, a contenda'," as Brando says in *On the Waterfront*. The best reason for education ever said or written and the best cinematic line ever in one listing! But I mean "somebody" in its educational and professional sense, since by faith alone, so many Francos were giants of the earth, gifted with amazing ingenuity, practicality, inventiveness, and can-do.

We set the tree up between the two windows of the front parlor, decorating as a family, except for busy, petite mom. Close to 5 feet, 10 inches, dad was fairly tall for a Franco, and until Bob passed him, he alone topped the decorations with the family's most prized ornament, a wired star for the peaking branch. If he delegated, "the chosen one" used a little stepladder - *un escabeau*. He used a bucket of anthracite to stand the tree in, adding water to preserve freshness and minimize fire hazard. At times he cursed under his breath about the entanglements of the lights in the storage box. And how many bulbs were dead after a year of cold or moisture in the unheated spare bedroom off the parlor! My folks called it *"la chambre fraite" (froide* - the cold room), where he stored his spinning jenny, barber, and cobbler stuff. We made use of only three of the four bedrooms in our cavernous apartment: the master bedroom, the three boys' room, and a third room for my sisters and *mémère* on weekends. Since ours was a cold water flat, the spare room with two outside walls was always cold at night, since the *chaufferette* (heater) was not on at night.

When we were children, they couldn't always attend the Midnight Mass, a strong Canadian tradition. But they always talked about it, and dad sometimes went alone if he bought a ticket, even for a church of 1,300 seats. In our culture, there was always at least one parent home. If there was a word for "babysitter" in patois, I never heard it except the verb *garder* (to keep). With what nostalgia she recalled how in Canada her family traveled to church by sled in the midnight cold. Her face lit up. It was pure Québécois! When I saw my first Currier and Ives scene, it was like theirs. Then they regaled themselves during *le réveillon* (New Year's Eve) on those traditional beef-pork pies - *tourtières*. When small town life was steeped in tradition and the faith in Canada!

Mom and *mémère* Emérance Fontaine (her mother) made them during the season, three at a time. A good cook in her own right, mom still deferred when it came to the crust. *Mémère*'s culinary art was like an unwritten recipe born of instinct and experience in baking for her large family in Canada as her women forbears had done since Nicolas Pion *dit* LaFontaine and Jean Morvan (her family) arrived in the New World. It was all "in the wrist." Mom said, "*Ta grandmère fait ses croutes avec une pincée d'ci et d'ça,* (your grandmother makes her crusts with a pinch of here and there)" a culinary mystery how a pinch here, a pinch there came out as savory delights. Part of their pie magic was a mechanical sifter and a rolling pin. Dad with his penchant for Chaplinesque humor chuckled whenever the Sunday funnies pictured a beleaguered wife chasing her sluggard husband with one. But imagine, mom always wanted dad to do less!

The Christmas Mass thrilled us with the joy of the Divine Birth and salvific hope. Because of Adam and Eve's sin, our faith and carols reminded us the world had lain in sin and darkness until He came, the second Adam. Even though we felt redeemed, the nuns gave us a sense of foreboding when they told us what would've happened if He hadn't come almost two thousand years ago when the world "lay in sin," as the lyrics said. Mom said the Nativity had a special significance for her people. Since they raised large families, the birth of a new child was a frequent and joyous occasion during the year. A newborn was "*un p'tit Christmas* (a small Christmas)," but especially *durant les fêtes* (during the holidays), like Bob's on December 26, 1925, she told me.

About family planning, I read Canadian farming families spaced their children in two-year segments, having their children away from the planting and harvesting seasons. Dad wasn't a farmer, yet the four of us were born in either December or January. But Ben, who became an avid landscaper, angler, and gardener besides carpentry, arrived in March, felicitously close to the Feast of Saint Joseph, the patron of his profession. I was only four myself, but I never forgot the day I saw him take his first steps (although mom said he had taken steps before) when *oncle* Henri *et* Laurence (Fontaine) Trottier had their wedding reception on Mailloux. A photo in the family album shows the company from our side of the street and our Demers neighbors across. Edgar Demers, Bob's age, was also in the navy during the war, and they're in a photo taken at Spring Lake after their discharge. I later counseled his kids for college. His brother, Norman, a talented goalie at the Academy, became a secular priest, author, and pastor in the diocese. Their sister was Thérèse.

French *Noël* hymns and carols with their just claim are among the most melodic, devotional, and stirring in Christian musicology and stirred everyone's faith. Almost *passé* like spoken French hereabouts, they still move the faithful in parishes "French" at one time. In my parish of Our Lady Queen of Martyrs – Holy Trinity, I laud the French carol renditions of organist and former Mount Saint Charles (MSC) counselee, John Guevremont. With their inspiration from the Divine Infant, Mary, the angels, shepherds, the Three Kings, and the Redeemer's saving mission, they carried the message of the Mass to ear and heart. That was an added blessing at a time when the Mass was largely a quasi-private affair between the priest and the faithful, with little interaction like today. The faithful were at the priest's back, as he faced East and Jerusalem. Older folks hardly ever looked at the altar. Heads bowed; many said their beads. But not us kids. The nuns insisted Liturgy, not beads, was more important, predating Church Renewal.

The most moving hymn was *Minuit Chrétien*: "O Holy Night." In solemn, devotional music, it expressed the joy and anticipation of Christendom at the birth of its Savior. When I was in the Order, only the most talented and deep-voiced monk was tapped to usher in the season. No one was more endeared to the role than Woonsocketer Brother Fernand Bérard, founding principal at Notre Dame HS in Fitchburg. He was also a Mount Saint Charles principal who acquired and helped build the Brother Adelard Hockey Arena, stage for the school's numerous hockey championships. Barrel-chested, his basso profundo "pipes" resonated throughout the chapel. His brother Rodolphe, also of Notre Dame, had a great voice too and knew so many Canadian sing-alongs to enliven our *soirées* (parties) and long bus rides to our annual seaside picnics and retreats. His other brothers were Peter Henry and George Edouard, a missionary buried in Africa. Four religious vocations in one family!

Because the whole family didn't usually attend Midnight Mass (only adults stayed up that late in pre-TV days) or have *réveillon* (Christmas Eve) after, opening our gifts was a morning affair. But to emphasize the religious significance of the day, we opened *nos presents* (our presents) only after we had all gone to Mass and wolfed down our usual hearty breakfast of pancakes, or French toast (*du pain doré*), or eggs with French *saucisse (sausage)*. You'll recall we had only one main meal Sunday with *le diner* at noon, since *le souper (the dinner)* was reserved for his famed fresh vegetable soup with French sticks of bread: *du pain sa sol. Sol* means "ground" in French, so perhaps how it was once baked. If we had ripped chunks of bread, imbibed dad's wine, and worn *bérets*, (a round, flat cap usually made of wool or felt) we could've dropped "Canadian" and been just "French." Dad had the good nose of a Frenchman, but no one else in the family. Does Mother Nature so adorn winemakers?

If our store-bought gifts seemed few and inexpensive, we've groused, never a Christmas came without knitted goods from *mémère* Fontaine, our third Santa or gift-giver. These were a stocking cap (*une tuque*); a pair of gloves (*des gants*); a pair or two of woolen stockings (*des bas de laines*, for winter and skating); or a sweater (*un gilet*), all made (*tricoté*) from yarn bought from dad's mill. Her gifts complemented the few my folks bought from McCarthy's, Najarian's, Kresge's, B.J. Farnum's, and Kornstein's, all stores anchoring the once vibrant Woonsocket Main Street, the downtown shopping center. And at least one Social clothing store (Baram's?) was run by Jewish merchants who spoke French: "*Ils parlent mon langage* (they speak my language)," beaming mom said. Since *mémère* Emérance was always knitting, if not praying, reading or baking with mom, we usually didn't know what she was making or for whom. Mom was silent! When at *tante* Laurence, she worked on our gifts. When with us, it. was for Claude or Ronald, or for *mon oncle* François *et* tante Blanche Fontaine's four children: Roger, Lucille, François, *et* Clémence. Trying to get a sweater right, she held it up against our chest or shoulders, approximating the difference for the intended receiver. Her knitting needles, protruding from her black bag when in transit between *les* Trottiers and us or in her hands by the stove, could've been symbols on her coat-of-arms. And speaking of armorial symbols, a Canadian amateur genealogist and Brother of the Sacred Heart, Herménégilde Tellier, who came to see me in the 1970's at Mount, told me a Tellier ancestor (LeTuillier: tile maker or the like) had three lizards on his coat-of-arms because his sons were "*grouillant*": overactive. Mom would've sympathized, since kids at home then weren't "tranquilized" by media and electronic devices. So dreamingly, did one of dad's ancestors have anything to do with Paris's *Les Tuileries*? Or was he from one of those other five families? If once blue blood, how did we go from the gravy train to the turnip truck, as people once snubbed those with no money, wardrobe, genteel manners nor education? Brother also told me there was *un judge* Tellier. but didn't say if he was "a hangin' judge."

So *mémère* too, like the good woman in the Old Testament, kept all her near and dear ones in warm clothing. Even the world's fastest prestidigitator (Houdini in her day; David Copperfield today) would've admired her incredibly quick hands. You swore she could do anything - pray, converse, eat, drink, without dropping a stitch, *"une maille,"* beaming mom said with pride, as if to say, "Hey kids, that's my mother, you know." Mom's and dad's affection for their own parents taught us the same towards them.

With her knitting and baking she easily saved hundreds of dollars to our related families, said dad. Because elders often lived with one of their children, their rich trove of skills, knowledge, piety, and wisdom was not untapped, like today. We cited poet Tennyson's line: "Old age hath yet his honor and its toil". Now with two-worker families or single parent households (41 percent plus) when their help would be so valuable and needed, they live mostly among themselves, yes, happily, quietly, and deservedly so, if wished. But one can speculate about the loss of their everyday wisdom and help. So now, is theirs a quieter response to poet Dylan Thomas' advice for the elderly? "Do not go gentle into that good night, / Old age should burn and rave at close of day; / Rage, rage against the dying of the light." But hearing that, how many now would say about "raging," I've toiled in the trenches of domesticity, but I've earned my day in the sun?" One told me, "I've raised my kids; I'm not going to raise my grandkids, even if I'll love and buy them things." One study said the happiest station in life for a married couple, or single grandparent occurs when the kids are raised and on their own.

But an article in 2012 revealed many elders still contribute much. Seven million grandparents are now raising children of "lost parents who have gone off to find themselves, have succumbed to demon rum (alcoholism), drugs, or serial monogamy." Only slightly more than half of absent fathers provide support. No wonder senior citizens are faring better than children in our culture! Politically, sixty million or more constitute a powerful lobby, AARP or not! By 2050 or even sooner, seniors will be one of the larger groups in the country (one in five). Will USA mean the United States of the Aging, with many thousands over 100 years old? A good thing about an aging culture is a drop in crime, usually the propensity of the 15-to-30 plus age group. Their mugs on TV every night and in the paper. Always hope they've caught the last one! The courts are soft on thieves, yet their crimes are premeditated and repeated after release. High incidence in RI.

Our poverty was one where with careful management of limited resources, self-sufficiency, make-do creativity, and domestic *savoir-faire* (know-how), life was "warm and comfy." It's why our Rule of Life in the Order (a sublimation of our French-Canadian life at home) became an easy transition, "detachment, not dispossession," said our vow book. Poverty of the spirit, not of the hand.

In the early Christian community, a writer hit it right, "Those who had much, didn't seem to have more; those who had little, didn't seem to have less." So unknowingly Francos were like the Christian community of apostolic times, living all the same way. No need for the Makeover people to come in. Something about a mill culture that equalized and immobilized just about everything. I related this fixity, this looking back, love of tradition, and *les bons vieux temps* (the good old days) infuriated their English conquerors in Canada. At one time, Anglos held them in very low esteem, deeming themselves more farsighted, ambitious, and acquisitive. It's appalling how after the battle of Québec the English dismissed their leadership talents, denied them education and a role in government, and stripped them of their lands. But they still held on to their language, culture, and faith, which many brought to America, especially New England.

But because of those restrictions "from their captors," small wonder most who came to the States were ill-prepared for little but unsophisticated, repetitive work, like most mill jobs: spinning, weaving, and cut-and-sew industries. As cousin Connie (Peloquin) Blais, born here, told me, "With the little education I received here, I couldn't get a job today." Yet, as Jean Charlemagne Bracq relates in *The Evolution of French Canada* and their Anglo-Canadian treatment before coming here, Québeckers had been so supportive of Britain in her efforts to keep Americans from conquering parts of Canada. Fortunately, minister Louis Fontaine (no relation), for one fought tooth and nail to get basic rights for his people - their birthright as British subjects. Another, dubbed "a son of French Canada," George Cartier, also fought for racial justice. We said Frenchmen came first to Canada, but the greater Anglo numbers and their alliance with the superior warlike Iroquois tipped the scale in their favor. Not to mention the venality and rapacity of the French King's ministers in the New World who kept selling back to France the very supplies he sent them. Like Judases, they undermined their own for "thirty pieces of silver." Friend Patrick Martin-Beaulieu and I were both dejected reading Robert Leckie's *Few Acres of Snow* about how one minister with those words consoled his French king about the loss of Canada. Champlain is universally admired in North America (more statues than our Washington), but his twice repulsing the Iroquois caused them to side with the British in the rich fur trade. He also tried to ferret out the two-timing business agents from France.

Mom's affection for her mother was shared by dad. His father Joseph lived down the street in our Peloquin cousins' two-story home, secure in the love and attention of his daughter Marie-Louise, husband Armand, and their eight children. I speak elsewhere of his sometimes supping with us. Dad told me mom's housekeeping was a backbreaking task for a small, asthmatic person like her, so *mémère* Fontaine lightened her load tremendously. Like him, she liked peace and quiet and reminded us when we got noisome. I liked the way mom called her *"Maan,"* (from *Maman*), as we used for her, but not so protractedly. She never ceased to retell how she had saved their lives in Canada and brought them to America. Who would've guessed it, looking at a smallish, slightly bowed, white-haired old lady next to the stove? She had been touched by the gods to pull that off! Enlarging on it, I was reminded of her when I read *Miracles at Sea* by Eleanor Anderson about her mother, Lillian Danielson, who kept all her six children alive after they were plunked into the South Atlantic Ocean by a German raider.

With three and sometimes four generations in one family, I said it struck me later how we unknowingly learned to respect elders, admire their wisdom, and revere their age. No special laws to save them from harm. In any given week two grandparents supped with us. The presence of elders in families prevented younger generations from being awkward, if not clueless, with them, either at leisure or at work. The culture was not youth-oriented, as it has become today, where businesspeople and telecasters fear to go past comic Jack Benny's perennial 39 years of age. "Silver threads among the gold" must be "Grecian-urned" to remain competitive. I applaud schools like the Academy where students in their Christian Action Program, visited and entertained the elderly. My wife Patricia, as religion teacher, directed it in her tenure. A memorable photo in the 1971 Excelsior yearbook shows seniors David Marcoux, now a leading internist in the state, and James Dunn motoring an older senior citizen basking in their attentiveness. Students told me how working with the elderly, akin to gerontology, was a special calling.

Presently students help first graders at the Bernon School. Public schools, like North Smithfield HS and Woonsocket HS also direct athletes and other students towards good works. Helping others, especially the needy, is America's saving grace. Why God loves the USA. Didn't Christ say even a glass of water given in His name will not go unrewarded. Militarily, we gave out $50 billion in war materiel to the 20 or more nations who fought with us in WWII; even to postwar ungrateful and scheming Communist Russia. What's called "suffering from justice's sake" when a good act gives you grief, not joy or merit. Some say we've yet unfathomed the Russian mind: part Western world, part middle East! Great talents, but also acts of cruelty and brutality (thousands of rapes in Berlin), and subterfuge.

Recall mom spoke of a special blessing for visiting Christ's crib or manger on Christmas Day: *"la crèche du p'tit Jésus* (little Jesus' manger)." With little socializing that day compared to New Year's, twice I went with her to St. Ann's where the manger was to our left of the altar. She explained how the Three Kings of the Orient, hidden that day by straw and trees, arrived *"plus tard"* or later. That is, on the Epiphany or Manifestation to the Gentiles, called *La Fête des Rois*, the Feast of the Three Kings or Wise Men, but not "Wise Guys," as a tyke said. She said it was the gift-giving day in Canada, more so than *Noël (Christmas)*. Once January 6, it's now the first Sunday in January after New Year's Day.

A Canadian custom, in the Order, the Brother who found a bean in his cake was *roi du jour* (king of the day). No "divine right" for me, a consummation mom who loved kings and queens would've told our family court. If crowned or sceptered, would I have absolved Brother John Louis Collignon *et mo*i (and me) from having to sweep like domestics the community room each day? In training if we did something "below our dignity" as future teachers, we quoted a saintly young Jesuit, *"Ad majora natus sum"* - born for greater things.

Also recall how deflated I was when dad said the Lafayette mill where he labored was probably my work destiny. Growing up, I shared the inherent dignity of all honest work, including millwork, the family's sole livelihood. But always there were the threats it brought to our lives. Colonel Theodore Roosevelt, in a nomination speech in 1912, lamented how many workers were sicklied by their work, besides lacking any kind of coverage, a concern too of President Wilson. Efforts were made to check the coal barons, steel-oil-cattle kings, railroad magnates, high financiers, and the monarchs of trusts, after all the vast free lands of the West had been gobbled up by financiers. If those barons had been left unchecked, said a professor, eventually one man would have owned every profit-making enterprise. Didn't the recession of 2008 revive the need to control businesses and banks and fine banks, for one, some in the millions, even as late as 2015!

Then, millworkers carried their family's economic survival solely on their often tired and stooped shoulders. From the start of the Industrial Age or Revolution, mill owners and governments were not yet attuned to the problems of the rank and file, a situation unions and labor strikes, at times bloody, eventually remedied. Joseph Pearce in *Literary Converts* reports, like the Bard did, on another author's seven stages of man from Whole Man in the image of God, to Renaissance Humanist, and finally to today's Economic Man, who is defined almost solely by his work. One pope decried Joe or Josephine Worker simply as a cog in the machinery of work.

As a royal watcher, mom knew the Magi brought gifts to honor respectively His kingship, humanity, and divinity. I wasn't surprised to find a few biographies of kings and queens in her effects, including the royal wedding of Charles and Diana (a gift from the Clark family), so unlike my parents in pomp and, yes, duration.

Because *Noël, le jour de l'an, et la fête des rois* (Christmas, New Years and Kings Day) were a trilogy of celebrations, the holiday season seemed longer somehow, because it didn't finish with today's Christmas commercial closure. Imagine, training in the Order we took the decorations down Feb. 2, the Feast of Purification, when all vestiges of the post-Nativity season were over. Now we end in early January.

Nearly all our decorations (*des courants* – currents, now a protected groundcover) were from our Harrisville woodlands of 1,400 acres, now nearly all sold off. People have now built homes across the street from the present Crystal Lakes golf course. Farm buildings and pastures are now fairways. When I later returned to teach novices and first-year collegians (Scholastics) in the 1950s, my Sunday task was "to take 'em for a hike" after Mass. So, I literally walked them all over creation in a lovely corner of RI, considered one of the healthiest in the state and best for hunting because of its rural feel and paucity of industry. Is that why Wallum Lake, once strictly a sanitarium for TB cases, was located there?

They say kings aren't what they used to be. Indeed "the biblical royals," who "annually" see his star in the East, find it "dark" when they finally arrive in the West, and merchants tell them their booking was for Thanksgiving Friday to Christmas Eve. The kings still come to give, but always hear the lament that sales weren't as good as expected!

Father Roussel: A Treasured Friend of Youth

LIFE FOR US KIDS at St. Ann's in the 1930's and 1940's would not have been as exciting if some priests hadn't foreshadowed Church Renewal of the 1960's. What John XXIII later called *Aggiornamento*, rendered as "Opening Up the Windows." Renewal would re-energize the church in the modern world and happily bring it back to the people in the marketplace, as Pope Francis emphasizes. This instead of a more stay-in-the-rectory ministry, since the misunderstanding with Luther, Calvin, Zwingli, Knox, Henry VIII, and other reformers over 500 years ago. Before them, Europe had once been largely unified, not only under one language academically (predominantly Latin, at least for the educated), but also one faith, until the Protestant Reformation over church abuses, royal malfeasance in some countries, and later the atheistic French Revolution. Instead of one faith, approximately 4,200 denominations now vie for people's worship.

Père Lucien W. Roussel was one of two priests who reached out to us in the new way. The other was Father Frédéric Moreau, Boy Scout Troop 4 founder-chaplain, profiled later. Tall, thin, energetic, communicative, and cheerful, he came to the parish in the mid 1940's and quickly became a visible force in our huge parish. His black-robed presence was a familiar sight.

In public, priests still wore a long, all-buttoned cassock with a Roman collar, *de rigueur* (traditional) like in my Order. Like families, he walked a beat. Hadn't Christ urged His disciples to go out with staff in hand and sandals on their feet?

With sports so dear to us kids, he called us to the rectory one day to form a baseball team. We usually spent all summer at swimming holes or playing street ball or at St. Ann's Park, a weather-beaten and wood-planked structure built by a pastor who was convinced "an idle mind was the devil's workshop." In fact, when Francos first arrived in numbers, clerical, civic, and business leaders in the community created numerous cultural, social, religious, and athletic clubs to sustain their heritage, language, faith, and family togetherness. Isolated in a confusing, challenging immigration experience, they received a sense of belonging or *déjà vu* from those community groups.

Dad belonged to some of them. He went at night to hear talks in the old St. Ann's Gymnasium (preservationists Phyllis Thomas and Larry Poitras could not save it due to its undermined condition) about his heritage, like the discoveries of Champlain *et* Jacques Cartier, and the two Canadian explorers of the Mississippi, Marquette *et* Joliet. Mom lauded relative and Wood Avenue resident *Docteur* Auray Fontaine, for his pioneering work, along with his neighbor, *dentiste* Armand Picard, in forming or directing some of those sports clubs, social or financial groups.

With our ripped gloves, coverless baseballs, 25-cent baseball caps, stinky sneakers, and dad's nailed-and-glued recycled bats, we were, minus Lucy, the forerunners of the Peanuts Gang. But not because other teams didn't show up, we did win at times. To this dynamic young priest, were we like those first Apostles with their torn nets, sturdy fishing boats, good hearts, and strong bodies that could grow in brotherly love, team spirit, and a force for good, as scouting did in the hands of *Père* Moreau? For him, the Scout Laws (12) were like the Ten Commandments plus two. We were never a well-equipped baseball squad because there was no money from the parish or our families for that. But for those pre-Little League or Babe Ruth League days, besides scouting, it was the first experience in team play a lot of us ever had, other than our group neighborhood games. I don't know exactly how far back the Catholic Youth Organization (CYO) movement went in Rhode Island, but if extant, it wasn't very active in the parish, as far as the gang knew. Besides, self-initiative was the earmark of childhood activity then. We always had something to do and some place to go, especially *pendant les vacancies d'été*: during summer vacations. When I saw the CYO flourish in later years, I thought of *Père* Roussel and *Père* Moreau as forerunners.

"A new breed of priests" wasn't coined, but the Gaulin gang knew he was different. I recall that gang of mine "standing on the corner" was *les* Peloquins, Carpentiers, Houles, Beauregards, Vandals, Lanoies, Laferrieres, Charrons, Courtemanches, Bourgets, Bérubés, *les autre*s (the other) Telliers, *et* Champagne. Nary a one whose parents came from the *Auld Sod* (one's native country) or once played for Knute Rockne and The Fighting Irish. All of us children of immigrants who, by parental choice, just missed being raised farm boys in Québec. *Père* Roussel was the kind of priest who came to your home turf, but not only for the parish two-year census or the Last Rites to the sick. Unlike the priests living in the rectory and ministering mostly in church (a liturgical priest as opposed to a career priest, one wrote) he projected an image of service in the parish.

His apostolic beat was St. Ann's, that is the flatlands of Social and those hills gently rising behind the church and capped by those tall tenements filled with people, symbolized by the twin towers of Faith and Family. We didn't realize how unique our experience was. In a way we were like everyone else, but earlier-come ethnic groups didn't always feel welcomed by America, as Jews, Poles, Irish and Blacks, especially, painfully discovered. But in fairness, Francos had a similar mindset when it came to their faith servers. Their faith bloodline or DNA had to be an unbroken sequence from *la belle* France, *la fille anise de l'église,"* (oldest daughter of the church) or *du Québec*(of Québec). Like us, earlier immigrants all came largely from countries of one ethnicity, faith, language, and customs. But some did not hold on to what they were as tenaciously as Canadians who came from just one skip, hop, and jump away!

I suspected *Père* Roussel was different when mom's antenna picked up static. Because I knew him, she confided some parishioners thought he mingled too much with the people: *"Y s'mélange trop avec le monde."* Of course, she knew the parish grapevine about each priest, always positive, because all were exemplary. But in pre-Renewal days, "the-church-in-the-marketplace" ministry was still waiting the coming of ecumenical Pope John XXIII.

About a later leap forward, religious orders like mine, who only taught boys in higher grades at one time, started teaching girls too. In fact, wasn't the Academy the first in the history of the Order (established in 1821) to go co-ed in the early 1970's? Even after ultra-conservative Bishop McVinney told Brother Paul Demers, principal, that a co-ed high school was, well, "cohabitation!" In my Order an older monk crossed the street if he saw a daughter of Eve coming his way! And some in authority even pooh-poohed your riding alone in a car with a woman, even your mom. But I never saw that in the late 1940's when I entered, except I recall that Brother Doorman fled to his vineyard when a woman and son showed up for Open House. Recall I inherited his job.

So again, why had our Church ever left this kind of active ministry and now needed to go back to it? A professor said the Catholic Church was hurt "from within and without" by criticisms and defections so it had closed in on itself, as any wounded organism does. Some 500 years would pass before the Catholic Church here and abroad began to talk with other denominations about common faith elements (instead of warring over dogmatic points, Küng wrote) and rediscover its goal of "mission, not establishment." Like the Brothers, religious Orders debated long and hard on that principle causing massive changes in religious life and the Church in general. "Opening up the Windows" a time to let fresh air and new ideas in and open new vistas of communication within itself and between faiths. But change is pain, and the debate still rages whether St. Peter's bark lists too much to the left. Newspapers especially love to label church personnel and practices as either liberal or conservative, as if political.

One author said the Church unfortunately relaxed some practices (but not its doctrines) at the same time the American culture experienced a lessening of the strict Protestant ethic (seven main churches) that long prevailed since the Founding Fathers. For many, trickles of change became a deluge of moral laxity, abandonment of church membership (so-called "Nones") and practices, and a kind of *laissez-faire* from the Vietnam era on when America lost its Christian moral stance. Popes generally encapsulated all these new bankrupt trends as "modernism." Or more severely, "the culture of death," with especially the twin specters of abortion and euthanasia, and to a lesser degree, "the death of marriage and family," the union of man and woman, as constituted by the Creator and honored for thousands of years in every culture on earth. Of course, other countries have also embraced this faithless secularism. But a point for us, we're seen as a somewhat reverent, God-believing country, if weak in church worship. Like in the commercial, the guy on a horse says, "Alone, got to be alone." Tellingly he quickly falls.

So, in his own way, *Père* Roussel was a bellwether or leader of that evangelizing theology of service to the people. Did he sense as Francos assimilated into the secularized American culture where church was no longer the central, magnetic piece in their lives, it again needed to go into the highways and byways to bring the Gospel ("the good news") to them? Hadn't Christ and the Apostles done it that way? After the Depression and eventually the new post-WWII economy of greater wealth and affluence, it became the pursuit of the Almighty Dollar, not just the Almighty! To keep up with the Joneses and beat inflation became a frenetic seven-days-a-week preoccupation. A preoccupation that in time gradually robbed many of the faithful, consciously or not, of the time and inclination to pursue those devotions and practices that had earmarked devout Catholics and all Christians before, a priest wrote. Symbolically, when everyone had a so-called "Sunday suit" or outfit! I'm surprised how often the Bible's Exodus mentions God's emphasis on a day of worship and rest. But people needing Sunday to rest from voluntary 50-to-60-hour workweeks for play and sports viewing and finding religious services dull compared to their daily electronic TV stimulation, all caused a serious drop in the Sunday Mass obligation for Catholics. You couldn't serve two masters, Christ said. The other master, Mammon (wealth) - "Greed is good," said actor Michael Douglas in the movie *Wall Street*, - seemed to overtake our culture and undermine the faith and morals of the progeny of those first immigrants.

As the Recession of 2008 showed, what a cruel irony that "overworked" Americans (on average 47 hours of work) have not profited at all, amassing huge credit card debts and little saving. Blissful sleep, which the Bard called "the balm of hurt minds." and "nature's second course in life," eludes many, especially those working indoors and sitting. One in five women are depressed and many overworked with home and outside work: from a 100 to 110-hour work week. Women now equally educated want to work, but unfortunately take on a heavy load, as many women have told me. Is that why in a 2013 report, women's longevity is declining a bit, and men's rising? Women are also into more challenging jobs, bearing with tensions and stress only men generally endured at one time.

American historian Scott Appleby said the Roman Catholic faith in the U.S. after the war moved out of its immigrant "ghetto Catholicism" into rapid educational, economic and social assimilation in the mainstream American culture. Presumably, those devotees all share the same workaholic syndrome (nine more work weeks a year than other Western nations.), as well as the features of the religion of Americanism." From my *Boston College* magazine, it reported Catholics now cohabit and divorce almost at the same rate as everyone else. And one wrote that ennui, as in boredom, is leading Americans to pay huge sums on gambling, entertainment, sporting events, *et al* to seek relief from overwork. Interesting theory! Sunday is no longer the relief, relaxation, and family togetherness it once was.

Figures vary constantly but Franco-American Catholics are about as devout as people in Québec (about 20 percent). Canadian historian Michael Gauvreau says "One of the most compelling problems of postwar Canadian history was the devastating evisceration (cutting out) in the space of one short decade between 1961 and 1971 of Québec's Catholic identity." *La*

Révolution Tranquille (The Quiet Revolution) in which the provincial government assumed control of education, health, and social services for the first time, replacing the church's storied and reputed overly dictatorial direction, besides moral lapses. About the Old Testament, I recorded my amazement how God's chosen people - the Jews - were only faithful in spurts, often relapsing, even with God talking directly to them or their faith givers. But the Book of Psalms often hailed their return to the faith of their fathers, as embodied in: Abraham, Jacob, Moses, and the prophets. Human nature is so finicky or changing, the so-called butterfly syndrome. Are we due for a mass return?

Entering the Order in 1947 and not returning for five years (my training in New England and Alabama over), I hardly had time to whine that "that old gang of mine" was gone when Father Roussel burst into our third-floor apartment with his usual energy to welcome me home with a movie. Even though we hadn't communicated much in five years, he kept in touch with news releases. He was still coming to you. It meant a lot to my parents and me.

Mom had been right about his apostolic drive when he came to the parish. In a slower time when sinking roots and forming lasting clerical bonds with parishioners were the norm, priests, pastors especially, carved out lifelong apostolic careers in one or two places. For example, whenever you mentioned Precious Blood Parish, symbiotically she said *"le curé* (the priest) Bédard,"; *curé* Morin *ou* (where) *curé* Forest was St. Ann's pastor; *curé* Meunier, St. Louis, all pastors for life. So, this permanence was why she knew so much about *"les prêtres des parwaists* (the priests of the parishes)." She knew the *dramatis personae* or stage cast of all the parishes. My siblings and I knew the names of a lot of priests we never met. If transfers occurred it was the talk of the parish like those big baseball trades before free agency. Like the mailman, grocers, teachers, beat cop, nuns, Mount Saint Charles's Brothers, insurance man, ice and fruit peddler, the men who wore *la soutane* (the cassock) were a fixture in our life, like the constant North Star, as the Bard wrote in *Julius Caesar*. I mouthed his line in that play and I'll never forget the sloppy ketchup mess on my toga when Brutus slew me. A confrère (colleague) told me how many eggs Caesar had for breakfast! *"Et tu, Brute."*

So we lived like in a theocracy (government by God, like Jews in the Old Testament and *"les vicaires* (the vicars)" had the same popularity and visibility as. "the man of God" for the faithful in Oliver Goldsmith's "The Deserted Village." Also in that poem, living in an age of inescapable illiteracy like many American immigrants did, the humble folk admired the book larnin' of their teacher and the parson's moral stature: Of the parson,

"Truth from his lips prevailed with double sway, / And fools, who came to scoff, remained to pray." And their teacher could only be "faulted" for his penchant for knowledge: "The love he bore to learning was in fault (me: as if too much); / The village all declared how much he knew."

I think of *Père* Roussel and others like him whenever I hear the words, "Whatever you did to the least of these, you did unto me." Our neighborhood was full of those little people with little of "the wealth of nations," but he had found us out. When Pat, Jim, and I came later under his pastorate at Our Lady Queen of Matyrs, he told us that besides the burden of coronary problems, he met with mild reservations from some founding parishioners about his coming, so endeared were they to his predecessor. Replacing a legend is not easy, and he was succeeding *le curé* Ronaldo Gadoury, the carpenter-builder for whom the school is now named. A wit said, "No one succeeds like a successor," but some thought he was responsible for the change, as if he had a thing with the diocesan personnel board to get OLQM! Later, a new curate told a priest his assignment was Our Lady Queen of Carnivals! Those carnivals, now restored, first ran for 50 years, boosting parish spirit, support for the parish, tithing for Christian groups, and a late summer community get-together for the city.

So coming to OLQM was more challenging than his coming to St. Ann's long ago, when he was received with open arms with "the oils of ordination still fresh on him." But he kept his hand to the plow and furrowed the field given him, even if lined with the "boulders and roots" of life. In February of 1981, he went to his rest as a faithful son of first biblical priest-king Melchizedek, who is rendered so well by Nincheri at St. Ann's. Like St. Paul in that sports analogy I like so well: he ran the race to win the crown. An athlete for Christ who in Heaven's Pantheon wears the laurel garland of victory! He won Mount Olympus gold, negating whatever failings he may have shared with all of us mortals.

Guido Nincheri: St. Ann's Michelangelo

AS IMPRESSIVE AS the original decor of St. Ann's Church was to me as a youngster, it underwent a splendid re-creation during the pastorate of *le Révérend* Ernest Morin, who came to the parish in 1929. In the 1920s Charles Lorin, a prominent stained-glass artist, had already replaced the original plate-glass windows with dazzling shades of red, blue, green, and gold.

In anticipation of the parish's golden anniversary in 1940 (counting the temporary school-church across the street), the pastor procured the talents of Guido Nincheri (1885-1973), a celebrated Montreal artist of Italian-Florentine descent, to redo the church's entire interior because he liked his work at St. Matthew's in Central Falls. But his Canadian connection is why if listening to mom, you thought he too was at least a second cousin or part French-Canadian. It's a feeling we had about people she often spoke about. If you were a new player in our world, you were soon on her scorecard, and like a good manager she knew his curriculum vitae (resumé) and a bit about his family life.

Small, hunchbacked, and with a bad back like Michelangelo of Sistine Chapel fame, the Raphaelite wannabe undertook a Herculean task as big as the *Bible*. The entire church was to be his canvas for the story of creation, redemption, glorification, and all its major players. His quest was to make St. Ann, a classical Renaissance edifice with Corinthian or Grecian architecture, one of the most beautiful churches in America. In mill town Woonsocket where workers like my folks at times found it hard to put 15 cents in the basket on Sunday! His vision was for an ever-curing "sermon in fresco" with freshly hued creations of the giants and events of the Old and New Testaments, like Genesis, Jonas (or Jonah) in the Whale, the Temptation of Adam and Eve, Christ's Resurrection, the Blessed Mother, the Last Judgment (his *magnum opus*), Major or Minor Prophets, *et al.* And in a tribute to troubled times, even a soldier and sailor of WWII.

On July 8, 1940, *Père* Morin signed a two-year contract with Nincheri for $25,000, but fate intervened and the project wasn't completed until fall of 1948. On September 30, 1946, the parish voted to award him an additional $5,000 to complete his work. Besides frescoes, his stained-glass masterpieces were another facet of his creative genius. In Montreal, for example, his renown stemmed largely from them as *le célèbre maître-verrier d'origine italienne* (the famous Italian window artist), as he was known. In RI alone, hundreds of windows in over twenty churches are adorned with his glass art, a genius he honed at the Academy of Fine Arts in Florence, Italy.

First with-the-story - mom found out his padre didn't like having one more starving Italian artist, even with Michelangelo-like pretensions or talent. "Not willing to put down his brushes," Nincheri went to live with his uncle. In imitation of the great masters, Nincheri, credited by some for introducing frescoes in North America, did his on fresh wet plaster to retain their vivid color forever. It also fixed their admirable perspective from any angle of viewing. He had the help of plasterers Paul Jacob, a Mohawk Indian from Québec; Jean Prampolini from Central Falls; and church sexton, Alphonse Lavallée, who all rose at 2 a.m. to lay down just the amount the artist needed that day. The night before, Nincheri prepared a small drawing and then a larger one using a piece of charcoal. Then Lavallée and Nincheri's wife, Guilia, traced each charcoal line with a perforation wheel to create a stencil of little holes on frames created by Gérard Noel. In church, the perforated lines were dusted with a bag filled with dry blue charcoal dye, now absorbed into the plaster. With the paper removed, the remaining outline of blue dots enabled the artist to begin painting. Isn't success ninety-nine percent perspiration, one percent inspiration?

As parishioner Paul Bourget, narrator of a video and author of the parish centennial book, said, "Nincheri had no margin of error." His drawing and execution had to be perfect each time, or he told the set-up men to plaster all over again. In charge when Nincheri was in Montréal to clear up suspicions of Fascist sympathies (think of the Japanese American internment during the war), Joseph Begnoche did several background scenes, along with Prampolini, who also rendered *des tableaux* (small paintings), picture frames, and medallions.

Nincheri's murals solidified to marble-like hardness over the years, while retaining their fresh-as-today appearance. As the years crept by, it's as if the ghosts of Nincheri *et compagnons-artistes* (and fellow artists) were sneaking in every night to freshen them up. Those borders, incidentally, like apples for Adam and Eve or fishes for Jonas, served pictorially to re-enforce the content of the murals. But why did mom only mention Nincheri and Begnoche at home? Were the others really "behind the scenes?" With her, he was a ten-year conversational piece. As I read about slavery at Jefferson's Monticello in Virginia, is there something about an oral culture that surpasses electronic media communication which negatively seems to foster a kind of social isolation instead of togetherness?

"In my closest brush" with a great artist of that medium, some mornings as I walked to school past the Peloquin home, I saw him coming down from Kendrick Avenue. He resided in a home on Wood Avenue owned by Edgar and Isabelle Ethier. Isabelle posed for the face of Eve in the Garden of Eden fresco in St. Ann Church. Their sons, Raymond *et* Edgar, were schoolmates and Boy Scouts with us. *Les* Ethiers lived across the street from *le docteur* (the doctor) Auray Fontaine, dad's doctor and mom's family line. But how I wished I had waved or said, *"Bonjour* (Hello)" at least once, as he walked with the same fixed look as the mill owning Lepoutres going to church.

But again, why was two years not enough time for Nincheri to finish the work? The war and his inability to work in winter or summer (the indoor or outdoor heat dried the plaster too quickly) greatly extended the project. Not ungrateful, but mom echoed the parishioners' annoyance about the delayed finish: *"Le projet prends trop d'temps* (the project takes too long)." But about European cathedrals, for example, Nincheri could've told the faithful that churches sometimes took over a hundred years to finish due to financial, artistic, or architectural reasons. Recall *"Vita brevis sed ars longa"* about life being short, but art long or enduring? Or in the making!

The task took so long, prime mover *curé* Morin didn't see the work completed, dying August 29, 1941. His death touched dad who often went to his church-sponsored cultural activities. "*Ça ya, le curé Morin est mort. Cée d'valeur* (That's it, Father Morin is dead)," mom in turn mourned. When Scoutmaster Walter Jannell asked us to be an honor guard in church where he was laid out, dad advised me to show respect. No need. Ours was a parish troop and he'd been our pastor. And we, whose parents were mostly renters, had our own meetinghouse near the church for scouting and a weeknight drop-in center.

Finally, Nincheri's biblical vision of salvation history was finished under the pastorate of *le Monseigneur* J. Adrien Forest. On October 22, 1950, he presided with Bishop Russell McVinney at ceremonies marking the 60th anniversary of the parish and the total remake of the church's interior, including a new altar and communion rail from the pastor. Mom had been overjoyed when on his first episcopal visit to St. Ann's, he spoke French: "*Il parle notre langage* (he speaks our language)." About the completion, "*en fin* (finally)," sighed the parishioners collectively since they could at last view church ceremonies unobstructed by scaffolding. For ten years, you couldn't get into the pews without banging into a metal leg or something. The faithful always wondered what he was working on. Even mom was befuddled, since her parochial *viva voce* news line didn't reach those obstructed cerulean or blue-sky vaulted ceilings towering over parish life, like the twin towers outside. But she always conjectured: "*mon idée*, (my idea)" because she couldn't be clueless if she met *tante* Marie Louise Peloquin on the way to church. If Poldine didn't know, no one did!

I was there that Sunday morning after Nincheri had swirled his last brush stroke. The faithful rubbernecked during the whole Mass, admiring how *l'artiste italien* (the Italian artist) captured all the biblical greats in a state of arrested motion. He got two thumbs up in patois: "*Ya baim faite; "Ya du talen*" (He did great. He's talented) echoed our resident critic with the understatement of the year. Not professionally educated or artistically trained (but great in manual arts), the faithful didn't stint their praise of those who were. They had incredibly curious, inquisitive minds, alert to their surroundings, personal or material. We chuckled when mom heard a performance, sung or played, and gave it a good review: "*Ya pas manqué* (didn't miss) *une note*," (a note, pronounced like "nut"). A quantitative analysis more attuned to dad's mindset.

When I counseled at Norton High School next to Wheaton College, I learned it was the first college ever to offer a liberal arts education to women instead of just domestic niceties like how to set a table or pack a suitcase. I pictured mom graduating from there as a teacher: "*J'ai mon diplome* (I have my diploma)," and wanting to impart her knowledge to thousands of kids. For many reasons it never happened, but siblings and I got lucky since her French-Canadian culture put a high priority on "home tutoring!" And gosh, we had another teacher in *mémère* Fontaine, whose classroom was in the 1880s in *Saint Francois du lac, Québec*. Imagine all the added education we would've received if brilliant dad wasn't stymied by a hand-to-mouth mill job! He who next to his faith valued education above everything else.

But some of the "naked splendor" of the artist's work quickly evoked a few conservative tut! tuts! in the pews. In the aftermath of the permissiveness and sexual revolution of the last decades, it's hard to believe his Resurrection of Christ and the Temptation of Adam and Eve stirred such a maelstrom or torrent in the parishioners' conservative teacups.

She told me objections were raised about the too unadorned Christ rising from the tomb, seen in the mural behind the main altar. Why, instead, of all those wrappings the Holy Women had modestly put around His body, only rays, a bit too diaphanous or *trop* (too much) Claire's conservatives said, swathed the youthful figure: Christ at the age of 33, once thought life's optimum state! In history, artist Caravacchio (1495-1543) had drawn the same complaint. Even though Nincheri could've argued the evangelist said the wrappings were neatly left in the sepulcher, he bowed to French-Canadian sensibilities about modesty in the human form, however divine and risen. So, he toned down "the habiliments of glory" to its present more modest form. He lost a round and perhaps "his composure" too: *"perdu sa façon* (lost his way)," mom said. Her favorite put-down or "perfect squelch" comment!

But even more controversial was his ceiling depiction to our right of the nave of the serpentine seduction of our First Parents. Adam and Eve were rendered a bit too comely and unadorned in their usual sylvan *parterre* or garden under the proverbial apple tree. Here supposedly too a few artistic strokes in the name of modesty rendered the former provocative scene a little less *"au naturel,"* especially of beauteous Eve! But another story, which Paul Bourget told me is the right one, says Nincheri balked at changing a biblical scene. St. Ann's French-Canadian morality be damned! He quoted Pilate when parties wanted INRI (Jesus of Nazareth, King of the Jews) stripped from the cross after his death: *Quod scripsi, scripsi,* meaning, "What I have written, stays."

Hadn't Nincheri taken almost ten years to do it all? Did they want him to undo it all stroke by stroke? Surely Nincheri, a latter-day disciple of Michelangelo (1475-1564), also knew his contemporary, Daniele DaVoltera, had, despite the Sistine Chapel creator's objections, covered up 38 nude figures with loincloths. This expurgating act was in keeping with proper 16th

Century taste and decorum. Four centuries later, parishioners - not untouched by Jansenism, Puritanism, or overwrought Catholic consciences, also wanted their art in full dress.

None of us kids at the time saw any reported change in the garden scene. Teachers told us about custody of the eyes with this scene especially. There was a lot of rubbernecking and raised eyebrows in church. You tried to see the painting without raising your head or neck. Trying to cop a sight while pretending to straighten your obligatory tie, you ran the risk of being caught by our vigilant and serge-garbed bastion of morality: *ma Soeur* (the nun). Al Savoie, brother of Bob's wife Millie, still enjoys retelling how he snatched some "reflected glory" with a mirror: "Curiosity killed the cat, but satisfaction brought him back."

True, we could have sneaked a look anytime we passed by the church. And that's something we did quite often in those days when we walked or biked everywhere, and I on my *Call* beat. Nuns and moms taught us to doff our hats or even drop in *pour une visite* (for a visit). Even in the pews, we were so programmed not to look, we felt a twinge of conscience if we did. We knew at birth we were given a guardian angel to watch over us, but you couldn't pull the wool over his eyes. Like my favorite radio character of yesteryear, Lamar Cranston (the Shadow), he knew everything you did. In our missals many had a holy card with a protecting angel hovering over a tyke at river's edge. But he wasn't going to save us despite ourselves, "*malgré nous autres* (despite us)," said mom.

You never wanted to tell Father Moreau anything in the confessional about the 6th or 9th Commandments, like "Forgive me, Father, for I've copped a sight," to quote Holden Caulfield in *The Catcher in the Rye*. We were always squeamish confessing transgressions against purity of body and mind. *Soeur Sainte* Émilie told us most sinful omissions in the confessional dealt with that. Again, would Brother Anthony in my Order have said, "How did she know?" That's why we should do that first when our resolve was at its highest. We had no qualms about confessing the old standbys, lack of charity and displays of anger and disobedience. Is that why Francos thought purity of body and mind was almost as important as Christ's essential message of loving God and your neighbor like yourself?

Like others, I had a hard time getting used to the doors of the church being closed during the week, long before the diocese closed them forever. Vandalism, desecration (once), and arson possible concerns? Who can forget the theft of a first-class relic from Saint Theresa's of Nasonville (village of Burrillville, RI), now magnanimously replaced by the Brothers of the Sacred Heart? Also, when heating oil was no longer seven cents a gallon, but a weekly hit of $1,000, so we read, it shut out daily visits, even if "heartwarming." And of course, people not going to Mass Saturday or Sunday certainly weren't going to drop in during the week: "Got to make the donuts," see a game on TV, catch up on sleep, make tee time, like all those in Christ's story who had an excuse and missed the wedding feast and were replaced by others. A cautionary tale? Should Francos who have wandered off into the mist be especially wary, since like the Jews in biblical times, they were first called to the faith in 4th Century Europe? Is theirs a case of "Many are called, but few are chosen?" Or choose not to be?

 About vandalism, recall my friend stole from the poor box (*pour les pavers*) inside the Communion rail. Was it unlocked or was he trying to jimmy it, as I pondered and prayed in the pews that no *femme de piété* (woman of piety/nun) came in during the devilish caper? He surely didn't know the line, applicable to houses of worship, about being "poor as a church mouse." Said he'd done it before, as if a heist gave you a pass to another. Later he got into trouble for his larcenous ways, and again I was with him. What a moral deterrent I was! Lucky not to be guilty by association! Mitigating factors were his parents who didn't always live together, a rare thing in Franco families. And he wasn't in scouting with us, again negating a good influence the rest of the gang had. But the Bard has a line about conscience making "cowards (fear of punishment) of us all," and so he grew up into a fine family man, now long departed. Compassionate mom gave him a pass, "*Le bon Dieu lui en a passe* (The good Lord has given him a pass)," supporting dad's belief that to understand was often to forgive. After all, didn't I say the Depression was also tough on us kids? Before my paper route, my weekly allowance was a buffalo nickel! Like the Prodigal Son, did he rationalize his tendency towards cupidity? "To work I'm unable; to beg I'm ashamed?"

 Isn't it a sobering time capsule that we dreaded more having to tell a priest, especially *Père* Moreau, than a police officer? I think priests in the confessional kept more kids "on the straight and narrow" than any other lawgiver in Social *Coin*. No need to have a Sockanossett reform school (now the RI Training School) in Woonsocket! Yet, a breakaway reformer in the 16th Century was convinced priests got in the way of the faithful and God! But that was like killing the messenger.

 But ah, "Fame, the last infirmity of noble minds," Milton wrote. How we wished Nincheri chose us as models for those 500 faces and 600 characters cavorting so airily in the church's stratosphere. Marguerite Forget, whom he sketched as he sat with the family on their porch, is rendered some 40 times. Maybe because I was too thin, without a round face, angelic looks, or healthy cheeks ("*les joues roses*," like Rachel had as a baby), I was not among the elect. To quote the Bard, had the Depression left "a pale cast of thought" over me, even if nutritionist dad was clever "*a nous donner un bonne table* (to give us a good table)," mom boasted? I never got the half-dollar (imagine, ten weeks' allowance!) or peanut butter sandwich the models he sketched received in payment. How did he say "Skippy" in Italian?

Bob's wife, Mildred Savoie, (married 64 years; died in June 2014) is rendered in a beautiful fresco above the main altar as the Child Virgin Mary flanked by her parents Saint Ann and Saint Joachim. Her portrait is now replicated on the Robert and Mildred Tellier family tombstone at the St. John Cemetery, Slatersville RI. Mom said the priests, *les Révérends* Morin, Forest, Moreau, Fournier, *et* Massicotte, were also depicted among the vaulted heavenly hosts or in some liturgical pose. Were they "bribed" with the four bits or peanut butter? *Père* Roussel was rendered in a vestry window outside the sanctuary.

In speaking about the artist Nincheri, Mom revealed an interesting little anecdote about who, besides those who were part of the Church Triumphant (heaven), got on those church murals in Christendom. Because *Il Duce* (Mussolini) had signed a Concordat of peace with the Vatican, made trains (*les chars*) run on time, and filled those swamps around Rome (refilled by the Nazis), some *Italiano* artists had literally canonized him in life, rendering his Roman face, aquiline nose, and square jaw on church murals. But in the war, his fall from grace was precipitous after we invaded Italy, shattering his dream of a "new Roman Empire." Mom, with no sympathy for sin and corruption, said, *"Ils l'ont faite effacé vite"*- they erased him before the paint was dry. A great one-liner! She often laughed at her own humor, her eyes filling up tear-like. She and *tante* Laurence were a terrific comedic duo. How could they forget their troubled past and at a moment's notice double up with laughter? But because so many Francos were jovial, was it a cultural genetic trait underpinned by a hopeful, joyous faith?

Nincheri, said mom, mis-stroked by picturing Mussolini in a Montreal church, causing his loyalty to be suspect. Hence his trips back to Canada. They say Rome moves slowly, but artists thought this great *Fascista* (Fascist) deserved a mural in the inner sanctum of saints. With very few exceptions, like the holy *Sainte Thérèse* of Lisieux (and now Pope John Paul II, *subito* (immediately), and John XXIII, and others), they forgot why the Church is agonizingly slow in conferring sainthood. A Jesuit author said literature must withstand the test of time to be called great. Likewise for the life, writings, and good works of saints. *Sainte Thérèse*, as one of our patrons, continues to do good in heaven for us on earth, as she promised. Of all the saints, a writer surmised she had the greatest devotion and love of Christ while on earth. Imagine, she never left the convent, yet became the patron of all missionaries, which she wanted to be. She also promised to pluck flowers off heaven's floor as proof of graces sent to earth. In the summer, I keep fresh roses before her statue in Patricia's memorial flower garden in our yard, including a plaster cast of two reading children, a gift from niece Jan (Tellier) Reale in remembrance of Pat's great gift in teaching that important skill. Pat told me principals liked that her students jumped two grade levels in one year in reading.

I wonder what artists thought when Romans hanged *Il Duce* upside down with his mistress, Clara Petacci? The photo was front page in all the newspapers; I had never seen anything so gruesome. True, in one dignified holy picture given us by the nuns, the saintly Saint Peter is seen crucified upside down because he felt unworthy to be laid out like Christ.

In the Order I heard the story - fact or fiction? - of St. Peter fleeing the city of Rome to avoid persecution. Meeting Christ, he asked, "Where are you going?" the *Quo Vadis* of book and movie. When Christ said he was going to Rome to be crucified again, tempestuous Peter got the message and re-entered the Eternal City for his fate.

We've never forgotten the pastor's sermon the Sunday when the project was *finito*. He spoke about the inscriptions beneath the murals behind and around the altars. To all non-classical parishioners, who like me spoke little true French, only passable English, and certainly no Latin, the inscriptions were "Greek to us." But one of them piqued my curiosity because the word "canine" was in it: *Panis Angelicus Non Mittendum Canibus*: "The Bread of Angels is not to be given to dogs" (the unworthy). The same language of the Mass next to French in our Sunday missal. I quickly forgot the translations the pastor gave but wanted to know what they meant. What joy eleven years later when I returned to visit as an English and Latin teacher! Now I like reading Latin mottoes on state shields, coat-of-arms, old tombstones, and older missals.

The pastor surprised the faithful by not talking at length about the paintings. They spoke for themselves! After church, mom gave the sermon her imprimatur or *nihil obstat*, that is, "print" and "nothing out of line," and "*Ya baim faite* (He did well). *Il nous falla la traduction* (We needed the translation)." Great news she could pass along to *tante* Laurence of St. Louis Parish and discuss with *tante* Marie-Louise of the parish. Those three had to be the most knowledgeable ETWN (Eternal Word Network) anchors the Church had in the city. In classical literature, would they have been the Greek Chorus commenting on a dramatic scene like in *Oedipus Rex*? Because those two were always "beaming" to her, is that why she knew so much about St. Ann's and St. Louis? They were like church deaconesses in their parishes. As their devout sisters do today, they would teach or run a CCD (Confraternity of Christian Doctrine) program, lector at Mass, minister the cup, and dress the altar. Didn't we say 70 percent of church volunteers are women? Didn't a teacher - pro-feminist or realist? - say more women may make it to heaven? But no gender identities in heaven and no more marriages, said Christ.

A writer counted some 15 women Christ knew and dealt with in His ministry. How he would've loved our moms too! How like during the Middle Ages had the church been so successful in making their lives such a faith-filled experience centered on worship, service, and salvation? For them and men too, there was no disconnect between Sunday worship and the rest of the week. Their loyalty to the church was matched by their piety and devotion. They were like members of so-called Third Orders, living their faith like religious priests, Brothers and Nuns, but without vows, distinctive habit, or communal life, save their large families. Bishop Tobin summed it up nicely: "Faith gives us a strong foundation of moral values on which we can build our lives 'in the here and now,' so that we're not tossed and turned by every politically correct fad that comes along."

About the vow of poverty in religious life, did I relate the comment of a poor mom who saw her son profess the three vows: "You have the vow of poverty, but I'm the one who practices it." Another, admiring the beautiful residence he lived in, said, "You've got a vow of property, not poverty." And one mom was ecstatic about her nun daughter loving the life; since all her letters had JMJ at the top. It meant Jesus, Mary, Joseph, but she thought it was "*J'aime ma job* (I love my job). " In the Order, I said we were taught that real poverty was detachment from possessions, not deprivations. But oh, how I hated throwing into the sports pile the professional glove Bob brought home from the navy! "My fielding average" took a dive when I drew a torn, pancake-sized glove.

Years after I left the parish for the Brotherhood, sadly mom told me about the death of Nincheri on March 1, 1973, in Providence, RI. He had shown parishioners an artistic and enduring vision of the incredible panorama of their faith. A faith arising from the Dawn of Creation (including that Adam and Eve scene: "All life began in a garden," says a writer) to the Last Judgment! He had literally put their faith on church walls for them to see. True, Christ told the Samaritan woman it didn't matter where you worshipped, but to them no spoken work or place was as eloquent as his artistic sermon. I wrote that faith comes from hearing (*ex airbus*) from parents, teachers, and priests but he took it out of their mouths, so to speak, and the pages of Scripture and manifested it before their very eyes. Unlike doubting Thomas who wouldn't believe unless he saw the Risen Christ and touched His wounds, those Francos and their rock-solid faith didn't need to see to believe, but Michelangelo's alter ego made it easier. With what joy mom burst out, "*On wé (voit) toute maintenant* (we see everything now)," echoing the Gospel's cured blind man, who not only saw the world for the first time, but also his God and Savior.

Unbelievably that faith would last longer than the parish. Believers throughout history have endured the pain of seeing their faith centers destroyed or closed. When Christ said even the gates of hell wouldn't destroy His church, He of course meant its spirit and message, not necessarily the church building where you were baptized or maybe married. Christ once chided doubting Thomas after the Resurrection, but not the parishioners. He knew they had come to the city in poverty, but with faith and generosity built their church with nickels and dimes and nurtured their belief through the Depression, health crises, and two wars. Theirs was a challenged faith that was, as a mystic like the great Saint Theresa of Avila called it, a kind of darkness of the soul, when for so long there was, like for *les* Fontaines, little or no light at the end of the tunnel. But they endured to see this day of unveiling, this new creation of St. Ann's, adding credence to Mom's oft-repeated line: "*On a passé à travers* (we got through it)," about passing through the crucible of poverty and suffering. And luckier than the three disciples at the short-lived Transfiguration, parishioners could now glimpse the glory that was, is, and will be every time they walk through its holy portals.

From a book in the Order about a person's lasting contribution, I thought of a Latin phrase, in part, for his monument, if Nincheri had been buried in Precious Blood Cemetery: "Truly, you have constructed a work more lasting than bronze," (*aere perennius*), a phrase Brother Paul Demers and I teased each other with if we did something good. Or the tribute a little old lady paid the artist indirectly when she saw me looking up after the funeral of *Soeur Ste. Émilie*: "*L'église est belle, n'est-ce-pas* (The church is beautiful, isn't it)?" Nailed it!

Nincheri's life makes one question if *Father Knows Best*. But of course, his father (padrone?) only wanted the best for his son. I was thrilled to attend St. Ann's centennial banquet ceremonies and see his grandson Roger introduced but didn't get to meet him. Isn't there a video biography of Nincheri called *Windows to Heaven*?[39] At Mass, did he find it hard to believe his padre finished this awesome opus so long ago? He surely felt his presence, his work still fresh, still curing, still enduring.

Humorously, did his dad teach him some of the patois he, Social *Coin's* favorite adopted son, picked up in his 10 years in the parish? But a sense of decorum prevents us from conjecturing what the sleep-deprived

---

[39] The *Windows to Heaven* documentary can be viewed online at: https://vimeo.com/23046664

plasterers may have "told" Nincheri when asked to redo a whole section again!

Shulla Sannella in *The River Valley Current* reported Nincheri decorated 220 to 260 churches and at least 5000 windows in his lifetime. Surely the Triune God has commissioned him to continue painting in the Church of the Triumphants! Are some of the sunsets his? As a latter-day disciple of Michelangelo, he believed "Perfection is no trifle; but trifles make perfection."

In a sense Nincheri brought all the masterpieces of the Vatican to Social *Coin*. Being Italian, Nincheri by his talent, heritage and artistic forefathers also helped make their French-Canadian faith truly Catholic (Universal), one of the four pillared foundations of Catholicism. Yes, one of the world's greatest fresco artists and stained-glass window makers lived for a whole decade in our aproned, blue-jeans city! How many towns and cities in America share that kind of artistic heritage?

Sadly, St. Ann's last Mass was on Sunday, October 19, 2001, before a thousand "unbelieving people" like me. As the faithful will long mourn the liturgical closure of this magnificent temple, isn't it ironic it was built when there was faith but little money, but ceased to be a church because, apart from shifting populations and prohibitive repair bills, there was more money, but not enough faith? "Who will save them?" a voice from Scripture once cried out in unspeakable despair? "Who will keep the barbarians (all we of little faith?) from the gates?" Yes, to erase St. Ann's is to erase one the most important chapters in the history of the coming of Francos to the city. Like the tubercular poet Keats (1795-1821) who worried about the script on his burial plot, historians of the parish will someday read "on the stone" of the church's history: "Here is one parish whose name was writ in water," meaning no lasting monument of St. Ann's in its spiritual and liturgical reality will be there. Again, is our cry the unbelieving tyke's "Say it ain't so, Joe?"

Since St. Ann's, like Precious Blood and St. Charles, was a founding patrimony of Woonsocket's faith, couldn't all local parishes and diocesan officials in Providence, the latter so inexplicably silent, have striven might and main to achieve the survival of one of their Mother Churches, one who gave so much to her children, but now needed them in her centennial senescence? But to be fair, cold reality is the city built too many "national" churches to serve the pedestrian faithful whose progeny in great numbers (the mill economy gone) now lives in the burbs and beyond where education and lucrative jobs have taken them. As Pat and I used to say, "It happened that way, moving west" from a Dick Powell weekly drama about people on the move.

Unfortunately, architecturally there is no fifth mark of our church like "Abiding" or "Forever." But it only allays the sorrow that it isn't just us (America and Canada) where decrease in faith is happening, like it did in Europe in centuries past and now also in Spain and Ireland. Like in the parable of the lost sheep, if those 40 percent in the mist return, the ecclesial bleeding may stop. I reflect the faith was at its peak when I was a youngster, but now only a shadow of its pristine glory. As in all events in history, the causes are multiple, but hopefully reversible. For the ancients did they have the advantage of the belief in "the second coming of Christ," giving them an enduring sense of hope?

Long ago, Horace wrote that poetry should both instruct and delight. But I believe that can be said of all the arts. So, if St. Ann's can no longer be a weekly visual teaching and liturgical text of the Catholic Church, perhaps the spirited work of the Saint Ann Arts and Cultural Center devotees can continue to delight and elevate us with its literary projects and musical programs. But it's comforting to reflect that Nincheri's never-aging "beautiful people" on the walls will always be in attendance, consecrated church or not, hoping against hope that someday the faith of our fathers will again be seen in the pews, as it was for a century. Is it ironical that while Nincheri's frescoes started curing in their ever-fresh mode, the faith of many started to dry out because like in the Parable of the Sower, their faith-seed was on shallow ground or choked by the briar entanglement of worldly cares and pursuits?[40]

---

[40] Chapter 7 in its original form appeared in *The Woonsocket Call* October 18, 2001, a day before the last Mass ever at St. Ann. I received letters from around the country expressing disbelief and sadness about the church closing.

8 - THE ASCENT TO TRUTH IN THE OLD SCHOOLHOUSE

Parochial School: "The Bishop Tells Me So"

As YOUNG SOCIAL *Coin* area parishioners, we were almost preordained to attend St. Ann's School, for us only a stone's throw from our Gaulin Avenue home. "Preordained" because every year, especially the Sunday before school started, the pastor used his "bully pulpit" to remind parents it was almost a matter of conscience to do so. A conference of Catholic bishops in Baltimore in the 1880s exhorted Catholics to attend if humanly possible, since people knew *Nul est tenu à l'impossible*, about no one being obligated to the impossible. The bishops knew a parish devoid of a school didn't nurture young people as strongly in the beliefs and practices of the faith. The ideal trilogy was family, church, and school to form the conscience of a good, moral person and practicing faithful.

Pastor Charles Dauray, so intimately bound with the early development of Precious Blood Church, was passionate about education for the faithful. So, his efforts led to the creation of St. Clare HS, Mt. St. Charles, and Sacred Heart College (*le petit collège*) in his parish, not to mention St. Francis Orphanage which served 12,000 children, orphans or not. And no less noteworthy, Hospice Saint Antoine, where my own parents spent their last years in a caring, loving environment. He was truly a pastor with "cradle to grave" concerns for the faithful.

In the evolution of American education, despairing at the incredible diversity of American religions, Horace Mann helped establish a public school system that, unlike some countries, was religion neutral. But interestingly, I discovered Massachusetts ended spending public monies to support private schools with an 1854 constitutional amendment. This occurred during a time of anti-immigrant prejudice sweeping the country, especially against Irish and other Catholics in the Bay State! The amendment applied only to parochial schools since Protestant-affiliated private schools received state help for another 60 years! Political forces in 1917 prevented the unequal legislation from being changed by the electorate. Did it reflect Christ's words, "They will hate you because of me." Paul Johnson in *A History of Christianity* affirmed his belief in a value-based Christian education: "But our system earnestly inculcates all Christian morals; it founds its morals on the basis of religion; it welcomes the religion of the Bible; it allows it to do what it is allowed to do in no other system, to speak for itself." One can only guess how far public education has departed from that Christian orientation, as well as in many families, with too many students growing up not anti-religious, but clueless about any belief system at all. The Bible anticipated it: "Who will teach them?"

Given the basically secular nature of public education, many students of Franco, Irish, Italian, Polish descent and others, like the Jews, for whom education and religion were an integral educational component, flocked to their Catholic parish schools, a tremendous saving for city and state. The rationale, as I saw written in one school's philosophy, was that "learning is taught along certain philosophical and theological beliefs instead of in a moral vacuum." As MSC says it, "Its mission and its founding charism - every student is known, valued and treasured - has never changed." Because schools were so much part of the parish, I said some Franco pastors feuded with the bishop when he sought funds to found diocesan schools. But those diocesan schools would also have mandatory religion classes and promote the faith and its practices in English.

I have mentioned that my friends and I had a vague, uncomfortable feeling about public school. If you misbehaved or did poorly in parochial school, your parents threatened to send you there. To us "boding tremblers," it seemed banishment into some academic dark place. Our school naturally reinforced that uncomfortable feeling. Another option for us boys before being "threatened" with public school was *le Petit Collège des Frères du Sacré Coeur* (the Little College of the Sacred Heart Brothers) on Hamlet with its tough discipline of the Brothers of the Sacred Heart. Mount St. Charles on Bernon Heights later replaced it and eventually went co-ed. Dad said the Hamlet school brooked no tomfoolery and kids boxed on Friday nights to lessen boyish aggression. Ben went, but by choice, as did cousin François Fontaine and Joseph Phaneuf, who both joined the Brothers. We trained together and after college at Spring Hill, Alabama, and St. Michael's in Vermont, we became staffers at the Academy. Not too forcefully, but there was another reason why dad "thought" about sending us to public school at times. Because our education was principally in French, we didn't progress as quickly in English, which irritated him. Of course, our inclusive Francophone neighborhood and the city's transplanted Canuck culture were largely responsible for that. He often chafed because we spoke both French and English badly. If the situation didn't change, it would hinder our education and career opportunities outside the mills. He reasoned fluency would come sooner in public school, even if by sheer osmosis alone. But he never wavered in his support of the Catholic school system and monthly paid the one-dollar tuition on time for each of us. Hard to believe, but some families couldn't pay it.

God, if we had gone to public school in our 'hood, we would've been the only ones. But for those who couldn't or didn't want to, there was "*le catéchisme*" (called CCD today) and release time for Catholic kids in public schools was allowed. Think about that bit of religious accommodation! Were the bigots of the early 20th Century nativism and anti-Romanism asleep at the switch, or thank God, had the religious intolerance of the previous century largely disappeared? Or to the city's credit, was it its great spirit of ethnic and church accommodation, always an earmark of the city?

So tight was our parochial enclave about Catholic education, I only knew one kid in public school. He wasn't a close friend but related to the Lanoies in our tenement. He had a lively imagination and brought a new dimension to our game of throwing baseball cards closest to a wall. Our cards were all dog-eared and without much value from rough handling and flipping. He never had many cards or any, so he suggested we pretend throwing them. But the gang didn't like his invisible cards being the closest. As Christ said, "The children of this world are often more clever than those of the light." So, we were dim bulbs to put up with him at first. But we quickly ostracized him. As the Brits say, "What we 'ave, we 'old." Yes, they too dropped their aitches, even when eating alphabet soup, Brother Hermas joked at MSC. There are no aspirated aitches in French.

In the parochial schools, the study of religion was numero uno in the curriculum and its raison d'être. For us Francos especially, if you forgot your French mother tongue, it would undermine your faith and its vigor: *Qui perd sa langue, perd sa foi* (Who loses his language, loses his faith). In the pamphlet *The French in Rhode Island*, the authors cite the *survivance* (survival) thrust to buttress this belief. Besides pulpit and school, this conviction was a recurring theme in local French newspapers, like *La Tribune*, (first Franco newspaper in the USA), *Le Travailleur, et La Sentinelle*. They found their way at times into many homes like mine. Even in my Order, founded in Lyons, France, 1821, but especially thriving in Canada and French-Canadian communities in New England. Before and after the war, I saw one or more of those publications, especially *La Sentinelle*. But in the 1950s they were read more for curiosity than support for any "Lost Cause" mentality. Beautiful French could be found in texts like a 1886 French edition of the Bible (Société Bibliqué Americaine), given me by my niece, Jan Reale from her friend Nancy Kaelin who found it in boxes. Who says Catholics don't read the Bible, as someone lectured me at Woonsocket's Autumnfest? I told him bibles were chained in churches to prevent thievery! And before translations, who knew the language of the Caesars? Luther caused an uproar when he translated the Bible into German. An English author did the same and was executed in a foreign country where he had it published to avoid King Henry VIII's wrath.

Canadian prelates implanted this fear of losing the faith into compatriots tempted to send their children to public schools in or outside of

Québec. *Mon oncle François* told me, as related in the Fontaine inferno story, that when living in Cochrane, Ontario, outside the pale of very Catholic Québec, the pastor "warned" parishioners. But one mother defied him. And when my grandmother spoke to him about coming to America after the forest fire, he tried to dissuade her. Obviously his and other prelates' caution had little effect on the 1,800,000 Canadians who fled to the New England mills and beyond. Canada's biggest export at one time.

Like the Irish of the 1840s, immigrants wanted "to keep body and soul together." *Mémère* agreed with the pastor that you couldn't live on bread alone but had the nerve to tell him you needed some to live. Unlike the Pilgrims or Puritans, religion had nothing to do with their coming. On the contrary, it's why the Canadian clergy tried to keep them home.

Exploration and conversions first motivated the first Frenchmen to North America, like Champlain (*Capitaine Ordinaire*), Jacques Cartier, and former apothecary-turned-farmer, Louis Hébert, who sired one of the great family lines in Québec. About him, Morris Bishop in his book *Champlain, The Life of Fortitude* says Hébert gave up the drudgery of compounding drugs in a sunless Parish shop for the bounties of Canada. The author extolled Champlain, a superb navigator and cartographer, his desire to explore new lands, meet new people, and find a way to China and the Far East. He founded Quèbec.

Hébert's dying words reflected the French-Canadian faith of old: "This life is brief, the life to come is for eternity. I am ready to go to the presence of God, my judge, to whom I must render an account of all my past life." France in the 17th century was in the golden age of its Catholic faith. And about Indians, he begged his family "to love them as I have loved them, to assist them according to your power. God will thank you for it and reward you in Paradise." The author called him "Canada's first habitant." It was wishful thinking when mom told me once we were descended from his daughter Guillemette's line. But how meritorious if our country had treated our American Indians like Hebert did in Canada. Ours is a great reprehensible stain on our Western expansion and Manifest Destiny impulse. The damage evident today on dispossessed reservations racked by unemployment and alcoholism. They were once Lords of the Plains! The open prairie horse culture was one of the greatest lifestyles ever, one wrote. No taxes, jails, or the thousand-and-one laws of modern societies. When the settlers first came, there were some 600 tribes and a million Indians, but the white man's greed, cupidity, mendacity or lies, desire for land, and viruses decimated tribes.

Since the Canadian clergy couldn't dissuade Canadians from leaving, priests followed them here to minister, establish schools with male and female religious, as well as hospitals, nursing homes, and orphanages. The faithful lauded them: "How beautiful upon the mountains are the feet of the messengers who announce peace," as eulogist Brother Demers cited at the funeral in 2014 of Brother Charles-Leo St-Amand SC, who spent years in Africa. Because those missionaries did their job so well, for a century or more they helped preserve almost intact the culture, faith, and language my parents and other compatriots had known in Québec. We said cataclysmic influences like WWII, the flight of the mills, the loss of their national churches and schools, the secularization of the American culture all "crept with their petty pace." It's a familiar story in history, as the "invaders" - French-Canadian in this instance - who initially "conquered" their new American habitats with their way of life, were in time mainstreamed. Like the Vikings were in Northern England (Danelaw), Normandy, and even Russia. But as good and inevitable as that was, it also meant for too many a decrease, if not a total loss, of *"la foi de nos ancêtres"* (the faith of our fathers) and their customs. Ethnically speaking, a writer said America's melting pot doesn't always melt fully. But when it does, it also vaporizes worthwhile ingredients put in there by various racial or ethnic groups. But King Baudouin I of Belgium was more positive: "America has been called a melting pot, but it seems better to call it a mosaic, for in it each nation, people or race which has come to its shores has been privileged to keep its individuality, contributing at the same time its share to the unified pattern of a new nation."

Again, about the loss of faith in America, sociologist James Davidson cited a change in status as a possible cause. "Protestants and Catholics are now similar in social status and the in-and-out groups that plagued them in the past are not as salient." Does it mean faith rises or declines depending on one's social and economic pecking order? With a lessening of the faith now for both denominations, is it a case of the biblical caution, "How hardly will the rich enter heaven." (Specifically, those unmindful of the poor and living scandalously.) And further, becoming fully Americanized and adopting fully its ethos of materialism, modernism, science as the only reality, and secularism. Yet, as mentioned elsewhere, people with education have been less likely to go faithless. To become a faithful practitioner requires a deep commitment of soul and mind.

In *Québec to New England: The Life of Monsignor Charles Dauray*, Ambrose Kennedy detailed how the Canadian prelate eventually decided to spend his apostolic career among Franco émigrés. Mom often retold his grittiness in helping develop Precious Blood church despite difficulties. Leave it to her to know that by special permission he was interred on church property. The on-site is *la Place Dauray*, said Ray Bacon of the Museum of Work & Culture, in his talk on Woonsocket landmarks. Like Dauray, other French-speaking priests initially came from Canada until an American-born clergy emerged. Alongside of them also came some 30 religious Orders of men and women. But eventually an American-born clergy with diminishing French speech undermined that linkage between French and faith for parishioners, especially in some churches.

Recall that telegenic Bishop Fulton J. Sheen in his *Life Is Worth Living* TV talks said this missionary élan works in cyclical ways. After initially sending missionaries to others, a country later becomes a receiver, as faith and call to higher service waxes and wanes, like now. Are we destined to become a missionary territory again in the future? Besides the aging of our native-born clergy, how many of our priests are now foreign born? Will our missionary priests mostly come, say, from Africa someday? A biographer said Pope John Paul II kept an eye on the continent visiting it nearly ten times. But in Europe where the faith is in serious decline, Poland is an exception with its many priestly vocations. Have 1,000 years of adversity as a nation between aggressive Germany and Russia somehow spawned a greater faith?

Unlike India, where Mother Theresa's community is also flourishing as well as others, priestly and male and female religious vocations in the USA are way down. Hopefully the ardent faith of the few faithful will surpass the tepidity of many so Christ may say of us here, "A greater faith in all of Israel I have not seen." And may our unequalled generosity be our saving grace!

The Mission of Catholic Education

HISTORIANS OF CATHOLIC education in America say the system was built largely on almost free labor (as my dad also said), nearly all of it supplied by teaching nuns, Brothers, and some priests too! We said some of those nuns were *les Soeurs de la Présentation de Marie* (the Sisters of the Presentation of Mary), the French-speaking congregation who taught at St. Ann's and elsewhere in the city. I said compassionate dad said they toiled for a couple of hundred dollars a year, a pittance even before the war. One Sunday when the pastor said they slept on straw mattresses, dad vowed to give what he didn't have. Mom's response after Mass was, we weren't sleeping on feather beds either! All her mild barbs about him were about the "faults" of his virtues. Other wives should be so lucky! She loved and liked this tall, somewhat shy and modest guy whose timidity once led him to skip their date. She was dressed to kill, a cousin told me. Proof that "a man chases a girl, until she catches him?" The story only came out later, otherwise we would have thanked her for staying the course. And because you "marry" his or her in-laws too, what joy for my siblings and myself that our spouses loved and liked them too.

Because we were children of mill town workers and first-generation Americans concerned with survival, we lamented that many grammar school graduates never went on to high school. Our nuns, however, were extremely competent and dedicated in their work with their first-generation children. Perhaps by today's professional standards not many had advanced or college degrees. This was also true of those in my Order when it came to St. Augustin Parish in Manchester, NH, in the 1890s. But through hard-earned classroom experience, examples of their fellow teachers, unswerving support of parents and parish, and their own professional pride, they achieved admirably. They imparted survival and competency skills, the tenets of the Catholic faith, the glories of our culture, pride in their Québécois speech, and initiation into the American way.

Of course, those teachers were, besides their ethnicity, the spiritual heirs of Constantine and Clovis who literally changed the course of history. Constantine not only stopped the Roman persecution of Christians, but proclaimed Christianity the official religion of the French kingdom in the 4th Century. Often, I've seen in churches and history books the Latin saying *In hoc signo vinces* ("In this sign (the Cross), you will conquer"), which embattled Constantine saw in the sky. He ordered his soldiers to put that on their shields or swords to win the battle, which they did. This is the faith that France in the second millennium brought to its New World explorations, especially to Canada, Lower Canada (New England Francos), Mobile, AL, and across the vast, future Louisiana Purchase.

I've pondered what might have been if history had played out differently. Yes, if only a latter-day Constantine and his army had been there on the Plains of Abraham when Québec and France's control of Canada dissolved when British General Wolfe defeated Field Marshal Montcalm in 1759. This led to a century or more of deprivation and second-class citizenship! Recall the little education Francos possessed when they came here which millwork perpetuated. After the loss of Canada, the French still maintained a strong interest in America and helped win our independence from England. But the Jay Treaty in the 1790s saw our gratitude towards France dissolve, much to their consternation, and then the Louisiana Purchase in 1803 hastened their exit. One author said it happened that way because most early Americans then were more "English than French" in language, customs, religion, and manners.

When you consider St. Ann's students only knew untutored French, a little English, and, as dad often said, were from a nationality that generally didn't or couldn't value education for its own sake or advancement, it was a tour de force for nuns to succeed with their large classes.

Classes at St. Ann's easily accommodated 35 or more students since I recall classrooms had at least six rows of at least six or seven desks. Dad figured we must've numbered over 1000 when my siblings and I went. Imagine! All from one parish with tuition of a dollar a month and no one was ever turned away! Mother Superior regularly passed along tuition reminders but was it like squeezing blood from a stone? Parents recorded payments on a little card. Nine dollars a year for each child! (I've read that in Harvard's first year in the 1630s, it was less than that!) But with nine grades, it was a rare family without several kids in school, a "heavy" tuition bill. But no matter the cost, because of Catholic instruction, we and our Peloquin, Fontaine, Trottier, Lebel, Brunelles, and other Tellier and Hantis cousins nearly all went to parish schools, as our neighbors and most Francos did.

Even if in our mill culture, boys were later destined to work in overalls and girls in cheap cottony dresses. But in school, shirt and tie were de rigueur for boys, and a conservative mode of dress for girls. Most boys' ties sat as awkwardly on their victims as a Sunday suit did on our fathers' mill worker frames. In the schoolyard *nos cravates* (our ties) were used to pull and drag a competing foe more than as a sartorial adornment. As the Bard wrote, those "ties were untimely ripped" during our horseplay. We wore knickers or short pants mostly, with mothers favoring corduroy for boys. Only when the knee area was worn smooth or over patched were they discarded after younger sibling use. Ditto for our overalls. Shirts were nearly always white, with ink stains from dipping pens always a threat from careless or mischievous students. Girls were subject to hair infestation, especially in lower grades. Did mom use kerosene to combat the menace? (It's why I wondered if that's how some girls got "flaming red hair?")

As in all Catholic schools, girls wore a prescribed outfit: *une costume*. Pictures of Rachel in the family album show a black or blue jumper with a white blouse. Long stockings, of course. But is it true girls were warned against wearing shiny, black patent leather shoes "for fear reflected light might reveal anatomical mysteries?" Since I've heard the comment several times in those stage follies, the story is perhaps fictional. Exaggeration is the essence of humor.

Mothers like mine liked the outfit regulation because it was relatively inexpensive to buy or make, which she did on her moulin - a Singer sewing machine which ran hot in August. When it wore out, I recall dad pounced on the motor! The uniform rule precluded today's costly me-tooisms and faddish imitations of other media goddesses, like Madonna, and Cher. When my wife Pat, a theology major, taught marriage to junior high girls at Mount in the 1970s, she was amazed these were their idols.

But if someone of the gentler sex dressed out of the ordinary for church, school, or public, she risked a verbal lashing by her denigrating peers: *Elle s'en fa craire*: she puts on airs. But even if ordinary, if female duds were worn with a *'tude* (attitude), you heard, "*Ai* (she's) stuck up." Or

"*Ai pincée*," as in too done-up or too tightly clothed. Similarly, *à la forme du corps*, meant she was poured into her outfit. (Didn't one starlet boast she wore "something she just threw on," to which someone replied, "and almost missed?")

Our wooden desks on metal legs were single or double seaters, bolted to a worn, usually scalloped, or uneven wooden floor from the trampling of thousands of students. They came with a glass inkwell whose ink splotched floors, clothing, and books. Accidents also occurred when filling the inkwells from a large four-liter bottle. *Sacré bleu*, had Carlo Rossi's vino once graced the convent table? Surely, they knew their Bible: *In vino veritas*: truth in wine, and *Vinum laetificat cor hominis*: wine rejoices the heart of man ...and woman too.

Initially, the Labor Museum memorialized the classroom of yesteryear with a mannequin priest, *sans ma soeur* (without sister). But the priest rarely came. So, The Nun Project, spearheaded by cousin Gene with help from religious and lay people, raised funds to display a nun mannequin with *Soeur Ste. Émilie* serving as the model representing the many hundreds of nuns who toiled in area schools. A listing by year of all religious personnel of all communities, nuns and Brothers especially, was computerized for research and remembrance in the Peloquin Room where high school yearbooks are also collected. I was also pleased to submit chapters from this narrative reflecting the toil and travails - sometimes frolicsome, sometimes painful, but always enriching - of our education at St. Ann's and Mount Saint Charles. Hopefully this book will also be included someday, an intimate and insightful American French-Canadian remembrance of the way we were, by one who lived it or was told by his parents how life once was in the city, aka *le Canada en bas* (the lower Canada).

Even though our education was rudimentary, we learned more than our parents, especially if they were farmers in Canada and mill workers here. As I saw at times with foreign-born children in the schools I taught or counseled in, some of them, despite obvious talent, were consumed with their family's priority in America: economic survival. Often, only the second American generation becomes fully educated when language and economics are no longer barriers. But exceptions are common. For Francos it came largely with WWII, media, the departure of the mills, the GI Bill, which all made possible "the full Americanization" of Francos in cities like Woonsocket. Long after the war, no wonder cousin Gene invited no less than 140 plus veterans to receive belatedly their high school diplomas. Their history book had been Europe and the Pacific, because the needed mill paycheck had kept them away from academe. It was largely our way of life, which Nancy Wartik in *The French Canadians* wrote about, to wit that "it has not been matched by any other European minority living in North America."

So, if you did go on after St. Ann's, say, to MSC, as I did with friends Paul Ducharme, Vincent Auclair, Armand Benoit, Normand Vaillant, Larry Laferriere, and others, you discovered how extremely sound you were in the basics, if poorly read. Because of time on those basics, reading was like a reward, like Friday afternoon one year in 9th grade, after we were drilled to death all week. But I mean reading for enjoyment rather than learning to read, which we did, student by student. Even with large classes, no student was forgotten, even if time consuming.

Girls going to high school went to Saint Clare HS or Our Lady of the Mountains boarding school in Gorham, NH, as sister Rachel, cousin Doris, and other local girls did. They also attended Woonsocket HS, like sister Suzanne, friend Madeleine Carle, *et cousine* Estelle Tellier. About St. Clare, did I hear a 100 or more entered the Jesus Marie nuns or other communities? But it was still a time when parents felt a future homemaker or *femme de maison* needed home-and-hearth skills more than book "larnin'." But who went to high school more: boys or girls? Was affordability a problem? I for one would have missed Mount and my career with the Brothers if I hadn't paid the tuition myself from my *Call* and Joyland Roller Skating Rink moneys.

Well taught by their mothers, young brides were usually good cooks. Since brides often lived across the street from their birth families (so thought my Midwestern Boston College counseling psych professor), if *leur époux* (hubby) wanted to talk to his *belle-mère* (mother-in-law) about her daughter not being *une bonne cuisinière* (a good cook), he didn't have far to go, he joked. But it was a rare happenstance. The husband who complimented his wife on her turkey stuffing, only to hear her say she didn't know it was hollow, probably hadn't married a French-Canadian girl! But good cooks like Mama Mia for one, spanned the whole ethnic immigration homemaking experience. Now, the emphasis is more on education, an equally cherished outcome, as women in college now outnumber men, and 4 out of 10 are now top earners in their families. But with opportunities in all fields, I still like Pope Francis' wish that women not overlook their genetic, God-given nurturing roles, however challenging both are in tandem.

Recall mom's advice to us boys, to wit, if we couldn't marry a "looker," - *une bonne mine* ("min") - we should marry "*un bonne ménagère*": a homemaker and good cook. Mom's advice sounds condescending or anti-feminist today, even from a woman. But she was being realistic about a woman's role then, affirming that "the way to a man's heart is through his stomach," and by extension good housekeeping. For instance, I never forgot the giant shrimp dinner I had the first time I met future wife Pat. She shared an apartment in New York with lifelong friend Donna (Schwarz) Tardif, a former teacher and Director of Social Services at Saint

Antoine Residence, and also a superb cook. They both introduced Marcel and me to the savory delight of sauerbraten (beef marinated for several days) and potato dumplings, not common here. Pat of German-Irish descent; Donna of Austrian heritage. Since marriage in those days was "until death do us part," mom was perhaps hinting that once espoused, "We should always dance with the girl we 'brung' to the dance." Québec may now have one of the highest divorce rates in developed countries, even if author Bracq says constancy was once the earmark of marriage there, as it continued here with first immigrants and their children.

My Boston College magazine reported 23 percent of adult Catholics have gone through a divorce, 11 percent have remarried, like all the U.S. population. Other statistics vary. Only 15 percent of divorced Catholics have sought an annulment; almost half granted one. The cost was once steep, but Pope Francis in 2015 eliminated time and finance hurdles. Two-thirds of espoused Catholics were married in church. An additional five percent tied the knot in civil marriages subsequently blessed by the Church. (Stats vary.) But many divorced Catholics, we said, are still estranged from the Church, reflecting a silent crisis in her ranks, since they and their children are without its spiritual support, pastoral preaching and instruction, and the graces of its sacraments. Even Christ dealt with the same problem when the Jews chafed him about his monogamous stance on marriage. He acknowledged Moses allowed divorce to his people, but only "because of the hardness of their hearts." Does Moses' allowance reveal some "give" on the matter? Another concern of Pope Francis is "people in the mist," and how the Church should look kindlier and supportingly towards them, even those with deviant lifestyles. In the South I heard "Who am I to judge my kind? The blindest groper of the blind." Christ spoke about seeing the mote in someone's eye, and not the beam in one's own.

In 9th grade, *Soeur* Donat taught us English grammar so well, many of us never needed any special help in high school or college. Through drills, repetition ad nauseam, diagramming, and parsing, she showed us the structure and form of the English language, the medium of our future careers. As she drilled us on parts of speech and the difficulty of English spelling (26 letters but 42 sounds) and pronunciation (especially those th's and aspirated h's), she inspired us to think big. I was later thrilled to thank her profusely when the Presentation of Mary Sisters concluded a founding anniversary year with a Mass at St. Ann's. I also had a photo taken with her at the Nun's Project dedication. Humble about her role, she said she just followed the teacher's manual. In the Order, we at times joked that's all you had to do to teach! In 2001, she surely went to the Heavenly Pantheon of Teachers for her merited crown.

Rene Tellier with *Sœur* Marie Donat, P.M., the inspiration for his teaching and counseling career.

I cited an Old Testament prophet who said those who taught others unto justice would shine like stars for all eternity. I'm glad to add my wife Patricia, former St. Joseph nun in New York and a 32-year school veteran, including posts in the city, MSC, and Bellingham schools until her death as first grade teacher at the Grove Street School. She shares the merited reward of thousands of women and men who taught so many for so long. Besides her B.A. in elementary education and an M.A. in reading, she also had an M.A. in theology. Mine in religion was from the Order, but we kidded ourselves about knowing religious laws so well that it left us no margin of error through ignorance!

I passed along her considerable collection of theology books to several college teachers, including Brother Demers, later ordained as a Brother-Priest, who administers at Bishop Guertin HS and also teaches at Rivier University, Nashua, NH He celebrated his 60th year of religious life in October, 2015. Also, Brothers Leon Cyr and Brother George Poirier were in my Novitiate class in Harrisville in 1955. Pat's devoted and talented assistant at the Grove school was Faith Guiney whose husband Carl, a gifted preacher, was pastor of First Assembly of God Church in the city. Why did I think those kids were learning more than their ABCs? They insisted on model behavior, friendliness, and classroom learning. Pat rewarded them with six parties each year. One first grader questioned why I married someone taller than me. "I married someone I could look up to," I said! Another tyke said, "You're a tall lady."

At the Academy, my sophomore English teacher, Brother Felician, later a professionally trained librarian for the Union Saint Jean-Baptiste Maillet Library, read to us in class. Recall, this was very contrary to norms since older students never, never saw or heard a teacher read to them in class. His reading for example of Alfred E. Noyes' *No Other Man* excited my reading curiosity. Perfectly fluent in English, his eyes sparkled, his big, white teeth shone, and his enthusiasm became infectious, as he conveyed the beauty of the language and the fascination of the story, a futuristic survival story after a global catastrophe. Was it a first of its kind? Daily we had to learn five new polysyllabic words we had never seen. Then he had us sit back and listen to a reading oration an actor like Charles Laughton would've been proud of.

Because my folks were great readers despite little education, there were constant exhortations and examples despite little reading materials to get the practice we couldn't get in school. In time, used schoolbooks, scouting's Boy's Life, and even dad's medical library filled the void a bit, and newspapers a lot. But I made no headway with bother Bob's navy pharmacist mate book! Going to Harris Library in town just wasn't for us French Canadians. The gang went once out of curiosity! Sister Sue received those movie magazines, which became a lifelong practice of putting name and face to movie and TV characters I saw. Confreres at Notre Dame Academy wondered how I got that worldly knowledge, not at all consonant with *The Lives of the Saints*! She also collected bandleader photos, including trumpeter and "Flight of the Bumble Bee" performer, Harry James, who I once sat next to at a casino bar in Las Vegas, sans wife Betty Grable, the G.I.'s favorite WWII pinup. He signed my glass napkin. It's still in my album. Other notables I learned about were Jimmy and Tommy Dorsey, Glen Miller, Woody Herman (saw him in N.Y.), et al. I never would have done it, but I couldn't read her diary because it was in Shorthand. Rachel also studied shorthand and later became, I said, my guidance secretary at the Academy. I saved time dictating to her, as she came into my office with her pad, just like Perry Mason's Della Street, one of two shows we were at first allowed to watch in the Order. Ed Sullivan the other. I felt both proud and humble at the irony of the two of us working together at the Academy, a school we saw every day as "poor kids" from our third-story window on Gaulin Ave. Who would've thought we'd go past the 8th grade and slip by the lure of the mill trade and help kids find their collegiate and professional destinies? As an educator and counselor, I personally wanted to give back what the Order gave me. I did it 3,000 times in three high schools, including nephews, nieces, and neighborhood kids. I once told an inquiring student my job was "to tell people where to go." But before counseling, I also taught English, history, Latin, catechism, and even geometry one year, staying a few pages ahead of the kids. "Religious wore many hats," was the saying; 13 one year at Notre Dame HS. If the phone rang, they knew it was for me, one monk told me.

For example, I recommended three of the four Cerrone automobile dealer family boys, with Rachel thinking my letter to Yale for Michael was my best ever. It was based on an Albie Booth character who always came through for his school. Michael, now a movie script writer in Hollywood, played hockey for the Bulldogs and a club in Sweden. If on a given day, I waxed eloquent, she said, "A Cerrone special." What a privilege during my stay to recommend so many other gifted children to college, like the Guays,

Martins, Guevremonts, McGhans, Mandevilles, Moreys, Berards, Wards, Dubois, Cotes, Morins, Lessards, Belisles, Gautreaus, and many other families, who entrusted their children to the Catholic and collegiate direction of MSC. Because of smaller families, the Academy now requires only four graduates, not seven, for parents to receive a plaque.

Boston College taught me never to deny a recommendation to a student wanting to continue his/her education. When I interviewed at Norton HS for a college placement counselor post, I nailed it when I answered what I thought was the mark of a good school. To wit, if a student graduated and wanted to continue studying, it meant the school had not stifled his learning curiosity but enlarged it. When I told the three interviewers I read that in a Cushing Academy, MA, publication, Principal Daniel Wheeler jumped out of his chair, "That was my high school." The superintendent, Dr. Maurice Splaine, "a Jesuit boy" like me told me I had the job, even if seven others were waiting to be interviewed. My Jesuit background was Boston College and Spring Hill, AL, his Holy Cross. (I mention it to stress the importance of reading.) John Atwood, my guidance boss and former North Smithfield resident, was indefatigable and ran a great Special Education program. By borrowing from the Academy's curriculum to initiate six curriculum changes, we raised our college acceptance rate from 39 to 92 percent. I used one of my so-called "white papers," which I wrote each year to make my school better. The Order taught us to always strive for perfection, and I read a school should be 2 or 3 percent better each year. Staff retention is crucial which Mount later achieved with better salaries, pensions, and medical coverage.

At a convention, I was speechless when a college said they had received my recommendations for close to 20 years but had never seen me damn a less-than-stellar student, preferring to be less laudatory, as well as stressing his or her need to continue maturing and developing the potential that was there. Three of those 3000 came back to see me the day they graduated, thanking me "for the recommendation I shouldn't have given them." My biblical inspiration was "not to break the bruised reed nor extinguish the smoking flax." That is to say, "where's there's life, there's hope." One of the returnees became a teacher himself. His grades weren't great, but his intelligence tests were, and he defended weaker kids bullied as frosh. And as Athletic Director at Notre Dame HS, it didn't hurt he played a gifted tackle on our Crusader teams! He was giving something back to the school. I had read colleges realized the commitment an athlete makes to his or her sport in time and energy, lessening reading time and SAT scores. But at Mount the two Guevremont student-athletes, David and John, amazed me with their SAT scores. They read waiting for hockey practice. Before becoming a counselor, I also wrote recommendations, one for a student who said no one else would. He wrote to me three or four years ago; now a lawyer, newspaper editor, and writer of theological themes. I also can't forget a football player at Norton HS. An advanced placement student, he was accepted as a sophomore at Harvard no less! Teasingly, Dr. Cottle at Boston College advised us "not to get in the way of those really smart kids who have a destiny of their own." A German exchange student at Norton HS thought he knew more than our best advanced placement history teacher: Fred Bartek. Was it that supposed Teutonic superiority? All exchange students, though, were bright and loved their rapport with teachers.

Like for people in 18th Century England, the newspapers for us also filled a void. We literally fought for the newspaper when it arrived at home. We became impatient if either mom or dad wanted it first. The paper and radio were basically our only link to the world outside our insularity. It was the fulfillment of a dream for me to write some 127 pieces for the *Call* as an education columnist in the 1980s, a paper which taught me how to read English well during the war. And with the encouragement of Brother Demers, principal, and *The Call* editor, Ed Berman, I also wrote several hundred releases to tout the Academy's new thrusts: co-ed, junior high, teacher-counseling, and greater student input in their own performance. Also, enrollment, that was undermined by the closing of the boarding element and rising tuition for day students, had to be expanded outside the Northern RI ring. Parents no longer sent their kids just because you taught religion. You had to tout your academics, character formation, athletics, and cultural activities. My pitch was "Early to bed / Early to rise/ Pray like hell / Advertise." Many outside of the city discovered or rediscovered the Academy. Ed Berman told me he mentioned my name in his Providence College class as an example of how to promote one's school. I asked *Call* co-owner Drew Palmer's benevolent city club to put up the first outdoor sign at Mount. It was a message of the massive physical and academic changes the Academy began to make towards becoming a top Blue-Ribbon School, recognized we said at the White House. As it was for us, if only more city kids could take advantage of an outstanding prep school in their midst.

Bob, Ben, and I always started with the sports page, a lifelong habit. In summer, if you read it first, you related how the Sox did. I eventually read the whole paper, including the editorial page and the obits like my parents did, and as people do (or should!) supposedly when they turn 40. But I learned what Negro pitcher Satchel Paige said, "Never look behind when you're 39, sumpin' may be catchin' up." And sadly, you begin to see death overtaking people you grew up with, schooled, or worked. In my 42 years, didn't I say some 12 students died: murder, suicide, accidents.

Again, I recall a student died in a car accident just a few weeks before graduation at Notre Dame in Fitchburg. Brother Robert Brassard, adviser of our award-winning Crusader yearbook, asked me to write the eulogy which I entitled "Graduation into Eternity." A former scholarship winner, now a dropout, was the driver and also a victim. He had put a Cadillac engine in a small Studebaker, morphing it into a "Studilac." A small car on steroids! The paper said the smashed odometer read 103, with the car wrapped like a U around a tree, puzzling police as to which way it was going. An entire town outside of Worcester lost power. Someone in Canada who read the obit was moved by the eulogy, which reminded him of one of Shakespeare's tragedies, so Brother told me. I also wrote one for a senior and a gifted runner who was killed at the beach in a firearm discharge. Every year his dad gave and presented the Best Trackman trophy in his memory.

The boys' race for the sports page was matched by our sisters' choice for comic heroes and the funnies. The men in the family were rabid sports fans, all dyed-in-the-wool Red Sox fans despite their late annual pennant swoon. If after supper you missed sportscaster Jim Britt's scores ("If you can't play sports, be one anyway, will you") on WEAN radio, tomorrow's *Call* was it. But we also liked comic characters like Scorchie Smith (an all-around good guy), Moon Mullins, Gasoline Alley, Little Orphan Annie, and others. We bought the Sunday papers for a quarter after Mass to keep up also with Mutt and Jeff, Prince Valiant, Dick Tracy, and wrinkled old Gravel Gertie. I've mentioned how we loved Tracy's wrist radio and its similarity to today's cellphone.

In the final analysis, if our grammar school days weren't a reading bonanza, our teachers did teach us to read well and whetted our appetite, the same curiosity I saw in my parents. About a reading apathy in students because of today's electronic gadgets, it doesn't allow those students to espouse the words of a Lincoln, to wit, that "his best friend was someone who gave him a book he hadn't read." A study in 2015 said you retain more from script than screen. Is it true grammar school kids read more books now than high schoolers? And in a recent year, a quarter of all adults didn't read a single book! Is America becoming paperless and readerless? Will we maintain our world status as a literate, educated nation?

No doubt we're now a "looking" age (and a busy one) rather than a reading one. "Trouble is," one educator said, "looking is not learning." It's sexist, but when a chorus girl got a book for Christmas, she wailed, "But I've already got one." But actually, young girls and women read more and the report "What's Wrong with Our Boys?" laments boys don't. Fifty-eight percent of young people's leisure time is spent on electronic viewing, up from 25 percent! In St. Michael's College (VT.) magazine, I read, "The habits of attention that we cultivate over time determine the nature of the world we inhabit - that is, whether it's populated by pixels or people." Is that the canary in the coal mine? Recently a teacher asked his students to participate in a "technology fast" for a week or so. Student comments were so positive: "less stress," "relaxing silence," "reconnecting and rediscovering," "face-to face personal time," "more sleep time," and "time to do other things." Some found they were addicted, even going to bed with their unit. One had sleep-walked with it! Why do young people have this need to connect? Are they afraid to be with their own thoughts, as an Old Testament prophet said?

In college I believed Francis Bacon's "Reading maketh a full man." Dad, the first person I thought of. He never went beyond the middle grades but became an intellectual giant. A full person! Like mom! In this context, it boggles my mind what they and other Canucks could've become professionally with more formal education. But recall what poet Gray said, "Chill penury (as in poverty) repress'd their noble rage," and the riches of education were a future legacy for their children and grandchildren. I rejoiced *tante* Laurence *et* uncle Henri saw their son Claude, a first generation American, get a Ph.D. in chemistry from Providence College, and son, Michael, in chemical engineering; my brother Bob and Millie's son Bruce, a second generation American, a DMA in music; and uncle François *et tante* Blanche's son Roger, first generation, continuing a Fontaine tradition of medical practice; and three of us college teachers: Jan Reale, Bruce Tellier, and the author. All from families in which grandparents didn't even go to high school.

Again, it's important for the reader to realize that however unrewarding, arduous, and sometimes unhealthy millwork was, my seeming deprecation of that honest toil is largely because it didn't coexist with education and coupled with child labor at one time. One author said the industrialization of America and all its "initial evils" blunted the Jeffersonian dream of a healthy, outdoor, self-sustaining economy in a land of unparalleled beauty and boundless natural resources. But he was not against some industrialization. A prodigious reader, his purchases caused his indebtedness. But later his volumes helped start the Library of Congress. I've boasted to some with education the early Franco-American culture would be ranked with the best.

Claude H. Trottier, MSC '56. First extended family member to earn a doctoral level degree - a PhD in Chemistry from Providence College. He's also authored his own study of his family lineage: *Trottier and Fontaine Family History: Courage and Perseverance: It's in the Genes.*

But eventually those mills would never again control the life and destiny of Francos to such an extent. After the war it seemed all my relatives were unemployed: *"en masse,"* said mom. People and industries started moving to the South and its "Ol Sol." Did I read 1,100 a day left RI? Like so many other communities, Woonsocket had put all its eggs in one basket. So, it became hard to bring in new industries and businesses: lack of land, no major highway connection (to Woonsocket, Central Falls, Coventry an article said) and untrained workforce.

We lamented our "brain drain" which has hit the state hard, since many of our best and brightest graduates leave for more fertile ground. Fifty percent! Yes, the state does attract its share of immigrants to combat the loss, but unlike the immigrant poor of yesteryear, like Francos, Irish, Italians, Poles, Jews, et al., whose public assistance was miniscule, if any at all, the newcomers' need now for much. Special education, health coverage, nutrition, locomotion, housing, and home heating are all more crushing. Especially due to the high cost of living in our state, which is also strained, like the nation, by Medicare, Medicaid, Social Security, as our people age and live longer, and of course taxes and fees. One magazine said the elderly are more and more without good Social Security pensions due to early divorces, so they resist change because they don't want to see their support diminished. As Louis XIV said, *"Après moi, le déluge:"* After me, the flood. What's the answer? ObamacareCare? Some politicos worry about the bill even if many do pay into it. Dad was right about the cost of living (*le coup d'la vie*) running ahead of Joe Worker's salary. Call them Occupiers if you will, but aren't young people starting to breed unrest? The wealthy, said the Providence Journal in 2014-5, have seen their purchasing power increase, but not the poor and the middle class. Usually both go up at the same time.

There's no free lunch; the money governments give you, is money you've given them, with dad adding that the dollar you send to Washington comes back as a dime. President Coolidge, for one, said taxation was money taken from the people. Read his bio to discover how unbelievably tight-fisted he was, like Andrew Johnson, Lincoln's successor. Dad often voted the person rather than party but said our state's single party-look and master lever (finally corrected in 2014) meant no one was watching the store, unlike the caution of our Founding Fathers to establish a bicameral form of government, and eventually the formation of political parties. Only angels can rule the affairs of men, said a saint, but they're never on the ballot! (But the new Catechism says one of the nine choirs of angels is the Authorities. If they ran with that label, would they win "with a wing and a prayer?")

Columnist Kathleen Parker, commenting on an address by Mitt Romney to Poland in 2012, saw a link with papal teaching (Pope John Paul's encyclical *Centissimus Annus*) and the inherent danger of big, central government and the welfare state: "Inasmuch as the welfare state is an instrument of centralized government, is it in conflict not only with personal freedom but also with Catholic teaching." There is also the thinking of a German theologian, Oswald von Nell-Breuning, who preferred smaller, simpler organization being based on the principle of autonomy and dignity of the human individual, which emphasizes the importance of small institutions from the family to the church, and to labor unions. The pope wrote the intervention of the state deprived society of its responsibility, which leads to a loss of human energies and inordinate increase of public agencies, which are dominated more by bureaucratic ways of thinking than by concern for serving their clients. They're also accompanied by an enormous increase in spending. A corollary if you will is newsman Bill O'Reilly's report that in 1962 some 6 percent received welfare, now it's 35 percent, with 100 million getting money from the government. This doesn't count Social Security and Medicare which are programs workers pay into. He concluded what we're seeing now is "the nanny state," not self-reliance and entrepreneurial spirit that made us the most powerful nation on earth.

Has "Where's mine?" taken root, he asked. Yet we have an obligation to the needy. Where's the happy middle? What will be our economic salvation in RI? Will financial services, computer technology, biotech, the arts, and tourism do it, and not gambling alone which doesn't produce wealth, but only redistributes money, especially from the poor to companies? Do we need a modern-day Aram Pothier for another economic miracle? But aren't all states competing to entice new businesses? Not an easy thing to do in a state dealing with unbalanced spending, high taxes, unsustainable benefits, struggling schools and dropouts, special education numbers above the national average, corruption, and a workforce not trained enough for modern technologies.

Baby Room: "*Bébé rum*"

AS AN EVALUATOR in the mid-1970s, I revisited the now closed St. Ann's Grammar School across the street from the church on Gaulin. It dawned on me I hadn't been in the building for over 30 years and ghosts of memories past flitted everywhere.

An early 20th century photo of St. Ann School on Gaulin Ave.
The foreground area is where St. Ann Church now stands.
(Courtesy of Woonsocket Historical Society)

How cramped everything seemed from the time I was there as a student from 1936 to 1944! The 600 students that day seemed to fill it more than our thousand in our day. Because of the daily rush of students, schools always show their age quickly, so the school was already into its architectural decline when we started in the mid-1930s. Later, small wonder its faded red bricks in an old neighborhood belied its near antiquity. Our initial step in first grade (*Bébé Rum:* "baby room" was mom-speak) was lining up in the schoolyard. Aren't lining up and keeping quiet the essence of grammar school years? As first graders (no kindergarten or *jardin d'enfante* then), we lined up on the Gaulin Avenue sidewalk, the second graders next to us, and so on until, I believe, you reached the ninth graders at the rear entrance of the school. Or was it just the opposite? It was going to take a long time before we got in first, like when it rained.

Even though we hardly recreated with girls in our 'hood, the first day of school was our initiation into the formalized separation of the sexes. True, grades were co-ed largely by alternate rows or at random in the classroom, but recess before and during school was segregated. The girls played and lined up on the other side of the building by "Pin Alley" (The origin of Locust St.'s nickname is unknown to me). And in church, priests faced the boys on the left and the girls on the right. Is there any biblical significance? The elects on one side and rejects on the other? Like at the Last Judgment. Both in Latin (*sinister*) and in French (*gauche*), "left" means awkward, not desirable, but in history great and talented people have been southpaws, even if schools once tried to change you. My wife Pat was left-handed, but when they tried to "right" her, she became ambidextrous.

For a long time, the diocese boasted all its high schools were single sex institutions. Recall I was in guidance at MSC when it became the first Catholic high school to go co-ed. Increasing pressure from alumni for their daughters to attend (due to the rumored demise of St. Clare HS) prompted Brother Demers, principal, to implement the bold move in the early 1970s. To say the least, we said conservative Bishop Russell McVinney was not supportive. Ultra conservative, he saw sexual overtones in the move. Soon after his passing in the early 1970s, the school enrolled its first and only girl, Jeanne Blanchard, whose father Walter, a Rhode Island College professor, was helping us implement our new student-centered learning plan. Then more came as thoughts of a merger - perhaps with the name "Claremount" – was not to be. Eventually La Salle, Saint Raphael, Prout, and Fatima (which closed June, 2012) turned co-ed too adding another dimension to their academic, cultural, and athletic achievements but not Hendricken. Providing a good alternative, Bay View has remained all female, and Bishop Keough is now part of St. Ray's, as of 2015. Since we went coed in the early 1970s, I asked Jeanne Blanchard how she felt being the only girl with 500 boys. She replied with a twinkle in her eye, "I liked the odds."

Teaching first grade class was our Presentation of Mary nun, the pint-sized and ebullient *Soeur* Saint Vital, already a legend as a superbly effective teacher of *les bébés* (babies). Considered ageless, she also taught Bob and Sue, older siblings of other students and even their parents. To several generations, she was the first teacher in their formal education. Their first Alma Mater, "fostering mother," as Webster says. She lived to be 101. The first school day was not without its tearful separations. With no nursery or pre-school experience, some were still tethered to their mom's apron strings. The more timid and frightened shed copious tears, as they sought to hide in the folds of their mother's dress when beckoned by the black-robed nun. *Ma Soeur* (My sister/nun) had a warm, inviting smile and manner. But how forbidding her religious habit was to 6-year-olds!

Curiously, I discovered during Renewal time in my Order that founders of women religious Orders wanted members to dress like the peasant women of their day. Secular dress, however, evolved (has it ever!) but religious garb didn't. So, what was initially a bond of similarity became a sign of separateness. If a child had never been to church with his mother, the nuns' black-robed presence was intimidating. It's why even a 14-year-old freshman boy couldn't control his bladder when he sat before me when I was black-robed Brother Alphonse at Notre Dame in the 1950s!

Since my family planned to move from its Cass-Mailloux apartment (the drunken revelry in the saloon below never ceased), I went to school at six going on seven. So, I was not intimidated by the nuns and felt no separation anxiety. In fact, Bob brought me to school, so eager was I to do what he and Sue did every day. Mom, a legendary non-worrier, always let us go into new situations without any trepidation on her part, so we usually acclimated easily. "*Il faut s'faire aller*," was her cry: we must let go so get off your duff and do something. Her Fontaine family post disaster battle cry!

Because of my grandmother, who was a teacher in Canada, we came to first grade knowing the alphabet, low numbers, and prayers, all in French. Ah, the wisdom of Franco families when three generations often lived under one roof. What we knew was considerable because homemaking mothers had a heavy load of domesticity. Large families, a plethora of household chores (sans modern appliances), the huge Monday wash, and serving three meals a day were all challenges, besides going to the store often due to tiny iceboxes. But did they also go to church often to hear Christ say, "Learn from me because my yoke is easy and my burden is light?"

But rudimentary knowledge of the alphabet and letter formation brought me my first ever academic put-down. Once given our seat, *Soeur* Saint Vital quickly taught us the letter "A." But with a *Speedibus Rex* (Speed King) complex, I raced ahead to write all 26 letters, surely violating all the rules of *The Palmer Method of Business Writing* the nuns excelled in. Despite her gentle reproach, I felt some icy reproof to stay between the lines (the challenge of everyday life!) and wait for the others.

But also had I violated the Franco canon (did Francos learn it from the Japanese?) of not singling yourself out from the group? So much for accelerated programs for alphabet learners in those days! It's what poet Pope obviously meant by "A little learning is a dangerous thing." Mom didn't mount up a snit, saying, "*Il faut pa(s) courir avant les autres*," don't run ahead of the others. How would she explain to other mothers in the hood if I had done all 26 letters, their prodigies only one? Would they have brought her down a notch with critical looks and arched eyebrows: "*Elle s'en fa craire*": putting on airs? Or worse, would they have been like Christ's detractors about my being just *filius fabri* - the son of a carpenter (mill worker in my case) and from a mill city. But really no one ever demeaned you for being that. Weren't we basically a one-job city? And honestly, who had book "larnin'" in our tenement? Until Sue graduated from Woonsocket HS, no one in the eight families had such an "advanced diploma!" But was this woman a relic of the Stone Age? - "I do not will him to be exceptional. It is the exception that interests the devil. It is the exception that climbs the sorrowful hill. Or sits in the desert and hurts his mother's heart. I will him to be common?" Had she read Milton's "Fame, the last infirmity of noble minds"?

About my first day faux pas, only later did I see the profession become comfortable with acceleration and enrichment and meet the challenge of those talented kids. Which, without false modesty, I wasn't. Just curious to learn and read like my folks. Incidentally, a sad commentary is these bright kids are at times called the newest "special needs kids" of the profession! Why? Spending sometimes never rises above the bottom or middle. Always there's the threat of excision facing honors and advanced placement programs, as mediocrity rules: "Come weal, come woe, our status is quo." One writer called it the curse of egalitarianism. That is, no one, it seems, has a right to achieve above anyone else, forgetting Lincoln's observation (reiterated by President John Adams) that "We're born equal, but don't stay that way." But luckily many schools, private and public in our state, have accelerated and AP (Advanced Placement) courses. MSC, for one, has continued to increase their offerings. As a counselor, I always knew if a kid did well in AP courses, he, she, would do well in college. So, I included that in my recommendation to colleges, even if on the transcript. It met the burden "Is he or she ready to do college work?" Presently in the state, too many kids aren't, say some state colleges about their applicants, whose courses were not rigorous enough. But can you believe one of my Boston College profs warned about the pitfall, if so, of having every one graduate from high school by watering down non-college prep courses especially! Is it also why there's resistance to testing where results, may reflect on schools and teachers? Absenteeism is a problem in inner city schools.

No doubt urban school systems with a lower tax base need more money, but in a relatively poor or strapped state like RI, how do we help them without unduly undermining systems in the suburbs and exurbs with their better scores? I wrote to several state legislators about drafting an equitable school formula for the state's 36 school systems. Or of merging all 36 into one! And what about vouchers to private schools for those trapped in chronically underachieving schools? Does (or doesn't) the state have a Tuition Scholarship Tax-Credit program, but capped at one million dollars? Do politicos fear it's like touching "the third rail," if they go against the public system? I believe some 10 states have more generous outlays with no teacher job loss. If it were done, would it reduce the need or desire for charter schools since so many excellent private schools already exist in RI? As someone wrote, doesn't the federal government grant money to both private and public colleges without hurting either one? Competition brings out the best. We should think of the kids first. The state helps private school kids with transportation and books, but the new governor in 2015 threatened a scalpel knife against that! Aren't those parents taxpaying citizens too who have a right to send their kids where they want to? Something crucial in communities with mediocre schools. Imagine thousands of private school kids flooding the public-school system overnight!

Again, not wishing to dispute its necessity in school systems, statewide are we putting too many kids in Special Education, rather than mainstreaming them into at least the basic curriculum track, so they can be recommended into Certificate (1 year) or Associate Degree programs (2 years) out of high school? Woonsocket recently admitted some 22 percent of students are in special education, almost ten percent above the national average! In Norton, if possible, I put challenged kids in our Basic Curriculum, and as I mentioned earlier, our college admission numbers improved dramatically. Was it a factor in my being recommended as an All-American counselor? Was the number I read accurate, 70 percent, of SPED[41] graduates have difficulty finding jobs in today's new tech economy? One child advocate wondered if we mistake boyish aggression (boys five times more likely to be placed in SPED!) as a learning deficiency! One day Norton Superintendent Dr. Maurice Splaine met with all of us counselors, because too many kids were being "Spedded," and 5 percent of the student body was eating up 30 percent of the budget. Other kids weren't even getting pencils! One child expert even said 4 or 5 percent should be the norm, but the national average is 12. No doubt it's a factor in the state's perceived unprepared workforce. This is not to demean the great work special education teachers do for students who are really learning disabled (not "conduct disabled," as one teacher lamented to me) and might not otherwise receive any education. But as Katie Mulvaney wrote in the *Providence Journal*, efforts to educate them must also include job preparedness. Germany is the best for job preparedness. It's done in school in cooperation with industries so graduates immediately have jobs. Is it why they have such technological superiority?

Even though one parent was always at home, large families and a mill town mindset and economy militated against homes as springboards to higher education. Mothers at times heard catechism lessons besides *l'histoire du Canada* (the history of Canada), but the rest of the curriculum was learned in class. So, no help was forthcoming in *la grammaire française*

---

[41] The reader is reminded that SPED is an acronym for Special Education. – ed.

(French grammar), geography, arithmetic, American history, and our English reader. And since a high school diploma was like a PhD for immigrant parents, college was hardly mentioned. We had constant spelling bees, multiplication table contests (I found my opponent always stumbled on 8 x 7, as "memory sags in the middle!"), catechism recitations, reading by turn, all time-taking tasks not as easily done today with society laying on many objectives besides pure learning. At Norton HS, principal Dan Wheeler counted 18 things society now wanted us to do besides academics, not a flattering reflection on the status of the family and society in raising children. But before anyone of us left grammar school for the mills, or high school, we knew our catechism, multiplication tables, basic computational and mental math, spelling, and practical reading; all "survival skills," negating the label of "functional illiterates," heard today of dropouts and some graduates. Optimistically, state and national testing are showing some results, but RI lags behind in New England. First generation students, poor language skills, uneducated parents, attendance, and poverty are causes I suspect, as they would have said about us Francos if in public school and tested. In the city, is absenteeism reason for failure and dropout, as we heard? Are parent(s) to blame? In one southern public system, schools are supported by the number of kids every day in school. So, the administration is vigilant. In another, a judge fined parents for wasting school money.

But again, my Boston College professor shocked us when he said a high school education for all was not realistic, since the curriculum has been so enriched now, looking more like first- or second-year college of yesteryear. He feared schools might "water" their curriculums and "resist testing," as seen in the state, so all could be "saved." Some schools in the South and one in New England I believe even altered test scores to avoid looking bad and putting jobs in jeopardy. To the causes for dropout, should we add broken families, instant gratification, lack of reading, and young people's obsession with electronics? A prof said a kid who wants money, car, or a serious relationship now is a dropout in the making. About the absence of fathers, out-of-wedlock births are at 72 percent in the African American community and 53 percent among Latinos, compared with 29 percent among non-Hispanic whites. In five years, dropouts are dependent on the state for support. Studies in 2011 showed 12.5 percent of kids drop out; 41.3 percent go to a four-year college; 22.3 percent to a two-year college; and 36.4 percent into the workforce after high school. The last statistic raises caution in today's economy. Untrained workers are the first to go in a downturn market. One has suggested adding two years of high school for job training for non-collegiates because private job-oriented certificate schools are too expensive for many, and some don't deliver on jobs. Their programs aren't linked to employers like in Germany.

At St. Ann's, the reason for our good spelling was *Soeur* Saint Vital's absolute adherence to the sound-out method of learning. Sight recognition of whole words, later popular, was disdained. Every day from huge, dog-eared standing charts, we sounded letters from looking at pictures in which an action depicted the sound., like, my favorite, the saw cutting wood for Z.

It was crucial we learn well and correctly, both in French and English, however little of the King's English we received. Schooling was our only shot at a career. It's why American educator John Dewey called for schools to be a kind of equal opportunity or democratizing vehicle for all students, immigrant or not. Dad knew that, but - think of it - religion was prime, and you didn't want the priest at your door and the neighbors saying, "Imagine *twé, y va à l'école publique*! (Imagine, he/she goes to a public school!) *Ya pas d'religion!* (There's no religion!)" Especially if in grammar school. No wonder the Sentinellist Movement's war room was in a Franco community like Woonsocket! The faithful thought their homogeneous way of life, language, culture, and religion had value not to be lost in an encircling sea of Americanism, as my sociology professor, Father Majoli, thought about we Francos at Spring Hill College in Mobile. (I liked it when teachers spoke about us. No doubt we were a sociological phenomenon. But they didn't know our ethnicity.)

But one wonders what more my generation in the city could have achieved with today's greatly educated teachers, programs, and facilities! One social theorist said that America's only caste system is education, that is, the diploma or degree system. Not with inherited wealth or breeding per se, but with education you have upward mobility, stature, and financial means necessary for careers in art, technology, science, architecture, business, industry, medicine, politics, the law, and a chance at "The Wealth of Nations." You also move up the echelons of authority and influence and have a good effect on people and society in general in your field of work. What John Milton called, "…a complete and generous education that which fits a man to perform justly, skillfully and magnanimously all the offices both private and public, of peace and war." Our Holy Grail!

But sadly, after great progress since the war, we said this quest for higher education is now receding faster than one can say ABC. Education now outstrips by far the spiral of inflation by a factor of 10, with reports that colleges are spending more for "brick and mortar," with some private colleges now costing over $60,000 per year, since education costs are up close to 500 percent over the last 25 years. McMansion facilities increased administrative staffing, hefty college president salaries (over 30 earning over $1 million a year); with the result that financial packages are now often two-thirds loans, one-third scholarships, the reverse of 20 years ago. Graduates with loans will be in hock until their mid 30s. Presently over a trillion dollars in debt, more than mortgage and credit card bills combined! Because of that, it's predicted more and more students will get their education from a screen at home. But of course, it's not free. I'm convinced what Americans want most - education, housing, health, home - the powers-that-be out there are making that impossible. Doesn't it seem every enterprise wants to retire on their last transaction? Like nativists once did, did they change "justice for all" to "just us" and "the devil takes the hindmost?" Dad predicted it, but he'd be shocked it's so widespread today, affecting even the basics of life, like shelter, heat, and food.

Discipline: A Gauntlet of Steel Under a Velvet Hand

WHEN LEARNING HOW to teach in the Order, experienced teachers often told us good discipline in class was like a gauntlet of steel under a velvet hand. Sort of like Teddy Roosevelt's advice: "Speak softly and carry a big stick." Appear gentle but be firm.

It's the advice I received my very first day in the now-defunct Sacred Heart School in Sharon. A wizened Brother Edgar, who also ran Camp Sacred Heart for 25 years, said, "Trust kids, but never take your eyes off them." Like a wise parent! Or the cop on the beat! Confidence and respect, but vigilance too!

No doubt as first generation Americans we had some rough edges in our collective personality and character, like a lack of savoir-faire, sensitivity, and polite manners. This despite good family influences, a strict neighborhood ethic, and our knowledge of the Commandments. Rough-hewn, if you will, but "*de bon coeur*," (with a good heart) mom said.

To curb our over-the-top exuberance, teachers like our parents still believed a bit in the 19th Century English adage: "Spare the rod and spoil the child." So, discipline was at times a smidgeon of physical punishment, verbal reprimand, and isolation tactics. But I said in our "theocratic-like culture" (government by God and church), parents and teachers in Catholic schools didn't let you forget the moral dimension of your conduct.

Even though our teachers were physically little women - some barely five feet tall, all were known for their discipline. For example, *Sainte Appolline*'s reputation (I heard "Attila the Nun?") evoked anticipatory fear. But in reality, she was a superb math teacher who tolerated no disorderliness in your behavior or inaccuracy in your numbers. With his fascination for numbers, dad never spoke of any other teacher. Mom knew about many of them, but not *Soeur* Donat our English grammar teacher.

Because classrooms were large, teachers restored calm quickly when unruliness broke out. Like rolling thunder, you heard an angry tirade or a stinging expression like *mon p'tit polisson*: my little mischievous brat, if a boy. Or you had to stand up in the corner or next to the teacher's desk. Or under her desk, a friend told me. And even if rarely, a stinging hit to your digits or arm, administered by a pale hand out of a rolled-up black sleeve blanched by chalk. At times "St. Michael's sword" was sometimes *une règle* (a ruler or yardstick) or a pointer for map or blackboard work, but the latter broke easily. Because teachers used the board a lot (the mark of a good teacher I was told in the Order), they usually held those in hand, accounting for their occasional punitive use. With no visuals, projectors, or whatever, chalk dust filled the railings below the blackboards by day's end. Later chosen kids created ghostly specters by banging erasers against our red brick building, competing with Nincheri's frescoes in the church for originality.

Teachers also had a clapper to move the troops in the hallway or playground. It was poetry in motion to see a *Soeur* Ste. Émilie lift her right hand and get a clear thwacking sound a foot over her head. All in one blurring motion, like a weightlifter's clean jerk! She didn't suspect she revealed a fleshly lower arm, pale like the little amount of skin you saw on the nuns' corpus not covered by their pre-Renewal religious habit. Usually, you only saw their faces and hands, so what did they look like outside of class? Their hair cropped short or completely shorn was like the third Fatima secret! Except for priests with their tri-cornered hat and soutane,[42] nobody in our world was cloaked from head to foot, not even our modest mothers. Later, my confreres and I were taught by Brothers in a cassock, as I wore for 25 years. I was at the Renewal meeting when we voted greater use of the black suit instead of the cassock and chafing Roman collar. Nuns wore a dress and no hood, especially after a nun at the wheel of a car lost her life because of impaired lateral visibility.

But again, physical reprimands, however mild, were the exception rather than the rule. Did their restraint and Christian patience stem from St. Francis de Sales' words I later heard in the Order(?): You caught more flies with a teaspoonful of honey than with a hundred barrels of vinegar (harsh discipline). But in training, there was always a class clown who piped up, "But who wants to catch flies anyway?" A monk also rang a bell in our class every 30 minutes to remind us we were in God's presence. Did we or God have a short memory? But we kids also had untold reminders we were also in God's sight: our active faith, Catholic school, church, catechism study, the faith of our parents, catechism every day, Sunday Communion and Mass, Confession once a month, the annual retreat from school, and evening devotions to Mary in May and October. We were also told we were temples

---

[42] A type of cassock: full length, single-colored garments worn by Roman Catholic priests. – *ed.*

of the Holy Spirit, and a guardian angel hovered over us constantly, as seen on a holy card. Was all this the reason no Franco kid was in juvenile court? A delinquent today experiences none of the above. No wonder religious vocations were numerous in Franco and other Catholic ethnic families. We were practically living the common life of a religious in the bosom of our large families, and our prayer and liturgical life were just as real, if not as intense or long. A chronicle about the Durand (my paternal grandmother's name) Family Association in Canada spoke about the desire for a priestly and/or religious vocation in every family. Often more than one. Lorraine Bourassa, a Boston College professor with roots in Manville, wrote about multiple vocations in her related family: Four of God's Chosen Ones which inspired other relatives to join. Also, the city's four Berard boys in my Order; those sister-nuns in France in the Martin family of St. Theresa of the Child Jesus, whose father and mother (les Martins) are now canonized.

About discipline, because of a strong family makeup, the nuns had the greatest disciplinary system going - informing your parents. In fact, teachers today whose careers began more than 40 years ago remember when parents automatically approved most disciplinary actions against their offspring. And doubled the dose at home! Obedience was one of the bedrocks of immigrant or post-immigrant life. The authority of the law, parents, and church was unquestioned.

The Latin *in loco parentis* (in the parent's place) was once held supreme and endowed teachers with quasi-equal rights and duties, including physical punishment, however mild, and verbal discipline. Even though teachers and schools couldn't be right every time, they were usually given the benefit of the doubt by parents. Student advocacy rights, the last social revolution, predicted my sociology teacher in the 1950s, were not as developed like today, and the rights of schools were almost monolithic and dogmatic. Good or bad, it made school discipline easier and unquestioned. There was also less teacher burnout!

Most homes, like our school, had no phone. I said the only exception I knew was our nearby Peloquin cousins whose father Armand needed one (the old, black rotary model) for his 37-record years as a business agent in the United Brotherhood of Carpenters and Joiners in the city. So, if disciplined, you brought the news home by word of mouth or note, with no one knowing about self-incrimination rights or taking the Fifth! And nothing was ever mailed (we're talking about a three-cent stamp here!), so no mailbox thievery, a practice that shocked me in my counseling career with its frequency.

In fact, sounding like "Here come da judge," I told the kids at Norton HS that stealing mail was a federal offense, but to no effect. At Notre Dame HS, a student started a fire in his desk, overstuffed with quarterly report cards not brought home! Were his failing grades incendiary? Besides, moms like mine were always at home, waiting for *le postillion*, the mailman. Strangely, ours was Irish, so how come he didn't have a North End route? Bob told me that's why his patois-speaking customers didn't chat with him, like with the iceman, coal, wood, milk, fruit, bread peddlers, and insurance man, who all came to the door. Who needed a car? They were all "at-large reporters" for inquisitive mom, who later informed *tantes* Marie-Louise *et* Laurence.

For us, mail from Canada and from my brother Bob while he served during the war sent us scurrying up to the third floor, as if mom had won the lottery. Mom, who wrote a lot, trained us well, and we all became letter writers. A vanishing breed! But how about the ploy a generous but frustrated grandma did to get grandkids to at least acknowledge their check at Christmas time? She didn't put the check in and got instant replies! (Humor: About generous grandmothers, I split a gut when in my I.Q. course at Boston College, I asked a student the meaning of "Grandma has a long stocking," i.e., generous. His response, "Someone's been pulling her leg." Hilarious, but I had to dock him. Different interpretations - from the obvious or superficial to a more profound meaning or understanding of a phrase or line - suggest levels of intelligence. Another was "Let sleeping dogs lie." Some saw nothing but slumber, not caution to avoid trouble.)

Schools once gave I.Q. tests (Intelligent Quotient), but these "overlooked" factors like home, ambition, drive, interest, opportunity, and chance. Minorities and/or poor people were often held back because of those tests. My nun professor at Boston College liked it when I brought in an article about possible other meanings of I.Q.: Interest Quotient, Innate Quirks, Inner Quest, all of which may lead to some form of achievement, intellectual or other. Some test makers have identified over 70 endowments or abilities, including athletics and movement. Others less than ten. In *The Rain Man* movie, weren't we fascinated with the "idiot savant syndrome," where a mentally challenged person is sometimes a compensatory genius, often in math and music? At Sacred Heart School in Sharon, one student could spell any word, but couldn't pass anything else.

Since almost every child had brothers and sisters in school, teachers had a secure line of communication with parents. With sibling rivalry, it was hard to dissuade very young sisters, for example, from being Cassandras or messengers of doom. Oh, how I dreaded to hear first or second grade Rachel tell dad if I did "bad" in the 'hood. One day she told him I hadn't broken any windows (baseball)! Did dad tell her you couldn't prove a negative as I hadn't done anything wrong? But despite the usual sibling chicanery, the five of us were tight and supportive, a feature in Franco families. For dad and *mémère* especially, domestic tranquility was a commandment. If reading, my mother tuned out *le bruit* (the noise). The afternoon sun flooded our apartment, and all was right in the world. After a day's work it was her downtime, *"prende ma chaise"* (I take my chair) she said about the window rocker.

Rene and Patricia (Smith) Tellier Wedding
St. Agnes Cathedral, Rockville, NY. April 10, 1976
Left: Pat's sister Margaret Misovec & Rene's mother Léopoldine
Right: Pat's father James Smith & Norma Kuffner

Teaching first grade at Grove Street School in the city, my wife Patricia did not tolerate first graders tattling. Influence peddling started early. Once when I served soda in one of the six yearly parties she gave and paid for, one little tyke asked why I wasn't wearing a wedding ring. I told him I lost it playing senior softball in the Baldelli League and was looking for it. But Mrs. Tellier didn't know. He jumped out of his seat and rushed to tell her. Guess what my next Christmas gift was! About her being taller than me I said I married someone "I could look up to." A flight of fancy! Poet Tennyson wrote "'Tis better to have loved and lost than never to have loved at all." But a wit countered, "Tis better to marry a short girl than not a-t-all."

However much our youthful flesh cringed from a slap or ruler to our hands, banishment to Mother Superior's office was like Murder One. In church, the scene of the Garden Angel expelling drooping Adam and trailing Eve captures the scene perfectly. How that little office on the first-floor evoked memories when I revisited it. To face withering criticism in the classroom in front of 35-40 students was one thing. But to stand on the carpet (figuratively) alone, face to face with the fearsome, intimidating *Mère Supérieure* (Mother Superior) was the coup de grâce, like the adulteress, doubting Thomas, or repentant Peter, all standing before Christ, or the Prodigal Son before his father, which my English professor called the best short story in all of literature for its touching dramatic elements. (Humor: A wit said it's not the older brother who was put out by the return of his wayward sibling, but the fatted calf! But more about local humor: a jokester was asked to write the parish Sunday bulletin. He wrote 4th graders were presenting "Hamlet," and parents were invited "to see this tragedy"; women should discard old stuff for the poor, but not forget their husbands; and hefty parishioners were advised to use the new double doors to the parish hall.)

But back to discipline, like parents and teachers, Mother Superior meted out verbal reproaches if you erred against a school law and threatened to warn your parents. It brought instant contrition and resolution. She knew our parents' greatest fear was being told their child was *"un mal élevé"*: an ill-brought-up kid. Families had a strong sense of honor, pride, and reputation, and no one, before God or man, was going to take that away from them. Working at the mill or running a comfortable home for six, seven, eight or more children wasn't their whole life. Parenting, as in rearing law-abiding, God-fearing, church-going children, was. If you sowed wild oats in your late teen years, you had to shape up or ship out, if incorrigible. The final judgment was *"Ya baim tourné mal,"* turned out badly, said mom.

But banishment, which mom saw more in Canada, was rare, because like Italians, Irish, English, Poles, Jews, et al, parents loved their children and reared them in a loving home. Less serious offenses were handled within the bosom of the family, *"entre nous autres,"* with mom adding "dirty linen" was kept on the rear clothesline: *"sa corde."* There wasn't much she didn't tell me. Like other *bonnes femmes de maison* (good housewives), she loved to talk, and I listened, which was what I had to do a lot in my counseling career.

Naturally nuns taught you how to prepare for Confession by going over the Decalogue (Ten Commandments). I recall the time a priest became annoyed with kids confessing as if they were reading from a shopping list, which they were. There were none the following month and waiting time was back to normal. One time, mom had me bring young, innocent Ben to Confession before his First Communion. The frustrated priest came out of the confessional and spotting me alone in church, said, "He didn't tell me one d... thing."

We were all from a neighborhood worth saving. Maybe that's why *le curé* (the priest) Henri Robitaille, said preservationist Phyllis Thomas (deceased 8/1/2013), lamented the liquidation of our parish digs. But defiantly, dwellers of *la petite* Gaulin in defense of what mom called *"leur chez eux"* (their home) when demolition loomed, reacted like hillbillies when a census taker came to the door: "You ain't takin' nuttin' off'n this prop'ty." In patois, someone wanting you to take a hike also said, *"Sac ton camp?"* So, their 'hood still stands today. Who says Woonsocket doesn't have a good track record in preserving "an immigrant corner of the past?" And we also have the city postcard collection of former Woonsocket HS history department staffers Ray Bacon and the late Martin Crowley, giving us nostalgically what was once "the glory that was Greece and the grandeur that was Rome," when the city was still largely in its architectural and mill working prime. MSC grad Robert Godin, 1960, also gave a photographic recollection of downtown as it was at one time, now nearly all gone. Nothing lasts forever. When in London, they showed us the one building left from Elizabethan times. Fire, as well as the Bard's "time and tide" all destroyers! Not only homo sapiens, but dwellings too have no lasting place here.

So, a practicing section of the parish (the rest of Gaulin) was undermined, dispersing long-standing and extended families like the Telliers, Peloquins, Carpentiers, Vandals, Carles, Turcottes, Lanoies, Houles, et al - some 800 - I was told, who were in the shadow of St. Ann's twin towers for many years, some close to a century. Speak about *les collines éternelles* (foundation columns), as said in the Order about early founders of religious institutions. We said they and progenies went to the suburbs, stripping the long-standing tenure of their once-anchoring roles in the parish. About the faith element, the Reverend Robert W. Hayman in *The Diocese of Providence, Rhode Island, A Short History* writes about this diaspora or migration. But for those who departed, was their practice of faith now more challenging, since they were no longer dwelling within the sheltering cocoon of the quadrangle of church, rectory, convent, and school that made the faith perhaps "too easy," as one wrote. But didn't Christ tell the woman at the well God could be worshipped anywhere? Its universality is one of the four marks of the Roman Catholic faith.

About imputing blame for a drop in church fidelity, is it as the Bard wrote, "The fault is not in our stars" (or location or work), but in ourselves we are underlings," that is, not up to the task. So, like everything that went into the nation's melting pot, you can judge its value by its fruits, the Gospel says. We said that whereas belief in God is high in America, church worship, which should be communal, is not. I often like to tell parishioners that their faith confirms mine. But at the turn of the 20th Century, was Cardinal John Newman too pessimistic about what he saw?: "The disappointments of life, the defeat of good, the success of evil, physical pain, mental anguish, the prevalence and intensity of sin, the pervading idolatries, the dreary hopeless irreligion, the condition of the whole race ...." But again, did the cardinal just describe the human condition as it has been, is, and always will be since the Fall? But if Adam and Eve's sin caused all this, why did the Germans, for one, observe their feast day Dec. 24? Recall the historian who said any century or period can be labeled as the best or worst since the dawn of history, like the last one. The same about the faith? And to which everyman and everywoman reply, "We were there."

The Fourth R: Religion in the Curriculum

BECAUSE THE LANGUAGE of our curriculum was mostly French, it's only natural, given the dictum *Qui perd sa langue, perd sa foi*[43], that religion, the fourth R, was at the heart of our curriculum. Called *catéchisme*, yes, it was the "cardinal" reason or *raison d'être* (most important reason for existence) for the Catholic school system. (The reader may find the following chapters religious, pietistic and faith-laden, but to know and understand Francos, the reader must know their commitment to the faith and heroic adherence to it and belief in the hereafter. Call it "The Faith of Our Fathers.") A history of most countries and their people reveals Faith was often a matter of life and death, as it was in Christ's own life, but now it's more indifference and dismissal, except in the Middle East. Are they going through what the Western World did for 500 or more years? One writer said religion incites the worst violence. Is it because of its soulful fundamentalism and belief in the hereafter? For example, our church can count hundreds or thousands who died for their faith. Did they believe too much and we too little? Overall, our curriculum as we advanced in grades must've resembled a typical Québec *écolier's* (schoolboy's). Along with *la religion*, I recall a bit of *l'Histoire du* (history of) *Canada*, the Palmer Method of Writing, *la musique, le dessein* (art), *l'arithmétique, la lecture* (reading), *la grammaire, et la littérature* (e.g., *Les Fables de La Fontaine*: mom proud of that), and in upper grades a bit more emphasis on English grammar and reading by rows, geography, and American history. Ahead of his time, Monsignor Dauray, pastor of Precious Blood, whom we touted as a farsighted administrator-educator, wanted his schools to teach English and French equally. The 1880s Synod of Bishops also wanted schools to give an education equal to public ones.

But at one time I knew more about Jacques Cartier, Champlain, Dollard des Ormeaux than about Washington, Lincoln, and other national heroes. A nun gave us a window placard about this Dollard. When his townspeople barricaded themselves in a house, he saved them from an Iroquois

---

[43] Who loses his language, loses his faith. – *ed.*

attack by running to the gun house for weapons. Mom liked the story because in her birthplace, Contrecoeur, heroine Madeleine (Madelon) de Verchères also saved her people the same way, once including *Sieur LaFontaine et famille contre les sauvages*. (Sir LaFontaine & family against the savages). Mom and a genealogist priest in Canada told me the first Fontaines always lived there in the Verchères region. The Iroquois (a name meaning "serpent") were always lurking. Because they sided with the British in the lucrative fur trade and became anti-French, they never forgot Champlain twice humiliated them in battle with a special gun made in France. They were also enemies of the friendlier, less warlike Hurons and Algonguins, friends of the French. One is amazed how much of New England, Canada, and Northern territories Champlain explored, sketched, and wrote about. Unlike two of his commanders who alienated Indians with their demeaning manner, and another for stealing their crops, he welcomed them and won their friendship. Besides their intelligence and judgment, he also found their physique better than his men's. In 2012, a monument and plaque in Champlain's honor were erected in Chatham on Cape Cod which he first visited in 1605 and again in 1606.

But to give them their due, the Confederation and Constitution the Iroquois established among their five tribes (Mohawk, Oneida, Onondaga, Cayuga, and Seneca) to halt killing their own inspired some of the Founding Fathers, like Thomas Jefferson, in writing our own. But their cruelty to missionaries in upstate New York and Canada was nothing short of disgusting, including victim René Goupil, my first patron saint. Their martyrdom was the first book I read in the Order, as cousin François included me in his reading circle. We followed the old boarding school schedule: Saturday morning classes and none Wednesday afternoons.

Even if Peck's law to make English the principal language of our curriculum was never fully implemented, it gave English more emphasis in non-public schools, however little at first. For example, mom, who never lost her accent, made me laugh when she recounted some of the wild responses given by *les femmes de maison* in citizenship classes at night. Was this an instance of the "coal calling the kettle black?" Born in Canada, Francos literally jumped from one culture into another in attending those classes on foot. I cherish her citizenship certificate with its youthful photo. "Wow," I said when as a tyke I realized mom and dad were once subjects of Britannia. Did that foster her love of royalty? Was it hard for her to give up that tenuous kingly (or queenly) link? (When I researched her brothers' WWI records, I received an invitation to become a Canadian citizen! I had written in French. If I did, I would have reversed what my folks once did, but of course only on paper? Dual citizenship. Recall what happened to the American missionaries, like Brothers Lavallée and André, who spent five years as POWs, because they had taken out Canadian citizenship papers (mother country England was at war with Germany) to get to Basutoland in South Africa. Not at war, but American ships didn't go into the South Atlantic at that time before Hitler declared war against us.)

About religion, before the massive new catechism, we had the little Baltimore one. In it, the greatest mysteries of the faith were put forth with simplicity and clarity in a Socratic question-and-answer method. A far cry from the new, voluminous over 800-page edition released in the 1990s, a two-year reading project. Teasingly, did the authors forget Christ chided the Pharisees for burdening the people with innumerable laws and practices? Isn't it reassuring Christ condensed the whole law to love God and neighbor? Imagine if still at St. Ann's when it came out! Instead of a diploma, perhaps a doctorate at graduation? But I appreciated its grand sweep over the entire moral and religious dimension of the faithful in their relation to God and each other. It takes a lot of learning to be a good Christian! It's also why it's shortsighted when some put up a misguided defense of some or all their actions or inactions, miffed about "the so-called interference of religion." Every human act has a moral dimension, one said. For example, is anything more shocking than a "Catholic public servant" exercising his or her role in a moral vacuum? Especially about abortion, banned in Exodus and the weight of history and morality, and same sex marriage, contrary to God's and nature's designs. For the former especially, some bishops even thought of denying Communion or at least a speaking forum in Catholic schools. Life at conception is one of the most basic truths of the Catholic faith. The Old Testament also says, "I knew you before I formed you in the womb"; "Thou has covered me in my mother's womb"; "I am wonderfully made ...and in thy book my members were written." Doesn't it answer all the questions about the viability and the right to life of the fetus? One wrote it's the new civil rights issue of our times, as slavery once was. We will overcome. God, the author of life groans, one wrote. Are the increasing and more terrible world catastrophes an indication, as some devout say who have had revelations? The only way God can punish mankind, another said. Didn't Jefferson write that life, liberty, and the pursuit of happiness are the inalienable rights of all peoples? If only he had said "in and out of the womb!" But he didn't need to then when abortion was considered an abomination. Weren't the founders of the first women's movement in upstate N.Y. also pro-life, so I was told?

And just as familiar as every Latin student once was with the opening lines of Caesar's Gallic Wars - *Gallia omnis divisa est in tres partes*: All of Gaul (now largely France) is divided into three parts - so did every student learn about those first questions of the catechism: "Who is God?" "How many persons in God?" "Where does God live?" "Why do we call God good?" "Why did He create us?"

A theologian wrote that theology (the study of God and His relation to the world, says Merriam-Webster) can't really be made simple, either for children or seminarians. But the Baltimore catechism was a great effort for Catholics, once largely uneducated, now schooled and in the comfortable middle class for many. With more education, Catholics sometimes joked at the simplistic explanation or pictures used in catechisms to explain complex and profound doctrines. For example, mortal or grievous sin was likened to a darkening of the soul, like pouring black ink into a milk bottle. In one of my beat-up catechisms, I said a "devilish schoolboy" also darkened the white bottle next to the dark one. St. Patrick himself used the trifoliate shamrock (un-theologically overlooking the one common stem, said my prof) to illustrate the notion of three separate, distinct persons in one God. Reportedly, St. Augustin also found the mystery beyond human understanding. He once asked a tyke by a seashore why he was trying to put all the water into an eggshell. The celestial wunderkind said he sooner would than the bishop could fathom the mystery of the Trinity. If the story isn't fiction, is it a case of "Out of the mouths of babes, Thou (God) hath plucked a truth." My prof said the Old Testament is largely silent about the Trinity, except at creation: "Let us make man in our own image, in the likeness of ourselves." That is, with intelligence and will. About the Trinity, my prof's take was God's infinite reflection of Himself from all eternity generates His Son (not creates, which implies a beginning), and the love between them generates the Holy Spirit. One God-nature but three persons is the mystery. For us it's one nature one person. Recall God saying, "I am who I am," so how can existence not exist, asked my prof?

In defense of simple comparisons, apologists wrote Christ in his parables used natural or everyday imagery, like birds of the air, the lost coin, leaves, the pearl seeker, the mustard seed, and the human family in *l'enfant prodique* (the Prodigal Son).

Because some explanations went over our heads or teachers spared us the knowledge of especially sexually sinful acts; learning was directive without discussion. We repeated it by rote. You had to know every word by heart, because not one iota of the law was going to be abolished, said Christ. In a history of Canada, I read even in the seminary that religion in the 19th Century was taught in a very doctrinaire manner, with no opposing opinion or belief mentioned or considered, even to reinforce the real truth by contrast. Another case of "Rome has spoken, let no dog bark!"

If you fumbled recitation, our nun suggested we have moms (never our mill working fathers) hear our catechism lessons. Ours never shirked her duty, saying, "*Sort-mwé ton catéchisme*" (Take out your catechism) from the homemade school bag she made. In how many Franco homes was there catechism learning after supper?

That soft cloth bag contoured your back as you walked. You used the long straps to helicopter the bag and smack someone with it. Passive learning! No doubt, hearing recitations helped parents emphasize certain rules of conduct; expand on a topic, and nostalgically recall stories of their own First Communion and Confirmation in Canada. Didn't we say a concrete example was dad twice asking us to return extra change to the store, once bowling over monsieur Choquette at Gaulin's Lavergne's Market. (Wasn't his son Woonsocket HS principal at one time?) The word *Justus* (Just) heard in the Order meant a person of great moral stature. Like mom, dad fit the label, as others did too. Barely holding back tears after his funeral at Assumption Church in Bellingham in 1982, I told Pat his only "mistake" in life was to grow old. I had given the pastor notes about his life for the eulogy. It's why a relative was amazed the priest knew so much about him! Someone who saw me with red cheeks said he heard the Telliers never cried!

I'm told Catholic students today are much more into liturgy and celebration, but less perhaps into the truths and dogmas of the Church. We, on the other hand, were walking encyclopedias of the faith. Except for altar boy service, our role in the liturgy was on the passive side, since altar and sanctuary were like "the holy of holies." We sat quietly in the pews with our mandatory missal, a Confirmation gift.

Besides the Commandments, we learned the Seven Capital Sins (pride, lust, cupidity, anger, etc.; a recent TV program said the number has gone up and down), and the Seven Gifts of the Holy Spirit (wisdom, knowledge, fortitude, etc.) And of course, the Seven Sacraments, more than the Protestants (Luther only kept two), *Soeur* Ste. Émilie told us with some one-upmanship; the 15 Mysteries of the Rosary (5 Joyful, Sorrowful, and Glorious). Is there any other religion with as many prayers or precepts, but amazingly with uniformity of doctrine throughout Christendom and the world? President Carter, dubbed our most religious president, said this lack of uniformity of doctrine is fracturing many Protestant religions. (A study of Protestant religions postulated that private interpretation of the Scriptures created hundreds of creeds. We recorded 4,100, as seen once! But no disparagement of Protestant believers is meant here, only our degree of separation. But now because interpretations differ from sect to sect, some believe in nothing at all. Catholicism's unity also stems from Sacred Tradition, the Sacred Bible, and the Magisterium (described to me as the sum of all church teachings). The Pope's infallibility when speaking on matters of faith and doctrine is a sore point with some religions and non-believers. Recall English converts at the end of the 19th Century, like Newman, Chesterton, Belloc, and Lewis were all drawn by that one, undiluted faith of Catholicism.

Amidst all the uncertainties of life, how comforting the absolute faith of our religion. In fact, Newman said a study of the faith history of the Western world can only lead to one conclusion: Catholicism. But as Hans Küng says in *The Church*, salvation is possible to all who are sincere that theirs is the right course, reversing, he added, a former church pronouncement from the Council of Trent. Called "freedom of conscience," it's why we should respect believers in other religions. I know some restrictions were put on Küng, but I have no particulars. His knowledge of Scriptures is the best I've seen. And what about his point that in the centuries, instead of warring about our differences, we should have spoken about mutually shared faith elements, as we do now since Renewal. Unfortunately, Protestants walked out of the Council of Trent, 1545, a major effort to reform the church from its abuses.

That's why a pervasive Catholic school system was so important for us since it bred well-informed practitioners. Ignorance of those rules today is probably as big as it has been in Christendom, especially now for Catholics who, strangely, are so much better educated otherwise, but have never attended Catholic schools or colleges or parish CCD programs. Is diminution of its school feeder system and faith-fostering families two major setbacks?

An article in 2013 said many families can no longer afford private Catholic education, whose tuition reflects the need to pay lay teachers a salary almost commensurate with public school teachers. I fought for that when I laicized at Mount and wrote that ten-page paper to the diocese. After I married and we adopted Jimmy, I couldn't live on my salary and went to Norton HS, as surprisingly a *Call* article and an artist's cartoon of me showed. But even in the 1940s some families couldn't afford Mount, even if it was only $75 a year in 1945. Tuition from boarders and students from North Smithfield "paid" for us. But now with aggressive fund raising and a tuition assistance program, the Academy hopes to address the problem, so hopefully no one who wants a college preparatory Catholic education (but open to all faiths) will be denied: a 99.1 percent college placement record, solid moral instruction, athletic and cultural programs, and the recognition of every single student for his worth and talent are high water marks.

(Humor: Amusing was a schoolboy's answer after learning Christ's founding words for all Seven Sacraments. About marriage he quoted Christ on the cross: "Father, forgive them, for they know not what they do." About avoiding getting angry, especially towards siblings, another quoted the 5th Commandment, "Thou shall not kill." But about the Bible and the Christmas story, "Pontius the Pilot flew the Holy Family to Egypt to avoid Herod's wrath."; and Joseph and Mary took Jesus to the Temple "because they couldn't get a babysitter." I used to collect them when teaching.)

Despite the great devotion and generosity of today's parish CCD teachers, understandably one session a week can't totally address the insurmountable task of turning out well-informed Catholics against the counter-culture of modernism, hedonism (the cult of the flesh and body), and moral relativism (no absolutes) of our times, i.e., Americanism. But thank God for them and the CYO, so strong in RI. The Catholic Church, for one, fighting a battle royal to preserve the one, true apostolic faith of Christ, as conservative Pope Benedict reaffirmed, touting it as unalloyed by fads and adaptations to modernistic trends. For us, John Paul II said Catholicism is the one true faith founded by Christ. But he too also stressed we should respect all religions since they have a portion of the true faith. One day when the apostles wanted Christ "to do something" about others preaching the faith, He told them, "Whoever is not against me is for me."

About the Commandments, *Soeur* Ste. Émilie said legislators passed a million laws for people to observe the Ten Commandments. A clever insight! Like Moses, who broke the tablets over his people's heads for their idol worship and disobedience, she showed the same cosmic urge against "our trespasses," lack of prayerful reverence, and uncharitableness. But like all nuns, "her divine wrath" was always tempered with mercy. And they took us to Confession monthly. As schoolboys we knew our side of the Confessional, but a friend and I peeked in once to see what was behind that sliding window grille. (Francos had quite a few Confession stories or jokes, like the one *mon oncle* François told us in his store. Also, during one football season, a Notre Dame University lineman confessed he had deliberately hurt a gridder from Southern Methodist University. Dismissively, the Irish priest said, "Son, start off with your mortal sins first!" And in one crowded church for confession, the priest announced he had an emergency and would only hear mortal sins. The church emptied in seconds.)

In correct French, mom said, *"Nous sommes tous les fils d'Adam"* (We are all the son's of Adam), about our fallen nature. Even though she often said, *"Le diable s'en mêle"* (like the devil getting into our stuff), I never heard her or anyone say in defense of those failings, "The devil made me 'dood it," as comedian Red Skelton joked. Judging by the numbers that went to Confession, if the faithful slipped, they confessed. St. Augustin said, "Confession is good for the soul." Recall Bishop Sheen, whose TV show was once number one, didn't agree with "sinners" opting for the psychiatrist's couch instead of the confessional. In the Order, we were allowed to hear him in the early days of TV. He joked one time when he said the airline TWA meant Travel with Angels. His cause for sainthood has started.

Was it profane humor when witty adults got a laugh by combining the first part of one Commandment of God with the latter part of another? This because those precepts were taught to us like proverbs or sayings in couplet style, with or without rime. Since one part might deal with sexual aberration or whatever, imagine the hilarity when joined with some other Commandment's imperative "to do it either at Easter time" or, say, "once a year." Mom said this verbal jousting was "sal" (dirty) or *"pas beau* (not nice)." Curiously, it was only seen in religion-based communities like ours. A sense of the sacred prevailed in our culture and everywhere, now lost in our neo-pagan times. But for many, like the foul-mouthed Holden Caulfield in the *The Catcher in the Rye*, I agreed with the critic that his was a lack of vocabulary and an empty mind, not ugly swearing. Like often done today for shock value. A poet called it, "The loud laugh that spoke the vacant mind."

We said the catechism got bigger as we moved up. We often recited it to chosen brighter students (girls mostly) in front of your row. Sometimes we garbled some gibberish to the interrogator, making veiled threats if a girl ratted on us. We were going to be saved even if it damned us! About observing God's law, I later read Charlemagne (742-814), Emperor of the West, imposed the death penalty for breaking fast in Lent and eating meat on Friday! (Is that why we thought it was just as important as Sunday Mass? Asked if he fasted in Lent someone said, "I don't eat any faster or slower.")

In some classrooms beneath a rendering of the eye of God were the words, quoted before, *Dieu Me Voit*, meaning God Sees Me. You were convinced you couldn't do anything without the All-Seeing-One looking on. It was like "Big Brother" watching you long before futuristic novelist George Orwell brought him into our lives with *1984* and *Brave New World*. During communism, Bob Hope won best joke of the year with the revelation people in Russia didn't' watch TV, it watched them! And added someone broke into the Kremlin and stole the results of next year's elections! But now, of course, electronic eavesdropping is everywhere with people "caught close to 15 times a day," a report said. It's why the TV show, *Person of Interest* is a big hit. At Norton HS, Peter Leddy, a science teacher who once worked Intelligence for the government, told me how much the government knew about us because of satellites and overhead flights. Grateful for my articles about his summer science grant travels, one year he brought me a Pravda edition of the day communism collapsed. When librarian at Notre Dame HS, I also had a copy of the day Lincoln died. And all National Geographic magazines from its inception, save one.

With nine choirs of angels on call, God selects one guardian angel for each of us at birth, causing St. Francis to say, "Make yourself familiar with the angels, and behold them frequently in spirit; for, without being seen, they are present with you." In the 1990s, angels became popular again in books, movies, and sitcoms to explain mysterious sources of help. Like the Boulder Dam worker whose sure-death fall was broken up by a supposedly "phantom worker" who had never worked there before, was not on the rolls, and never seen again. Or the young woman with a child facing exposure and death on a lonely, snowbound highway in the Midwest, who was told how to start her disabled car by someone who in no way should've been there, unless AAA means three angels!

Even in public schools at one time, can you believe 90 percent of all text materials in certain subjects had a moral tone or message? It's now, less than 10 percent! With a tremendous slippage in moral behavior, especially in young adults, it comes as no surprise there's a movement in some states like California, military academies, and law and business schools to initiate ethical studies acceptable to all. As a counselor, I visited all three military academies, and two of them were reeling from breakdowns in their Honor Code. Ethical instruction is controversial in a pluralistic, morally relativistic culture, but nevertheless necessary. Why? A TV anchor opined that since schools are rapidly taking over many familial, societal, ethical roles in raising children, it's now an important "academic task." Especially since families, churches, and neighborhoods don't or can't speak as one on matters of ethical conduct, as they once did.

Because many sexual transgressions are no longer a matter of law, many people eventually seduce themselves into personal, family, and civic disasters, as seen in letters to advice columnists and newspapers. Did it all come about because "you couldn't legislate morality," which for some lacking training at home or church affiliation have been left with no training in self-control or restraint in their make-up?

About Jefferson's opinion in a private letter regarding the separation of church and state, again, moralists aver his intent was freedom of religion, not freedom from religion. Patrick Conley, noted historian in the state, explained forcefully that one of the principal meanings of the nation's separation of church and state is that government will not interfere with people's right to worship as they please. Other rights propounded by historians is no state obligatory religion, as first settlers from England in New England, labored against. And that religion, however, should not be torn from the national fabric. John Milton Cooper, Jr. in *Woodrow Wilson: A Biography* quotes him, a Presbyterian: "Our civilization cannot survive materially unless it be redeemed spiritually. It can be saved only by becoming one with the spirit of Christ and being made free and happy in the practices which spring out of the spirit." President Coolidge said good government came from religion. How far have we gotten away from all that? For example, in 2012, how sad and completely mystifying was a decision to remove a Cranston West HS banner by one single atheistic girl and the ACLU, because the title or content had a moral, quasi-religious message, which expressed the right of people to do so. The now beatified Cardinal Newman said no self-made morality can long sustain itself if not founded on an established ethical system and religion. Morality without religion, he added, was like trying "to moor a ship with threads," or "quarrying marble with a blade!" He made a deep impression on me. Again, it's why Pope Benedict wanted people to return to religion and church to uphold their faith in God and the moral code.

Should we not give more credit to parents of old or now for insisting on a fourth R (as in ethics or morality) in their children's education? Without it, Brother George-Aimè said you risked instructing kids only, but not educating them. Because of its time-honored insistence on this moral substratum in the curriculum, private schools, especially those in tune with their religious history and founding philosophy, are now in the vanguard of national school reforms stressing character formation, values, and standards of conduct. Some public schools too with students oriented towards good works we said. Otherwise, it's a weapon's check at the door, metal detectors, cameras, police on site, and, sadly, shootouts like at: Columbine, Newtown, and Colorado. Where has the little red schoolhouse of yesteryear gone?

The Good Nuns: Lifeblood of the Parish

A 1946 EDITION OF the Brothers of the Sacred Heart publication *Entre Nous* (Among Us) lauded teaching nuns: "*La religieuse enseignante dans l'obscurité de sa classe est comme la racine de la paroisse, de la cité, autant dire de l'Eglise et de la nation. C'est elle qui pompe regulièrement la sève nourricière de la culture humaine et de l'esprit chrétien et la rend assimilable.*"[44] [*see footnote for translation*]

The above is a superlative praise of teaching nuns, extolling their moral and cultural impact in the life of those units so important to Francos and other nationalities in parishes, municipalities, churches, and nation. One wrote they established the largest private school system in America. They far outnumbered teaching Brothers and priests, who also performed their role in equally meritorious fashion. But how often did my confrères and I feel belittled or unappreciated when speakers, who lauded Catholic schoolteachers at conferences or seminars, omitted the work of teaching Brothers

---

[44] "The religious teacher in the darkness of her classroom is like the root of the parish, of the city, in other words of the Church and of the nation. It is she who regularly pumps the nourishing sap of human culture and the Christian spirit and makes it assimilable."

in the orders of the Sacred Hearts, Christian Brothers, Marists, Marianists, et al.

Yes, unlike St. Theresa of the Child Jesus, we couldn't always be completely selfless. Our Manual of Perfection or Vow book in the Order cautioned us that even in the best selfless intention, there's always a scintilla or canker of self-interest at the core. Alexander Hamilton concurred about all men. But we still needed that pat on the back.

St. Ann's teachers were among those devoted nuns, many legends at a time when religious teachers sank roots in parish soil and became beacons of knowledge and faith for immigrants and future generations. Recall *Soeur* Saint Vital, perennial first grade teacher, who, like Saint Theresa, possessed that rare Gospel-like quality of being childlike herself, but not childish in guiding *les bébés* (the babies) into the world of learning. However traumatic it was beginning your schooling in a huge building with black-robed teachers who appeared stern to a tyke, it was reassuring when parents said you'd have her. The Good Housekeeping Seal in teacher selection! We saw tears the first day, but they soon dried up in the warmth of her motherly touch. After St. Ann's I was never to see her again, yet her bright morning face is still fresh in my mind. Unlike the kids in Goldsmith's "The Deserted Village," we could not read "the day's disasters in her morning face." In the Order, we considered equanimity, that is, equal temper or virtue in good and bad times, one of the greatest virtues. She had that gift, not an easy attainment for teachers and parents affected by the ebb and tide of children's behaviors and moods, especially in this age of young fragile psyches.

I thought of her in a story about a legendary first grade teacher in a Canadian Province. When an inspector visited a Brother's class (Canadian stories about schools often dealt with evaluators: *inspecteurs*), a tyke was standing in the corner. "Little boy (*petit garçon*), why has *le Frère* punished you?" Replied the wunderkind, "Our teacher doesn't punish us. He corrects us." As Art Linkletter said, "Kids do say the darndest things." And didn't Christ say, "If they be silent, the stones will speak." He so loved children and life, He would be against the death penalty today, but said a molester should have a millstone tied around his neck and flung into the sea! (Check the size of the millstone on Main Street where McCarthy's used to be!)
Knowing children's passion for sweets, she quickly introduced us to the delights of homemade taffy (*d'la tire*). We sold it for school causes, a penny a stick, but I recall it was also a reward, along with pictures of saints, medals, and those playground-doomed penny rosary beads for going to Mass during Lent and First Fridays of the month.

"If a good beginning is half the battle," how fortunate to have her as our first pedagogue with her enthusiasm for learning, and personally as a future teacher, her love of teaching and opening young minds. Career selection often comes from imitation. What a fierce, loving heartbeat in her tiny body! After her long career, she retired to the Order's St. Joseph Residence, Manchester, NH, returning to the city for reunions. She too surely glories in Heaven's Pantheon of Teachers. If it's one's destiny, what amazing saintly and amazing people one will meet in heaven. One teacher said God sometimes let the elect know the doings of people on earth. We pray for them; they for us. Those miracles we can't explain?

It was a sad farewell, but I recalled the passionate zeal of *Soeur* Ste. Émilie at her Memorial Mass, September 10, 1983, after her death in Manchester at 84. A former student and missionary priest highlighted the 50 years she toiled here after vows in Saint Hyacinthe, Québec. She taught religion, French, Canadian History, the Palmer Method, drawing, and school music. She retired in 1973, one year after being feted by 500 people, with a representative from each of the 50 classes she taught. Can you imagine all that time in the classroom? Chalk dust instead of blood in her veins? It was once said anyone who taught for 30 years or more in large classes probably didn't have a nervous system intact! I did 42, but more than half as a counselor talking to kids one at a time apart from the so-called "thundering herd!" My sociology studies told us how different solo conduct is from gang behavior. It's so sad when a less threatening member of an urban gang is indicted for murder, say, even if he was influenced by one of the member's amoral, vicious thugs, like five of them once were in Providence. Mistakenly, they shot a teenage girl.

Character-sketching praises from her eulogist were "a good faithful servant of the Lord," "a dedicated teacher," and "a person who gave her life and talent for the students of St. Ann's." They all re-fleshed in my mind the person who "had come into the fiber of our being and whose shadow had now fallen and gone." People like her were in the trenches when the Catholic system was created to teach school and the faith to immigrants and their offspring. They stand tall alongside the secular schoolmasters and schoolmarms of yesteryear who crop up in American and English Literature and the history of education. With little esteem and pay, they taught the rudiments of learning in sometimes drafty, bare, unfurnished settings. Because it was "a calling," young, single, secular women, for example, had to give up dating, socializing after 5 p.m., marrying, clean their own classroom, and survive on a pittance. And see part of their salary held back "in case they didn't have enough sense" to save for the summer months or their declining years." When my Norton HS secretary Ruth Church showed me an article about those times, I now understood why people thought teachers were paid in the summer. In fact, to abolish the perceived economic injustice of withholding part of one's wages without permission, or finally destroy the myth of paid summer teachers, school systems now offer the option of full pay during the school year. Some teachers, however, still prefer the old way, knowing the human propensity - so American - to spend now what's in hand. My wife Pat loved those summer checks.

Soeur Ste. Émilie had that indefatigable body and mind to teach first generation kids for so long. When you entered her classroom and saw her rolled-up sleeves already whitened with chalk, you saw the fire in her eyes, like boot camp Sergeant Lou Gossett's orbs in the movie, *An Officer and a Gentleman*. You sensed a coiled spring about to unwind. A rigid disciplinarian, she, as Rachel and friend Maurice Aubin (retired Globe Park School principal) recalled, didn't even tolerate coughing in her classroom. What's called "staying on task." She wanted you to pinch your nostrils to stem the rheumy blast!

Mistress of her domain, she kept her class on the alert with her quick pace, darting eyes, and sharp tongue. That speech organ froze you into immobility if she preceded your last name with *monsieur*. Her eulogist said she taught a multitude of subjects because teachers then were like all-knowing Renaissance scholars "who wore many hats," as said in my Order. But she took on the dimension of an Old Testament prophet when teaching the famed little catechism. It's why she wore the habit and taught large groups in her career. A charter member of those teachers who came to the states ("*qui sont venues aux états*," mom said) to fill the parish units of school and convent. Again, what a citadel of faith and prayer (and learning) in Social *Coin* with over 40 nuns (three also in the rectory) and 5 priests in our midst. And from 1924, MSC in the Bernon Heights District had some Brothers who taught students from America, Canada, and South America. Was Woonsocket ever more God-centric? A golden age of faith and learning transmission!

But academically, *Soeur* Marie Donat was my most influential mentor. Since we left after 9th grade for the Academy, she formed the last and deepest impression. A sparse-looking woman with an unfathomable air like the Mona Lisa, she was unique, because she seemed equally comfortable in English and French. Was that because she was born in Phenix, RI (1902), and not in Canada like our parents and her fellow teachers?

Given our Franco ambiance, we were fortunate to have her as a teacher of English and a model of bilingualism, along with Scoutmaster Jannell, Father Moreau, and later Father Roussel. They were Francophones who mastered the country's native idiom. That meant they had little or no evidence of those words and pronunciations we were often mocked for outside our ethnic cocoon, stumbling over those th's and not aspirating our h's.

Also legendary was *Soeur* Jeanne Leber, who taught religion and French for 43 years. She implanted and directed the J.E.C. Movement (*Jeunesse Étudiante Catholique*: Young Catholic Students) and *La Croisade Eucharistique* (The Eucharistic Crusade) for the religious formation of young people. Some couples met as a result and students loved her unfailing good humor and equanimity. My brother Ben and wife Gloria (Landry) met through the KBG (Kappa Beta Gamma), another community-wide group outside the parish for young people to socialize.

If not for *Soeur* Donat, how ill-prepared we would have been if we'd gone to high school and college without the rudiments of English grammar, a working vocabulary, and a bit of literature. Because we learned French first, hers was a Herculean task, because unlike today's Hispanic, Portuguese, and Asian kids, we didn't go back after school to an English-speaking neighborhood and pervasive English media. Years later, when my son Jim played Pony League baseball with kids like them, I marveled how they switched accent-free from their own idiom to English while their mothers encouraged them in their native tongue. Was it those ESL programs (English as a Second Language)? Or by the 1970s or earlier, was the city basically monolingually English outside the home?

At the Academy in the 1970s, for instance, I was amazed how quickly an Asian student picked up the language. He jotted down every new word he heard. A likeable kid, he quickly caught on when teasing students purposely used "dirty words" around him. I recommended him to URI for engineering. St. Agatha's Parish sponsored him. In a way, it reminded me of my non-Catholic star basketball player at Notre Dame HS (Freddie Gillis; Division 3 All-American at Fitchburg State College) who "reprimanded" teammates whose language was not "orthodox" in the locker room after a loss. An honor roll student, he aced his religion classes with the Brothers. Now with a national trend of more non-members in private Catholic schools in the country (20 percent), their mission is of course not to convert those of different faiths but develop in them a solid core of moral beliefs and behavior and appreciation of religious diversity. One mother, not a Catholic, told me she appreciated that. I only recall one Jewish student being excused from religion at the Academy in the 1970s. He was going to the synagogue.

What a great opportunity to sharpen our English skills in the Order when we trained with recruits in Mobile from the Provinces of New York and New Orleans in the early 1950s. More attuned to hunting and fishing than we land "lubbing" Ocean Staters, southern Brothers also taught us how to pick up crabs, lobsters, and marvel at porpoises on Mobile Bay. One young Brother, however, got 20 stitches from a stingray, a fish that never swam in the Blackstone River! (Truth or fiction? - a southerner told me a porpoise once flipped a shark over as he was attacking a Brother in the water! In Greek the letters of the word fish render Christ's name. Was it monkish humor to think the porpoise was properly "schooled" to recognize one of Christ's own?) Unlike some of our older brothers in WWII, we already spoke better English, but it was a great opportunity to perfect our American dialect. Like rolling our "r's" in words like "park" and "car," not always accenting the last syllable, or putting r's at the end of words ("idea-r"). We also omitted r's ("chowda," "Rhode Islanda"). It's called "Rhode Islandese." We did all this without picking up a drawl in two years! My religious class of 1949-50 was so incredibly fortunate to be the first American recruits to receive a full degree before teaching. Since I paid $75 to attend MSC, no way as a layman could I have gone to Providence College where the tuition was around $300. I'm greatly beholden to the Order for bestowing on me what was denied to many of my French-Canadian generation. I also got to know religious confreres from the NY and New Orleans provinces which along with New England, became the United States Province in July, 2014. Brother Mark Hilton, former MSC and Bishop Guertin HS principal, served as first provincial.

Before us, older New England American Brothers fluent in English and French were admired in the Canadian Provinces. They spearheaded the complete Americanization of the New England Province (minus Maine at first), which became a non-Canadian entity in 1945. Some of these Brothers - Victoric, Claver, Hermas, Ulric, Honorius, Felician, Eugene, Eymard, Paul-Albert, John Joseph, et al - were at the Academy in the mid-1940s. How they helped the fluency of thousands of French-Canadian kids! It's no wonder the new New England Province had to pay "a release fee" for a few years to Canada which lost a fertile recruiting ground, as the Southern Province had once lamented before the century.

An incident forever endeared *Soeur* Donat to me as a concerned teacher. Always a willing student, I had resolved my last year to be successful, but to have a blast. My seat in the middle of the last row with kindred souls made my foolish resolve an easy task. Thus, I partook in a succession of little covert actions, like teasing girls in the next row; speaking out of turn for a laugh; jabbing students with pencils; careless with ink; and all the usual antics of your typical attention-seeking clown of the 1940s. Enduring the charade for a week, she asked me to stay after class. Wasn't I good that day? "Rene," she said in a disarming voice, "Do you have any idea the record you've established since first grade?" I honestly said no because I had no idea schools kept records. I thought they threw stuff out like we did with our books in June, thinking September was never coming back. She showed me a stiff yellow card (Didn't all schools have them?) with all my yearly grades, along with flattering comments about my conduct (*bonne conduite*), desire to learn (*ambitieux*), etc. Letting me catch my breath, she added, "This is what you're undermining with your foolishness. Don't you want to build on this good record?" If you pardon the grossly unequal comparison (my knowledge of the Bible!), like Paul, future Apostle of the Gentiles unhorsed at Damascus, my conversion was immediate. But thank God, I wasn't on a horse and didn't lose my sight, as he did temporarily. My eyes were immediately opened. My epiphany! Don't we all have one episode like Paul in life with varying degrees or urgency?

In my professional life, I used the sobering effect of having one's entire academic life brought back into focus. As a guidance counselor, I did it to students many times and often with the same effect. Since students are by nature existentialists (here-and-now people), they don't realize in the long term their record is a resume for further schooling, jobs, promotions, entrance into the military, etc. *Soeur* Donat, who later retired to Arctic, RI, was the first to tell me "Experience runs an expensive school, but fools will learn in no other."

With education now a cradle-to-grave experience, students who didn't go on after high school at Norton HS often returned for academic counseling within a five-year period, as I told actual students. How I also enjoyed advising returning adults (many women as it turned out, including two would-be masseuses in one week), who now had the maturity and means they once lacked. But in two other schools, even well-educated and salaried career people came in for a career change: an embalmer depressed over two infant deaths in a week and an accountant tired of traveling to visit clients. Statistics reveal Americans now have a 42-year working life on average (I hit the mark), four career changes, and twelve jobs. Evidence we live longer and need more education to adapt to those changes. At times the choice is not ours, as companies go belly up or outsource, as dad predicted. One pope chastised companies for doing that and putting people out of work.

(Four more humorous anecdotes: One day one of the prettiest girls ever to graduate from Norton HS came in to look into nursing. A rare day when my work was caught up, I gave her a couple of hours, as strangely, a stream of students and faculty members walked by my windowed office! Curious, the next day I asked a student who said the buzz was "Miss America the Beautiful" was in Mr. Tellier's office for all that time! I once recommended a girl for a college beauty contest. She never told me how she did! Also, in the Order we were taught to see Christ in our students. Even after laicizing, I did that. A girl with family issues came in for the third day in a row when I was swamped with recommendations, recruiters, testing, and reports. Exasperatingly I barked, "Christ, are you here again?" She ran out! And about being Christocentric, cousin Frank, a storyteller like his dad, spoke about a drunkard who claimed he was Christ, telling a doubter to follow him to a bar. When the bartender saw him, he confirmed it: "Christ, are you here again?")

In the Order, you heard, "*Si jeunesse savait, si vieillesse pouvait*": if young people knew, if older people could. But in my career, even if some kids knew how the world operated and had the talent to succeed, they didn't profit from it. It's now prompting the question, "What's wrong with our boys?" Far more boys than girls show learning problems (5 to 1), drop out of high school, or opt not to go to college or finish. We already reported lack of ambition, absenteeism, effortless lifestyle, electronic addiction, and often the absence of fathers. Is it genetic with Americans to want it now? One theorist said for too long we thought girls had a problem. Their lack of self-esteem or confidence in 8th or 9th grade, as evident and reported at one time, was more the absence of a level playing field in education and opportunity. Can anyone doubt the 21st Century is the Century of the Woman? For example, isn't it revealing the nation's shortage of nurses stems partly from more women now in med school? Law, dental, and business schools are nearing parity. Engineering up to 17 percent. We said millions of husbands are now homemakers because wives make more. The recession made more men jobless.

Many parochial schools are now gone or diminished. But the work of those teachers with generations of students is a rich legacy in the country's school history. Fortunately, lay people have stepped into the breach in Catholic schools. MSC, for example, imperiled with the drop of its boarding element and fewer Brothers, soon became vibrant again with Brothers, lay teachers, and a Religious of Jesus and Mary nun working together to educate a strictly commuter population of 650 or more from over 40 communities, including over 20 from Asiatic countries. A richness for the city, as His Honor Charles Baldelli told me about boarding students coming to Mount at one time. About the cost of Catholic education, the administration, for one, is sensitive to that, we said, and is trying hard to help struggling students, especially from the city, with its Sacred Heart Scholars Program. Funds are limited but growing, and parents needing help are asked to fill out an FAF form (Financial Aid Form), as students do for college. Parents of means are also encouraged to aid partially or totally needy students. And about recruiting parents with kids at Mount are proving to be effective also as some 25 new students in 2013-4 proved. I try to speak about Mount at least once a day when I'm in the public domain. Hopefully, the challenge will be met, especially when the academic and physical needs of the school, campus, and arena, have been met. (I fantasize which successful grad will be the school's first million-dollar donor? When I attended a conference in

Chicago on how to establish a fund-raising alumni association in Catholic schools, I learned people give more for education than any other reason.)

It bears repeating MSC has already undertaken a $5 million dollar academic, athletic, and arts expansion in the last few years, along with a new science wing and technology lab, a West Wing (integrated computer facilities and relocation of the library), new front stairway, modernized classrooms with tech boards, renovation of floors and hallways, improved rear entrance, a new gym complex, the new fine arts wing, gas heat to cut heating costs, gradual improvements for the Brother Adelard Arena, and tennis courts across Logee St. With giving from alumni, parents, and other benefactors, President Herve Richer has been indefatigable in expanding the whole Hilltopper experience. The new Mount. An Excelsior experience, which more city kids should experience, as my generation did.

Encounter With the Gendarmes

WHO WOULD HAVE thought St. Ann's School, a veritable bastion of morality, would be the scene of our too close encounter of the first kind with the city's finest? We did the usual pranks in the neighborhood, especially at Halloween, like levitating a stuffed dummy in the middle of the road and sending unwary drivers into cardiac arrest; flinging water-filled balloons at houses, and at cars from the top bleachers at St. Ann's Park; shooting pea-propelling missiles at people's windows and doors; and knocking over (but never stealing) pumpkins and lanterns.

Also walking to and from school twice a day was tempting, but the Age of Ripping People Off hadn't dawned yet, because the 7th and 10th Commandments of God (not damaging or stealing your neighbor's property) were heavily emphasized. Because people had so little then, stealing was almost like taking the Gospel widow's last mite. Or a man's horse in the Old West, a hanging offense. England at one time had 150 capital offenses on the books (300, another said), including stealing a loaf of bread.

It was still an age when doors were left unlocked, bikes left about, and a driver's registration or license was wrapped on the steering column, like neighbor Mr. Houle did. God, all this must've been before Adam and Eve's fall from grace! The Age of Innocence! Like the biblical rivers of Tigris and Euphrates girdling the Garden of Eden, did the Blackstone River drain an unsullied Northern RI? But in truth the city at one time had its share of political shenanigans, like illicit gambling, which necessitated reforms, meriting it an All-American City honor. Dad welcomed the change and told his advice seekers "to vote the 'bad-uns' out." It meant voting Democrat (or a reform party) which he did, and not the party in power. People often asked him, *"Ti-Phonse, pour qui j'devra voter?"* (Ti-Phonse, who should I vote for?) Equally well-informed, mom had her own voting insights, not always consonant with his. Honesty and integrity both high on their list. They always voted. Our confrontation with the law occurred because of a tree in the Dumas family's yard near the convent on Elm Street atop Pin Alley. During our lunch hour, the succulent fruit (so we thought) that seduced Mother Eve almost got us thrown "out of the garden" or school. A couple of us climbed the inviting tree with its leafy embrace, only to have the splintering crack of a good-sized limb fill us with terror.

We scooted like bats out of hell, because unlike our primal mother, we couldn't blame the serpent ("passing the buck") as she did. And the administration couldn't pin this on the Kendrick School kids. This was a parochial school caper, proving "*L'occasion fait le larron*," about opportunity spawning mischief. This arboreal seduction was very close to the girls' segregated schoolyard. But crime or mayhem like drinking, drugs, stealing from banks, and bad behavior was not an "equal opportunity employer" for girls then. If Homo sapiens had descended from trees, monkey-like, well, boys were more likely to indulge in this kind of simian behavior. But did someone turn in state's evidence for a lighter sentence? "Murder will out," poet Chaucer said, and five of us boys were called to Mother Superior's office with the future chief of police himself, Edgar J. Turcotte. But why would "one of the city's finest" come to St. Ann's for a couple of purloined or stolen Macintosh Reds?

All of us, nine or ten years of age, looked up at the bigness of the man, his intimidating blue-black uniform, gleaming badge, and holstered revolver. And shivered in our little culottes (pants). Not that Mother Superior's accusing look was less threatening. After all, everything the school stood for, why the school was founded was on the line. And in her administration! How would she account for this with Mother Superior in Hudson, N.H? Was hers Cicero's famous lament? - "O tempora! O mores." (O what times! O what morals!) Yes, how in time did morality go so far south? Which of the building blocks of our impregnable culture - church, school, family, neighborhood, scouting - was undermined by venality or empty stomachs? Where were the guardian angels assigned us at birth? Where were the biblical "sentinels at dawn?" But with proper respect to our initial presumption of innocence, the dour duo began the grilling in French. Turcotte knew he wasn't with the Irish in the North End or Italians in Diamond Hill: "*Êtes-vous coupables?*" (Are you guilty?) In our collective stammering and stuttering, we went from initial denial to a protestation of just having fun (don't all misbehaving kids say that at first?), then abject contrition, and, as we did in monthly Confession, a soulful promise to be good from now on. We knew the drill. The penance? Nothing like a couple of Hail Marys from curates Fournier *et* Massicotte. Christ said, "Render to God what is God's and to Caesar what is Caesar's." No doubt *le* policeman drew his check from "the togaed one." Gospel-like, he didn't so much want the denarius of repentance, but the shekel of good conduct for the future.

More terrifying was our parents could be told. Recall parents held fast to two cardinal rules in running a home and raising children. One: no child of theirs would engage in immorality, voluntarily harm anyone, or steal anything; two: if a child did that, no one could ever accuse them of condoning it. The success of their role as parents was the good conduct of their children. And not their own personal or career advancement or their children. Your life was a moral testing ground for salvation, so you tried to live a good life. And wrongdoing jeopardized that, because unless forgiven in Confession, St. Peter wrote those failings "on the debit side of his sky-blue ledger." Christian art always pictured him with it and the Keys of the Kingdom. Up there, everything "went by the book." "The door to salvation" had its own lock and key to record good intentions and actions. Seventeenth Century Calvinists were on the same page with us on that.

St. Paul said nothing in life mattered except winning the race to salvation. An unbelievably grandiose vision, it gave profound meaning to what a cynic today might call their humdrum, commonplace lives. A controversial, but famous Jesuit geologist and theologian, Pierre Teilhard de Chardin, was convinced the whole universe had purpose and strove to be one with Christ, the alpha and omega of all things: first and last. But wrongdoers, said a writer, now experience only shame when caught, not guilt like in the old days. And they speak about "a lack of judgment," and not "rancor (sin) in their immortal soul," as the Bard says in a play. But speaking about prominent, high-salaried individuals also committing crimes, Father Eugene Hemrick of Catholic News Service asked, "When does 'wanting' and 'having' get out of hand?" Is it the Bible's *Radix malorum est cupiditas* about money (and anything that glitters) being "the root of evil?"

Writers have said those who ignore history are condemned to repeat it, since it doesn't teach us anything, but only reminds us of the same mistake. We kids didn't know that. So, it didn't cure us completely from climbing more trees for non-edible chestnuts and apples. We helicoptered those chestnuts at the end of rope bands dad brought from the mill. Those hard-shelled enticements were between Elm Street's Chateau Gaulin and relative *Docteur* Auray Fontaine's Wood Avenue home. Another time we again broke a limb on the way to Harris Pond through the yard of the now Soucy Insurance Agency on Rathbun. Like Lady Macbeth washing away the king's murder with a little drop of water, we laved our misdeed with a swim. But we now made sure after our encounter with the Woonsocket PD that our Cro-Magnon acts weren't around St. Ann's trinitarian redoubts of church, convent, and school. Yes, we feared a guilty verdict from officer Turcotte, but more that our folks might be told. We innocents didn't fear juvenile courts, judges, and detention centers, as a wayward teen might today. Detention in Cranston (Sockanossett Boys Training School) was as distant to us as Devil's Island. Nobody we knew had ever gone there. For us, the buck stopped with our parents. Besides Confession, they were the last judgment this side of heaven. There was little or no appeal, and ignorance of the law didn't cut it. Luckily, Turcotte's sentence was just a warning our folks would be told the next time. A policeman at our door would've been like Louis XVI and Marie Antoinette being fetched to be taken by tumbrel to the guillotine!

Another boyish challenge was an iron picket fence near the church. You tested your "mettle" by trying to bend one of those mini spires. But only Blackie could, a kid from around Cumberland Street. With a bodybuilder's frame and powerful muscles and hands, he strained to "bend it like Beckham." We gaped with amazement, much like the 98-pound weakling in those Charles Atlas ads on the back cover of our comic books, "*Popular Mechanics*," and "*Boy's Life*."

He popped up again in my life when I taught novices in Harrisville in the 1950s, spying him at a distance with that build. Shovel in hand, he was digging the foundation for the Order's eventual Provincial and Retirement Home. My brother Ben, future co-owner of RITE Contractors and later Dean College factotum, was also on the project, cutting his carpenter's teeth on framing tasks. Seeing Blackie brought back fond memories of those golden rule days, those comings and goings from school on foot. They were packed with so much more excitement than today's soporific rides (a one-hour ride each way, my sister Rachel once lamented about her son David). The fence still stands today, not misshapen, but still evocative of those days when the opening bell drew 1,000 children! Was it the densest spot in the second densest state in America? All going to St. Ann's to keep faith and language together and get *d'instruction* before the mills and homemaking beckoned. Apart from a Murphy kid, a polio victim, I swear we were all Francos. Forty-nine thousand and nine hundred and ninety-nine more and they would have said of us, "Fifty thousand Frenchmen can't be wrong," once a popular saying.

Our "student march" to school was like a peaceful rumble on the periphery of Social *Coin*, shades of our fathers' trek to the mills. No worry at all about vehicular traffic then! Streets were mostly for binding sidewalks from side to side, pitch and catch, and a macadam-evening ballgame under a dim light. The auto culture only came after Ike.

We said some "holy fear" played a role in our being good, but also a certain Gallic pride was an extra incentive for us scouts. I mentioned earlier that Judge Jalbert rarely saw a Franco kid in juvenile court. Since we were a majority of the city's kids, was he idle like the Maytag repairman? We felt good about it and stiffened our goal to maintain *une bonne conduit* (good behavior). Of course, mom knew about him. With women now marching in protest "to take back the night," I don't recall any kid in the 'hood or school whose behavior warranted police action regarding sexual matters. No doubt the 6th and 9th Commandments (purity of mind and body) received more emphasis than others. (Humor: a schoolmate told me a nun caught him after school in a broom closet with a girl, so he was "swept out of office" from volunteering to do the halls, as some of us did. Where was he, I wondered?) Respect for the opposite sex was an inviolable commandment, so we were taught the dignity enveloping the mystery and sacredness of sex, if not the knowledge. Teachers, we said, even shunned any discussion of the nature of their violation: the Bible's "Let evil not even be mentioned among you?" So, our Catholic education was holistic or all-encompassing, since all the major players of our world were "teachers" in or out of the classroom. As Bishop Peter A. Rosazza, Auxiliary Bishop, Hartord, CT, wrote, "By equipping our young people with a sound education, rooted in the gospel message, the person of Jesus Christ, and the cherished Catholic traditions and liturgical practices of our faith, we ensure that they have the foundation to live morally and uprightly in our complex modern world." If basically Christian, isn't any school also concerned with character formation and civic duties as the best safeguards against juvenile delinquency? A kind of Christian Humanism.

If any of our churches had been built with four lofty spires, like Saint George School in South County or Gasson's at my Boston College Alma Mater, it could have been symbolic of those four vital units in our Catholic upbringing. Our instruction touched our whole being. Thus, it was the real meaning of education for us Catholics, which in Latin means to lead out of darkness and ignorance (*ex ducere*) into the knowledge of God's and society's laws, and not just academic instruction, however important and enriching.

We said how blessed were those missionary teachers who followed our folks to America! No less meritorious are those who still heed the call to foreign lands to evangelize and convert. As Jesuit St. Francis Xavier, Apostle of India, said, "He who saves a soul, saves his." How fitting the city's Museum of Work & Culture has recorded for posterity the names and years of service of all the Orders and members who worked in the city: the Franciscan Missionaries of Mary, Religious of Jesus and Mary, Sisters of Assumption of the Blessed Virgin, Sisters of Divine Providence, Sisters of Mercy, Sisters of Presentation of Mary (Manchester), Sisters of Presentation of Mary (Methuen), Sisters of Presentation of Blessed Virgin Mary, the Sisters of Sainte Anne, the Sisters of Saint Joseph, the Franciscan Bernadines, and the Brothers of the Sacred Heart, with whom I taught and counseled for 25 years, eight at Mount.

If our mothers taught us how to walk and talk, devoted religious teachers taught us how to fly and orient our lives towards our ultimate destiny, as lay people also do now in greater numbers in Catholic schools. In addition to teaching, I read no one ever ran hospitals, nursing homes, and orphanages as well as nuns once did and still do. And as postwar children of immigrants thirsted for higher education for their children, many communities, besides grammar schools, also founded great centers of academic learning at the college level, negating the prejudice at one time that "Catholic scholarship" was not on par with secular institutions.

Mount Saint Charles Academy, Woonsocket, RI

9 - HILLTOPPER BLUES

Scaling Bernon Heights

IN THE 1981 BOOKLET *The French in Rhode Island: A History* (a publication of the *Rhode Island Ethnic Heritage Pamphlet Series*) the authors touch upon Mt. St. Charles' embattled beginnings and mission. "In 1924, the Woonsocket preparatory school was opened, offering still another institution apt to instill pride in French Rhode Islanders. Although Mount was from its formation caught-up in the swirl of controversy over its designation as a diocesan high school, and therefore abhorrent to the '*Sentinellistes*,' it must be emphasized the school has been clearly identified as a Franco-American academy, ably directed and staffed by the Brothers of the Sacred Heart. But eventually other ethnic groups were almost on par with the Franco element at MSC, the result of its boarding element at one time and its continued reach into some 40 RI and Southeastern MA communities, especially now as a strictly grade 6 through 12 coed college prep commuter school of all ethnicities and faiths.

MSC has been an important player in the education of French Canadians in the greater Woonsocket area as is the current Regional Catholic School System and as the former Saint Clare HS once was. We related the first presence of the Brothers in New England was at St. Augustine Parish, Manchester, 1889, with four staffers, including a Brother Alphonse from

Mobile. The Order stayed for 47 years. Dining in a restaurant there I spoke to two ladies who knew about the founding.

Among the boarders at Mount were Canadian students. *Frère* Adélard, the *Père d'Hockey* (Father of Hockey) discovered they were *des bon patineurs* (good skaters) on the frozen lakes of Québec, where the Order ran many schools. Other boarders were from numerous New England towns and cities, some African Americans from Washington D.C. and even a few from South America. For us, a diverse student body like that was an education. In mom-speak, it was going to school "*avec du monde pas comme nous autres*" or "*le restant du monde*," that is, we were interacting with people not like us, ethnically speaking. From 2012, even foreign students from China and South Korea began to attend and board with area families. (One article said more Chinese, with their billion plus population are now learning English than Americans.)

But with all their inbred Franco conviviality and close-knit camaraderie, was it simply an instinctive, initial immigrant thing to associate and speak mostly with your own kind? Besides, who else knew your language and ways? In Roman history, for example, if you weren't a citizen (*Civis Romanus*), they considered you a barbarian (*barbarus*), an outsider if you will, but not with the odium and put-down the word now means. I love the name Barbara, but always think of that when I hear it. But as Shakespeare said, "A rose by any other name would smell as sweet." But doesn't an incestuous kind of bellicose Islamic racism still prevail today, especially in the Middle East? Not absolving the West, didn't racial purity and language inspire Hitler's megalomaniac fantasies? And just a century or more ago, wasn't Europe enmeshed in extreme nationalism, a primary cause of WWI, causing empires to fall and 10 million to die? But about the Middle East, will it take a WWII-like bloodbath to bring peace rather than terror to thousands? It took Europe almost 2000 years to coin "Europeanize." When will the Middle East come together as some form of Middle East Union or whatever? But their history and penchant for violence doesn't inspire confidence or predict cohesiveness. The West is West, and the East is East, and never the twain shall meet? Even the Roman Empire split because of innate differences.

Crucial in securing Mount's foundation was the New England appeal by the Woonsocket-based *l'Union St. Jean-Baptiste*, a fraternal benefit insurance society (once solely owned) which again showed its generosity with a monetary gift of $50,000 in 1974, the school's golden anniversary. Its centenary in 2024 is now eagerly awaited.

Initiated in 1923, recall the Sentinellist Movement was an attempt by French-Canadian purists to resist diocesan control over schools like the Academy, destined to be under episcopal rather than parochial oversight.

Many of these reactionaries, called ultra-nationalists by some, were obviously "dyed-in-the-wool" believers and propagators of *la Survivance* in their efforts to preserve their faith, culture, and language, especially in Little Rhody's Woonsocket. For different reasons, both sides in the tussle were convinced the "rapid assimilation of immigrants would take place," with English the language of the classroom. The face-off was between English-speaking diocesan officials and parochial Francos. People in Québec, I've read, were more accustomed to greater local control of Catholic institutions, like churches, hospitals, and schools, as I also read about France over 200 years ago. Immigrants were not comfortable with losing that oversight, even if parish clergy already ran the day-to-day operations. Their souls, identities, and ways of life were largely tied to their schools and churches.

So, purists felt this diocesan control was suspect because the episcopal administration was assimilationist. Did some, therefore, see some anti-Gallic sentiment in taking away local school control? However much the renegade nationalistic survivalist movement was just a distant memory by 1972, how many old-timers warmed to the name and person of Reverend Louis Gelineau from Vermont to lead the diocese as bishop as he did for 25 years? (I treasure an 8 x 10 photo of his first visit to the Academy. Dad once commented to me on the ethnicity of our bishops, but only to re-enforce his conviction others moved ahead of us because of more education. Only mom spoke about the Sentinellist movement.)

Farsightedly, Bishop William Hickey was convinced the burgeoning Catholic population required schools beyond the size and scope of parish schools, however much it was a thrust against the armor-clad vanguards of the people's culture and language. But apart from its necessity, the disappearance of parochial schools presaged a great drop in church loyalty, faith, and practices. Mom always spoke about the brouhaha in that hushed tone adults use with children around. With St. Ann's the epicenter or fault line, Catholics arose in rebellion against the bishop. Their goal was to keep their institutions purely French by continuing parish control run solely by French-speaking priests and teachers. This was America, but they still thought of "*Québec, le pays de mes amours*" (Québec, the land of my loves), mom's nostalgic phrase. Because they had kept their faith and French, the shock of immigration in some ways had been far less than others. But now the gloves were off.

They had come here for economic reasons (jobs), and not because of famine, disease, persecutions, economic hopelessness, and religious intolerance like Anglos, Irish, and others. In affection and memory, they were umbilically tethered to "*les petits villages òu nous sommes nées*" (the small villages where we were born), mom added. Is it why they consciously resisted assimilation for a record-setting one hundred years? Like the Amish and Germans in Pennsylvania, as I read, did they try imperceptibly to establish "a nation within a nation?"

So, in the latter-day shoes of a Jacques Cartier *et* Samuel *de* Champlain, were they looking to found another Québec, another Montreal? Historians, who credit Champlain for first seeing Cape Cod and New York, wrote that only the vagaries of chance prevented France from being their colonizers ahead of the British and Dutch. All proportions kept, was it somewhat like the intent and blueprint of Sir Thomas More's book *Utopia* to establish "a place of ideal perfection" in America like Anglos once had in rural, pre-industrial England? And Francis Bacon's wish too? A Frenchman, Charles Fourier, tried to do that in the Bay State and in New Jersey. People would only do jobs suited to them, besides living life in common like the early church. Was it social engineering? It failed.

Here since 1904, 12 years before mom and more a thinker and a predictor, dad thought we had to learn English better, go to school longer like other ethnics, and assume leadership in politics and church. That sounded like a ringing endorsement of Bishop Hickey's plan for diocesan control of Catholic high schools. But unlike mom, I think he had no Tellier family left in Canada, so there were no letters from there and no wistfulness about his birthplace, not even about *le grand air* (the open air) whose lack in the mill caused his bronchiectasis lung disease. He wanted us to be American in language and education. Even if a lot of mills were Francophonish, was it still easier to amalgamate as a worker by mixing and mingling daily in American life more fully, unlike our housebound, full-time moms? Was nothing more "Canadian" here than *une bonne femme de famille dans sa cuisine* (a good housewife in her kitchen)?

I said I wrote my master's thesis - *Artistry and Character in Willa Cather* - because I marveled at her portrayal of the travails and courage of immigrants in the Southwest, Minnesota, and Québec in her books: *O Pioneers!, My Àntonia, Death Comes for the Archbishop,* and *Shadows on the Rock.* By association, I felt Cather also spoke for all French Canadians who came here with the same heroism, endurance, character, and fidelity to Old World values. Initially those pioneers still spoke in their native tongues and worshiped like their ancestors, but their children slowly grew out of that patrimony. About pioneers in America, the non-Catholic novelist wrote, "Where there is great love, there are always miracles." And I believe eventual change and integration were two of those miracles. Even if catastrophic, WWII also brought greater assimilation. But recall in my education at Boston College and Spring Hill College in Mobile, professors had doubts about us Francos. Were they intrigued by our die-hard, irresistible immigrant hold?

Because Mount was one focus in the foray of school change, in this chapter we reiterate and enlarge on some of our previous notes. The Sentinellists were chagrined ("*boulversés*," said mom) when the bishop started a parish-based drive in the diocese to found these schools. This was akin to dismantling their way of life, lock, stock, and barrel. Because it dealt with religion, language, and the education of their children, has any other immigrant group, save perhaps the Irish, ever faced greater pressure to assimilate with the prevailing culture? As seen in a photo, protesters by the thousands rallied. Nowadays, only a pope draws crowds like that.

The opening salvo occurred soon after Bishop Hickey announced his million-dollar drive in 1923. Immediately, Elphège Daignault, a city lawyer and head of a protesting group, rose to the challenge and sent a letter to the Sacred Congregation of the Council in Rome to protest the drive's financial burden and its implied threat to parishes' school autonomy. Believing in the persuasive power of the printed word, in 1924 he began publishing *La Sentinelle* (The Watchdog or The Sentry) to air the group's grievances about loss of governance in Hickey's "takeover." He also hired canon lawyers in Québec and an Italian lawyer who knew his way around the Roman Curia. He steamed when the opportunistic bishop authorized parishes to dip into their own funds pro tempore (I want the money now!) if their quota wasn't met. Many parishes in the city had schools, and two objecting pastors were removed. In a related case, as touched upon in *The Diocese of Providence, A Short History*, during the time of Bishop Matthew Harkins (1887-1921), "the judge upheld the bishop's right to use parish funds for the good of the whole church and the local parish." Isn't precedence and/or possession nine-tenths of the law?

Daignault also sought relief in civil court. Gotcha, he thought! But again, to no avail, as Hickey also won in Superior Court. Deciding things had gone far enough, Hickey ordered the penalty of excommunication (*ex cathedra*) for the major instigator and 55 other recalcitrants. He placed the French publication on the now-gone *Index*, a centuries-old compilation of publications banned for Catholics. Jocularly, it's today's "Banned in Boston," recalling its Puritan heritage.

When at Spring Hill College in Mobile in the early 1950s, it was a standing joke that "every good Jesuit" had at least one banned book in the *Index*! Their Order had locked horns with the Vatican after Ignatius of Loyola in Spain founded them around 1540. His conversion occurred as he recuperated from war wounds, becoming a soldier for Christ. Interestingly, because the Brothers of the Sacred Heart modeled their religious habit on theirs - "Imitation, the sincerest form of flattery?" - and adopted some of their "Rule of Life" counsels, I heard in the South we were at times called "the little Jesuits." But not "the little Jebbies," as collegians called them on that flower-festooned campus in the Azalea Capital of the World.

These Jesuits always gave the annual, obligatory one-week summer retreat in our province, usually in hot, uninsulated MSC. Kids playing baseball outside on Brother Michael's hallowed field was a torture for us as we did the Spiritual Exercises of Ignatius, which we knew too well. One year a Canadian retreat master used a pet expression ("et puis, et bien," i.e., "thus and so" or "well and then') so often that math teacher Brother Gregory Bouley, later Director of Welfare in the city, counted some 157 reiterations. In Mobile, we swam with their trainees destined for ten years of training as future college teachers, authors, and scientists, like seismologists in Weston, MA. Was I told rightly the Brothers came to America in 1847 on the same boat they did? Pope Francis in 2013 was the first Jesuit ever to occupy Peter's Chair. In the city and on loan from Boston College, Father Gerald Finnegan was pastor of St. Charles until 2015-16. Since I graduated from two Jesuit colleges, one Boston College, I've enjoyed talking to him. We spoke about one of the founder's mottoes: *Agere Contra* (Going Against the Grain), one of our favorites. The Jesuits are known for their active apostolate. They think our highest faculty is the will; for the Dominicans it's intelligence.

Brother Ignatius, our formation director in the South, said a bishop invited us to run an orphanage in Mobile, but it didn't exist. He showed us the little second-story space where they made-do. Did those four French Brothers lament they initially had nowhere to rest their head, cursing the bishop in vitriolic French about *manque de vérité*: stretching the truth? I saw on a small monument in Mobile that Canadians or Frenchmen were involved in its founding and history. So unlike tenements here, how I loved those antebellum (fashionable before the Civil War) colonnaded homes, azalea bushes, magnolia trees, and Spanish moss. A newcomer was tricked into thinking they would remove it from trees.

In a final note on the Sentinellist crisis, I spoke to someone whose grandfather was the very last one of the 51 to return to the fold. Mom was glad Daignault and others came back to the church: "*Ils sont revenues à l'église*," like those dramatic deathbed conversions she told me about. Though sympathetic for trying to preserve her way of life, they went too far: "*Yon t'été trop loin*." Like the Irish, the clergy was the nobility of their life, calling from the faithful obedience and respect, but not generally, as a wit said, just "to pay, pray, and donate." Like the Jews in the Old Testament, they spoke for God: "*Ils parlent pour le bon Dieu*," she said. They had gone beyond the faith of the coalman: *la foi du charbonnier*," - the workingman's unquestioning belief in what the bishop or priests said. "My deaconess mom" always held the company line! Everyone has these crazy fantasies.

Mine was to be there at her private judgment in the New Jerusalem. God surely welcomed her. A Confessor (preacher) with apron strings! Unlike Henry VIII (before his breakup with the church, named "The Defender of the Faith" by the pope for his treatise on the Seven Sacraments), she never had a title here, but she remained true to the faith of old and an apologist against those who didn't. On a final note, a speaker at the Museum of Work & Culture opined the bishop should've been more conciliatory, less forceful in dealing with the Sentinellists as in "You catch more flies with a teaspoonful of honey than a barrel of vinegar."

How did the world get so complicated since that time? Is it as Pope Benedict XVI championed, supported by Rev. David Lewis Stokes, Jr.[45] who wrote, "Benedict has argued that Christian faith and human reason, far from being at odds, share a mutual responsibility of trying to articulate the rationality that undergirds the order of things." He added "too much noise and not enough silence and simplicity." Did Francos then with their simple, unpretentious life understand that more than we now do in our hectic, troubled times and diminished faith? How ironic for earlier Francos their crisis was not losing the faith, but hanging on to it *"comme autrefois,"* the way it was. Faith or faithlessness and "thin partitions do their bounds divide," as a poet said about genius and folly.

So, the Academy was built (Bishop Hickey's picture still hangs in the reception room), a high school apart from any parish or diocesan support, as eventually the Brothers assumed total ownership of the school. We said after its inception it quickly became a veritable League of Nations, at least in its boarding element. I did have a commuting Irish kid from the city in one class. The only kid in school with a car, he was always late for class, causing Brother Hermas to wax sarcastic: "The closer you live and the more transportation you have, the more you're tardy."

Surely as others had done before us, my friends and I faced for the first time the cold steel of that language and cultural melting process feared by *les Sentinellistes*. Very parochial and somewhat pusillanimous or timid (said of many Francos at that time), we were going to scale the altitudinous Bernon Heights. Even mom, who thought our street *à pic* (steep), huffed and puffed when we walked up there to register. How many other parents walked as far or as steeply (from *la Grosse* Gaulin off Cass and Cumberland Streets) to register a son? Our American acculturation stood like Mount Everest, and like it, that lofty, rocky hill was the loftiest peak in our quest for a Catholic secondary education. In one respect, it too added to the city's reputation of Mills, Stills, and Hills. Remember that my dad had figured in all three labels,

---

[45] Anglican convert and professor of theology and humanities at Providence College.

even if practically a non-imbiber. Nothing is ever easy for immigrants and their first-generation offspring. It was indeed rarefied air with no Sherpa guides (aka counselors) to lead us! We hoped this unalloyed mainstream of American life coursing through its teacher and student ranks wouldn't bruise our sensitive skins too cruelly on the shoals of derision and mockery. Leaving our parish school, we were coming out "*de notre nid*," she said, about leaving the nest of our ethnic cocoons. "Be Prepared," our Scout motto also advised.

Our immigrant parents had faced a lot of firsts; now it was our turn. Did she rejoice that there'd be no bobbin boy's job for me at the mill for $26 a week? But the tuition was, I said, $75 a year from my War Bond savings earned climbing the city's cliff-dwelling tenements to deliver papers. With my two pneumonias as a tyke, she feared the mills for me. She knew dad had no choice. Our lives depended on that little brown envelope paycheck. I cite negatives of millwork here and there, even if it was the family's only lifeline.

Friends and I could have stayed another year at St. Ann's, but wanted to attend all four years in one high school and break out of the linguistic deficiency dooming so many Francos. Of course, we were learning some English (grammar especially) at St. Ann's, especially in *Soeur* Donat's class, but like *My Fair Lady's* Professor Higgins, dad chafed at our mélange of French and English: Franglais. Always he lauded Jews especially, Irish, Italians, Poles, et al for sprinting out of the academic blocks faster. Jews had done it for thousands of years, said city editor Ed Berman of *The Call*. Dad knew his English deficiency, lack of education, and family poverty cost him a medical career. He was, I said, a Homo sapiens' sapiens: a man who knew he knew. I was intrigued the first time I saw it written that way. He was not blissfully ignorant! He never said, "I know nothing me" and was more a victim of education deprivation, like others.

He could never understand anyone turning down an opportunity for education. But did he fantasize himself dispensing health care and nutrition guidelines to his patients? With his millwork, it was always "Sixteen tons and what do you get? Another day older, and deeper in debt," as balladeer Tennessee Ernie Ford lamented. About reading - practically his only muse - unknowingly he reflected Lincoln's words, already quoted, "His best friend was someone who gave him a book he hadn't read." Unlike mom who was on a book-and-magazine swap with *mémère* and aunts Laurence and Marie-Ange, he had none. About his limited command of English, once he had learned enough to chide two of his grand kids, "What for you do that?" They chuckled. He was thinking French while trying to speak English! We'd all been there. It was the first and only time I ever heard him speak English. As second-generation Francos, the grandkids no longer understood French well, except for a few words mom taught them while playing cards, giving them lunch, or when babysitting when they lived in Bellingham. This while Sue and Guil Bouffard ran their upholstery and curtain business in a converted garage on their Freeman Street property. Sue had encouraged them to take the second floor above them. With their thriving business, they found resources to encourage their kids - Patricia, Julie, Denis, Claude, and Christine - to further their education as far as they wished, as did my other siblings for their kids. The war ended the tragedy of no high school or college education for many of the children and grandchildren of its warriors.

Speaking of education and ambition to advance "*dans les affaires du monde*" (in world affairs) mom often eulogized the late *Gouverneur* Aram Pothier, a notable exemplar among our people. She always commented on his "*génie et talent*" (genius and talent) when visiting *tante* Laurence and "conducting" one of those Sunday afternoon cemetery tours from 520 Rathbun. Didn't I say *les* Telliers (Alphonse *et* Léopoldine,), *les* Trottiers (Henri *et* Laurence), *et les* Fontaines (François *et* Blanche) bought their tri-family plot in the shadow of his monument as a kind of "we're-with-him" move? With *mémère* Emérance *et tante* Marie-Ange Fontaine, it's also where my wife Patricia awaits the resurrection, as will Guil and Sue Bouffard and son Guilbert. For added clerical support, the plot's also in the shadow of *le curé* (the priest) Ronaldo Gadoury's family mausoleum! *Oncle* François *et* tante Blanche, however, were eventually buried in their son Roger Fontaine's and wife Janice's plot in St. Paul Cemetery, Blackstone, MA.

Pothier did so much to create the city's great factory ascendancy for so long. As cited in a guest editorial in *The Call* by the late industrialist Jacques Staelen, he realized his vision of making Woonsocket the Queen of the Blackstone Valley. Now a monument to honor his achievements stands before the Museum of Work and Culture. Claire Quintal authored his biography in a book of 2,000 outstanding ethnic Americans. Mom must be unbelievably proud committee members - chairman Al and Jackie Auclair, Ray Bacon, Terry Riley, Roger Petit, Staelen, Phyllis Thomas, Al Klyberg, Dr. Gerald Lamoureux, Aram P. Jarret and daughter Alicia Curran, and I - spoke about raising funds for the memorial and offered suggestions for a fitting inscription to the industrial giant. I wrote a grant (unsuccessful) to obtain funds, but the project got done. Was it the last great endeavor for Auclair - businessman, officer, legislator, WWII combatant, family man - for the city, state, and nation he so greatly loved and served?

For many boarders at MSC, we were now the "people not like them," as mom said often. But after Mount, remembering how the progeny of "the first Americans" from the Mayflower" once resented our speaking French in their midst, as a lover of language I welcomed the multilingual harmonies of Portuguese, Cape Verdeans, Hispanics, Southeastern Asians and others in the city and elsewhere. In the late 20th Century, they all became, like the earlier French Canadians trying to make it here, intrepid and committed to embrace the country's language and ways. With some Spanish in college and aided by a lot in print and television, I have a leg up. Since French, Italian, Portuguese Spanish, and Romanian (so-called Romance languages) are "children of Latin," one can recognize altered words from the language of the Caesars. "Romance" meant it was once the language of heroic tales, as later mocked by Cervantes' Don Quixote who jousted at windmills and rescued "fallen damsels," who, a wit said, didn't want to be rescued.

So, at Mount we heard a common refrain, "You're French, aren't you?" But credit to those who didn't mind a little self-deprecation when belittled for their speech. When I returned to the city after a twenty-two-year hiatus, I no longer heard it, since English was now largely "the official language." The King's English finally prevailed in Canuck centers in the state. We cited war, media, and education as critical factors and the historical phenomenon of "the conquerors" becoming "the conquered," like in the poem, "Those who came to scoff, stayed to pray," like the marauding Norsemen who settled in northern England and parts of Normandy, France. So besides Native American genes, do Francos also have recessive Norwegian and Scottish genes? Didn't someone say every child is the product of a thousand years of generation? Also, about gradually being acclimated to an all-American ambiance, was it like the business maxim: "When you're in the store, you're 50 percent sold"?

My generation and the next saw our once French-Canadian dominated culture in the city evolve into a more American one. Transformation is a painful experience, but how exhilarating and fulfilling it was "to Americanize fully." Again, our only lament is we've lost or seen diminished some truly magnificent cultural treasures of our way of life: the faith for some, our quaint but useful patois, regular church attendance, stable marriages, large, loving families, and joie de vivre. Like Chartier, many *patriotes* ("defenders," if you will) in cities like Nashua, Lowell, Manchester, Worcester (the French Institute at Assumption College), Lewiston, and others fought hard to prevent that, but English was of course America's destiny. Not an easy victory, considering all the languages that fought for supremacy.

Besides English, we were drawn to the Academy for other reasons. Faculty members *Frére* Adélard, the Father of RI Interscholastic Hockey and winner of ten State and three national crowns, and Brother Michael, resident student supervisor and baseball field builder, had, for us, star power. Like mom, everyone used an ethnic label (but not in a derogatory way) about the hockey legend and his thrift as treasurer. Also, two now deceased classmates and boyhood and scouting buddies, Paul Ducharme (later a renowned architect and cartoonist in the war and MSC Hall of Fame inductee in 2013), and Vincent Auclair, later Oblate Haitian missionary for 25 years, were magnets. Until they signed up, I wavered between Mount and a mill paycheck. But as Frost wrote, "Oh, the difference to me." Sadly, how many didn't have the option mom gave me to make it possible? At age 16, helping your family was a priority for many kids of mill working fathers. But I chuckled I didn't know the caution: "A self-made man is someone who has no one else to blame but himself if he fails!" Mom always kept repeating, "*L'instruction cée (c'est) beau*" (Education is good). But her competitive slip showing a bit, mom exhorted me to do as well in school like my Peloquin cousins down the street. She left no stone unturned to motivate us. Imitation the sincerest form of flattery, she was saying nice things about cousins who were more like brothers and sisters to us. I knew I had to be on the fast track to keep up with Roger *et* Doris in my class, the latter jumping a grade at St. Ann's by studying under the covers at night with a flashlight! With thirteen children between them, mom and *tante* Marie Louise enjoyed chit-chatting a lot.

The Peloquin Family
Front: Armand – father, *Sœur* Doris, P.M., Marie-Louise (Tellier) – mother
Back (l to r): Constance, Raymond, Gerald, Normand, Eugene, Roger, Rita

Perhaps not as loud or outlandish as *The Honeymooners*, a classic TV sit-com needs to be written about those fabulous *femmes de maison* (housewives) of yesteryear. "How sweet it is" or was! They elevated raising children to an art form. How did they do it with so many children and so few resources? Is it partly, as I read, that children once cost little to raise, since Catholic grammar school education was a dollar a month, clothes were handed down, and mills hired youngsters? So, parents made money raising kids, as farming did in Canada. But even if so, it never lessened their love of children themselves and the joy of family life, one of the strongest features in their culture and best gift to the nation.

God works in mysterious ways His wonders to perform, like helping me get a job that strengthened my resolve to continue my education. That summer at the mill in Manville I mentioned earlier, I found myself working alongside three dropouts, an unwed pregnant girl (rare in the late 1940s) and boys passing around risqué pictures. It showed me my life had been blissfully sheltered. Religion-bred and thinking *Soeur Sainte* Émilie was still catechism-thumping at St. Ann's, the prospect of not getting to heaven if I stayed there came to mind. In the fall, I went back to Mount and my destiny with the Brotherhood. Every day I saw Mount from our Gaulin third story window, raising my sight above the LaFayette and French Worsted mills to see my future. *Ad Astra*, looking up to the stars, as said in the Order.

Mom spoke about the Academy's once superb field and grandstands, almost destroyed by the 1938 Hurricane and the double play combo of Wear and Tear. They claimed even major league greats barnstormed there (since poorly paid) against the area's best in the late 1920s. She even told me stories about a few priests and religious with Babe Ruthian baseball prowess who gave up team flannels or woolens for clerical garb. Imagine, her news antenna even penetrated the city's sports scene! Housekeeping for her was not a closed, out-of-touch existence from the hustle and bustle of city life.

It was a mild clerical task, but school registration was tense. Upon arriving, mom and I were shown the office of *le Frère* Simon, whom I was to know later, even inheriting his spring jacket when he died. A man of extreme punctiliousness in his manner and speech, he quickly told me his office etiquette. Leaning forward to sign the application on his "mahogany foxhole" (guidance boss John Atwood at Norton HS loved that expression for bureaucrats), I placed my left hand *à la* Palmer Method above the paper and on his Windex-clean glass. "Young man," said he, with chiseled speech like actor Clifton Webb in movies *Cheaper by the Dozen* and *Mr. Belvidere*, "You're dirtying the glass of my desk, and no one does that." Turning to my avenging angel, I whispered in patois, "Ma, I told you I should have gone to the mills. This isn't going to work out." When people got huffy, she usually said, "*Qu'il mange une peanut*," as in "Let him eat crow!" but his religious garb kept her tight-lipped.

For her, authority was sacrosanct, and parents rarely gave bad example. And they taught us obedience and respect for authority was the stuff of the Fourth Commandment. Besides, MSC had a special cachet for her, because, as I said, the Academy's architect was Oliver Fontaine, son of Walter who with his wife was swept out to sea in their beach home in the 1938 Hurricane. He had also designed St. Ann's Church. We weren't related, she added, but his family name like hers made father and son more than just players in her Franco universe. She puffed I was going to a high school designed by "*un* Fontaine." When she first brought me to St. Ann's Church, she pridefully pointed to Walter's name on a metal plaque at the entrance.

With no Parents Nights, mom or dad never saw the inside of the Academy again. Education was the job of the Brothers. I later joined the Order in the spring of 1947 as a junior, proving *Frère* Simon's initial rebuff had no effect on me. But was it Divine Providence my not getting him for Latin! Friends bemoaned his workload and "test-iness" (no pun intended) in trying to make them perfect classical students. I commiserated but didn't say I could've told them so. Who you got for teachers was the job of the Prefect of Studies, *le Frère* Honorius, not who you were, unless *deus ex machina*, like divine favor or improbable chance intervening.

Frère Simon, I later learned, brought that same meticulousness to his hobby of making or restoring furniture. Nowadays with advanced degrees, the Brothers are full-time academicians with advanced professorial skills. But at that time, with less emphasis on teacher erudition and college diplomas, and with most of their schools elementary, the majority taught very young students (except Mount with grades 7-12), while others were caretakers, minders, and jack-of-all trades. One Brother in Canada was even an embalmer, causing me to wonder if he was known as "the last friend to let you down," as undertaker character "Digby O'Dell" often said in an old William Bendix TV show?[46] His farewell was "I'm shoveling off." Brother Simon was perhaps the last of a vanishing species: a master craftsman for whom an eighteenth of an inch was like a mile. They did what my brother Ben, the contractor/carpenter in our family, calls "finish work." Unbelievably meticulous, he started a casual conversation and took you back some 15 or 20 years, with a total recall of names, places, and events. All were linked in his mind somehow to any conversational opener, even the day's weather, my opener once. He even coached hockey, a game of inches. Even if learned, he exemplified the great Franco oral culture and the prodigious memory of many. In our world Order, I heard some Brothers also had great

---

[46] A very popular character in the radio, TV, & movie versions of *The Life of Riley*. Digby "Digger" O'Dell was known as "the friendly undertaker." The series ran from 1944 – 1951. – *ed.*

retentive minds in other provinces. Was religious life with its intense studying fertile soil for great retention feats? A Brother in France memorized 1,800 lines! Hearing that, I thought of the centipede when "asked" which leg it moved first ... if that Brother was asked to recall one particular line? My novice class in the early 1950s at Harrisville dug up these historical tidbits for History of the Order week, well received by all the trainees. Growing up, I so liked "Believe It or Not" by Ripley in the *Providence Journal*. But many would-be world beaters today are into frivolous things.

Teachers like Brothers Simon, Odilon, Ulric, Eugène, Hermas, Felician among others and non-Gallic students like Boylan, Cassidy, Brauer, Offenheiser, O'Connor, Finnegan, Seminare, Kennedy, Czerwinski, Cononnese et al were transforming agents in our efforts to Americanize more fully. I wanted to prove the air on the Mount wasn't too rarified, what with its motto of Excelsior: Webster's "higher." Later when in the Order, Brother Morel and I shared an expression when we failed to grasp something we should have: *Lenti ad intelligendum*, which Christ leveled at "slow-on-the-take disciples," even after being told. The Sea of Galilee was their book, not the Temple scrolls. But largely a maritime culture, one writer said fishermen were probably high on the economic scale. A boat Peter used sat ten people, sign of a good business! Jesus' earthly father, Joseph, was a woodworker, so Christ's detractors mocked He was only *filius fabri*: son of a carpenter. One writer wondered if Joseph had other trades since trees are not abundant in Israel! Did Joseph teach Jesus to make, say, a table, He who made the world!

Mom wanted us to be bolder to succeed. But if you wanted too much too soon, she said, "*Les yeux plus gros que la panse*": your eyes are bigger than your stomach! But later in college I learned aiming for the stars was not a bad thing. To quote Browning, "A man's reach should exceed his grasp, or what's a heaven for?" (English Literature really acquaints you with the beauty and grandeur of the language.) If you did a good thing, mom said, "*Ta (tu as) faite une bonne chose*." Perhaps like a kid going off to a faraway college nowadays, going to high school then was for some a quantum leap in a mill culture. We said survival was always the bottom line, not education. Imagine hearing your folks talk about having enough to live and them not knowing you're picking that up. With seven people in the living room, conversations were always "public." I chose to listen; I didn't have to. For ten years, it was a game of chess on how to beat the Depression. Careful husbandry was crucial, since theirs was not the wit's line: "Live within your means, even if you have to borrow to do so!" One cause and effect of the 2008 recession, did we surmise? Credit card debt was $8,000, but even higher now! Are we too acquisitive to live in a credit-card culture, with the divide between rich and poor now seismic, as *Providence Journal* statistics recently showed? (Over 60 percent of the federal government's $19 trillion budget (and climbing) now goes to social welfare programs!)

Rene Tellier was inducted into four honor societies at Norton HS in 2000
From left: Dolores Robbins, English; Veronica Gagnon, art; Bob Maher, language; John Atwood, guidance and Sped Director.

    Joblessness was often the curse of dad's life. He'd be amused that nothing's changed, even if we're richer and better educated today. Not to demean our Native American brothers, but do we have "too many chiefs and not enough Indians?" I often told my seniors not to disdain so-called blue-collar jobs - plumbing, electricity, automotive, construction, computer tech - so much more remunerative than today's clerical jobs, with too much sitting and thus some obesity. But nearly all jobs now require some college training too since skills and practice are now acquired in the classroom. Recall at one time even medicine and law were learned on site, like Lincoln and Coolidge did. I took a few jibes for it, but my goal was for every senior, if not military-bound, to consider one - or - two, or four-year school programs after high school. When my Norton HS white paper for more math, languages, science, and better attendance, increased our college acceptances, other schools wanted to copy our policy to corral senior let-down, like allowing only one failure to graduate no matter one's prior record. I wanted them to go to college upbeat. I did have a bright, two-sport student lose his acceptance to a top college because of his drop off in the second half of the year. But because he had become angry and laissez-faire after his father died, I was able to get him reinstated. Respecting his privacy, I told seniors every year their June report card had to be as good as the one in the previous fall. At a funeral of one of the Brothers in Harrisville which he attended, I told him his story helped so many others. About the military, I encouraged those interested, especially for the education bonus. One MSC counselee did two whole years of college in his four years in the Air Force and got money for the remaining two when out. I got a letter of commendation from the military for my work in that regard. But some students left notes on my desk against the military, a result of post-Vietnam blues! Some colleges even ousted the ROTC. But proudly, Woonsocket HS has a crack high school unit which performs annually on Veterans Day at the Museum of Work & Culture. Most colleges have brought it back.

The Melting Pot Boils

IF, LIKE MY SISTER Sue, I had gone to Woonsocket HS in the 1940s instead of the Academy, I'd have found the total English-speaking milieu to hasten my complete Americanization. But oddly enough, one of Sue's complaints was you were required to cultivate a kind of Parisian accent in French class. A challenge and change from the nuns' proper Canadian accent and certainly the city's patois. As mom often said, "*Cée du monde qui parle pa(s) comme nous autres*," that is, the difference between how the literati or enlightened speak and us. It seemed nobody spoke like us. I suggest no blatant racism, just realism. Insularity protected you "from the slings and arrows of outrageous fortune," aka, "the bad world," but also barred you from the academic and financial richness of the world at large. As said elsewhere, if lack of education wasn't the bane of our culture, it would've been one of the greatest ever, given its great human and familial values, morality, and Christian faith. All great cultures have largely had a substratum of values, often religion-based, like Egypt, Greece, and even Israel under conquest. Any doubt countries now basically pagan with unbelievable violence seem to be in a self-destructing downward spiral? Empires like ancient Rome fell from within. But despite the annual pressure from priests not to attend public school and avoid the "Protestant Y," (YMCA) MSC wasn't the only option for us boys. Friends like André Carpentier, Maurice Bouley and his brother, later ordained, and others went to Enfield, CT, where the LaSalette Fathers (famed for their Marian Shrine and Christmas lights in Attleboro) trolled for vocations. I said no because they translated Latin into French, not English, which dad insisted we needed. Another option was Canada's Berthierville school. And still others like Ben's friend, Robert Laplume, clothier Phil Auger, René and future attorney Paul Fontaine, sons of *Docteur* Auray Fontaine, and dentist sons of French-Canadian pioneer Docteur Picard - Jean *et* George - all went to Assumption Prep, Worcester, where French was more de rigueur. The tornado in the early 1950s that killed one priest there first passed by our school in Sharon. Brother Savio, Camp Sacred Heart director in the summer, saved our main chapel window with a huge wooden crucifix-like block. What a sight when he lifted it into place in the sanctuary window!

But my first French-Canadian bilingual model, Scoutmaster Walter Jannell, once had doubts about the Academy. He told me he almost left for LaSalle Academy because in the 1930s there just wasn't enough good English spoken by students and teachers. At least not for someone destined, like him, to work for his father's New England-wide truck body business. I considered his opinion because he was always goading us to speak good English. I once spoke at LaSalle about MSC's new curriculum and teacher counseling. It eventually went coed too. Their hockey rivalry with Mount is one of the fiercest in RI sports! Like the Brothers of the Sacred Heart, the Christian Brothers were founded to teach orphaned children during and after the French Revolution in the 1790-1821 years. Just trades at first, then academics.

Mr. Jannell spoke fluently with no trace of Canuck. He monitored our schoolwork, so I told him the King's English was completely in at MSC. So, he sent his son Walter Jr., who later ran the business on Cumberland Hill Road (now sold) after his mom and dad died in an airplane crash on Mt. Fujiyama, Japan, in 1965. Later, Junior's death also saddened us. Twice on vacation with him, I mentioned what mom said about his dad: "*C'tun bon homme. Il aime la jeunesse*" (He's a good man. He loves youth).

At Mount, we acquired new words, like "procrastination," used by Brother Hermas, the dictionary buff (a page a day), everyday idioms, and some fluency and correct pronunciations. We even had some initial success with the dreaded "th" and the aspirated "h." But still hardly a week passed without someone asking, "You're French, aren't you?" No wonder Francos held on "to their identity" for a century! Didn't I say Brother Hermas likened us to Englishmen who dropped their aitches in their alphabet soup! But like Brother Honorius, he had a perfect accent and a deep, resonant voice like James Earl Jones' Darth Vader.

The school's South American students were sons of wealthy families in shipping or other commerce. A half dozen or more, like us they naturally stayed by themselves at recess. But they had a great ear for English and put us to shame, which some teachers teased us about. Better traveled and surely exposed to other languages more! Some of us from the city had never even left the Social Flatlands unless scout camping at Yawgoog. But sadly, Guillermo Socorro, '56, close to a family in the city, perished at the end of the schoolyear with members of his family. Heading home after graduation, their plane crashed over New York while jettisoning fuel for an emergency landing. The news came to us on retreat at the Academy. Academically, those students were good students. Later, was I told rightly one of them wowed the audience by delivering the valedictorian address in English, French, and Spanish? The latter language was a curricular offering at MSC in the 1940s, perhaps because of them. With us Francos, however, French and religion were gimmies on the academic green, thanks to our nuns in grammar schools.

Un tableau d'honneur (An honor roll board) hung in the main entrance and Prefect Brother Honorius raffled cash awards in the gym to honor roll students. Winning $10, I raced home on my Schwinn bike, but dad deflated me about not having a higher honor grade. A Bill Belichick-like response! Aren't dads especially prone to relive their youth through their sons especially? Moms with their daughters? In the 1970s, a girl came to see me because her dad, whom I knew, was on her case about her algebra grades. Later, I checked his grades in the school records and yes, the weakness was "genetic." I never told her.

Leaving Mount in my junior year to enter the Order, I was honor-bound like other recruits "to seek perfection," a mystery at first. Brother Floribert, Director of the Juniorate, had a good laugh at my expense when I told him after three weeks in the Order I hadn't reached it! With parents like mine, I was too goal-oriented and time-conscious. But he passed along a fascinating saint's thought I never forgot - you didn't need to get all virtues at one time. If you progressed in just one, you did so in all others by moral osmosis, like getting a whole bunch of grapes when trying to get just one. Ditto with faults if you conquered only one. It's probably what St. Paul meant by "cupidity," as in "greed, the root of all evils," as if it's really the only sin. Wanting something you shouldn't. For example, my Shakespeare prof had us notice his characters were basically good people, with just one fatal flaw. Scary, if you think of it! It's why we're shocked about the downfall of good, well-known people; so-called "pillars of society" who are overcome by one flaw that resonates with the above "cupidity."

Unlike the nuns, the Brothers weren't known for the Palmer Method of Writing. With many curriculum objectives, they splashed their thoughts quickly on the blackboard. At home, mom's letters had a kind of sweeping Spencerian flourish, akin to John Hancock's! A touch of grandiosity? Did our *mémère* teach her? Mom loved to write letters (she made a virtue out of necessity!), a source of comfort to us. She wrote with that quick nervous flair and cursive abandon. Novelist Willa Cather said we write what we are. It changes every day. Mom's darting energy, curiosity, and knowledge about her world filled her missives. But sadly, as an editorialist noted, we've lost the immediacy, fullness, and emotional content of letter writing, becoming slaves of staccato electronic pulses in a truncated, one-syllable manner, which has killed cursive. When I think we kids didn't even know block writing! Is this progress and its so-called "unintended consequences?"

I recall a report said kids are losing the practice of eye contact by not communicating personally with their own. Overall, Professor Cottle at Boston College said teenage boys are always the least promising segment of the population. Will it now be true of girls too, with their faster rising crime rate? But in the same breath he said most boys grow up to be model citizens, heads of families, and contributors and innovators in their field. As girls are also doing now in careers, professions, and families. He thought it was often just curiosity, the desire to know and experience, not malice, that oftentimes led young people to mischief. He said parents hoped their youngsters wouldn't commit any unredeemable act of violence or thoughtlessness, jeopardizing their freedom and sometimes their life. Like nowadays in the guise of opiates, speeding and texting at the wheel, and possessing guns. Other negatives about us are drinking while driving, high infant mortality, lower birth weight, more HIV AIDS, climbing opiate deaths, more chronic lung disease, more disability, shorter life spans, and poorer health - all from U.S. Health in International Perspective. (Statistics have their place, even if there's a saying about the three kinds: "Lies, more lies, and statistics. Americans learn little from history, largely hidden because of the profit motive. Are we like Broadway where one manager said, "The show must go on, otherwise we'd have to give refunds at the box office?")

In Professor Cottle's "Adolescent Psych" class, he advised parents not to blame themselves if their children's waywardness occurred despite their doing all the right things. He was particularly sensitive to mothers in the room. As a wit said, Adam and Eve raised "Cain as best as they were "Abel," but surely they regretted desiring the "knowledge of the tree of good and evil." But how come one boy turned out all right, but not the other? For Adam and Eve, was it the first coulda', shoulda', woulda'? Are you curious too about their life after their ouster from the garden, which some think was between the Tigris and Euphrates rivers in Iraq? It's not dogma, but a teacher theorized their initial idyllic existence in Eden left them ill prepared for the pain, suffering, and death they experienced afterwards. So perhaps understanding of those was given them by God later. Fascinating! But they lost that perfect existence and we too. But as related elsewhere, Christ - the new Adam – didn't give us back those gifts of that perfect life in Eden (what are called preternatural gifts), but rather, supernatural grace. I've read several theology books, but never any mention of that theory. Having all those gifts and still do what they did makes it even more difficult to understand why!

I read an opinion that the second-class treatment of women throughout history was an unjust reflection against Eve for first succumbing and then involving Adam in the Garden tragedy! You know, blame the messenger! But is that why the French coined, *"Cherchez la femme"* (Look for the woman), when things went wrong? Or is simply the mistaken notion that "might is right?" But a sainted nun (Emmerich), who recorded visions of heaven and hell, said she saw a depressed Adam, but didn't say where. She felt bad for him and Eve, since they were "preordained," as it were, to be in that situation in the garden, but still with free will like Judas. But aren't we also tried in our time on earth like them? It's why in the Our Father we ask Him "not to lead us into temptation?" A retreat master at St. John's in Slatersville compared asking forgiveness to a guy walking on ice. Even if he and God know he may fall again, he marches on. Recall Peter felt magnanimous when he asked Christ if he should forgive seven times. Then Christ said seventy times seven!

Of course, Franco students at MSC from the rest of New England had a much better command of English than we did. Their towns and cities, like Nashua and Manchester, NH, Lowell, MA, Putnam and Meriden, CT, to name a few, had assimilated faster than, say, Woonsocket, Manville, Central Falls, et al. But other die-hard preservationist strongholds in Maine, where the Brothers once had schools, were Lewiston, Biddeford, and Madawaska, the latter where the Order ran the public school. (And provided cousin Frank a chance to hunt deer. He got lost once but had the wisdom to stay put. A James Michaud from Maine was in my first class in Sharon. His mannerisms and accented speech reminded me so much of us Francos at one time.)

Like sons of the soil, in training in Harrisville we shared 1,400 acres at one time with pigs, cows, chickens, and a few horses. Our morning Mass was twice interrupted because the cows had broken loose on Lapham and Steere Farm roads. The Brothers also grew their own tobacco, and I enjoyed smelling the aromatic leaves piled high in the barn. But as a Tellier whose mother was a Fontaine - two respiratory challenged families - it's as close as I got to the "noxious weed," as Virginia named it after it ruined its soil. As an adult in the Order, I said in my evening walks I sometimes smoked one cigarette. Studies said smokers come from smokers, so we were lucky, since our dad smoked no more than a pack a month. But Sue and I never saw him smoke. Only once was I asked to buy a pack of Lucky Strikes for him.

One day as I showed the folks where I slaughtered diseased chickens, I recall I found an 1805 coin in the dirt. The farm was part of a land grant from one of the Stuart kings of England to the families of Thomas Harris, the Laphams and the Steeres and others around 1630. Besides lands in Rhody, the grant also encompassed parts of Connecticut and Massachusetts. The Brothers in 1933 initially bought over 500 acres from a Mr. Birch who had purchased it from General Hunter Carson, a man of great education with a great library. The Order bought more acreage, including a cottage for the chaplain's residence and control of the entire Suckers Pond where we swam and boated. It was later named Brothers Pond and now the Crystal Lake Golf Course and dining/function facility. I groan that we unknowingly tore up precious first edition English works in our ancient house to repair worn-out religious books. Until Route 102 was extended, few knew the Brothers had the only private pond in the state. In training when no challenge was beyond our aquatic prowess, we swam the whole length once. We also boated in the pond's recesses in homemade *chaloupes* (rowboats). Historical is the family cemetery overlooking the lake, with tombstones going back hundreds of years, with infant mortality sadly high. The property, with only 100 acres, is the Motherhouse and retirement home for the Brothers. I love to visit the Brothers' cemetery and reminisce about my life with so many of the departed, recalling interaction in our careers. When my class helped build it, the woman next door took us to court for "unsavory cemetery spillage," draining on to her property. The decision? Any spillage was from her property onto our lot! "Don't throw the first stone unless …" It happened to me in North Smithfield. A neighbor thought my fence was on his property. But his was on mine, which I told him I didn't mind one bit. Later friendly, he even gave me a new pitchfork when he saw I broke mine in the garden. They loved watching me.

Young Brothers in training in Harrisville, RI, 1951.
Seated (l to r) are staffers Bros. Marcellus, George-Aime, Allyre, Theodore.
Second row: Bros. Dupuis, Pelletier, Tellier, Phaneuf, St. Armand, & Sicotte.
Third row: Bros. Martin, Leduc, Boucher, Roy, Fontaine, Proulx, & St. Germain.

Once heavily recruited, those Canadian *patineurs* (skaters) at Mount spoke excellent Canadian French. But they didn't mingle much with us. I did, however, enjoy the company of Montrealite skater Gerry Jean Tremblay in my religion class. Tremblay was so forlorn he couldn't play in the school league, a move to curtail the Academy's domination in hockey. The Academy "retaliated" by playing a private school schedule, but the draw was poor and the travel long. That's when the drumbeat for the school's own arena grew louder, culminating in construction of a military surplus hangar in the early 1960s. It restored the Academy's state and national reputation for excellence in the sport. And generated 20 NHL players under the tutelage of my classmate Coach Bill Belisle '48, greatly assisted by his son Coach Dave. Before the ban, one year the Mounties had a Canadian triune of Roy, Cabana, *et* Gagnon, who terrorized the league with their speed, scoring, and hard shot. But after hockey season was over, some of these Maurice Richard look-alikes *"qui avaient traverser les lignes"* (who had crossed the border) as mom said, re-crossed the border since Québec outdoor ice lasted until April.

African American students like football player Ed Bradley of "60 Minutes" fame and hoop Hall of Fame great Lionel Jenkins came from Washington D.C., New York, or the South. They were a new school experience for us. Were there any blacks at all in the parish or public schools of the 1930 and '40s in the city? Obits in *The Call* chronicle their migration from around 1951, many were from a community in South Carolina.

When at Mount, my first disease scare occurred when dad revealed FDR's "hidden affliction": polio. After his death, memorialists had a quandary: should they show him with or without his wheelchair? His impressive Washington memorial amidst cascading waters renders both postures. Also shown is his wife Eleanor, first U.S. ambassador to the U.N., whom mom said was smart, but not attractive, as if it was a requirement. She was also a gifted writer and speaker. But when FDR was President, the feeling was people couldn't bridge the gap between physical disability and leadership. Today it's about shortcomings: can leadership and moral slippage coexist? One is inclined to say yes, judging from what we now know about the private lives of many "challenged" presidents. FBI director J. Edgar Hoover with his Gestapo-like spying always knew their secrets and it helped with his budget requests. At Thomas Jefferson's Monticello home, which I visited twice, the widower had six children with Sally Hemings, a beautiful black servant-girl whom he took to France. Critics called it "concubinage." DNA in modern times proved it, but none of the offspring are buried in the family cemetery behind the home he built. One said when he dined with his gifted friends, it was the greatest assemblage of talent ever. Except when he dined alone! I liked his invention to copy his letters while he wrote them, his day clock, and a mastodon fossil found west of Virginia. While on their trek to the Pacific, Lewis and Clark also sent back live animal specimens.

THE WAY WE WERE

According to former music director Brother Henri Peter Lussier (HP) who, despite a heart condition, volunteered and later died a missionary in Africa, one of the brightest kids ever to attend Mount up to the 1970s was a black student. He was a brilliant student, accomplished musician (learned in two days to triple-tongue an instrument to replace an ill performer), football player, poet, and perfect SAT scorer. He taught himself physics in three weeks and got a perfect Achievement score to get into a blue-blood college. Brother Lussier was also proud he helped one of his finest musicians ever (Nedo Pandolfi, '46, deceased in 2009) start a music program with MSC-used instruments at Ponaganset HS of the Foster-Glocester school system. I reminisced with Pandolfi when my wife Pat was at RI Hospital for the first of her two brain surgeries. I wrote the story for *The Call* as an example of the mutual support between private and public educators and schools. Some town fathers had nixed having a band at the high school. He told Brother, "If I could put on just one concert." It was a smash! Surely, he's a future MSC Music HOF member.

About Lionel Jenkins, after I left for the Brotherhood, this tall, African American super athlete brought basketball fame to the Academy and later helped Providence College's rise to national hoop prominence under Coach Joe Mullaney. Jenkins, '54, who stayed in RI after graduation, and other ethnic kids nearly all had the one physical attribute we Franco kids lacked and envied: height. Attending a PC hockey game in 2002 with friend, former Mount teacher, and hockey moderator, Marcel Tardif, I heard a fan seated in front of us talking about his Washington D.C. mother sending him to a private Catholic boarding school in the city. Could it be? I tapped him on the shoulder, and, yes, it was Jenkins; talkative, friendly, and now retired after personnel work. He was proud of his military service, Civil Rights work, and volunteerism. I told him he was a legend in MSC hoop history who once dropped 42 points against the Villa Novans. He said he had his hoop skills before he came and was proud to be involved in fundraising for the school. He was inducted to the first MSC Athletic HOF in 2012 and passed on in 2015. Later inducted into the RI Heritage Hall of Fame.

Other MSC HOF inductees were Dr. Jean Guay' 48, hockey team physician for over twenty years and father of five hockey players; Brother Adelard, founder of RI high school hockey at Sacred Heart School, Central Falls in 1912, and Director of Hockey at MSC from 1929 to the mid 1950s with many national and state titles; Tommy Songin '72, baseball, hockey, Boston College HOF; Joe Couture '76, hockey, baseball, and especially soccer with all-N.E. Honors, all-time scorer, and HOF at St. Anselm's College; Gus Galipeau, '40, hockey on state and national champions, MSC coach, professional hockey and baseball player, and backup to the Dodgers' Roy Campanella in Nashua; Gilles Baillargeon '51, baseball, football, and hockey All-Stater in his senior year; Gerene Boisvert Mabray '86, 12 varsity letters in cross country, basketball, softball and Providence Journal Honor Roll Award; Marc Dubois '86, tennis, perfect season on the '84 team, RI College HOF and highest .933 college winning record; Brian Lawton '83, All-Stater in hockey and first American-born high school player chosen number #1 in the NHL entry draft, 494 NHL games, and sports analyst for Rogers Sportsnet; Meghan McCooey '06, tennis, All State all four years, two times national champion in doubles at Tufts U.; Mathieu Schneider '87, hockey and Stanley Cup winner with the Canadiens in 1993, the Olympics in '98 and 2006; 1,289 games in the NHL with ten teams and twice All-Star; Garth Snow '87, hockey, Olympics, '94, Vancouver Canucks goalie, NHL Executive of the year 2006-2007, former general manager of the NY Islanders; Alan Tenreiro '92, soccer player and three times Coach of the Year, RI College HOF, national principal of the year in 2015 at Cumberland HS, and president of MSC; Wayne Wagner '06 track and MVP in baseball, all-time hits leader at Westfield State; the 1939 Hockey Team with RI, New England, and national titles; the 2002 undefeated Varsity Girls' Tennis Team led by Coach Dick Lawrence, six on the All-State First Team: McCooey, Andrea Lee, Nicole Breting, Lisa Cerrone, Emily Bowen, & Kaitlin Kelly, with Sarah Ballou & Christina Pimental on the Second Team; William Coffee, first lay coach and winner of state titles in three sports: football, basketball, and baseball.

 On May 6, 2014, MSC inducted its second class into the HOF: Coach Bill Belisle '48, multiple hockey state championships and national titles and over 1,000 wins; Keith Carney '88, NHL player for 1,000 games, twice All American at UMaine, Stanley Cup playoffs, 101 wins at Mount, and baseball player; Angela (Martinelli) Burke '96, outstanding cross country runner, 1,000-point scorer in basketball, softball player, Quinnipiac U.; Michele Leigh (Merten) Diodati '91, 1,738 hoop points and 1,000 rebounds, a .400-plus hitter in softball, and twice NCAA All-American at Babson College; Al Thurier, unmatched 50-goal scorer in hockey and 16-year pro career in the AHL and NHL; Richard Rondeau '39, only MSC player in the U.S. hockey HOF, led Mount to local, state, and national titles, Dartmouth NCAA record for most hockey goals (12) and assists (11) in one game; Marcel Peloquin '41, MSC and Assumption College baseball, batted .400+ three times, coach and long-time Woonsocket vice principal and athletic director; Lise-Anne (Wante) Lepine '82, premier cross-country runner, won all her meets in her junior and senior years, Northeast 8 Conference honors from 1983-1985 and assistant cross country and track coach at Bryant U; John Harwood '70, Mount's only Providence Journal Honor Roll male student, outstanding baseball and hockey athlete and leading hitter, high scorer, and All-Ivy hockey player at UPenn; Brenna Leveille '03, three-sports star, first ever girls hoop state championship, 1,000 points in basketball, volleyball talent, and MSC Female Athlete of the Year in 2002-3; Tony Garganese '82, outstanding first baseman, and Bryant U player of the year in 1986, N.E. All-Star in 1986-7, NCAA All-American in 1987, and record holder for batting average, hits, runs scored, home runs, triples, & doubles. Single game records for hits-5, doubles-3, and triples-2; Sarah Gervais '00, MSC Female Athlete in 2000, five-sport athlete, All-Class in track, basketball and soccer, Brown U. MVP as soccer goalie, All-Ivy team in 2002 & 2003, and Regional All-American; David Roy '98, all-time basketball leading scorer with 1,947 points and 1,200 rebounds, twice Academic All Stater, a state representative in the European Junior Basketball Tournament, basketball at Vassar; The Spirit of Sport Award went to Father Charles Quinn, league founder and junior high boys' soccer coach from 1982-2011, 9 state titles, 13 division titles, and also junior high boys' tennis coach, school chaplain from 1982-87, a member of the teaching faculty, volunteer chaplain, and liturgical service at the Brothers' Motherhouse in Harrisville.

Mount Saint Charles' 1977-78 Hall of Fame Hockey Team

The 1978 Hockey Team was inducted into the third MSC athletic Hall of Fame. This is the team that produced Coach Belisle's first state title in a record string of 26 consecutive state championships. With 307 goals for the season, this team averaged 8.5 goals per game, making it the greatest scoring team in the long and rich history of Mount hockey. The team compiled a record of 35 wins, 1 loss and no ties. They won the state championship defeating LaSalle by an 8 to 2 score in the first game, suffered their only loss of the season by a 2 to 1 score in the second game but bounced back in the final game with a 7-1 victory. The New England Championship came with three overpowering victories as the Mounties beat Concord in the first game 5 to 1, LaSalle in the second game 8 to 2, and St. Dom's in the final game by a 9 to 0 score. That year, they were selected 2nd in the nation. This team had 3 All-State players, two future professional players and 14 players that would go on to play college hockey. Team members were Marc Sarazin, Joel Guay, Bruce Kraftcheck, Mark Lester, Denis Plante, Marc Beauchamp, Tom Anchukaitis, Ron Deziel, Mike Samborsky, Dan Potter, Him Colucci, Bob Edwards, Mike Hodson, Ed Lee, Ken Fargnoli, Mike Gouin, Paul Guay, Pat Manocchia, Bob Carignan, Dave Guevermont, Mike Picard, Marc St. George, Tim Plante, George Pisaruk, and Barry McColgan. Coaches: Head coach Bill Belisle, assistant coaches Larry Tremblay and Philip Cerrone and moderator Brother Leo Labbe.

In 2005, Providence Journal sportswriter, John Gillooly, published *Pride on the Mount ...More Than A Game* highlighting Mount's 26-year streak of state titles in hockey. Now 44 all told. In 2012, Charlie Mandeville '68, authored the book *Mount Saint Charles Hockey: How It All Started*, featuring players, coaches, Brother moderators, like Marcel Tardif, state and national records, Coach Bill Belisle, and Coach Dave Belisle '77. This was soon followed by *A History of Mount Saint Charles Hockey* by Brian Ethier in 2013.

Returning to genealogy for a moment, interestingly more and more French Canadians, like friend Patrick Martin-Beaulieu, Anne Conway of the Museum, and others have told me they've discovered Indian blood lines in their genealogical search. That also includes over 40 percent of Canadians and many Francos in America. Genetics tells us that human history is fraught with *métissage* - the mixing of two or more races. This mixing was not without hazard, however. I've read all of Lewis and Clark's men had sexual relations with Indian women, many of whom had been infected with venereal disease by earlier European explorers. This necessitated the use of a special remedy brought by the farsighted duo to combat venereal outbreaks. It's speculated that many members of the Corps of Discovery eventually died of VD. I'm envious that they saw most of America when it was still one of the greatest natural wonders of fauna and flora on God's earth. Fortunately, they survived some 15 near misses that could've ended their lives and fabled trek and thus delay the settling of the West.

Proof that French Canadians explored most of America are names like Labiche, Drouillard, Cruzat, Dorion, Faufon, La Liberté, and of course Toussaint Charbonneau (a lousy shot, he hit one member in the buttocks, but kept the corps alive with his superb cooking), and his Indian wife, Sacajawea, who was kidnapped from her tribe years before, incredibly found her chieftain brother and tribe during the expedition. On the trek, she gave birth to a son, Jean Baptiste, later adopted and educated by Clark. My pride in that trek is matched by eight of our Presidents having French blood, including John Tyler. A Roosevelt ancestor's French name "de la Noye" evolved into the Delano of FDR's middle name. Other notables are Etienne Brulé who discovered Lakes Huron and Superior; Jean Nicolet, Lake Michigan;

Joliet and Jesuit Jacques Marguette, the Mississippi; and de Pierre Gaultier de la Verendrye, the Rocky Mountains. Still others too with French ancestry are John Adams, Presidents Garfield, Taft, Coolidge, and of course other Roosevelts. Also, from the world of letters: Longfellow, Whittier, and Freneau. Paul Revere was a Rivoire, and a *Monsieur* Boncoeur "lent" his name to Bunker Hill. Interestingly, all descendants of La Fayette whose funds and leadership helped us win the Revolutionary War are by order of Congress de facto citizens of the United States. Also, refugees from the French Revolution: Talleyrand, Liancourt, Volney, de Noailles, Cazenove, who, with their great wealth, invested in millions of acres in Maine and the Appalachian Mountains, expanding our nation at a time when the federal government had no money to do that.

Brother Adelard, born Alphonse Beaudet, February 5, 1884, St. Jean Deschaillons, P.Q., was just a mite above five feet, like perhaps his first Sacred Heart HS skaters in Central Falls, RI, in 1912. Dad had tall people on his side of the family but speaking of French Canadians in general, mom often said, "*Les Canadiens sont du monde de moyenne taille*": Canadians are short. Irish kids, boarding at Mount and scouts at Yawgoog were taller than us Francos; Italians stockier.

But altogether, except for occasional jibes about our accent, there was no unbearable racial or ethnic tension at the school. As is still true today, one report said the mix in private schools is often greater than in many public schools, especially if segregated by real estate values or forced busing. The latter resulted in "white flight" from Boston, as I saw on school records of kids from Bellingham at MSC in the 1970s, even if the bishop denounced transfers. I read about the struggle in a book given me by my wife Pat's niece. Some mild division existed in the faculty between dayhops and boarders, who of course lived there and went to Mass every morning with the Brothers. As Tardif told me, the one real casualty was some extremely athletic boarders played in persuasive Brother Michael's intramural leagues after school, hockey excepted. Some did baseball too. Otherwise, the Academy might have fielded better grid teams especially. Their most potent foe was Gus Savaria's Villa Novans in football and other sports. Brother Adelard's cry, "We nevair lose" was mostly about hockey.

Hockey, we said, brought together a mix of Canadian blue chippers and at times good homegrown talent and outstanding boarders. Sadly, Gary Coyne, one of the best multi-sport athletes ever to attend Mount, was killed in Korea. He was found with ten dead Chinese around his machine gun emplacement. George Goulet was also a great athlete at the time, along with his brother Roger. Before the arena was built, practice was early in the morn at the old arena in Providence, as well as games too, one with LaSalle attracting 6 or 7 thousand.

Brother Adelard, SC, director of the Notre Dame cafeteria, Fitchburg, MA with staff. From left: Brother Leander, Mrs. W. Fohy, Mrs. W. McNeil, Brother David, and Mrs. H. Hauler.

I never missed a baseball game at Cass Park. The Mounties had good teams with a talent pool of boarders and skilled athletes from Manville, Albion, Woonsocket, Blackstone, Cumberland, and North Smithfield - all areas with a proud sandlot and semi-professional tradition dating back to pro players like Napoléon Lajoie, Gabby Hartnett, Lou Lussier (saw him pitch at St. Ann's), James Connolly (the 1914 Miracle Braves), and the two Lepines. And besides MSC's Gus Galipeau, the Villa Novans' Clem Labine gained fame as a reliever and spot starter with the Brooklyn Dodgers. Labine was part of the team that won the Dodger's first world series and went on to win two more. Deceased in 2007, in 2015, Richard Elliott, who knew him well, wrote *Clem Labine Always A Dodger*. Through the courtesy of his stepdaughter, Attorney Susan Gershkoff, Labine signed three of his cards for my son Jim, adding to his overall collection, besides his complete Nolan Ryan set, minus his rookie card. In the pros, Galipeau roomed with Newcombe in Portland, Maine, the first time a black and white player did so and was the backup catcher to Roy Campanella with the Nashua Dodgers in 1946 and '47. Professor Neil Lanctot, a city native and college teacher, authored a Campanella biography and spoke about Galipeau at the Museum of Work & Culture. A serious car accident ended his career.

Those days were still a time when baseball was truly the national pastime. We said towns, cities, clubs, businesses, industries, ethnicities, all had teams, as seen in Ken Burns' TV documentary. National Park Service ranger Chuck Arning's talk at the Labor Museum on the sport in the Blackstone Valley highlighted that. A patch of open field, bat, ball, pancake-like gloves, and makeshift bases fit the bill, especially if young, cash-poor millhands played the game under an open sky. As America's first non-media stars, the game gave them a chance to show their physical prowess, speed, and agility, and separate them from unathletic, "run-of-the-mill" workers. And for a few, professional careers at some level.

Before the advent of so many other sports, wasn't baseball every kid's first career fancy? Along with a church missal and a bike, a new or used glove was a godsend for us Francos. Recall how my larcenous friend rewarded clueless me when we went downtown on a $25 spending spree? We didn't know that only one player out of 44,000 made it to the majors, like the area's Rocco Baldelli. Out of 500 drafted each year, only four or five will get more than "a cup of coffee in the majors." But, as poet Pope said, "Hope springs eternal in the human breast," like in Mudville where eager Casey at the bat swooshed nothing but air in his bid for sandlot immortality. Writers have waxed poetic when comparing the game to life itself. Until you make an out, you're still alive. No time constraints. Some have called it the best game ever invented for its marvelous complexity, rare occurrences, and mix of individual and team achievements. (Comically, army careerist and cousin Norman Peloquin told me the story of a Brit who at his first game was baffled when one batter walked to first instead of running. When told he got "four balls," he, sympathized in typical British understatement saying: "Yes, that would impede one." He called a bat a piece of willow, and bases, cushions.)

The 'Sting of French' at the Academy

DISCIPLINE AT THE ACADEMY was a mite tougher. We were all boys, older, tougher, and perhaps more prone to academic mayhem. Maybe because the Sentinellist movement failed, the Academy wasn't like a parish parochial high school with largely mill town lower middle-class pedestrian kids like us. There were boarders with varied backgrounds from the entire socio-economic, ethnic, and cultural spectrum of the Northeast, the Washington D.C. Beltway, Québec, and even South America. But again, we went willingly, unlike much later the Irish kids of Boston who objected to being bused out of "Southie," as told in a fascinating book given me by wife Pat's PhD MIT niece, Kathy Misovec. It made the system one of the most segregated in

America. The Irish had built a germane community of churches, schools, and local customs which they wanted to keep.

Kathy Misovec, M.I.T. PhD engineering graduate (2nd from right) visits (l – r) Rene Tellier, Donna and Marcel Tardif and Jim Tellier

Not only students, but the staff also took some getting used to. For example, from my brother Bob, I was aware of massive Student Minder Brother Elisée's reputation. A huge, mountainous man with double the girth of Robin Hood's Friar Tuck, he waddled rather than walked. The size of his monastically round face, tonsured haircut, bulbous features, large hands, and basso profundo voice all enhanced his Paul Buyaneske "enforcer" notoriety. Since, like Brother Michael in the junior section, he wasn't a teacher but looked after the boarders when not in class, I expected to escape his touted "biblical wrath," if I walked the line. "*Écoute les Frères*" (listen to the Brothers), mom said after registration tensions with fastidious Brother Simon.

As we milled around on opening day in 1944, we waited in the senior rec room (boarder territory) for our schedules. Weary from the altitudinous climb to school, I sat sidesaddle near the middle pocket of the pool table. But swoosh, all my 98 pounds was lifted two feet off the floor with my tie chafing against my Adam's apple. When I corkscrewed my head in the direction of the suspending force, I saw Brother Élisée's massive face. Had I met my Maker prematurely? Is this what an avenging God looked like? When he deposited me back to terra firma, he boomed possessively, "Nobody sits on my pool table, especially a day hop - another pejorative term boarders called us, besides "frogs. (How does one get labeled? Even Queen Elizabeth I referred to a French ambassador with the "frog" sobriquet, as

Leoni Frieda relates in *Catherine de Medici: Renaissance Queen of France.*) So, the enforcer didn't allow boarders to sit on "his" pool table. But it verified that MSC, with 200 or more boarders and some 400 commuters, had a dual persona. Great changes would come only later in the early 1970s, when principal Brother Paul Demers and I, guidance counselor, and department heads met to make revisions. Dealing with the end of boarding, in a day-long meeting with the faculty, all expressed their support to go coed, remain strictly college prep, initiate teacher-counseling, expand the commuter population, enrich the curriculum, and re-introduce the junior high, all critical decisions that literally saved the Academy, along with an initial Alumni Association, now the Office of Advancement, which Brothers Bob Croteau and Ray Reinsant, Annette Blair, and former Director Donald Demers developed into the fund-raising source it is today.

But in the 1940s the net result of this dualism was students split the faculty as pro-boarders - *les pensionnaires*, or pro-day students - *les externs*. So-called "minders," like Brothers Elisée and Michael, wore their allegiance on their sleeve, as expected. A demanding job, it kept those monks away from the community, its prayer life, socializing, faculty dining, except holidays and summer. For school recess in winter, one bowling lane and a pool table were pitifully inadequate to keep boarders occupied, apart from the gym. Another reason for building the ice arena in the early 1960s. When I taught at Sacred Heart School in Sharon, the provincial said no to television discouraging minder Brother Savio who was desperately trying to deal with hundreds of young boarders in one rec room during inclement weather.

Eventually the New England Province of the Brothers stopped accepting boarders in two other schools: Sharon and Andover. But since their tuitions were the lifeblood of the New England Province, repercussions occurred. At MSC, boarder tuition had kept day-pupil rates extremely low. Their demise caused day tuition to rise which resulted in a severe drop in enrollment. That's when Brother Demers gave me the green light to reach out to students all over RI, and Southeastern MA, and fund an annual flyer mailed widely to schools and CCD programs. Many Italian kids, for example, started coming from Johnston, North Providence, Providence, and Smithfield, as well as Irish kids from Cumberland, who once went solely to Bishop Feehan in Attleboro. Pat Manocchia, hockey all-stater, later Brown U. player and J.F. Kennedy Jr. roommate, was an outstanding recruit who in many ways helped Italian American kids find their way to Mount with the help of staffer Phil Cerrone. His father Smokey, a car dealership owner, was generous to the arena and school. He, wife Maryann, and I visited scores of colleges and 5th year prep schools to pave the way for student-athletes. She closely monitored the schoolwork of their four Mounties, and Phil, Al,

Stephen, and Michael all graduated later from college. We traveled to Sweden in the early 1970s with the Andover Prep School hockey team. The family's Christmas Eve party in Cumberland included many of the state's political and sports luminaries. Their tennis court helped many granddaughters win state tennis championships at Mount like previously mentioned Hall of Famer Lisa Cerrone '03.

Former MSC staffers at Jan and Tom Reale's home in Chelmsford, MA. From left: Rene Tellier, Director of Guidance; Terry Riley, first volunteer guidance secretary; Brother Paul Demers, principal.

Quickly the school became "cosmopolitan" again, with over 40 communities represented. Initially I was shocked many parents and students outside the city didn't know where Woonsocket or the Academy was. At the time, politically and otherwise, it seemed Northern RI, was in the state but not part of it influence-wise. It's as if route 146 North was a road to nowhere! In the 1970s and later, I wrote many letters to the DOT and state and local officials about upgrading its drivability. North Smithfield Town Administrator Paulette D. Hamilton eventually told me work would begin in the fall of 2012, with state rep Brian Newberry also fighting for it. At one time, did the prevalence of Francos in the area with their mill culture, minimal education, and Canuck speech create some negativity with sneers of "backwater" and "side by each" from detractors in the press and TV? But eventually the city did assume greater clout with political luminaries like former counselee Lt. Governor Roger Begin '71, Mayor Gerry Bouley (I was honored to write his election platform and inaugural speech); state political officials: Brian Newberry, Al Auclair, Marc Cote, Al Brien '57, Lisa Baldelli-Hunt, Paul Kelly, Gerry Martineau '78, Barbara Burlingame, Nancy Benoit, Roger

Badeau, Charles Baldelli, Roger Picard, et al. With a large voting bloc in the city, any politician able to deliver the vote for a gubernatorial or other statewide candidate was wooed. Hillary Clinton even came to the Stadium once for a gubernatorial candidate.

As for the boarders vs. day student conundrum, was it puffery to think day students were better? But no doubt, boarders also had their bright academic and athletic lights. So, the much greater talent pool in the classroom, court, field, and ice was another big adjustment. From smaller parish schools, day students realized if they had once been "top shelf," they were now swimming with sharks in a bigger pond. The school was no longer a French language haven. But as much as Brother Elisée ruled the senior section with an iron hand, boarders knew he loved them, and under that rough facade beat the heart of their father away-from-home. I recall I saw his gentleness firsthand when we were both stationed at the old Sacred Heart Novitiate in Harrisville in the early 1950s. On his side of the old historic house, he directed a small cadre of Brothers who ran the farm, like those English founding families did for centuries. He died there of a diabetic seizure and heart attack and rests in the Brothers' cemetery on the property. The link between MSC and the farm became closer when boarding ended in the early 1970s, and Cor Jesu Terrace, built originally as a training site and motherhouse, briefly became a resident option for students under Brother Leo Labbe's principalship. Later, the sale of most of its 1,400 acres greatly helped the New England Province solidify its financial footing.

Novice Master Brother George Aimé and we trainees built the cemetery for the New England Province in Harrisville, in addition to landscaping the entire property and erecting the impressive grotto to Our Lady and other monuments. (For me, this fostered a love of landscaping, a relief from intense schoolwork.) Clearing trees from the cemetery site one day, *Frère* Germain sped forward too quickly with our first-ever army surplus tractor. This caused a tree he was pulling to land on his head! He shrugged it off. Leathery and tough, we thought he could walk through a wall or glass door without feeling it.

A post-mortem! One day I got ample proof of Brother Elisée's put-on boarder sentiments when I saw two students, resident and day, wrestling on the floor of the recreation room where I had once been "uplifted." He walked over like "a sheriff from Dodge," bellowing, "No fighting! Especially if a boarder is getting the worst of it!" He was their "corner man," and Mount was their home court. In an age when school children mostly came from Father-Knows-Best families, there was a rumor some were disciplinary problems or in the grip of the juvenile detention system. But my records disproved that.

I'd never seen so many Irish and Italian kids at one time, especially from the Boston urban ring and the Nutmeg State. They were kids whose families passed up the local school system for the academic discipline and religious values of private, Catholic boarding education. In Sharon I recall almost every kid's grades went up 10-15 points.

About the minders, many boarders formed great attachments with them, as did other students also with teachers and coaches. As many athletes will tell you, the latter are often the ones they never forget. Why? Because of the time they spent with them, and as Olympic announcer Jim McKay used to say, "through the agony of defeat, and the thrill of victory." Classrooms usually don't touch those emotional highs or lows. Yet about teachers, many also became unforgettable, touching a responsive chord in the lives of students, as *Soeurs* Donat *et Sainte* Émilie did with some of us at St. Ann's. The ones that make you stand up and say, "Where would I be today if not for them?" Later in the Brotherhood, it was Brother George-Aimé in my formative religious career and later in his retirement. He even asked me to write his biography, but I begged off. I proofread some of his writings on the history of the Province and helped write a short resume of his career positions and achievements before his death. As Provincial, he was at the epicenter of the greatest expansion of the New England Province into Canada, England, and Africa. After the war and his captivity by the Germans, he fulfilled his dream of going to the African missions in what were then Basutoland and Rhodesia (now Lesotho and Zimbabwe). He was also the founder of the Province's school in St. Albans, England where he also served and directed.

Women teachers have always been predominant in the history of American elementary and middle school education especially, but for us kids whose grammar school was staffed solely by nuns, an all-male staff at MSC was a first. With their taller and heavier presence, sterner voices, and greater classroom mobility, Brothers and laymen Arthur Pard Jr., Albert P. Lavallee, and coach Lionel Ferland got your attention. Unlike the nuns, the Brothers had long ago given up wearing rosary beads around their waist. More embroiled with older kids, did they shed some religious armor for speedier deployment? Didn't St. Paul write the race belonged to the swift? When there was trouble, you could hear the nuns coming but not the Brothers. It's why I said I got caught trying to skip out early after class at day's end. Ah, the wages of sin: *speculum peccati* - another phrase Brother Morel and I liked.

Once I was rendered mute when a teacher dealt with a listless student by backing him up against the blackboard causing chalk dust to fly out of the edges. The poor kid told me he was in Providence till the wee hours and struggled to stay awake, as the teacher droned on with French articles *le, la, les* (the, that, they). It soon ended, but it was still a time when mild corporal punishment in school was considered an extension of parental authority - *in loco parentis*. In England, it's "Spare the rod, spoil the child."

In fact, when the Order opened its school in England, Brother George-Aimé told me parents expressed concern an American form of discipline, like staying after school, might replace "the headmaster's paddle." Obviously, Brits still wanted children "to respect them as brought them up by hand," a writer said. At Norton HS, I never saw kids do much in detention but sleep, shuffle their feet, and wait for deliverance.

But imagine my "parochial fear" when I questioned a grade I received in tall, stentorian-voiced Brother Hermas' civics class. A test had netted me a mere 76, which would keep me off the honors list and ruin my chance at winning money and having my name in the school foyer (what price vanity!). "So, you think I made a mistake with your paper?" he said incredulously. But before I retracted, he said he'd look into it. The next day he told the whole class I had an 86. My fortitude pleased me more than my honor roll clincher.

Mountie, talented goalie, Catholic priest/pastor, and author, *Père* Normand Démers '50 later told me there was a belief that economic, academic, and linguistic inadequacies at one time bred an inferiority complex and a non-confrontational attitude in Francos. An article confirmed it. No Franco at that time wrote a best seller like "Success Through Intimidation." And not too many local Donald Trumps in boardrooms said, "You're fired." How many of us fought that Morty Meekle or Caspar Milquetoast[47] humble feeling? In Sharon, a cartoon in a Lewiston, ME, paper showed a guy letting pee run down his leg, not to call attention to himself in the lavatory! About timidity, I once met an Edmundite miracle worker priest in Mobile, but I was too shy to speak to him. To spite bigoted Louisiana politician Huey Long's memory, he introduced us to a young black orphan whom he named after Long. The Edmundite Fathers, whom we later had at St. Michael's College, VT, missioned there.

Our jump starts in French and catechism meant more time in English, math, science, history, and Latin or technical drawing for some. With French in the afternoon, you felt good and got paid helping boarders with their French homework during dinner recess. Looking for last-minute help, they didn't say, "Frenchy," but pleaded like a hungry cat in the kitchen at suppertime. It was the first time I ever taught. I wondered how they had money. But I endured a setback in one of my classes. In our sophomore year

---

[47] Both were popular newspaper comic strip characters in the mid 20th century. Morty had a low-level office job and the comic strip featuring Caspar was *The Timid Soul*. – ed.

the Troop 4 scouting gang - Paul Ducharme, Vincent Auclair, Armand Benoit, Normand Vaillant, Bill Belisle, *et moi* (and me) - found itself in the same class. Perhaps a smoker, the teacher spoke inaudibly and frog-voiced, but God bless, he often got off the subject and homework. This especially if anyone questioned him (which we did with pretended seriousness) about planetary bodies and weights and measures. No one knew why he had those disparate interests. When I was in the Order with him, in another case of Franklin's Waste Not, Want Not, he even salvaged bent toothpicks on the grounds at Mount. Some monks wondered if they reappeared at the table! Or was he building his own *Tour d'Eiffel* (Eiffel Tower)?

With exams coming on, I was "volunteered" to ask our almost mute oracle to speak a little louder about what to review. Which I did without sarcasm! Since he had a habit of looking right over his black-rimmed glasses and I sat to his left - I failed to see menacing storm clouds on his thick shaggy brows. Ignoring me, he continued to teach in his usual relative whisper, creeping meanwhile towards the fourth seat of the second aisle where I was sitting, unaware Doomsday was at hand. But this stroll was a calculated, seek-and-destroy Rambo mission! When almost behind me and out of the corner of my watchful eye, he grabbed me by the shoulders and dragged me to the floor, pulling on the threadbare tie I wore every day for two years. The same sartorial adornment *Frère* Elisée almost ruined on my first day at Mount. Every day after school I loosened it and put it on my bedpost. Was there a faculty attraction to it, like the Bard's "Blessed be the 'tie' that binds?"

As I lay prostrate, no biblical verbal thunderbolts rolled from *le maître* (the teacher). Just white anger! I was stunned and twisted like a pretzel around the leg of my seat. Daring a look, I saw him staring speechless at me as he nudged me with his foot. His anger spent, he pointed to the back door with a long, bony finger, like the angel banishing Adam and Eve from Eden. I left disheveled and dusty from wiping the floor, but not hurt. But that tie was ruined. Would mom say, *Quesquia arrivé à ta cravate?"* (What happened to your tie?) A kid's tie cost a quarter, an amount good for three pounds of bananas, dad said. Later in the Order I learned that "self-justification is not from God" (St. Augustin), I thought of protesting the injustice, but didn't. But if the operatic duo of Gilbert and Sullivan were on the scene, would they have encored *The Mikado's* "The punishment should fit the crime?" After I joined the Order, I was amazed at the constant stream of holy cards he sent me. I had not been that close to the man before or after the incident. Did he think he overreacted? Maybe he thought: "Hey, if he answered the call, he can't be a bad kid. Did I beat up a recruit who someday may teach next to me when I can no longer defend myself?" (We teased each other a lot, but we only fought "the devil.")

I didn't spend all my 42 years in the classroom but did lose my temper a couple of times. Which teacher hasn't? In my first year in Sharon, I let slip a curse from my Confederate confrères in Alabama. The fifth grader was stunned like his mates. Our training in New England was more ascetic by far, more Canadian if you will than American! For example, our Southern mentor, Brother Ignatius, told us Northerners that listening to popular songs was not really against the spirit of monasticism or its founders. Of course, lyrics and performers at that time were clean, with no suspicion of crotch-grabbing antics and risqué outfits. Even a beer at a picnic on Mobile Bay was better than soda, he said. It took us a few weeks and a paternal lecture to get over the notion we weren't "going to hell in a handbasket," if less French-Canadian. The war had "Americanized" a lot of French-Canadian soldiers and now the South was doing the same with us New England recruits. I thought of those four French Brothers and their "anglicized baptism" when they arrived in Mobile to run that orphanage that didn't exist in the 1840s. The South was not a healthy place to live then, and some were victims of epidemics that struck about every ten years. One Brother drowned in the Mississippi, weighted down perhaps with gold (legal) in his pockets, as confirmed to me by new provincial Brother Mark Hilton of the U.S. Province. I said my novice class in Harrisville had dug up interesting facts during History of the Order week. Brother Leon Cyr, one of my student Novices, is the historian for the once New England Province that is now one with NY and the South. Brother Paul Demers, future principal at the Academy and ordained, was in the 1955 class, along with now missionary Brother George Poirier and five others who laicized. I asked him to write the Mass if Brother Polycarp, first Provincial of the Order, is canonized.

Our arrival in Mobile portended a hurricane that very night, as if we were Northern carpetbaggers again invading Southern soil after the Civil War. But the sound was more than the fury. Once settled in, on Saturdays during our in-house chores we even listened to opera, even if faithless lovers always seemed to beguile swooning heroines, often beset by consumption. Late afternoon, Brother Ignatius in his best Mister Clean pose came around and passed his finger over furniture and door frames. Compared to our spartan training and nutrition in New England, we appreciated our new residence near Spring Hill College, fabulous meals like our mothers made, daily showers, and no hard, physical work like in Harrisville. I put on some avoirdupois consuming a milkshake between meals and, yes, wine before supper. I also wrote my first piece ever for a newspaper. But our fellow trainees weren't all Southerners. Some were Irish from New York neighborhoods, once a great source of vocations until families moved to wealthier burbs. But of course, some Southern confreres teased us about our accent and our winning the War of Northern Aggression, aka The Lost Cause, as modern rebels once called it.

But back to my setback at MSC, teachers told me they especially liked one feature in teaching boys. That is, they quickly forget and move on. I reflected briefly about justice and fairness, which one psychologist wrote are the two rights young people know first or instinctively. One teacher surmised how often I may have been wrong and gotten away with it. We had sidetracked Brother quite a few times, with the gang exchanging smirking, 'got-him' glances. But long-dormant Mt. Vesuvius was ready to erupt, and I walked into the stormy blast. But he held no grudge, and I did well on the test. But I got no thanks for "taking one for the team." But was I like the ill-fated Julius Caesar who was done in after his self-effacing words (literally) about impending danger? "What touches us ourself shall be last served." Boys and men should beware of volunteerism, as recorded elsewhere.

As a guidance counselor, I often used the incident when counselees came to me about perceived injustices from their teachers. Since a counselor's major role is student advocacy (the so-called "third ear," that is, to listen and empathize), I really tuned in with genuine concern. But instead of telling a student I'd fight his battle and speak to the teacher; I asked the aggrieved to do it himself. Invariably, he or she got another viewpoint of the incident from the teacher's point-of-view and their challenge to maintain order and make quick decisions in class.

Teachers as Bilingual Role Models

I SAID EXCEPT FOR Scoutmaster Jannell, *Soeur* Marie Donat, and Fathers Moreau and Roussel, kids like me at St. Ann's and in scouting had few people in our lives fluent in English and French. Was it because between the wars someone said you could almost live your whole life in the city, especially in Social *Coin*, without hearing any or little English?

But at Mount, we found a cadre of bilingual models among the Brothers who, we said, had previously staffed schools *dans* (in) *la province de Québec*. In New England, their American birth and English fluency were so important when the New England Province finally became whole with Maine. Despite collegiate studies done mostly in French, either in the Order or Canadian colleges, they had retained or developed their fluency in English, providing badly needed role models for Francos like us.

These American-born Brothers came from your typically devout family, an invaluable source of vocations for the secular priesthood and religious orders! In my Order, the word *pépinière* (nursery) described this fecundity. Archivist Brother Cyr showed me statistics that Woonsocket and Lewiston, ME, for example, sent numerous candidates to our community.

Both were Francophonish, along with Central Falls. Later, many vocations to the priesthood and Brotherhood also came from Notre Dame HS in Fitchburg, with its Cleghorn section, many with roots from Nova Scotia.

Few Brothers were mocked by fluent students for that unmistakable French cadence and crude phraseology. In an age when not every recruit in the Order was trained to be a teacher, degrees of fluency in English did exist. French was the official language of the Order since its founding in Lyons, 1821, by *Pére* André Coindre. As the Academy nears its centenary in 2024, evoking in students their memories of past and present teachers. I'd like now to "wake up the echoes" of the voices and actions of staffers in the 1940s when I was a student. Surely any school is the embodiment of all its teachers and of the knowledge, devotion, and wisdom they imparted to thousands of students. Teaching is a precious calling since its fruits are far reaching and everlasting, as Christa McAuliffe, space shuttle Challenger victim, said so eloquently.

Mellifluous, like honey if you will, and bombastic were the image and spate of words projecting from Brother Stephen, (born Joseph Desmarais from Central Falls)[48]. He railed big time against the slothful and slovenly habits of ill-disciplined students. Pity the student who was the object of his tirades. A wave of mild epithets washed over the classroom miscreant. Obviously, he read voraciously, feeding the unfathomable wellsprings of his mock and serious teacher tantrums. But he was a learned, jovial and gentle person. His return to self-composure belied his quick, theatrical temper, which he used sparingly. But no teacher had the genius tag put on him more by students than taciturn, enigmatic, and gifted Brother Eymard, (Philip McManus of Norton Mills, VT). His accent was definitely American. As a math teacher, students said he taught himself complex engineering and mathematical concepts. He reflected Goldsmith's line from "The Deserted Village": "And still they gazed, and still the wonder grew, / That one small head could carry all he knew."

A hard marker, he was never guilty of grade inflation, that is, giving higher grades than deserved, as if, like humorist Garrison Keillor says of Lake Wobegon - "All students are above average." In my Algebra 2 class, one student had less than zero for the term! As I waited for my grade, a frustrated *bonne femme de maison* (good housewife) lamented her "Gaston" had a minus five for the term. She wailed, "*Mautadit, si j'lava garder à maison, yara pas moins qu'zéro*": If I kept him at home, he'd have no worse than zero! Brother knew French, but remained Sphinx-like, immutable, mut-

---

[48] Religious in many Catholic Orders relinquish their birth name and take a new name to signify their new life. – *ed.*

tering perhaps *Je ne sais pas quoi* (I don't know what). In one of the highwater marks of my student math career, I was one of two students who passed with a modest 78. When Brother Eymard later suffered a non-debilitating stroke that left him even more enigmatic, was he still his inscrutable old self beneath it all?

Because reading for pleasure was unheard of at St. Ann's, I said only at the Academy did I develop a love for it in Brother Felician's English class (Lionel Letourneau of Dodgeville, MA). A future master's degree recipient in English and library science, he interspersed the teaching of grammar and spelling with his reading of spellbinding novels. For the first time I began to feel the power, beauty, and majesty of English words. As a teacher, I found the practice of reading practically non-existent in schools. Why? Reading has always been something teachers assign. Students never see teachers or other students read. Credit him for also teaching whole bodies of work like novels and read from them, breaking up the usual, piecemeal anthology method of an author-a-day. Because reading for pleasure or learning is unpracticed in schools, it's understandable students don't see the connection between reading and learning. When years ago, Bryant College President Ronald Machtley added a Humanities dimension to the business programs, he was grateful for my five-page paper on how to make business majors read more and better. I did suggest professors read in class and test somewhat frequently, rather than on the whole book. In his letter to me, he said he told all department heads to implement my ideas.

At St. Ann's *la Soeur Directrice* (Sister Director) was visible in the day-to-day governance of the school and, even if strict, students held her in awe. But because Mount was a junior and senior high school with teaching and governing roles very separated, principal Brother Claver, born Claver Gingras of Marieville, Québec, was not very visible. But "he went by the book," the kids said and judged people and situations with firmness, as I saw later in the Order. But my incident didn't get his attention. And I always respected the man and his office. At the time, the same Brother was both school principal and director of the more than 40-resident Brothers, a 24/7 commitment. A split came in the 1970s, when lay people became administrators, like assistant principal Julien Mitchell, and Herve Richer, '74, first principal and then president when he replaced Brother Robert Croteau who had been named Provincial. Present assistant principal Edwin Burke replaced Richer. I saw the move coming in the 1970s when Catholic colleges started to name lay people to lead their institutions. Even with fewer religious, MSC's Catholic commitment is still "to provide our students with the quality education, spiritual formation, co-curricular, and athletic activities that have made the Mount name synonymous with Excellence," wrote Donald Demers, former Director of Institutional Advancement.

Mount eventually became a Blue-Ribbon School, attesting to its excellence and recognition at the White House. Indeed, if a college preparatory school sends 99.1 percent of its graduates to college, it does what it says it does, besides developing the whole student. But again, regrettably, because the city is in some dire financial straits, the school only draws 8 percent of its kids to a decorated school that compares with other premiere high schools in the nation. When it was a boarding school, perhaps 80 to 90 percent of the commuters, like me, were local. Implementing a kind of parental school choice program by the state, as some states do, would eliminate that gap and boost the city's education stats and reputation. Since tuition at Mount is somewhat less than what some state budgets allow per student, a saving would be realized. I've read that no public-school jobs would be lost. Private schools generally attract brighter pupils, but an educator who researched it, surprised me when he said slightly less talented and motivated students need private schooling even more because of strict attendance, academic discipline, and the college-oriented atmosphere. Attendance is the curse of many public schools, with 24 percent of high school students chronically absent. Elementary school students (12 percent) and middle school students (l5 percent) are somewhat better. Absent students are three times less likely to go to college or stay. As a scholarship judge for a local military post, I know Woonsocket HS has a good college prep track, yet ranks low among the state's public schools. Is this due to high absence and dropout rates?

Again, about principal Brother Claver, I found him warm and personable when he spoke to me as a student and as a confrère. But in a seven-day retreat at the Academy in the summer, he called me in because I was answering communal prayers too loud and a nanosecond before other monks. I got the volume and timing down, but another greyhound saw an opening and took the lead.

His administration had long passed when I arrived as Director of Guidance in 1970, but one final crack-in-the-cloister tidbit. At the time, forbidden by our rules were your own radio, pocketknife, and camera. But alerted by "an ingratiating monk," Brother Claver slipped into an "offending staffer's" bedroom to remove a portable radio. When the "aggrieved" discovered it was missing, like a second-story burglar he slipped into the principal's office and got it back. A canonical Vatican standoff!

His administration was enhanced by Prefect of Studies, Brother Honorius - born Joseph Courcy in Uxbridge, MA, an intellectual giant who read and wrote prolifically. Since at times we all received our grades, especially if failing, one by one in the huge school gym before the entire student body, he presided like the Inquisition's Torquemada at those convocations. (There were no privacy rules then and report cards came later.) In an age when a student was thought to succeed by his own volition and efforts (the only learning disability was laziness), he praised achievers but riveted failing students through the hardwood gym floor. Deep voiced, he spoke perfect English, using well-turned phrases in a completely American accent. For us kids, his fluency made you forget substance for style. But I felt bad for failing students he singled out.

Even if I liked my English classes, I experienced an emotional kind of grief, one rooted in my French-Canadianism, as I was falsely named the culprit in a plagiarism case. After all, wasn't I the kid who at 12 told his scoutmaster in a Tenderfoot test the country's mother tongue was French? When I lent a book report to a procrastinating friend (so he could "get an idea what Brother Eugene wants"), he copied it word for word. I had told him to bring his in with mine, with nary a thought of plagiarism. (I only learned about "plagiarism" or copying when I was in college. A wit said, "If we college kids copied an author, it was plagiarism; if an author did, well, that was research.") I was accused of copying his paper and informed that he was getting a passing grade and I, an F. Mine was poet Shelley's lament: "I fall on the thorns of life, I bleed." Incidentally, copying in school, a recent TV report said, has become pervasive with today's obsession with success and technology an aid. In balmy Mobile at Spring Hill College, we saw a kid during a test throw a paper out of a first-story window. Later, the paper flew back in. When we Brothers reported the cheating, the Jesuits were angry hearing it from us. And academically, other collegians "resented" us since we shattered the usual grading scale with our superior grades. One year they thought too many of us were in the same easy philosophy class, so we were transferred to another, with three big papers to write. A year later when at Sacred Heart School in Sharon, a student called to ask if I still had one of them! No, but I gave him some ideas. Was I known to his fraternity? I've admitted that for Brother Frank and me, both English majors, writing and testing were easier than most. I always tried to give a little more on each question, some from outside reading. (Humor: In one class I gave eight replies to a lengthy question, but still wondered if enough. The proctor said I needed 12. So, I came up with four more! Teachers, I discovered, taught their notes, but I always read the textbook, besides taking good notes. When at Boston College for my Counseling Psych degree, a couple of girls offered me dinner for a copy of my notes.)

In my college placement work in three high schools, I stressed seniors should write a meaningful essay, the only subjective part of the admissions process. When some kids had no clue, but I knew them well, I rattled off what I would say, but laughed one time when a senior told me to slow down, so he could take it down! I stopped. Often, they didn't realize their own meaningful life experiences, like Nicole Maher at Norton HS who taught special needs kids in a Marion, MA summer camp and found them smart and grateful. A great topic I told her. She got into Bowdoin and is now a PhD in environmental and ecological sciences and has been quoted in the New York Times. And at a time when it wasn't always done, I got the idea from her more challenging courses to advise colleges according to their academic weight: Advanced Placement, College Prep, Standard, Basic, Special Ed. Because I always enjoyed working with known families and siblings, I also counseled her brother Stephen and sisters Lauren and Courtney. Robbie, who graduated from Xaverian in MA, became a talented boatman, a tradition in the family, which later moved near Buzzard's Bay. Their dad Bob, a former Christian Brother who taught at De La Salle in Newport, headed the language department and coached tennis, with son Stephen a star player. Like other mothers, his wife Jean, later a nurse at Salve Regina, appreciated the work we counselors did to recommend their kids. I found mothers more involved than fathers in their children's schoolwork and college applications.

But back to my plagiarism debacle, I admit the copier had a better command of English. But was I going "to suffer for justice's sake?" I complained, but at first Brother was unbending, since I was "dumb enough" to give someone my paper. I thought his decision too quick, but he let me tell my side of the story and he raised that lowly grade. Later when he too like Brother Felician got a master's degree in English, he became a role model for me in the Order. Some fifty years later at his wake, I spoke about his fairness, not mentioning what mom had told me: "That's what you get for taking 'a foreign language." As a Brother religious, I learned the meaning of "*suffering* for justice's sake," that is, enduring pain even when doing good, even if it doesn't appear so. I suspect it happens to many in their lifetime. A poet comes close to describing the dilemma: "Great wits are sure to madness near allied / And thin partitions do their bounds divide." Like truth and falsehood at times.

But a good thing from that fallout! Later teaching English at Notre Dame HS, I caught three seniors whose book report was only the movie version of *To Kill a Mockingbird* by Harper Lee who disguised her femininity for a better reception. I was merciful because they 'fessed up. About movies, because Jewish theater manager Ben Gold was a friend of the Brothers, I too had seen it. In the 1960s, he told me any movie the Brothers saw was the best two-thumbs-up rating he could give the public. Now an R rating is sought by movie producers, however!

Another time I went to see *The Robe* about Christ's crucifixion. But it was still a time when generally you couldn't go to the theater. But God, I saw *confrères* (colleagues) in there who had asked permission from the Superior "to take a long hike" on a school holiday. But saints preserve us, a radio reporter put a mike in my face as I exited. It went all over the city because of the big promo buildup. Facing Principal Brother Frederick at the residence, I proffered a "fait accompli": Was it all right if we did what we did? With so many rules then in the Order (someone counted over 800 before Church Renewal), it was your only defense if caught with your hand in the cookie jar.

Also on the staff were Brothers Sebastian Ferland *et* Robert Brassard, science and technical drawing teachers, respectively. Their influence in my career, however, wasn't at the Academy, but at Notre Dame HS. I was in Brother Robert's technical drawing class for all of ten minutes in the late 1940s, quickly switching to the classical course and Latin because drawing tools were $18 and the folks and I didn't have it. That was only 75 cents short of the school quarter's tuition. Yearbooks have always been award-winning creations in Brothers' schools, and as yearbook advisers they were both legends.

Brother Sebastian with his photographic skills and Brother Robert with his eye for layout design energized my writing crew (I was literary editor and theme creator) to produce annual editions unique among schools in the country. Our winning formula featured a yearbook theme, which ran through the whole school experience each year, drawing constant parallels through script and photos. For example, the school received local and national acclaim with themes like "The Classical Ideal of Greece and Rome," "The Medieval Crusader," "Around the School Year in 180 Days" (from the movie of Jules Verne's book *Around the World in 80 Days*), "The Sound of Music," "A Man for All Seasons" (The story of St. Thomas More). The Jules Verne topic helped popularize a trend at the time of photos and bios at the end of the book after 180 days of schooling. But I became more wizened when I went to see the movie on my summer vacation when asked to be in the wedding party of Patrick Martin-Beaulieu (a cousin of sister-in-law Gloria Landry Tellier) and Ali Plante. Ali is the daughter of Joseph Plante who I lauded earlier as an investor, humanitarian, and voice for justice for ill-treated employees during his mill career.

But if my movie going was again "caught" in Fitchburg, it would've required a creative imagination to convince the Superior of its "religious significance." Ah, a poet said, "Oh, what a tangled web we weave, when first we practice to deceive." Phil Gorman, Providence College English grad and energetic assistant principal at Norton HS, often cited the line in dealing with kids. English majors love to throw lines hither and yon. One guy in college told me I always cited others but "What do YOU say?" Didn't the bible say, "There's nothing new under the sun," so we repeat what others have said? And hopefully, as Pope wrote, "What oft was thought, but ne'er so well expressed." Other expressions I've enjoyed are "Let's Roll," as 9/11 passengers prevented their plane from possibly smashing into the White

House in 2001. And in WWII a pilot on patrol uttered the memorable line: "Sighted sub; sank same." "Apt alliteration's artful aid," critics say about that figure of speech. With all of today's dull, truncated electronic chattering or faddism, will any "memorable line" or invention survive?

About "heavenly discourse," marriage is of course a Sacrament. We all know Christ went to weddings (Cana, scene of His first miracle), but not funerals, as He told the young man who wanted to delay His call to bury his father. We did just the opposite in the Order then, at least in training. But when Notre Dame HS staffer Brother Louis Jules Berard was asked to deliver a wedding address, he asked me to write it. It was well-received and I found it 40 years later in my files. Like my mom, I keep everything. But speaking of marriage, a woman "with too many kids" heard a young priest preach about the blessed state and sighed, "I wish I knew as little about it as he does."

But ah! the perils of writing, as I learned at *The Call*. When at Mount in the 1970s, I wrote a dedicatory piece ahead of time since I was going to a fund-raising convention in Chicago for Catholic schools. (This led to the founding of the initial MSC Alumni Association when I returned.) It's also where I saw later-disgraced Vice President Spiro Agnew and rioting outside. My piece appeared in *The Call*, but the event was not held, because Brother Adelard, the intended honoree, was indisposed! Even before reading Walter Cronkite's book - *A Reporter's Life* - I knew snafus occurred often, as Ed Berman, former *Call* editor, told me when I was publicist for the Academy.

Sadly, Brother Sebastian (Ferland), Notre Dame HS principal and former Mount staffer, became the first Alzheimer's victim I knew. Besides award-winning yearbooks, in his career as a physics teacher and administrator at Notre Dame he was expert at involving parents and others in the service of the school, mining them for ideas about management, finances, improvements, and fund raising. Since the days of "*la p'tite école* (the little school) were long gone, he wanted his school to look professional, modern, and innovative. He was related to the Ferland construction family which built housing in Woonsocket. His brother Lionel taught and coached at Mount along with Arthur J. Pard, Jr., and Albert P. Lavallee. This at a time when secular teachers were rare in Catholic schools mostly staffed by religious.

About finances, as athletic director at Notre Dame I once reported I was robbed in our residence "by a second story thief" of hundreds of dollars from the sale of sports jackets. Brother Sebastian said, "That explains why money is missing from my desk too, but not the candy drive money from my dented locker." Only months later did several monks reveal they too were robbed but had kept silent. The Order hadn't caught up yet with monks driving and needing money for gas, eats, and repairs. Before Renewal, our strict vow book said a religious with a penny wasn't worth one: *"Un religieux qui a un liard ne vaut pas un liard."* But what about the prudence of future provincial, Brother John-Louis Collignon, who was puzzled by Brother Leo Labbe's closed bedroom door, usually always left open. It had been open when another brother had been at the residence just before him. Had "prudence been the better part of valor?" The thief must've been inside!

When a nun in New York, my wife Patricia came face to face with a would-be robber coming up the convent stairs. She yelled and he fled. Proof "the cloth" is no safeguard and no one is safe anywhere, especially with the proliferation of guns and knives in our culture. Of three Brothers I lived with at one time, two were murdered and another stabbed within an inch of his life. Brother Albert, who with others fled France in 1903 because of anticlericalism, was past 80 when killed at Sacred Heart School in Sharon. Because each culprit knew where the treasurer's office was, both attacks occurred in separate schools by dropouts who knew our daily schedule. Visiting during the day, both crooks jimmied the treasurer's door to prevent it from locking. Fortunately, Brother John Joseph, who went to check his office after night prayers at Sacred Heart School in Andover, survived the knifing. Later, a young Brother in my English and history class in the scholasticate (college) at Harrisville was killed in Boston by a hitchhiker. All three perpetrators were caught and convicted.

But can you believe I said no to Bishop John Wright (later a Cardinal in Rome), who at a teachers' convention in Worcester asked me for parking meter money? I had the dime, but before my fellow confrères I couldn't say yes and resorted to "a mental reservation!" Because of my monkish dilemma about our vow and money, I could've put a future Prince of the Church - an unbroken episcopal linkage to St. Peter himself - in the clutches of the city's finest! I pictured mom saying, *"Ta pa été baim smatte"*: I was a dim bulb for missing my 15 seconds of fame? At Notre Dame HS he had laid the school cornerstone and delivered the first graduation address in 1956, a gem on the pursuit of excellence. How improbable a former Woonsocket tyke, son of a pedestrian mill worker, was asked for parking money by a future cardinal! When the Church renewed itself in the 1960s, religious Orders eliminated archaic rules unsuited to modern necessities.

We said Brother Adélard was a household name for his famed exploits as a winning hockey coach of state and national titles. As a student at MSC and later co-faculty member at Notre Dame, every day I heard the broken accent, saw his legendary thrift, and felt his infectious joie de vivre. All qualities which endeared him to thousands of people, including mom, who often spoke about him and the now sainted Brother André, a religious Brother, former mill worker, and miracle worker who cured two relatives.

As an Academy founding staffer (1924), he typified the Canadian immigrant of the turn of the century who didn't let his speech, modest education, and *moyenne taille* (average size) deter him from carving a piece of the American pie for himself and the community. What an inspiration to live with him for ten years at Notre Dame where, as bursar, he curried favor and support for the school using chunks of cheese (government issue of course) from the cafeteria. I recall a state official told me his was the only school operating in the black in the Bay State! An octogenarian, he sold lunch tickets and counted the money with religious diligence. "Puts it 'ere," he told kids. He saw they got a good meal, and many kids bought two meals for a participation rate of 110 percent. He really knew how to handle kids. By not posting the menu for the week on Monday, he denied finicky ones a chance to pass up good nutrition just because "the menu didn't look appetizing." He was of the old school: kids should eat what you give them and not just what they think is good. No junk food or soda, something now followed by schools to combat obesity in children. I was honored to cover for *The Call* his 100th birthday celebration, February 6, 1984, at the Cathedral in Providence! Imagine, the first centenarian in the Order since 1821. He lived six more years in full possession of his faculties, dying literally of "old age," a doctor said. I recalled the day at Notre Dame when I came into his office and he was crying and bleeding from a severe urethra or prostate condition. I had never seen a man cry. "*Je suis fini*" (I am finished), he lamented. But after surgery, he lived some 20 plus years with only a residual incontinence problem.

The secret of his longevity? Confrères in Fitchburg thought he moved so slowly, if death caught up with him, it would pass him by. We kidded him he'd live forever, since "very few people died at his age!" When the Director didn't let the community get up from supper until everyone was done, seventeen of us shuffled our chairs, hoping the old monk got the message so we could get on with our lives! Even the lowly green pea he cut in two. If the faculty boarded the school bus for morning Mass and you were behind him, would you get there only at Communion? It was hard to believe he ever coached a speed sport like hockey! But critical in our religious life, it got us accustomed to living with the elderly who stayed in the trenches until a retirement home was built in Harrisville. Like General MacArthur said about old soldiers, they didn't die (retire), they just faded away. He lived by one of the Order's slogans, *Festina Lente*: Make haste slowly. About hurrying, we often rushed in our residence when the bell rang for prayer. But one Superior said being on time didn't mean running but starting on time. But one time when all of us monks rushed to go to the chapel for the rosary, the Northeast Blackout of 1965 occurred! It gave us a rare prayer break and my niece, Christine (Bouffard) Spielberger, was born that night.

Sometimes I couldn't believe I was once a little kid in the city who marveled at Brother Adelard's exploits. Like the time I sneaked into St. Ann's Park for a Mount game with Woonsocket HS, lying on top of the enclosed ticket box where below he was selling tickets. Wow! This guy had been born in the l9th Century, some 10-12 years before my folks, and he was still dealing with *le dur quotidien* (the daily grind), shopping, counting money, running the cafeteria, and raising money for the missions with his raffle. He epitomized Browning's "Old age hath yet its honor and its toil."

Brother George Adélard Gagnon, who terrified weak-kneed geometry students, also bridged the culture gap brilliantly between America and Canada. Rhode Island-born, he became a master of the French language *et littérature*. Like the great French masters, he wrote poetry and essays in *la belle langue française* (the beautiful French language) comparable to the rich, sensuous imagery of their Romantic poets. He broke through the Order's initial Francophone timidity to pursue advanced college degrees. A brilliant high school teacher, he once taught biology, chemistry, and physics the same year at Madawaska HS in Maine! When he taught French at Notre Dame HS in a peppy Socratic manner (the question-and-answer method), students learned to converse with him regardless of their accent. And no one dared mock! In 1970 I featured for *The Call* his work as a gifted translator for the Order's General Chapter in Rome. He brought back a small Discobolus (marble disc thrower) statue, which has stood on my desk for over 40 years. I was also proud to do his retirement story on his last day at the Academy when he came into my office to tell me. I never did a release so fast for next day's *Call*. For people like him, the story wrote itself.

A man whose refined taste in *belles-lettres* (fine literature) included a discriminating taste in the brandies and scotches infrequently served on feast days, the Brothers roared one night when he gasped at the first gulp of his spirituous drink. *Le Directeur* had exchanged an inferior product in a bottle of known quality. "This is ratgut," he bellowed, as he propelled the ersatz or inferior offending liquid into the air. At MSC when he taught geometry, he wanted students to solve problems with their own proofs, as if they were the second coming of famed French savant Pascal, who wrote his own geometry book as a teen. I dodged another bullet that time by landing in an easier class. Just figuring out a straight line is the shortest distance between two points was challenging enough for me.

When I ran a 2,000-member monthly raffle which earned a $1,000 monthly profit for Notre Dame, he did "my books." For his help, I, who once couldn't give a future cardinal a dime to park, kept him "in fine spirits" with, of course, a French cognac. He also liked a good cigar. In his last hospital stay he confided with a devilish twinkle in his eye that he sent up too many smoke signals in his life. I recall we had a tongue-in-cheek quote in the Order that it was better to be regretful of the consequences than sorry about missing a good, allowable opportunity. For example, even after a late hour event, you still had to get up at 5:30 - "the entertainment tax." In our "Manual of Perfection," a saint said if you were tempted, it meant the devil was still on the outside trying to get in. But we didn't subscribe to the devilish opinion of English bon vivant, wit and author Oscar Wilde whose strategy to end temptation was to submit to it. Once banished to the Continent for some Victorian Age deviancy, he did convert on his deathbed. These deathbed conversions were big stuff for Franco women like mom. I liked telling her about our religious life, activities, celebrations, teaching, and special events. She wrote to us, so we all reciprocated.

Like the nuns, the Brothers were messianic in spreading the faith in religion classes. At one time, few, if any, had a degree in theology, but many taught catechism as a natural outcome of their religious life. Like French, it was an important part of the curriculum in Catholic schools. In an ironic twist before I joined, my last religion teacher at the Academy was Brother Charles Edward. The class was in a study hall, later the school library and final repository of the former chapel's thick oak benches. He taught it with so much sincerity and conviction. During my novitiate training he died relatively young of cancer, mumbling a catechism presentation in his deathbed delirium. Confrères and I laid him to rest in the cemetery we built in Harrisville. Old Brother Josephus (known as *Père* Phus when he was the founding principal of MSC) threw a handful of dirt on top of the casket in the ground. It was the first time I saw that old custom. Were his words from Ash Wednesday of yesteryear when the priest signed your forehead: *Memento homo, quia es pulvis et in pulverem reverteris*: "Remember man, thou art dust and unto dust thou shalt return." Lorraine Durand who, with Stefanie Lachance of the former Mezza Luna pizza family, is part of the breakfast crowd Tuesday morning at Danny's on Cass Avenue still remembers it in French. Now it's "Turn away from sin and be faithful to the Gospel."

Long before the Order allowed some Brothers to be ordained and say Mass, diocesan priests filled those roles. Two brothers - *les Pères* Oscar *et* Christian Guilbault - served the Order as great liturgists and preachers, one also a teacher. Since the Guilbaults were related to my brother Bob's wife, Millie (Savoie). I once went with them to *Père* Oscar's Scalabrini retirement home and recalled his chaplaincy at Mount where he taught Latin, English and History to cousin Gene, one of his Homeric students. His brother Christian was in Harrisville. Before entering the Order, I said mom gave me the option of altar boy or scouting, but I chose the latter, engendering a hilarious incident in the Order. In my first Mass at St. Patrick's in Burrillville, I came to ring the bell at Consecration and realized my co-server, the former Brother Clarence (Gerry) Proulx, had dismantled it. So, I grabbed the loose clapper and smacked it against the bell. When the padre turned around at the unfamiliar sound, I wish I had known John Donne's famous line, "Ask not for whom the bell tolls, it tolls for thee."

But whenever I served Mass for perfectionist *Père* Christian, he always chided me for some lapse, like not giving him his tricorne (three-cornered) hat correctly. Priests were never without it in public! Kneeling one day beside him at the end of Mass for prayers to St. Michael and Mary, his mind went completely blank. A senior moment? An attentive prompter, I whispered the next few words with no one, I was told, noticing his *lapsus mentis*: mental lapse. *Le Frère* Alphonse (my religious name) could do no wrong from that time on. (I chose Alphonse to honor my dad and St. Alphonsus Liguori, a great orator, and founder of the Redemptorists.) And I finally did learn how to properly give him his hat.

I know it's a senior thing to think times and people were better then. But only God knows if we were just better catechized, so perhaps more culpable if we slipped. Now that I'm an octogenarian who has lived most of my life in the city and the Bay State, I miss the warm, devout, Christocentric touches that are gone. Like crowded churches, faith-filled everyday speech, devotions, big devout families, greater public decorum and behavior, and the humor and camaraderie of Francophone people in the city. But in a plus for our modern times, James F. Keating, associate professor of theology at Providence College, said, "The United States is a developed country with such pluralism - ethnically, religiously, even morally" ... the implication being we're good people, diversity and all. But another wrote that people and nations with basically one ethnicity are more law-abiding, because of the one culture, language, traditions, and beliefs. Much like the Franco neighborhood I once lived in. But I still favor the rich, immigrant tapestry that is America. Aren't we unequalled among nations on earth in giving time, talent, and treasury for our own and the world's poor and tragedy-stricken? Providentially, charity covers a multitude of sins and is a source of forgiveness. And didn't Christ say the basis of our Last Judgment destiny will be our corporal and spiritual works of mercy, like helping the needy, visiting the sick, feeding the poor, and, yes, helping the recently arrived. I recall mom cited *le curé d'Ars* (the priest of Ars - Saint John Vianney) about great surprises on the day of Final Judgment for all of creation. A Negro spiritual we sang in the South proclaimed it: "I want to be in that number when the saints go marching in."

Personally, in a script my family could never have imagined, I later lived and taught with these same men who made it all possible. Their huge footsteps made the journey so much easier. Like in that story, I, like others too, walked in the sands of time alongside of them. But when there was only one set of prints, they (like personifications of Christ himself in the story) hadn't vanished, they carried us on their shoulders. A Greek philosopher said that any student who didn't surpass his teacher was a fool, since knowledge builds on the past. But just trying to equal them was a challenge. When I was a kid and knew little or nothing but wanted to be a teacher (or a journalist), I wondered how that could happen. Like the nuns, they were our models, our vanguards. Imagine, on all of upper and lower Gaulin, initially only Andre Carpentier, my sister Sue, Madeleine Carle, and I went to high school out of some 70 kids. (Later Pierrette and Ghislaine Bérubé, Gene and Doris Peloquin, my sister Rachel, Maurice Vandal, and the Lanoie brothers also.)

In 1947 I left the Academy in the spring of my junior year to join the Order, graduating in 1948, while in training with the MSC-affiliated school in Sharon. A prized possession is my 1948 Excelsior yearbook, truly a work of art with Duce's (Paul Ducharme) pictorial renditions of school classmates. Among those "immortalized" are lifelong friend Coach Bill Belisle and the late Dr. Jean Guay who was a premiere hockey booster, benefactor, and team doctor. He and wife Marilyn sired the greatest family hockey dynasty ever at MSC, which now includes granddaughter Denyse St. Germain who has a state championship banner with the girls' team. Do they have more state titles than any other family in the state and country? I had the honor of counseling their seven children: Paul, Thomas, Joel, Marc, Michelle, Lise Anne, and Bruce. Also, sons David and John of the Belisle family. I'm proud three of our class of 1948, whose lives were so enriched by the Brothers, have served the Academy in our careers. While still in the Order, my career brought me back to MSC in 1970 as Director of Guidance, to which I added publicity, recruiting, admissions, and fund raising. This was a time when the existence of many Catholic schools like Mount was threatened so many took on extra duties. I was humbled by my induction into the Excelsior Hall of Fame in 2010. President Herve Richer, a counselee of mine, called to inform me as I was working on my book.

We've lauded lay teachers who are still bringing great witness of Christian commitment in their personal and family lives, besides great teaching. The last principal of St. Clare High School, RJM Sister Jacqueline Crépeau also served with great distinction as teacher, curriculum coordinator, and occasional publicist until 2014. Volunteer secretary Terry Riley helped me mail thousands of annual recruiting flyers to tell people about the new revitalized Mount, again primed for greatness. When she passed on, I eulogized her in the Valley Breeze, as I did Jeanne Biadasz who also volunteered before taking on nursing duties at the Motherhouse. In fact, when "*La Nurse*," as engraved on her stone, died, the Brothers allowed her to be buried in the Order's cemetery, alongside many retirees she had ministered to. That's when my sister Rachel became my paid secretary with her exceptional typing, shorthand, and office-managerial skills, besides her savoir-faire in welcoming visiting college recruiters.

Mount Saint Charles Guidance Director Rene Tellier and his first paid secretary, Rachel Clark, check whether a college has received a student's financial aid form. Mount became coed in the early 1970s.

When recruiting, I said many had never been to the city or didn't know where MSC was. Father Theodore Hesburg, famed President of Notre Dame University and model for my efforts, said Catholic institutions once lagged far behind their secular counterparts in recruiting and fund-raising. His mantra: "You are as good as what you could go out and get." He wrote Catholic schools once drew the first wave of Catholic immigrants and their children by the sheer osmosis of faith, but today's parents, besides moral and character values, were now seeking Blue Ribbon excellence and college readiness for their children. Other private high schools soon imitated my newspaper releases, circulars, Open House, and two testing dates to attract students. When a mother once came in with her son, I asked why she chose us? She had read all those articles in *The Call* about what MSC kids were doing. When kids still walked to school, another mother said she recognized a Mountie by the bulging book bag!

Rene Tellier '48, right, inducted into the MSC Hall of Fame in 2010 with, left, Brother Robert Lavoie '52; Brother Robert Croteau - Provincial and former principal; Donald Bibeault '59; and Robert Ayotte '59.

Again, that's why I thought the Academy should be in any history of the city and its people. Its founding, development, progress, and achievements are so much a part of the glories of the city's Franco culture and of other ethnics too. It's a light of the faith on the Bernon mountaintop, and the unparalleled values of a college preparatory education for all jobs and professions. Since 1924, it's been a beacon of knowledge to six thousand students or more from Woonsocket, many states, and several countries including the Far East. Adding to the city's once national fame as a mill center, the Academy has also won laurels for scholarship, charitable work of its students, professional work of its graduates in many fields, and record-setting state and national championships either in hockey, baseball, tennis, soccer, volleyball, and basketball. No other high school has had 20 graduates sign NHL professional contracts! Hundreds of Brothers and lay teachers have imparted their wisdom and knowledge to those thousands of students and created a lasting impression of selfless academic service and devotion in and out of the classroom. Some 40 still living Brothers who taught at Mount were honored at the 90th anniversary banquet in 2014. Other schools in the city, past or present, have all added glorious chapters to the city's history, especially St. Clare HS and Woonsocket HS.

Bishop Hickey had envisioned a truly American school, as he held firm against the onslaughts of *les Sentinellistes*, those fractional isolationists whose name mom could only whisper. No doubt his spirit continues to cast a protective eye over the initially embattled Mount, especially now with its curricular, co-curricular, and physical expansion, co-ed commuter status, huge sports programs, and enlarged Christian work in the community. Catholic high schools like Mount are all heirs of those former, small parochial grammar and secondary school units of yesteryear who laid the foundations for greatness.

I secularized from the Order in 1973, donning the same counselor attire as a layman. In 1976, I married Patricia Smith, a former Saint Joseph nun from New York, and we were both on staff at Mount when we adopted newborn son James in 1977, later an MSC '96 grad. One of my most endearing prides in my seven-year tenure, besides working with staffers to go co-ed and restart the junior high, was, with the invaluable help of Brothers Henri, Gladu, Michael, and Euclid, the creation of that initial MSC Alumni Association. With the devotion of Herve Morisseau, founding president, and the Association, we funded over 30 scholarships, promoted a gala alumni ball each year, and renovated the rear campus and baseball field. I proudly count myself as part of that alumni group which also included Patrick Beaulieu, Larry Tremblay, five times president Ray Denis, Charles Gallant, Marcel Fagnant, Marcel Nadeau, Robert Hamel, Bob Bentley, also president, Aldo Rossi, Ed Goryl, Roger Begin, Bill Belisle, Cam Belisle, Roger Brissette, Hubert Choquette, John Gregory, Leo Gartsu, Jacques (Jack) Staelen, Bertrand Bibeault, Laval Lachance, James Clancy, Montcalm Cote, Roger Demers, Joe Gill, Livian Gionet, Ernest Godbout, John Brodeur, Normand Vadenais, John Harwood, Al Valière, Larry Sutherland, Ralph Savaria, Leo Taillon, Edmond Laflamme, Gerald Pelletier, Cornelius O'Leary, Robert Menard, and Larry Laferriere. I must also mention the valuable legal advice we received from Omer Sutherland. One of five recommendations when I left for Norton HS promoted the idea of a permanent full-time development office. All charter members of the fledgling association are listed at the base of the Sacred Heart statue in the front oval. Gail Bryson directs alumni activities and reunions with great organizing skills, filling a post once unknown in Catholic schools.

Arriving at Sacred Heart School, Sharon in the early 1950s, my first job was weeding the flower bed around the Sacred Heart statue that's now at Mount. I could not then have imagined the reach of the Order's patron over my professional career at the Academy. Looking at the statue now brings to mind the beginning (1952) and the end of my teaching and counseling career with the Brothers when Norton HS beckoned in '77. If I take in a soccer game at the lower field, I linger and pray for those alumni founders, living or dead, whose vision, hard work, and leadership helped the Academy expand its financial reach after boarding ended. To me the involvement of the alumni in the school's renewal and expansion mirrors the church's efforts to involve the faithful more in its governance and mission. Now retired, I'm involved with private recruiting for the Academy, gardening, landscaping, flowers, playing Baldelli senior softball until Pat's death in 2000, reading, researching, writing guest columns, and finally, this, my over 600-page tome: *The Way We Were*. Once as I pulled weeds around the statue, I scared a burrowing animal into his hole and saw two deer brush by me before the front steps. We commuters in the 1940s came in from the beautifully landscaped front, and not the rear campus: boarder territory. We had a bike rack, which I sometimes used. In my very first bike trip home as a frosh, I changed my mind at the last second about not stopping at Manville Road before the Davison Ave. underpass. An 18-wheeler barreled through at that very moment! If walking in the winter, I used to throw big ice and snow chunks from the Hamlet Avenue bridge into the Blackstone River. I spoke of the irony of going to Mount from the same bridge that took my dad to his Lafayette mill job which cost him what he wanted most in life: an education and a career in medicine, as he tearfully told me.

Rene Tellier, '48, reads the names of the founders of the Alumni Association on the base of the Sacred Heart statue in front of Mount Saint Charles Academy.

We've already described Mount's new look. Let me add here that the Music Department while under the indefatigable leadership of former director Marc Blanchette, who was honored by the diocese for his work with young people, was finally provided the facilities, and privacy it so richly deserves. Aren't a fourth or fifth of the Academy's 600 plus students in the music department or graphic or related arts, drama, and choral programs? Is it so that the Academy is the only one with all four of those arts? The departments first Hall of Fame induction was in 2013 under Marc's and John Guevremont's organization. Besides Ducharme '48, the first inductees ever were Ronald Blais '70, Roger Bultot '70, Maryanne Donohue (founder of the modern MSC musical theatre),

George Lessard '62, Brother Henri-Pierre Lussier, SC (former band director), and Julie Gramolini Williams '93. The Academy's expansion has been greatly aided by the annual Walkathon, increased giving by alumni and friends, a $100,000 gift from Mark Hebert '70, and $200,000 from Mr. and Mrs. Jerry Knueven, grandparents of Mounties, past and present, making possible an LCD projector and interactive Smart Board technology in classrooms as well as hallway renovations. Adelard Arena is also undergoing needed upgrades like a new sprinkling system, locker rooms, and new solar roof. (A critic once claimed Mount often won at Adelard Arena because players knew how to play the puck "off the chicken wire." Unfortunately, money given for a professional installation in the 1970s was not spent for that, angering a big donor!)

Athletic Director Dick Lawrence, who among his many awards was inducted into the Hall of Fame of the RI Soccer Coaches and the RIIL High School Athletics in 2013 has also been honored nine times as *The Call's* Coach of the Year and recognized by the University of Chicago as an Outstanding Teacher. In 2013, he welcomed the new tennis courts on Logee for an even stronger program for boys and girls. Winner of 52 matches in a row at one time and multiple state championships with the girls' and the boys' teams, he's also been a winning coach of soccer and basketball teams. But humbly he said, "I've been inducted into a variety of Hall of Fames in the past, but the work I've done in promoting sportsmanship I consider very, very, important." Additionally, his children were All-Staters, especially in tennis and soccer. He now assists with the boys' and girls' teams.

Going coed, the Academy delivered a powerful message about the academic, co-curricular, and athletic talents of young women in private Catholic high schools in the diocese and everywhere. As a college recommending counselor, I saw women even surpass their male counterparts nationally in college attendance, M.A. degrees, and a higher graduation rate. One writer opined that co-ed, which once meant women, may now mean men in former all-male colleges. As a Princeton U. classical wit opined, "Young men will know, 'It's 'nais' (nice) to sit with Thais (goddess) on a dais (platform)." Car dealership owner Al Cerrone and former Boston Bruin player, Eddie Lee, are among those I recommended there as well as others from my three high schools. It has a gorgeous campus. I enjoyed a weekend there with the Cerrone family and boated with Al's rowing coach. Al also pitched for the Tigers. Continuing his dad's philanthropy, his dealership has helped many civic activities.

I prefer to win my debates with the cogency of my ideas rather than with the volume of my voice, and so in the 1970s I spoke at a faculty session that, despite a drop-in enrollment, MSC should remain college preparatory. At religious life renewal talks to New England Province delegates in the

1960s, Msgr. John Geoghegan, superintendent of Catholic schools, spoke convincingly about Brothers' schools not abandoning their present mission with the grandchildren of immigrants. Even though their destinies, he said, were no longer in unskilled work, but largely in the professions and skilled trades, there was still the challenge of infusing modern life with their Christian faith and values in a secular culture now bereft of its Christian center or mooring. For many Francos of yesteryear in a lower-class economy, an English language deficiency, minimal education, and hand-to-mouth existence, they had, to cite Christ's parable, but one biblical talent to work with (a natural gift; the gospel speaks of five overall). But now, their post-WWII progeny have three, four, or five talents. Responding to the Gospel admonition, "To whom more is given, more is expected," today's students, the monsignor emphasized, "needed schools like the Academy and its teachers and counselors to orient them towards higher learning." When he died in June 2006, I wrote a eulogy for the RI Catholic: "Recalling the Day Msgr. Geoghan Saved Mt. St. Charles." Only after his passing did cousin Gene tell me his last wish and trip outside Hospice St. Antoine was to see the expanded Academy. He helped keep it faithful to its mission right on the cusp of its rise to a nationally acclaimed Blue-Ribbon School. Now in its ninth decade, its history is being recalled in the "Mount" publication. Since I graduated and staffed at Mount, lived with founding Brothers Josephus and Adelard, spoke to an alum who was also there the very first day, and with an in-law, class of 1927, God willing, I hope to be there "when the Saints go marching in" for the centenary celebration in 2024.[49] Graduate Armand Laprade, '26, will have been the first of thousands who came to be "Excelsiored," that is, uplifted to greater achievements and guided by "the light atop Bernon Heights," which from its beginning, as the Gospel advises, "has not hid its light under a bushel."

About my going to Mount, as Wordsworth once said about his formative life, it was "a blessed seedtime," especially when I joined the Order. I was visiting cousin Frank in training in Harrisville when Provincial Brother Jean Marie spoke to me. (Later, sadly, he was an auto accident victim the day after I ran an in-house errand for him in Sharon.) He called the Academy "to go after me," said my recruiter, Brother Paul Metilly. Initially I couldn't leave my family and my gang, nearly all in scouting with me, and whom I loved so dearly. But one day as I was battling for a spot on the baseball team, the coach (like the movie's "I'm mad as hell and I'm not going to take this anymore") couldn't find even one "lousy baseball" on campus. So, I went to my homeroom and told Brother, "I'm joining the Brothers' team." (He

---

[49] Sadly, the author of this book, Rene M. Tellier, passed away in 2019 at the age of 89. – *ed.*

later became a missionary in Africa before secularizing. He died in 2013 at 92. He too, like Brothers Odilon and Ludger, had an unforgettable laugh.)

Mount Saint Charles 1970 staff picture
Everyone was asked to bring items that were
Indicative of their work or department.

But it took some 50 years before I received my diploma from the Academy. Entering the Order as a junior, I kept in touch with classmates and when laicized helped organize our 35th reunion in 1983. But I never saw that diploma. So, I endured my disappointment and jibes from those who knew my age and college studies. And mom's zinger! Even if grateful to the Order, she jabbed me a couple of times, *"Ta pa ton diplome de l'Académie"* (You don't have your diploma from the Academy). For my parents' generation, a high school diploma was a giant leap forward at a time when many mill workers' children didn't even go to high school. But in 2009, Sue Tessier, head of the guidance department, who has my gratitude, gave me my diploma. Unlike the legal dictum, "Justice delayed is justice denied," my half century-plus wait has not dimmed its value.

But all's well that ends well and on Sunday, June 7, 1998, 31 of the 102 grads of my '48 class received their golden anniversary diploma during the 1998 commencement. Oh, it was so long ago when I registered in 1944, and *le Frère* Simon icily told me to keep my left elbow and right hand on the registration form and off his squeaky-clean desk. That glorious June day, returning boarding students from all over the country, reminded me how important they were to my education and other Francos from the city. Many commuter students in my class had worked and raised their families within the shadow of the school. And I had counseled and directed many of their children to college, a chance not given to many of their parents.

If mom had been in the audience, I would've raised my diploma and shouted, "*Ça c'ést pour vous, Maan*" (This is for you, ma). She had brokered the deal for me to go: "*On va payer pour le reste*," about my parents paying for expenses outside of tuition, as she displayed that steely determination to overcome any obstacle. She and dad had faced immigration, the Depression, two world wars, the Spanish influenza, the flight of the mills, near homelessness, and lung problems. Nothing was ever easy for them, which is now the norm again for many as dad predicted. But for mom's Fontaine family, after getting out alive from that fire in Canada and arriving here with only the clothes on their backs, they had been through too much to roll over dead before threadbare poverty and the acculturation experience. And for dad's family the loss of their mother who left ten children, which later led to the angst of their dad's second marriage! I've told sister Sue I never tire looking at those singed, fire-salvaged daguerreotype photos of our maternal grandparent's betrothal. Their family's "flight to the Promised Land" started when that fire had consumed their home and farm. But oh, how I would also like to have *le cinquante sous mémère* (the 50-cents grandmother) despairingly told God He could take back when she flung the coins into the ashes because he had taken everything else. Just as the first Fontaine in Canada, Nicolas Pion *dit* Lafontaine, came *avec presque rien* (with almost nothing), they too left the same way, prompting mom to say, "*Il falla tout recommencer* (We had to start over again). *On nava rien* (We had nothing)." In their life's Monopoly, they kept losing all their possessions before arriving at Go, forcing them to move. Yet she married a man who liked to move! Don't women crave stability and economic sufficiency more than men do because of the working incapacity which birthing brings, as an author noted?

About the Brotherhood, I later thought God put the tag on me with the hidden ball trick! But why me? Was it because baseballs were my prized possessions as a kid! Do our lives wind and unwind one thread at a time like those baseballs I once picked up at St. Ann's Park? And in literature, didn't Theseus' wife Penelope in the Trojan War do the same, winding and unwinding a ball of thread, like a symbol of the passing of time, as she put off suitors in a 20-year wait for her war hero? And mundanely, what about the lowly onion and its many layers, so symbolic of life's multifaceted journey and changes "in this world subject to futility," as the 14th Sunday in Ordinary Times reminds us at Mass.

10 - SCOUTING AS A FRENCH-CANADIAN KID

A Rite of Passage

WHEN WE BOYS reached 12 in our neighborhood, besides learning how to throw a quoit and hit a baseball, joining Troop 4 of the Boy Scouts was another rite of passage.

Because *Père* Frédéric Moreau was founder and chaplain, signing up was like being baptized again or confirmed in our faith, because many of the earliest moral precepts from home, school, and church were going to be enlarged and strengthened by our practice of the Scout Law and Oath and his printed catechism-like reminders. Joining wasn't obligatory of course, but it seemed so exciting and virtually the only game in town for many of us whose parents had no car nor income to travel. Ironically, today's many competing activities, especially sports, are competitors. Mr. Jannell told me a scout's tenure lasted until reaching working age (not college), late adolescent dating, and the call to service during the war, especially for older scout leaders. Joining was also like family since many older siblings had done that and whetted one's appetite for wearing the uniform, camping locally on weekends (a strong earmark of Troop 4), day trips, Camp Yawgoog in summer and winter, parades, wartime paper drives, Monday night meetings, leadership training, and indoor games. For us whose pedestrian *marche-à-pied* (walking) world was a microscopic speck of Little Rhody, it was a Leviathan step.

Like Nancy Sinatra's boots, our shoes were made for walking, not for adornment or athleticism. We often walked to the trinitarian shrines of our youth: school, church, and scouting, including our scoutmaster's field on Cumberland Hill in summer.

The fragmentation of today's world, so bewildering to young people, just didn't exist for us since everyone in our mill town seemed to read from the same script. We were all part of the E Pluribus Unum gang. Because of our hand-to-mouth economy and mutual faith, language, and culture, our lives were remarkably similar. The Romantic poets of the 18th Century had foreseen us: "We're born originals, but we die copies." But that was okay with us! Isn't "imitation the sincerest form of flattery" in its best sense?

Poverty for us existed till the war, but also evidence of an earlier America with pristine values of thrift, industry, and moral rectitude. Under that dull gray landscape of poverty and limited means, no one saw or predicted a well of untapped greatness lay hidden. Mysteriously, were scouting, a plethora of other youth activities, and the Depression itself seedbeds or building blocks towards a burgeoning national character of great potential? Yes, by the mysterious weave of cause and effect, it took millions of lives to reveal the courage of those sons and daughters who joined to fight after their families survived the greatest economic downturn in American history. About character and ethics, Albert Speer, Hitler's favored architect, in *Inside the Third Reich* cited historian Spengler's *The Decline of the West*: "Perhaps nations which have passed through infernos will then be ready for their next age of flowering." And so, the nation did bloom, becoming the richest and most powerful country in the world after the war, the world's policeman against communism and brutal racial or ethnic conflicts in Europe and the Middle East. But contrarily, nations who experienced the war on their own shores were now as poor as our nation had been before the war. It's why by choice or necessity, we assumed a leadership role among nations on earth implementing programs like the (George) Marshall Plan which helped rebuild Europe after the war. In providing character-building and ideals for young boys, did Boy Scout founder Lord Baden Powell ever dream his brainchild would help thousands of pocket ethnic youths like us develop a greater awareness of our own country's founding principles, all of which have molded and transformed over 100 million kids since 1910.

But as Francos trying to become fully American, some scouting steps were painful. Whenever we camped in August or winter at Yawgoog or in the local area, we heard: "You're a French troop, aren't you?" We were different and didn't speak English "trippingly," as the Bard advises in *Hamlet*. It was almost like having *Je Me Souviens* on the back of your scout shirt (Québec's motto: "I Remember"). Non-Franco scouts couldn't resist teasing us. But our scoutmaster didn't want us to get even. We weren't brawlers, and other "national" scouts always seemed bigger than us. But adversity has its merits, empowering you to improve even without Mary Poppins' "spoonful of sugar to make the medicine go down." Our scoutmaster wanted us to speak "the King's English," not our patois. When we spoke like old hens or frogs, as others said, he bellowed, "Hey, speak English. This is America, you know." He wanted us to master the American idiom. But every Troop 4 scout in my day was a first generation American whose parents had been born on farms or small villages in Canada speaking only French.

Reading *The Forgotten Soldier* by Guy Sajer, a Franco-German soldier in the Wehrmacht's crushing retreat from Russia, I was surprised how worldwide the epithet "frog" was. Despite heroic fighting, his fellow Krauts called him that with some mockery. Does French or patois really make a croaking sound? Is there a lilt to an Irishman's brogue? Is German guttural like a guy clearing his throat or speaking to a horse, a notion that chagrined Brother Alton Voelker, a German American Southerner in training with us in Mobile? Or thinking of Dean Martin, Mario Lanza, or Caruso (mom's favorite), is multi-voweled *Italiano* the language of *amore*? But in *The Story of Language*, author Mario Pei lauds French for its purity and precision. It has always been an official and working language of The United Nations.

Deep down many of us hoped to be like Mr. Jannell. Who else in our everyday world showed us it was possible? The city of course had a modicum of professionals, educated and well-spoken, but because our priests and nuns were esteemed more through the prism of religion, our scoutmaster played a critical role in our mill culture. He was a University of RI man whose business family had money to pay for college, since his lifestyle was not hand-to-mouth like ours. In the history of a family's climb to middle class respectability, with access to comfort, enriching culture, learning, and truly gainful employment, one must do the initial, grueling spadework. It's basically how your successful immigration story is written. Some do it quickly, but we Francos didn't because of farming in Canada and millwork here. As dad lamented, neither one was fiscally nor educationally rewarding.[50]

Our scouting apparel was no better than our speech. Compared with troops outside the city, I noticed at Yawgoog we were like "second-hand Roses" in appearance. But always impeccably dressed in his khakis, our scoutmaster, in pants compared to our knickers, advised us to get our mothers to use their stove-heated iron (I still have mom's - a wedding gift in 1923) to add a little pick-me-up to our appearance. How did he know we didn't have an electric iron in our homes?

About our lower middle-class economy, dad guffawed when he told us all the foodstuffs a five-dollar bill bought. It's not hard to believe when our own weekly food-shopping bill at the Belhumeur store was about $8 for a family of 7. Because he believed bananas were the best food ever, we always got a bunch, three pounds for a quarter. "*Le potassium*," mom added.

---

[50] About our European ancestry, the France of our forebears had a higher standard of living than the English, but because they still came primarily for economic reasons and not religious liberty (except for the Huguenots), more went back. One Europanized Indian even questioned *un Gallois* (a Welsh) why he came, since he knew living in Europe was better than in the wilds of the New World. Several Montagnais Indians were taken to France in friendship and upon their return helped relations *avec les colons* (with the settlers). When the English came, they mostly stayed and quickly built outstanding colleges like Harvard (1636) and William & Mary (1693), as well as the prep schools of Andover, and Exeter, MA et al. Canadian Francos were more intent on conversions of indigenous people and exploration, so they tended to emphasize seminaries, convents, and lower schools. (Humor: about school origins, Prime Minister Margaret Thatcher once spoke at the College of William & Mary, Williamsburg, VA. "God, she joked, created Harvard first, but then realized He could do better, so He created William & Mary.")

Dad said if he were stranded on an island with nothing else, he'd want that. But because his salary was fixed, he detested inflation and wanted prices to stay the same. "*Toute ai (est) figuré à la cenne*" (Everything is figured to the penny), mom said. Recall dad's prediction in the 1940s that Americans would regret chasing the inflationary spiral, hoping to beat it with more pay. In the 2012 elections, it was revealed some 100 million Americans receive something from the federal government, but many do pay taxes. But the problems are so massive, it's hard to cut back! Those beset by tragedy, sickness, lack of ambition and without a good education or job can hardly afford to live here. They're caught in a state of dependency, helping to create our massive federal debt. But we also can't forgo our military expenditures to avoid our unpreparedness in past wars. Like in RI's out-of-control Medicaid spending, is medical/hospital care vastly overpriced, which the state government is looking into? Reading President Coolidge's life, I couldn't believe the federal debt until WWI was only $30 billion! Now it's over 20 trillion!

Again, is there a middle ground between needed government spending and some necessary level of self-sufficiency? In *This Time Is Different: Eight Centuries of Financial Folly*, economists Carmen Reinhart and Ken Rogoff wrote, "The true legacy of financial crises is more government debt ... associated with slower growth. If growth is curtailed by soaring government debts, job creation will be sub-par." But balance that with the Catholic social teaching principle of subsidiarity, which insists higher levels of government and social organization must act and do what individuals and smaller groups cannot do for themselves." But how long "can one give what one doesn't have?" The trouble is, Washington doesn't need to balance its budget. From my readings about presidents, before FDR all were against national indebtedness. WWI started the precedent, later aggravated by the Depression and WWII. But Truman restored a sense of restraint. A happy middle is elusive, since times are so different now and our population so large and diverse. In Woonsocket alone, one stat said 42 percent live under one level of poverty or another; many on food stamps. For us Depressionites, is it déjà vu all over again? But unlike then, we now "borrow from ourselves" to get out of it, like kicking the can down the road. As one said, "What does it matter, we owe it to ourselves?" Recall what Louis XIV said in financing one war after another: "*Après moi, le déluge*." - The deluge is after me. Passing the buck is not new! The last three generations are leaving heirs more money than ever, but also the largest national debt ever.

My own scout uniform was typical, mostly hand-me-down stuff from my brother Bob who was taller and bigger at a comparable age. The droopiness of my outfit came from years of use and hand washings with strong Octagon soap. If parts of the uniform were missing, you got the rest at McCarthy's downtown, or bought a piece from a former or older scout. I even wore stuff Bob bought second-hand. A quarter got you a nice shirt. When finally in full uniform, the family took a picture of Bob in a baseball uniform and me as a scout across the street on Gaulin.

Our scout wooden meetinghouse, demolished after the flood of 1955, wasn't "high rent" either. Since most parents were "*des rentiers*" (renters), said mom, we appreciated the church giving us our own place. It stood alongside a rat-infested brook called the Peters River across a wooden span past the rectory on lower Gaulin Ave. And like those old one-room schoolhouses of yesteryear, it was heated by a wood burning stove. Before the Monday night meeting, a "brave" volunteer got a crackling fire going to dispel the winter chill that snuck in with every scout. Because it was uninsulated, we appreciated outdoor summer meetings. I said "brave" because for his good deed, Lucien St. George had to get the firewood from an unlit crawl space by a trapdoor and wooden steps. Since the cavern was level with the river, it was dank, dingy, and rat-infested. I went down only once in five years and saw a rat coming up for Tenderfoot training! Later my younger brother Ben bravely performed the same "hazardous" tasks. On my paper route, I saw too many on the river side of Cumberland Street and the hospital garbage barrel shed.

Shooting rats was a pastime for us kids near the brook off Cumberland Street. Whenever "a courier" reported the rats were running - "*Les rats courrent*" - the gang, armed with BB guns (every kid had one), ran down the hill like the Colonials after the British. A few shots and the varmints scampered back into the undermined wall lining the canal. Did they ever violate the rectory's "canonical security" and terrify the heavily- robed nuns? Even we on top of Gaulin, parallel to Cumberland St., had the varmints. Our meeting hall accommodated leaders and 50-60 scouts in patrol units. There was room in the middle for plays, skits, scouting practices, and group games. It was a safe, instructional, and relaxing haven for us. It beat hanging around that lower Social Corner poolroom, even if those foul mouths were tame by today's standards. We cited a writer who said Catholic countries swear much more, "invoking" the names of God, saints, church vessels, and the like.

Like all first-generation immigrant children, we weren't like today's indoor kids. We spent our leisure days bicycling, playing baseball, neighborhood games, skating, swimming, and fishing. We didn't know about Tom Sawyer and Huck Finn, but we roamed and played carefree like them. To fish we made homemade poles from small branches, and lines from our mothers' sewing machine threads, using diaper pins for hooks. We dug worms for bait and angled in the Cass and Sylvestre ponds. Later in college I learned Izaak Walton (1593-1683) wrote the first "how-to" on fishing: *The Compleat Angler*. In the Order and our Sacred Heart summer camp where I was publicist and lifeguard, I sent a release to *The Sharon Advocate* about our "compleat angler" who caught the most fish one week. When the paper came out - you guessed it! – the old English spelling was changed to "complete." The editor must have thought: "This publicist can't spell." Weekly director Brother John Rosaire, for whom I also did office work, asked me to help campers write home - a reassuring touch for parents. A mom with two boys was amazed both said exactly the same thing! They had copied my "suggested letter."

Besides the Monday night meeting, the scout center was open one day a week. There were no fast-food havens, pizza places, and electronic gadgetry parlors to while away our idle time. When you think of those drop-in centers today to keep kids off the streets, Mr. Jannell and our chaplain were farsighted in opening it up. You sharpened your scouting skills for merit badges, played Ping-Pong, and Kingers, wooden discs slid over a long table to target spots, at which later future-contractor Ben was predictably very skilled.

Again, in the Order while in training, Ping-Pong skills brought me a championship and in tennis too by using the same stroke. But did my 15 minutes of fame in table tennis (as the pros prefer) cause the loser in the title match to abandon his calling? He left the Order the next day. I got a new paddle from treasurer Brother Ludger, whose accounts I did in his office by hand since he had a balky adding machine. Sadly, he later died helping with the construction of the Adelard Arena at the Academy. (I was a bit older and it's why I think I got those jobs. I came in later in my junior year from Mount, not as a school frosh.)

Since we only had two tennis courts in Sharon, *le Frère* Floribert, director, said you kept on playing if you kept on winning. That motivational directive made up for our lack of seminal talent! Hey, how many inner-city kids played the sport in those days? Or had a racket and knew where the courts were? Looking at a tennis racket, did unfamiliar old timers think they looked more like the snowshoes of those famed *coureurs de bois* (fur traders) in old Canada? Tennis was more the Great Gatsby's game in Newport, RI!

I asked myself later if I subconsciously joined the Order to expand my "field of dreams?" But no, dad said I'd have a chance to study with a lot of great kids and decide if I wanted the life of a religious teacher. He was the first and best counselor I ever had. In all humility, as a guidance counselor I prayed to walk in his shoes, as he dispensed advice on almost every aspect of the human experience. But not the Renaissance man he was, my field was largely restricted to college choices, financial aid, and career fields, besides personal problems. No kid ever asked me about inflation, the national debt, political candidates, making medicine, tapping shoes, cutting hair, buying the best cuts of meat, making soup, toys, or woolen baseballs. He had the wisdom to judge things insightfully, not always conferred by education. He not only had common sense, but that rare "sixth sense" or intuition. That alone is a mark of great intelligence because it requires wisdom, judgment, instinctive knowledge, and the valued use of experience beyond the five senses, says Webster. He also had compassion. I recall that like his dad Joseph, his belief was "You can't always justify what a person does, but sometimes you can explain why!" Wow! A spiritual writer said almost the same thing, adding why God is forgiving.

With the city's flood control project, the brook was eventually covered. But going by there, one hears echoes of our scoutmaster calling to order a bunch of loud first-generation kids in hand-me-down uniforms. He had us pledge fidelity to the ideals of the Scout Law: "loyal, helpful, reverent...." A kind of Christian Humanism at its best, anchored in self-control and service to others: The Golden Rule. Also, there's a happy marriage between religion and scouting because both are grounded on the inviolability and dignity of the human person. Something reaffirmed by recent popes, our Constitution and Thomas Jefferson. I also liked the belief that man - God's creature built in His own image - is "just a little less than the angels," as I entitled a play in the Scholasticate[51] in Mobile. My only other mini-play was for a Clark nephew about one of the great happenstances of all times: Sacajawea finding her brother in that 5,000-mile Lewis and Clark Expedition trek! But recalling the meeting site stirs up more than nostalgia for cousin Gene Peloquin, Eagle Scout and Scoutmaster after my time. Living nearby at 205 Gaulin, he thought Troop 4 Boy Scout equipment stored there might be vulnerable during the Great Flood of 1955, so it was relocated to higher ground. The deluge was the legacy of Hurricane Diane ("a beautiful name for a terrible hurricane"), which dropped eleven inches of rain. When he opened the door, he put on the lights and got zapped by an electrical shock. Because of the flooding, he was standing in water! But he avoided the fate of John Keats, a young tubercular Romantic poet, who feared his tombstone script was going to be: "Here lies someone whose name was writ in water, that is, not lasting." My prof said all the Romantic poets who streaked across the literary firmament like flaming comets died young (Keats, Shelley, Lord Byron, Coleridge, et al) except William Wordsworth. Why? Might it be the lack of a wonderful wife and domestic felicity? As also emphasized by PhD cousin Claude H. Trottier in *Courage and Perseverance: It's in the Genes*,

---

[51] A college-level school of general study for those preparing for membership in a Roman Catholic religious order. – *ed.*

single men in the colonization of Canada were, for survival's sake, pressured to marry one of the Daughters of the King, *les filles du Roi*, like our ancestor. Even today, a 2012 study said single men die sooner than married men, even if women undergo more hospitalizations. When Pat died, I had to learn to keep medical and dental appointments, payment schedules, and healthy practices. Things mothers normally keep track of with their steel-trap memories. Like knowing where everything is at all times in the house! One even said God made mothers because He couldn't be everywhere at all times!

My cousin Gene, a retired North Smithfield Halliwell School principal, Naval reserve officer, and chosen cultural envoy to China in 1988 for his promotion of art and music at the Halliwell school, also helped recover about 50 bodies and caskets awash in Social *Coin*. They were uprooted from an eroded section of Precious Blood Cemetery off Rathbun St and Diamond Hill Rd when the dam broke because of the bloated Harris Pond. His mom burned all his clothes when he got home. Did she, who could turn a phrase as good as my mom, tell him, "*Coup donc, Eugène, tu sens comme un revenant*" (Eugene, you smell like a ghost.)? Not alone in this "undertaking," Walter Lauzon, Explorer Post Adviser, and Troop 4 Explorer Post Scouts Paul Lauzon, Gerry Baillargeon, and Milton Wilbur all did their "good deed for the day." Other Troop 4 Scouts who chipped in to help evacuate the neighborhood were Assistant Scout Master Ray Bacon, and Scouts Robert Charron, Gerard Sabourin (now Monsignor Sabourin in Exeter RI), and Armand Poisson. What new scout ever thought joining would involve such "grave" work?

The Lafayette Worsted on Hamlet, dad's mill for 39 years, never reopened. The RI Plush Mill on River Street and the A&P Market on Cumberland St, where my family shopped, also closed permanently. The recovery saga later reminded me of the Black (or Bubonic) Plague, though, of course, not as historically horrific. (It killed a third of Europe's population over two centuries.) A woman who was presumed dead was stacked up with the corpses. Waking up, she ran home to her husband who thought she had perished. He quickly "undertook" to dismiss her because he didn't believe in ghosts. A relative convinced him to take her back, however. In nationally reported disasters in 2010 and 2012, people also "came back to life." And in one of her can-you-believe-it stories, mom also told me about a Canadian cousin who saw her "dead" infant son move after a service. What a captivating memory? The rescuers' hardest task was to extricate a woman's corpse stuck in a window on East School Street. Since the dead could not be returned to their own plot, internment was in a mass grave at St. Jean-Baptiste Cemetery on Wrentham Road. Years later and near the burial site, Pastor John Allard of St. Agatha and Precious Blood parishes blessed a monument donated by the Caron Rock of Ages Memorials. Relatives hope to have the names recorded eventually.

Not only a man of the cloth, but also a blue-collar worker, *Père Moreau* worked alongside the Army Corps of Engineers to rebuild the crumbled cemetery wall. Hadn't tentmaker apostle St. Paul said even those who preached should do a day's work? (He should try running a parish today as a single pastor!) One report said, "Caskets floated all over the city, undermining walls and crashing into textile machinery." Yes, even in death "the lash of the loom" nipped at their remains? English history speaks of workers who destroyed machinery they thought would take their jobs away: Luddites (half-witted). In France, saboteurs used their *sabots* (boots) to jam the machines. But God forbid, when they found an old lady's body downriver at Ann & Hope in Cumberland, the RI Catholic newspaper picked up on "my grim humor," when offhandedly I said if she was *"une femme de maison sans auto"* (a housewife without a car), she perhaps never traveled so far in life! (One never knows when the "mike" is on.)

But knowing the everyday life of the city, mom also spoke about an unknown returnee, *un revenant* (a ghost), like the rescued Fontaines in Cochrane, Ontario, who made a sepulchral visit to St. Ann's Church. Sounding like poet and storywriter Edgar Allan Poe, mom only knew it was a woman who had promised in death "to bedevil" her husband who had made her life a purgatory on earth: *"son purgatwère (oire) sa terre,"* confirming that "Hell hath no fury like a woman scorned." A "grave" mistake on his part! (Humor: friend Maurice Trottier, who taught with me at Notre Dame HS, told me another ghost joke about a casket that ended up near two drugstores in Social Corner and pleaded, "Can you do anything about my 'coffin'?")

Even before an obit was published, mom always seemed to know when someone died. It's as if these *femmes de maison* kept a daily count how many Francos out there were still trying to make it here! The paper confirmed what they already knew. With the immigration spigot in Canada drying up in 1929, did people like mom keep track of those who were still one with them in culture, language, and religion: *"qui sont encore en vie"* (who are still alive). Again, the miracle of oral transmission of their pedestrian life!

If not a tall tale, was the woman who promised to haunt her husband completely innocent in that domestic drama? Or at least, as the poet said, "Was she more sinned against than sinning?" Mom didn't know all the particulars in this case, but she often thought alcoholism by husbands "whetted" by poverty caused marital tensions among the poor. Because separation or divorce was usually not an option due to poverty and the church's stand on the indissolubility of marriage, great hardship befell those families. You stayed on the Bard's "rising tide of grief or ebb of despair" until death did you part! Mom knew a few *buveurs* (imbibers) "who could hoist a few." But if there's a positive, did imbibing enliven the conviviality of, Francos, Irish, Italians, Germans, and others? Francos said, "*Un p'tit coup, c'est agréable*" (A little shot is nice). I read men in an Arctic mission were becoming morose until liquor lifted their "spirits." (Madeleine DeRoche, a Landmark Hospital volunteer, said another coffin with the name of Viola St. Germain was spotted on Cumberland Street. But apparently this woman had no vengeful intent against her husband!)

    I didn't ask mom if the country was better off with or without Prohibition. Hey, even dad was "proof" you couldn't stop people from making or drinking it, even if he was too health conscious to imbibe very much. My sociology prof thought some who couldn't afford the psychiatrist's couch for their problems tried to find a solution at the bottom of a bottle! (Humor: a comic reported a depressed man filled his swimming pool with liquor. The deeper he went "the more his spirit was lifted.")

    When the Brothers ran Sacred Heart Academy in Central Falls and walked to Mass, they went by no less than nine bars in one-quarter mile. Everybody there told you that. The community's judgment on drunkards was always about men, since serious female imbibers were virtually unknown. When we entertained the Tellier clan Sunday nights, the women only drank dad's wine; the men, a beer and a shot of whiskey (*du fort*: strong). Another male addictive problem was smoking, especially before it was considered harmful. Before entering the Order in 1947, I had never seen a lady smoke. But later, tobacco companies targeted women with advertising lines like, "You've come a long way, baby" and started a 20–30-year period when women began to smoke. It was revealed in 2003 that for the first time in our history, more women than men died of lung cancer and respiratory diseases.

    I saw scores of men in the Order give it up cold turkey. But at Notre Dame HS, I related how I dreaded chapel because my seat was in front of an addicted "Nick O'Tine" who coughed incessantly into the back of my neck. I didn't pick up the one carton every 15 days we were allowed but if I did, would my folks have sent a bus to come get me? In their mind, lung disease seemed the only mortal danger the Telliers needed to fear!

    Long before it became law, I began a STOP campaign of my own by writing to restaurants. Besides the health hazard, I wondered why a restauranteur allowed smoke to spoil his menu and Pat's and my dinner. At first, owners complained about a loss of revenue, but studies proved them wrong. Adjoining smoking and non-smoking sections were a joke. "How can you chlorinate only half a pool?" a wit said. And second-hand smoke was proven to be even more hazardous, with some 50 carcinogens.

But back to the flooding "comeback-from-the-dead story." I kinda' took it as gospel truth, because even dad knew the story. Did he react with his Chaplinesque slapstick manner and single guffaw? But Ray Bacon told me a few fictitious stories went around during the flood. But in a talk at the Museum, a Main Street Najarian store saleslady related, if I recall correctly, how a buried parishioner or unknown casket did wind up on St. Ann's steps. Also, when the flood chased people out of their homes in the Social district, the pastor offered the church's newly-renovated hall. But no one took him up on his antediluvian (as in before the flood and the Ark) offer. It quickly became a "repository" (so fittingly Catholic!) for up to nine feet of water. Had God omitted Social *Coin* in His promise never to repeat the deluge? A wit said the faithful avoided a second baptism, this time by immersion.

Besides Confessional jokes, Francos told stories how Saint Peter caught up with you at the pearly gates if you were *un pécheur*: sinner. But if our story isn't all fiction, is it a case where the deceased "sainted old lady" decided to get her post-mortem (no better use of this Latin term!) judicial licks in first? It's what mom called solving problems "*en famille*" (with family), however belatedly. Francos were poor but jovial nevertheless.

About the problems that beset immigrant families like mine, would mom, for one, have crumbled in despair, if she had foreseen the future? Because of Christian charity, neighborliness, or kindness, sometimes one hears good things about one's family. What pleased me most was its unfailing serenity, as cousin Connie (Peloquin) Blais said about my parents. Like St. Paul, they put up with the good and the bad, but fortunately few if any were in three shipwrecks like him. We were landlubbers all astride the shores of the Blackstone River!

Even if the Bible says, "The earth is subject to futility" (like Murphy's law!), are the victors survivors of the thousand-and-one cuts of daily living? Ponder the line, "Cowards die a thousand deaths; the brave die only once." Did many courageous first-generation Francos only die once? But if mom had known anyone "who died more than once," would she have said, "*d'la luxure*," that is, it's expensive and beyond a millhand's salary? (Sorry, mom!)

Monday Night 'Not the Loneliest Night of the Week'

ON MONDAY NIGHTS, people in Social *Coin* swore a lot of teenage boys went to night school, but not like our Canadian-born parents "*pour devenir citoyen*" (to become a citizen). It was our scout meeting.

Like our fathers going to the mills or people to Mass on Sunday, 50 or 60 of us came down from the hills of Gaulin Ave., Kendrick, Burnside, Dulude, Wood, Elm St. or from Social *Coin* and the streets off Cass Avenue, et al. We walked and picked each other up. Nobody got dropped off, because even if a few fathers had cars, tires and gas during the war were *rara avis*: a rare bird. Like foot soldiers, we owned the streets, not vehicular traffic. Just like kids in poor cities did at one time, playing Stickball in N.Y. City.

I recall no one ever knocked, since only company and vendors did that. And no one called ahead of time since Ma Bell didn't speak patois. So, from the sidewalk or front porch you yelled out the scout's name we were there to collect. In our hand-me down uniforms, we were the second coming of the Bonus Army, the one that marched on Washington D.C. demanding early payment of their WWI bonuses. We jumped over anything. Even the railings of first story porches - *les galleries*, even if no scout lived there! Mom called it *"avyerre du front,"* unmitigated gall! She warned us, *"Le propriétaire va vous chasser,"* about the owner chasing us out like pesky gnats. Wise about our simian tactics, Mr. Jannell also cautioned us about our peripatetic mayhem on *le bien immovable*: real estate. In winter, he outlawed snowball throwing at each other and public and private school kids, an offshoot of our yearlong love affair with baseball. Snow gripped the city for days then.

He also exacted attendance and punctuality too as if part of the Scout Law. Since the door of the meetinghouse opened almost dead center in front of his desk some 50 feet away, you felt humbled if you were late, especially if you gave landlords fits. He gave you a mild put-down. Since it was Washday Monday, tongue-in-cheek he asked if you had hauled in mom's laundry from the clotheslines: *"le linge sa corde."* Wash was only once a week, but imagine the load for a family of seven or more, even if many boys like us didn't change daily. "One-and-done" would have looked like Mt. Everest. Hauling in those sagging clotheslines was a ritual repeated in thousands of homes at dusk, removing a pall that blanked the city. They defined the city skyline, like white ghostly specters or domestic canvasses waiting for painter Grandma Moses' homespun strokes. Like the Saturday bath (*prendre son baim le samedi*), *le lavage le lindi (lundi)* (washing on Monday) was an "ordained" (again fittingly Catholic!) ritual like Sunday Mass. There was some comfort in the routine.

By tradition, we surmised French-Canadian families looked patriarchal, with the paterfamilias' authority traditionally primo, but loving. With families sometimes having a grandmother, unmarried aunts, or older sisters, womenfolk often had plurality on their side in domestic decisions and governance. With birthing occurring often, I said I loved the expression mom used when someone helped a new mother for a week to get back on her feet: "*Ai (est) venu me relever.*" But why was recovery so much longer? I was amazed a few years back when a neighborhood woman, a former Academy counselee, delivered in the morning and picked up her other kids at the bus stop that afternoon! In mom-speak: "*Une forte* (a strong) *constitution.*" Didn't Indian squaws give birth unattended in the woods? So, no reported warrior faintings were ever seen in smoke signals!

When we lived on Cass across from the hospital, besides our parents our household consisted of *mémère*, my unmarried *tantes* Laurence *et* Marie-Ange, three of us boys, and Sue, later dubbed by mom "*la seconde mére*" (the second mother). Rachel was born later on Gaulin Ave. We boys had many authority figures to contend with, but we really didn't notice it. On Gaulin, we did what mom and dad asked of us, like setting up the Monday wash, going to Sweet Avenue for ice, running errands, hauling coal up three floors, and repairing the clothesline when dad left it to Bob and me. Besides errands, Sue and Rachel also had household chores, especially the dishes.

About the clotheslines, I never thought of heights until adulthood and the Order. In fact, one summer we young monks painted fire escapes three or four floors up in one of our schools. We were cautious to avoid a fall, hoping "hymnally" if we slipped that "He will (would) carry you up on angels' wings and on the breath of dawn." I did slip but grabbed the railing. Academicians doing steeplejack-like work! Also, in the Order, after a hurricane an insurance man told me the Brothers, unlike nuns, saved a lot of money by doing their own painting and repairing. But he wondered why we didn't count our work more or at all in filing a claim! Many Brothers had craftsman skills in those days. But just a few years ago, how I marveled when workers walked so carefree over the coursing Blackstone River when the Court Street Bridge was rebuilt. Bob and I witnessed the demolition of the old see-through metal bridge, which I feared as a tyke.

But not to avoid painting more fire escapes, after lifeguarding at summer camp in Sharon for a few years, I asked to go back to college to finish my master's thesis on American novelist Willa Cather, who once lived in Jaffrey, NH, not far from Notre Dame in Fitchburg. A word purist, she didn't want her great novels to be "Hollywoodized." Her model was the French author Flaubert and *le mot juste*: word economy. No selling her books "by the pound."

Scout meeting dues were only a dime, but some boys were penniless. Our scoutmaster urged us to be thrifty but knew the challenge of mill families. It wasn't a question of prioritizing an expense, but of sparing money for something desirable but not necessary. But no one was ever turned back. He and *Père* Moreau, who alone financed 10 Mount tuitions (dad didn't ask), knew our parents were challenged by the one-dollar-a-month school tuition and even the 15 cents Sunday collection. But compared to the recession of 2008, I think the necessities of life were still more affordable for poor people then than in today's overpriced economy where food, education, healthcare, home, transportation, and heat are beyond the reach of many. Wealth is not intrinsically evil, but the gap between the haves and have-nots is reported bigger than in the past. Pope Francis calls it the "idolatry of wealth" when it's not shared. One of the biggest questions of our time is finding the dividing line between self-sufficiency and government help. I spoke of the great irony of our lower middle class and poorly paid dad spurning government help in favor of self-support. That's hard to do today. In the excellent seven-part Ken Burns series *The Roosevelts*, it gave credit to FDR for expanding the presidency from just administering to supporting the people. And the towering figure of his wife Eleanor, who was indefatigable in her efforts for the poor. FDR's predecessor, Hoover, was insensitive to the plight of the people during the Depression believing help should come from private sources rather than the government.

When kids at Norton HS dropped pennies in the hallways, I picked them up, remembering eleven cents got me into the Laurier Theater. One teacher picked up discarded soda cans worth five cents to help put his two kids through college. Who says teachers are overpaid? In college I read Ben Franklin's *Poor Richard's Almanac* which inspired the saying: "A penny saved is a penny earned," and remembered my childhood Christmas money purse had a penny slot. But since it now costs more than it's worth to make a penny, Canada, for one, has done away with it. If still made of copper, would lowlifes rob young school kids of their lunch money? But have I lived to see the day when some stores keep pennies on hand to round out your bill?

The scout meeting agenda was drilling on essential skills of scouting life: First Aid, knot tying, semaphore (flags) or Morse code, folding the American flag, camping lore, and learning merit badge requirements. Memories of folding the flag is why I was moved at the Tomb of the Unknown Soldier and when I saw it done at the interments of cousins Ray Peloquin and Romeo Tellier. The ritual is so redolent of country, valor, and devotion. Could I still get it so right and tight? It's so moving when bereaved members hear the gratitude of a nation for a fallen veteran who once faced the fires of hell, but with God's grace returned to loved ones or served well stateside. And now all await the Resurrection when "the call to arms" will be replaced by the joyful clarion blasts of angels, and not the clashing of arms of "warring nations by night," as poet Arnold lamented. I read a lot about wars and wonder if more people have died from strife, including civilians, than from natural causes? Many of the 60 million deaths in WWII were civilians, like in Dresden, Hiroshima, Nagasaki, and London. It was so unlike the Civil

War's Battle of Gettysburg where 50,000 soldiers died in just three days, but only one civilian woman in her kitchen from an errant bullet!

Since our scout leader knew our competitive nature, he kept the score of patrol units' achievements on a movable blackboard. And during the year, like on Columbus Day, he took the winning patrol to places like the Mohawk Trail in MA, La Salette Seminary in Enfield, NH, or some military base. He told us the Daniel Boone Patrol (we Gaulinites) was unbeaten for years. What a thrill for us pedestrian kids to ride out of the city, since our world was circumscribed by our shoe leather. Again, about walking, how often in my case I went by the Lafayette Mill where dad was giving up his life so we could have one. I never forgot the evening when mom was close to tears when she called my attention to his telltale cough from the master bedroom. How she must've loved him for putting up with *le dur quotidien* - his daily martyrdom. Long after we all had left home, for over 30 years she provided care during his lung disease, patiently enduring his raucous expectoration regimen to free his infected lungs. Hadn't life been tough enough, he now lived with chronic illness? She told me if he had served in the war he might have received medical help to remove part of a diseased lung. But would he have survived the poison gas trench warfare which partly disabled our neighbor, Mr. Charron, whose sons, Robert and Roger, were in our gang? And what about the Spanish influenza, which killed as many doughboys and other combatants as trench warfare with its vermin and rats! The Germans alone lost 500,000 men to the disease: the British, 400,000. Some 10 million soldiers of all nations died: 8 million civilians, 20 million wounded. A great non-combat hero of WWII was Winston Churchill who wrote five volumes on the war. When young, he was an overactive and mediocre student, but his great memory, we said, once enabled him to learn 1,200 lines of poetry. Once when not ready for an exam, he only studied one part, which turned out to be the test. Like the unprepared kid at St. Michael's College, VT, who answered "False" on all 50 True or False test questions and got them all right, foiling his prof's "testy" trick. Mom never said what kind of a student dad was, but in their oral culture, his recall (and hers) caused people to shake their heads. It gave our house the feel of a domestic newsroom, with bulletins every minute about the world's events.

A born teacher who knew "All work and no play makes Jack a dull boy," Mr. Jannell included parlor-like games into our meeting agenda. With complete relaxation but fierce competitiveness, we played musical chairs but without music; (jokingly, most of us only "played the radio"); stealing the bacon; do-this; do-that; and passing the stick around (you'd hold or pass it upon command). These were games of an early industrial America. Fatigued but refreshed in spirit, we resumed the meeting agenda set by patrol leaders and him at Sunday morning meetings held at patrol leaders' homes. The meeting was always after the obligatory Sunday Mass - the 13th Scout Law in a Catholic troop. With coaching from dad, I hosted my first meeting, set up extra chairs, served them his fabulous root beer, and introduced them to my family. What pride to have Mr. Jannell in your own home and in our holy of holies - our parlor. He once lived near the old Woonsocket HS at Park Place across the Kendrick Street Bridge and up Villa Nova Street.

St. Ann Troop 4 Boy Scouts during WWII
Taken after a Sunday morning meeting at the Peloquin home, 205 Gaulin Ave.
Front row (l to r): Robert Lemoine, (1st name unknown) Valois, Vincent Auclair
Back: Oscar Laferte, Scoutmaster Walter Jannell,
Rene Tellier, Roger Peloquin, Paul Ducharme.

Absent for those meetings was *Père* Moreau who said one of the four or five Masses on Sunday. He told cousin Gene there were six thousand in the parish. Didn't I say the practice of our faith was like living in a fishbowl? Absolutely everyone knew if you did or didn't practice. It was a kind of public support, and lately popes have emphasized how worship should be communal. I recall what a sight it was to see an army of believers gravitate towards the centerpiece of their faith – St. Ann. How God must have loved them all for their devotion and obeisance to the Third Commandment: "Remember to Keep Holy the Lord's Day," so often repeated in the Old Testament. Our Sunday clothes - *habits du dimanche* - were a sartorial symbol of our reverential feeling for Him. Our dads rested from work; we from school; mom cooked only two meals, not three because of dad's famous Sunday vegetable soup. For six days God created, and on the seventh He rested (like Sunday once was), a symbol of eternity after creation, "the day without end." I liked mom saying if it was for God, nothing was ever good enough.

No wonder He loved those *femmes de maison* who served Him and their families so well, which for us kids was the biggest anti-delinquency plank in the whole Franco-American culture!

In defense of no women disciples, a writer said Christ related closely to some 13 women in the Gospels, besides of course choosing one to be His Mother. With typical English understatement, Anglican poet Wordsworth said of Mary, "Our tainted nature's solitary boast," a hint of her unique calling and our fallen nature from its original state. I was struck twice by what Cardinal Newman said about God not having created the world as it is, because after each creation day He said initially, "It was good." Some catastrophic fault had to occur. But about the problem of evil and suffering on earth as if God's fault, a writer rebuffed the complaint of "Where was God?" with "Where was man?" Writer C.S. Lewis theorized man is responsible for some 80 percent of the earth's problems. In the U.S. alone, don't we have more than two million in jail? Teens by themselves are responsible for 30 percent of crimes, adding $5 billion in court costs. And 30 percent of adult criminals "graduated" from teenage crimes.

With the Industrial Age and capitalism, was it inevitable, a writer theorized, that eventually religious and family activities made Sunday dull for Americans who wanted excitement and more money? You now see hard physical work on Sunday! (Roofing especially "floors" me!) Men once took a Sunday afternoon nap, a real luxury in a farming or mill economy. And in season, dad like others loved a ballgame at St. Ann's Park, *"au grand air"* (in the open air). Now it's the living room or den on Sunday afternoon in a sedentary and munching state; more than four hours sitting at one time, a harbinger of cancer and other ills, an author penned.

Before the "chaplain's minute" at 9, Mr. Jannell mixed praise and gentle prodding. He always knew where he wanted us to go and how to motivate us to get there. There was no ranking of scout troops, but he wanted his "French troop" to be second to none. To be all we could be! Was he conscious of our minority mindset, having to do more or better to equal others, like other minorities in sports and music at one time, and the glass ceiling for women? It was great to have two languages and cultures. But it was a time when "unum" (one) and not "pluribus" (many) held sway. This was the case between the "Mayflower pedigreed" and we later arriving Francos who spoke in a foreign tongue: our patois. Yes, for some nativists the Pledge of Allegiance ended, "with liberty and 'just-us' for all."

Knowledgeable about troops around the state, our leader cited examples of good to imitate and bad to avoid, especially in camp. First, being good scouts was our way of thanking him for his confidence in us; second, by acting morally straight, as our Scout Oath said; and third, by moving up in scouting circles. We had no or few esteem-boosting venues. Recall in the war around 40 percent of the recruits in the country had never even been to high school. Some couldn't read. Contrast that with Germany where a full high school education was the norm since the 1870s! Was that the seedbed of their achievement in music, philosophy, mathematics, and weaponry? But "pride goeth before a fall," so negatively, was it also the root cause (perversely?) of their superiority complex, Theodore Roosevelt wrote? Twice in 25 years they fell under the sway of a tyrant: the Kaiser, then Hitler. The magnetism of leadership and oratory! In the 19th century in Europe, nationalism drove countries thirsting for expansion, domination, and control. It's why Theodore Roosevelt felt the Germans would eventually upset the balance of power in Europe. They also displayed a Teutonic penchant for strict order and a mania for record keeping, which providentially after the war helped convict many at the Nuremberg trials: *Verba volent; scriba manent* - Words fly away, but writings remain.

Johnson, in his book *A History of Christianity*, does question the near appeasement Pope XII and bishops took towards Hitler, fearing otherwise he would abolish Catholicism which was doing well in Germany. But Hitler still destroyed much of the Catholic leadership. Sixty million deaths in WWII taught us appeasement rarely works. Of course, Catholics aren't alone with questionable faith and morality. In fact, 25-30 percent of the concentration camp guards were Catholic! So, for them too was it, "It's up to us to do or die, and not to ask the reason why?" A writer wondered who really knows the right or wrong of what your leaders are doing, if not demonstrably obvious! That was the dilemma of the Nuremberg Trials after the war. It's why I love to read history. But one writer thought the German people knew or should've known about the concentration camps! As in all things, some did, some didn't. Some lucky Jews fled but were not generally welcomed here in the USA.

How proud you were on scout promotion nights when he called your name and you received a promotion card, pin, or emblem from him and the chaplain. You went from Tenderfoot to Second Class, First Class, Star, Life, and finally Eagle. I was at the Life level when I joined the Brothers. Like Mary, our moms treasured all these things. The family albums show *Call* articles and photos of these awards nights, with us looking more like "young sprouts," than scouts. "Time the subtle thief of youth," a poet wrote.

Camping at Yawgoog, the troop "misbehaved" one winter, failing what later in my Order was Grand Silence after lights out. I guess we were giddy about sleeping in another universe 50 miles from home. He brought us back before the weekend was over. As the leading patrol, my gang had taken the loft through which the big fireplace chimney ran. Later, I saw the same gabbiness in Sharon when at summer camp especially, some kids couldn't lie down and sleep. One kid got up during the night and woke up in somebody else's bed. And there was never a night without bed-wetters, as if they hadn't gone all day. But I never forgot a charity case the Brothers took in during the school year. Jovial Minder Brother Bellarmine, who once got a letter addressed to "Brother Blasphemy," told me he hadn't washed in weeks. They consigned him to the shower for a half hour. Since the faculty used the same showers at a different time, I always battled athlete's foot. One day water came down my third story bedroom wall as I was shaving. The school, a roofless orphanage purchased from a Boston bishop, was weathered. I often banged on the walls when I heard rats scurrying through them.

When summer came and the heat was unbearable in our meeting house, we met at Mr. Jannell's truck-body business on Cumberland Hill Rd. At the rear of the building was a large field that sloped to huge rock outcroppings at one end. Every meeting was like an outdoor minicamp where we sharpened our skills, the sign of a good troop, he told us. No hothouse scout leader was he! We were a vigorous, active, young America. We sang under the stars and enjoyed a roaring campfire with the obligatory marshmallows from him and hilarious creative storytelling. A scout would begin a fictitious tale that would be embellished by each succeeding scout according to his own imagination. Little thought was given to Greek Aristotle's three literary canons of a beginning, middle, and end. For us kids who read little, this was creative. Like Yawgoog, it was like the romance of the wild, with young scouts sitting around in a circle, fire crackling, crickets chirping, sky darkening, stars twinkling, and a full moon enfolding like a scene from a western movie. No school the next day. O where have all the flowers gone? No urban kid had a better childhood and all for a dime a week! A time when you never heard, "If you need to know the price, you can't afford it."

He had us play King of the Hill where you tried to steal a team's flag after stripping defenders of their belt-worn kerchiefs, like Flag Football! The play was tough on our already threadbare hand-me-down shirts and pants. But stocky Mr. Jannell, a former football lineman at the Academy, loved it. He hoped for "transfer of training" from our rough play, since he thought we were not aggressive enough in speech, ambition, and action in our life. He was not your off-the boat immigrant with eyes lowered and hat in hand. Whatever promoted aggressiveness, he encouraged. It was like Mathew 11:12, "The kingdom of heaven suffers violence, and the violent take it by force."

Of course, there were some perils camping! Never having seen a serious accident before my first camping trip in Burrillville, he teased me when I got faint at the sight of blood. A camper in another troop mishandled an axe and dripped blood as he was led by our camp. But later when another camper bled at Haffenreffer Field in Bristol, I was like an ER pro.

Unless we walked it, we biked home with the downslope of Cumberland Hill to our advantage. If we went off to the meeting with an extra nickel or dime, we alighted at an ice cream parlor on Cumberland Street or on Brook Street. Back home, I hit the sack awfully quick after peeling off my dirty clothes for next Monday's wash and hoping my stuff was dry for the meeting. One time on a cloudy Monday, I wore damp clothes. "*Trempe*" (Soaked), mom shrugged, as she put on that "What-do-you-want-from-me" look, what with the laundry pile looking like the Johnston Landfill. What a contrast between her gorgeous wedding photo and her Monday washday look as she wore dad's beat-up hat and an unraveling sweater *mémère* had once knitted. Another "I Could Have Danced All Night" moment! What a load immigrant women of mill workers took on when they married! I heard a young mother complain to her mom who had warned her about "bad times," but never about "worse times," like raising a large family on a hope and a prayer and the now-you-see-it, now-you-don't little brown envelope from the mill on payday. But thank God, the cost of living was not absurd like today.

Recall even Peter asked Christ why people married if it was such a challenging station in life. But despite the failure of half of all marriages, a writer said Americans still believe in the institution with second and third marriages common, even if their breakup is more complicated when children are in the mix. In 2010, even with so many redefinitions of family, only 51 percent of the 18-to-21 age group (the most marriageable age) were married, the lowest ever. RI has the highest marrying age: men (29), women (27). Our high rate of unemployment is a cause we reported. It's why college grads, for example, marry more and with their own kind because it's better financially. Unmarried live-in couples (60 percent now break up, once 40) and single parent households outnumber nuclear families! As mom said, immigrant poverty and a less hectic lifestyle somehow made affection more durable and the biblical indissolubility of marriage easier. And Christ's words, "What God has put together, let no man put asunder," as He elevated marriage to a Sacrament. Several quasi-religions in history nixed marriage and of course soon declined, one of which, I believe, was condemned by Catholicism. Another, the Shakers, is known for their unique, fine line of furniture.

Our parents were glad scouting helped fill the long summer. There were few jobs for teens outside of peddling newspapers or selling produce for touring vendors. Families rarely got away. Francos who did often went to Canada, causing mom to say, but without envy, "*Comment les autres vivent, ceux qui ont une machine*": how others live, those with a car. That's why one day we asked dad about getting a car. His reply: "What do you want to trade for it, food, or shelter?" With a little Ford, would he have lost his reputation as: *"le grand maigre qui marche partout"*: the tall thin man who walks everywhere?

The family was in awe when Bob got his first car after the war. A Hudson, which a Brunelle cousin later displayed at an antique show in MA. Did we look like the Beverly Hillbillies when we piled in? The Telliers as *nouveaux riches* (newly rich)! *"Du swell"* (Wealthy people), did mom say? In Newport one day with Pat and Jimmy, I met Buddy Ebsen, star of the Barnaby Jones and Beverly Hillbillies TV series. He joked in "Roe-Dye-lindese" he was here for "lobstahs." Later at the Brenton Point Tower behind the dilapidated horse barn, I recounted seeing Fred Astaire, the dancer extraordinaire. I wanted to ask him whom of his four partners - Ginger Rogers, Cyd Charisse, Rita Hayworth, and Leslie Caron - he liked best, but Pat shushed me! He died a year later. A bit of a gate crasher, I was the first to shake Ted Turner's hand after his America's Cup victory in Newport. And I said hi to HOF hoop coach Rick Pittino at 30,000 feet in one of his recruiting jaunts. Sue's Hollywood mags made me a curious celebrity hound. But unfortunately, many of today's media stars now enjoy a less than deserved cult-like status we once reserved for historic greats and for us Catholics, saints and living meritorious people. But imagine if I had reminded Astaire about his first screen test results: "Can't act; can dance a little." Would he have said, 'Who in the hell knows that in RI?'

Mom approved of Mr. Jannell keeping us busy: *"Il vous tient occuper."* Of course, she knew where his family fit into the Francophone universe, where and when it came from Canada, and other census-type tidbits any chronicler should know about someone spending time with your kids. The background check of an oral culture and a feature of Franco minority life. Their life was so much more personal than ours today, where time, overwork, money, travel, electronic chattering, and caution against crime limit relationships. A TV special on ten electronic gadgets which have changed our world said we now lack concentration, focus, and are bombarded twenty-four hours a day with pure drivel, justifying an Old Testament prophet's "Man is in trouble for not thinking enough." *TV Guide* wonders if the sacred hour of evening news and its stars may disappear! Oh, the irony of growing up without phones! Now, with 300 million in circulation, one can't even speak to a real person in the business world without first being asked by an automated voice to press "one, two, or three." And then hearing "Your call is being recorded for quality assurance." My patience thin, I've complained to companies about that and even hung up at times. Perhaps it was just immigrant self-sufficiency, but along with love of children and fidelity to church and country, theirs was also an incredible grit, ingenuity, patience, and make-do in sustaining themselves during hard times with little assistance. Was it all summed up in "Character is what you stand for; reputation what you fall for?" Unfortunately, it bears repeating that individual or family self-sufficiency is largely impossible for too many today because of modern challenges: family disunity, the high cost of medical care, the disappearance of industrial jobs, an aging population, the high cost of living, the need and cost of advanced education, the growing disparity between the haves and the have-nots, all spawning an ever-growing dependency on the federal government, causing huge deficits for future generations and creeping federalization. About education, the Bay State has much better school scores: a higher living standard and more college degrees.

Despite some critics, Francos never rejected the American culture, but did the poet's line apply to them? - "Those who came to scoff stayed to pray." Some stayed temporarily while others delayed Americanization, especially language-wise. But mom's and dad's families reflected all the choices. The first Telliers in 1904 all stayed; in 1916 two Fontaines didn't come and two later went back. Not having to recross the Atlantic was a plus, one historian wrote. Biblically, recall the liberated Jews wanted to go back to bondage for the fleshpots of Egypt. Hitler, for example, knew a lot of people of Teutonic origin and language would overlook his abolition of civil rights for a mess of pottage (work, the next meal, better times). Beginning anew is the most critical trial of the human experience. "Habitude" is not in our genes. With or without humor, wasn't Jack Benny's perennial age of 39 once thought to be the time when people also stopped creating, experimenting, and moving in favor of consolidating one's gains, as I once read? But luckily for us, many Franco immigrants never went back, especially when the Depression hit. But Canada's imprint was to remain in *Le Canada en bas* here in New England, one of the theses of this book. And why we're tops in genealogy research! Once farmers in Canada, many knew how to implant "roots" deeply.

Father Moreau: Black-Robed Scout

CHILD PSYCHOLOGISTS SAY in creating behavior patterns and career aspirations, young people imitate active role models rather than just pay obeisance to spoken or written instructions. True existentialists all as movers and shakers in their developing world! Movies and video games aside for the moment, television especially explains why children are so enthralled with athletes and other media types coming live to them. Even in serious drama, a professor said you're drawn to the person doing something, even if his or her actions aren't always legal or moral: today's so-called anti-heroes! But we wrote it was once very different in movies of old, which featured simon-pure actors like Roy Rogers, Gene Autry, the Lone Ranger, et al, who basically reflected a more simple, lily-white culture. In movies, the bad'uns didn't cut it. Dressed in black, they weren't and didn't look "good." (But is it true "black" once meant "holy" in the 14th Century?) Consequently, we were doubly blessed in Troop 4. The friendship of our scoutmaster and chaplain bridged the gap between the secular and the divine. At the time, however dutiful a priest was in his ministry, he was usually apart from us and ministered mostly in church. He wasn't as public as today's priest is and needs to be. Like Father Roussel, Father Moreau was very much in the parish mix.

    I first met him when he opened the door to the rectory when I delivered *The Call* and when he walked on Cumberland Street to visit a sick or dying parishioner. But it was in scouting I saw his full apostolic dimension as a friendly, dedicated person, a counselor of youth, and sacerdotal recruiter. He was also founder of Troop 4. Tall, spare, and scholarly looking, he made us see scouting as a humanistic dimension of Christianity's Golden Rule. That is, doing unto others as they to you. While Mr. Jannell was concerned with scouting rules and practices, our chaplain reminded us by word and example of the giving and helping we should do in and out of uniform. We orbited Father's black-robed presence at his weekly minute at 9 p.m., which he never missed. He always wore his black cassock, with as many buttons as my brother Bob's bell-bottom navy trousers. Those metallic, felt-covered buttons ran all the way down from his Roman collar to the hem above his shiny, pointy shoes, rare in a blue-collar city.

    As a religious for 25 years, I can attest the collar was an irksome, easily cracked and sweaty neck-chafing irritant. Relaxing monks still in their cassock often removed their collar for relief, carrying it in their left hand. (Humor: I once heard a monk say a confrère wore a "roaming collar," because he got around so much!) Taking it off at night was like slipping off the hangman's noose. A permanent ring around your neck! When church renewal came, the black tie and suit became an option, which I voted for at a renewal meeting. At another renewal meeting where a speaker for every school had to justify "its role of mission," I was asked to speak for Mount, even if I had not yet transferred there. But I'd always been an advocate for the school, my Alma Mater since 1944.

    About good-looking shoes, shoeshine boys did their spit-and-polish thing in Social Corner. But Father surely did his own. Before I delivered papers, I wanted to do that. I also wanted to set bowling pins at St. Ann's Gym lanes until I learned those pins doubled as body-seeking missiles. About shining shoes, dad said his homemade box (I still have it) was strictly for the house, not for the street. Those shoeshine boys looked forlorn sitting on theirs, ready to defend their turf. They waited for a rare Beau Brummel ("*un coq fière*," mom said: a proud rooster) looking to add luster to his glad rags by buffing up his Bostonians, perhaps bought at Gagné's Shoe Store in

Social where even dad bought quality shoes. Yes, even on his meager salary, because two of his economic principles were "The best is the cheapest" and volume buying: *acheter en gros*. I loved hearing those maxims. Near that shoeshine corner was a hat shop and a Chinese laundry. If the gang dared a look, we quickly took off, as if a Ming dynasty soldier was after us. How did they ever get to Woonsocket? (Humor: But can you believe at a Scout assembly at the old Woonsocket HS, the speaker asked us scout leaders if we knew "How long (Long) is a Chinaman?" He got all kinds of numbers, until he revealed jokingly it was the laundry owner's name. Turning serious, he then asked us scout leaders if someone could do a better job than us in our troop. He really tore into those who said yes. His message: you're a poor leader if you thought someone could do a better job!)

Despite Père Moreau's "ascetic look," recall Bishop Keough had recognized him as being good with young people and sent him in 1935 with Father William Delaney (first Camp Yawgoog chaplain) to a Youth Leadership Conference at Notre Dame U. So, both men became vanguards in the development of scouting and CYOs in the diocese. As one was Irish and the other French-Canadian, they reflected the breadth of the diocese's concern with all youths, since like Poles, Italians, and others, those groups were large and Catholic. Our chaplain drew parallels between the Scout Law and Christian morality. Obedience to parents, teachers, police, and other authority figures, he said, was an extension of the same submission to God and church. I said he was not content with our catechism in school, so he also required you to relearn religious doctrines from the Baltimore Catechism. The scouting treasure trove my brother Ben gave me included booklets about the cardinal virtues of Faith, Hope, and Charity. There was no separation of Church and State in his Troop 4! The troop was 100 percent Catholic and Franco, a felicitous marriage of ethnicity and faith. But, of course, you didn't have to be or speak French (everything was in English) or be Catholic to join. But at that time, wasn't it largely the only DNA in the Social area? And about raising kids, our leaders and parents knew their Bible: "Train the young in the way they should go; and even when old, they will not swerve from it." Is this less true now? For example, "good" young people fleeing to the Middle East to join brutal, murderous and false Islamic cults.

Living as we do now in a different age of faith (Catholic in the context of this narrative) with dissenting voices, how did our immigrant Catholic culture at one time ever achieve such unison in all its players and doctrines, even after a severe 16th Century fracture and the growing faithlessness of the modern age? Overall, in 2012 we said figures revealed more and more Americans are "Nones," as in no religion, and that once-religious America is no longer "a Protestant country," with only 48 to 51 percent belonging to the "seven sisters of liberal Protestantism.[52]" Catholics are 21 percent of the population, down from 25. But despite its diminishing numbers, Catholicism is still distinguished by its four unchanging marks: One, Holy, Catholic (universal) and Apostolic? Heresies and breakaways have always existed: 103, one prof told us. But for 1,500 years, a writer noted that the Western world was largely Christianized. Johnson, in his book, lauds America as the only country initially or eventually providing both religious liberty and representative government. Elsewhere, for thousands of years, because religious liberty was unknown, people were under the tyranny of single despotic rulers who established the religion of the land. Often inflicting suffering or death for non-conformists. For example, the Spanish Inquisition, King Henry VIII, "Bloody Mary" (she tried to reverse Henry's breakaway from the church), some kings of France, Russia, and now some Middle East countries. The world long awaited one of President Roosevelt's Four Freedoms: worship. Of course, one should hold to what he or she thinks is the true faith, and not deny or persecute those who differ. Freedom of conscience. Roger Williams was the first in our state to fight for religious choice, no matter one's politics, as seen in *Roger Williams and The Creation of The American Soul* by John M. Barry. How long will it take for the Middle East to achieve tolerance and freedom of religion like in the Western world, which, however, took almost two millenniums to achieve? Roger Williams, however, did hate Baptists and Catholics.

But despite our diminished faith in contrast to the church in the East (some 375 million adherents; Roman Catholics over a billion), John Allen Jr. in "Discovering America" praised our faith-community worship and spiritual activism. On the other hand, a Vatican reporter said the European faithful now gravitate towards church mostly for sacramental moments like baptism, marriage, and death! We cited the "Hatched, Matched, and Dispatched" practitioner of our day! The once-falling observance of Sunday as a holy day by Catholics in America seemed for a while to stabilize and even increase a mite due to Hispanic immigrants, but no longer so. Half a million Hispanics have switched to more Pentecostal-like religions. But even if our religion boasts that it alone was founded by Christ, some of our "devotees," have been shockingly irreligious. Surely, it's a sign, one wrote, our religion, like all others, is one of people with human foibles and weaknesses, so evident with the Apostles initially. But in contrast, what extraordinary devotion, holiness, and commitment is found in many priestly and secular followers to service, even to the acceptance of death. Priest Maximillian Maria

---

[52] From Father Edward St-Godard of Holy Family Church in his weekly *Call* newspaper column.

Kolbe, for example, volunteered to go to the gas chamber for a family man during WWII.

Having spent my whole career in education, I do bow at its shrine, but I've never equated its pursuit with causing moral slippage to follow in its wake. Contrarily, isn't it truth that sets you free? Nevertheless, today's Catholic, little educated in the faith and with weak if any religious practices, is more prone to abandon the faith (at least its practice) as irrelevant, inconvenient, and contrary to the prevailing culture. Again, 23 percent of whites, ages 25 to 44, neglect worship monthly, whereas 46 percent of college-educated whites of the same age are frequent churchgoers. The American Sociological Association reported "Religious institutions tend to promote a family-centered morality that values marriage and parenthood as well as traditional middle-class virtues such as self-control, delayed gratification, and a focus on education." Add to that, Father Peyton's belief, "A family that prays together, stays together." About the curse of Modernism (that science is the only truth) or America's religion ("Americanism," as in greed and acquisitiveness), I was emboldened to label a columnist, "The High Priest of the Church of Accommodations." If it was doable, he was for it. Orator Bishop Sheen once called those ultra-liberals Flat-Heads, so unbalanced or uncontrolled in their thinking. Let's hope modern erudition and spiritual beliefs will usher in a revival of sorts in the 21st Century. But like the Gospel parable of the wedding feast, I fear "Many are called but few are chosen." The three Fatima children confirmed that. And St. Paul cautioned, "Let him who stands take heed lest he falls." Did architect Speer in *Inside the Third Reich* have Hitler in mind when he wrote "One seldom recognizes the devil when he is putting his hand on your shoulder." In Rhode Islandese, is it, "Hey, I know a guy?"

A man of charitable speech, conservative thinking, and impeccable personal appearance and behavior, *Père* Moreau challenged us to display an outward personal cleanliness along with purity of mind and body. Unlike today's young people whose purity especially is bombarded by suggestive songs, sex without commitment, drugs, salacious magazines, movies, videos, and cyberspace crimes, we were rather naïve until very late adolescence. But because we came from rather large families with little education, we loved to engage in horseplay and showed rough edges. He and our scoutmaster safeguarded our innocence while giving us some external polish and advice. With his rather tall presence, you felt he was always watching and listening to you, but not invasively. Was he looking for recruits? I went to the rectory once for advice about a Life Scout merit badge, and he called my attention to my fingernails being "in a state of mourning," as said in the Order. Our dusty playgrounds? Dad, with his damaged lungs, was amazed the amount of dust we lived with. Of course, not everything was paved and our mill culture was fueled with coal, not to mention chimney exhaust. Pollution from the industrial heartlands of Middle America also found its way to RI.

Kids saw mothers and sisters do their nails, but it wasn't something male mill workers especially spent much time on. Did they know Will Rogers, America's best-known humorist, said, "Americans need dirtier fingernails but cleaner minds?" But because of his job and hygienic sense, dad kept his clean and short to avoid entanglements with mule-spinning threads. He used scissors from mom's sewing machine.

When the local Works Progress Administration (WPA) - one of FDR's New Deal initiatives, put in a new sidewalk across our street, I watched the men wield shovels, picks, and sledgehammers all day amid spiraling dust and debris. Clean fingernails not a priority! Mom said even dad helped build Cass Park, one of our playgrounds. A patch of green in macadamized tenement-city Woonsocket! Because of our large parish, we said all priests were on deck Sunday mornings. No lay person in the holy of holies except altar boys, so to Mr. Jannell's chagrin, Father rarely stayed overnight with us when we camped on weekends. We worked on our outdoor skills, but never succeeded in starting a fire by rubbing sticks or from flint sparks. So, we bent the rules by using wooden matches from home. He caught us once. Where was the Greek god Prometheus who brought fire to earth? Did he snuff out our efforts because we knew some French, passable English, but no Greek? Pantheistic, the Greeks like the Romans had a god for everything, but not to start a campfire.

But our "black robe" often arrived at our campsite Sunday afternoon. About the Lord's Day, if for our parents camping meant missing Mass, scouting would've been "cast out into the darkness where there is gnashing of teeth." It was our most serious obligation as practicing Catholics. Mr. Jannell always knew where the church was if we weren't at Yawgoog in August. He never took "a traveler's pass," a reasonable option at times nowadays. Mom, for one, probably didn't know the line, "*Nul est tenu à l'impossible*," about nobody being held to the impossible, but her own version: "*Ce qu'on ai (est) capable.*" Reasonableness said Christ, who chided the Pharisees lambasting the famished apostles who ate sheaves of grass on the Sabbath. My Gospel favorites are always about His humanity, goodness, and compassion: Lazarus, the young girl from the dead, multiplication of the loaves (prefiguring the Holy Eucharist), sparing the adulteress from the stone throwers, the blind man, the woman with the issue of blood, and the promise of heaven for the Good Thief, the very best. Biblically, he and Mary are the only two mortals we're sure are in heaven, one wrote.

Not only were we "road Catholic scouts," but we also attended Mass in a group if leaving Sunday morning. But our leader, who knew about the efficacy of prayer, but also irony, chuckled at times how the Lord of Fair Skies turned a deaf ear to our plea. No camping group was ever cursed with so much foul weather. With no nightly weather reports, we didn't know about the fickle New England climate. We could've used dad, a superb forecaster, who claimed he could smell bad weather. But not endowed with his proboscis or nose, I tried once, but failed. Are all wine makers blessed with that olfactory sense, like one who detected a copper nail in 100 gallons? Did he *whine*, "There's a coppery taste?"

Putting up with the cold was hard. I for one hated to be cold at night. When once I crossed America with a few Brothers and a friend, we chose a midland route and slept comfortably, especially at Yosemite where even without a reservation we got the last campsite. But squirrels got to our foodstuff at night. I was nearly dehydrated after crossing the Mohave Desert without air conditioning. We couldn't wait to swim in the Pacific Ocean, but Murphy's Law - a cold rainy day - followed us out there. We were "Silent, on a peak in Darien," to quote a poet who was wrong about the real discoverer of the Pacific (Balboa, not Cortez). One of the great lines in literature for the mood and imagery it evokes. Two others are "A thing of beauty is a joy forever," and Moabite Ruth "shedding tears amid alien corn," which for Francos evokes so nostalgically their immigration story. "Wherever you go, I will go," she told her Jewish husband. How many women said the same to their husbands who wished to better support their family away from dirt-poor farms in Canada, like *pepère* Joseph Tellier to Angélina in 1904? Savvy mom said, *"La terre était epuisée"*: the earth was exhausted. She knew and spoke of his family history more than he did. He, the strong, silent type.

If in summer we scouts camped in tents on platforms at Yawgoog, or in winter in a log cabin with a fireplace, we were okay. But if outdoors in the fall, our leader knew our survival limits and brought us back home early if disaster threatened. Like the time I arrived home early one Sunday at mealtime and told the family how brutal the cold was. The wind had blown our tents down and snuffed out our fires. Our own Valley Forge in Rhody. It's partly why I too like my brother Bob would've preferred being a navy sailor (*"un matelot,"* said mom) for service in the Pacific, not Europe. In *Armageddon*, the author blamed the last brutal winter of war in Europe on cannon exhaust. Like weekday industrial emissions bringing rain more often on the weekend, said an article!

Since *les* Telliers weren't big people, mom said we were *frileux*: easily chilled. Warmth was always a perennial quest for her equally tiny Fontaine sisters. Unlike Canada, where it was colder but dryer, the New England dampness got into *"la moelle de nos os,"* the marrow of your bones, she said. At Yawgoog one weekend, we told Mr. Jannell that scouts were tenting by the pond in brutal, near-zero January weather! He gave them shelter for the night in our log cabin in front of its blazing hearth.

Our chaplain also kept a constant watch over our progress in school, serving as parish director in support of *la Mère Supérieure* (Mother Superior). For him, it wasn't a given we'd wind up in the mills like our parents. But like my dad and Francos, he saw it as good and honest labor. But as a man of education, he wanted us to move up the ladder. We were fortunate, since outside of his and our scoutmaster's encouragement to do well in school, parents, yes, knew the value of schooling, but little about how to do so. Planning for their children's future was not a top priority. Besides Father Moreau helping kids go to Mount, we also praised the nuns and Brothers. Their vow of poverty and support of their Orders made tuition possible for mill workers' children at MSC, Saint Clare HS, and parochial grammar schools in the city and the state. The so-called "contributed services." Currently, some two million Catholic school students (figures vary) are saving $24 billion for the American taxpayers. They still pay taxes for the public-school system, a fact not recognized by some myopic politicians and parents.

When at Notre Dame HS, Brother John Collignon and I went to Boston College for a pittance for our master's degree in Counseling Psychology. Unfortunately, those deep discounts don't exist now because for one, Catholic schools and colleges serve all religious denominations and strive to keep up with secular institutions. And religious teachers are far fewer. But like high schools, hopefully Catholic colleges will retain their Christian character, unlike many former denominational Christian colleges founded in our early history, now secular. A Christian Brother penned a book about the slippage of faith instruction in some Catholic institutions with popes concerned about that. As said, I'd like RI to fund a Choice or Voucher system, as do 12 other states, so parents may have that choice.

Is that why there's a thrust for charter schools and academies? Fifty-six percent of Rhode Islanders support the voucher system, but if it still exists, it's only funded $1 million, if at all. Indiana's program, for one, saves $4.2 million for local districts since most private schools charge less than your usual public school-per-student state allotment. A $2,000 difference in RI? About supporting both public and voucher systems, a writer said it's no different than the federal government aiding private colleges alike with loans and scholarship moneys. Competition breeds excellence. I mention elsewhere our government till the mid-19th Century used to help all denominational schools also. How much better would many school systems be if a nationwide support system, public and private, had been retained? The poor especially are badly served by underachieving schools in many states. Some not well funded.

Sadly, we said, the rising cost of private Catholic education is now out of reach of many. The reason stems from faculties with more lay teachers who, like their public-school counterparts, need and deserve a living wage, pension, and medical coverage. Mount is addressing the challenge with a Sacred Heart Scholarship Fund for needy qualifying students. Especially those from the city, which is beset, like others, with financial problems due partly to a poor populace with 40 percent on food stamps. Other needy students may also qualify for aid by filling out an FAF (Financial Aid Form). When on the MSC staff in the 1970s, I wrote a ten-page paper to the Superintendent of Catholic Schools in Providence to boost lay salaries and other benefits. Catholic academies like Mount, St. Ray's, LaSalle, Hendricken, Bay View, Prout, St. Patrick (diocesan supported), not forgetting Catholic grammar schools, are run by fewer if any religious and more and more lay people. In the annual diocesan drive, Anchors of Hope provides scholarships to needy students in the diocese. But no doubt the state's loss of many of its Catholic grammar schools is a major reason for diminution of church membership and practice.

Unfortunately, the drop in enrollment is occurring at a time when Catholic schools have never been better. How often in my tenure at Mount I saw students, not initially good college material, become so when surrounded by other serious students for four or more years. Didn't President Reagan say, "A rising tide lifts all boats?" All high schools have good students and solid academic tracks, but some kids can only succeed in a tight, academically oriented school culture where absenteeism, rowdyism, indifference, and willful failure are more evident. Sadly, in some non-private comprehensive schools, impressionable students fail to imitate good students, preferring to hang out only with the less motivated. As Brother Floribert said when I entered the Order, "Birds of a feather flock together." Yes, teachers in those schools are as good as any, but the challenge is greater. We cited a study where the biggest influence now on a growing child is not his parent(s), but the world outside his home, including school. Good teachers and a solid curriculum can only do so much in the face of unmotivated, indifferent students, so said a national educator a few years ago. I've already highlighted the importance of regular school attendance! TV reported last year that a school in the South receives only money for kids who show up. A daily count is reported. In a late 2015 report, Woonsocket HS had 36 % of students absent 18+ days the previous year.

But if dad was right about others jumping ahead of us educationally from 1900 on, one can believe Francos have made tremendous academic strides since the war. Nationally, Catholics are now among the better educated and salaried, so I read. Like the Irish, we're no longer "an uneducated, immigrant church." But Woonsocket isn't or has never been a greatly moneyed municipality. With its, mills gone, subsidized housing above the mandated average, people of limited means, many nutritionally challenged, and parents with limited English skills, it's unfortunate that local and state support for education can't meet all those challenges. Schools are usually close to 70 percent of civic budgets, so if a municipality is poor and tax revenues lower, schools must depend on the state or on other communities, so to speak. Hopefully, mutually agreed adjustments in pensions, COLAs, and retirement plans will assure sufficient support for education and other vital social services and needed infrastructure work. Does "no maintenance" Rhody still have the worst roads in the nation? Imagine, only 7 cents of our gas tax go to roads. (Also, a report said that not all federal revenues we receive for roads are used for that purpose!) But now the city's roads are being addressed by Mayor Lisa Baldelli-Hunt. Former state attorney Arlene Violest has been exposing the road scandal in some of her weekly Valley Breeze articles. Changes are needed at the top.

But to the extent they can, communities must be realistic in shouldering their local share of the education bill, a judge told Warwick voters. Reasonable tax increases yearly to match inflation and rising health costs are necessary, unlike what happened for almost ten years in the city. For about ten years, starting in 2000, the city increased its tax just a mite above one percent, said one report. That was not enough to keep up with inflation. Because I saw a similar situation in Fitchburg under the mayoralty of a tightwad, re-election-conscious mayor, each year I predicted to my son Woonsocket's coming fiscal bind. Imagine, even pension deposits were not kept up. But the city is not the only one to make that mistake.

Communities have many needs, but taxpayers and politicians must consider education a top priority as well as roads and public safety. The state average for school support from communities overall is 67%, but only 21% in Woonsocket, not a ringing endorsement for education. But can it do any better, one said? Is merging the state's 36 school systems into one the answer? But doesn't funding already come out of the same pot? You'll recall I mentioned excessive "spedding" (Special Education) of students may be one reason for what the *Providence Journal* calls our lack of worker preparedness? Is more technical training for these students the answer?

I spoke of my sister Sue going to Hill College in the city after Woonsocket HS, with naysayers telling mom it's *"une dépense d'argent"*: a waste of money. Her education later allowed her to be secretary, estimator, and accountant for her husband Guil's Bouffard Upholstering in Bellingham and publicist for the Mt. St. Charles Mothers Club and Assumption and St. Blaise parishes. Always two or more grades ahead of me in school, she unknowingly challenged me when she told me how tough it was going to be.

The Bouffards encouraged all their five children to go beyond high school. "Uncle Rene" was glad to provide guidance help. After years of counseling, knowing well the 40 or 50 college admissions counselors I often dealt with helped me to intervene when more than a written recommendation was needed. One time a remedied failing grade was not reflected on a student's transcript. The admissions counselor at Assumption College changed a rejection to an acceptance. He once told me I sent so many there it was the "Mt. St. Charles of Worcester." The student graduated and the family was grateful. At two other colleges, two high-achieving senior girls were "waitlisted," but when I intervened, they were later admitted and became doctors. As my Boston College prof said, "The kids will define your role."

We had a thought in the Order how a religious should recruit one candidate to replace him and another to increase its numbers. My recruits were Brothers Robert and Roger Marcotte (secularized), another student, and Thomas Greer, a veteran staffer and multi-degreed religion teacher at the Academy, speaker, and Zambian missionary. Recruiting is a crucial endeavor, especially now in an age when religious and priests aren't replacing themselves. In approaching some of us, *Père* Moreau was zealous for the priesthood. He was disappointed when I told him the teaching Brotherhood attracted me more than the pulpit. I did identify with him and Mr. Jannell in their work with us kids, but, as I heard in the Order, teaching was the role Christ chose on earth. And didn't I quote a prophet who said those who taught others unto justice (truth and rightful knowledge?) would "shine like stars for all eternity." In *Inside Heaven and Hell*, Thomas W. Petrisko speaks of a mystic who in a vision saw the back of that same light in the recesses of heaven itself! Teaching is also one of the many gifts St. Paul says the Holy Spirit endows us. Every human is unique, I told kids. (Humor: But one day when a kid asked me why, I jokingly told him God doesn't make the same mistake twice! A bit of levity and sports topics also helped establish a comforting interview.)

Our chaplain made us realize there was once a defining career decision to become what he and other curates were. Expectedly, most of us had a hardwired career mindset as children of mill workers. Girls were often jobcast solely for homemaking or clerical work, as one told me, but the good nuns also cast a wide net to attract them, which they did superbly. Nuns from numerous religious Orders, not discounting teaching Brothers and some priests, created the largest faith-based school system in America: 180,000 nuns at one time, but only about 80,000 now; 40,000 or fewer Brothers. The Vatican at one time, but no longer, was concerned about the nuns's diminution and the stand of some on controversial issues of the day, like a female priesthood. But the Vatican report in 2014 praised their call to holiness and service. Like the Brotherhood and Priesthood, the Sisterhood's declining numbers reflect more outside forces, like diminished faith, loss of church membership, and smaller families than any internal community cause.

Parents like mine were always defining peoples' roles in our life and culture. One time, *ma tante* Blanche and mom saw a play where cousin François uttered, *"Nous sommes les hommes de demain"*: tomorrow's leaders. Visiting them on Ross Street near Front Street where my uncle ran his little variety store, they reminded us about that line. *Père* Moreau's recruiting did influence Vincent Auclair, an Oblate missionary in Haiti, Normand Demers, diocesan pastor and author; and Lionel Trudel, a missionary priest. Having him as a counselor was ideal because the Academy had none when I went. It was like many Catholic high schools at one time, since few of the first and second generation went on to college, especially Francos before the war. But even with my parents' love of education and our chaplain's encouragement, I would've missed college if the Brotherhood hadn't beckoned. Similarly, cousin Gene, retired school principal, seaman and Naval Reserve officer, told me he went to Providence College because a friend suggested it to him one late summer. He was working with my brother Ben on a housing project in the city. Higher Ed in the 1950s and '60s, especially with the G.I. Bill and the death knell of the mills, was now within reach. But we lamented the cost is now prohibitive, going up ten times faster than the cost of living! Not surprisingly, fifty-seven percent of the grads of 2011 said their education was not worth the money or the debts incurred. Is that why we now rank 12th in the world in college students? Again, one of mom's one-liners is apt here: *"pour les riches seulement"*: for the rich only. Many Ocean Staters can't even afford CCRI (Community College of RI). Many drop out with finances as one reason.

Didn't a millionaire in 2010-11 give smart kids huge sums not go to college, but to invest? But I'm still a devotee of Cardinal Newman's *The Idea of a University*: "Knowledge is its own reward." Especially the fruits of a liberal education that teaches you to think, speak, and write, to know the broad outlines of world history, its great literature and philosophy, and the role of Christendom in keeping the torch of learning lit during the Dark Ages between the fall of Rome in 476 and the Renaissance in the 14th and 15th Centuries. For example, Providence College with its Humanities Program is renowned for these studies and has built a new facility for more growth, bucking the trend of colleges towards "how-to" courses.

For other ethnics, the thrust towards education once they got here came from "within," unlike from "without" for us. So would-be millhands finally extricated themselves from those entanglements of woolen and cotton fibers that had bound them for so long, an article said. Not as cruel or debilitating of course but think of the shocking classical sculpture in art books of the Trojan priest Laocoon, who with his two sons is strangled by sea serpents. Since a wit said, "No good deed goes unpunished," he too had warned the Trojans against the wooden horse trick. But again, to be fair, for all their low pay, layoffs, and health hazards, the mills were better economically than those depleted farms in Québec. Their sons and daughters would eventually storm the bastions of learning, like the Bastille was stormed by their French ancestors July 14, 1789, if only for tax relief and bread.

Again, about economics, in William Manchester's magnificent biography of Douglas MacArthur - *American Caesar* - he cites Wendell Willkie who thought FDR was undermining people's sense of self-sufficiency and can-do. But did recipients tell ultra-conservatives you couldn't eat "self-sufficiency" and "can-do?" But isn't it disheartening when often help, goods, and services don't get to the poor, as corruption, inefficiency, and inertia all take their cut? Haiti the latest example? No wonder the Bible says, "We shouldn't be weary of doing well," with Christ adding "the poor will always be with us." It's not hard to comprehend given the human condition. Especially in a loosely controlled capitalistic economy like ours which breeds a have, have-not situation. I touched upon Theodore Roosevelt's fight to initiate controls, as seen in *Colonel Roosevelt* by Edmund Morris, but I didn't like his efforts to remove "In God, We Trust." (Humor: A wit who ran a business told customers about that motto, adding, "All others pay cash.") Stats in 2011 revealed the economic gap, for example, between whites and Hispanics and Black Americans is 15 to 20 percent. Francos were once like them, but then the basics of life were not expensive. It now makes the immigration experience an unenviable challenge, but they still come, because it's worse elsewhere. But one outcome of our lack of jobs and high prices is illegal immigration has been cut in half from Mexico! Many returning. A lot of our unskilled jobs went there (NAFTA), which Americans didn't want to do, but some have now changed their opinions. *60 Minutes* cited another growing national problem. Some people who have lost their job and exhausted benefits now falsely claim physical disabilities with the help of shyster lawyers, a specialty, in parts of West Virginia and Kentucky, whose economy is based on it.

But is there a job for every man, woman, and adolescent boy or girl in the nation's economy? I shudder reading that mostly we've never had prosperity without war. At least at one time, one stat claimed 52 percent of all Americans worked in some government-related job! In 2104 more of the federal budget is going toward interest payments, leaving less room for investments in energy, education, infrastructure, low-income support, and research, health especially. In the next ten years our interest payments will go from $220 billion to nearly $800 billion, and in a few years all the government revenues will go to payments! Hard to believe, if so. Our national debt now: 19 trillion! With the Romans, we said the policy was to give people *panes et circenses* (bread and circuses: amphitheaters) to keep government spending high and the citizens happy. Do we Americans have to choose between "guns (government contract s) and butter," the choices between war and the more peaceful life at home, but not as lucrative? It's why I love to read political and military history years after the fact, when the "the real truth" is finally revealed. In my war chapters, I quote Ike who may have shocked war hawks (and weapon makers) when he said the resources we spend on arms - "the cross of iron" - are moneys not spent on human needs: education and health. We can't afford the government we have now.

Saying Mass, Père Moreau showed a prayerful deliberation, with unhurried, well-intoned prayers, as he reenacted the Last Supper and the miracle of the Eucharist. With his elongated frame, unlike most Franco priests he cut a nice figure at the altar, so mom observed. When Mass vestments seemed heavier and more enveloping ("Roman" versus "Gothic"?), he still wore his with a certain grace. They didn't smother him, like the other priests who showed little but the back of their head.

My folks loved his preaching because they could hear him. The others with their weak or gravelly voices went partly unheard. The echoes from the lofty, vaulted dome accentuated their muffled pronouncements from the pulpit and altar. So many went to Mass with a missal to read the liturgy? But parishioners who didn't speak or read good French too well (no missal in patois) didn't cotton to Latin either. (Humor: A parishioner boasted he knew every language but Greek? When asked about Latin, well, that was "Greek" to him too!) We spoke earlier about the poor sound system, with many priests lacking an audible speaking voice, and lectors rarely adjusting the tiny, single mike to their mouth, unlike stage and TV performers who practically swallow theirs. I've called it our church's information gap, advocating training, better sound system for us aging parishioners, and neck-strapped mikes. Not yet in church, but lately I've seen people get up at meetings to ask more volume from speakers or to raise the mike. One said the microphone has killed oratory. Shakespeare, whose medium was the written word, did speak about "A woman's voice being sweet and low, a fine thing in a woman." But not in a lector, I told a diocesan communications person recently. And negatively, men's voices get muffled with age. Unlike Protestant churches, the size of ours doesn't help. One should go to the Mormon Chapel to see how sound, without a system, can be as good as someone next to you. Or the curved wall which traps the sound at Princeton University. Only those retreat masters of old beat the poor systems.

Like dad, many aging mill workers developed hearing problems because of ear-busting noise at the mill. In my Manville mill summer job, I couldn't believe the noise the first day. Is that why dad wanted peace and quiet at home? "Sadly," he had gone from the natural quietude of farm life to the clatter and roar of textile machinery. But again, if only the voice of education could still have been heard about the roar of the mill engines! The thousands of mill workers who offset all the negatives of their trade in producing great work deserve our praise. They and others who were at their machines when America's work ethic was the world's best, said one report. When work was making something!

So many rated priests on their pulpit oratory, aka clarity and volume. If someone was not good, mom's critique was "*Yé pa(s) bon en chaire*" or "*Y parle pas franc*: weak pulpit voice. Have I said two priests even admitted to me the noted oratory of so many Protestant preachers stemmed from their emphasis on the spoken word, in contrast to our Mass and the Real Presence in the Eucharist? But didn't Christ's urge his disciples "to speak as one having authority?" In the political arena, for example, a writer said Senator Kennedy spoke in a loud, clear, and forceful manner, as a "Lion of the Senate" should. What did a Greek orator do to become one of the best? Demosthenes overcame a poor speaking voice by learning to project with rocks in his mouth. "Marble Mouth" in the Greek Senate? I said Eleanor Roosevelt learned how to speak in public, reversing the opinion at one time women weren't good pulpit speakers.

Recall it was a no-no for us kids to assume the men's "three-point landing" posture in the pews. Men's minds may have been on the Mass, but their elbows on the top of the pew and their derrière on the edge of the bench. Hey, if some men at the mill like dad walked close to ten miles a day (Claude Trottier wrote it was "25" in his book), no wonder they "parked" anywhere on weekends. And if like the apostles during Christ's agony at Gethsemane, they sometimes "slumbered and slept," they always came. He couldn't blame them for "not watching one hour with me." Women had missals, but few men did, unlike the mill owning Lepoutres. Before dad retired to Hospice Saint Antoine, I admired him for reading his Sunday Mass missalette when he couldn't attend due to his damaged lungs. And mom when going to Assumption Parish in Bellingham on foot, if not driven by the Bouffards, fell once, bitten by a dog, and jostled by a young bicyclist, but never missed. I guess she didn't know *Nul est tenu à l'impossible*, that is, only the Marines do the impossible, even if takes a little longer.

Some men of course swore, drank, or got angry, but if a paterfamilias didn't go to Mass, well, that was scandalous. We said at St. Ann's they were known by Père Moreau. (Recall *mon oncle* François's story about a habitual criminal who was indignant about being asked if he missed Mass: "Hey, Father, do you take me for a Protestant?)

Exiting Mass early was also an irritant with priests admonishing those unmindful of Yogi Berra's "It ain't over till it's over" or "until the fat lady sings." But Ben still wonders why the quick exit, since at St. Ann's anyway, no one was rushing to a parking lot and car that didn't exist. Or else were they heading to Belisle's Bakery on lower Rathbun for cream puffs and wickedly good chocolate cakes? Unlike the Old Sod, bars weren't open in the city on the Lord's Day then, at least not "for the thirst," as novelist Frank McCourt said some of his intemperate imbiber friends did.

About walking, did a pedestrian city like ours help Francos live healthier and longer, helping delay, as Shakespeare said, "shuffling off one's mortal coil?" (If the reader wants to live 10 to 15 years longer, *The End of Illness* by David Agus a must. I'm on my second reading.) But about quotes, a prof said if you're asked to identify a saying, say Shakespeare, Alexander Pope, or the Bible, and you'll be right 70 percent of the time. Pope is not as well known, but his "Whatever is, is right"; "A little learning is a dangerous thing," and "Hope springs eternal in the human breast, Man never is (happy), but always to be blest" are all keepers. We emphasized Sunday was the Lord's Day, jokingly not today's NFL ("No Faith Left?") Day! How did God lose the contract after a championship run of 1500 years or more before severe defections in the late Middle Ages? Why, for one, are France's ("oldest daughter of the Catholic Church") many great churches just cultural attractions, like St. Ann's now? In the history of the Providence Diocese, the author relates that at one time they couldn't build them fast enough to accommodate faith-endowed ethnic immigration waves.

Hard to believe but my Boston College magazine reported Confessions used to outnumber Communions. Many people went before Mass or on a Saturday afternoon, like my folks monthly. A sacramental grace. James O'Toole, Boston College professor, said the monthly penitential practice practically vanished in the mid 1960s with the erosion of the notion of sin, Saturday Masses, shortage of priests, and a drop in attendance. But Communion is way up. Gone is that hang-up (again by one of my profs about us French Canadians especially!) you were unworthy to receive unless you fessed up just before. He added Communion for them was once considered more "like a reward rather than spiritual nourishment." Imagine, even saintly Thérèse of Lisieux needed permission to receive. But historically it was not common to receive often, and only mandated once during Easter Season. Mom and dad received every Sunday, but one Sunday, I heard him say it was for his Easter duty. A clever teaching moment! The obligation was confused with Confession; the regulation being only if one had committed a mortal sin and not yet confessed. Several times priests told me how it felt hearing a sinner "unload," say, after some 20 years. In modern times, stigmatist Saint Padre Pio heard confessions for hours, as did St. John Vianney (Curé d'Ars). Our Confession is auricular, to the ear, unlike Protestants, in secret to God. One theologian said *Ego te absolvo* (I forgive you) is an audible assuring sign that one's sins are forgiven.

But in a pedestrian city like ours, a lot of those ethnic churches were built within walking distance of each other, such as Precious Blood (French-Canadian) and St. Anthony's (Italian); St. Ann's and St. Louis, which we mused could be blessed at the same time by a priest with a vigorous holy water stroke. St. Louis later became All Saints when Our Lady of Victories and St. Ann's were merged with it. Since the city became overwhelmingly French-Canadian (70 percent, a Québeckian wrote in 2014), Irish St. Charles is now partnered with All Saints, as is Holy Family and Sacred Heart, and Saint Theresa with Our Lady of Good Help, both in Burrillville. I mentioned with true Hibernian hospitality that St. Charles parish once warmly welcomed Francos before and during the building of Precious Blood. I like to think also only mild tension existed between Irish and Franco at the mill, if so, where some Francos I read were willing "to work on the cheap," or avoided taxes by going back to Canada to put crops in the spring or pay debts.

A publication, *Monument de l'Amitié* (Friendship Monument), designed and promoted by Jacques E. Staelen of the city, cited the celebration of the 400th anniversary of Québec's founding (1608-2008) and the phenomenon of many Québécois working in both countries at the same time: *"Ils vinrent donc travailler en usine durant la periode froide pour rentrer l'eté à la ferme."* (They came to work in the mills during winter and return to the farm in the summer.) But because of lower attendance, will Woonsocket - veritably The City of Churches, like Mobile in my estimation, - lose that unofficial and honorific title, a testimony to its great faith for so long, alongside its Protestant, Polish, Orthodox, Middle East churches, and Jewish synagogue. Too bad faith waxes and wanes, like the whole human experience.

Mom especially esteemed our chaplain for his "Scout Law Reverence" and solicitude towards his own mother, who lived *"sur la petite* Gaulin" (on little Gaulin) behind the church. The grapevine reported her aging condition and his visits, a sign of loving tenderness with family-loving Francos. They absolutely loved that in their priests because affection and care for one's parent(s) was like a commandment of God. They too were part of that strong and vibrant community and family ethic whose absence is lamented today.

For Francos, *le presbytère* (rectory) was (still is) a vital unit in the lives of the faithful. The Holy Name Society, the Conference of St. Vincent

DePaul, and the recently formed Men of St. Joseph and the Women Growing in Faith at OLQM-Holy Trinity all provide material and spiritual help. The rectory is *L'Hotel de ville* (town hall) of their spiritual life! The priest shortage today has intensified the intrinsic residential singleness of sacerdotal parish life and service. That's why at Notre Dame in Fitchburg, for example, we often invited our parish priests for fellowship, a meal, and, yes, chess. We were 18 on our faculty, they, two at best, in parishes (except St. Joseph's run by a religious Order) with the usual 30-40 age gap. As the '59 Crusader yearbook said about ours, "Father Charles Gendreau, the school's founding chaplain, has been a continued source of spiritual guidance and inspiration to the young Crusaders" and faculty.

After 1947, I saw Father Moreau just once more. One day mom wrote, "*Yé transféré à une autre parwaist.*" (He transferred to a new parish.) The year was 1950, and after 17 years at St. Ann's he was called to Our Lady of Good Counsel in Phenix, RI. He died of cancer in 1959, less than a year after parishioners of St. Jean-Baptiste, Warren, feted him on the 25th anniversary of his ordination. Cousin Gene went to see him in his last illness and related his condition to his mom who told mine.

Despite the rapidity and severity of his last illness, he, like my wife Pat later, was willing to meet the God he served so well. Once out of what poet Tennyson calls "our bourne of Time and Place," surely, he heard, "Whatever you did to the least of my brethren, you did unto me. Enter the kingdom of heaven." When my parents moved to Hospice Saint Antoine, I found a Christmas card from him, with his neat, precise signature and title: *prêtre* (priest). A reminder of all he had done in the parish, before planting, watering, and harvesting in a different field. (Said of a harvester or *un moissonneur* in my Order, I chose the name for a newsletter I later started in the New England Province at Harrisville, with a reporter in every school.)

He would always be a legend in the history, if not the living structure, of the once vibrant but now silent parish territory! Another giant who once walked in our midst with a steady tread that was not loud, but deep. Somewhat like Manchester who quotes MacArthur in his farewell to the cadets at West Point, "My days of old have vanished, tone and tint; they have gone glimmering through the dreams of things that were. Their memory is one of wondrous beauty, watered by tears, and coaxed and caressed by the smiles of yesterday. Corps, Duty, Honor." *Père* Moreau was truly an exemplar of *Sacerdos secundum Melchisedech*, the first biblical priest called by God, whom Nincheri renders at St. Ann's. "Thank we all our God" for *Père* Moreau's comet blazing through St. Ann's cosmos when it was the faith epicenter of Social *Coin* and encircling hills.

THE WAY WE WERE

Camp Yawgoog: The Call of the Wild

A *Providence Journal* article on scouting at Yawgoog reported "city kids come out in the country to camp and fish and swim, to shoot guns and bows and arrows, to cut wood and sit around fires wide-eyed and whispering, talking about what growing boys talk about when they're alone."

We were some of those city kids - French-Canadian boys from Woonsocket - in the 1940s. Even if we weren't from large inner-city playgrounds, our curiosity for things natural and wild was no less impoverished by the narrow confines of tenement living, mill town poverty, gravel playgrounds, and the myopic effect of a lower middle-class pedestrian life. For many, opportunity didn't knock twice, not even once.

One of the oldest camps in America founded in 1916, Yawgoog was only six years younger than scouting. For untold generations of kids, it quickly became "a lush terrain of woods and water where Boy Scout traditions and ideals never die." At least 50 miles from Woonsocket, the 1,800-acre camp in Hope Valley, Hopkinton, RI, was the farthest place some of us had ever traveled. We traversed into a parallel universe! But how do you pay to go when a beginning mill worker didn't make $30 a week? Imagine the angst of families like mine to get up the $10 for the week. Our scoutmaster, Mr. Jannell, pushed us all year round to hoard pennies, run errands, save birthday money, and sell rags, newsprint, and especially copper wire to salvage places on Elbow or Privilege Streets. He and the chaplain were concerned about empty pocket scouts they couldn't leave behind.

So, because some families had more than one scout at one time, Yawgoog was near a week's pay. So, a vacation is something some parents took only once in a lifetime, like a honeymoon. Welded to the earth's iron core by the gravity of limited means, they, we, were generally immovable. My only vacation ever in 17 years was Yawgoog.

As we arrived for our week, the 800 scouts settled in one of three camps: Three Point, Sandy Beach, and "our" Medicine Bow. Mr. Jannell boasted it was tops in natural beauty, swimming facilities, and sleeping quarters. (I never saw the other two sites until much later when Jimmy and I visited one anniversary day and left unfinished scouting chapters in a 2015 capsule.) We jostled to get the bottom or upper bunk. But oh, how those late summer nights were nippy by the pond, always the second week of August, so we had something to look forward to in summer. I thought of my family's kerosene heater (*la p'tite chaufferette*), but our scoutmaster snuffed that idea out!

At day's end, we welcomed the rustic comfort of our bunks. They were slung over with canvas, stretched to the breaking point in the corners by heavier scouts. If you chatted after lights out, you braved the displeasure of Mr. Jannell who made chronic offenders run the gauntlet. It consisted of scouts straddling their legs and hitting your backside with the flat of their hands as you crawled through on your knees. Like in Irving Berlin's "You're in the Army Now," the 7 a.m. bugle was early compared to rising at home. I never got up earlier to skinny-dip. But with the clear morning water sparkling off their bodies, some early rising scouts were completing their bathing when we stirred out of our waterside bunks into the chilly and dewy morn. And like Romantic poet Browning's sight of "the lark on the wing" at daybreak, even for us Francos it was an Irish "top-of-the-mornin" feelin." But unlike home where the gang had to plan its day, the camp had it all mapped out.

Unless the mess hall crew prepared a meal for a hike to some "faraway place with a long-sounding name," we ate in a big, cavernous hall, oblivious to the din and table slovenliness of hungry youngsters. To us kids whose mothers were full-time homemakers and terrific cooks, the fare was just palatable. But we weren't the finicky eaters like some today, with little money for the canteen. A weekly nickel allowance only bought you a candied orange slice, ice cream cone, Drake's cake, or a mini pie. The choices of the poor are always slim and none.

As kids from a blue-collar city, camp gave you a chance to advance in scouting lore, because at home we had trouble finding professionals to prep us for special skills merit badges. You didn't see 14- or 15-year-olds becoming Eagle Scouts like today. We appreciated the expertise of camp counselors in archery, metalworking, swimming, and First Aid. When a veteran camper, you could fold the bottom of your scout pants. A first-year scout in another troop did and was thrown into Neptune's lap.

In the summer we swam in local swimming holes, but it was mostly shoreline bathing with no instruction or depth conducive to aquatic mastery. But for the merit badge of athletic fitness and performance in camp, like throwing a ball for distance or broad jumping, we Gaulinites did that in our backyard over the Laferriere stoop. Our throws wowed the judges, because we played ball all day at St. Ann's Park, below the hospital sandbanks, and near the Bell Spinning Mill across the Kendrick Bridge off Cumberland Street. And in winter we threw a million snowballs. I had a sore arm most of the time as a kid, but it was "the wages of sin," so parents weren't told. One time at the city dump, the gang found twelve dozen eggs (a gross), precipitating an egg war. But some broke in your hand and splattered your clothing. But for me, it escaped mom's detection on washday. Her favorite saying was *"Les enfants, il faut qu'c a grouille."* Kids had to play. Unlike today's organized sports, our play was carefree and spontaneous, but you couldn't miss family meals. (Recent studies reveal children who have at least two family meals a week do better in school than others. (Education by ingestion!)

During leisure time in camp, we wove a plastic-like gimp into a ring, bracelet, or whistle holder. My brother Bob made one and it still holds the same whistle, which became mine when he joined the Navy, and Pat at Grove Street School. We bought the material at the canteen, even if nickel candy bars were more tempting. But you couldn't eat one without your famished friends wanting a piece of your Snickers, Mounds, Babe Ruths, and Caramels. Kids then had no money to eat between meals because moms didn't have it or wanted you hungry for the family supper. Overweight kids were very rare.

The waterfront was a big part of our day, with instruction in the morning and free swimming and competition in the afternoon. We never dove in the city, but with expert instruction from lifeguards from future North Smithfield attorney and Judge Scott Keefer and others, we held our own in competition. We loved watching him and others compete against Three Point and Sandy Beach camps. A Woonsocket HS and college grad, you saw why he was a talented high school and college athlete. I was thrilled that he, Clem Labine, Herb Rowey (who noticed my sister Sue at school in the 1940s) were inducted with others in the Villa Novan Hall of Fame, including friend and gridster Tedio Ciavarini and postwar teammates. Labine graciously said yes to a photo of us. I saw him pitch in high school when he also hit the top of the leftfield fence at St. Ann's Park. When he passed on, Jim and I attended his moving memorial service at Kirkbrae in Lincoln. Bob played ball for the Red Raiders in the Vin Carney League when Labine, later a Dodgers relief ace and spot starter, pitched for the Bernon Pelicans. And Paul Pryor, later a minor leaguer and pro umpire, hurled for the North End Dodgers. Few went to college, so the city abounded in young players.

Even if raised "on the shores" of the Blackstone River, and the ponds of Cass, Sylvestre, and Harris, no one had ever boated or canoed until Yawgoog. Kayakers now skim over the clearer waters of the Blackstone, but we never saw any craft on its dark, effluvium-filled surface, the cesspool of a dying industrial age! (When Pat got her brain cancer, the oncologist shocked us when he said there's a 7 percent above-average cancer incidence in Cumberland, Woonsocket, Lincoln, and North Smithfield through which the river runs! The ten feet of pollution in the Blackstone River, he theorized, affecting our air, soil, and water in ways we don't know?) Reports also say the jet stream from the industrial Midwest brings their pollution over the state after first smearing Ontario, Québec, New Hampshire, and Maine. If so, it's frightening that New Englanders, said an article, are ten times more likely to be afflicted with respiratory diseases! And more cancer? Southerners do live two years longer, but have more obesity, diabetes, and, yes, crime. We cited Obama's efforts, nationally and internationally, to cut emissions by 30 percent in the coming years.

When you became a good swimmer and could hang on to a capsized rowboat or right an overturned canoe, staffers allowed you in the evening to shout "anchors away" and head out to alluring places like Phillips Island, The Shallows, Devil's Slide, and other ports of call. For us mill town boys who during the war breathed coal dust from factories layering dirty soot over our colorless world, it was good to be alive and breathe deeply. Like Lewis and Clark and the Corps of Discovery, we too shouted "O what joy!" like they did when they saw the mighty Pacific. In their trek of several thousand miles, they marveled at an unspoiled, untainted American wilderness. I rarely read a book twice but have gone back to the saga six times in different books. I imagine seeing what they saw. What a special relevance now living as we do in a petrochemical culture since 1870 with its pollution and the acceleration of extinction of flora and fauna a thousand times faster than ever before! Ours compares with the four great extinctions of mankind, including the Cretaceous era 66 million years ago and the extinction of dinosaurs. What a sad commentary that among all living things, we're the only creatures, said a writer, unable to conserve and live in harmony with the rest of creation, adding we've misinterpreted God's command to Adam and Eve "to fill the earth and, erroneously, subdue it." Needed is wise management, not obliteration, a concern of Pope Francis who wrote an encyclical about it. One of the worst incidents: the killing of some 50 million bison, mostly for sport, with 500 accredited to Buffalo Bill in one day! "The Lord of the Plains" sacrificed to women's hats in Europe! Others gave disease-infected robes to Indians. (By breeding bison with cattle, sportsman financier, capitalist Ted Turner has thought of marketing "beefalo." It's much healthier than beef and more resistant to disease and severe climactic conditions. Would love to see it at the market.)

Scout Commissioner Williams was quite a raconteur. One time I thought I was again hearing *Soeur* Ste. Émilie about custody of the eyes! Our 6th and 9th commandments said circumspection was key in maintaining purity of body and soul. As my *"Paradise Lost"* teacher said, "What's a man's chance against a glance?" Williams related the ordeal of a good but voyeuristic man (a Peeping Tom) who at night couldn't refrain looking through his window at his neighbor's naked form. After he unburdened himself in the confessional, a curate was not punitive but practical: "Just close your shade." But as Christ cautioned, "The spirit is willing, but the flesh is weak," so the voyeur came back with another mea culpa (my fault). "But didn't you pull turn down your shade like I told you to?" asked the curate. "I did," he said, "but she didn't turn down hers."

I don't know if Williams was Catholic, but that was one more Confession joke to remember. It was indicative of the total faith impregnation of our lives. As a result, a lot of Franco humor dealt with Confession, Communion, marriage, Mass, priests, nuns, God, heaven, St. Peter, hell, and even The Way of the Cross. Even conservative dad had two good stories about Christ's painful via dolorosa (walk to Calvary). In one, a devout Lothario or "lover boy" combed his hair before doing the Fourteen Stations. Asked why, he said he was looking to meet *les saintes femmes* (pious women) at the 8th Station; the other was about a Wrong-Way Corrigan (a true college football story) who did the stations in reverse. When told, he replied, "*J'pensa qui en prena pour le mieux*," about Christ looking better, not weaker, with each station. Always, a single guffaw from dad. Along with Red Skelton's zany facial contortions and Jack Benny's wounded dignity look, it's my best memory of his comedic face. Their lives were so hard, it was good to see adults like him laugh.

During those Yawgoog campfires and truck rides, we had a lot of sing-alongs, like "The Bear Went Over the Mountain, "A Hundred Bottles of Beer," "My Name is Yon Yonson and I Come from Wisconsin." Except for "Frère Jacques," we sang in English. Our Camp Medicine Bow song is:

> Oh! I'm a hayseed
> My hair is seaweed;
> And my ears are made of leather
> And they flop in rainy weather.
> Gosh, O hemlock!
> I'm tough as a pine knot
> For I come from Medicine Bow,
> Can't you see? Hey! Hey!....

Our youthful energies spent, we sat entranced besides a dying fire. Repairing to our own campsite, Mr. Jannell called for "Taps" from the bugler and his dented instrument: "Day is done, gone the sun, / From the lake, from the hills, from the sky, / All is well, safely rest, / God is nigh." (I've read several versions of its Civil War origin, with Rachel telling me about an authoring Union father for his deceased Confederate soldier-son.) Then with only the crickets and the frogs breaking the quiet evening spell, he gave us our scorecard for the day: a measure of praise and recommendations. He told us what the new day would bring, write home, and say our prayers. It was still a time when kids in Catholic schools and homes too were reminded to pray every night and make it a lifelong habit: three Hail Marys, an Act of Contrition, and prayer to your Guardian Angel to keep watch over you. In

French of course. Like its canticles, French prayers have a warmth that nourishes your soul.

At home, if Bob, Ben, and I made noise in the boy's bedroom (*la chambre à coucher des garçons*), she piped, "*Faisez vos prières du swère (soir) et couchez-vous*" (Say your evening prayers and go to bed). Franco moms who bookended our lives from morning till night kept those practices alive. Our scoutmaster also suggested we thank God for another great day and ask blessings for our folks sweltering in their uninsulated apartments. He knew there were no air conditioners for French Canadians, said mom.

It may be mundane but a beer commercial sums up those days: "Guys, it just doesn't get any better than this." Our families were somewhat poor and generally not well educated, but solid and strong in their core values, giving the church and nation citizens of character, moral and religious stature, great work ethic, love of family, and service to country in peace and war. All bedrock values of immigrant practices not destined to wither and die completely for 100 years from internal weaknesses or the nation's growing moral bankruptcy in the 1960s and on.

But to be fair, even if I'm not blind to the larcenous and murderous propensities of our present gun and drug culture, to the world community we're still a nation of values, the legacy of those families of yesteryear and many of today's. Their gift to today's American family is showing signs of rejuvenation amid the myriad kinds of family structures that now abound. Christ spoke about bringing out good things from the old (*vetera*) and the new (*nova*), so hopefully both will cause "the desert to bloom again, valleys filled, and crooked paths made straight," as the Advent liturgy says.

A couple of incidents stand out about Yawgoog. As a Catholic troop, we never failed to attend a holy day Mass, August 15, the Assumption of Mary into Heaven. But why did Father Delaney ask a troop's skit players to show up for Confession before Mass the next day? The night before, they entertained the whole camp with a hilarious marriage ceremony. A "fourteen-carrot" ring didn't upset him too much, but when the faux-chaplain asked the audience if anyone objected to the union, well, out came a wild-eyed screaming wife with a couple of kids about this bigamous marital mélange. We all roared. But it struck him as disrespectful, if not sacrilegious. Living as we do now in an age when absolutely nothing, sacred or not, and no one, president, prelate, pedestrian, institution, is beyond derision or buffoonery, it's like a time capsule of the way manners were then in society. When reverence prevailed, and no Rodney Dangerfield needed lament, "I get no respect." Respect, which the late George Nasuti, A.D., and principal in the city's school system, so highly esteemed and promoted in young students, athletes or not. Like the Golden Rule: give it to get it.

In my chronicle of Woonsocket at war, recall at war's end I jubilantly stroked an oar on Yawgoog Pond and soaked Phil Carpentier. The news was highlighted by the tallest bonfire in my young life. The ones I'd seen at Cass Park on the feast of Saint John the Baptist, June 24, couldn't compare. We were missing the jubilation in Social *Coin* (mom saved the paper for me) but rejoiced with scouts whose lives were possibly spared. As it was, a lot of fuzzy-cheeked soldiers did the fighting and dying in 1944-45 since many older warriors had already given "the last full measure of devotion" or were now unfit with "their million-dollar wounds." Units were so bloodied, most had turnover figures way over 100 percent, like the 83rd Division of cousin Raymond Péloquin, brother-in-law Eugène Godin, and friend Normand Malo.

Since I was now a veteran camper, Mr. Jannell nominated me and two others for the Knights of Yawgoog and the secretive Order of Winchek. The latter meant, I was told, an all-night initiation, eating night crawlers, drinking unsavory liquids, and staying in the woods at night. I hesitated at first, but the reality was much less threatening. Nothing made us prouder than to get a bold handshake from him, see that gold-capped pearly grin, and being warmed by his praises.

He often told us a troop was as good as its leaders. He was a great leader because he talked the talk and walked the walk. The relationship between a troop's worth and its leaders was no different to me when mom spoke how a good pastor begot good parishioners: *"Un bon curé, une bonne parwaist (oisse)."* Another of her pearls of wisdom about the interrelationships of all players in our lives, secular or divine.

I said constipation for dad was a concern. A good healthy organism had a good elimination system. He took a purgative "Serutan," ("Natures" in reverse, the ad said), and kept our icebox stocked with facilitators, like prune juice, dried prunes, figs, and dates. And to avoid colds at breakfast we also hand squeezed oranges from a glass juicer with fluted sides coming to a point. The fruits were from Gardella's in the city for mom's touted *vitamine Cée*.

Well, unknowingly sharing dad's concern for regularity with us 52 campers, Mr. Jannell expanded what little English we all knew at 12 or 13. At day's end at Yawgoog, he lined us up and asked if we had a bowel movement since arriving. No one said a word. Puzzled at the silence, I stepped forward and said I played volleyball that day! He smiled broadly, like the time in my Tenderfoot test he caught me saying French was our mother tongue. With mock seriousness, he told us a bowel movement was not a sport. But no one teased me about it. No one knew the word either. Weren't we a French troop? At home my folks used the expression: *Aller à la selle* or *faire caca* (Have a bowel movement or poo). We children used number 1 or 2 for what and how long we'd be "occupied." As big as our tenement was, we were seven using a postage stamp-sized bathroom. But at least we had a bathtub! So, I picked up another English word, but didn't tell them, because all maladies, labels, functions, and the like would always be in French. But I'm so glad I had the chance to learn two languages in monolinguistic America! For all immigrant families, there's so much history and life, sometimes heroic, tragic, humorous, embedded in the language. Some have even equated language as the very culture itself. And for us Francos, a necessary adjunct to the faith.

When friends Paul Ducharme, Vincent Auclair, and I were hiking once at Yawgoog, we found a huge boulder or glacial erratic at a precipitous edge overlooking a fall of 75 feet or more. Like Ice Age wanderers, we desperately wanted to hear it crash on the forest floor below and planned to topple it our next camping trip. Like escapees, we hid chisels and crowbars in our bedrolls from Mr. Jannell's circumspection. Back at the site, we chiseled, pried, and pushed against the huge mass, and moved it a mite. But it settled again, stoically retaining its magnificent perch over the yawning chasm. We abandoned the project. (Didn't some boys in RI get in trouble in 2013 for dislodging a boulder with geologic significance?)

With his rather short, somewhat rotund frame, Mr. Jannell never hiked with us. Older scouts did that. Unlike our dads, his life's work was on four wheels or at a desk. Education, business, and capital all moved you up on the locomotion tree. But thanks to his trucking business, I think we picked up more scrap metal and newsprint for the war effort than other troops. Safety aside, what joy riding atop a loaded truck! Like many parents working on war materiel, we too were part of the war effort. Unlike Vietnam or Korea, the war united young and old, and, for one, made me an investor.

I wonder if like the fantasies of youth, I could find that boulder again! Or did other scouts find it and succeed? I marvel in our youth we tried to move what geologic forces left behind when the last Ice Age receded 10,000 years ago! Shelley wrote about youthful fantasies in his "Ode to the West Wind": "I were as in my boyhood, and could be / The comrade of thy (wind) wanderings over heaven, / As then, when to outstrip thy skiey speed / Scarce seemed a vision." Do children still try to outrun a moving cloud, as Lucien Laferriere and I did when coming home from school? Like Wordsworth, Saint Francis also considered nature a great teacher. There should be "a Yawgoog" in every childhood.

Mom worshipped "*le grand* (fresh) air." So, when we were infants, she bundled us up in winter and put us on the porch of our Cass-Mailloux apartment, deflecting remarks from "cribbed, confined, and cabined"[53]

---

[53] Another quote from the Bard - Shakespeare.

neighbors about the threat of sickness. Hard to believe she once knew nothing about raising kids but from experience, readings, and advice, she became, with dad's help, one of those thousand immigrant-moms who raised healthy families on a wing and a prayer.

Troop 4 presented me a scroll and gifts at a surprise farewell party, March 11, 1947, when I left for the Brotherhood. The pen and missal, symbols of *Père* Moreau's Troop 4 mission about school and church, are long gone. But was I the last ever to receive a missal as a going-away gift? Did my fellow scouts know in the Order, I'd go to Mass every morning (six times one Christmas Eve and Day in Mobile)? But I cherish the scroll with its scripted message that I was a brother to them. And even if on a solitary career trail, I remained with them in spirit, never forgetting we marched together "in the pleasure of the pathless woods," one of my favorite Romantic lines of poetry.

Not emotionally affected, I was excited to join the Order of my Mount teachers and study with cousin Frank. No less than three Brothers, including recruiter Brother Paul Metilly, came to my home one Sunday afternoon to bring me to Sacred Heart Juniorate (high school) in Sharon. Accustomed to leaving home for scouting trips, I was eager to become a boarder, enjoy academic plusses (library and resident staffers), baseball fields, ping pong, tennis, and swimming at Lake Massapoag. Since dad always bought apples by the bushel, I also enjoyed Frenchman *Frère* Jean's apples from his 110-tree orchard whose fruits became pies like mom's. Imagine, we were six at a table in the refectory, and one time Brother Gregory Bouley used a protractor to make sure each one had an equal cut! Like dad, *Frére* Jean was also a winemaker, who, like later murder victim *Frère* Albert, left France at the turn of the century when anti clericalists seized power and schools.

I got homesick a year later, suddenly missing all the things of my boyhood: like a case of Thomas Wolfe's "You can't go home again?" Some recruits went through that the first or second week. But I wasn't 14 or 15 like most, but 17. Was I going to be like that young man in the Gospel who Christ asked to follow Him, but he backed off to bury his father or take care of business? I stayed, but it would've been easier if I had known St. Augustine's thought about the young man probably not making it to heaven because he rejected a clear call from Christ. But no, too harsh a judgment, say writers. Why, the saint even thought unbaptized children went to hell! Ordinarily Baptism only comes in one of three ways - water (sprinkling or immersion), martyrdom, and desire, but now some tout God's mercy for those dying before any baptism. Abortion victims?

The call to the priesthood also hit me later in training, but novice master Brother George-Aimé convinced me to stay the course. A thought in

Latin in the Order was "fearing to miss the grace that passes me by." Like that young man did! For me it was a call to the Brotherhood. How I would've missed the commitment, friendship, learning, holiness of many hundreds of men dedicated to Christ's own teaching mission on earth!

Wisely, Director *Frère* Floribert allowed me to visit home, and since everything I had left behind was still there, I was immediately okay. Like a military on leave, I was warmed by the admiration of family and friends. I thanked the good Lord for the unbelievable impact the decision had on my faith, education, and career. Not only for those 25 years, but also in my second vocation as a Catholic layman-counselor. Fortunately, counselor-dad had advised me to give the Brotherhood a try. He cited the chance at an advanced education denied him, schooling with kids from all over New England, Canada, South America, and enlarging my faith.

The latter especially happened in the novitiate, a year-long study of religious life, the three vows of poverty, chastity, and obedience, the four Gospels, and the three levels to a greater love of God that all saints go through: purgative (penitential, like I think most of us), contemplative, unitive. I later taught the 1954-55 class, which celebrated its 60th anniversary in 2015. I thought every Christian should have the same opportunity in whatever station he or she was in. Religion requires such a profound grasp of eternal verities, even if Christ reduced its practice to love of God and neighbor. Theologians are aghast at the little knowledge of many Catholics today. We said the severe diminution of the nation's Catholic school system is one reason. Locally, while not absolving them for their defiance, the Sentinellists knew too well the disappearance of their parish-based schools and eventually their national churches would jeopardize not only their language and customs but for many, their faith. Even if Americanization was inevitable and desirable, one can still pine for the rich patrimony that was once theirs from their ancestors in Québec and France, but now only a shadow of its pristine glory. The high and low tides of the faith.

But my family was in last analysis the bedrock or wellspring of the faith and wellbeing of my siblings and me. "No river rises above its source." In my 42-year teaching and counseling career, my wish was every child should experience the kind of loving, nurturing family support that was for most the earmark of all those French-Canadian immigrant families who came to live, work, and worship at "America's templed hills."

Finis Coronat Opus: The End Crowns the Work

DID THE STORY get away from him? A financially strapped novelist of the 18th Century, Sam Johnson wrote a book to pay for his mother's funeral, admitting his conclusion didn't conclude anything. Perhaps the first lexicographer or dictionary writer of the language (and a witty one too), he was once approached by a lil' old mum who praised him because she hadn't found any dirty words in it. Bemusedly he said, "Why, madam, were you looking for them?" His famous biographer Boswell said his corpulent and bibulous idol - known for his blotched, bloated face - was often between a rock and a hard place: "He could abstain, but not moderate." (Isn't it a question everyone in our bibulous society must ask oneself? The slaughter of young people on our highways for one thing. At a Christmas Eve party one year in Sweden, a young man told me Stockholm adopted a radical solution to solve the problem. Anywhere you went, you could not drink if you drove. If you did, you got "court" and a jail sentence. What about drugs now?)

And so, it is with these *mémoires* (memories) of the way we were when Greater Woonsocket was *le petit Canada ou le Canada en bas* (the little Canada or the lower Canada). No conclusion or end is at hand because recollections, either oral or written, are a kind of enduring heritage binding the past to an ever-unfolding present. About that linkage, poet Tennyson said it best in "Ulysses": "I am a part of all that I have met. Yet all experience is an arch wherethrough / Gleams that untraveled world, whose margin fades / For ever and for ever when I move." In Blood, Tears & Folly about WWII, Leigh Deighton cites poet T. S. Eliot about the mysterious circle of life: "And the end of all our exploring / Will be to arrive where we started / And know the place for the first time."

If our precious dead gain a measure of immortality by being remembered in the hearts of loved ones, so also do *mémoires* of the past achieve a life of their own, as they also ruminate in people's minds and hearts. And more so when eventually some of these oral histories become part of a people's written history. If ever we're tempted to think of those times as no more, recall as we did in the beginning of our chronicle that 'Gone' like in the novel doesn't mean forgotten. In fact, Nancy Wartik in *The French Canadians* noted, "That reverence for their past has been a potent force in the phenomenon of French-Canadian survival." For example, the Museum of Work & Culture joins hands yearly with devotees of "*la francophonie*," a celebration of the diversity and vitality of the French-speaking world, especially for us in New England and Québec, forever strengthening an unbreakable link.

That's why words like culture, tradition, heritage, ancestry, *et les bons vieux temps* (and the good old days) remind us they're not only precious vessels of the past, but also "seeded evidence" giving birth to new ways and new forms of life, as our dedication poem says. Maybe like those "thousand points of light," the elder President Bush spoke about.

As highlighted in its 1988 Centennial Year, Woonsocket remains a rich treasure trove for French Canadians and other nationalities of their forebears' "seeded evidence," now deeply rooted in the fertile soil of their first American experience. Jubilantly, the city marked its 125th Anniversary in 2013 from Market Square to Monument Square, under the mayoralty of Leo Fontaine.

Even if a third-generation French Canadian, for example, hears less and less *le patois* (the dialect) of the city's immigrants from Canada, and notes the passing of their folksy ways, still so many threads of their lives remain in the rich weave of the city's ethnic tapestry. As is the focus of our book, a lot of the city's history and character was profoundly shaped by the language, culture, and religious values of French Canadians, as by others too. As a result, their impact will linger longer than many epochal events in the annals of the city, state, New England mill towns, and even the nation. In *An American Story*, for example, cousin J. Robert Brunelle wrote about the travails and triumphs of his NY family after leaving Woonsocket in the 1930s, one of many families who eventually settled first out of Canada and then out of New England.

Is there a special historical line on Francos? An authority on how geography affects history, English historian John Keegan in Fields of Battle says, "The Canadian was an Americanized Frenchman, a man assertively independent." When those approximately two million plus "independents" came to America, from 1840 to 1929 they brought that subdued but steely assertiveness with them. While steadily maintaining pride in their heritage, they finally convinced doubters they were All American, fought in its wars, and contributed mightily to its rise as the world's greatest industrial nation. Doesn't the common man often harbor the seeds of greatness, as said of the Greatest Generation of WWII, touted as the best ever?

In the city and especially across the land, even if Americanized more and more in pronunciation and sometimes in spelling, the names of remembered heroes, streets and churches, place names, buildings and monuments, schools and parks, still bear witness to their French-Canadian origin and traditions. Recall my earlier discussion that Bunker Hill and Paul Revere were names of French origin. So no less than 3000 place names in our country bear witness to the discoveries and explorations south of Canada by French Canadians. Champlain, who crossed the Atlantic 27 times, was the first known European to see Cape Cod, New York, and Canada. Fellow navigator Jacques Cartier sought passage to the East and is also prominent in the discovery of Canada.

Wartik also writes French Canadians are "A people whose loyalty to mother tongue, ethnic roots, and religious faith has hardly been matched by any other European minority living in North America." Great tribute. But since other ethnic groups have also left their mark, no single epic story from one racial stock or people can be written about America. As E Pluribus Unum makes clear, our history is from "many, one," In our home, mom spoke of *"Toute la gang"* (The whole gang), with local and national implications. I am proud she was the first woman I knew who knew the history of her people.

It bears repeating that far more precious, if intangible, French-Canadian cultural traditions of the golden past remain in evidence here and elsewhere where *les habitants* settled. These are love of family and children, respect for the elderly and all authority, great moral fiber, deep filial piety, joie de vivre, fierce attachment to country and Mother Church, patriotism in answering the country's call to service, and now a nostalgic remembrance through research of the country and people of Québec especially.

And no less unforgettable is their work ethic that helped make this country, especially the Northeast, an industrial giant in the manufacturing field through the initiative and wisdom of mayor, governor, and twice envoy to France, Aram Pothier. Also, their love of sport and competition epitomized in the heroics of Nap Lajoie and Gabby Hartnett, both enshrined in the Baseball Hall of Fame. And reliever extraordinaire, Clem Labine. And no less unforgettable, despite the travails of their recent past, was their tenacity to survive and even prosper. The word survivance was well coined on the anvil of endurance and tenacity with our mom boasting: *"On a passer à travers,"* about going through the crucible of suffering or the Temple of Doom in cinematic language.

It was so fitting when Woonsocket celebrated its centennial as a city and highlighted one historical tale from so many different immigration chapters, either political or ethnical. By association, it recalled the chapter of the first Americans of English stock who first harnessed the power of the Blackstone River, especially its textile-producing potential; Roger Williams, first to fight for religious freedom apart from the body politic in Rhode Island; the Canadians who came to live and work in the mills and brought their language, religion, and culture to a degree unsurpassed by others.

And the chapter of the Italians who passed through the golden door at the turn of the century, gracing a corner of the city and bringing their strong faith, political and culinary talents, and stone artisan skills too. And nationally, no less than 38 soldiers of Italian descent won the Medal of Honor in WWII. And the early Irish who first worked in the mills, dug the canal to Worcester, and laid tracks, while also erecting St. Charles Church and the stately homes of the North End. And gave us Edwin O'Connor's *The Last Hurrah* and *The Edge of Sadness*. And the indefatigable entrepreneurial drive of rubber titan Joseph Banigan whose benefactions to education and religious institutions providing care were outstanding; Eileen Farrell, Met opera star; Dave McKenna, jazz artist and pianist. And other ethnic greats mentioned in the book, like Jewish Israel Goldstein, a paper supplier who with his four sons started the mega-pharmaceutical giant CVS, and our Jewish brethren who brought their biblical and monotheistic faith to the city's synagogue, our first "brothers in the faith," as the Bible says, *fides ex Judeis*.

And the chapter of the Afro-Americans who came from the South to find work "up Nawth" after WWII and sired large families and demonstrated their work ethic, faith, musical talent, and athleticism; the chapter of the dispossessed Southeastern Asians who sought refuge here from decade-long conflicts of the 1960s; the coming too of the Poles, also the Scotch-Irish, Scandinavians, Germans, Austrians, Ukrainians, and others, in small or large numbers, at different times; and finally the chapter from countless other shores of the globe, with people of Mexican, Cape Verdean, Hispanic or Portuguese heritage in the main. When Mayor George H. Grant in his inaugural in 1888 traced the city's formation from different surrounding districts, could he have foreseen that its populace in the next century would arrive more from "cosmopolitan districts" in the truest sense of the term?

In conclusion, I again caution the reader not to think this chronicle has been solely the story of *les* Telliers, Fontaines, Morvans, Trottiers, Bouffards, Clarks, Peloquins, Brunelles, Lebels, Hantis, Villeneuves, Villemures, Houles, Carpentiers, Beauregards, Turcottes, Bérubés, Lanoies, or other families mentioned. Or of the author, alternately a participant or interested observer, recorder, and commentator of what can only be an infinitesimal part of the vast Canada-to-America saga. If only my mother could have written it. An old television show about New York City reminded viewers that its weekly story was just one of eight million. If 1,800,000 Francos did come to America, we may never know the whole story, unless the story of every voice is preserved. And especially, as was my intent, to let us know what the immigration and acculturation experience was like in the deep recesses of their hearts and minds. American novelist Willa Cather said that all you needed for a great story were four walls and one emotion. But I suspect their one emotion, if so, had many facets, but perhaps the greatest was Rhode Island's motto HOPE. Love is the only virtue that lasts forever, Christ said, but hope, buttressed by an unshakable faith, brought them to it. One wrote, "Of all the forces that make for a better world, none is so powerful as hope. With hope, one can think, one can work, one can dream. If you have hope, you have everything." Like all immigrants, Francos had it.

Every day we learn families like mine were lucky to have an oral historian in their midst who, like Christ's mother, "kept all these things in her heart." True most historians have been men, but don't women harbor special remembrances because they're about loved ones in good and bad times? No one needs to tell them, "Get it together." Their story, especially about French Canadians in the case of this book, was never lost, because their center always held and they never gave up on America, even if *"le pays de mes amours"* (affectionately their birthplace, mom said) always stirred fond memories and at times allurements to return.

In our immigration trek involving three countries (France, Canada, America), one should not be surprised their story was embroiled in the sweep of world history, its great men and women, ordinary people, tragic and comedic literature, war and peace, tensions of labor and capital, travail in the industrialization of America, the crucible of religion and the faith, the Depression, and finally acculturation and pursuit of higher education after the war. All stuff of high drama, often masked sometimes by ordinariness and at other times by violent economic disruption and world conflict.

As is true of every person in every nation on earth, the life of the French Canadian was and still is a microcosm of Everyman and Everywoman, reflecting by and large Shakespeare's seven stages of life in one of his plays, no matter the geography or time. Perish the thought that their lives were menial or insignificant. In ways we may never know, theirs is the truism in the Bible that the meek do inherit the earth, while the mighty, proud, and criminal are often ground to dust, like Hitler, Göring, Himmler, Goebbels, Stalin, Mussolini, Hirohito. For French Canadians, theirs was never the claim of a so-called master race, but just good, decent people "just trying to make it." Like that beautiful essay on Christ as a man, son of a carpenter, who never led armies, never conquered nations, never wrote books, or built pyramids, yet has exerted the greatest impact ever on all of history, as expressed by Bill O'Reilly and Martin Dugard in *Killing Jesus*. Far less grandiose of course, but in their own little sphere, earlier and later Francos may have left an impression more for what they were, than perhaps what they did, evoking poet Thomas Gray's "the short and simple annals of the poor," which we said was Lincoln's favorite line.

Even if you changed their names and the stories of those I've written about, this anthem - *The Way We Were: Growing up French-Canadian in Woonsocket, RI, Le Canada en Bas* - would still reverberate with the same melody. But because of their remarkable unity and conformity of thought, faith, and language, their cast of characters may often seem like carbon copies, with only the *mise en scène* - the staging or locus of their lives - differing in small ways depending on time and locale, as is true of the human species. But if one makes the mistake of stereotyping French Canadians of old as all from the same mold in a negative sense - poor, educationally deprived, submissive, unambitious, as their critics alleged in Canada and here - I prefer to take Lincoln's spin about the poor people of his day: "God must love them, He made so many of them." Their wealth was more in the Gospel's Pearl of Great Price: their faith and their goodness.

In summation, I repeat the words of King Baudouin 1 of Belgium: "America has been called a melting pot, but it seems better to call it a mosaic, for in it each nation, people or race which has come to its shores has been privileged to keep its individuality, contributing at the same time its share to the unified pattern of a new nation." He sounded the right note, "*le mot juste*," as French writer Flaubert said. Or as our mom often added when something was just right: "***la bonne note***," as we fittingly allow her the last word among the many "pearls of wisdom" she uttered during the saga of her *séjour* (stay) or time with her loved ones and compatriots in Canada and the United States.

For updated information regarding the ancestry of the Tellier and Fontaine families, the reader is directed to p. 666. – *ed.*

The Way We Were...

Author Rene Tellier (left) and his cousin François Fontaine in the 1930s. Both entered the Brothers of the Sacred Heart and taught at Mount Saint Charles.

And Many Years Later...

Friends and ex-Brothers of the Sacred Heart, from left, Patrick Beaulieu, Marcel Tardif, and Rene Tellier. All retired from teaching in 1995 after 123 years of collective service in RI and MA schools including England for Patrick.

GLOSSARY

Common French words used frequently throughout the text and not always translated.

coin – corner. e.g. – Social *coin,* or in patois: *Coin Sochelle.*
et – and
femmes de maison - housewives
Frère – a Brother, monk, of friar who is a member of a religious order.
frère – brother, male sibling
le-la-les – All are forms of "the."
les - them
ma, mon, mes – All are forms of "my."
mémère - grandma
mère – mother or mom
oncle - uncle
patois – a dialect of the common people that differs from the standard language. French-Canadian patois borrows heavily from English.
pepère - grandpa
Père - a Catholic priest. Commonly addressed as: "*Père* (name)"
père – father or dad
Québécois – people of Quebec
Sœur – a nun of Sister who is a member of a religious order.
sœur – sister, female sibling
soutane – see "Religious Terms"
survivance - survival
tante - aunt
un, une – Both are forms of "a"

Religious Terms

cassock – a full length, single-colored garment worn by many male Christian clergy.
soutane – French for cassock.
He – When capitalized, the author is referring to God
"Nones" – people not affiliated with any religion.
salvific – leading to or bringing salvation

Note: When the author capitalizes Brother(s)/*Frère*, Sister(s)/*Sœur* or Father/*Père*, he is referring to someone who belongs to a religious order. Only when not capitalized is he referring to a blood relative.

Education terms

HS – high school
MSC, Mount, the Academy – Common names for Mount Saint Charles Academy in Woonsocket, RI.
SPED – special education.
"spedded" – to place a student in special education.
Prof – short for professor
the Bard – refers to William Shakespeare

Brothers and Priests

The "Brother" in the Catholic Church is a man who is vowed to poverty, celibacy, and obedience like any priest who is a member of a religious congregation. All are involved in various ministries in fulfillment of the vowed commitment.

All priests are ordained by the Sacrament of Holy Orders to administer the Sacraments of the Catholic Church. The priest is called to this important ministry and fulfills it in a variety of ways and places.

Brothers do not feel called to receive the Sacrament of Holy Orders and therefore do not administer the Sacraments of the Catholic Church. The brother is called to minister in other ways, including educational ministries and missionary work.

In recent years some Brothers have been ordained to administer the Sacraments of the Catholic Church but remain Brothers.

Brothers of the Sacred Heart (Frères du Sacré-Cœur)

A Brother of the Sacred Heart is an ordained man in the Catholic church. The Brothers of the Sacred Heart were founded in 1821 by a priest by the name of Andre Coindre in Lyon, France. The first Superior General, Brother Polycarp, saw a new field of ministry in the new world and sent Brothers to Mobile, Alabama in 1847 and then populated other southern towns, moving north to Canada and New England. The Brothers built and continue to manage and teach in schools located in the United States and other countries.

BIBLIOGRAPHY

EDITORS' NOTE: This bibliography was compiled after the passing of the author. Thus, it was not possible to confirm exact sources of many of the works he cited. Because of this, it was decided to cite the original publication date and publisher of each source if they were available.

- Agus, D. B. (2012). *The End of Illness.* Free Press.
- Allen Jr., J. L., (2005, Fall). "Discovering America." *Boston College Magazine.*
- Ambrose, S. (2000). *Nothing Like It in the World: The Men Who Built the Transcontinental Railroad 1863-1869.* Simon and Schuster
- Anderson, E. (2000). *Miracles at Sea: The Sinking of the Zamzam and Our Family's Astounding Rescue.* Quiet Waters.
- Aquinas, T. (1485). Summa Theologica.
- Aubin, A. K. (1988). *The French in Rhode Island: A History.* (Rhode Island Ethnic Heritage Pamphlet Series) pub. The R.I. Heritage Commission & The R.I. Publications Society.
- Bacon, F. (1612). "Of Marriage and Single Life."
- Bacon, F. (1625). "Of Studies."
- Bacon L. (1944). *The Fighting Sullivans* [Film]. S. Jaffe & R. Kane.
- Barry, J. M. (2004). *The Great Influenza: The Story of the Deadliest Pandemic in History.* Penguin.
- Barry, J. M. (2012). *Roger Williams and the Creation of the American Soul.* Viking Adult.
- Bekker, C. (1966). *The Luftwaffe War Diaries: The German Air Force in World War II.*
- Benedict XVI, Pope (2007). "Charity in Truth." (*Caritas in Veritate* – lat.)
- Beyer, R. (2013). *Ghost Army.* [Film]. Rick Beyer, PBS.
- Bishop, C. (2011). *The Lion and the Journalist: The Unlikely Friendship of Theodore Roosevelt and Joseph Bucklin Bishop.* Lyons Press.
- Bishop, M. (1979). *Champlain: The Life of Fortitude.* Octagon Press.
- Bishop, M. (2001). *The Middle Ages.* Mariner Books.
- Bonier, M. L. (1997). *The Beginnings of the Franco-American Colony in Woonsocket RI.* (Claire Quintal Editor/Trans.). Institut Francais Assumption College.
- Bourget, P. A. et al. (1990). *Towers of Faith and Family: St. Ann's Church, Woonsocket, RI – 1890 – 1990.* St. Ann's Church Corp.
- Bracq, J. C. (1924). *The Evolution of French Canada.* Macmillan.
- Bradley, J. (2000). *Flags of Our Fathers.* Bantam.
- Bradley, O. N. (1951). *A Soldier's Story.* Holt.
- Brault, G. (1986). *The French-Canadian Heritage in New England.* McGill-Queens University Press.
- Brokaw, T. (1998). *The Greatest Generation.* Random House.
- Brooke, R. (1914). "The Soldier"
- Browning, R. (1841). "Pippa Passes" (aka "Pippa's Song")
- Browning, R. (1855). "Andrea del Sarto"
- Browning, R. (1864). "Rabbi Ben Ezra."
- Buck, P. S. (1931). *The Good Earth.*
- Bunyan, J. (1678). *The Pilgrim's Progress from This World, to That Which is to Come.*
- Burns, K. (1990). *The Civil War* [Film documentary]. K. L. Burns (Florentine.)

- Burns, K. (1994). *Baseball*. [9-part documentary film series]. National Endowment for the Humanities.
- Burns, R. (1786). *The Cotter's Saturday Night*.
- Butler, A. (1995). *The Lives of the Saints*. Tan Books, reprint ed.
- Capra, F. (1947). *It's a Wonderful Life* [Film]. Liberty Films.
- Cather, W. (1913). *O Pioneers!* Vintage.•
- Cather, W. (1915). *The Song of the Lark*. Mariner Books.
- Cather, W. (1918). *My Ántonia*. Houghton Mifflan.
- Cather, W. (1923). *A Lost Lady*. Alfred K. Knopf.
- Cather, W. (1927). *Death Comes for the Archbishop*. Alfred K. Knopf.
- Cather, W. (1935). *Lucy Gayheart*. Alfred K. Knopf.
- Chang, I. (1991). *The Rape of Nanking*. Basic Books.
- Chant, C. (1996). *Warfare and The Third Reich*. Smithmark Pub.
- Chaucer, G. (ca. 1381-83) "Parliament of Fowls" (original title: "Parlement of Foules")
- Chaucer, G. (1387-1400). *The Canterbury Tales*.
- Chartier, A. (1999). *The Franco-Americans of New England: A History*. Institut français of Assumption College.
- Cooper, Jr., J. M. (2009). *Woodrow Wilson: A Biography*. Vintage.
- Crane, S. (1895). *The Red Badge of Courage*.
- Cronin, V. (1975). *Louis and Antoinette*. Morrow.
- Dante (1430). "Divine Comedy."
- de Marchi, J. (2009). *The True Story of Fatima: A Complete Account of the Fatima Apparitions*. Self-published.
- DeBrosse, J. & Burke, C. (2004). *The Secret in Building 26: The Untold Story of America's Ultra War Against the U-Boat Enigma Codes*. Random House.
- Demers, N. (1995). *Revolution in Quebec: A Past Rejected, A Future in Doubt*.
- Desbiens, J.P. (1962). *Les insolences du Frère Untel* (The Impertinences of Brother Anonymous). Harvest House.
- Diamond, J. (1997). *Guns, Germs, and Steel: The Fates of Human Societies*. W. W. Norton & Co.
- Dickens, C. (1843). *A Christmas Carol*.
- Doenitz, K. (1958). *Memoirs: Ten Years and Twenty Days*.
- Donne, J. (1624). *Devotions Upon Emergent Occasions, Meditation XVII*.
- Donne, J. (1633) "Death, Be Not Proud." Sonnet 10 in *Holy Sonnets*.
- Dryden, J. (1681). *Absalom and Achitophel*, pt. 1, l. 163.
- Dufford, R. (1975) "Be Not Afraid." Robert J. Dufford, SJ, & OCP Publications
- Dunwell, S. "The French-Canadians in New England." [quotes William MacDonald, from a l898 ed. of the "Quarterly Journal of Economics"]
- Dunwell, S. (1978). *The Run of the Mill*. David R. Godine.
- Eden, A. (1976). *Another World 1897-1917*.
- Edwards, J. (1741). "Sinners in the Hands of an Angry God" [Sermon].
- Elder, G. (1998). *Children of the Great Depression*. Routledge.
- Elliott, R. (2015). *Clem Labine Always a Dodger*. Page Publishing.
- Emerson, R. W. (1841). *Essays: First Series* – "II. Self-Reliance."
- Ethier, B. (2013). *A History of Mount Saint Charles Hockey*. The History Press.
- Fénéon, F. (2009). *Novels in Three Lines*. [translated with intro. by Lucy Sante] NYRB Classics.

- Fleming, V. (1939) *Gone with the Wind* [Film]. Selznick International Pictures & MGM.
- Ford, J. (1941). *How Green Was My Valley* [Film]. D. F. Zanuck.
- Fournier, C. (1989). *Les Tisserands du Pouvoir*. Table Ronde.
- Frank, W. & Rogge, B. (1956). *The German Raider Atlantis*. Ballantine Books.
- Franklin, B. (1743). *Poor Richard's Almanac.*
- Frieda, L. (2006). *Catherine de Medici: Renaissance Queen of France*. Harper Perennial.
- Frost, R. (1914). "The Death of the Hired Man."
- Frost, R. (1916). "The Road Not Taken."
- Fulghum, R. (1989). *All I Really Need to Know I Learned in Kindergarten*. Ivy Books.
- Furstenberg, F. (2015). *When the United States Spoke French: Five Refugees Who Shaped a Nation*. Penguin Books.
- Gannon, M. (1990). *Operation Drumbeat*. Harper Perennial.
- Gerard, J. (2012). *The Autobiography of a Hunted Priest,* Ignatius Press.
- Gerstle, G. *Interpreting Woonsocket History (1875-1955): Working in the Blackstone River Valley: Exploring the Heritage of Industrialization.*
- Gillooly, J. (2005). *Pride on the Mount …More Than A Game*. Lyons Press.
- Goldsmith, O. (1770). *"The Deserted Village."*
- Gray, T. (1751). "Elegy Written in a Country Churchyard."
- Grondin, M. (2018). *The Art and Passion of Guido Nincheri*. Véhicule Press.
- Guderian, Heinz (2014) *Blitzkreig in Their Own Words: First Hand Accounts from German Soldiers 1939-1940*. Amber Books.
- Gurney, D. F. (1913). "God's Garden"
- Halberstam, D. (2007). *The Coldest Winter: America and the Korean War*. Hachette Books.
- Hammerstein II, O. (1927). *Showboat*. [Song lyrics from: "Ol' Man River"]
- Hawthorne, N. (1850). *The Scarlet Letter.*
- Hayman, R. W. (2000). *The Diocese of Providence, Rhode Island, A Short History*. Editions du Signe.
- Henry, O. (1907). "The Last Leaf" published in *The Trimmed Lamp and Other Stories*.
- Henry, O. (1907). "The Ransom of the Red Chief."
- Hersey, J. (1946). *Hiroshima*. Knoph.
- Hochschild, A. R. (1997). *The Time Bind: When Work Becomes Home and Home Becomes Work*. Metropolitan Books.
- Horace. (19 BC). "Ars Poetica"
- Housman, A. (1896). *"To an Athlete Dying Young.*
- Howell, R. (1977). *Cromwell*. Hutchinson.
- Hugo, V. (1862). *Les Misérables.*
- Ivory, J. (1995). *Jefferson in Paris* [Film]. Touchstone, Merchant Ivory.
- Johnson, P. (1976). *A History of Christianity*. Touchstone.
- Johnson, P. (2002). *The Renaissance: A Short History*. Modern Library.
- Jonson, B. (1616). "Epitaph on Elizabeth, L. H."
- Joyce, J. (1922). *Ulysses.*
- Kahn, D. (1978). *Hitler's Spies: German Military Intelligence in World War II.*
- Kay-Shuttleworth, J. P. (1970). *The Moral and Physical Conditions of the Working Classes Employed in Cotton Manufacture in Manchester* (England). A. M. Kelly.
- Keats, J. (1816). "On First Looking into Chapman's Homer."
- Keats, J. (1818). *Endymion*, Book I.
- Keats, J. (1819). "Ode on a Grecian Urn."

- Keegan, J. (1998). *The First World War*. Hutchinson.
- Kempis, T. (1418-1427). *The Imitation of Christ*.
- Kennedy, A. (1948). *Québec to New England: The Life of Monsignor Charles Dauray*. Bruce Humphries.
- King, H. (1943). *The Song of Bernadette* [Film]. William Perlberg.
- Kipling, R. (1910). "If."
- Klein, M. (1984). [Playbill notes of play: *Joe Turner's Come and Gone* by A. Wilson]
- Korda, M. (2007). *Ike: An American Hero*. Harper/Harper Collins.
- Kukor, G. (1964). "*My Fair Lady*" [Film]. Warner Brothers. Song lyrics from: "The Rain in Spain" lyrics by A. J. Lerner.
- Kulik, G. (1982). *The New England Mill Village: 1790 – 1860*. (R. Parks, T. Penn, Ed.). The MIT Press.
- Küng, H. (1976) *The Church*. Image Books.
- Kurson, R. (2004). *Shadow Divers*. Random House.
- La Fontaine, J. de (1664). *Les Fables de La Fontaine*. University of Illinois Press.
- Lanctot, N. (2011). *Campy: The Two Lives of Roy Campanella*. Simon & Schuster.
- Lang, W. (1950). *Cheaper by the Dozen* [Film]. Lamar Trotti.
- Lavallee, G. A. *Marking Time Behind Barbed Wire*. Unpublished.
- Lean, D. (1957). *Bridge on the River Kwai* [Film]. Horizon.
- Leckie, R. (2000). "*A Few Acres of Snow*": *The Saga of the French and Indian Wars*. Wiley.
- Madhavan, A. (n.d.). "Come weal, come woe, my status is quo." (Paraphrased by the author.)
- Maher, F. M., (1980). *Florentine Raconte*. Domino.
- Malcom, A. (1987). *The Canadians*. Paperjacks.
- Man, T. (1833). "Picture of a Factory Village."
- Man, T. (1835). "A Picture of Woonsocket or the Truth in its Nudity."
- Manchester, W. (1978) *American Caesar*. Little, Brown and Co.
- Mandeville, C. (2012). *Mount Saint Charles Hockey: How It All Started*.
- Marshall, G. (1947). *The Perils of Pauline* [Film]. Paramount.
- McCarey, L. (1941). *Going My Way* [Film]. Leo McCarey.
- McCourt, F. (1996). *Angela's Ashes*. Scribner.
- McCullough, D. (2001). *John Adams*. Simon & Schuster.
- McCutchen, B. (1961). *History of a Free People*. Macmillan Co.
- McElvaine, R. (1984). *The Great Depression: America, 1929-1941*. Time Books, Random House.
- McPherson, J. M. (1996). *Drawn With the Sword: Reflections on the American Civil War*. Oxford University Press.
- Merton, T. (1999). *The Seven Storey Mountain*. Mariner Books
- Miller, M. R. (2005). *Envoy to the Terror: Gouverneur Morris and the French Revolution*. Potomac.
- Mills, D. (2007). *Renaissance and Reformation Times*. Angelico Press.
- Milot, A. (1992). *Childhood Memories*. Claude Milot.
- Milton, J. (1644). "Tractate on Education."
- Milton, J. (1645). "L'Allegro."
- Milton, J. (1667) *Paradise Lost*.
- Milton, J. (1693). "Lycidas."
- Mitchell, M. (1936) *Gone with the Wind* [Book]. Macmillan Publishers.
- Molloy, S. (2008). *Irish Titan, Irish Toilers*. University of New Hampshire Press.

- Montgomery of Alamein, B. L. M. (1958). *The Memoirs of Field-Marshall Montgomery.* World.
- More, Sir T. (1551 English ed.). *Utopia.*
- Morris, E. (2010). *Colonel Roosevelt.* Random House.
- Mukkerjee, S. (2010). *The Emperor of All Maladies.* Scribner.
- Neame, R. (1956). *The Man Who Never Was.* [Film]. André Hakim.
- Newman, J. (1864). "Apologia pro Vita Sua."
- Newman, J. H. (2015) *The Idea of a University.* Aeterna Press.
- Nickerson, L. A. (n.d.). "Ancestors."
- Nickerson, L. A. (n.d.). "Sequential."
- *Northland Post* – now known as *Cochrane Times-Post.* [Newspaper] Cochrane, Ontario, Canada.
- Noyes, A. E. (1940). *No Other Man.* J.B. Lippincott.
- O'Connor, E. (1956). *The Last Hurrah.* Little, Brown.
- O'Connor, E. (2002). *The Edge of Sadness.* Loyola Classics.
- O'Reilly, B. & Dugard, M. (2011). *Killing Lincoln: The Shocking Assassination That Changed America Forever.* Henry Holt.
- O'Reilly, B. & Dugard, M. (2012). *Killing Kennedy: The End of Camelot.* St. Martin's Griffin.
- Orwell, G. (1932). *Bold New World.* Chatto & Windus.
- Orwell, G. (1949). *1984.* Secker & Warburg.
- Overy, R. (1998). *Russia's War: A History of the Soviet Effort: 1941 – 1945.* Penguin.
- Overy, R. (2001). *Interrogations: The Nazi Elite in Allied Hands, 1945.* Penguin.
- Palmer, A. (1st ed. 1894) *The Palmer Method of Business Writing.*
- Pearce, J. (1999) *Literary Converts: Spiritual Inspiration in an Age of Unbelief.* Ignatius.
- Pei, M. (1965). *The Story of Language.* Lippincott.
- Petersen, W. (1981*). Das Boot* [Film]. G. Rohrbach.
- Petrisko, T. W. (2001). *Inside Heaven and Hell: What History, Theology, and the Mystics Tell Us About the Afterlife.* Saint Andrew's Productions.
- Petrisko, T. W. (2001). *Inside Purgatory: What History, Theology, and the Mystics Tell Us About Purgatory.* Saint Andrew's Productions.
- Plath, S. (1962). "Three Women: A Poem for Three Voices." A radio play in verse.
- Poe, E. A. (1845). "To Helen."
- Pope, A. (1709). "A Little Learning."
- Pope, A. (1733). "An Essay on Man."
- Prange, G. (1982). *At Dawn We Slept.* Penguin.
- Randall, J. (2003). *No Spirit… No Church…* Koinonia.
- Reinhart, C. & Rogoff, K. (2009). *This Time Is Different: Eight Centuries of Financial Folly.* Princeton U. Press.
- Rice, G. (1941). "Alumnus Football"
- Robb, G. (2007). *The Discovery of France: A Historical Geography.* W.W. Norton & Co.
- Roscoe, T. (1983). *Pig Boats: The True Story of the Fighting Submarines of WWII.* Bantam.
- Rubin, R. (2013). *The Last of the Doughboys.* Mariner Books.
- Sajer, G. (2001). *The Forgotten Soldier.* Potomac Books.
- Salinger, J. D. (1951). *The Catcher in the Rye.* Little, Brown, & Co.
- Salmon, J. & Farina, J. ed. (2011). *The Legacy of Pierre Teilhard de Chardin.* Paulist Press
- Santé, L. (1996, May 12). Living in Tongues. *The New York Times.* Section 6, p. 31.
- Schoenbrun, D. *Soldiers of the Night: The Story of the French Resistance.* E. P. Dutton.

- Shelley, P. B. (1820). "Ode to the West Wind."
- Shirer, W. (2008). *The Nightmare Years: 1930 – 1940*. Birlin.
- Showalter, D.E. & Deutsch, H. C. *If The Allies Had Fallen: Sixty Alternate Scenarios of World War II*. Skyhorse.
- Sides, H. (2001). *Ghost Soldiers: The Epic Account of the World War II's Greatest Rescue Mission*. Doubleday.
- Smith, B. (1943) *A Tree Grows in Brooklyn*. Harper & Brothers.
- Speer, A. (1997). *Inside the Third Reich*. Simon & Schuster.
- Specter, R. H. (1985). *Eagle Against the Sun: The American War with Japan*. Vintage.
- Spector, R. H. (2001). *At War, At Sea: Sailors and Naval Combat in the Twentieth Century*. Viking.
- Spielberg, S. (1998). *Saving Private Ryan*. Steven Spielberg et al.
- Spengler, O. (1991). *The Decline of the West*. Oxford University Press.
- Steinbeck, J. (1939). *The Grapes of Wrath*. Viking.
- Steinbeck, J. (1962). *Travels with Charlie: In Search of America*. Viking.
- Stennett. R. (1999). *Day of Deceit: The Truth About FDR and Pearl Harbor*. Free Press, Edition: Touchstone ed.
- Stevenson, R. L. (1880). "Requiem."
- Stevenson, W. (1976). *A Man Called Intrepid*.
- Stone, O. (1987). *Wall Street* [Film]. American Entertainment Partners, Amercent Films.
- Stone, O. (1994). *Natural Born Killers* [Film]. Regency Enterprises.
- Taylor, B. W. & Taylor, C. E. (1990). *Miss You: The World War II Letters of Barbara Woodall Taylor and Charles E. Taylor*. (J. Litoff, D. Smith Ed.). University of Georgia Press.
- Tellier, R. *Artistry and Character in Willa Cather*. unpublished thesis.
- Tennyson, A. L. (1833). "Ulysses."
- Tennyson, A. L. (1842). "Break, Break, Break."
- Tennyson, A. L. (1849) "In Memoriam H.H.H. Canto 27."
- Tennyson, A. L. (1854). "The Charge of the Light Brigade."
- Tennyson, A. L. (1889) "Crossing the Bar."
- Thayer, E. (1888) "Casey at the Bat: A Ballad of the Republic, Sung in the Year 1888."
- Thomas, A. P. (1976). *Woonsocket—Highlights of History*. Woonsocket Opera House Society.
- Thomas, D. (1951). "Do not go gentle into that good night."
- Thompson, F. (1893). "The Hound of Heaven."
- Travis, M. (1946). Sixteen Tons [Recorded by T. E. Ford] Los Angeles: Capitol. (1955).
- Tremblay, R. [Quoted by M. A. Briottet, in "l'Union." A publication of L'Union Saint-Jean Baptiste, Woonsocket, RI. Excerpt available in: Tremblay, Remi (1883) *Caprices poétiques et chansons satirique*.
- Trottier, C. H. (2018). *Trottier and Fontaine Family History: Courage and Perserverance: It's in the Genes*. CreateSpace Independent Publ. Platform.
- Troyat, H. (2000). *Catherine the Great*. Phoenix Press.
- Turner, F. J. (1921). *The Frontier in American History*.
- Tyldum, M. (2014). *The Imitation Game* [Film]. Black Bear Pictures.
- Uris, L. (1963). *Armageddon: A Novel of Berlin*. Dell Books.
- Uris, L. (1976). *Trinity*. Doubleday.
- Virgil (19 BC). "The Aeneid."
- Waller, D. (2010). *Wild Bill Donovan: The Spymaster Who Created the OSS and Modern American Espionage*. Free Press.
- Walters, C. (1964). *The Unsinkable Molly Brown* [Film]. L. Weingarten.

- Wartik, N. (1989). *The French Canadians.* Chelsea House.
- Watkins, T. H. (1993). *The Great Depression: America in the 1930s.* Little, Brown.
- Weintraub, S. (1991). *Long Day's Journey into War: Pearl Harbor and a World at War–December 7, 1941.* The Lyons Press.
- Weir, A. (1972). *The Six Wives of Henry VIII.* Grove Press.
- Werfel, F. (1942). *The Song of Bernadette,* [Book]. Hamish Hamilton.
- Wilder T. (1938). *Our Town* [Play]. Harper Perennial Modern Classics.
- Wolfe, T. (1940). *You Can't Go Home Again.* Harper & Row.
- Wordsworth, W. (1798). "Tables Turned."
- Yellin, E. (2004). *Our Mothers' War.* Free Press.
- Zinnemann, F. (1952). *High Noon* [Film]. Stanley Kramer Productions.
- Zinnemann, F. (1955). *Oklahoma* [Film]. Arthur Hornblow, Jr.

Web Sites Referenced for Historical & Genealogical Information

Discover Canada – Canada's History. (Last updated 2015-10-26).
https://www.canada.ca/en/immigration-refugees-citizenship/corporate/publications-manuals/discover-canada/read-online/canadas-history.html

Encyclopedia Britannica. (n.d.). *Sorel-Tracy, Quebec, Canada.*
https://www.britannica.com/place/Sorel-Tracy

www.familysearch.org This genealogy site is operated by the Church of Jesus Christ of Latter-Day Saints. It is a free membership site. Web pages referenced on the site by the contributors/editors to obtain information regarding the author's ancestry are too numerous to list individually.

~~~~~~

To visit St. Ann Church and experience the beauty of Guido Nincheri's amazing frescos, go to: http://www.stannartsandculturalcenter.org/ Their website has information about tours of the church that has come to be known as "The Sistine Chapel of America" as well as schedules of upcoming events.

Wedding portrait of the author's parents, Alphonse Tellier and Léopoldine Fontaine, St. Ann Church, November 19, 1923

THE WAY WE WERE

Tellier Family Tree

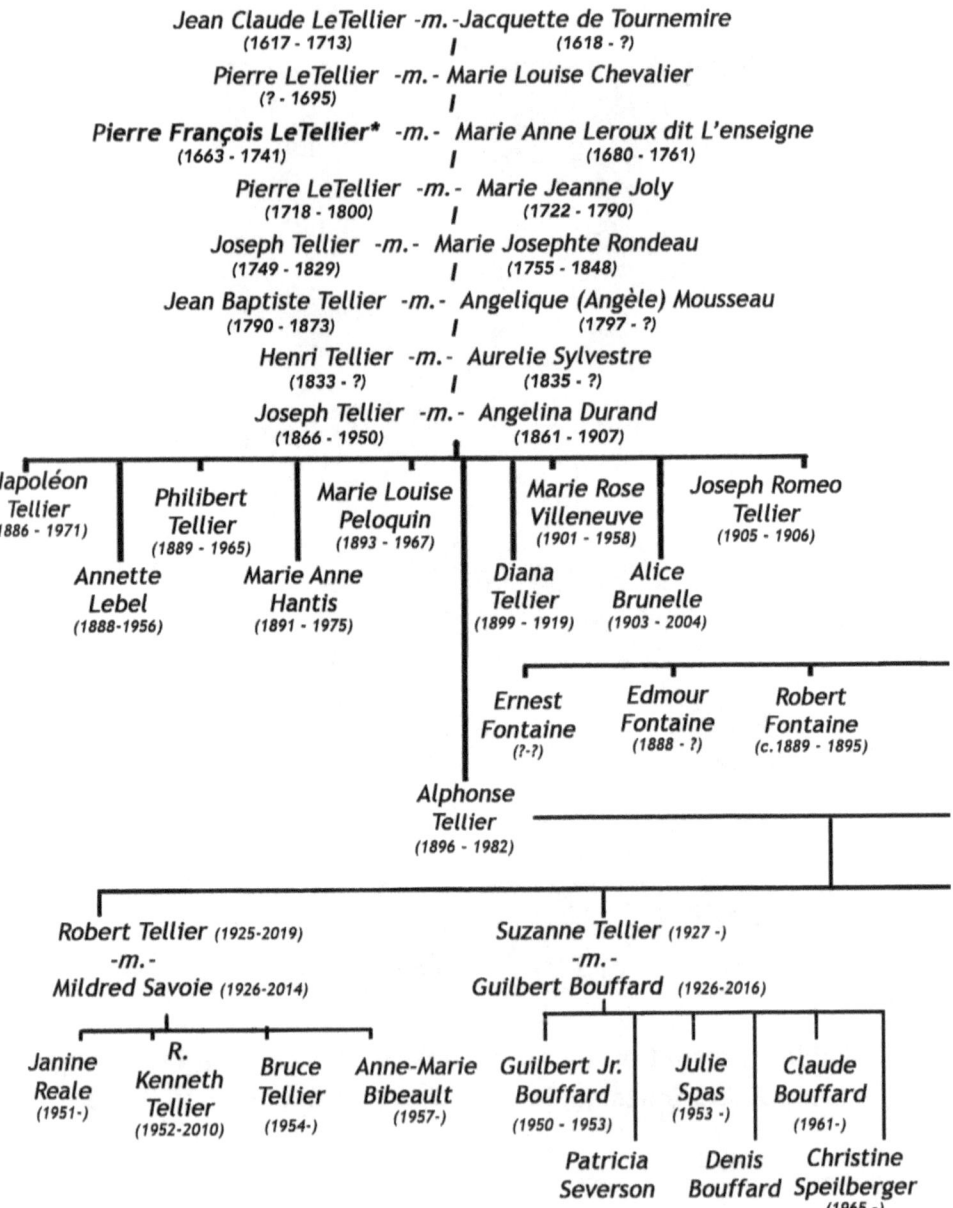

***First ancestors** to immigrate from France to Canada (New France).

THE WAY WE WERE

Fontaine Family Tree

Nicolas Pion dit LaFontaine -m.- Catherine Bredons
(1598 - 1677) | (1608 - 1662)

Nicolas Pierre Pion dit LaFontaine* -m.- Jeanne Amiot (Amyot)
(1634 - 1703) | (1651 - 1745)

Maurice Pion dit LaFontaine -m.- Marie Therese Chicoine (Chione)
(1684-1727) | (1688 -1764)

Jean Louis Pion dit LaFontaine -m.- Marie Marguerite Guertin
(1727 - 1769) | (1727 - 1774)

Jean Marie Pion dit LaFontaine -m.- Marie Charlotte Casavant
(1749 - 1793) | (1752-1838)

Jean Felix Pion dit Fontaine -m.- Marie Louise Claire Charron (Cabana)
(1773 - 1855) | (1775 - 1853)

Louis Pion Fontaine -m.- Audace Eudoxe Gaudry dit Borbonniere
(1805 - ?) | (1811 - 1875)

Louis Jacques Pascal Pion Fontaine -m.- Aurelie Meunier (Minier) dit Lagace
(1829 - 1910) | (1833 - 1890)   (Lagasse)

Louis Jacques Pascal Fontaine -m.- Emerance Morvan
(1861-1914) | (1864 - 1949)

| Emile Fontaine (d. 2y) | Yvonne Villemure (c.1893-?) | Auray Fontaine (1895-?) | Urgel Fontaine (1897-?) | Francois Xavier Fontaine (1900 - 1994) | Marie Ange Fontaine (1902 - 1968) |

Leopoldine Clemence Fontaine (1898 -1988)

Laurence Trottier (1905 - 1993)

Rene Tellier (1930-2019)
-m.-
Patricia Smith (1936 - 2000)

James Tellier (1977 -)

Bernard Tellier (1934 -)
-m.-
Gloria Landry (1936 - 2020)

Donald Clark Jr. (1959 -)

Rachel Tellier (1937 -)
-m.-
Donald Clark (1936 - 2019)

David Clark (1960 -)

Christopher Clark (1966 -)

Michael Tellier (1961 -)   Marc Tellier (1962 - 2019)   Alan Tellier (1971 -)

Additional Family Genealogy Information
Contributed by Bruce Tellier

As noted earlier in this book, the author's initial finding that his family descended from Jean Baptiste LeTellier who arrived in New France (Canada) in 1665 has proved to be inaccurate. Further research done following the author's death has revealed a different lineage that has been included in the preceding family tree. As is common in genealogy, discrepancies in the spelling of names are frequent. On the preceding family tree pages, variations in names that were discovered are included in parentheses. Also, in tracing the Fontaine family, there were instances where records showed that the (La)Fontaine surname was missing. These records ended with "Pion." What follows is additional ancestral information and as our author noted, accuracy of this information is always subject to revision.

Tellier Family Tree__

• Jean Claude LeTellier 1617-1713 and his wife Jacquotte DeTournemire b. 1618 are the earliest LeTellier couple on record. Jean Claude was born in Court St. Etienne which is now part of Belgium. At the time of his birth, however, the area was referred to as Southern Netherlands or Catholic Netherlands and his town was part of the Duchy of Brabant. At some point during his long life, he moved to France where he died in Ramecourt.
• Pierre LeTellier died October 9, 1695 - Église (Church) de Saint Eustache, Paris, France which is less than a mile from the city's Notre Dame Cathedral. A source lists his occupation as *commissionnaire-voiturier* - a carriage driver who was a messenger or delivery man.
• His son, Pierre was born in Paris in 1663 and died in Montreal in 1741 making him the first paternal Tellier ancestor to settle in New France (Canada). He married Marie Leroux January 7, 1700, in Notre Dame de Quebec (in Quebec City – it's now a Cathedral). While it's possible he was a soldier and his wife a *filles du Roi* (Daughter of the King), no evidence of that was discovered.
• Pierre Tellier 1718-1800 (Yes, a third Pierre!) is listed in an online source as being born in Sainte Anne de la Pérade, Champlain, Quebec. However, St. Anne de la Pérade is a church near the Sainte-Anne River just north of where it enters the St. Lawrence River and Champlain is a community about 10 miles southwest of the church on the north shore of the St. Lawrence. It's most likely the church is where he was christened. He marries Marie Joly June 8, 1740, in that church and dies in Saint Cuthbert in 1800 – the place where the author's father would be born 96 years later.

- Joseph Tellier is born in 1794 on Île Dupas, an island in the St. Lawrence River, near Saint Cuthbert. He passes away in Saint Cuthbert in 1829. His marriage to Marie Rondeau was celebrated there January 30, 1775.
- Jean Baptiste Tellier 1790-1873 was born in Saint Cuthbert. Two communities near St. Cuthbert: Sainte-elisabeth, and Joliette, are listed as where he married Angèle Mousseau on June 17, 1816.
- Henri Tellier, born 1833 in Saint Cuthbert married Aurelie Sylvestre there on August 4, 1857. They had 9 children.
- Joseph Tellier 1866-1950 was also born in Saint Cuthbert and married his first wife, Angelina Durand there August 25, 1884. They had ten children. He immigrated with his family, which included the author's father, to Woonsocket, RI in 1904. He had no children with his second wife.

Fontaine Family Tree__

Two additional generations of Fontaines were discovered who preceded Nicolas Pion and Catherine Bredons, the first couple on the preceding Fontaine Family Tree page.
- The earliest Fontaines on record were Nicolas Pion, born c. 1545, and his wife Renée Lemaître, born 1550. Both were residents of Tours, France.
- They gave birth to Nicolas Pion in 1574. He and his wife Jeanne Roy were lifelong residents of Tours.

[Much of what follows is information gathered by the author's cousin, Claude Trottier.]

- Nicolas Pion dit LaFontaine and Catherine Bredons were married in St. Pierre du Boile. Today there is a St. Peter's church in Tours which might be where they were married.
- Their son Nicolas (1634 – 1703) is the first Fontaine to immigrate to Québec as a soldier in 1673. That same year, he married *fille du Roi* Jeanne Amiot. Two locations were found for their wedding. Claude Trottier's research indicates it was Richelieu, St. Pierre du Sorel, Quebec. The French built Fort Richelieu in 1642 where the Richelieu River joins the St. Lawrence River. A primitive missionary church built there c. 1670-1672 may have been where they married. Another source indicates their wedding was in Notre Dame de Québec (City). Québec City would have been Nicolas's first stop while sailing up the St. Lawrence so it's plausible that he met and married his *fille du Roi* bride there before continuing another one hundred plus miles upriver to Fort Richelieu/Sorel. Since the fort experienced numerous attacks by the Mohawk tribe of the Iroquois Confederacy during the 17th century, it's doubtful many women lived at the fort.
- Maurice Pion dit LaFontaine (1684 – 1727) has two communities listed as

his birthplace: Contrecoeur and Verchères, Québec. Both are on the southeast shore of the St. Lawrence River about seven miles apart. He marries his wife Marie Thérese Chicoine on January 22, 1713.

•Jean Louis Pion dit LaFontaine (1727 – 1769) married Marie Marguerite Guertin February 19, 1748 in St. Francis Xavier Church, Verchères. They had six children.

•Jean Marie Pion dit LaFontaine (1749 – 1793) may also have had Louis as one of his middle names. He married Marie Charlotte Casavant on November 16, 1772 in Verchères.

•Jean Felix Pion dit Fontaine (1773 – 1855) is the first of the author's ancestors to be born a British subject after The Treaty of Paris in 1763. He married Marie Louis Charron on February 8, 1796 in Verchères.

•Louis Pion Fontaine (b. 1805) is the first Fontaine in three generations not to be born and marry in Verchères. He is born in St. Hughes and marries Audace (Eudoce) Gaudry dit Bourbonniere on January 13, 1829 in St. Hyacinthe, Québec. They had twelve children.

•Louis Jacques Pascal Pion Fontaine (1829 – 1910) married Aurelie Meunier (Minier) Lagasse (Lagace) on June 12, 1860 but disagreement was found as to where. One source indicates St. Hughes, Québec while another identifies St. Henri which is south of Québec City. Since St. Henri is just over one hundred miles from the area where the previous six generations of Fontaines lived, St. Hughes appears to be the most likely location. Louis and Aurelie had ten children.

•Louis Jacques Pascal Fontaine (1861 – 1914) was born in St. Hughes and died in Cochrane, Ontario, Canada. He married Emerance Morvan on July 18, 1887 in Saint François du Lac, Québec. They are author Rene Tellier's grandparents. Widow Emerance emigrated to Woonsocket, RI with four of her eight children in 1916 following the destruction of their homes in Cochrane by forest fire. The author's mother was one of those children. The communities mentioned above where many generations of Fontaines lived are relatively close to each other. When the Fontaines started their journey from Cochrane to America, relatives who still lived in some of those communities took them in for a time.

•The story of how the author's mother, Léopoldine, got her unusual name bears repeating here. According to her children, their grandparents wanted to name their mother Pauline. But when her godparents took her to be baptized a few days after her October 28 birth, the priest thought Pauline wasn't dignified enough, or more to the point, it wasn't Catholic enough. So he looked at a wall calendar that listed saint feast days for each day of the month and saw that St. Leopold's feast day would soon occur on November 15. To feminize the name, he added "ine" and that is how she got her name.

It should also be said that this was a time when good French-Canadian Catholics did not question the authority of their priest – even when the priest displayed exceptionally poor taste in selecting a child's name!

Rhode Island 1905 Census form of the author's father Alphonse Tellier at nine years old. This is the first census taken for his family in the United States as it indicates they had only been in the US for eight months (8/12). Since the Tellier family numbered eleven at the time, the additional two members that resulted in thirteen being listed must have been relatives who had taken them in until they could get their own apartment. It's interesting to note that RI conducted its own census every ten years on the half-decade year from 1865 through 1935.

1910 U.S. census of the Joseph Tellier family.
Joseph's wife Angelina died in 1907 so he is listed here as a widower. (The four columns following each name indicate 1. Sex, 2, Race, 3. Age, & 4. Marital status.) It must be noted that there are significant errors in this census. The fourth name should be Marie Anne; but as our author tells us in chapter 3, the family pronounced her name: "Marionne" It's clear no one in the family spell-checked the census taker. She was also not born in Rhode Island (4th column from the right). The last column lists the year each family member immigrated to the US and all those dates are incorrect. The entire family immigrated to the US to establish permanent residence in 1904. Only their father Joseph is known to have temporarily visited Woonsocket prior to 1904.

1911 Canadian Census of the Fontaine family

This census was taken while the family resided in Trois-Rivières (Three Rivers), Québec, Canada. The author's mother, Léopoldine was twelve at the time (Line 46). The incorrect spelling of her name as "Leopauldine" must be pointed out. It could be speculated that this mistake occurred because the family told the census taker the story behind how she received her name (p. 670). Since Léopoldine's father Louis would pass away in 1914 in Cochrane, Ontario after he had established his lumber mill business there, it can be assumed that not much time elapsed between the taking of this census and the move of the family to the far northern region of Ontario.

ABOUT THE AUTHOR

RENE M. TELLIER (1930-2019), was born in Woonsocket, Rhode Island. He was the third child and second son of Alphonse and Léopoldine (Fontaine) Tellier who emigrated to the United States from Quebec, Canada in the early 1900's. Most of his youth was spent living in one of the many tenements on Gaulin Avenue, which is behind St. Ann Church, with siblings Robert, Suzanne, Bernard and Rachel. He grew up speaking a patois that was a French-Canadian dialect of the common people of Québec. Since it was the primary language of his family and neighbors, he used it with translations throughout this text.

Rene's primary education was at St. Ann School in Woonsocket where he was taught by the Presentation of Mary Sisters. He then entered Mount Saint Charles Academy, also in the city, and in his junior year, decided to join the Brothers of the Sacred Heart. The Brothers made it possible for him to earn two bachelor's degrees and a Master of Education degree in Counseling Psychology from Boston College, Class of 1971. His first years teaching were at Sacred Heart School in Sharon, MA. He then taught English and Latin at Notre Dame High School in Fitchburg, MA while also serving as Athletic Director. Turning his education career to counseling, he returned to his alma mater, Mount Saint Charles, as Director of Guidance in 1970 and was instrumental in helping transition the school from an all-male student body to a co-ed program, also expanding the recruitment of students beyond the city and bringing back the middle school.

Rene left the Brotherhood in 1973 and in 1977 departed Mount to become Guidance Counselor at Norton High School, MA. Over his 42-year career in education, Rene helped send over 3000 students to college. He took tremendous pride in his profession and the role he played in the continuing education of his students. He felt that every child should have a chance at higher education and fought for every single one.

Rene married Patricia (Smith) Tellier on April 10, 1976, in New York and welcomed their son Jim in 1977. He was later blessed to add a granddaughter, Mackenzie Briggs, to the family. Pat died on December 10, 2000.

Rene's Catholic faith, which stemmed from his parents, was the core of who he was. He was also a gifted storyteller, taking special interest in his family's history and genealogy. He recorded stories told by his parents, especially his mother Léopoldine, and details of his life growing up during the Great Depression, World War II and the post-war years. He was an avid WWII buff, reading many texts about this event that affected the Tellier family and so many others mentioned in this book. Even during challenging times, Rene maintained a sense of humor he shares with the reader. Over the years he often contributed to the *The Call* and *The Valley Breeze,* writing about the family or current events. He also enjoyed gardening and landscaping.

Writing this book, *The Way We Were,* was a labor of love taking over 40 years to complete. Besides recording priceless family memories, Rene personalizes the immigrant experience, the French-Canadian culture, life as a textile mill worker and the importance of family, faith and the Church. Rene lived in North Smithfield RI until his death on September 8, 2019.

Thank You, Rene, for giving us this gift.

www.ingramcontent.com/pod-product-compliance
Lightning Source LLC
Chambersburg PA
CBHW030211170426
43201CB00006B/52